WIND ENSEMBLE SOURCEBOOK
— AND —
BIOGRAPHICAL GUIDE

**Recent Titles in
the Music Reference Collection**

WIND ENSEMBLE SOURCEBOOK

—— AND ——
BIOGRAPHICAL GUIDE

Marshall Stoneham,
Jon A. Gillaspie,
and David Lindsey Clark

Music Reference Collection, Number 55

GREENWOOD PRESS
Westport, Connecticut • London

Library of Congress Cataloging-in-Publication Data

Stoneham, Marshall.
    Wind ensemble sourcebook and biographical guide / Marshall
Stoneham, Jon A. Gillaspie, and David Lindsey Clark.
        p.   cm.—(Music reference collection, ISSN 0736–7740 ; no.
55)
    Includes bibliographical references and index.
    ISBN 0-313-29858-0 (alk. paper)
    1. Wind ensembles—Bibliography.   2. Wind ensembles—Bio-
bibliography.   I. Gillaspie, Jon A.   II. Clark, David Lindsey.
III. Title.   IV. Series.
ML128.W5S76   1997
016.7848—dc20   96–22021

British Library Cataloguing in Publication Data is available.

Library of Congress Catalog Card Number: 96–22021
ISBN: 0-313-29858-0
ISSN: 0736–7740

First published in 1997

Greenwood Press, 88 Post Road West, Westport, CT 06881
An imprint of Greenwood Publishing Group, Inc.

Printed in the United States of America

The paper used in this book complies with the
Permanent Paper Standard issued by the National
Information Standards Organization (Z39.48–1984).

10 9 8 7 6 5 4 3 2 1

Contents

Preface

If you wished to buy recordings of Beethoven's complete symphonies, you would know which works to expect. His "complete wind music" would cause you more problems. Indeed, all the recordings available at the time of writing omit some of his original music for wind octet (**LVB-3** in our referencing scheme) and many include wind music written mainly by someone else (**LVB-5**). If someone wanted to know the scoring or the date of composition of Gounod's *1st Symphony* (hardly one of his most popular works) there would be no problem. Yet the same searcher, turning to Gounod's *Petite Symphonie* for winds, perhaps his most commonly performed and recorded work after *Faust*, will usually find a wrong date of composition and incorrect scoring, both dependent on the source used. If you hoped to know why Mozart's piano concertos were written, despite the gaps in what is known, there are many suggestions, discussions, and assessments; for the masterpieces for wind ensemble he wrote at much the same time, there is very little guidance. If one were an opera lover, or a player of a popular instrument, a violinist or pianist seeking interesting novelties to perform, there is a wealth of literature. Yet the wind player who wants to know what is available for her or his ensemble will have a daunting task to find out just what is in print and what its merits are, let alone what works remain unpublished in libraries throughout the world.

This sourcebook is intended for the many players and listeners who wish to gain a wider appreciation of wind music, and especially those who enjoy the serenade music which delighted Mozart's contemporaries. It is also an attempt to fill a gap in musical history. There are many general guides to "The Opera" or "The Symphony" in which the reader can assume the raw facts (like dates) will be right, works will be properly attributed, and there will be a sound historical context and musical perspective. The reader should make no such assumption for wind music. Wrong dates and misattributions abound, even for well known composers. As for the contexts and perspectives of wind music, there is hardly a possible error which has not actually been made. It would be over-optimistic to assume our own volume is free from error. However, we have used primary sources wherever practical, so we hope we have avoided many of the major traps. We have made great efforts to check original sources and also to know works at first hand from our own performances and those of other ensembles.

Music for wind harmony (which we shall define, but typically for an ensemble of four or more winds, mainly in pairs, e.g., 2ob 2cl 2hn 2bn) is as enjoyable to play as to listen to. This has important consequences. One is the great revival in the playing of wind ensemble music in recent years, in the availability of printed music and of recordings, and in the reappearance of wind ensembles outside the concert hall, in informal settings similar to those for which such music was intended two hundred years ago. Another change has been growing interest in the background of music and the social aspects of its origin. Wind ensemble music fulfilled clear but varied social functions, and is rich in source material, much difficult to find. This music was a part of many lives, and reflects what amused or moved a significant fraction of those in the Western world. The music often has links to specific people or events. These personal features remind us that real people were involved: the music was not an academic exercise for some ideal wind band, but with specific players in mind, some with their weaknesses, and for a patron whose views mattered. It would have been easy to write a far larger book, and we are well aware of many potential research projects.

Any social background leads inevitably to the asides of musical history. In preparing this book we encountered the link between what Beethoven wrote for two eyeglasses and the prehistory of the metronome, the origin of the cigarette, how Casanova contributed to da Ponte's libretto for *Don Giovanni*, the associations of wind music with magic and the supernatural, the mystery of Gounod's second oboe, and why Seiber's excellent *Serenade* caused such an upset in Budapest. We have had to address such issues as musical borrowings (even by Mozart) and just who might have written the parthia containing the *St Antoni Chorale* (the standard suggestions of Haydn or Pleyel cannot be taken seriously). We have had to balance evidence for works dubiously attributed to major composers. Sometimes there is a convincing case (e.g. from Haydn to Hoffmeister); wherever we can only speculate, we have tried to make this clear.

What we have attempted is a systematic survey of music for wind ensemble. We leave out much of what is already well known about, say, bassoons or Beethoven. We omit music for the separate genres of large concert or military wind bands and of wind quintets or smaller groups of solo winds. Even so, we mention approximately 12,000 works by 2,200 composers. Our sourcebooks comprise three linked volumes, each able to stand alone. In the present volume, *Wind Ensemble Sourcebook and Biographical Guide,* we try to give some structure to this rich resource. The detailed scorings and locations are listed in a companion volume, *Wind Ensemble Catalog,* which includes appropriate music from the late 17th century to the present day. Much is unpublished. This second volume identifies arrangers and arrangements, as well as original works. A third companion volume, *Wind Ensemble Thematic Catalog,* gives incipits and lists movements for works composed before about 1900, to make identification of specific works easier. Its appendices list lost works, works for major configurations, and a glossary of dances found within wind harmony.

The three volumes include details of the music, the composers or arrangers, where the music is to be found, and of many recordings. What we leave out by intention is discussed in Chapter 1; we hope our readers will inform us of omissions by default. The *Sourcebook* surveys a genre of music for which most standard sources are silent or unreliable, details of recordings, and lists of music both in print, yet whose availability may be transient (not forgetting "ghosts," announced but never published) and in archives. These archives stretch over the traditional geographical and political boundaries and over the traditional (and illogical) catalog divide between pre-1800 and post-1800 dates. Despite great efforts over many years, we must be realistically modest about any claims to completeness, and do not claim this study is final. We believe this field is beginning to flourish. Even more works are coming to light again, and new compositions are appearing. Our hope is that players, publishers and recording companies will gain from a wider repertoire. We also hope that scholars will benefit from recognizing the range and scale of wind harmony and from its background.

Our efforts have involved many libraries and national music information centers, to whose staffs we express our gratitude, and our volume two includes a full list. Our text identifies those many specific cases where individuals were able to give us special help or guidance. We provide reasonably full references. It is appropriate, nevertheless, to single out three sources which we have found particularly important. The first is the magisterial series on Haydn by Professor H C Robbins Landon, notable both for his discussions of Haydn's wind music (available largely through his own efforts) and for his description of the context of so much of the music of that time. The second source consists of the writings of Dr Roger Hellyer, initially in his Oxford University thesis, which provided the first detailed, wide ranging and careful discussion of the 18th and early 19th century wind music. It was his editions which brought to our attention just how good Krommer's music was. Thirdly, the compilations of Dr David Whitwell (which also cover some areas outside our scope) have been a formidable source, not least for checking the completeness of the ensemble music we discuss. Since these sources appeared, Eastern Europe opened up. Many further archives proved to be rich sources of wind music. This has led us to a very different picture of wind harmony, both in extent and in associations with more familiar musical forms.

No one working in this field could ignore the players of wind music in their acknowledgments. We have gained especial insight from a number of recorded groups: the pioneering recordings of the London Baroque Ensemble, the London Wind Soloists for their Mozart and Haydn, the Netherlands Wind Ensemble for their Strauss, the Nash Ensemble for their Krommer, Dieter Klöcker's Consortium Classicum, who have shown just how good the less famous works can sound when played with skill and affection, and the Czech groups, notably the Collegium Musicum Pragense, for their recordings of Bohemian wind music. Other major influences have been those friends with whom we have been able to play so many of the works discussed and in so many settings, and especially the Dorchester Wind Players, for their continuing encouragement.

It is a pleasure for us to thank those who have made a special contribution to the book. Robert Eccles not only made many constructive suggestions, but also resolved issues of fact, translated texts from many languages and guided our use and accenting of the foreign languages we encountered. Charles Barnard provided valuable assistance with the figures. We thank Dr Volker von Volckamer (Fürstlich Oettingen-Wallerstein'sche Sammlungen) for permission to reproduce the famous silhouette. We are grateful to the Ermuli Trust, which partly funded two of Jon Gillaspie's many visits to Eastern Europe. The insight of Marilyn Brownstein (of Greenwood Press) led us to a conception of the book far better than our original ideas. We are enormously grateful for the continuing encouragement we received from her, Mary Blair, Alicia S Merritt, and from our Production Editor, Lynn Zelem, and Copy Editor, Charles Eberline. We are particularly grateful to Alicia Merritt for her support and encouragement, especially when our work seemed set to grow out of hand as we identified more and more (and in one case, purchased) large and rich collections of wind music. Finally, we thank our friends and, above all, our families for their tolerance of our eccentric enthusiasms.

NOTES TO THE READER

One part of our notes covers the obvious basic information: abbreviations, major references, and those library sigla which we reference explicitly in this volume (a fraction of the archives we have used in our survey). The other part of the notes was added bcause we know that many readers will be unfamiliar with the background and range of wind harmony. In our main text, Part 1 is organized by countries and by sphere of activity. We have provided a chronology to show general trends, and to make clearer some of the international similarities. Likewise, we provide a summary called "Facts and Myths," which makes some of the main points to emerge from our survey.

Chronology 1650–1900

Numbers of arrangements quoted relate to original works with known dates, irrespective of how often they were arranged.

1650–1700 La Musique de la Grande Écurie adopts oboes and bassoons. These start to replace shawms and pommers in French orchestras and in town and military bands.
Cornetts and sackbuts play in London for the restoration of the monarchy.
1680–1700 The fashion for Hautboisten bands spreads east and north from France. British waits bands start to adopt oboes and bassoons.
1700s In France, La Musique de la Grande Écurie grows in importance.
Hautboisten bands reach Austria. The German bands at Gotha and Gottdorf are described as "türkische." Krieger's *Lustige Feld-Musik* (1704) uses the term "Parthien."
1710s French wind bands celebrate the end of the War of the Spanish Succession.
Born: Alcock, T A Arne, C P E Bach, J Stamitz, Wagenseil.
1720s The first known use of the term "Harmonie."
The Prussian Military School of Music founded. Horns enter Saxon army bands by 1729; this configuration 2ob 2hn 2bn becomes known as the "Sachsische variante."
Born: Asplmayr, Gassmann, Starzer.
1730s Born: J C Bach, Dittersdorf, Dušek, J Haydn, M Haydn, Mysliveček, Vanhal.
1740s War of the Austrian Succession (1740-1748) and the Peace of Aix-le-Chapelle.
Handel's *Music for the Royal Fireworks* and smaller pieces for 2ob 2hn bn and 2cl hn.
Wind bands noted in processions in London. Ranelagh Gardens open.
Wind music composed by J Stamitz for Paris.
Early Harmonien were formed at Melk, and probably Regensburg, Brno and Kroměříž.
Wind bands in processions in Prague.
Born: Druschetzky, Dibdin, Eichner, Fiala, Kozeluch, Kreith, Paisiello, Pichl, J Reicha, Schacht, C P Stamitz, Stumpf, Went.
1750s The Seven Years' War (1756-63).
First official reports of 2 UK regimental bands.
Wind bands play for funerals in the German states.
Wind music for an Imperial visit to Kroissenbrunn described by Dittersdorf.
Born: W F E Bach, Blasius, de Croes, Feldmayr, G F Fuchs, Hoffmeister, Krommer, V V Mašek, Mozart, Pleyel, Righini, Rosetti, Salieri, Sperger, A and J Stadler, Vanderhagen, Wineberger, Winter, P Wranizky.
1760s Russia and Turkey at war from the late 1760s to 1774.
There are signs of the core band changing from 2ob 2hn 1/2bn to 2cl 2hn 1/2bn.
Clarinets and horns play at Ranelagh and in Dublin. Winds and stage bands used by Arne in his operas. The Royal Artillery band is founded, 2ob 2cl 2hn 2bn. There are first reports of 22 British regimental bands.
The Garde Suisse founded, with clarinets. La Pouplinière's band ceases. Roeser, in Monaco, composes, arranges, and writes his *Essai d'Instruction*. Gossec composes wind music for Chantilli. Rameau's operas use winds extensively.
Haydn composes wind music (1760); the Eszterháza Harmonie is revived on his arrival. Dušek and M Haydn also write for winds. A wind band is established in Hesse-Darmstadt. Asplmayr composes and arranges for the Pachta Harmonie (Bohemia).
Born: A Wranizky, Cherubini, Danzi, Gyrowetz, Mayr, P Mašek.
1770s The American War of Independence (1776-83); England and France also at war.
The rise of classicism; this was the period known as Sturm und Drang.

The core band of 2cl 2hn 2bn is established, with octets appearing later in the decade. The Russian Imperial Harmonie adopts the configuration of 2fl 2cl 2hn 2bn; Paisiello composes for it and for stage bands. There is a rise of "Turkish" music. Early wind music journals and periodicals are published in Britain, France and the German states. Church bands common in Britain, playing music by Alcock, Dixon and others. The first reports of 19 regimental bands; new Guards bands are formed. Wind bands perform at spas like Bath. Three wind bands play for the Regatta on the Thames.

Harmonien popular in central Europe courts (such as Batthyáni, Clam Gallas, Schwarzenberg, Thurn und Taxis, Wallerstein) and at monasteries of liberal orders (Brno, Melk, Osek). There are theater wind bands at Regensberg. Eszterháza wind bands celebrate the Duke of Milan's visit. Mozart, Myslivecek and Salieri compose for Milan. Wind music by J C Bach (London), Asplmayr, Mozart, Dittersdorf, Salieri, Myslivecek, M Haydn's *Missa Sancta Hieronymi*. Born: Beethoven, J N Hummel, Küffner, Sedlak, Starke, Triebensee, Witt. At least 21 opera and 15 ballet arrangements made for winds.

1780s Austrian religious reform. War with Turkey (1787-91). French Revolution.
Further journals are issued, with arrangers including Beinet, Ozi and Vanderhagen.
Shield, Kelly and Storace use stage wind bands. Wind music continues in the London pleasure gardens. Wind band concerts in Philadelphia and Providence.
French bands flourish, their musicians surviving the early part of the Revolution.
The Imperial Harmonie founded in Vienna; the octet (2ob 2cl 2hn 2bn) becomes standard in the Austrian domains. Went establishes octet arrangements of operas as a major part of Austrian wind music. A Wiener Tonkünstler Societät concerts includes wind music by Starzer. Schwarzenberg Harmonie thrives (2ob 2ca 2hn 2bn). Donaueschingen expands to full Harmonie; Bonn Harmonie changes; Liechtenstein Harmonie formed; Thurn und Taxis and Wallerstein Harmonien at their peaks. Expansion of wind music in public settings, for both civilian and military bands.
Music by Druschetzky, Mozart (K.361, 375, 388), Pleyel, Rosetti, C Stamitz, Went.
Born: Bochsa père, Castil-Blaze, Gambaro, Sellner, Spohr, Vogt, C M von Weber.
At least 70 opera arrangements made for winds.

1790s The French Revolution becomes the Terror. Wars with France.
Many British militia bands formed. US Marines band founded. Wind concerts in Boston.
Gossec, Cherubini, Méhul write music for the Fêtes nationales. New French bands are formed, including the Garde Nationale and the Garde Directoire. The Conservatoire de Musique is founded to train bandsmen. The Magasin de Musique des Fêtes Nationales is formed, mainly to issue music for small bands and patriotic songs. The core military band configuration remains 2cl 2hn 2bn in France and several other regions.
Bands in the German states begin to add some form of flute. Some Austrian court Harmonien (such as Schwarzenberg) disband, probably due to real or perceived economic pressure from the wars and French expansion. Others develop (Chotek, Kinský, Lobkowitz), and the Esterházy and Liechtenstein Harmonien flourish. Wind bands are found in many recreational settings, e.g., lemonade stalls in Vienna. Music publishing expands, both in manuscript (Traeg is very active) and in print, following Senefelder's invention of lithography.
Wind music by Beethoven, Druschetzky, J Haydn, Krommer, Triebensee, Went.
Born: Donizetti, Rossini, F L and F P Schubert.
At least 111 opera and 16 ballet arrangements, many by Went, Stumpf and Fuchs.

1800s The Peninsular War; the Battle of Trafalgar. The beginnings of Romanticism.
Probably several hundred British bands active at this time, including those of the Prince of Wales, the regular army, and the militia. Many marches written and published, as well as Dibdin's *War Songs* and Schetky's *Airs, Reels and Strathspeys*. The Philharmonic Concerts start, and include wind ensemble music by Mozart. In America, the Moravian

communities begin to play wind harmony. New journals begin in Britain and France. The French invasion of Italy stimulates the formation of wind bands and conservatories to train bandsmen.

The Austrian reformation of the monastic system leads to the closure of monasteries, and hence of their wind bands. Rampant inflation, military occupation and deaths of patrons bring an end to many court Harmonien, such as Clam Gallas, Esterházy, Liechtenstein, Thurn und Taxis, and Wallerstein. Others began, including Lippe (Detmold), Hohenlohe, Löwenstein (Wertheim), Mecklenberg-Schwerin (Ludwigslust) and Sondershausen. Count Festetics buys a large collection of wind music for his music school in Keszthely. The Sondershausen and Lobkowitz Harmonien give public concert series for winds. Band configurations vary from place to place, leading to local arrangements of classics, like Mozart's operas, to fill gaps in repertoires.

There is increased use of small clarinets in E♭ & F across Europe. Many Austrian bands add tp and cbn; German bands add b-tb; French bands add a pair of flutes.

Wind music by Beethoven, Fuchs, Gebauer, Krommer, Sedlak, Triebensee, Weber. Born: Lachner, Lucas, Mendelssohn.

At least 121 operas and 25 ballets arranged, dominating the wind music market.

1810s French invasion of Russia and defeat; the Battle of Waterloo.

Spa bands and the Band of the Prince Regent continue and grow in size. The enormous fall in militia bands in Britain leads to a collapse of the market for printed wind music. Moravian wind bands at Bethlehem, Lititz and Salem flourish. Many bandsmen remain in north America after the War of 1812; they begin to train musicians.

Large band works written by P Mašek and others to celebrate Napoleon's defeat. The Austrian Imperial Harmonie plays in Paris. In the aftermath of the War, many Austrian court bands cease, partly from financial problems; survivors include the Imperial Harmonie and the revived Liechtenstein Harmonie under Sedlak. Wind music becomes dominated by arrangements, with most sales to regimental, town or pleasure garden bands. Many German courts establish or retain Harmonien, and many flourish for decades. Their varied configurations meant that much music was of local origin.

The Tsar presents higher pitched instruments to an Austrian band, with lasting consequences. Russian horn bands become familiar in the West.

Music by Donizetti, Gambaro, Küffner, Mayr, Scholl, Sedlak, Starke, Triebensee. Born: Gounod, Gouvy, Schumann, Wagner.

At least 90 opera and 13 ballet arrangements made for wind harmony.

1820s Peace in Europe, but most countries maintain strong armies, even in France as occupying troops leave. The first railways. South American states gain independence.

Larger military bands move to having more than one instrument to a part and a related increase in brass instruments. Early brass bands are formed in Britain.

The Vauxhall Gardens orchestra replaced by a military band, playing works by John Parry and others. Owen's wind band plays for Model New Lanark Mills.

New journals founded (Berr, Louis, Marchal, Münchs; Küffner's *Pot-Pourris*); those in France and Germany often use the same plates. Arrangements and short military pieces dominate markets; there is little demand for major new original works. Some original works (notably Krommer's published Harmonien) remain in use for decades. German court Harmonien flourish, often where a full orchestra is not maintained.

Austrian church music for funerals and processions grows, often with a core band of 2cl 2hn 2bn. Such bands continue throughout the century, especially in small communities, where the bands probably played for civic and secular functions as well.

Wind music by Beethoven, Küffner, Mendelssohn, Sauer, A Schneider, Walch and Weber. Born: Bruckner, Raff. At least 50 operas and 9 ballets arranged for winds.

1830s Spa wind bands continue at Cheltenham and Bath; their repertoire is similar to that of their contemporary German bands. All-brass bands in the UK include a private band at Cyfarthfa Castle. Some British brass bands started as bands with woodwinds. British military bands in India play opera arrangements.

New York considers a civic military band. The first Canadian militia band in Quebec. Berr becomes director of the French Gymnase de Musique Militaire; works by Krommer continue to be used in conservatoires.

German court bands flourish. Many works for Darmstadt written by Mangold and by Rinck; the Hohenlohe and Lippe Harmonien thrive; however the Löwenstein, Schwerin, and (probably) Liechtenstein Harmonien end.

Band grow in size in armies and major urban centers, a transitional stage between Harmonie and present-day military bands. Wieprecht standardizes Prussian army bands. Austrian regimental bands keep a core of 2ob 2cl 2hn 2bn cbn, often with 2tp and b-tb. Wind music by Lucas and Mendelssohn. Born: Brahms, Hartmann. At least 48 operas arranged made for winds.

1840s Revolutions in Berlin, Milan, Naples, Palermo, Paris, Prague and Vienna.

Most military bands are now much bigger (from 35 to over 100 members) than the earlier Harmonien, but the functions and types of music played remain as before. Smaller wind bands continue in rural communities. Saxophone and saxhorns invented. French military bands reformed on German lines.

The Bavarian Court Harmonie ceases. Probable end of the Austrian Imperial Harmonie, reconstituted as the kk Militärkapelle. Some wind music with the earlier configuration is still written for special patriotic church services by F L Schubert. Harmoniemusik continues to flourish at the Augustinian monastery at Brno, encouraged by the enthusiasm of Abbot Napp, and also at Schlawentzitz (the Hohenlohe Harmonie).

Elsner's essay on (Polish) military music classes military music as "chamber music". Wind music by Berlioz and Wagner; smaller works are published by Batiste and Leye. Born: Dvořak, C H Parry, Taffanel. At least 31 opera arrangements for winds.

1850s Vauxhall Gardens closed. Kneller Hall opened as a school for military music. The top UK wind bands become brass bands (Bess o'th'Barns, once Peter Wharton's Brass & Reed Band; Black Dyke, once Clegg's Reed Band, both still top brass bands). The Hohenlohe Harmonie ends. Detmold remains as the only Harmonie which kept for most of the century a configuration close to the earlier Sondershausen band. Lachner's *Octet* and Gounod's *Hymne á Sainte Cécile* composed. Born: d'Indy, Janáček, Roentgen.

1860s American Civil War. Darwin's *Origin of Species;* Karl Marx's *Das Kapital.*

Janáček becomes a chorister in 1865 at the Augustinian Monastery, Brno, just before its Harmonie disbands. The Lippe Harmonie, Detmold, remains active. Many small town bands of Harmonie size remain in the Austrian Empire and in parts of North Italy. Some works (by Cianchi, Mabellini, and others) are published in Italy for conservatory use. Japan opens up to Western military band methods.

Born: Nielsen, Nováček, Pierné, Sibelius, R Strauss.

1870s Custer's Last Stand. Telephone invented.

Parry writes his *Nonet*, a pioneering work in the revival of wind harmony. Taffanel's Société Moderne des Instruments à Vent, an expanded wind quintet. Wind music by Dvořák, Elgar, Raff. Born: Hahn; Holst; Reger; Vaughan Williams.

1880s Taffanel's ensemble strongly influences composers and other ensembles. Wind music by Gounod, Gouvy, R Strauss. Born: Berg, Enesco, Jacob, Villa-Lobos.

1890s Panama, Kiel and Manchester Ship Canals open.

Regular Wind Chamber Music Society concerts at the Royal Academy of Music, London. Nearly 150 named bands in Oxfordshire, probably mostly wind bands; estimates suggest more than 5000 UK brass bands. Enesco hears Romanian wind bands. Wind music by d'Indy, Sibelius. Born: Hindemith; Ibert; Martinů; Milhaud; Poulenc.

Library Sigla

A-Sca   Salzburg: Museum Carolino Augusteum, Bibliothek
A-Wgm   Vienna: Gesellschaft der Musikfreunde in Wien
A-Wn   Vienna: Österreichische Nationalbibliothek, Musiksammling
B-Bc   Brussels, Conservatoire Royale de Musique, Bibliothèque
CH-E   Einsiedeln, Benediktinerkloster
CH-Gpu   Geneva, Bibliothèque Publique et Universitaire de Genève
CZ-B   Bakov nad Jizerou, Pobočka Okresního archivu v Mladé Boleslavi
CZ-Bm   Brno, Moravské Museum, Ustav dějin hudby.
CZ-K   Český Krumlov, Státní Archív Třeboň
CZ-KRa   Kroměříž, Zámecký hudební archív
CZ-Pnm   Prague: Národní Múzeum, hudební oddělení
D-B   Berlin: Staatsbibliothek Preusseischer Kulturbesitz
D-Bds   Berlin: Deutsche Staatsbibliothek (formerly Köningliche Bibliothek;
         Preussische Staatsbibliothek; Öffentliche Wissenschaftliche Bibliothek)
         Musikabteilung. Now being merged with D-B.
D-Dla   Dresden: Staatsarchiv (formerly Sächsisches Landshauptarchiv)
D-DO   Donaueschingen, Fürstlich Fürstenbergische Hofbibliothek
D-DS   Darmstadt: Hessische Landes- und Hochschulbibliothek
D-DÜl   Düsseldorf, Landes- und Staatsbibliothek
D-F   Frankfurt am Main, Stadt- und Universitätsbibliothek
D-HR   Harburg über Donauwörth, Fürstlich Oettingen-Wallerstein'sche Bibliothek
         now in D-Au, Augsburg Universitätsbibliothek
D-Mbs   Munich: Bayerische Staatsbibliothek Musiksammlung
D-Rtt   Regensburg: Fürstlich Thurn und Taxis'sche Hofbibliothek
D-SWl   Schwerin, Wissenschaftliche Allgemeinbibliothek
         (formerly Mecklenburgische Landesbibliothek)
D-Tl   Tübingen, Schwäbisches Landesmusikarchiv (in D-Tmi)
D-Tmi   Tübingen, Musikwissenschaftliches Institut der Universität
D-WEMl   Wertheim am Main, Fürstlich Löwenstein'sche Bibliothek (most of the wind
         music is now in the possession of Jon Gillaspie, GB-Ljag(w))
DK-Kk   Copenhagen: Det Kongelige Bibliotek
F-Pn   Paris: Bibliothèque Nationale (also F-Pc, Conservatoire Nationale de Musique)
GB-Lbl   London: British Library, Music, Manuscript and Reference Libraries
H-Bn   Budapest: National Library, Országos Széchényi Könyvtár
H-KE   Keszthely, Országos Széchényi Könyvtár "Helikon" Könyvtára
I-BGc   Bergamo: Biblioteca civica Angelo Mai
I-BGi   Bergamo: Civico Istituto Musicale "Gaetano Donizetti"
I-Fc   Florence, Conservatorio di Musica "Luigi Cherubini"
I-Mc   Milan, Conservatorio "Giuseppe Verdi"
I-Vsmc   Venice: S Maria della Consolazione detta "Della Fava"
NL-Z   Zeist, Archief van de Evangelische Brodergemeente
PL-LA   Lancut, Biblioteka muzyczna zamku w Lancucie
RF-Sk   St Petersburg: Biblioteka Gosudarstvennoj Konservatorii imeni N A Rimskogo
         Korsakova
S-Skma   Stockholm: Kungliga Musikaliska Akademiens Bibliotek
UKR-Ku   Kiev, University Library
US-BETm Bethlehem, PA, Archives of the Moravian Church, Northern Province

Abbreviations

Individual works also have a unique reference number. Thus, **AXB-1**, given in boldface, would be by a composer whose family name begins with B, and whose first name usually begins with A; AXB is unique to the composer. These numbers provide a cross-reference to the lists in our companion volumes. The works are numbered in decreasing size, grouped and labelled where helpful by a suffix. Thus an arrangement by this composer might be **AXB-1a** (and unrelated to **AXB-1**), a doubtful work **AXB-1d**, a vocal work with winds **AXB-1v** (**AXB-1vt** for a funeral piece), and **AXB-1m** military music.

A	Alto voice	obdam	oboe d'amore
a-	alto (e.g. a-fl, alto flute)	oblig	obligato
Auto	Autograph	oph	ophicleide
B	Bass voice	org	organ
b	(basso) unspecified bass instrument	Pc	Published edition, historical (usually printed, but including early manuscript editions)
b-	bass (e.g. b-cl, b-dr)		
Bar	Baritone voice	perc	percussion
bar-	baritone (e.g. bar-sax)	pf	pianoforte
basso	undefined bass, e.g. bn	pic	piccolo
bc	basso continuo	Pm	Printed edition, modern
bn	bassoon	pn	plate number
bomb	bombardon	quart-	at 4th above/below
bthn	basset horn	quint-	at 5th above
C	Canto (male soprano)	RISM	Répertoire International des Sources Musicales
ca	cor anglais		
cb-	contrabass (e.g. cb-cl)	S	Soprano voice
cbn	contrabassoon	s-	soprano (e.g. s-sax)
cel	celeste	sax	saxophone
cl	clarinet	sd	sine dato (i.e. no date given)
clar	clarino (trumpet)	sd-dr	side drum/snare drum
crt	cornet	serp	serpent
cym	cymbals	sl	sine loco (i.e. no place given)
db	double bass	Sm	Sammelband
dr	drum	sn	sine nomine (i.e. no name given)
euph	euphonium	T	Tenor voice
f./ff.	folio(s)	t-	tenor (e.g. t-sax)
fl	flute	tamb	tambourine
fldam	flauto d'amore	tb	trombone
glock	glockenspiel	terz-	at the 3rd above
gtr	guitar	timp	timpani
harm	harmonium	tp	trumpet
heck	heckelphone	tri	triangle
hn	horn	tu	tuba
hp	harp	vla	viola
hpcd	harpsichord	vc	violoncello
kk	kaiserlich-königlich	vl	violin
M	mezzo soprano	vlne	violone
MS	Manuscript	xyl	xylophone
ob	oboe		

References Abbreviated in the Text

Burney   Charles Burney (edited P A Scholes 1959), *Doctor Burney's Musical Tours in Europe;* Oxford University Press (reprinted 1975 Greenwood Press). It comprises the texts of Burney's 1771 *The Present State of Music in France and Italy* and his 1773 *The Present State of Music in Germany, the Netherlands and the United Provinces.*

Catalog   Jon A Gillaspie, Marshall Stoneham and David Lindsey Clark 1997 *Wind Ensemble Catalog;* Westport, Connecticut: Greenwood Press.

Cobbett   W W Cobbett 1929 *Cyclopaedia of Chamber Music;* Oxford University Press.

Deutsch   O E Deutsch 1966 (translated Eric Blom, Peter Branscombe and Jeremy Noble) *Mozart: A Documentary Biography;* London: A and C Black.

Grove V   (edited Eric Blom) 1961 *Grove's Dictionary of Music and Musicians, Fifth Edition;* London: MacMillan.

New Grove   (edited Stanley Sadie) 1980 *New Grove's Dictionary of Music and Musicians, Sixth Edition;* London: MacMillan.

Hellyer   Roger Hellyer 1973 *Harmoniemusik: Music for Small Wind Band in the Late 18th and Early 19th Centuries;* D Phil Thesis, Oxford University.

HCRL/1-5   H C Robbins Landon *Haydn: Chronicle and Works, Vols 1-5;* London: Thames and Hudson. The volumes are *HCRL/1* 1980 *The Early Years; HCRL/2* 1976 *Haydn at Eszterháza 1766-1790; HCRL/3* 1976 *Haydn in England, 1791-1795; HCRL/4* 1977 *The Years of the Creation 1796-1800; HCRL/5* 1977 *The Late Years 1801-1809.*

MGG 1&2   F Blume (editor) 1949-1986 *Die Musik in Geschichte und Gegenwart;* Kassel.

Mozart Letters   W A Bauer and O E Deutsch (eds) 1962-75 *Mozart: Briefe und Aufzeichnungen;* Kassel: Bärenreiter, 7 vols. See also: *Letters of Mozart and his family,* edited and translated by Emily Anderson 1975; London: Macmillan, 3rd (revised) edition.

Pierre/MF   C Pierre 1899 *Musique des Fêtes et Cérémonies de la Révolution;* Paris: Imprimerie Nationale.

Pierre/HC   C Pierre 1904 *Les Hymnes et Chansons de la Révolution;* Paris: Imprimerie Nationale.

Sainsbury   J Sainsbury 1825 *A Dictionary of Musicians from the Earliest Times;* London (reissued 1966 New York: Da Capo Press).

Salmen   W Salmen (editor) 1971 *Der Sozialstatus der Berufmusikers vom 17. bis 19. Jahrhundert;* Kassel. Translated: H Kaufmann & B Reisner 1983 *The Social Status of the Professional Musician from the Middle Ages to the 19th Century;* New York: Pendragon.

RISM   *Répertoire Internationale des Sources Musicales: Printed Works pre-1800;* 1970 onwards, Kassel: Bärenreiter-Verlag.

Scholes   P A Scholes 1970 (10th edition, edited J O Ward) *Oxford Companion to Music;* London: Oxford University Press.

Thayer   Elliot Forbes 1970 *Thayer's Life of Beethoven Revised and Edited by Elliot Forbes;* Princeton: Princeton University Press.

Weinmann   A Weinmann, various dates, *Beiträge zur Geschichte des Alt-Wiener Musikverlages;* Vienna: Universal Edition.

Weston/CVP   P Weston 1971 *Clarinet Virtuosi of the Past;* London: P Weston.

Weston/MCVP   P Weston 1977 *More Clarinet Virtuosi of the Past;* London: P Weston.

Whistling   Carl Friedrich Whistling 1817 *Handbuch der Musikalien Literatur* with supplements to 1827; Friedrich Hofmeister 1829, 1832 *Supplements* (In Commission bey Anton Meysel: Leipzig). Reissued 1975 New York: Garland Publ Inc.

Whitwell/1-9   D Whitwell 1987-1990 *The History and Literature of the Wind Band and Wind Ensemble Vols 1-9;* Northridge, CA: WINDS.

Dance Movements

The many dance movements found in works for wind bands can be obscure or have several forms. The *Wind Ensemble Thematic Catalog* includes a fuller glossary.

Bolero Spanish dance, related to the polonaise; used by Castil-Blaze and Jadassohn.

Contredanse "Contra Dance: A dance where the dancers of the different sexes stand opposite each other, instead of side by side" (1811 *Dictionary of the Vulgar Tongue;* reprinted 1984 London: Bibliophile Books). *Scholes* disagrees. Dittersdorf, Süssmayr and others write *contra*danse; Mozart and others use *contre*danse; usually in 2/4 time.

Cotillion/Cotillon J C Bach's 4th *Wind Symphony,* has an attractive example. "Cotillon" means petticoat, but the dance was more genteel than suggestive.

Ecossaise Similar to the contredanse and to the Czech polka. There are no verified links with Scotland. Beethoven wrote an *Ecossaise* for winds, WoO 22.

Englese (Anglaise, Inglese) Any brisk dance in duple time, similar to a cotillon, and without obvious English character; as used in Vincenc Mašek's *Partita* **VVM-27**.

Furiant Swaggerers' Dance, in 3/4 or 6/8, usually vivace, and with cross-rhythms, e.g. the splendid Trio of the second movement of Dvořák's *Serenade,* and Vanhal, **JKV-1**.

Gavotte A slowish dance in 4/4 (sometimes 4/8 or 2/4), often starting on the third beat. Common in neo-classical music, like Strauss's Op 4, but also in Mozart's K.240.

Gigue (Jig) Some jigs are modern in idiom, as in Goddard's *Fanfare, Romance and Jig,* but most are neo-classical (in 6/8 or 12/8), cf. Ibert's *Concerto for cello and wind.*

Ländler Rural ancestor of the waltz, based on a dance from Styria, Bavaria and Bohemia. Usually in 3/8 or 3/4; often slower than the Viennese waltz. Examples are found in Mozart's *Gran Partita* and the sextet attributed to Krommer, **FVK-1d**.

Minuet (usually Menuetto in German areas, and Menuet in France) The 3/4 minuet exists in two forms. That dating from the early 18th century is gay and fast, but with three beats in a bar. The dignified dance appeared later; it often had aristocratic associations. A contrasting trio (or "alternativo") is common; many early wind works have trios for 2ob bn alone. Sometimes there are two trios, as in Mozart's *Gran Partita.*

Musette Like a gavotte, for which it was often used as a trio, often with a drone mimicking the small French bagpipe of the same name. Sibelius uses a musette for winds in his *King Christian Suite.*

Polonaise (Polacca, Poloneso, but not polka!) A Polish 3/4 dance introduced to Germany during the partitions of Poland in the 18th century. Like the March and the Minuet, two main forms exist. The slow stately dance is found in Haydn's **FJH-9**. The fast version is noted for its cross-rhythms. Good examples appear in the first movement of Mozart's K.252 and in the superb finale of Krommer's Op 57 *Parthia.*

Polka A Czech dance in 2/4 popular from the 1820s. The finale (mis-named "Rondo") to Krommer's Op 69 *Parthia* is an early polka.

Reel Scottish dance, usually fast and in duple time and in two strains, each repeated with decoration. Schetky's Reels are in a collection with Airs and Strathspeys.

Siciliana A slowish 6/8 or 12/8 dance, often in a minor key and often pastoral in spirit. Examples: Mozart's K.252, Handel's *Music for the Royal Fireworks.*

Strathspey A Scottish dance of moderate tempo (slower than a reel), often in duple time and using the "Scotch snap" rhythm. Examples by Schetky date from around 1800.

Tango An Argentinian dance (perhaps with African roots) which spread to Europe via France. Popular particularly after it was denounced by the Vatican in 1914.

Waltz This dance in triple time became especially popular early in the 19th century. Mozart's *Gran Partita* and one of Mayr's sextets contain examples. A letter in *The Times* of 16 July 1816 referred to the waltz as "indecent."

Facts and Myths

Wind Harmony (Harmoniemusik): Music for small wind band including pairs of wind instruments, typically an octet (2ob 2cl 2hn 2bn), or sextet (2ob 2hn 2bn; the 2cl 2hn 2bn ensemble was adopted earlier than the octet and, for many purposes, outlasted the octet). The genre is distinct from works for large wind bands or works for solo winds (including the wind quintet of fl ob cl hn bn). There is a vast body of music for this genre (our lists identify some 12,000 surviving works), including much well-written, unknown music, by over 2400 composers and arrangers, known and unknown.

Wind Harmony Bands were sponsored from all parts of society from around 1750 onwards: royal courts; courts of the nobility; churches large and small; civic bands and those of places of entertainment; military bands. At the critical period, around 1800, there were several thousand wind harmony bands in Europe. This range of support gave wind harmony music special social links in a rapidly changing society. Part 1 of our book describes the context of wind harmony and its various forms in different parts of the world. It gives examples of where and when it was played, and how it fits into other developments in music.

Wind Harmony has wide links across music: to the major areas of classical music (opera and the symphony), to early entertainment music (e.g., the waits), to the military (both early bands and recent bands), to the church, the theater, and to courts and ceremony. Wind harmony was at its peak when mainstream music was changing in many ways, and when instruments and instrumental technique were evolving rapidly. Part 3 of our book describes these technical changes.

Wind Harmony Music falls into six main groups: (i) "Parthias," serenade music for various purposes (perhaps 2500 surviving examples), (ii) Arrangements, usually of operas (an industry in itself; we know of nearly 2000 surviving examples), (iii) Marches and other military music (several thousand surviving examples), (iv) Religious music (several thousand surviving items), (v) many isolated movements, typically dances, and (vi) the wide range of modern music for wind harmony, some in exotic forms.

Our book also comments on some of the common myths:

Myth 1: Only court bands played wind harmony. Probably the main purchasers of wind harmony at its zenith were military bands. Many other bands played wind music, including those in pleasure gardens and the like, town bands and those associated with monasteries and churches.

Myth 2: Court bands developed from military bands. Players often were members of both civil and military bands. The two types of band had common origin, rather than one evolving into the other.

Myth 3: Only composers like Mozart and a few court composers wrote wind harmony. Of the many composers whose works we list, only a minority of those born before 1850 held court appointments. Some were professional arrangers. Part 2 of our book gives biographical information on many of these composers and arrangers.

Myth 4: Hardly anyone listened to wind music except as background music. Entertainment was a major aim, certainly. Yet there was plenty of serious music. The arrangements were also a means to become acquainted with the greatest music.

Myth 5: The genre disappeared c.1820. Much continued after 1820, though other forms evolved, like brass bands.

Myth 6: There was no "music industry" until after the genre had vanished. The arrangements industry 1800-1820 is a classic example of commercialization.

Part 1
THE PHENOMENON OF WIND HARMONY

1

Common Ground:
Music for All Occasions

WIND BANDS WORLDWIDE AND THEIR SETTINGS

In many cultures, from the Far East via the Himalayas to the Indian subcontinent, from Africa to the Andes, from North America to Europe, wind bands are found at the center of celebrations, ceremonies, and funerals. All of these cultures recognized how effective the sound of wind bands can be. Most of what we shall term *wind harmony* dates from the three-quarters of a century between Bach's death in 1750 and the death of Weber in 1826. Its peak matched the zenith of a conservative aristocracy and the growing intellectual enlightenment of the Age of Reason. The Napoleonic Wars and the Industrial Revolution brought change. Tastes shifted to larger bands, to public music instead of music at court, and to exhibitions of virtuosity which easily tended to excess.

Composers in the classical tradition knew how well wind groups sounded in the open air, whether in the everyday performances of the brass music in 16th-century Germany, the wind music of the English Waits, or Handel's compositions for grand occasions. Some wind music was written to divert, some for marching, and some to augment those occasions for which extravagant pageantry was essential, whether to welcome an Imperial visit or to precede "a large Cargo of Malahyde Oysters ... brought into the City in Grand Procession" (1). Some works for winds show the same serious intent as any symphony. Wind harmony had wide influence. Compositions were often in the vanguard of woodwind technique, and the scoring and rich sound soon reached the opera house and the concert hall. The recent revival of classical and modern wind harmony by professionals and amateurs testifies to its character. Its composers aimed to please both audience and players. Players spread the composer's reputation; an appreciative listener might provide the next commission (2). Many commissions were for specific occasions, and the reasons for composition can give a novel view of the period and how composers worked. Yet a look through modern eyes alone would mislead, so even the brief contemporary comments which we shall quote can be illuminating.

The wide appeal of wind bands bridged cultures within nations too, such as the gap between the serious and the popular. Today one has this week's popular music, soon to be forgotten, and standard classics which dominate public concerts of serious music. Two hundred years ago it was rare to hear works of previous generations: the greatest works could be ephemeral. Yet even the most serious-minded composers wrote music to entertain: works with titles like *Divertimento, Parthia, Harmonie, Serenade* and *Notturno*. Urban Europeans spending their evenings at pleasure gardens expected music. Bands of players were heard at formal meals at any well-appointed Court. Such music for pleasure could be heard in all kinds of places, from royal palaces to windswept streets. It was played by musicians from all social classes: royal amateurs (3), virtuoso Bohemians (e.g. *Burney* vol 2 p 133), and charity school orphans playing to demonstrate their musical training (*Burney* vol 2 pps 52-54).

WHAT IS WIND HARMONY? SCORINGS AND NOMENCLATURE

Much of what we call *wind harmony* is for two or more pairs of winds: oboes, clarinets, horns, and bassoons. Sometimes these were joined by other woodwinds, brass or percussion; at times one or more string players were added. In France and the German-speaking countries, this music came to be known as *Harmonie,* from the euphonious blending of the wind timbres. In Italy, the corresponding term is *Armonia.* We adopt the phrase *wind harmony,* though the term did not really take root in the English-speaking countries. The term *Harmonie* is more specific than wind band, and is not simply military music. A survey of some five hundred Viennese wind works from 1782 to 1825 (4) suggested that *Harmonie* referred only to the standard octet, with different words *(Tafelmusik* or *Blasorchester)* for other configurations. However, Viennese vocabulary was not typical, perhaps partly because the conservative Viennese only made the move from sextets to octets in the 1780s, after many other places had done so. The term *Harmonie* is used for larger bands in the 19th century (e.g., Mendelssohn, Op 24) and earlier for small ensembles (*Forest Harmony, ... a Collection of the most Celebrated Aires, Minuets and Marches; Together with several Curious Pieces out of the Water Musick, made on purpose for two FRENCH HORNS By the Greatest Masters. N.B. These Aires may be play'd on two German Flutes, two Trumpets, or two Violins ...* [GB-Lbl, b.4]). Our own examination of titles in Bohemian and Moravian archives suggests no special distinctions according to ensemble size.

We have looked at the titles of over 2,000 works from the main period of wind harmony, omitting arrangements and straightforward marches. While numbers are inevitably imprecise (a title may not show that the work is really an arrangement; some titles refer to collections and others to single movements; titles from publishers' lists may differ from printed titles) the statistics lead to striking conclusions. We have looked at both the general form of title (so *Parthia* includes all spellings, e.g., *Partita, Barthia)* and qualified forms like *partitta di campagna.* Listed numbers are not exclusive, so *Suite d'harmonie* is included under both key words. For Europe as a whole, and so dominated by Austro-Hungary, Bohemia, and the German states, 1479 of the sample of 2440 use the title *Parthia* or something similar; 242 are called *Divertimento,* 114 *Suite,* and 104 *Harmonie.* For France, of 220 works sampled, 101 are called *Suite,* 38 *Divertimento,* 20 *Harmonie,* and 17 *Symphonie.* The 67 works from Great Britain use the word *Military* in the title in 55 cases, *Divertimento* for 23 cases, and 34 are called *Concerto.* The French used *parthia* very rarely (even then with possible German links) and the British not at all; the German use of *Stücke* (pieces) is rare. Overall, *Parthia* and its equivalents dominate the German states, Austria and their ex-dominions. Turning to specific forms of title, the modern forms are *Parthie* (German), *Partita* (Italian), and *Partie* (French). All mean a suite or group of movements, rather than the various alternative meanings. We have encountered 16 basic forms (54 forms when prefixes and other descriptive phrases are counted, like *Partia ala camera* [sic] or *Feldparthie.* The commonest additions are those indicating indoor nature (such as *alla camera*; 22 cases) or outdoor character (*Feld-, di campagna, pastoralis* (5), and the like; 43 cases). Of the original 1,479 examples, ignoring these prefixes or qualifications, we find 961 cases close to the modern German form, 414 cases close to the modern Italian form (*Partita* 153, *Partitta* 261) and 104 close to the modern French (*Partia* 66, *Partie*

38, though few seem to be French works, since the French preferred *Suite* or *Pièces,* just as the British chose *Pieces).* One rare but evocative British term is *Night Pieces* (the scoring is strictly outside our range: James Oswald's 1758 *Forty Airs for Two Violins, German Flutes, or Guittars [sic]. Consisting of Tattoo's [sic] Night Pieces & Marches as They Are Perform'd in the Hessian and Prussian Armies).* The French *Nocturne* is rare as well (Vern; also G F Fuchs, a German), but the German *Nachtmusik* is more common, and there are 55 *Notturnos.*

What works do we include? Many works we mention are ensembles close to the standard octet of two oboes, two clarinets, two horns and two bassoons. The commonest ensembles are for pairs of clarinets and horns, with one or two bassoons; the best known works are the octets for 2ob 2cl 2hn 2bn. Where do we set the limits? For larger works, we usually omit those with more than 18 players, which allows us the big Strauss works (16 players) and the wind ensemble of a standard orchestra (2fl 2ob 2cl 2bn cbn 2tp 4hn 3tb tu). For smaller works, we exclude those which lack pairs of instruments, notably wind quintets (fl ob cl hn bn), and usually ignore those for fewer than 4 players. We are aware of a further unnamed subgenre of wind harmony, which we term *half-harmony.* Scored for single wind instruments to give the impression that pairs of instruments are being used, such works are distinct from those wind trios, quartets and quintets which emphasize the contrast rather than the blend of timbres. We include works for wind harmony and voices. Most of the vocal works in our lists were for the Church; much was written for revolutionary regimes, when substitutes for religion were needed; a few works were written for secular or military settings.

What works do we leave out? First, we omit works for large wind bands. This is not simple. A Sousa march is certainly different from Stravinsky's *Symphonies of Wind Instruments,* but what about Holst's *Suites* for Military Band? Both *Suites* are carefully scored, free from the indiscriminate doublings of many wind band works. Here we must make a subjective judgement. Secondly, there are small works for winds. We have consciously omitted all but a few wind quintets. But again, some works raise difficulties. When d'Indy writes for fl ob 2cl hn 2bn, his approach allows us to include it with little hesitation. When Janáček writes for fl ob cl b-cl hn bn, we use our authors' prerogative to include it, not least because a regular wind ensemble might wish to keep *Mládí* in its repertoire. Our concern rests primarily on the work's particular sense of ensemble. In wind harmony, one is aware of both the pairings of instruments and the relation between pairings. The blend of instruments typifies the sound of wind harmony. Some works which lie outside our guidelines (less than one percent of the total considered) are useful as context, and are mentioned in the biographies.

Scale: How much of wind harmony music was there? It is tempting to believe that little was written beyond the well-known works by Mozart and Beethoven, and that what was written was all for world-class ensembles in imperial courts. Both views are wrong. Our lists of music include some 12,000 works by over 2,200 composers; from this and other information, it is clear that many hundreds of wind bands bought this music. The numbers of these bands increased steadily in the late 18th century, with more rapid growth as armies were mobilized. Numbers of bands declined as armies went to war or were disbanded. Commercial practice matched demand with many hundreds of wind arrangements of operas, ballets and symphonies. Sometimes the editions were large. On 15 February 1794, the Comité de Salut public in Paris approved funds to provide 550 copies of collections of music "pour servir dans les fêtes civiques"; later that year, funds for 12,000 copies were provided (6). Such cases were exceptional. Printed parts took over from manuscript in the early 19th century, which made economic sense only for sales of more than 50-150 copies. Such numbers are consistent with the list of 41 subscribers for the *10 Märsche* CYF-1m published by Carl Fischer in the 1830s (7).

Who bought printed wind music?   The markets for wind music point to the place of wind bands in society. At the top were court bands of the best musicians available. Such bands gave concerts, played for entertainment and for court functions; a few may have had military duties too. Almost without exception, the finest wind works were written for these ensembles. We do not know for whom Mozart's greatest works were written, but he could draw on a pool of outstanding professionals. But sales to court bands, especially in Great Britain, could never have justified printed editions. Beneath the top ensembles were wind bands of the pleasure gardens and the better regimental bands. Entertainment was the full-time task of civilian musicians, and took much of the time of military musicians too. Collectively, officers could afford bands beyond their personal resources, and they could afford to purchase a wide range of music. Many arrangements of popular operas were intended for them. Such bands correspond more to today's better dance bands, reproducing "hits" rather than creating music, and catering for popular taste with recognizable music which does not demand the sustained attention of the listener. The remaining markets for printed music were talented amateurs, town and church bands, and bands of the lesser regiments and militia. For them, the music had to be both enjoyable and technically practical, criteria which can conspire against the writing of great music. Overall, regimental bands seem to have been the major purchasers of wind music around 1800. This had wide implications, not least because peace brought the dispersal and loss of their musical archives.

Who supplied wind music? Commercial perspectives and publishing industry.   The music trade took over from music patronage as wind harmony was evolving. In earlier days, many bands used locally-prepared material only, perhaps marches arranged from piano scores; indeed, such scores were often written in C to make arrangement easy. As sophistication grew, so did cooperation: agents ensured that the better material was sent to friends or associated bands. Haydn's music was circulated in the early 1760s; we know of von Beecke's role at Oettingen-Wallerstein and of Pichl's role as agent for Eszterháza (8). Important changes followed. "Publishers" provided music, sometimes as agents, sometimes in manuscript copied to order from a single house copy, sometimes simply pirated. These publishers issued lists of what was for sale. Whistling's collations of lists for the Frankfurt Book Fair from 1817 to 1827 were a natural consequence. The next stage was especially significant. From the 1780s, it had been realized that regular issues encouraged regular purchasers, and were good commercial practice, whether or not payment was prepaid or on receipt. "Journals" of wind music could succeed whenever the market was big enough and uniform enough to support the large regular issues which customers wanted. What were the advantages? There was a guaranteed market once a subscription was paid; there were savings on distribution costs; publication could be made a more continuous process; above all, the customers paid for some works which they might not have bought separately, so the income was greater. In the three decades from 1800, a number of journals started, then ceased, whether from lack of business skills or as a result of the instability and turmoil in Europe.

British bands around 1800 (9-14) offer an important area of study. Much of the printed music is still accessible because of the early copyright deposit laws. The market for wind music was largely self-contained. Sales overseas seem to have been negligible, and very little British band music of this period is found in archives outside the British Isles. There can be little doubt that most printed wind music in Britain at this time was aimed at the military market and its priorities. Camus (14) gives dates of origin and configurations for about 60 British infantry bands in the period 1775-1785. Our own lists of surviving wind music, mainly printed between 1790 and 1810, include works naming about 40 militia bands. Other sources (like marches which survive only for piano) suggest that there were at least 20-30 further militia bands during the Napoleonic period. With the bands of the regular army (including the cavalry and artillery), the number of British military wind bands must have been as high as 100-150. This number is not well defined, for some bands may have come together only for specific occasions, and others may have been civilian bands, like the waits, playing under a different name. These 100-150 bands formed a market for printed band music which lasted for several decades. Some music, like Busby's marches (1798-1801) and Dibdin's *War Songs* (1803-1804), appeared as journals, which ceased when peace or fighting intervened.

The same principles held in France and Austria, though the records are less complete. Wars in Europe dispersed or destroyed many continental libraries, so we know of some material only from catalogs or advertizements. Journals flourished early in France from the 1770s; in the Austrian Empire, Triebensee was a pioneer with his 1803 series. Some of series were printed, others were only in manuscript. Again, a printed version would be uneconomical unless 100 copies or more were sold, so top court wind bands could not have been the sole market. Printing gave other gains. Steiner's 1810 *Journal für neunstimmige Harmonie* observed "The arrangements for wind instruments will all be made from the original scores with special care and detailed knowledge of instrumental effectiveness by famous and acknowledged masters. Their price will amount to a maximum of a half of that of the works in manuscript. Further, these printed editions will have particular advantages over the manuscript editions in respect of their correctness: the close and careful proofreading that can be undertaken with engraved copies under the direction of the composer himself is simply unthinkable with multiple copies, as each copy would demand such exacting and diligent effort as no composer could exercise on every proofreading."

WIND HARMONY IN THE MUSICAL SCENE

Wind Harmony and the Mainstream of Music. The golden age of wind harmony at the end of the 18th century coincided with major developments both in instruments and in the structure of the orchestra (15-18). The instruments became both more refined and more flexible technically. Musical forms changed: the suite, a set of contrasting dance-derived movements, was superseded by the symphony; the concerto grosso gave way to the solo concerto; the trio sonata developed into the string quartet. Changes in content matched changes in form. Polyphony became less important as sonata forms developed which exploited the contrasts between different keys. Wind harmony straddles this musical revolution, and has features of both earlier and later periods. Many divertimentos included dance movements, and many of them had more movements than contemporary symphonies or quartets. Yet individual movements adopted later compositional styles, consistent with a title like *Symphony*. Some of the developments in wind music parallel those in orchestral music; others point to different functions, whether as a source of color in the theater, a part of church ceremony, or a relaxing background for court and pleasure garden. By long-accepted practice, the same music could be used for major stage works and small entertainment works; thus Handel's five-movement *Overture in D,* basically a serenade, anticipates his famous *Arrival of the Queen of Sheba* from *Solomon.*

Demand for wind harmony rose rapidly in the 1780s, when even small courts could afford a modest ensemble. The rise continued in the 1790s as armies were formed, but less often deployed. Composers born in the mid-18th century were at the height of their powers when wind music was most sought after. Players and publishers alike turned their hands to writing. Some of this music is, to be charitable, very modest. Yet much is well constructed, elegantly written and imaginative. It may lack the originality and power of Haydn or Mozart, but compares favorably with many symphonies by codifiers of the classical movement, rather than its innovators.

Wind harmony encouraged imaginative instrumental writing instead. Special effects like echoes (used by composers such as Asplmayr, Druschetzky, Hoffmeister, d'Ordoñez, Seyfried and Triebensee) probably seemed highly original. New ideas in the use of wind instruments cross-fertilized genres: the new sounds of wind harmony influenced opera and, in turn, the new dramatic operatic styles affected wind harmony. Mozart's writing for winds and, later, Weber's sensuous melodies and characteristic orchestral wind color must have seemed a revelation to listeners. The impact can be heard in works for full orchestra too. Typically, a few percent of the playing time of orchestral works is for winds alone. Apart from stage bands in opera, there are three main forms In one form, often chorales, the winds can suggest an organ or wordless choir more than a wind band. Examples range from the *Introduzione,* a separate movement in the choral version of Haydn's *Seven Last Words,* to Berg's *Violin Concerto* (3cl b-cl), Raff's *5th Symphony,* many of Mahler's symphonies (usually brass chorales) and perhaps the deeply-felt slow section near the end of Beethoven's *3rd Symphony.* Marches are a second form, as in the finale of Beethoven's *9th Symphony,* Hindemith's *Symphonia Serena* and the *Scherzo* of Vaughan Williams's *8th Symphony.* The third form adopts the wind harmony sound itself. This can be heard in Haydn's symphonies Hob I:42, 55 and 84, in Mozart's *Piano Concerto* K.482, and in later works like the *Musette* from Sibelius' *King Christian Suite,* the little waltz in Act I of Richard Strauss's *Der Rosenkavalier,* and in several works by Brahms: the opening of his *St Antony Variations,* the slow movement of his *Violin Concerto,* and the *Minuet No 1* of his *Serenade in D,* Op 11.

Issues of Quality: Why Are There So Few Masterpieces?   Since so much wind music was written, why are there so few works recognised as masterpieces, comparable with the best symphonies and quartets? Technical limitations of early instruments are not the reason, for there were exceptional virtuosos. Nor is it simply that most wind music was meant to entertain a casual listener. Perhaps one expects too much. Carse (16) asks how many symphonies it takes to produce a good one, and concludes that it requires hundreds. On this scale, our 12,000 works should yield 60 really good ones. There are certainly tens of very good works, many little-known. Yet, in judging them, one should remember that "art" and "greatness" are the province of the critic, and "entertainment" in all its forms, including uplifting the spirit (be it humanist or religious), is the concern of the composer. Writing music was the way composers chose to make their living, and artistic "immortality" is a concept less than two centuries old. In the great period of wind harmony, most active composers wrote music which they hoped would appeal to their time, rather than music to appeal to all times.

The Pick: Composers of Quality.   Of all those who wrote wind harmony before the mid 19th century, a few composers and arrangers (Haydn, Mozart, Krommer, Triebensee, Went, G F Fuchs and Sedlak) stand out above all the others. Later wind harmony is less well defined, with Richard Strauss one of the few composers writing more than a single distinctive work. Mozart's achievement is unrivalled. He was the first composer to realize the potential of the then-new wind instruments, the sheer beauty of sound, the range of expression, the variety of tone, and the blend of the sound of winds with each other and with the human voice. Haydn was a pioneer, not the first to write wind harmony, but one of the first to bring real originality to the genre. The vitality of his fast movements, and the serenity and nostalgia of his slower ones, make his music remarkable for its time. Haydn's works were written for pairs of oboes, horns and bassoons, before the clarinet had found its proper role; Krommer's music was written when wind harmony for full octet and contrabassoon was at its zenith. His music shares with Haydn's a verve and a robust and earthy character, but owes much to the maturity that Mozart brought to this music. His mature works are strikingly novel, and are far from being simple background music relying on elegance. He even exploits surprise: no sooner is a mood established than the listener is startled by an unexpected modulation or change in dynamics, or by a movement appearing to start with a closing cadence. Haydn, Mozart and Krommer all wrote excellent *wind* music. Good music arranged for wind may not be good wind music. The idiomatic use of wind harmony as a proper medium in its own right characterizes the best wind music. There is a great gulf between the composers who achieved this and the hacks who seem to have regarded the octet as a poor substitute for the orchestra or the organ. What makes Went, Triebensee and Sedlak special is that their arrangements are imaginative transformations of works. In their works, the wit, the drama, or the nobility of the original emerges once more.

Wind Harmony: The Crop.   Social pleasures, not just musical fashion, helped to shape wind harmony, so there are many pieces worth exploring, even if few are masterpieces. Works by well-known composers can show the roots of their greater achievements. Many lesser-known composers left reminders that the famous did not write all that is worth hearing. Some such pieces are by composers, like Mayr, who had substantial influence on the development of music; other composers had little influence on anyone else at all. Yet all of them, minor and major alike, helped to fulfil the demand for wind harmony. What was published was a pale reflection of what existed, but does show what sorts of pieces could be expected to sell, and how successful such pieces were. The earlier composers, typically those born before 1730, tended to write suites of simple movements which, while lacking the complexity of counterpoint or the scale of sonata form, often prove unpretentious and pleasant. Such unsophisticated works could be used equally well by the military, by a church band, or at a formal dinner. Such versatility encouraged a move away from a basso continuo and, by this change, the link between wind harmony and the baroque was weakened. Here the influence of Johann Stamitz was particularly far-reaching. As Einstein remarks (19, p 121), the leadership in the development of both the symphony and sonata form left France when Stamitz moved from Paris to Mannheim. Stamitz's personal approach to wind music, combined with the freshness and simple directness of melody favored by South German and Austrian composers, provided the key to what became the classical serenade style.

Opera and the Arrangements Industry.   Opera flourished throughout the major period of wind harmony, and points to three links between the modest-sized wind bands and the most expensive of arts. First, wind writing devised for wind harmony found its way into opera orchestral scoring. Stage wind bands became common. Secondly, many players in opera orchestras were also members of wind ensembles. Thirdly, as the arrangements industry developed, the best tunes from the latest operas could be heard by a wider audience or appreciated in social contexts other than their original one.

Arrangements for wind harmony increased in importance from the 1770s, and stayed significant until World War 1. They dominated the French market from 1770, and gained similar importance in the Austrian Empire by the 1790s. Arrangements made it possible to disseminate works which otherwise might have been heard rarely in smaller towns, if at all. Arrangements made it possible to perform works in a wide range of settings and for equally diverse audiences. When wind harmony was at its peak (1775-1830), composers and publishers drew little distinction was made between original works and arrangements. Even Beethoven may have supervised Sedlak's arrangement of *Fidelio.* The best arrangers, like Fuchs, Went, Triebensee, Sedlak, Starke and Scholl, produced works with the depth and excitement of the originals. Less able musicians produced transcriptions, possibly redeemed by the quality of the original music. Large-scale works would be published in piano reduction and other arrangements: wind ensemble, string quartet, duets for flutes or violins, guitar, and various exotic scorings. The Archduke of Tuscany's collection in Florence (I-Fc) includes many cases for which there is a wind band arrangement as well as a string quartet version.

The Surviving Arrangements.   We have analysed data for some 677 arrangements for wind harmony from our lists. The sample includes 551 operas, 83 ballets and 43 symphonies arranged. Overall, output peaked in the period 1790-1820. Opera arrangements rose rapidly in the late 1770s, peaked in the 1790s and fell off after 1840. Ballet arrangements peaked later, in the first decade of the 19th century, disappearing after the 1820s. Why did people want arrangements at all? One reason why opera arrangements were wanted is much the same as the reason for wanting serenades and not just symphonies: people want to be entertained. Opera arrangements were especially popular because they often contained the best tunes. They were needed too when the opera was simply not available. Thus Verdi's *La forza del destino* reached England in a brass band arrangement five years before a British performance of the opera itself. Arrangements helped people to get to know an opera, to remember it, or to hear it from another angle, just as Liszt's reminiscences of operas are still played.

   Why were some famous operas never arranged? Now-forgotten successes like Holzbauer's *Günther von Schwarzburg* were never arranged. There is only one Haydn opera arrangement, despite the fame of his operas for Eszterháza. Perhaps this was because they were written in the wrong decade, before the peak in the 1790s. Timing may explain why Mozart's *La Clemenza di Tito* is his most arranged opera, yet certainly not his most popular. Other operas may have been written in the wrong place, away from the major arrangers; still others may have been arranged and lost.

How Did the Arrangements Relate to What Was Arranged?   Journals of wind harmony point to a demand for music to give pleasure, and especially music which transformed the best tunes from theaters into high-quality divertimentos. Such transformation needs skill: the musicianship needed to provide good entertainment music is rare. It is one thing to arrange a single especially popular item, quite another to make an effective suite of ten or twenty pieces. Several features emerge from the many examples we have studied. First, the order of movements of the original may be changed, and sometimes caused the arranger some trouble. A fascinating example is to be found in CZ-K, where Asplmayr's *La sposa Persiana* is found in both its original form and in an arrangement (probably by Went). The arrangement starts with No 10 of the original and, while many of the items which follow are in broadly the original order, there are other displaced movements. Several movements are linked ("Segue") in the new version, and the closing movements show obvious thought and reorganization. Secondly, even if the movements are in the same order, their emphasis may change. Almost all the dramatic sections are omitted in Triebensee's arrangement of Mozart's *Don Giovanni,* notably Don Giovanni's spectacular demise. Yet some of the most complex parts - like the three orchestras playing three different dances simultaneously - are arranged very effectively. Audiences for the wind music were happy to hear virtuoso display, less so to follow a drama. This means that keys can be altered, often to C, presumably to reduce demands on horn players' stamina. Mozart's *Don Giovanni* is of special interest because it includes wind harmony within the opera. Some composers, like Went, were happy to rearrange this wind music; others, like Triebensee, ignore it, concentrating on other parts of the opera. Thirdly, several different works may be combined. No version of Haydn's *Symphony No 102* uses the original slow movement (Hoboken is wrong on this point). Probably the movement's subtle rhythm was considered unplayable by most wind bands; one wonders whether orchestras substituted an easier slow movement too. Fourthly, there are cases where works by more than one composer are intermixed. These include opera and ballet pastiches. An interesting example is an arrangement of Bianchi's *La villanella rapita,* where Mozart's *Symphony No 32* (K.318) appears as the Overture. The interest lies in the fact that Mozart's *Symphony* was indeed used in opera houses as an overture to Bianchi's opera: the wind arrangement simply reflects operatic practice. Similarly, Angelica Catalani's insertion of music by Rode in Rossini's *Il Barbiere di Siviglia* appears in the wind version. An arrangement can be based on a version of a work not now familiar. Thus Druschetzky's arrangement of Mozart's K.455 *Variations on Unser dummer Pöbel meint* may be based on a now-lost version of these variations (20). Finally, there are Potpourris, the medleys of tunes strung together without reference to the original order, and often with tunes from several works.

Developments from 1870 to the Present. There is a watershed in the better-known music for winds in the mid-19th century. This gap is more apparent than real. Much wind harmony continued to be written, but it moved into conservatories as the new forms, like brass bands, created their own public audiences. From about 1870, a new generation of composers emerged: Mabellini, Raff, Dvořák, Parry, Strauss, Gounod, and others. The ensemble expanded: flutes, contrabassoon, and extra horns were added to match contemporary orchestral wind sections. The intention to entertain remained; happily, bombast, regrettably common in later romantic works, is far less prevalent in wind music. Suites and symphonic structures were preferred to the latest fashions in serious music, at times with an almost anachronistic sense of elegance. Nationalism and neoclassicism emerged, as did more widespread uses of the wind ensemble with soloists or choirs and in theater music. Other changes stem from the demise of the aristocratic patron, the rising cult of the soloist, and broader problems of identity in modern music.

MILITARY AND CIVIL WIND HARMONY: COMMON ORIGINS

Private and Public Music. Wind harmony was heard occasionally in concert halls in the 18th century. Public concerts were a small part of the musical scene at first, though their popularity grew rapidly (21). The sound of wind instruments, outdoors, on a fine evening was enjoyed throughout Europe. Music to be heard at dinner was a common pleasure, both indoors and out. Favored guests at Eszterháza (8 p 218) and elsewhere were awakened by wind music. On visiting Württemberg in the 1760s, Baron von Wimpffen wrote (22) "Amid pleasures we went to sleep; amid pleasures we awoke. Two separate bands of music gave the signal to rise." Military bands matched their civilian counterparts. In Leipzig in 1726 "Every morning the hautboists perform a little morning music [ein Morgen-Liedgen] in front of the officers' quarters, a march which they enjoy, an overture [Entrée] and a few minuets, for which the commander has a special liking" (23). Standard bugle calls, evolving at the same time, offered a ruder awakening, though even these sounds would have been gentler than the impact of a pipe band at dawn (24).

Military Music.   Military music (9-14, 25, 26) is not the direct by-product of wind harmony, nor is wind harmony a civilian derivative of military music. The two forms have common origins, common sponsors, and a shared community of musicians who contributed to both forms. In the 18th century, J C Bach's marches could, and did, fit naturally into his *Wind Symphonies.* Handel's two fine *Arias* are clearly "military music." Whether they were written for the changing of the guard at St James's Park, for inclusion in stage works, or as typically English "military divertimentos" (27 p 135) is not clear. Handel's famous march from *Scipio* (9, 10) is rumored to have been written first as a parade march for the Grenadier Guards, and the equally famous "See, the Conquering Hero Comes" from *Joshua* (inserted in later editions of *Judas Maccabeus)* became a popular band work soon after it was written. Popular soldiers' songs, often played by bands (28, 29), had connections to stage music of the same sort, including Purcell's "Britons, Strike Home!" from *Bonduca.*

Military bands and wind harmony took somewhat different directions in the 19th century. The military bands expanded their brass sections. New and original music evolved, with impressive works from Sousa, Alford, Fučik and others. Some parallels continued. Military band concerts still included arrangements of classical symphonies; public demand ensured yet more arrangements of operas and musical shows. But differences are marked: Richard Strauss's marches are wholly distinct from his wind harmony music, and it is very hard to conceive a march which would fit comfortably with Stravinsky's *Symphonies of Wind Instruments*, though Stravinsky might just have managed it for the right fee. Successful civilian bands changed in much the same way as the military bands. In England, the Stalybridge Old Band started in 1814 with 2cl bn and percussion, growing later that year to 4fl 4cl 2hn 2bn tp bugle-hn b-hn serp perc; by 1848 it was all brass: 2hn 6crt 2bugles 2tb b-tb 2bar tu oph bomb perc. Examples of the many links between military and civil wind bands center on four main issues to which we shall return: Who paid? Who played? Who taught them? What did they play?

Who Paid for It? Why Did They Think They Needed It?   Who paid the band? Often the same source - whether an individual noble, or a civic council - would have both the obligation to raise a force on demand and the wish to provide musical entertainment. If both needs could be met by a single band, economics and quality could both benefit. Even today, military bands are frequent performers in public parks. Whenever standing armies were small, and the raising of armies was a responsibility of privilege (30), both musicians and soldiers would be a matter of keen concern to the one who paid the bill. Many early wind bands were expected to play for the regiments of their employers. Only patrons as wealthy as Prince Nicolaus Esterházy the Magnificent could afford separate horn players for his hunt, his military band, and his serenade music. For others, a single wind sextet might have to fulfil every function. Yet one should not assume that music was only commissioned for the great. We have been struck by how much music was written for the funerals of private citizens in Bohemia and Moravia.

At least two monarchs standardized their bands throughout their realms. In 1670, Louis XIV of France formed a band of 2ob taille bn perc (31); this grouping proved to be so effective that even as late as 1747 J S Bach wrote a march *Pour la Première Garde du Roy* (32) for a group differing only in having the taille replaced by a trumpet. Frederick the Great reorganized the Prussian bands in 1763, choosing the standard octet of 2ob 2cl 2hn 2bn (33), replacing the previous 2ob 2taille 2bn tp and an even earlier band of 2ob taille bn tp. Many of the finest players in Europe passed through the school of military music at Potsdam, founded in 1724 by Frederick William. Matters developed more slowly in England: regimental bands were recognized officially only in 1803, and standardization had to wait a further half-century.

It should be no surprise that rulers took a personal interest in their military music. Only in the 18th century did rulers withdraw from the field of battle, making way for professional soldiers. Charles XII of Sweden, George II of England, and Prussia's Frederick the Great were among the last warrior kings. George IV wrongly believed that he had fought at Waterloo with the 10th Hussars (34), and few later heads of state even considered military direction from the front. Writing music for their bands was a quite appropriate activity for men or women of culture. Probably the Duchess of Kent wrote the *Royal Artillery Slow March,* although perhaps it was scored by George McKenzie. Officers could be inspired by the Muse, including General Reid (1721-1807) and Kuno, Graf von Moltke (1847-1923). Even if marches such as *Der Hohenfriedberger* are wrongly attributed to Frederick the Great (a very capable composer), there is no reason to doubt the authenticity of works by his two sisters, Anna Amalia (1723-87, Princess of Prussia) and Philippine Charlotte (1716-1801, Duchess of Brunswick-Wolfenbüttel). Nor are their marches any worse than those by professional bandmasters. In the present century, King Bhumidol of Thailand, musician as well as monarch, has written a *Royal Guards March.*

Who Played in the Bands? British bands of the 18th and early 19th centuries included civilians, militia conscripts, and professional soldiers. Regimental bands provided a pool of skilled players, in the same way that present-day players from the top forces bands are among those who deputize in opera and symphony orchestras. The mix of civilian and military personnel caused problems. Lord Cathcart, recently appointed Lieutenant-Colonel of the Coldstream Guards, wished its band to play "during an aquatic excursion he had formed to Greenwich." The band, a wind octet "selected from the King's and patent theatres" declined, this being "incompatible with their respectable musical engagements." The consequences were profound. The officers wanted a band under their control, not just in their pay. They wrote to the Duke of York, then in Germany. He in turn recruited some of the first of the foreign bandsmen who were to have such an impact on British bands in the early 19th century (35, 36).

Foreign bandmasters in England often assumed that they needed to do no more than direct music, and some felt no need to go to war. Johann Gottfried Lehmann (35), Bandmaster of the Cambridgeshires, brought from Hanover in 1794, regarded himself as a civilian, and had serious disagreements with his regiment over playing without leave at a private house some two years later. His position was not unique, and the problem was not confined to players of a single nationality. For the bandsmen who had come from the continent, Britain was an admirable place to be: relatively prosperous, and free from invasion and revolutions. They found the same advantages as did composers like Handel and J C Bach, who spent spent much of their lives in Britain, or like Haydn, Weber, W F E Bach, and Mendelssohn, who visited for extended periods. In much the same way, the United States has been enriched by foreign players (37).

Fortunate was the player who could stay in one wind band for a full career. Those players who did try to leave their employer to take up a solo career, like Fiala, often succeeded only with difficulty. For many players, the major changes in the year would be moves from city palaces to summer palaces. A band might change because the new ruler brought his own players. This happened at Bonn in 1784, on the arrival of Elector Maximilian Franz as Elector of Cologne (22, 23). Some new players came from Vienna, such as oboist Georg Libisch and the Welsch brothers, one an oboist, the other a bassoonist. One new member, horn player Nicolaus Simrock, left later to establish the publishing house bearing his name. Sometimes a band changed because it left older players behind, as when the Mannheim orchestra moved to Munich in 1778 with Elector Palatine Carl Theodore (there are extensive descriptions in *Burney* and in Mozart's letters). Other bands ceased to exist through economies or soon after the death of an enthusiastic patron, as at Oettingen-Wallerstein, or in England when George IV died.

Soldiers as Musicians and Vice Versa.   Military bands did not play only for their employers' pleasure. In peacetime they had parades and similar duties; in war they needed military skills. Even in the 8th century, the English chronicler Bede is said to have observed "music ... rouses [men] to battle, it exhorts them to bear fatigue, and comforts them under labor." Frederick the Great's bands were expected to follow their regiment's colors into the thick of battle. They seem to have done so without conspicuous enthusiasm: "Just as the swallows are seen in the Autumn and reappear in good health in the Spring," remarked one general, "so the oboists [bandsmen] are seen before the battle and again after it, without anyone being able to divine where they have been in between" (38). Enterprise is another side to bravery, and one can only praise the bassoonist who repulsed his pursuers by pointing his instrument at them (39). Farmer (11) lists bandsmen who won the highest honors for their bravery.

The main military needs were fanfares for signalling (40), support for morale, and an aid in precision on parade (41). Some musicians had more to do. Bernard Kupfried, of Kassel, Regimental Kapellmeister to, Prince Waldeck, had both musical duties - conducting 11 or 12 hautboists and writing music for them - and serious military duties (42), for "in 1741 he led a convoy from Arolsen to the regiment in Hungary and also returned a released Turk to Turkey." He took part in eight campaigns until the peace in 1748. Heinrich Baermann (1784-1847), the great clarinettist for whom Weber composed, led his band with the defeated Prussian army at the Battle of Jena (14 October 1806); he was captured by the victorious French, but escaped to Berlin. Christian Haupt (1844-1912), the horn player who directed Sibelius's early wind music, was wounded in the Franco-Prussian War of 1870. The bands of enlisted men in British armies were directed to stay with their companies in battle and to assist the wounded. In Wellington's army they were found at the front, albeit as non-combatants with a reputation for impartiality, plundering the dead and wounded from both sides.

Who Taught These Players? Who Were the Organizers?   The Church was one great trainer of singers, organists, and wind players. Outside a few major centers, it was often army musicians who trained wind instrument players during the expansion of the armies in the late 18th century. Many of the important oboists and clarinettists spent time in regimental bands. Since instrumentalists were often composers as well, this military experience formed part of their common culture.

The Role of the Bandmaster.   Bandmasters had two main functions. On the military side, they were responsible for discipline, military skills (if any), the recruitment of musicians, and the acquisition and maintainance of equipment and music. Their civilian role was concerned solely with the music: what was played and how well it was played. No doubt they also arranged extra engagements and negotiated payment. Much of the repertoire must have been specially arranged, such as by Roeser and Fuchs in France, by Eley, and Christian Kramer in England, or by the many forgotten but practical bandmasters throughout the world. Haydn, at Eszterháza, supervised uniformed civilian musicians, ensuring that their instruments were in good order and other duties fulfilled. Overall, the bandmaster was a military version of the Kapellmeister.

Among their minor but practical considerations was how music was held for the players to read. Clips (known as "lyres" from their shape) seem to have been used from the late 18th century (43). Lyres were not universal, however. Some pictures show bands without music; others show that one duty of junior band members was to hold the music for their seniors to play (44). Children of private soldiers could be given preference as drummers (45); they also acted as mobile music stands. The parts for trumpeters and drummers, simple rhythms and fanfares, suggest that they were intended for soldiers who might play by rote, rather than for trained musicians.

REPERTOIRE: WHAT DID THEY PLAY?

Fundamental questions remain about what wind music was played and by whom. The information is patchy, despite the huge number of works surviving, and despite extra information available from publishers' lists (some lists are found on individual parts, especially on pages which would otherwise be blank) and from purchasing records. Information on publishers' lists is given in the volumes of Weinmann (46) or in the collected publishers' catalogs issued by Whistling and Hofmeister (47). The catalogs from the warehouse ("zu Wien, in der Singerstrasse Nr 957") of Traeg (48) appeared from 1794 until about 1818. They list many works which have not survived, especially early works, and so are the source of musicological problems. Johann Traeg (b 1747 at Gochsheim, active in Vienna from c.1782) was both copyist and employer of copyists. It seems that most of his publications were issued in manuscript. He may well have held only a single "house copy" of items advertized, from which copies were prepared to fulfil orders. Traeg may have acquired the house manuscripts of Lausch.

Archives: What Is on the Shelf? There is no guarantee that what survives is typical of what was played. Some archives contain copies in virtually mint condition. Were these replacements of favorites, or had they simply gone out of fashion? Nor can one be sure that the most popular music has survived. Some may have become unusable through wear and tear; other parts might have been thrown out when regiments merged, or when a band changed configuration or was disbanded. Wars and fires destroyed many collections. Even major works have been lost. Mozart's piano concertos survived precariously (49); mature works by Haydn (50) and Mendelssohn (51) were lost despite their composers' fame. Knowing what survives is a further problem, for Union catalogs are still in their infancy, especially for music in manuscript, or for music after 1800.

Our own survey (which include manuscripts) suggest that, for court bands, the repertoire for winds might be from 10% to 25% of the total musical holdings, though it was as high as 40% to 50% for the Löwenstein and Hohenlohe Harmonies. For church collections, the figure was far less, perhaps 2% to 5%. Books of military band parts say only what was available to play, not what was popular. One sample (52) shows four types of march. Some are famous, like Beethoven's or the *Grosse Kurfürst* march by Kuno, Graf von Moltke. A few are based on operas. Most of the remainder are by professional bandmasters, with a few (no worse in quality) by royalty: princesses, countesses, and even a king. Were these played as much, or merely included to boost sales? There are a few catalogs of music collections which appear to reflect what was played. Yet catalogs of surviving collections can confuse as well as help, with works misidentified (53) or given titles so obscure as to mislead (54). In the same way, publishers' lists (55) need the qualifications that they may contain "ghosts," works promised which did not materialize. Concert programmes, even including oddities like Panharmonicon concerts (56), point to only a small fraction of wind harmony.

Examples of What Survives: The Eszterháza and London Royal Music Collections c.1800. We may compare two widely different but similarly sized collections from opposite ends of Europe. When Hummel compiled the Eszterháza catalog in 1806 (57) the musicians, though somewhat isolated, knew that they belonged to a leading ensemble. They were aware of the musical world outside through Haydn and through their own contacts. The catalog lists only current works; early material (including Haydn's own) is missing, perhaps from loss by fire, perhaps from a systematic culling to remove older works for smaller ensembles. In London, the Royal Music lacked a major name to give it European prestige, but it was more secure financially. The purchase orders of Henry Pick and Christopher Eley (27) show what music was bought in the early 19th century. The London and Eszterháza lists are interestingly similar in character, if not in quality. Eszterháza has parthias, serenades and variations; London has military divertimentos, sinfonias, and grand or favorite pieces. Both lists name plenty of stage works (more in Eszterháza), including opera and ballet. The tastes are similar.

Further Comparisons across Europe: Repertories from East to West. Similarities and contrasts emerge from an analysis of some major collections: D-DO (Donaueschingen: Fürstenberg); D-HR (Oettingen-Wallerstein); D-Rtt (Regensburg: Thurn und Taxis); D-SWl (Mecklenburg-Schwerin); I-Fc (Florence, Conservatorio); PL-LA (Łancut, Poland, where the collection from the associated court at Tulchin is found); CH-Gpu (Geneva). There are several hundreds of works at D-Rtt, D-DO and I-Fc; the collections at D-SWl, CH-Gpu, D-HR, and PL-LA are smaller, but still sizeable. There are interesting differences in emphasis. Parthias (however named) are plentiful in D-Rtt, D-HR, D-DO and D-SWl, but are relative rarities in I-Fc and PL-LA. The collection from Tulchin, now at PL-LA, contains many individual pieces for 2fl 2cl 2hn 2bn, which could be made into suites as needed. Geneva's collection is from the Conservatoire. Unusually, some of the music in Geneva has never been played, and remains in mint condition. Of the 47 items, most are arrangements: 33 operas, Haydn's *Creation,* and 7 instrumental works (4 volumes of Haydn symphonies, and an arrangement of Mozart's *Gran Partita)* together with a few original military items. Opera arrangements dominate at I-Fc, whereas D-SWl has very few, which suggests a firm preference of someone important. The German choice of parthias and the Italian choice of operas might reflect national characteristics, though probably some of the works in Florence date from Archduke Ferdinand's period in Salzburg. D-SWl has many marches; one cannot say whether other courts managed without them, or merely that they had separate march collections.

NATIONALISM, GEOGRAPHY AND ETHNIC ISSUES

The European Perspective. There were accepted and distinctive differences of style between bands from different countries. This is seen from titles like "In the French style" (as for Anton Wranizky's marches "auf französisch Art" [sic] **AYW–2m**), and from "battle" works in which different wind bands represent opposing forces. Beethoven's *Wellingtons Sieg,* has both the obvious differences (like the use of national tunes) and subtle ones (so only the French band uses C clarinets). Yet there was common ground. We can see this when we compare marches from three different countries: England (**WZB–1v**, attributed to Willoughby Bertie, 4th Earl of Abingdon [58]), France (Gossec, **FJG–18mv**), and Austria (Beethoven, **LVB–8m**). All have the same scoring (2cl 2hn 2bn; the first two have optional chorus parts); all were composed in the 1790s. What is striking is their similarity, not least the use of some standard formulae. While Beethoven's modulation is better judged, the English amateur has original touches - like the moving first bassoon line - and is by no means outclassed.

A Common Threat, a Common Style: The Turk in Europe. Turkish armies penetrated so far into Europe as to besiege Vienna, first under Solyman in 1529, then under the third vizier, Kara Mustapha, in 1683. The second failure ended the career of the vizier: one can still see in Vienna the silken thread with which he was garotted by order of the Sultan. The war continued. Turkish-occupied Hungary did not fall to Austria until 1699 (59); territory continued to change hands until the accession of Maria Theresa in 1740, and hostilities began again as late as 1788. The Schwarzenberg crest, with a raven picking the eyes of a beheaded Turk, shows how profoundly the Turkish threat was felt. The individual, but seemingly primitive, Turkish sound would have been known by many musicians at first hand. Composers of marches and wind harmony would have known those alive when the Turkish threat was at its height. In more peaceful years, early in the 18th century, the Sultan sent bands of about a dozen musicians each to the courts of Poland and Russia as gifts (9). Turkish percussion caught on in Western music, first in Eastern Europe in the 1740s, reaching England by the 1790s. Tambourines became a specialty of West Indians attached to the Guards bands, part of a long tradition of black musicians. They may have influenced the popularity of the tambourine in minstrel bands of the 1840s. Many composers used the then-exotic combination of triangle, cymbals, bass drum and "Jingling Johnny." Jingling Johnnies ("Johnny" imitates the Turkish name, chagána), were poles with cross-pieces on which pieces of metal were loosely fixed. They were proud trophies for regiments who captured them at war (60); later they were used in American jug and string bands. The other conspicuous legacy of the Janissaries' bands is the adornment (including tigerskins) adopted by modern military drummers.

The label "Turkish" implies a particular musical idiom, with prominent percussion. The exotic coloring was perhaps the 18th-century equivalent of the 19th-century "Hungarian Gypsy" sound and of Latin American rhythms in our own century. Yet the Ottomans also enjoyed their wind bands in settings familiar to Western audiences: in pleasure gardens, on boats, and in conjunction with firework displays (61). Other Turkish influences are found too. Both Mozart's *Rondo alla Turca* (K.331.iii) and the Scythian Chorus from Gluck's *Iphigénie en Tauride* are based on the same Turkish tune used by the Janissaries on their tax-collecting missions (62). "Turkish Music" became very popular throughout Europe. In Pressburg on New Year's Eve, 1774, "a new Symphony by Herr Glanz, Kapellmeister of I.R. Karol Regiment" was performed, which "consists of all Turkish instruments, most of them obbligato. There are no string instruments at all" (63). More important examples include Mozart's *Die Entführung aus dem Serail,* Beethoven's *Symphony No 9,* Weber's operas *Abu Hassan* and *Oberon,* and Spohr's *Notturno.* The three major band works by Paul Mašek (**PLM-1** *Die Schlach bey Leipzig,* **PLM-2.1** *Die Besitznahme von Paris,* and **PLM-3** *Oesterreichs Triumph*) give an interesting snapshot of the way Turkish bands were used c.1815. His large ensemble, described on the title pages of **PLM-1, -3** as "Harmonie mit Türkischen Musick [sic]" includes a Harmonie group (2ob 2cl[C] 2hn 2bn cbn tp) and a Turkish group (pic 2fl cl[F] b-tb serp perc). The Harmonie does play alone; the Turkish group never does so. Modern Turkish marches are recorded on Turkish Art Products KKB.86.34.Ü.014.

Nationalism. Nationalism in music has several strands. There is music for formal state occasions, including the musical symbol of a nation known as its national anthem. There are traditional tunes and songs termed "ethnic" or "folk" music which have formed the musical language of a group of people. There are also works of nationalist sentiment, especially of a minority culture or a conquered nation with a distinctive culture.

Nationalism: national anthems. National anthems are a relatively new phenomenon. The British "God Save the King" was one of the earliest. It was first used in 1745, when the Scottish troops under Prince Charles, the Pretender, were pushing their way south, and the outcome of the Jacobite Rebellion was in doubt. Some twenty members of the cast of the Drury Lane Theater stepped in front of the curtains and sang the "Loyal Patriotic Song," arranged by Thomas Arne. There have been many settings since, ranging from ones by Hummel and Weber to that of the desperate-looking wind band (the Dorsetshire Militia, perhaps?) in the sea at Weymouth, encouraging the recovery of George III as he bathed (64). Other anthems followed, such as Haydn's Austrian anthem, *Gott erhalte Franz den Kaiser* of 1797; this anthem has been arranged for winds by composers such as Krommer and Triebensee. Rouget de Lisle's *Marseillaise* existed in wind versions from its early days, with wind arrangements including that by Fuchs and the extravagant setting by Gossec for performance by hundreds of wind players. In the 19th century, many national anthems were written, including Lachner's for Bavaria, and one by Giuseppe Donizetti (brother of the more famous Gaetano) for Turkey, where a new anthem was written for the accession of each Ottoman ruler. Some nations are fortunate in having additional unofficial musical symbols; the British have Arne's *Rule Britannia* and Elgar's *Land of Hope and Glory*. We presume that all national anthems exist in wind versions, though usually for larger wind ensembles.

Nationalism: folk song. The famous *St Antony Chorale* and the Trio of Beethoven's *Seventh Symphony* are both thought to be based on Austrian pilgrim chants. Traditional tunes and characteristic dance rhythms are common ingredients of wind music. Yet a traditional tune need not be a "folk" tune in any populist sense. Many sophisticated, composed tunes passed into common use (65) and became identified with "folk", for example the dance music of Oswald and Gow in Scotland. Schetky's *Scottish Airs, Reels and Strathspeys* (JGS-1, c.1800) includes examples of traditional melodies.

Folk songs are used in more recent works for winds, such as those by Gordon Jacob. Other composers adopted the idioms of traditional music, rather than its melodies. Dvořák's Op 44 *Serenade* is clearly Bohemian in its dance rhythms, but wholly original; Enesco's *Dixtuor* attempts to catch the flavor of Romanian music. Seiber's use of the verbunkos dance form in his *Serenade* exploits Hungarian Gypsy music as a source of color. Gipsy music has a long history, which includes the *Racouzy [Rákóczi] March*. This march, dating from the early 19th century (66), was named after the leader of the 1703-1711 Hungarian insurrection. The first written version (NQS-1m, c.1820) seems to be that of Nicolaus (Miklós) Scholl, bandmaster of the Esterházy Regiment in Pest. He, in turn, based it on János Bihári's version of the Rákóczi song. Could Scholl (who also made opera arrangements c.1811) have been the bagpiper in the Bihári gypsy band who later became a clarinettist in the Esterházy Infantry Regiment (67)?

Nationalism: national style. Nationalism was a major political force in Europe in the 19th century. The smaller nations of Eastern Europe were especially affected: those under the shadows of Russia, like Finland; of Turkey, like Romania; and of Austria, like Bohemia, Moravia and Hungary. There are hints in earlier music, for the Turks were not forgotten, as in Druschetzky's *Zrini Ungaria* and in some of Beethoven's incidental music for *The Ruins of Athens*. The extraordinary music written in France in the years following the Revolution was not for musicians of a regular army, but its character is nationalistic and militaristic, if not military. Many of these big revolutionary works show how hard it is to write well on a large scale without strings, and they also show failings equally evident in the music of 20th century revolutionary regimes.

The turmoil in Austro-Hungary in the mid-19th century, reflected in the music of Liszt and Erkel, heralded a change of attitude. Overt nationalism was coupled with wider political activity and with the rising liberal intellectual atmosphere which, in 1867, gave rise both to Disraeli's Reform Act in Britain and to the first volume of Karl Marx's *Das Kapital*. Sibelius composed his *Aténårnes sang* (*Athenians Song*, originally for boys' and men's voices, saxhorn septet and percussion) shortly after Governor-General Bobrikov's February 1899 Manifesto removed Finnish political autonomy. The composition was a "tableau" (a scene with costumes and scenery, but static), and the text was nationalistic to the point of advocating open rebellion: "Splendid is death when you fall courageous leading the onslaught... Rise to fight for your country..." Stravinsky, realizing soon after the 1917 Revolution that "God Save the Czar" could no longer be used as the Russian national anthem, produced a wind version (ITS-1a) of the "Song of the Volga Boatmen" as a nationalistic substitute, anticipating the former Soviet practice of removing L'vov's Tsarist anthem from Tchaikovsky's *1812 Overture.*

IS NEW MUSIC NEEDED FOR WIND HARMONY?

Past predictions of the future of music have the reliability and credibility of long-term weather forecasts. We concentrate instead on how the growth and enjoyment of wind harmony might be encouraged.

New Music. As long as good ensembles based on the classical octet exist, new works will be needed to complement the classical repertoire. Without this input, wind harmony could become a historical curiosity. Adding to the repertoire is not easy. A young composer is far less likely to be crowned in glory or buried in money for writing new wind music than for a new symphony or opera. Yet there is a growing market for good wind works, with the possibility of substantial performance returns to a composer who recognizes the social background of the wind band and is prepared to continue that pattern. Music is enriched by imaginative new works, rather than extreme experiments of forced novelty. Composers like Milhaud, Stravinsky, Françaix and others have shown ways forward, and other composers are extending the genre. New compositions and arrangements are needed to fill gaps in the repertoire and to match those major works for which there is virtually no other music using the same instrumental forces, for example Mozart's *Gran Partita,* Dvořák's *Serenade* and Bruckner's *E minor Mass.* A novel idea, implemented at Glyndebourne in 1991, is to commission wind works to be played before each Mozart opera, outside the theater. The works are by Stephen Oliver (for *La Clemenza di Tito*), Nigel Osborne (for *Così fan tutte),* Jonathan Dove (for *Figaro),* Robert Saxton (for *Idomeneo)* and Jonathan Harvey (for *Die Zauberflöte).* Another approach is to link cultures. Small wind bands, in their various forms, are a worldwide phenomenon, spanning many cultures. Thus, in a 1996 concert series, the Bournemouth Sinfonietta Wind Octet joined with the One World Band, musicians from many countries and backgrounds in an interesting cross-cultural experiment.

New Arrangements. In the second half of the 19th century, arrangements for winds were mainly for brass bands and larger military bands. Only recently have arrangements reappeared to diversify the repertory of small wind ensembles. While an arrangement of, say, *Madam Butterfly* might not succeed, works like Dvořák's operas would transfer well to wind harmony. Arrangers can provide works for specific contexts too, such as for use in small theaters where the orchestra pit allows only a few players, or for amateur or professional opera companies whose budgets rule out a full orchestra. From our own practical experience, fl 2ob 2cl 2hn 2bn db offers an admirable substitute. For smaller-scale or classical operas, an even smaller ensemble, such as wind quintet and harpsichord, works well, provided the arrangement exploits the style of harmony music. Wind ensembles also prove very effective in accompanying choirs.

New Music: Availability. Here there are opportunities both through recordings and sheet music, where new technology has simplified matters. The production costs of compact discs have fallen to the point where it is possible for ensembles to produce their own recordings in short runs, thereby avoiding the heavy front-end costs and the problems of storage. Well-produced cassettes still remain a viable option. Distribution and promotion can still be problems, but direct sales of recordings at concerts can prove a useful source of revenue. The photocopier and desk-top publishing make practical small editions of previously unavailable music, since there is no need to produce copies from a master until an order is received (a situation reminiscent of Traeg's methods c.1800). In preparing masters for photocopying, we remark on three routes. (1) *Original to photocopy.* Direct copying is possible either from clean parts or by cut-and-paste from a photocopy of the score. Note that badly aligned parts irritate performers. (2) *Manuscript masters.* The very highest standards (68) must be adopted, as many musicians find manuscript harder to read than printed sources. Bar lines and stems should be ruled. It is unhelpful to use abbreviations for repeated bars. (3) *Computer-generated masters.* Relatively cheap, user-friendly systems (69) allow one to extract parts from a score, to try various layouts and different transpositions. The typesetting system should match needs; many simple systems are intended for popular music, and cannot produce a pick-up bar. Likewise, printers which are excellent for print may be poor for crescendo "hairpins," and it may prove best to use a large format printer, only reducing the image at the photocopying stage.

Should any reader be considering a small publishing venture, we make three basic points. Copyright law must be obeyed: the possession of a photocopy from a library does not imply permission to publish. Secondly, the main aim is to aid performers, not merely to save space. Music produced by photocopy is far cheaper than music produced conventionally, so one or two more pages will not affect your profits greatly. Apart from legibility, the one great demand made by performers (and often forgotten by publishers) is that page turns should be practical, ideally between movements only, or in any case in reasonably long rests. If this means using less than the full number of staves on the right-hand sheet, or starting a work on a left-hand page, the performer will not complain, and may thank you by prefering to buy your editions (70). Reduced-size printouts are not popular. Thirdly, editorial integrity is important. It makes sense to inspect as many copies as possible and to reconcile differences, since there are many cases of human error by copyists, and of corrupt texts "improved" by a local musician.

Exploiting the Older Repertoire. A major obstacle to finding surviving wind music is the huge amount of accurate cataloging still lacking. It is virtually impossible to get information from some key sources. Often we have felt that serenade music is being dismissed as "ephemeral." Much of the work of location, identification, transcription, editing and publication has been done by players of harmony music, not catalogers or musicologists. This has led to works being wrongly identified; we give many examples in our biographical information. Happily, much wind music has become available in recent years, including the rescue of wind music partly lost (like Weber's *Trauermusik*) or left incomplete (such as Beethoven's *Quintet* for ob 3hn bn). Clearly performers unaided cannot do all that is needed. As interest in wind bands grows, music educators could take advantage of wind harmony for training in ensemble techniques, as the basis of a good orchestral wind section, and as a component of courses in composition, arranging and orchestration. Surely it is time to set up an international organization for wind ensemble music, with proper scholarly involvement through conferences and research papers, supported by research grants. Irrespective of academic developments, the future of wind harmony is secure just because wind players enjoy playing together. For them and for their audiences, wind music in the open air on a summer's evening will remain a special pleasure.

JOURNALS OF MUSIC FOR WINDS: THE COMMERCIAL SIDE OF WIND HARMONY

Publishers had varied associations with individual composers or arrangers. One group of publishers had what one might call "house arrangers" who worked for them routinely, if not always regularly. Thus Franz Gleissner arranged for André (Offenbach am Main), Sedlak for Johann Cappi and possibly later for Mechetti (both Vienna), and Goepfert for Simrock (N Simrock, Bonn and H Simrock, Paris). Stumpf's relationship with André remains unclear but we note that his major series of arrangements was for this publisher. Other publishers seem to have treated certain composers with sympathy (like Sedlak with Artaria and the Chemische Druckerei, or Starke with Artaria and Mechetti). A composer might publish solely with a chosen publisher, like Kreith with Eder. Lausch (the Viennese manuscript house) issued all of Went's works; there is a strong possibility that this firm was taken over by Traeg sometime after 1791. Traeg had agency agreements with André, Breitkopf & Härtel and Simrock; thus some of Went's music ended up with Simrock, and Stumpf's *Recueils* were sold in Vienna by Traeg.

To publishers, regular and loyal customers were desirable. It made sense to encourage regular purchases by issuing sets of works which appeared predictably at times of year to match the need for new music. Some publishers responded by giving editions similar titles and formats, e.g., the Berault/Durieu/Imbault *Suites d'Airs d'Opéras Comique.* Many, but not all, such regular issues were called "journals." Subscribers could have advantages over purchasers of single issues: de la Chevardière in Paris (with Castaud in Lyon) offered a 20% discount to subscribers for all 12 issues of Vanderhagen's *Suites d'Amusements militaires.* Such journals had to cater for a standard band. Most of the journals of the 1770s and 1780s chose 2cl 2hn 2bn as a core band, with extra instruments optional to some degree; this remained the standard core military (and often civilian) band throughout Europe until the 1840s, despite the attractions of octets. M J Gebauer's *Nouveau Journal d'Harmonie* was available in a small band form for a much lower price than the full version (42 francs versus 60 in Paris; 45 francs versus 66 in the provinces). Moreover, even for irregularly issued works, a series title acted as a "brand name", indicating both the nature and quality of the contents.

The commercial climate for series of printed publications for wind bands could only exist where the market was sufficiently standardized to allow many sales. In practice, this meant that most series were scored for a core band of 2cl 2hn 2bn. When other instruments were added, many works have them labelled as *ad libitum* or as *ripieno*. The availability of this printed music led many bands to adopt the same core configuration to fit the music. It is common to find printed works for wind sextet even in the archives of bands with unique configurations, for which much of the music would be composed or arranged by the Kapellmeister or local musicians.

The emerging picture is that regimental bands were a major part of the market for journals, and they probably made the difference between profit and loss. This is fully consistent with the situation across Europe, where there can be little doubt that army bands were the dominant market for wind music. Regimental bands must have bought enough entertainment music (as well as parade music) to shape the market. Sadly, much of the music of the regimental bands across Europe was dispersed or destroyed in the wars, when instrumentation was changed, or when regiments were (literally) disbanded.

Journals of wind music were pioneered in France in the 1770s. Perhaps the first was the (lost) *Amusements Militiare* whose three issues were listed in a 1771 catalog by Sieber (père). Short runs were a common feature. Many journals folded after a single year, probably from the usual marketing, sales and distributions problems. War and revolution made long-term plans difficult, but also created a demand, cf. the five

Harmonies by Fuchs celebrating victories in the French campaign in Belgium in 1792, Dibdin's *British War Songs,* and perhaps Busby's series c.1800. Here we describe some of the main French, German and Austrian journals, generally omitting those which survived for only a few issues or which are known only from catalogs.

France

The history of the journals in France is especially complex, and we omit here most of the major analysis of plate numbers, dedications and biographical information needed to rationalize the information. Series are described in chronological order.

Suites d'Airs d'Opéras Comique   Published initially c.1773 by Madame Berault and continued by Durieu and later by Sieber (père) through successive purchases of the plates, this series for 2cl 2hn 2bn was the pioneer. The first 46 issues comprised arrangements by Valentin Roeser, who may have been the originator of this genre of wind music. From its beginnings in the 1770s it reached either issue 67 or 84 by the Revolution (both are listed in a Sieber catalog c.1788 but it is impossible to determine whether the latter is merely forward planning); it certainly had reached No 91 by early 1791. The series continued throughout the Revolution, including arrangements by Vanderhagen and Fuchs, and into the Consulate period. The last issues we have traced (115, 116) are livres 8 & 9 of M J Gebauer's arrangement of *Così fan tutte.*

Suite des Amusements Militaires Contenant un choix d'Ariettes Tirées des Opéra Comique [continuing as] Pièces d'Harmonie Contenant des Ouvertures, Airs et Ariettes, de Opera, et Opera comiques [sic]   The related series of Vanderhagen's arrangements of operas for 2cl 2hn 2bn began with the 12 issues by de la Chevardière (Paris) and Castaud (Lyons) from 1774-1776. Leduc purchased the firm in 1784, reissuing the first set and issuing a further set of 12 issues from 1784-1786 under a new title, but commencing with No 13. Most were opera arrangements, but No 18 consisted of 8 Marches and 6 Pas redoublés; this issue may correspond to Vanderhagen's lost *2 Suites de pas redoublés.* Leduc's 1786 "Catalogue N° III" lists the series under the alternative title, "Journal Militaire"; however there is no evidence that this title was used for any of the numbers issued.

Journal de Musique Militaire (Strasbourg 1784-86, Jean Reinhard Storck). It has been suggested (6) that five numbers of this series correspond to the Leduc series. We find no evidence for this, and suspect it is just a coincidence of titles. The *Avis* of No 1 describes Storck's journal as for regiments with small six-part bands, as well as for those with up to eighteen players. The scoring confirms this: a core of 2cl 2hn 2bn, with extra parts for 2 "petite flûte ou fifre", 2cl 2tp serp and percussion. It was ambitiously planned, with monthly issues, each to be about 40 pages (and perhaps as many as 48 pages, if it sold well), to contain overtures and airs from new operas, a selection of pieces from symphonies and concertos, rondeaux and sets of variations, followed by a march and an allemande. We know of only one surviving copy, an apparently unused copy of No 1 in Schwerin. The overture is from Mozart's *Die Entführung,* with an Air by Grétry, and a March and Allemande by Müller.

Nouveau Suite de Pièces d'Harmonie Contenant des Ouvertures, Airs et Ariettes d'Opera, et Opéra comiques [sic]   The 32 sets of arrangements by Ozi for 2cl 2hn 2bn were issued by Boyer from 1783 until around 1791 (the last piece in set 32 being Rouget de Lisle's "Marche de Marseillois [sic]". Each issue generally comprised 8 selections from various operas; the exceptions are set 27 & 28 (c.1789/1790) which each comprise 12 original marches and dances. Boyer's firm was purchased by Naderman in 1796.

Suitte d'Airs d'Harmonie [sic]   Only No 21 of Le Roy's series survives; it dates from 1783-84 and consists of opera arrangements for 2cl 2hn 2bn by Vanderhagen.

Ouverture Arrangée Pour Harmonie   Imbault ran several simultaneous series of overture arrangements, including Harmonie, string quartet, violin duet, flute duet, clarinet duet, piano, and harp. Generally each series bore the same plate number with a different prefix (Harmonie: "O.H.H." or "O.H.") although their use tended not to be consistent. The earliest Harmonie arrangement is No 74 (Bonnay's *Les Curieux punis*, of 1786); the latest, No 201, dates from between 1806 and Imbault's death in 1811. There is no guarantee that all titles appeared in all of the series; 10 wind arrangements are known from catalogs only and another 16 survive. The titlepages show how a publisher could economize: each uses a split plate with the top part bearing the information that could be used for every series and the bottom portion bearing the specific information for the individual series. Most of the arrangements are by Fuchs, scored for 2cl 2hn 2bn until No 199 when 2 ad lib flutes are added. Imbault also issued collections from the operas as well as the overtures, under the names "Airs", "Airs choisis" or "Morceaux choisis". Scorings varied and the plate numbers are erratic.

Amusemens [sic] Militaires   4 sets of 12 arrangements by Beinet for 2ob/fl 2cl 2hn 2bn (the first known French set for octet) were issued jointly by Boüin, Castagnery and Blaisot in 1786-87. The reissue by Imbault in 1793 suggests for the first time that he purchased the firm of Boüin.

Magasin de Musique des Fêtes Nationales   On 15 February 1794, a Parisian Comité d'Instruction et de Salut public accepted a proposal by Sarrette to produce each month an issue of 50-60 pages containing "une symphonie, un hymne ou choeur patriotique, une marche militaire, un rondo ou pas redoublé et au moins une chanson patriotique". This structure (possibly based on Storck's journal) greatly influenced other military journals. In return for funding of 33,000 *livres* the Comité were to receive 550 copies for distribution. The series was administered by a committee including Gossec, Ozi and Méhul, who were to be assisted by fifty of the musicians of the Garde nationale.

When Sarrette became Director of the new Conservatoire in 1797, Ozi took his place (although Sarrette continued as a "silent partner"). In 1799, the Magasin de Musique, now the name of the publishing firm as well as the military journal, adopted the imprint "Ã l'Imprimerie du Conservatoire de Musique", which had used as an alternative from 1796. 1804 saw a further change to "Ozi et Cie". On Ozi's death in 1814 it changed again to "Magasin de musique du Conservatoire, tenu par MM Charles, Michel, Ozi, S. et Cie"; the "S." of the imprint was, of course, Sarrette.

Funding on this scale - with free distribution and the participation of most of the composers from the Garde Nationale - had great impact on other publishers, for it was tantamount to a monopoly. In 1795 & 1976 Imbault, Sieber (père), Naderman and others complained. Rouget de Lisle, appointed to adjudicate, not surprisingly found in favor of the officially approved *Magasin*. This monopoly collapsed in 1799 when Napoleon overthrew the directory, enabling other journals to compete again.

Journal de Musique Militaire ("Redigé par une Société des Artistes", for 2fl(F) 2cl(F) 2cl(C) 2hn 2bn tp serp b-dr), continuing from Livraison 7 as the *Journal d'Harmonie* ("Composé par une Société des Artistes" for 2fl 2ob 2cl 2hn 2bn tp serp timp). Other changes with Liv 7 include the titlepage, engraver and the Paris agents. Pierre Leroy's first issue from Lyon dates from 1806. He offered the "Suites" at 9 francs each, or 60 francs for all 12. These 12 monthly issues (67 items), are ordered thus: *Ouverture; Rondeau* or *Andantino* (always an arrangement of a Haydn work from Liv 7 onward); *Marche; Allemande; Walze[r]* or *Fandango; Rondeau* or *Pas Redoublé*. The *Ouvertures* are extended works, often like the first movements of symphonies. Serious instrumental music is also included, some from previous decades. Composers includes Louis Jadin, Blasius, Bochsa (father and son), and minor figures like Leroy himself (who provided many of the smaller works, including two fandangos). A few pseudonyms are included, e.g. "Rondeau Finale par H.D." and "Marche by LXXX". Haydn is strongly represented by movements from his symphonies (Hob I/72ii, I/92ii, iii, I/94ii, I/100ii, iii, I/101ii, I/104ii); these arrangements may be by Carl Bochsa (père) who made arrangements of Hob I/91 and I/102. This series was initially distributed in Paris by Pleyel; from Liv 7 the Parisian agent was the joint firm of Cherubini, Méhul, R. Kreutzer, Rode, Isouard & Boieldieu. A certain confusion exists between the first 2 Livraisons and items in the von Sydow & Werckmeister *Journal de Musique Militaire* of late 1804. It appears that Fleury's *Ouverture,* Leroy's *Pas de Manoeuvre* (as "Pas redoublé) and the "Walze" by Haydn (*Symphony* Hob I/101iii, Menuet) were taken from the German journal. Leroy himself claims authorship of the Haydn in his journal; if the German editors had taken the work from Leroy, it is unlikely that they would have identified it as by Haydn. However, we cannot explain the presence of a work by Leroy in the earlier journal.

   Nouveau Journal d'Harmonie   Edited by M J Gebauer and published by P & J-J Leduc, this series, dedicated to "Monseigneur le Maréchal d'Empire Bessières" appears to date from 1808-1809. The 4 issues include 25 items, scored for fl(F) cl(F) 2cl 2hn 2bn tp serp/tb b-dr cym tri (but playable with fl 2cl 2hn 2bn serp). The title offers "un choix d'Ouvertures ou Symphonies Andante Airs Rondeaux Marches Pas Redoublés et Walzers [sic]" from the works of famous composers. The first two sets are mainly marches (some by Gebauer, including a "Drapeau") with arrangements of Viotti, Haydn (strictly Roman Hofstetter, for one "Walzer" is taken from the *String Quartet* Op 3 No 2 once attributed to Haydn), Paisiello and others. The third issue consists of works by Fuchs; the fourth is an arrangement of items from Solié's 1808 opera *Mademoiselle de Guise.*

   Musique Militaire was issued by Gambaro in 1814 and 1815, the time of the fall of Napoleon. Each of the 4 Suites includes 6 items, usually marches or waltzes; although Suite 3 includes three movements of Haydn's "Imperial" Symphony (Hob I:53). Suites 1 and 2 came out in the second half of 1814, probably in response to the need for new military music after the Restoration. Suites 3 and 4 seems to date from after the "Hundred Days" and Waterloo in 1815. Most are scored for pic(C#) cl(F) 2cl(Bb) 2hn tp serp b-dr, i.e. without bassoons, although there are signs that they might have doubled the serpent. The puzzling lack of separate bassoon parts is found in other works of this period, such as the marches by F Gebauer and J Frey.

   Harmonie Militaire Contenant Marches, Pas Redoublés, Rondeaux et Walze [sic] Composed by Frédéric Blasius and dating from 1815-16 (the year between the Restoration and Blasius' retirement), each Livre comprised four movements, scored for fl(D) cl(F) 2cl(C) 2hn 2bn tp b-tb serp b-dr. The dedicatee was the Duc de Gramont, Pair de France (also the dedicatee of F Gebauer's *Six Marches et Pas-redoublés Composées Pour le Garde Royale).*

   Journal d'Harmonie et de Musique Militaire   The complex history of this journal is confused by misnumbering, by a change of composers, and by the missing Livraisons 2-4 [10-12] of Année 3. It was issued every three months. The first series of 4 numbers (Année 1, Liv 1-4, from c.1820) offered "2 Marches, 2 Pas Redoublés, 2 Waltz, 3 Morceaux, Harmonie Militaire." These were composed, seemingly at random, by the Chevalier F Louis, Conrad Münchs, and François Marchal, all directors of regimental bands. The scoring was usually fl(Eb) cl(Eb) 2/4cl(Bb) 2hn 2bn tp tb serp b-dr.

   After the first year, Frédéric Berr replaced Marchal. The general title did not change, but the journal now offered "1 Marche ou Allegro Militaire, 3 Pas Redoublés, 2 Valses, 3 Morceaux d'harmonie formant une Messe[:] Un Ouverture[,] Un Andante [&] Un Menuetto ou Rondo." The division of labor was carefully organized with each composer taking 3 movements (Marche/Allegro, Pas redoublé, Waltz; 2 Pas redoublés & a Waltz; the 3-movement Harmonie) in rotation in the order: Berr/Münchs/Louis, Louis/Berr/Münchs, Münchs/Louis/Berr. The first six movements were generally scored for pic(D) cl(E♭) 2/3cl(B♭) 2hn 2bn tp 2tb 2serp b-dr. The Harmonie, however, adopted a less military scoring of fl(C) 2ob/2cl(C) 2cl(C) 2hn 2bn tp tb cb(ad lib). Année 2, Liv 1-3 were dedicated to Baltazar d'Arcy, Maréchal de Camp, Colonel 1er Régiment de Garde Royale; Liv 4 and Liv 1 of Année 3 (the only surviving Livraison) were dedicated to the Duc de Bellune, Ministre de la Guerre from 1821 to 1823. Berr took up the post of second clarinet at the Théâtre Italienne in 1823. He may well have withdrawn from the journal at the end of its third year, and this may have precipitated its closure.

The various sections of the each Livraison were reissued from the original plates by les Fils de B Schott (Paris, Mainz & Antwerp, 1828) with the consecutive plate numbers 3006-3029 added. Each set of the small pieces (1-3, 4-6) was issued as a different Cahier as *Musique Militaire,* and the 3-movement Harmonie (7-9) was issued separately as *Grande Harmonie.* The issues by Louis and Münchs comprise 5 Cahiers and 3 *Grand Harmonies;* those by Berr comprise 6 Cahiers and 2 *Grande Harmonies.*

Journal de Musique Militaire Authorisé par S.E. le Ministre de la Guerre Frédéric Berr applied his experiences from the collaboration with Louis and Münchs when he prepared his own journal in 1826. Published by Gambaro, the title of Livraison 1 (the only one to survive) provides a wealth of information: "Nota: Ce Journal paraîtra à partir du 1er. Janvier 1826. chaque Souscripteur / recevra une Livraison tous les Trimestres, contenant 6 Morceaux. / Le Prix de l'Abonnement est de 30 Francs per Année (conformément à la Circulaire de S.E. / le Ministre de la Guerre en date du 22 Juillet 1825) payable en recevant la 2e. Livraison. / [MS: 1e] Livraison. Prix: [left blank] Régiment [left blank] / A PARIS / chez GAMBARO, au Magasin de Musique." Liv 1 comprises a march, 3 pas redoublés, a polonaise and a Waltz scored for fl(E♭) cl(E♭) cl(B♭ solo) 2cl(B♭) 2hn 2bn tp(crt) b-tb serp b-dr+cym t-dr. The inclusion of a separate solo B♭ clarinet part was characteristic of Berr's arrangements from the mid-1820s.

Nouveau Journal d'Harmonie et de Musique Militaire Publié sous L'Autorisation de S.E. Le Ministre de la Guerre Münchs, like Berr, prepared his own journal. Of the original four issues, only Livs 2 and 3 survive. They have the same format as the original journal (Marche, 3 Pas redoublés, 2 Waltzes, and a 3-movement Harmonie); since one Pas redoublé is based on Rossini's *Semiramide,* Liv 2 must date from after February 1823. In Liv 3, the Harmonie consists of three works **FXB-3.1** arranged or composed by Berr, later issued by Schott, but hitherto unlinked to any journal.

Journal de Musique Militaire Only Année 1, Livraison 1 survives of this journal prepared by F Louis and C Münchs after the Revolution of 1830. By this time Louis had his own shop and publishing house. Münchs joined him as a partner from 1832 until his death in 1835. The inclusion of an ophicleide as an alternative to serpent also supports this dating. Intended to be issued every three months, the journal was a far more modest affair comprising one *morceau* by each composer: "Pas-redoublés, Marches, Valz [sic], Polonaises, Pas de charge[s]". There are no attributions for the two Pas redoublés in Liv 1 but the widely varying scorings of the two works suggests two composers working with different, non-standardized regimental bands.

Great Britain

As in France, the 1770s saw a burst of periodical publications in Great Britain. Everything from piano music and songs to symphonies was offered at regular intervals.

Military Concertos by Different Masters Dating from c.1770, this series printed by James Bremner was sold not only by him but also at the branch shop run by his brother, Robert. This is the series also advertized by Breitkopf (acting as agent) in Leipzig in Supplement 6, Part IV of the 1771 catalog ("Concerti Militari di diversi Maestri, *intagl. in Londra. /* a *2 Oboi o Flauti, 2 Corni, 2 Clarini [i.e. clarinets] & 2 Fagotti.*"). In keeping with periodical publications of the period, the pagination is continuous through the series. The announced scorings for "Two Hautboys, Clarinets, Flutes or Violins. Two Horns, and Two Bassoons" has led to considerable confusion, not least because two separate Bb clarinet parts were included; however these were merely oboe parts transposed. It appears that plans were altered after the second issue, possibly due to a change in composer. The titlepage states that the Concertos were "To be continued Monthly"; although 13 Concertos were printed, these comprise only 8 issues. The single works of issues 1 & 2 (5 and 4 movements, respectively) give way to a pair of three-movement works with the third issue. The bassoon parts were separate in issues 1 & 2 (although in issue 2 they were printed on a single part with the only divisi appearing in the second half, "Allegro 2do", of the second movement); from issue 3 the part had become "Fagotto" although two copies were provided. It is unfortunate that composers are not named. Adam Rathgen may well have contributed; J C Bach and Abel are less likely (although we note a untraced "Divertissement" by "Bach and Abel" in Madame Berault's 1776 Paris catalog). Only one copy survives, in Schwerin (D-SWl).

British publishers preferred to issue band works in single issues, either single works or collections of pieces. There were brief forays into periodical publications at times when Napoleon's victories were causing alarm across Europe. The scores of *10 Marches* by **Thomas Busby** were included on an irregular basis over the run of the more general *British Military Journal* (London, Richard Phillips; the marches bear the additional imprint, "Published as the act directs ... by Hookham & Carpenter[,] Bond Street"). Nos 1-9 appeared between October 1798 (Vol I, No 1) and August 1799 (Vol I, No 11); the tenth did not appear until March 1801 (Vol III, No 30). All have titles such as "The Field of Honour" and "British Valour." The scorings fall into several configurations: 2fl/pic 2cl 2hn bn serp 1/2tp (Nos 1, 2, 4); 2cl 2hn 1/2bn serp 2tp (No 6); 2cl bn 2tp timp (No 10); 2cl 2hn (2)bn (Nos 8, 9), 2cl 1/2bn with a piano reduction (Nos 3, 5, 7).

British War Songs   Charles Dibdin's short-lived periodical publications of 1803-1804 is discussed extensively in part 2. Here we merely note that, like the French *Magasin de Musique des Fêtes Nationales,* they were subsidized by the government to increase patriotic fervor. The songs, first sung in the composer's one-man entertainment, *Britons Strike Home!,* were issued with accompaniments for orchestra or for piano and (without voices) for a small band of either 2cl/ob 2hn 2bn bassi or 2cl 2hn bassi.

The German States

Series publications did not appear in the German States before the mid-1790s. Apart from Breitkopf's agency advertizement for the *Military Concertos,* there seem to have been no Harmoniemusik journals; publishers evidently preferred to offer works by single composers at irregular intervals.

Stumpf's *Pièces d'Harmonie*   Stumpf's 20 Recueils of opera arrangements (all for 2cl 2hn 2bn, and containing 6 movements without overtures) and his three Recueils of original works first appeared between 1795 and c.1801 (André: Offenbach am Main). Second editions of at least the first 12 sets were published between 1809 and 1813. Due to André's agency relationships (Traeg in Vienna, Sieber père in Paris), Stumpf's set is the most widely distributed throughout Europe; copies are even found in the collections of the Moravian Brethren in America.

Journal Militaire   Published by Johann Michael Götz (Munich, Mannheim & Düsseldorf), Gleissner's arrangements for 2cl(D) 2cl(A) 2hn 2bn could date from as early as 1788 to 1792, but are likely to be from the early years of the 19th century.

Journal de Musique Militaire   A series, edited by de [sic] Sydow and Rudolphe Werckmeister in "Orangebourg" (Oranienburg, near Berlin), and first advertized in the

Allgemeinische Musikalische Zeitung in December 1804 (for "Hautboisten," a late usage of the term). The series was in two parts: "La Première Moitié renferme des Pièces d'Harmonie à Plusieurs Parties" (in fact, for 2ob 2cl 2hn 2bn tp); "La Seconde des Pièces pour la Musique Turque" (2pic 2quart-fl 2cl[C] 2hn 2bn 2tp serp b-dr s-dr cym). Copies of both parts survive in Prague and Kroměříž, and show parallels with the Storck, Leroy, and Gebauer series. The *Première Moitié* comprises: (1) C Fleury: *Ouverture in C;* (2) Schmelling: *Marsch;* (3) Haack: *Walse;* (4) v[on]. Sydow: *Pas redoublé;* (5) Himmel: *Pas de Manoeuvre.* In the *Seconde Moitié:* (1) R Kreutzer: *Lodoiska, Ouverture;* (2) B A Weber: *Marsch;* (3) Leroy: *Pas de Manoeuvre;* (4) Haydn: *Walse* (in fact, the Menuetto of Symphony Hob I:101iii). As noted above, these journals served as a source for some early works in Leroy's *Journal de Musique Militaire.*

Journal de Harmonie [sic] Composed by Karl Heinrich Meyer and published by Hofmeister in Leipzig. One issue survives from 1808, and is "Collection XV, Livraison II", containing items 13-24. If all the previous issues contained 12 pieces, the numbers imply there were as many as 360 items, so sales must have been strong and stable. It seems unlikely that more than 3 Collections (6 Livraisons, 72 items) were issued each year, so the series would have started c.1806. Although many of the items are short marches and dances, the size of the project makes one wonder if it incorporated music from other (possibly defunct) journals. The surviving issue, dedicated to clarinettist W L Barth (1774-1849), is scored is for a core band of terz-fl cl(E♭) 2cl(B♭) 2hn tp b-tb, with ad lib parts for 2bn serp timp b-dr s-dr cym.

Musique Turque (Küffner) Küffner's series comprised 15 Recueils, each of 7-10 movements, without opus numbers. They were published by André in Offenbach am Main between 1812/1813 and 1818 (and with at least 3 duplicated by Les Fils de B Schott in Mainz). They were generally scored for pic 2cl(E♭) 2cl(B♭) 2hn 2bn 2tp b-tb serp b-dr s-dr. Küffner's 11 *Potpourris* were issued by Schott between c.1818 and 1826 with scorings rising from fl 2cl 2hn 2bn to 2cl(E♭) 3cl(B♭) 4hn 2bn 5tp 2tb serp b-dr s-dr; issued with opus numbers and consecutively numbered, there is no indication that they were anything but an occasional series.

Journal für mil[itärische] Musik Issued by Hofmeister in Leipzig, the 5 known issues include works by Hummel (vol 3, 1817, arranged Rose), Marschner, Rothe and Theuss.

Sammlung von Märschen für vollständige türkische Musik zum bestimmten Gebrauch der Königlich Preussischen Armee (Schlessinger: Berlin). Here the two series are "Türkische" and "Trompeterchöre." The Turkish set is listed in Whistling from its start, but the number are not systematic; perhaps the series was not fully established in 1817-1818: the 1817 entry is under "Militz" rather than "Sammlung." From 1821 all looks clear, except successive years to not yield numbers in the same order, but this could be a matter of distribution rather than publication. The last number is 66. The Trompeterchöre set is much clearer, with volumes as follows: 1824 (1-4), 1825 (5-12), 1826 (13-15), 1827 (16, this issue includes an item by J H Krause).

Pièces d'harmonie pour Musique Militaire (Walch) Walch's occasional series, invariably comprising 12 pieces (marches, dances, and other single movements) was published by C F Peters between 1818 and the mid-1840s (except Liv 12, c.1828, published by Schott). The first 2 Livraisons were issued without dedications; scored for fl(E♭) cl(E♭) 3cl(B♭) 4hn 2bn 2tp 3tb serp b-dr s-dr, with the option of a reduced band of about 10 musicians; signal horn is usually included in the scoring from Liv 2 onward. Between 1819 and 1827 five more were issued, with royal dedications, but without the reduced option (although this remains a distinct possibility throughout the series); from Liv 8, many of the dedications are to well-known musical directors or musicians (Barth, Berr, Braun, Lindner, F Müller, Richter of Stuttgart, Weller). Liv 27 (c.1840) is dedicated "Au Corps de Musique de la Vielle-Garde de Washington à Philadelphia."

Walch's *Potpourris* prove to be part of the same series. Issues are known from 1819, c.1828 and 1833. Their Livre numbers and Peters plate numbers (apart, perhaps, from the early 1819 *Potpourri*) fit exactly the gaps in the *Pièces d'harmonie.* Only Liv 16 (c.1830) of the *Variations et 4 Pièces d'Harmonie pour Musique militaire* has been traced, published by Peters with similar scoring to the *Pièces d'harmonie.* Many of the surviving copies of these series are in the Moravian Archives in Bethlehem, US-BETm.

The Austrian Empire

Periodical publications of Harmoniemusik came relatively late to the Austrian Empire (post-1800), and we have not found *any* journals with *explicit* military links. The few series issued either in manuscript or print tended to exploit the concert repertoire, although enough marches were included to fill the needs of regimental bands. Marches were published occasionally, but never in a periodical form. The lack of standardization of bands may have also been a factor. Many marches published in Vienna, even those derived from a particular regiment, were issued only in piano reduction, possibly for rescoring for local needs.

Triebensee's two series   These important series are known from advertizements, from archive catalogs (notably those of the Imperial and Esterházy Harmonien) and from a few surviving copies which together to make up complete sets. Both series were issued in manuscript only. Some surviving copies are either pirated versions or compilations from various issues.

Harmonien Sammlung   Triebensee's 1803-1804 series, issued by the composer at Feldsburg (Valtice), pioneered high-quality wind music in this format. Triebensee led the Liechtenstein Harmonie throughout much of the 1790s and early years of the 19th century. Yet it was only in 1803 that he began to publish for himself, rather than through established Viennese manuscript houses. Subscriptions were sought in the *Wiener Zeitung* of 16 November 1803 and in the *Allgemeine musikalische Zeitung,* January 1804, No 6, for the "best and most recent operas and ballets and also original parthias arranged [gesetzt] by Josef Triebensee." There were to be 6 Lieferungen (issues) in each year (Jahrgang). Only two issues appeared, one comprising Triebensee's *Partitta in B[b]* and Winter's *Das Labyrint,* the second comprising Triebensee's *Partitta in Eb* (only in the Lobkovic catalog is this given as "Es") and T Weigl's ballet, *Baccus und Ariadne.* Why did this first venture seem to fail?

One possibility is simply that there were too few real subscribers. Only two sets are actually labelled "Harmonien Sammlung," namely those for the Schwarzenberg (CZ-K) and Esterházy (A-Ee) Harmonien. All other sets are incomplete and/or without a series title. Probably many of the surviving copies were purchased *via* Traeg, or were pirated copies. Another factor may have been pressure of work. Triebensee had much to do as Liechtenstein'sche Kapellmeister, and he might have found it hard to meet deadlines with new works and arrangements. Some works could have been ready in advance, such as Winter's opera, performed on 12 June 1798 in Vienna. This was not the case with Weigl's ballet, first performed 13 December 1803, just a month after Triebensee's advertizement appeared. The original *Partittas* may have been earlier works. The 1804 *Erste Nachtrag* issued by Johann Traeg und Sohn includes on page 27 ("Harmonie pour 2. Clar. 2. Ob. 2. Cors & 2. Bassons.") the entry "Triebensee Jos. Parth. Nro. 1-5. a 2 fl[orins]." A third possibility is that the mix of original works and arrangements did not prove popular. One noticeable absence from the subscribers is the Imperial Harmonie, whose repertoire was dominated by arrangements.

There is another puzzle associated with this series. Clearly, it was hard to prevent copies being pirated. A stamp was prepared to indicate authentic copies. It consisted of a border of dotted lines in a diamond shape with the inscription, "J / Har / J monien T / Samlung / W." J/T must be Triebensee's initials, and surely J/W must be the initials of Johann Went, Triebensee's father-in-law. Was this series originally planned jointly with Went? Was the arrangement of Winter's opera actually one of Went's, which Triebensee inherited on Went's death in 1801? The stamp is the only documentary evidence, and it raises tantalizing questions on authenticity and intent.

Miscellannées [sic] *de Musique*   If there are doubts about the success of Triebensee's first attempt at a periodical publication, there are none about his second series, which ran to 32 issues between 1808 and 1813. Although undated, we can deduce a chronology of issues of the *Miscellannées* (the title misspelling appears in almost all copies we have seen). First, Prince Johann Esterházy authorized payment for the opening issue (Jahrgang I, Oeuvres 1, 2) on 6 August 1808. Some of the works arranged had their first performances in 1807 so the likely launch date was June/July 1808. These first issues were unusually well produced, in cardboard folders, with the title written on a shield of colored paper pasted on the front. Secondly, the final items in the first Jarhgang (Oeuv 11, 12) date from February 1810: Triebensee's receipt (bill) to Prince Esterházy is dated 15 March 1810; Hummel, then Kapellmeister, adds a comment that the music has already been delivered, and the authorization for payment by the Prince is dated 27 March 1810. Thirdly, the first numbers of Jarhgang II can be dated from the Lobkowitz copy; the date is partly obscured by a wax seal, but can only be June or July 1810. The printed slip, *not* a dedication as has sometimes been suggested, states "This document with its attached seal guarantees that the present collection is my own work, and is published by me. At the same time I request and expect my respected customers to be so good as to confine it to their personal use, and not permit or tolerate illicit copying, as I would thereby suffer financial damage. Vienna, Joseph Triebensee, Director of Music to the courts of Liechtenstein and Hunyady ['fürstlich Lichtenstein= [sic] and graeflich Huniadischer [sic] Kapellmeister']". Fourthly, the first two issues of the third Jahrgang were advertized by Stegmayer (as agent) in the *Wiener Zeitung* of 3 October 1812. Finally, the Imperial Harmonie copies in A-Wn bear these copyright notices on many of the issues, although many appear to have been signed in batches and given to the copyists.

What, then, can be deduced? Obviously "Jahrgang" does not mean issues with a twelve-month period, any more than "journal" indicates a daily issue. Further, each issue comprised two Oeuvres. The picture emerging is of three issues per year: early summer (June/July), to fit the outdoor serenade season and court moves to summer residences; fall (October/November), for the social events of the winter, including Christmas, New Year and the pre-Lenten Carnival; and early spring (March) for the social season following Lent. In only one case (Jg II, Oe 5. 6) does the copyright notice seem to predate this schedule, and only by 2 or 3 months; this may simply confirm our view that Triebensee signed and dated batches of notices. The series continued through the disbanding of the Liechtenstein Harmonie in 1809, without delays in issues. Nor did the 1810 start of the Chemische Druckerei *Journal für neunstimmige/sechsstimmige Harmonie* seem to alter the schedule. However, the issues of 1811-1812 are confused, with surviving copies of Jg I, Oe 9-12 including the same works but with inconsistent numbering (and in the case of Oe 10 in A-Ee, an arrangement of Paer's *Numa Pompilio* was substituted for the scheduled work). The corresponding numbers are:

A-Wn	Jg I/9	Jg I/10	Jg I/11	Jg I/12
A-Ee	Jg I/11	*(Numa)*	Jg I/9	Jg I/12
Lobkovic	Jg I/12	Jg I/11	Jg I/9	Jg I/10

There are other minor differences as well. Thus the Imperial Harmonie (A-Wn) copy of

Oeuvre 9 includes an additional Marsch (No 17) not found in the other copies; as with the other 16 pieces, Triebensee's name appeared as composer, but this has been scraped off and replaced with Steibelt's name. Using the A-Wn set as a reference, Oe 9 comprised original works by Triebensee, Oe 10 an arrangement of Süssmayr's *Solimann der Zweyte,* Oe 11 an arrangement of Himmel's *Fanchon,* and Oe 12 separate works from a number of sources. Given the confusion, and the shift to arrangement of full operas and ballets, we believe that Oe 9 and Oe 12 were intended as the fifth issue of Jg I and Oe 10 and 11 as the sixth.

There is a possible gap in the series in July 1812, at the same time as a similar gap in the Chemische Druckerei *Journals.* Perhaps schedules were upset by Austria's 12 March 1812 alliance with France and the promise to provide an army for Napoleon. There was, however, no similar gap near 8 February 1809, when Austria declared war on France; possibly by 1812 Triebensee knew better how his market would respond. The passing of the position of Liechtenstein'sche Kapellmeister from Triebensee to Sedlak might have been a further contributing factor, since it could have placed unexpected demands on Triebensee's time. The *Miscellannées* seem to have ended with the 32nd issue (November 1813). The reasons may have included Austria's declaration of war on Napoleon (12 August 1813) and Triebensee's appointment as opera conductor in Brno.

While the Chemische Druckerei *Journals* did not affect timing, it may have affected the contents of the *Miscellannées.* The types of work included changed substantially with the passage of time. In the first three months of Jg I, for instance, there were movements arranged from symphonies by Mozart (K.543i, K.425ii) and Haydn (Hob I/102iv, 97ii-iv) and from chamber music by Beethoven (Op 16), Pleyel and J B Cramer. Arrangements of symphonies became rare after the middle of Jg I, the last being Haydn's *Oxford Symphony* (Hob I/92) in Jg II/11. Original compositions, apparently all by Triebensee, were published in the second half of Jg I, amounting to at least 26 movements. Apart from the *March on the [Haydn] Austrian Hymn* (Jg II/6), a *Parthia* (Jg II/4, Nos 7-11) and an *Echo Partita* (Jg II, Oe 8, Nos 8-10), no more were evident. Instead, the market was offered (and presumably demanded) popular operas and ballets. The major shift, from the beginning of Jg II, appears to coincide with the start of the competing Chemische Druckerei *Journals,* and possible market pressure. In both cases, the operas and ballets arranged are those currently popular; works from earlier decades were only included if they had been recently revived.

Triebensee *Miscellannées*	Chemische Druckerei *Journal für 9-/6-stimmige Harmonie*	
	A-Wn copyright dates in [ ]	*Wiener Zeitung* advertizement dates
I/1, 2	July 1808	
1/3, 3	Nov 1808	
8 February 1809: Austria declares war on France		
I/5, 6	Mar 1809	
I/7, 8	July 1809 [20 ?May 1810]	
Miscellannées numbering confused: I/9-12		
I/9, 10	Nov 1809 [10 June 1810]	
I/11,12	Mar 1810 [10 June 1810]	(J9/1) 30 May 1810
II/1, 2	July 1810 [10 June 1810]	(J9/2) 12 Sep 1810
II/3, 4	Nov 1810 [30 Dec 1810]	
II/5, 6	Mar 1811 [30 Dec 1810]	(J9/3) 17 Apr 1811
II/7, 8	July 1811 [27 Aug 1811]	(J9/4) [no advert: ? Sep 1811]
II/9, 10	Nov 1811	
II/11, 12	Mar 1812	
16 March 1812: Austria promises an army for Napoleon		

1812: Sedlak succeeds Triebensee as Liechtenstein'sche Kapellmeister

III/1, 2	3 Oct 1812	(J9/5) 23 Sept 1812
III/3, 4	Mar 1813	(J9/6) 23 Sept 1812
III/5, 6	Jul 1813	

12 August 1813: Austria declares war on Napoleon

III/7, 8	Nov 1813	
[No further Miscelannées issued]		(J9/7) 10 Aug 1814
		(J9/8) 24 Nov 1814

An obvious question is: What were Triebensee's sources, especially in Jg I where many single numbers appear to be unusual choices? We find that about half of the arrangements in Jg I (A-Wn copy: Oe 1-4, 5-8, 12) correspond to works issued with piano accompaniment in Johann Cappi's *Musikalisches Wochenblatt,* a weekly miscellany published in Vienna from 3 October 1806. In Triebensee's Jg I/1, 8 of the 10 works correspond; in Jg I/8, 9 of the 10 match. If our suggested order for the confused last 4 Oeuvres of Jg I is right, the only exception is Jg I, Oe 5, an arrangement of J Weigl's *Kaiser Hadrian;* perhaps this work from 1807 proved so popular that Triebensee felt he had to include it. We have found no evidence whatsoever that Triebensee was merely exploiting his old arrangements for the Liechtenstein Harmonie as it was winding down.

The *Miscellannées* served as a model for other Harmoniemusik collections. Some of the collections of pieces by Krechler for the Lobkowitz Harmonie also employ the same title (although his commercially-available manuscript copies used the title "Harmonie") and there a number of similarly-titled collections made by the members of the Augustinian monastery Harmonie in Brno.

Journal für neunstimmige (sechsstimmige) Harmonie   This was first advertized by the Chemische Druckerei publishing house in Vienna as follows: "A Series of favorite operas, ballets and other works, arranged for 6- and 9-part wind ensemble, will be published every two months, commencing at the end of May 1810 ... In addition to these journals, the following wind works have recently been published by us, and will be added to at short intervals according to the demands of the royal and imperial regiments, and of various respected amateurs". In 1809, Siegmund Anton Steiner and Rochus Kranitzky joined the firm founded by Senefelder in 1804, and may have been at least partly responsible for the increased proportion of Harmoniemusik issued. Steiner became the sole proprietor in 1812, being joined by Tobias Haslinger in 1814; Haslinger became the sole proprietor in 1826. Thus the Journals were issued in the years for which Steiner was the major influence.

Despite the initial statement, the Journals did not come out every two months, but rather twice a year at first (advertized in the *Wiener Zeitung* on 30 May and 12 September 1810, 17 April 1811, and possibly on September 1811) and then less frequently (one advertized 23 September 1812, another issued possibly mid-1813, and the final two in the second half of 1814). Detailed examination shows that the 6-part version was produced first, and a plate number assigned; generally the horn and bassoon parts bear not only that number but also the subsequent one as well. The route to the 9-part version was carefully (and cleverly) planned to reduce production costs. The horn and bassoon parts remained the same in both versions (indeed the bassoon II part of the 6-part version is labelled "Fagotto 2do e Contra" although no divisi are given). The two clarinet parts of the 6-part version were adjusted to produce the four parts for the oboes and clarinets in the 9-part version; the oboes are often silent for the opening tutti, and the second oboe parts are largely ripieno and unrewarding for the performer.

Given the competition, it is not surprising that there was duplication with Triebensee's series. The five cases (sometimes given under alternative titles) are:

J Weigl *Die Schweizerfamilie* (1809): J9 No 1 (30 May 1810); Triebensee (July 1810)
Spontini *La Vestale* (1810): J9 No 3 (April 1811); Triebensee (Nov 1811, March 1812)
Isouard *Cendrillon* (1810): J9 No 4 (c.Sept 1811); Triebensee (Nov 1811)
Boieldieu *Jean de Paris* (1812): J9 No 6 (Sept 1812); Triebensee (March 1813)
Duport *Zephir* (1812): J9 No 7 (Aug 1814): Triebensee (July 1813)

Steiner was often slightly faster to the market. Steiner's series also included Seyfried's *Saul* (No 2), Spontini's *Fernand Cortez* (No 5) and Hummel's *Die Eselshaut oder Die blau Insel* (No 8; unlike the others, this arrangement by Sedlak was not issued in J6 series).

While only eight issues were formally part of the *Journals,* the second pledge of the first advertizement was honored and other works addressed similar markets and are similar in many respects. Examples include two symphonies by Beethoven, dating from 1816 (when several other versions of these works including string quartet, piano trio, and piano were also published) or from 1817: Symphony 7 (?arranged Sedlak; 6-part pn 2562-2563, 9-part pn 2563) and Symphony 8 (6-part pn 2572-2573, 9-part pn 2573). A further attempt to establish a periodical, the *Neue Journal für Harmonie und Türkische Musik* began and apparently ended with its first number, an arrangement for large band of Beethoven's *Wellingtons Sieg* (pn 2368; first advertized in the *Wiener Zeitung* on 6 March 1818).

Journal militärische Musik in monatlichen Lieferungen We include Friedrich Starke's series with some reservations, for it may have been a series of separate issues, not a journal. Yet it is hard to see how such a large series could have been marketed successfully without some of the methods associated with journals. Remarkably few items survive. As to its periodical nature, there are only two sources of information: *Whistling* (which normally listed only printed music, and none is known for this series) and CZ-Bm, where only one item uses "Journal" in its title *(Journal der Musik enthaelt Eine Ouverture von Rossini[,] eine Nazionale-Polonaise und ein beliebtes Thema nebst 4 Variationen mit Nachspiel und Coda [sic]).* The later stages of this substantial series are documented in the supplements to *Whistling* where, in 1829, "Heft" numbers become opus numbers. Virtually no wind music appears in Starke's Op 1-60, numbers which are missing from *Whistling;* it is entirely possible that what was perceived as a journal is really separate compositions and arrangements. Examination of Starke's entire surviving works shows that at no time is there a duplication of a known opus number with any of the Hefts listed in *Whistling.* The 1818-1820 supplements list these works as "1 und 2 Jarhgang jeder von 2 Heften, Wien, Autor, Traeg". If Starke's works really do constitute a journal, 1816 is the logical start date.

Two types of works are listed: those for Harmonie, and those for Turkish music. Sometimes an item appears in both forms, sometimes only in one. This can mislead, as when an arrangement appears in two or three sections, with the 1st "Abtheilung" for Harmonie and the "2te, 3te Abth" for Turkish music. Were later parts issued for Harmonie too? Or was this a definition of genres made by *Whistling?* Where works *have* survived in several parts, it has invariably been the Harmonie version.

In 1821, the first year where individual titles are given, there are 16 items for Harmonie, and 6 for Turkish music (hereafter abbreviated H and T); presumably some were issued in earlier years but remained unlisted. One finds the following works listed (in some cases, works are not given a genre): 1821, "Hefts" 61-82 (16H, 6T); 1822, Hefts 83-95 (9H, 8T); 1823, Hefts 97-104 (7H, 1T); 1824, (no entries); 1825, Hefts 108-120 (7H, T); and 1826, Hefts 124-141 (9H, T). The numbers suggest that this series delivered Hefts approximately monthly, as promised. In many cases, the individual numbered Hefts contain six or eight works, often in groups. Thus Heft 81 is named "Sächsisches Journal"; it comprises "1 Polonaise, 3 Märsche, 2 Walzer, 1 Quad[rille] u[un] Ecossaisen". There are many opera arrangements, and also a few more serious works: the 1822 entries includes a *Fugen Parthie* in Heft 91, arranged from several composers, including Spohr. One other interesting feature is the way the prices evolve. Starting from 5 or 6 florins in early 1821, these fall to 4 or 5 florins in late 1821 and 1822, rising again for 1823 and staying at 6 florins through 1825; in 1826, however, the price drops to a mere 3 florins.

By the 1820s, few courtly Harmonien remained other than the Imperial and the Liechtenstein. Sedlak appears to have had the "monopoly" for both of them. Starke's works were clearly intended for the military market. Since so few have survived he has been largely neglected, which is regrettable because of the generally high quality of his works. In many cases, his adaptations are truly arrangements rather than mere transcriptions, placing considerable technical demands on all players.

Musikalischer Sammler [sic] für Harmonie N: 2   Again, we list Nicholaus Scholl's "58tes Werk" with reservations. Was this really another journal? The only known copy, from the Harmonie of the Duke of Modena (I-MOe) comprises arrangements from three operas, the latest dating from the spring of 1827. The scoring is similar to both Sedlak's and Starke's from the 1820s (2ob 2cl 2hn 2bn cbn 2tp) and appears while Scholl was Kapellmeister of the Lob: K:K: fürst N: Esterházy 32ten Linien Infanterie Regiment. Only two other Harmoniemusik works by Scholl have been located so it is impossible to assess his impact either as a competitor to the two better-known composer/arrangers or as a serious contender as a journal producer and publisher. This clearly represents an area of potentially fruitful research for the future.

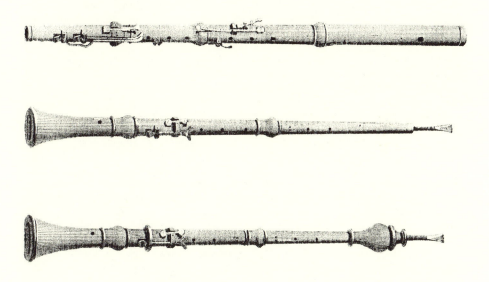

Figure. Wind instruments, as shown in the original steel engravings in Abraham Rees 1806-1820 *The Cyclopaedia; or, Universal Dictionary of Arts, Sciences and Literature;* London: Longman, Hurst, Rees and Orme. This figure is a montage from originals in the possession of Marshall Stoneham. The original caption identifies the instruments as Improved German Flute with additional Keys and [two] Hautboys.

2

English-Speaking Countries

THE BRITISH ISLES AND ASSOCIATED TERRITORIES

British wind harmony has received far less scholarly attention than that from the German-speaking countries or France. If the music is less sophisticated, its social background is more familiar, national boundaries have been stable, and important archives have survived. As in other countries, wars seemed to encourage wind bands and their music as well as disturb traditions, especially the American War of Independence and Napoleon's threatened invasion two decades later. In 18th century England, Handel dominated the whole musical scene. His diverse works for winds range from the familiar and mighty *Music for the Royal Fireworks* (71) to the barely known *Overture* for 2cl hn and various movements for 2ob 2hn bn. Yet, even with a composer as famous as Handel, so much of this music and its origin is unfamiliar that one can still approach British wind music with fewer preconceptions than with the music of Paris or Vienna.

Wind Music in Public Places

Early Developments: The Waits. "Waits" has three related meanings: the watchmen who patrolled the streets, the pungent-sounding oboe-like shawms they played, and the bands of musicians who played for civic occasions (perhaps from the town hall balcony, as in famous pictures by Holbein and Dürer) or for private hire (72, 73). Waits sang; they played string instruments, but their wind instruments gave the volume and tone quality needed outdoors. The wind bands of the Waits were precursors of wind harmony.

Records exist for about seventy such bands prior to the English Civil War (74). The best bands gave pleasure; the worst sought a fee to be silent (72, 75-77). These bands may have been enjoyed more outside the cities. Emily Brontë's *Wuthering Heights* describes a welcome visit of a wind band during a dance in rural Yorkshire: the Earnshaw's housekeeper recalls "Our pleasure was increased by the arrival of the Gimmerton band, mustering fifteen strong: a trumpet, a trombone, clarionets, bassoons, French horns and a bass viol, besides a singer. They go the rounds of respectable houses, and receive contributions every Christmas, and we esteemed it a first-rate treat to hear them" (78). Among the many civic bands, one finds examples such as these:

Edinburgh Waits. By 1696 the "Tounis Minstrels" had replaced their earlier cornetts with "French hautboyes" (79).

Norwich Waits. This famous band was established by 1408; by 1622 it comprised 16 players, including three recorders, four hautboys, two tenor cornetts and four sackbutts. Sunday playing by the Norwich Waits was restricted soon after the Restoration.

Nottingham Waits. Established by 1501, they played for civic banquets and processions. On July 27, 1787, the Mayor paid out "to Drummers 15 Shillings and the Trumpeters 10 Shillings for the Day of Thanksgiving for Drumin & trumpetin yt Day [sic]" (74). This fee, one assumes, was either a benefit or a payment for some longer period of service.

York Waits. The York Waits were formed as early as 1272, so they may have been the first of the municipal bands, and certainly they were among the earliest.

London Waits. In 1606, the London Musicians Company enacted that its members should not appear in bands of less than four, "in consort or with violins," at banquets within the City of London or its precincts. Under Puritan control in 1642, the city authorities decided that the waits were not to play at the Royal Exchange on Sundays. A survey of the events for which they played provides glimpses of their functions.

1661. On April 23, Charles II passed through London on his way from the Tower to Westminster Abbey for his coronation (the Restoration of the Monarchy). In addition to the King's Trumpets (augmented for the occasion) which went with the procession, there were six fixed bands along the route: at Crouched Friars, eight waits on a stage; at Aldgate, six waits on a balcony; at Cornhill Conduit, eight nymphs and trumpeters; at the Royal Exchange, three singers dressed as sailors; at the Stocks, a military band; at Great Conduit, Cheapside, eight nymphs accompanied by wind music (27, 80).

1662. On December 29th, while the King entertained the Russian envoys, there was "Wind Musick playing all the while in the Galleries above" (80).

1667. At Windsor, on April 23, at the lower end of the hall where the Feast for St George's Day was taking place, the diners were entertained by winds and "on the balusters above the Wind Musicque [sic], trumpets and kettledrums" (80).

1692. The *Gentleman's Journal* (81) noted that "while the company is at table (in Stationers' Hall), the Hautboys and Trumpets play successively. Mr Showers [John Shore] hath taught the latter of later years to sound all the softness imaginable."

1742. An anonymous contemporary plate (27) of the Lord Mayor's procession (82) shows both the King's Trumpets (comprising two trumpets, two oboes, bassoon and kettledrum) and the City Music (three oboes, two bassoons).

1791. Haydn noted that, at the Lord Mayor's Dinner, "The Lord Mayor was escorted according to rank before and after dinner, and there were a good many ceremonies, a sword was carried in front of him, and a kind of golden crown, to the sound of trumpets, accompanied by a wind band" (83 p 252).

1792. Haydn again noted that Lord Claremont "ordered the wind band to play the well-known song 'God save the King' in the street during a wild snowstorm. This occurred on 19 Feb[ruar]y 1792, so madly do they drink in England" [sic] (83 p 135).

The waits were not formally disbanded until the passing of the Municipal Reform Act of 1835. They had been in decline for half a century (74, 84), especially in the larger towns. As they declined, the military bands grew in numbers with the colonial and Napoleonic Wars. Probably many players moved from the one type of band to the other.

The Pleasure Gardens and Spas. The public pleasure gardens were places for music, whether full orchestra with singers, wind bands, or just organ. Writers like Dr Johnson and his contemporaries praised the gardens' beauty and elegance, at least when weather permitted, and admission fees kept petty criminals and common whores out. "I could have thought myself upon enchanted ground, had I spirits more gentle to associate with. The hautbois in the open air is heavenly," wrote Fanny Burney (85). Other countries followed the British example: "Vauxhall Gardens" appeared in cities as far afield as New York and Charleston, South Carolina, in the New World, and "Ranelagh" and "Vauxhall" (with variously spellings) in Paris and St Petersburg in the Old World.

Vauxhall is associated with Handel's magnificent *Fireworks Music,* originally written for large wind band to celebrate the Peace of Aix-la-Chappelle. The first performance (if, indeed, it was all performed) was a disaster, with rain, accidental fires, and an outraged designer who threatened the organizer with a sword (little has changed in the commerce of music except choice of weapon). Sixteen years on, Leopold Mozart declared, "Vauxhall seemed the Elysian fields, with its beautifully lit gardens, laid out with such imagination, and with music from the organ, from trumpets and drums, or from that idyllic combination, clarinets, horns and bassoons" (86). Vauxhall's reputation continued, with contributions from James Hook and J C Bach. From 1821, a military band replaced the concert band; oboist W T Parke left in consequence. Presumably the (lost) music by Thomas Powell (noted in *Sainsbury*) and John Parry's arrangements of songs by Hook were for this band. Natural decay and changing tastes took their toll, assisted by moves to suppress pleasure of any sort on Sundays. Vauxhall finally closed in 1859. Its raised "orchestra" (bandstand) was demolished and the site built over.

When J C Bach used arrangements of Gluck and Boccherini in his *Wind Symphonies* of the 1770s, he may have been adapting ideas he had heard in France. He gave no sign that the music was arranged, but nor did Asplmayr or Mozart always say when they arranged the music of others. The pleasure gardens would have been a natural place for arrangements. Sadly, we have little idea of what was played, but it can hardly have been all original music. Those few arrangements which survive from the 1780s and 1790s (such as *Non più andrai* arranged by Eley, and versions of Dibdin and Pleyel by Brooks) suggest there were isolated movements within divertimentos, not extended suites from operas. The Royal Music accounts point to changes between 1800 and 1805, when copies were bought of opera and ballet arrangements by Cimador, Cimarosa, W Müller, Paisiello, Salieri, and various British composers, mostly now lost. Arrangements for winds survive from operas by J C Bach, Dittersdorf, Martín y Soler, Paisiello, and Storace. These examples may have led Zwingmann to publish his *Airs and March* from Steibelt's *La belle laitière* in 1805. The few such works published between 1805 and 1815 (by Eley, John Parry, and others) are a mere 1% of the total published output, far less than in France or Austria. More music may have been configured for specific bands, such as for the bands of the Prince of Wales, which played arrangements, such as Haydn symphonies. The programs of spa bands and military bands of the 1830s and 1840s were similar to those in continental Europe, but probably less sophisticated.

Ranelagh seems to have adopted the "idyllic combination" of winds in the early 1760s when, between the four parts of the evening concert, "French horns and clarinets played favorite pieces in the Chinese Temple while the ladies and gentlemen took the air in the garden" (88 pps 117-118). The Chinese Temple, a sign of the fashion for all things oriental, was a modest pavilion across the canal which, like the Rotunda, was a feature of Ranelagh. The format proved popular, and even in the late 1770s it was still "Horns and clarionets at 7 and the band at half past" (88 p 131). The music would have matured; certainly J C Bach's *Wind Symphonies* fit the time and description, in 1781, of "modern instrumental music which blended with the heavy grandeur of the ancients" (88 p 138). Times became harder in the 1780s, not only because of the uneasy peace with America but also because of mundane problems, such as the poor quality of the refreshments offered. The fortunes of the gardens also depended much on the fame of their singers. The year 1788 proved exceptionally bad, for Ranelagh opened without singers at all, though there was an extra band of wind instruments in their place.

Other London gardens offered the same sort of entertainment (87, 89, 90) and presumably the octets heard were by such composers as W F E Bach, Eichner and Weilland. Visitors to Marylebone Gardens in 1766 would have heard "choice pieces on the Clarinets and French Horns played by Messrs. Frickler, Hennig, Seipts and Raythen" (89). Less pretentious gardens, such as Finch's Grotto Gardens, followed suit.

The musicians of the pleasure gardens in summer were often the same musicians who played in opera houses and theaters in winter. Not surprisingly, the special effects of wind harmony found their way into opera as well. English composers applied these effects with skill: works such as Arne's *Artaxerxes* (1762), which Mozart may have heard in London, certainly foreshadowed Mozart's use of wind harmony in his mature operas. How far Arne's style was typical is difficult to judge, for full scores and sets of parts of many subsequent English operas were destroyed in London theater fires. Certainly Arne used a stage wind band as early as 1761, in *Thomas and Sally.* Later British composers such as Michael Kelly, Stephen Storace and William Shield employed wind music, sometimes under or behind the stage, typically for marches (as in Shield's *Siege of Gibralter* [sic]) or for scenes of the supernatural. Shield used pairs of clarinets, horns and bassoons to accompany the serving of the feast during the finale of his 1784 opera, *Robin Hood,* a precursor of the band in Mozart's *Don Giovanni.*

Open-air wind music was not confined to London. Dublin was early to encourage concerts by wind bands, such as those at the Floating Orchestre [sic] at the City Bason (1, 91). The developing provincial spas followed many of the traditions of the London pleasure gardens too. In Bath, the second most important center of musical and social life in England in the 18th century, the "Band of Horns and Clarionets" which had made its appearance in the 1760s continued to play both in the evenings and at the public breakfasts well into Jane Austen's lifetime (92). When the Prince of Wales and the Duke of York visited Bath in 1797 - the last great royal visit before Brighton eclipsed Bath as the fashionable English resort - Dr Henry Harington wrote a new set of words for the march in Charles Burney's 1751 entertainment *Queen Mab,* and the music, arranged as a three-part glee, was performed "accompanied with Horns and Clarionets at Dinner" (93). An anonymous poem "A Peep at Spring Gardens: on a Public Evening" (perhaps by R B Sheridan) in the *Bath Journal* of 2 July 1778 evokes the Spring Gardens Vauxhall:

> The Flutes, Horns & Clarinets ravishing sound,
> In soft modulations re'echo'd around;
> The Goddess of Pleasure threw open the gate
> Which display'd all the Beaux & the Belles - tête-à-tête.

Mention of flutes and omission of bassoons may be poetic license. It is probable that there was a bassoon with the Band of Horns & Clarinets in the following year, for the announcement of the band's Benefit Breakfast Concert in the *Bath Journal* (20 May 1779) lists the members as "Messrs. Cantilo, Loder, Stevens, Whitehead & W Cantilo." A more Italian emphasis followed from the mid-1780s, under Venanzio Rauzzini. Yet the wind players of the Bath Theatre Royal were good: visitors to the Pump Room in the 1830s noted "the high enjoyment afforded from the recently introduced first-rate military band which performs daily during the season, from 2 till 4 o'clock, choicest productions of Rossini, Auber, Strauss, and other composers, aided occasionally by first-rate artistes from the Metropolis" (94). Other bands visited Bath as well. In 1873, Henry Falconar wrote to his mother describing the Floral Fête in Sydney Gardens, "We had the Horse Guards who were conducted by Charles Godfrey and the Hanoverian Band; they both played better than ever they did in Bath before, at least Papa, Harriette and I thought so" (95).

At Cheltenham Spa in the 1830s, the Montpellier Band, claimed to be one of the finest provincial bands, played every evening from about seven to half past nine. The band, led by the clarinettist, Mr Murphy, with the flautist, Mr Davies, Mr André on serpent and Mr Klussman as the first horn - with other wind players to a total of about fifteen - played "the most celebrated and scientific compositions, as well of ancient as of modern times, appropriately arranged, and which are played with great taste and ability" (96). In the 1840s, the mixture was much the same, although some of Mr Murphy's colleagues had changed; the clarinets were Cox, Best, Graham and Donegani; flutes Davies and Cox; P Jarrett played bassoon, his brother, trumpet, and Ryale, horn; Hatton and Cox were trombonists and Collins played serpent and ophicleide. The music was by Auber, Strauss, Donizetti, Bishop, and by composers less well known. These bands of the 1840s selected their material along the same lines as the Viennese ensembles had done fifty years earlier. By 1846 a full band, twenty strong, played each morning and for evening promenades. The setting brought comments reminiscent of those of the earlier pleasure gardens: "the Rotunda and Promenade Room, as well as the Grand Walk, are brilliantly lighted up, producing a beautiful and diorama-like effect upon the appearance of every object ..., more in harmony with the fairy scene" (96). Not all band music was of this caliber. The Town Band of Tunbridge Wells in 1889 was known as the "Thirsty Eight", presumably for reasons we encounter in part 3.

Private Bands, on the Water and Elsewhere

Court Bands, on the Water. The outing on the Thames for which Handel composed his *Water Music* was by no means the first of its kind. In 1501, the water pageant along the Thames celebrated the wedding of Prince Arthur to Katherine of Aragon, "with the most goodly and pleasant mirthe of trumpetts, clarions, shalmews, tabers, recorders and other dyvyrs instruments, to whoes noyse uppon the water hathe not been heard the like"[sic] (97). Almost two centuries later, King William and Queen Mary heard "wind and trumpets on the river", on the Thames near London in 1689. On a larger scale, during the spectacular Regatta on the Thames in 1772, "three select bands of the most eminent masters on wind instruments" were hired to "entertain the Company while on the water and at the time of disembarking" (96 pps 117-118, 98). The journey to Kew was popular too. Mrs Papendiek, recalling her years in the service of Queen Charlotte, mentioned several times bands on the Thames opposite the Prince of Wales's house. In the spring of 1781, she observed, "The nobility, on fine afternoons, came up in boats, other boats being filled with bands of music, to take the Prince to the promenade at Richmond" (96; see also 99).

Court Bands. The Prince of Wales, later Prince Regent, and then George IV, kept his own band to play for him when he wished. He was a talented musician, a keen lover of music, and indeed an enthusiast in his various loves and hatreds. J C Bach, Haydn, and Carl Stamitz wrote marches for him. Despite the marches and the many arrangements which must have existed, he inspired little original works of real substance, presumably because of his reputation for not paying debts. "Perhaps you may also be able to point out to me how I can recover from the Prince Regent the cost of transcribing the *Battle Symphony* on Wellington's victory at Vittoria, to be dedicated to him, for I have long given up hope of receiving anything from that quarter," complained Beethoven to Salomon, "I have not even been deemed worthy of an answer as to whether I am to be authorized to dedicate the work to the Prince Regent" (100 p 836, 101).

One must distinguish between bands like the King's Band, the Prince Regent's Band, and bands of the armed forces, whether of the regular army or of the militia. Such distinctions can be deceptive. The directors of the King's Band were professional musicians (Sir William Parsons, from 1786 to 1817; William Shield, from 1817 to 1829) but many band members were not; it sufficed for them to hire deputies when needed.

The Prince of Wales's bands evolved in several stages (102). The first was the Band of the 10th Hussars, formed shortly after 1795. This band performed primarily at Carlton House, the Prince's London residence. The Prince of Wales's Private Band followed. It included F André, the serpent virtuoso, later associated with the Montpellier Band at Cheltenham and with Queen Victoria's Private Band at Windsor. The Prince Regent's Band, active from 1811 to 1820, was usually based at the Pavilion, Brighton. On 5 February 1811, the Prince was sworn in as Regent; by the next year, it was clear that King George III could not be expected to recover, and this meant that the various financial constraints on the Prince Regent had to be formally removed. The ceremony took place on 18 February 1812, accompanied by "God Save the King" and "martial airs" played, interestingly, not by the Prince's band but by the Band of the 1st Regiment of Guards (103). In 1818 the Prince Regent's Band comprised thirty-four players: 3fl 2ob 8cl 4hn 4bn 4tp 4tb (s-tb ["canto" in some scores] a-tb t-tb b-tb) 4serp (one solo and three ripieno players) and timpani. With the death of George III, the Prince Regent succeeded to the throne as George IV and the band's name was changed to The King's Household Band to reflect his new status. The band was active throughout his reign (1820-30), based at Windsor. This band boasted a still larger ensemble: 3fl 3ob 12cl 4hn 2bn 4tp 6tb (a-tb t-tb 4b-tb) 2serp 2timp. It is probably this band which is shown in John Nash's famous folio publication on the Brighton Pavilion (104, plate 14).

Economy was not one of George IV's virtues. The band cost £6,000 per year, exclusive of uniforms, to play for balls and to entertain guests each night. It was directed by Christian Kramer (104, 105), once a pupil of Peter von Winter. Whatever was thought of Kramer's arrangements (he was described by contemporaries as "a musician of the very first water" and as "an insignificant hack" by a modern scholar seeing Kramer's adaptation of a Mozart opera [106]) or his improvements in serpent design, he filled his band with some of the best players in Europe. Kramer was born in Hanover in 1767, and must have been one of the first of the foreign bandsmen to arrive in England; he played the clarinet and flute, joining the service of the Prince in 1803 and leading the band from 1813. A quiet, gentlemanly person, Kramer understood the future George IV to perfection; when Sir George Smart asked him how he managed to choose tempos for Haydn symphonies to satisfy such an exacting master, he replied "Why, His Majesty always beats time to every movement - I watch him and beat the same time to the orchestra." This mutual sympathy was probably aided by a common affliction: both monarch and musician suffered from gout. In 1829 Kramer became Master of the King's Music, after the death of William Shield.

Other Private Bands. "Four beautiful cabinned pinnaces, one for the ladies, one for the gentlemen, one for the kitchen and servants, one for the dining room and band of music, weighed anchor, on a fine July morning, from below Crotchet Castle, and were towed merrily, by strong trotting horses, against the stream of the Thames" (107). Water music still held its charms in 1831. Haydn enjoyed the experience too when, in August 1791, he "went with Mr Fraser up the Tems [Thames] from Westminster Bridge to Richmond, where we ate on an island. There were 24 persons in our party, besides a Feld Music" (83, 108 p 95). The entertainers and entertained were kept comfortably apart by putting the musicians on a separate vessel: "We rowed up the river as far as Richmond," wrote Mrs Delaney, "and were entertained all the time with very good music in another barge. The Concert was composed of three hautboys, two bassoons, flute allemagne and young Grenoc's trumpet" (98 p 47). The wealthy found many reasons to hire bands. When General Burgoyne (whose surrender at Yorktown effectively ended the American War of Independence) organized a Fête Champêtre in 1774 to celebrate the marriage of the 12th Earl of Derby he chose as composer François Hyppolyte Barthélémon, who wrote wind music for Marylebone Gardens (109). French horns saluted guests as they arrived; a "capital band of music" lay concealed behind the orangerie. The guests heard a "harmonious sound from the instrumental band which, being conveyed to the company through the orange plantation and shrubbery, created a most happy and pleasing effect, and which was still the more heightened by the company not being able to distinguish from which quarter it came."

Church and Masonic Bands

Sunday observance speeded the decline of the pleasure gardens and their music, but encouraged music of its own. The fortunes of English church bands varied over the years. After the Restoration, bands flourished for want of good singers; by the mid-18th century, good players were in short supply, and organs replaced bands. Even so, amateur oboists and bassoonists were common in country churches in the 1760s (4, 110-112).

Systematic studies of records show that church bands varied widely in constitution (112). Many had strings and winds; most had a bassoon or other bass instrument. Early bands included oboes and flutes, but those active after the 1830s preferred clarinets (always in C). Most music was read from choir parts. Among the few full scores for winds are those by William Dixon, of Liverpool, and John Alcock. Dr Alcock's delightful *Let chearful [sic] Smiles in ev'ry Face. A favorite Hymn for Christmas Day 1779* (**JYA-1v**) includes substantial opening and closing sections for 2ob bn. The same instrumental forces are used in *Six New Anthems* (1795; **JYA-2v**) by Dr Alcock and his son, John Alcock the Younger. Dixon's 1792 *Four Services in Score for the Use of Country Choirs* (**WYD-1v**) includes a note: "N.B. Let the Oboe accompany the Tenor, and the Flutes the Alto and Treble throughout" (the bassoon part is independent).

Bands of the regular army, like that of the Royal Artillery, played for church services (11). The expansion of the militia bands in the 1790s may have given a new lease of life to the church bands. Certainly there are works suggesting a link between the military and the church, like the march *Hallelujah* (c.1793, attributed to Willoughby Bertie, 4th Earl of Abingdon) whose title page shows trumpet, flag and weapons, linking church and state. The link is evident in another march by the Earl of Abingdon, in his setting of the Funeral Service. As all the choral parts are unaccompanied, or with organ only, one presumes that this funeral march was for the outdoor part of the ceremony.

In the 19th century, the enthusiasm showed by these church bands was beyond praise, but their sound could be beyond belief: "The bare walls ached with the screech of their discord ... it was the only part of the service in which no one could sleep" (113). Hardly wind harmony, but one can regret the demise of these well-intentioned bands. The spirit is nicely caught by a verse on a bassoon c.1810 from Hawridge Church, now in the County Museum, Aylesbury, England: *I hear some men hate music - Let them show in Holy Writ what else the Angels do - then those that do despise such sacred mirth are neither fit for Heaven nor fit for Earth.* Not all disappeared quietly: in 1866 the band of Walsingham, Norfolk, objected so strongly to the new organ which was to replace them that they threatened to blow up the church with gunpowder (113). The bands themselves could be in danger: the Salvation Army bands were attacked many times; at Eastbourne, UK, on 22 November 1891, the crowds tried to drive them into the sea.

Wind music was not confined to the Anglican Church: in the 1820s, Robert Owen founded a wind and brass band at his Model New Lanark Mills for an interlude in two-hour sermons (114). By the mid-19th century, civilian brass bands were also emerging, generally linked to the great industrial establishments. At first the intentions behind this new trend had more to do with encouraging abstinence from liquor and violence than inculcating a love of music. In much the same spirit, missionaries in Papua New Guinea are said to have encouraged bands as a substitute for headhunting.

Masonic Music.   English Freemasonry differed from continental freemasonry in many ways. One difference was in its music, perhaps because organs were more common in England. James Boswell (115) described an excursion by Samuel Johnson and a Mr Langton "to see a freemason's funeral procession, when they were at Rochester, and some solemn music being played on French horns." Johnson said "This is the first time I have ever been affected by musical sounds," adding that the impression made upon him was of a melancholy kind. Not all Masonic music was sad; Thomas Ebdon's *Favorite March* was performed at the installation of William Henry Lambton, Esquire, as Grand Provincial Master of Free and Accepted Masons for the County of Durham.

Military Bands

The American War of Independence and the Napoleonic Wars led to the growth of military bands as the militia and regular forces expanded. At the same time, trade and ambitions for empires took armies and their bands to distant parts of Asia and Africa, establishing further musical traditions. The militia, usually organized on a county basis, comprised largely amateur bodies deployed for defense rather than offense, and officers acquired their commissions through land qualification rather than purchase. Units of volunteer militia aspired to the ceremony of the regular army, so a band was considered more a necessity than a luxury. Bands of lesser regiments and provincial militia thrived; now, their music can be the only memento of regiments long vanished. Examples of such marches are recorded by the London Military Ensemble, Classics for Pleasure CFP 40230; Grenadier Guards Band/Parkes, Decca SB 706; London Bach Ensemble/Sharpe, Saga 5417; and Royal Military School of Music/Beat, Music Makers MMC 0632 and 0633.

British Army Bands. Many early bands were simply parade bands of civilians, paid for by the officers of the regiment. "If your regiment should not be provided with a band of music, you should immediately persuade the captains to raise one. This, you know, is kept at their expense, whilst you reap the principal benefit" wrote Grose (116), tongue-in-cheek, in his 1782 *Advice to the Officers of the British Army*. He added, "the band will if properly managed, serve to raise you a considerable interest among the gentlemen of the country and, what is more, among the ladies." Grose's suggestion that English officers should establish bands fell on fertile ground. The costs of bands - borne by the officers - could be considerable. In 1767, over the full year the thirteen captains of the 3rd Guards paid out a total of £119; the officers of the Oxfordshire Militia paid £231 per year in 1778 (117). The bandmaster received by far the most (two guineas per week in the Oxfordshire Militia) but had, of course, duties to match. Costs could vary considerably, depending on the number and quality of musicians: the cost of players and instruments for the Cambridgeshire Militia in 1781 was only £60.

Bands of the Regular Army. Parade bands began to appear regularly in England in the 1750s. Handel's music was among the best played by the earlier bands, and his music was never forgotten for long: the "Dead March" from *Saul* and "See, the Conquering Hero Comes" have long and sometimes strange military links. However, the "conquering hero" was not written for the Duke of Cumberland after his victory at Culloden; while found in *Judas Maccabeus*, composed to celebrate the suppression of the Jacobite revolt, the chorus was a later interpolation from the oratorio *Joshua*. "See, the Conquering Hero Comes" was played by the band of the 12th Regiment when the siege of Gibraltar was raised in 1779 (see also Shield, **WYS-1m**), and was a favorite composition for victories such as the fall of San Sebastian during the Peninsular War (1813) and the arrival of Sir Robert Napier after the fall of Magdala, which effectively ended the Abyssinian campaign in 1868. In 1840, it was the piece chosen by Queen Victoria to accompany the entrance of Prince Albert at their wedding. When the Thames Tunnel was opened in March 1843, this same piece was performed by the Band of the Fusilier Guards (118).

The first enlisted band was formed by the Royal Artillery in 1762, with its eight musicians playing ten military instruments (two oboes, two clarinets, two horns, two bassoons and two trumpets), expected to double on flute and strings without embarassment. Bands remained small until the 1780s. Robert Hinde's 1778 *The Discipline of the Light Horse* describes the basic cavalry band as 2cl 2hn 2bn. In 1783, an octet of civilians provided music for all three regiments of Guards; their duties amounted only to accompanying the daily journey from Horse Guards' Parade to St James's Palace and back. The Coldstream Guards acquired its own band in 1785 following the disputes with civilian musicians mentioned earlier. The fashion for foreign bands was begun in the mid-1780s when twelve men arrived from Hanover (two oboes, four clarinets, two horns, two bassoons, trumpet and serpent); trombones and a "Turkish" percussion section followed soon after. Christopher Eley was appointed Music Major, a post he held until 1818. Eley acquired a reputation as a skilled arranger. One satisfied customer was Michael Kelly, who remarked that the march from his opera *Bluebeard* was arranged "most delightfully" (119). Regimental tradition has it that the Coldstream Guards adopted Mozart's "Non più andrai" from *Le Nozze di Figaro* (the aria arranged, rather than the wind march within the aria) as the regimental slow march as early as 1787. Tradition may be right, but we do not know of a published version earlier than 1792. Early publications of "The Duke of York's March, perform'd by the Coldstream Regt" (**CFE-1am**) are in Eley's name, without mention of Mozart.

Most regular regiments had their own bands (9, 117), many founded during the years 1747 to 1769 when some 24 bands were mentioned for the first time (9, 14). Even the navy had its bands: at the Battle of Trafalgar (1805) there were several private bands (120 p 36). The players were civilians, so their presence sometimes led to friction. The civilians were not always volunteers: press gangs claimed some; others were spoils of war, such as French deserters from the Peninsular War, or the band of sixteen German, Danish, and Italian musicians captured from the Dutch fleet by the HMS *Windsor Castle* in 1799 (two years after the British victory over the Dutch fleet at Camperduin which inspired Steibelt's *Combat Naval,* later arranged by Goepfert, **CAG-9a**).

Mobility of Players. In the United Kingdom, there were few court bands like that of the Prince of Wales. There were town bands, successors to the waits; there were bands associated with the church, though these were less sophisticated; there were bands of pleasure gardens and theaters. There were also military bands; in the United Kingdom, these were an important link between sectors. Players could move from one ensemble to another. As *A New Musical Directory for the Year 1794* (121) shows, many bandsmen from the Regiments of Guards played for the pleasure gardens, for theaters, for the oratorios, for musical charitable organizations (like the Royal Society of Musicians, or the New Musical Fund), or for "grand performances in Westminster Abbey." Examples include the following:

Theaters. *Astley's Theater:* Tamplin (tp, 2nd Regt of Guards); *Circus (later Surrey Theater):* William Jackson (hn, 2nd Regt); *Covent Garden Theater, Oratorios:* C F Eley (cl, 2nd Regt), Robert Munro (ob, fl, cl, 3rd Regt), William Jenkinson (bn, drum, 3rd Regt); *Drury Lane Oratorios:* J C Flack (tb, hn, 1st Regt), C F Eley, (cl, 2nd Regt); John Hawton (tp, 3rd Regt), Sickel (serp, db, 2nd Regt), John Zwingman (tb, 2nd Regt).

Pleasure Gardens. *Apollo Gardens:* Counts [Kauntz] (cl, 2nd Regt); *Ranelagh:* William Jenkinson (bn, drum, 3rd Regt).

The members of the Guards' bands were a select group of musicians. It is no surprise that several of them were composers: Flack, T Smart (1st Regt of Guards); Eley, G Kauntz, Elrington (presumably the flautist William Elrington [1st Regt] rather than Elrington Jnr [2nd Regt]), Zwingman (2nd Regt); John Mahon (3rd Regt). Zwingman's arrangement of Steibelt's *La belle laitière* (London, c.1805) is for a configuration very close to that of his regimental band (2fl 2cl 2hn 2bn tp buglehorn serp).

The Militias. The regulars of the British Army were distinct from their part-time associates, the militia, the yeomanry, the fencibles and the volunteers. There were similarities in who paid for the bands, who organized them, and in what sort of music was played, though differences arose in the course of time. The militia were only mobilized when need arose in the American War of Independence, the Napoleonic Wars, the Crimean War and other periods of tension (120, 121). Thus the Oxfordshire Militia (117) was embodied only for five main periods: 1778-1783, 1792-1799, 1803-1815, 1854-1856 and 1857-1860. The regiments of militia were used sparingly, mainly for minor military operations, like the dispersal of Colonel Tate's abortive invasion in February 1797, repulsed by the Pembroke Volunteers and Yeomanry and the Fishguard Fencibles (122). Not all performances were military. *Jackson's Oxford Journal* of 8 November 1856 notes that the Oxford Militia Band "under its able leader, Mr Viesohn, played during the dinner to celebrate the roof-rearing of the new mansion" of Oxford brewer James Morrell. The mansion was later used by Robert Maxwell, publisher.

Organizational Matters. British War Office General Regulations regarding bands tended to appear during outbreaks of peace: in 1786 prohibiting musical accompaniment to marching, in 1835 prohibiting the use of foreign marches, and in 1883 systematizing the bands. We are indebted to Mr Christopher Duffy for pointing out that marching in step was not normal in the early 18th century. The Neapolitans introduced it, but it became common only after changes in military discipline under monarchs like Frederick the Great. One even finds 19th century marches whose natural musical speed is not appropriate for the physical act of marching (see also Section 3.3). Change occurred quickly, mainly because the Turkish percussion sections made disciplined manoeuvres much easier (11). The entry in Fanny Burney's *Diary* (123 p 282) for 23 May 1815, just before Waterloo, says "my ears were alarmed by the sound of military music, and my eyes equally struck with the sight of a body of troops marching to its measured time."

Scale of Activity. Not only did the army grow (74,000 in 1748; 110,000 during the American Wars of 1776; 200,000 in 1807) and the number of bands grow, but also the bands began to grow in size. "New" instruments were added: the flute from about 1790 and the trombone from about 1800. Numbers of other instruments were increased to maintain balance, with clarinets being normally about one quarter of the total. In the 1760s, two clarinets sufficed in an octet; in the 1820s, ten clarinets were normal for a band of around forty, and the larger bands of the 1880s had similar proportions. This expansion of bands, from one player per part to several players per part, began the move from wind harmony to the modern military bands and large wind bands.

The military activities of regulars and militia were matched by musical activity. Our lists show that in UK collections there are nearly 200 surviving items or sets of items in full score or parts, amounting to well over 700 items; this excludes the many published only in keyboard versions. We know of many lost works, some published at the time (like John Marsh's *Chichester Volunteers' March* and his *Overture* and *10 Pieces,* or several of John Parry's works).

Looking through the lists, we see that marches were written for regiments of most counties in England or for their major cities. Marches are named for specific officers (by Attwood), special occasions (not necessarily military, such as Ebdon's Masonic march; this is consistent with our remarks about the way wind bands were involved in several sectors of society) or specific people (by Biggs, Dittrich). Armies encamped, mobilized but not yet at war, provided an important market (works by Busby, Dibdin, and McLean). Some marches were for volunteer regiments (Bridgemen), others for regulars (like Eley's works for the Guards). Scottish regiments were well catered for, and India was not forgotten (Abington, Williamson, and Anon [A-55.3m]), with a few marches explicitly for Europe (Barthélémon; J C Bach). The many reductions for flute, guitar or piano may have been intended for loyal amateurs, families and sweethearts. Songs with band are rare. Davy and Schroeder wrote examples (Dibdin's military band versions of his *War Songs* omit the vocal parts), but their texts are really not ones for soldiers to sing. Purcell's "Britons, Strike Home" could be and was sung at the front line (as in 1791 when the 52nd Foot rushed the breach at Savandroog, India [13 p 11]). This would not be credible for Schroeder's *Since Virgil Wrote in Yeoman's Praise.*

The Concert Tradition

The English concert scene kept in touch with developments in wind harmony during the 19th century. This can be seen from the programs of two of the long-lived series of London concerts, those of the Philharmonic Society and the Promenade Concerts. Some efforts were made to follow the initiative of Reicha in presenting the wind quintet as an alternative to the string quartet. Yet, despite early performances of Reicha's works in England, the wind quintet also lapsed as a viable form until its revival during the late 19th century. Oddly, it was his quintets with cor anglais which were mentioned by *Sainsbury* (124, under "Reicha"), even though they were not published until nearly a century and a half later. The ensemble which played the works by Reicha may have been the "Classical Concerts for Wind Instruments" (125), namely the Bohemian flautist Jean Sedlatzek, the French oboist Apollon Marie-Rose Barret (1804-1879), the English clarinettist Thomas Leslie Willman (1784-1840), the Belgian bassoonist Friedrich Baumann (1801-1856) and the Italian hornist Giovanni Puzzi (1792-1876).

The first Philharmonic Society concert, on 8 March 1813, included a serenade by Mozart, played by clarinettists John Mahon and James Aldwell Oliver, bassoonists Holmes and Tully, with the brothers Joseph and Peter Petrides on horns (126). The serenade is unidentified, and it is just possible that it was a spurious work (127). A week later, the concert contained a "Notturno" for octet, also by Mozart, the players being joined by oboists Friedrich Griesbach and M Sharpe. This can be identified from the surviving copy (GB-Lbl Loan 4.1874); "The original and only copy in score for Wind Instruments of Mozart's celebrated Notturno as performed at the Philharmonic Concerts" proves to be second, third and fourth movements of K.388. The sixth concert included arrangements of unspecified Mozart works for winds and piano. The Society was a sponsor of the very best in music from its inception. Even in the relatively barren 1850s, the Philharmonic Society continued to champion Mozart's wind music (128).

The transition was easier in the less formal Promenade Concerts whose atmosphere and setting had more in common with the pleasure gardens. In both London and Paris, they shared with the gardens an unsavory reputation from those who did not come for the music. In London the term "promenader" became a euphemism for a prostitute; in Paris, they were known as "Musardines" from concerts pioneered by Philippe Musard. Musard's success in London was followed in the 1840s by Jullien (who had 35 forenames from his father's fear of offending any member of his orchestra by selecting one as godfather) (129, 130). Jullien's Promenades featured large wind bands, giving rise to musical excesses, with a huge orchestra augmented by four military bands, "monster bass drum" and "monster ophicleide." It is hard today to realize that once Musard was known as "The Paris Strauss" and Jullien as "The London Strauss."

Sir Henry Wood's success in establishing a great annual series of such Promenade Concerts is thus all the more remarkable (131). His initiative went far beyond what a farsighted pleasure garden proprietor might have imagined. Many wind works received their English premieres there: d'Indy's *Chanson et Danses,* for example, was featured on 23 September 1899, very soon after its world premiere in Paris on 7 March of that year. Some works were specially commissioned, like the successful *Suite Miniature de*

Chansons à Danser of Madame Poldowski, the daughter of Wieniawski and pupil of d'Indy. Nor was the standard repertoire forgotten: works by Mozart, Beethoven, and Richard Strauss were given. What is standard now was not familiar around 1900; the erudite composer and musicologist Ferruccio Busoni did not recognize Mozart's *Gran Partita*, K.361 (**WAM-1**), though he did appreciate Mozart's genius in his use of clarinets and basset horns: "Those legato arpeggi are wonderful. Some of our younger composers can afford to learn much from Mozart" (132 p 203) - an observation as true today as in 1906. Even though the Queen's Hall Orchestra boasted an outstanding wind section, Sir Henry Wood found that the smaller-scale works "did not go down well with the public. My young stalwarts who will stand still for forty or fifty minutes will not do the same thing for seven or eight players. I suppose they feel they are not getting their money's worth" (132 p 154).

Developments from 1815 to the Present

Political revolution and Napoleon's wars affected both major institutions and the way of life of private citizens. In England, the Industrial Revolution changed both the landscape and the distribution of wealth. Shifts of fashion affected both Court ceremony and the fashions of entertainment. George IV's famous band ceased when he died. Later monarchs supported music less lavishly. The violin, piano, and harp were in the ascendant; amateur music making became largely a feminine pursuit. Public taste was pandered to by giant bands, by facile and flashy instrumental variations, and by sentimental vocal ballads, rather than by elegant (if sometimes facile) wind harmony. The sensibility of romanticism shifted taste away from an appreciation of ensemble - one of the most vital features of wind harmony - and substituted such metaphors as the individual's (the soloist's) heroic, but inevitably doomed, struggle against fate (the orchestra). Wind harmony and its music declined, apart from rarities like the *Septet* of Charles Lucas (qv), whereas larger brass and military bands developed vigorously.

The role of professional musicians also changed. Styles of composition and band configurations altered. Military bands grew ever larger and took on more ceremonial as well as genuinely military functions. Players, released from what often amounted to near serfdom (more so in Europe than in England) sought other patrons. With the rise of commercial and some civic concerts, many players preferred the life of itinerant virtuosos. Technical dexterity was a saleable commodity. Survival was not easy and many succumbed to drink (part 3) or supplemented their income from music in other ways. As an example (124), Montague Corri, born c.1784 into a family of musicians, planned to be a painter, but later ran away to sea. Turning to music as his profession, he then dislocated a finger, so that he could not play the piano. Close to poverty, he had to augment his income by work as a painter and a fencing instructor. He could still arrange music for military bands, and was an able composer and arranger of theater music. This had other risks as well: he survived shipwreck when returning to London from Newcastle, where he had been arranging music for regimental bands.

Original music for wind harmony developed more slowly. Parry's 1877 *Nonet* was one of the first seriously written wind ensemble works of the modern revival. Later works point to the range of wind music which has evolved. There is music based on folk songs (Jacob's *Old Wine in New Bottles),* works with a lighter touch (Cole's *Serenade for 9 Winds),* works with conscious neoclassicism (Jacob's *Divertimento*), occasional works for formal ceremonies (Arnold's *Trevelyan Suite),* occasional works for very special occasions (Jacob's *Variations on "Annie Laurie"* for the Hoffnung Festival [133]), and works written as serious modern music, notably Maxwell Davies's *St Michael Sonata,* and several of Birtwistle's works. Lutyens's *The Rape of the Moone* shows that wind harmony survives in a lively and contemporary form, not just as a basis for nostalgia. The 1980s and 1990s have seen more fine works, including a set of pieces designed to be played in the gardens at Glyndebourne to precede the Mozart operas. Perhaps a more important development is the rediscovery of the art of arrangement, with many fine works arranged by Campbell, Gillaspie, Sheen, Skirrow and others.

Music for military and brass bands, though outside our scope, has been important too, especially in Britain and America. Some of the music, like that of Alford and Sousa, shows real originality and range. Larger bands tempted major composers more than did wind harmony: Elgar, Holst, Vaughan Williams, Percy Grainger, and many others showed wide sympathy for larger bands. The techniques of brass writing were absorbed into choral music too, a fine example being Sir Arthur Bliss's Op 116 *The World Is Charged with the Grandeur of God,* for 2fl 3tp 4tb and chorus.

Empire and Commonwealth

British bands, especially army bands, travelled throughout the colonies and beyond (134-137). Their main purpose was to meet the musical needs of the armed forces and expatriate civilians, and the sort of music they provided was very similar to that heard at home. But the bands did more than this. They established traditions which lasted after their departure (39, 136) and absorbed some of the musical culture of the indigenous musicians. This gave an interplay of cultures, unlike developments in North America, where the imported music thrived because there was no substantial musical tradition, and unlike the impact of the Turk in Europe, where there was already a strong and receptive musical tradition. Music could even be a tool of diplomacy. In Tibet, the band playing English tunes "not too badly" in a procession (138, p 226; 139, p 296) presumably used instruments sent after Sir Charles Bell visited the Dalai Lama in 1920-21. Traditional music for Tibetan trumpets continued undisrupted.

The indigenous wind bands varied in form. The Pitt-Rivers Museum (Oxford) has instruments from a traditional Nepalese temple band (1870), with two oboes, two long horns and percussion. Traditional Tibetan music, based on oboes, long horns, cymbals, drums, bells, and chanting in which the voice produces three note chords, was broadcast and illustrated in the *Radio Times* (BBC, United Kingdom, c.1989) in a series on music of the royal courts. A Korean counterpart was heard in Seoul in 1989 (140), when the last Princess of Korea, Lee Pang Ja, was buried amid the plaintive sound of conches, musettes and trumpets. Such music could travel to unexpected places. Thus a Buddhist wind band was reported in the late 1940s in a Chinese community in Havana (141).

Cultural exchanges. Indian tunes were used in marches written in the early 19th century (A-55.3m, for the 33rd Regt, includes *Chundah's Song Hindostan Air* [sic]; 28 p 205 notes some other cases) or for Indian regiments (like the marches by Attwood and Williamson). Such tunes added color, but were less influential in Europe than the Hungarian Gypsy sound. In India, Western wind music coexisted alongside the traditional forms. Some Indian musicians took Western music to heart. An unusual appearance of "See, the Conquering Hero Comes" happened in the Indian Mutiny (1857-1858) when 10,000 sepoys besieged the small British force at Lucknow. Many of the rebels were still in their original units, including native regimental bands, and gave regular concerts. They amazed the defenders by a stirring performance of "God save the Queen" (142). In the later years of the Raj (136), "In Mysore, every ceremony or festival was always heralded by the nagaswaran (a clarinet-like wind instrument [actually double-reed]) ... There was also a Western band and orchestra ... with a wind and brass section which played during the Dassara Darbar and parades." The Nizam of Hyderabad had several bands in European style, one a band of women musicians (39).

In Japan, soon after it was opened to Western nations, foreign bands were stationed at the port of Yokohama. These included a British marine band and a French army band. When the Emperor Meiji (1852-1912) moved the capital from Kyoto to Tokyo in 1868, part of his progress along the Tokaido Road was to the sound of "The British Grenadiers," played by a British military band (135). The first Japanese military band (143) was organized in 1869 under an English bandmaster, John William Fenton (b 1829). It became the Japanese Navy Band in 1871. The Japanese Army Band was formed in 1872 under a French bandmaster. The different British and French national conventions caused minor problems of notation and scoring when the first official Japanese national anthem was composed (by a Japanese and a German bandmaster) in 1880.

British Military Bands Overseas.   The bands overseas seem to have maintained musical contact with home. The regimental bands based at Poona, India, were able to play extracts from Bellini's *I Puritani* (first performed in 1835) as early as 1839 (137). Skills did not always travel well, as shown by a review of a December 1834 concert in Sydney, Australia, by a Mr Lewis and the Band of the 17th Regiment: "With respect to the performances, there was a melodious sort of noise, but no real music. The band being placed under the gallery, the tones were flat and dull, and such as issue from an unbraced drum, or a dry flute which has not been oiled for a long time. We shall not find fault with the paucity of the violins, and with the music being military; it was unavoidable where the public will not attend in such numbers as to pay for proper concert music, supposing it could be had." While the anonymous reviewer managed to praise the band for its accurate performance of the overture to *William Tell,* he ended: "God Save the King concluded the evening's entertainment, and was about the best piece of the whole, especially when the audience joined in the chorus" (144).

The most accessible records of wind bands are the reports of funerals (134). Thus in 1802 "the band of His Majesty's 86th regiment [2nd Royal Irish Rifles, formed only in 1799] and the [Bombay] garrison band were playing the dead march, and other appropriate solemn music ..." for the funeral of James Rivett-Carnac, member of the Presidential Council. In Madras in 1833, "The Surgeon requested the Commandant to let the dead be buried quietly without music or firing, as the almost daily repetition of the 'Dead March' had a depressing effect on the sick and dying." It was the band which was disturbed at a Hyderabad funeral some years later, when it aroused swarming bees.

WIND MUSIC IN OTHER ENGLISH-SPEAKING TERRITORIES: NORTH AMERICA

Public Music in North America

When one finds references to civilian wind band music, there is often a European connection, for many immigrants brought music or musical traditions with them. Most of the British army regiments in America had their own bands (14). When their tours of duty finished, many bandsmen settled, earning their livings as teachers or from musical commerce. Their bands played for dances and outdoor promenades. It is no surprise that music for winds in the New World paralleled its Old World forms. In the present century, the influence has been in the other direction, such as through music for larger wind bands. American marching bands, symphonic bands of the highest quality, and popular dance bands have had a major impact throughout the world (25).

In 1786, Vincent M Pelosi, proprietor of the Pennsylvania Coffee House .in Philadelphia advertized "by the desire of several gentlemen, he has proposed for the summer season to open a Concert of harmonial Music, which will consist of the following instruments, viz. Two Clarinets, Two French Horns, Two Bassoons, One Flute. To begin on the first Thursday of June and to continue every Thursday till the last Thursday of September" (146). Gottlieb Graupner, the Boston publisher, announced in the *Boston Gazette* (4 May 1801) that his Benefit Concert would include "Harmony for oboe, clarinet, horn and bassoons by Rosetta [sic]" (the Rosetti pieces in Bethlehem, Pennsylvania have different scoring). American composers, like Uri K Hill, Oliver Shaw, and clarinettist Samuel Holyoke, wrote marches, dances, and small band works. The first band music collection published in America (147) may have been Holyoke's *The Instrumental Assistant* (Exeter, New Hampshire, 2 volumes, 1800, 1807), based on his experience with "The Instrumental Club," an amateur group in Salem, Massachusetts.

In America, the theaters were major employers of musicians: "Almost every secular composition we possess from eighteenth century America is by a man we can place in the theater orchestra of some city" (148 p 83; 149). As in England, the pleasure garden bands were largely made up of musicians who played in the theaters during the winter months. The gardens came into their own in the summer, where breakfast and evening entertainments best fitted a climate with hot and humid afternoons. English names were adopted for the gardens: in New York, both a Vauxhall Gardens and a Ranelagh Gardens were founded by 1762. In 1797, New York boasted two Vauxhalls (one renamed Ranelagh the next year after yet another Vauxhall was opened). A Columbia Gardens was added in 1800, to be followed a few years later by Niblo's Gardens. At least one of New York's Vauxhalls survived through the middle of the 19th century in competition with Niblo's. Concerts were also given in pleasure gardens in Baltimore.

Private and "Court" Music in North America

Thomas Jefferson aspired to wind harmony. In 1778 (150) he wrote: "The bounds of an American fortune will not admit the indulgence of a domestic band of musicians, yet I have thought that a passion for music might be reconciled with that economy which we are obliged to observe. I retain, for instance, among my domestic servants a gardener, a weaver, a cabinet maker, and a stone cutter, to which I would add a vigneron. In a country where[,] like yours[,] music is cultivated and practised in every class I suppose there might be found persons of those trades who could perform on the French horn, clarinet or hautboy & bassoon, so one might have a band of two French horns, two clarinets & hautboys and a bassoon, without enlarging their domestic expenses." This idea recalls the practice of European courts like Oettingen-Wallerstein, where rank-and-file players were also employed as servants-in-livery. Jefferson failed to establish a Harmonie at Monticello, but he helped found the United States Marines' Band. In 1798, an Act of Congress allowed the Marine Corps a band of "one drum major, one fife major and thirty two drums," based in Philadelphia, with William Farr its first Drum Major. The band moved to Washington in 1800, and grew to include oboes, clarinets, horns and a bassoon. It performed for the first time in the White House for President John Adams on New Year's Day, 1801.

Church Bands in North America

Religion and wind harmony mixed well in North America. The Moravian Brethren made one major contribution. Music played an important part in the original community at Herrnhut (Upper Lusatia, Saxony), and this tradition was carried with the Moravians, first to Zeist (Netherlands), then to the New World settlements of Bethlehem (1741) and Lititz, Pennsylvania, and then to Salem (later Winston-Salem), North Carolina, where they established new roots for their European musical traditions. They maintained the highest possible performance standards and encouraged their own composers (6, 151-154). At first wind music was performed by a choir of trombones, often in the evenings from the roof of their Brethren House (a flat-roofed building, now the Music Department of the Moravian College). Close connections were maintained between these communities and Herrnhut. When Harmoniemusik became fashionable in Herrnhut, probably in the 1780s, it was natural for the music to find its way to the New World. Some of the music was from European sources (e.g. the *Divertimento* attributed to Haydn as Hob.II:B7 [FJH-17d] and to Mozart as K.C17.09 [WAM-18d] and, in the Moravian archives, to Joseph Morris); other music was by their own local composers, notably David Moritz Michael, who wrote sixteen works for this purpose.

Michael worked with the community at Nazareth, Pennsylvania, from his arrival in 1795. It is difficult to know exactly when wind harmony began in this area, but we note the arrival of two clarinets and a bassoon at Bethlehem in 1805. In 1808, Michael moved to Bethlehem to begin the rebuilding of the Collegium Musicum. The Moravian wind band at Bethlehem, Pennsylvania, organized by Johann Friedrich Peter (1746-1813), included clarinettists John Ricksecker (1780-1827) and David Moritz Michael, hornists (Jacob) Christian Kuckenbach (1785-1852) and (David) Peter Schneller (1787-1842), and bassoonists (Johann) Samuel Krause (1782-1815) and Jacob Wolle (1789-1863).

Michael, who arrived in the United States in 1806, organized a Whit Monday water music program (c.1809-1813) with wind music to suit each phase of the boat trip on the Lehigh River. The music included two suites by Michael, whose titles suggest the setting: *Parthia bestimmt zu einer Wasserfahrt auf der Leche* (for a boat trip on the Lehigh River), and *Parthia bey einer Quelle zu blasen* (to be played by a spring).

One unusual feature of the serenading tradition at Bethlehem was the rescoring of wind works for a Serenading Party, a band of strings and winds. Probably the works were adapted from 1850 onwards. It is very rare to find adaptations in this direction.

Military Music in North America

The wind band in America was associated both with the military and with bodies whose activities included marching, such as the Washington Benevolent Society of Boston, whose march was published by Graupner around 1803. Not much is known about what was played, though there are records (149) of early militia bands, such as the Salem (Massachusetts) Brigade founded in 1806 and the Militia Band of Bethlehem (Pennsylvania) founded in 1810. A few part-books and individual parts survive, including marches by Krommer. A survey of music extant from before or around 1800 (155) lists an abundance of music for fifes, but identifies very little music for more than one or two players. Among the few examples are a commonplace book of marches by Hervey Brooks and a copy book compiled by Silas Dickinson, Second Master of a band active at Amherst, Massachusetts, c.1800 (the First Master was Isaac Gleason). Most of the music which survives from the early years following the War of Independence consists of marches published in piano reduction, though the score of Uri Hill's *Governor Sullivan's March* calls for the unusual combination of clarinets, tenoroon and bassoon.

The few reports of performances of wind band works in the New World in the 18th century (147, 149, 155, 156) include performances in Salem and Portsmouth in 1783 (when Colonel Crane's Artillery Band, later the Massachusetts Band of Musick, played "several overtures, simphonies, military music, several songs, and several duets on the French horn"), in Boston on 20 May 1788 (clarinets and horns), and by an unidentified band in Santo Domingo, Cuba, in 1794. In the 19th century, many fife and drum bands were superseded by regimental bands, which still maintained a relatively modest size well into the 1830s. Alvin Robinson published in Exeter, New Hampshire, his 1820

Massachusetts Collection of Martial Music for fl 2cl bn. Camus (145) observed that military bandsmen in America were expected to play for social, religious, and formal occasions, as in Europe. In surviving collections, five-part compositions are most common; the third edition (Hallowell, Maine) of Ezekiel Goodale's 1829 *Instrumental Director* is for 2fl 2cl 2hn basso.

Civic Military Bands.   An article in the *American Musical Journal* (New York, October 1835) shows especially clearly just how wind bands were regarded (157):

> The state of military bands in New York is not very flattering to our city pride. With respect to these bodies we must yield the palm to our Boston friends. We have some tolerable bands, but not one of a superior kind, such as would be accounted good in a regular regiment, or equal to one or two of the Boston bands. But what may appear singular, our bands are not so good at present as they were formerly; this is partly to be accounted for, as occasioned by the attempts made a few years since, in some of our regiments, to introduce black bands. This, it is well known, occasioned much disturbance, for no body of respectable white musicians would march in line where there was a body of blacks placed as their equals. Many of the white bands performed their duty for their respective regiments until the forming of the brigade line, when, in consequence of some of the regiments having black bands, they would quit in a body, and most of our citizens will recollect one 25th of November, when the military parade looked like a long funeral from this cause. Those who witnessed this march, were forcibly impressed with what it is that gives animation and brilliancy to a military parade. The attempts to make black bands answer, has been abandoned as impracticable; but not until they caused the breaking up of nearly all our city bands. Another cause has been in operation lately, viz: the revolution or rather the transmigration which these bodies have been undergoing to the state of brass bands, which seem at present to be all the rage. Brass bands, when they play in tune, are good things to march after; but it is not in the nature of things that they can produce the beautiful effects of the old bands.
>
> We very much desire to see in this city an independent and complete band formed solely with the view of improving military music. We have associations for promoting the practice and knowledge of almost every species of music, and why not one for military music? A spirited and good body of this kind would be of the greatest utility, as constituting a standard, and exciting a spirit of emulation in others. That there is [sic] amateurs enough to be found with all the requisite capabilities to form such a band or association we believe, and there is sufficient public spirit and city pride for the purpose, we hope.
>
> A full band ought to consist of 8 Clarionets, 1 E♭ do, 1 Pic[c]olo Flute, 2 Horns, 2 Trumpets, 2 Bassoons, 2 Trombones, 1 Serpent, 1 Bass Horn, 1 Bass Drum, 1 Pr. of Cymbals, 1 Muffled Drum, 1 Triangle; Total 25 Instruments. Bands in Europe sometimes are much larger than this, but then the parts are increased in the above proportions. Sometimes oboes are employed in bands, but this is generally in cases where the music written for a theatrical orchestra is arranged for bands.
>
> Regular practice say once or twice a week under a good leader would soon render a band of amateurs really excellent. Plenty of appropriate music can easily be obtained, and the individual expense to members would be but trifling.
>
> There are various occasions on which the services of a band of this kind might be appropriately rendered. We think we can suggest one source of employment. On our fine summer evenings when the inhabitants of our metropolis flock in crowds to enjoy the sea breeze on one of the finest spots it was ever the good fortune of any city to possess, the Battery, this band might once a week serenade our citizens,

which would be both an appropriate praiseworthy and public spirited occasion for the exercise of their talents. What a delightful and gratifying sight would it be to see along those shady walks, with the moon peeping through the dense foliage of the stately elms and the waving willows, the young and light-hearted thousands promenading with measured and stately step to the music of a grand march, or on the light fantastic toe tripping to the r[h]ythm of the inspiring dance. Such a scene we can view in imagination, and it brings to mind those happy arcadian times that poets tell off [sic]. We hope some of our amateurs will take the subject into serious consideration and act upon it with spirit.

Wind Bands in the United States.   In the 20th century, the best US bands stand comparison with any in the world. This was not so in the emerging nation two hundred years ago. One interesting parallel between the British and American experiences concerns foreign bandsmen (158). Jefferson felt the Marines' Band could be improved. He arranged through Lt-Col William Ward Burrows, the Corps commandant, to seek Italian musicians to form a second band. This was achieved only with difficulty by Captain John Hall, of the USS *Chesapeake*. Bandsmen from Syracuse, Sicily, were able but uninterested; those in Gaetano Carusi's band in Catania, Sicily, were persuaded, together with others from Messina. Their passage was eventful because of war at sea, and their reception at Washington on 20 September 1805 was less than encouraging: the new Corps commandant knew nothing of the orders or arrangements for the bandsmen. In his view, "the Secretary of the Navy can never consent to allow two military bands for one Corps." Nevertheless, some players formed the nucleus of a new band. One was Venerando Pulizzi, who later led the band. Others planned to return to Sicily, including Carusi, but the plan was thwarted when a battle en route between the USS *Chesapeake* and HMS *Leopard* made it necessary to return to Washington. Recruitment from Europe continued, despite the varying fortunes of the band. Francis Maria Scala, later to lead the band, recalled in 1903 how he was recruited as a third class musician in 1841. Then the band had one flute, one clarinet, one French horn, two trombones, one bugle, one bass drum, and one pair of cymbals. The musicians came from America, Germany, England, Spain, Italy and Austria, and only five could read music (158).

Wind Bands in Canada.   In Canada, perhaps the earliest all-civilian band was formed by the Children of Peace, at Hope (later Sharon), Ontario, as a community band in 1820 to play hymns and sacred instrumental music during services at their Meeting House. The band, directed by David Willson, comprised flutes, flageolets, 3/4cl 2hn 2bn and sometimes trombone and drums. It was one of the first bands to include women (147).

The first properly Canadian militia band was founded in 1831 in Quebec City by Jean-Chrysostome Brauneis (1785-1832), who had come to Canada around 1814, with the 70th (East Surrey) Regiment of the British army. He left it c.1818 to become a teacher and seller of instruments. The band he founded was attached to the Régiment d'Artillerie, lasting just six months until Brauneis died of cholera. In 1836, Quebec-born Charles Sauvageau (c.1804-1849) revived the band (then pic 3cl 3hn bn 2tb tu timp perc) as La Musique Canadienne. It led the procession to the cathedral during the first celebration of Saint-Jean-Baptiste Day, 24 June 1842, and played patriotic music at the evening banquet. The band was dissolved in 1849 on Sauvageau's death (14, 159).

3

France

BEFORE THE REVOLUTION

Gardens and Street Music

"Whenever there is some discontent among the people, the police double the music of the streets, and it is prolonged to two hours later than usual. When the ferment increases, ambulatory music is let alone in the intersections, the drum resounds from morning to night; gunshot on one side, clarinets on the other" (160 p 199). Subtlety and sophistication might not have top priority, but music to control dissent worked both before and after the Revolution. Paris had its "Wauxhall" Gardens: the "Summer" Wauxhall on the Boulevard St Martin survived from 1764 to 1780; the "Winter" Wauxhall at St Germain lasted from 1769 until 1787. In May 1779, at the Cirque Royal, Boulevard du Luxembourg, a wind band accompanied dances in the Rotunda, a Maypole, tilting games, and fireworks; Varinière's fireworks exploited the emerging science of electricity. At Ranelagh (Paris) in October 1783 a wind band, rustic dances, fireworks, and even a balloon were reported (89 p 32). The fireworks, as in London's Marylebone Gardens, were supplied by Giovanni Battista Torré. Pleasure gardens survived the Revolution. In 1802, the gardens included the Tivoli, Bois de Boulogne, Luxembourg, Arsenal, and Soubise. In the garden of the Palais Royale, "The odour of exquisite ragouts ascends in vapours to the air ... and you may dine to the sound of musical instruments and French horns played by girls who are *not* nymphs of Diana" (161 p 73).

Private and Court Bands

Classical wind music owes much to the court of Louis XIV, where greatly improved oboes and bassoons were first produced. As Michel de la Barre noted, the oboe only became fit for concert use after Jean Hotteterre and Michel Philidor had "spoiled great quantities of wood and played great quantities of music" (162). Skilled wind players were available to provide an incentive to such experiments, notably the ten oboists and two bassoonists who constituted the Douze Grands Hautbois de la Grande Écurie (163, 164). Composers soon had reason to write elaborate wind parts for players whom they could trust. As instruments evolved during Louis XIV's long reign (1643-1715), so did the music for festivities expand (164, 165). In 1664, fireworks, plays with music, staged illusions, and trumpet fanfares were provided at Versailles - nominally for Queen Anne's visit, but perhaps more for the King's affair with Louise de la Vallière. In 1669 the celebrations for the inauguration of Louis XIV's statue in the Place Vendôme, Paris, included a mock battle on water, with boats full of players of drums, trumpets, flutes and oboes. By the time that the Treaty of Utrecht was signed in 1713 the oboes were preeminent, with contributions from "Les Hautbois, les Trompettes et les Tambours de la Grande Écurie."

The wealth of France before the Revolution made Paris the first city of European music. Foreign composers gravitated to Paris, and the influence of foreign musicians was strong. Two such composers especially encouraged the use of winds, both within the orchestra and in wind ensembles. One was the Belgian, Gossec. The other was the Bohemian, Johann Stamitz. Stamitz later created what *Burney* described as an "Army of Generals," the Mannheim court orchestra of the 1770s. Around 1750, Stamitz showed Paris just what a well-rehearsed orchestra could achieve (166, 167). He was one of the innovators who introduced the clarinet to the orchestra. Rameau, always ready to take advantage of new opportunities for orchestral color, exploited the potential of the clarinet, and many of his later operas, especially *Les Boréades* of 1764, show striking use of woodwinds (168). Rameau and Gossec, and lesser figures such as Valentin Roeser, clarinettist to the Prince de Monaco (perhaps a pupil of Stamitz), established the clarinet as the main melodic instrument in French bands, replacing the oboe adopted in central Europe. Wind bands of clarinets and horns appeared in the middle of the 18th century (105, 166, 167, 169), shaping the wind bands of such notables as the Duc d'Orléans, the Prince de Condé and the Prince de Monaco.

The court ensembles were the pioneers in playing arrangements, rather than original works. Valentin Roeser, who led the Grimaldi Harmonie in Monaco from about 1763, made early arrangements for wind band. By 1771, the market justified the publication of these arrangements for 2cl 2hn 2bn. Competition from Vanderhagen began around 1776, and they shared the market until Roeser's death c.1782. The gap this created was filled by Ozi's arrangements, from c.1783 to 1794, when Ozi became director of the Conservatoire. G F Fuchs arrived in France in 1784, and was recognized as one of the finest arrangers. Bisch, Devienne, Ernst and M J Gebauer made a few arrangements; others may have done so as well, like Eichner and Macker.

The Concert Scene

Gossec organized his long-running series of concerts in the years before the Revolution, usually including a mixture of large scale and small scale music. His Concerts des Amateurs (for music lovers), later the Concerts de la Loge Olympique took place at the Hôtel Soubise. They included his own symphonies for winds, as well as first Paris performances of major works such as Haydn's "Paris" symphonies (Hob.I:82-87). Concerts in Paris had featured wind music as early as 1735 when oboe and bassoon duets were played with great success by the brothers Alessandro and Girolamo Besozzi. Wind bands appeared in public concert performances in the Concerts Spirituels of the 1760s and 1770s, greatly increasing the popularity of the genre. The Concerts Spirituels took place in the Salle des Suisses in the Tuileries during the great religious festivals when the Opéra was closed. After the restoration of the monarchy in 1815, wind harmony continued to be played, with works still being composed by lesser figures like Berr, Blasius, Castil-Blaze, Gambaro, F Louis and C Münchs.

MUSIC FROM THE TIME OF THE REVOLUTION

Political changes had their effects on music. The period 1794 to 1799 was dominated by the large-scale festivals and an emphasis on patriotism and propaganda. Arrangements languished, but recovered with Napoleon's rise and army mobilization from c.1800. The major arrangers were Vanderhagen and Fuchs, who had lost his Conservatoire post in a reorganization. A new generation of arrangers included Blasius, E F Gebauer, and M J Gebauer; Vogt contributed the occasional arrangement after 1810. From 1815, wind sextets (2cl 2hn 2bn) virtually disappeared from publishers lists. France was occupied by foreign forces (1815-1820), French armies greatly reduced, and military bands curtailed. Demand rose only with the revival of the French army c.1820, especially for larger works. Fuchs contributed a 10-part arrangement of Rossini's *Il barbiere di Siviglia,* but was unable to follow up this work. It was Frédéric Berr who did most to revive arrangements for winds. He did this not during his period as director of the band of the Garde Suisse, but from about 1823 when he took up the post of second clarinet at the Théâtre Italien. By this time, flute, Eb clarinet and trombone were established in military bands, which often had 3-4 Bb clarinets. Instrumentation was not standardized, so Berr's early works offer a 7-part arrangement with ad lib parts. At this time, there were a few other arrangers, such as J Mohr. Soon after Berr's death in 1838, French military bands changed radically in instrumentation, size and character.

Religious and Revolutionary Music

The contradictions of the Revolution show in its music too. Quasi-religious texts and quasi-religious ideals are seen at a time when the church was under attack, combined with military fervor and display. Judged as concert music, the repertoire of the Revolution is harmonically and rhythmically banal, with good tunes a rarity. The music is so "fanatically diatonic ... a dominant seventh seems like an impious strain" (170) that an average Victorian oratorio seems adventurous. Judged by public impact, however transient, and by its effect on a huge scale where any sophistication was almost impossible, the wind music of the Revolution possessed outstanding qualities to gratify audiences, combining bombastic grandeur with directness and simplicity. Gossec, Méhul, Catel and Cherubini wrote fine works and could be trusted to maintain professional standards, with real inspiration in a few cases (171). Some of the best wind music of the French Revolution is recorded by the Wallace Collection/Wallace on Nimbus NI 5175; Garde Républicaine de Paris/Boutry, Conifer 2C 069-16316 (the Garde Républicaine has also recorded "Révolution Française" on EMI CDC 7 49473 2), and Les Gardiens de la Paix/Dondeyn, Nonesuch H7-1075. Serp MC 7033 and MC 7034. Music for Napoleon's coronation is recorded on Philips Universo 6518 012.

The Revolution - or the series of revolutions: the Orléanist of 1789, the Girondist of 1792, the Jacobin of 1793, the Thermidorean of 1794, and the several minor ones - attempted many forms of radical politics. In music, too, experiments were made, though more in form than in content. Small wind ensembles remained active, so new works were still written for them. Attempts to employ enormous groups of performers became common, transforming French music. The ultimate founding of the Paris Conservatoire de Musique, originally intended to maintain the standards of bandsmen, was due primarily to two individuals: Gossec and Bernard Sarrette. Sarrette, a minor military figure before the Revolution, possessed an enthusiasm for wind music and proved to be just the right able administrator for the musicians of the newly formed

Garde Nationale (a citizens' army, with elected officers, established in August, 1789, with Lafayette as its first commander). It was Sarrette who persuaded the authorities to fund the Magasin de Musique des Fêtes Nationales, the massive exercise in music publishing, notably of new music for wind bands. By his unflagging efforts, Sarrette managed to steer the band of the Garde Nationale through the tortuous political and ideological changes of the various revolutions. He championed the use of French musicians and campaigned against bringing in German musicians, although he consistently defended the interests of those foreign musicians who were already resident in France and actively supporting the Revolution.

If Sarrette was the major administrator and Gossec the principal composer of revolutionary music, it was the painter Jacques-Louis David who inspired occasions and venues which established the importance of wind music in the public consciousness. The champion of the return to the classical values of Greece and Rome, he masterminded the vast Fêtes Nationales, popular adaptations of earlier royal masques and spectacles. With the resources of the nation at his disposal, David enlarged both the noble proportions and the gross vulgarity of the spectacles, producing in Paris some of Europe's greatest-ever public events. The first of these major festivals, the Fête de la Fédération, was held on 14 July 1790 to celebrate the first anniversary of the fall of the Bastille. This festival set the fashion for subsequent ones. Their links with political power gave a sense of instability, rarely reflected in their music. These spectacles cost more than Napoleon would tolerate, and ceased soon after his rise to power.

The Fête de la Fédération took place in the presence of Louis XVI, but clearly real power had changed hands. It began with an immense parade which wound its way to a colossal amphitheater. The Champ de Mars, which could accommodate 400,000 people, was completed by volunteers after money had run out. The procession of some 40,000 people was headed by the mounted trumpets and drums of the Garde Nationale. Next came the Parisian citizens elected to the États Généraux, the third component of the Fédération (the others being the nobility and the clergy). The Garde Nationale and its band followed, leading the senior governmental administrators and officials. Only then did Louis XVI appear, albeit with the President of the National Assembly at his right hand. Other bands appeared at many places in the order of march. After this display, following a suggestion of J J Rousseau, came 100 babies carried in their mothers' arms; then, as now, no parade in the name of political ideals was complete without those still too young to know why they were marching. After them came 400 children aged eight to ten. Lesser officials followed in their usual abundance, then soldiers and sailors of the regular forces, followed by veterans. Bringing up the rear were some 14,000 Députés and a final detachment of the Garde Nationale.

The ceremony in the Champ de Mars began with a solemn high mass celebrated by Talleyrand. General Lafayette then preached a sermon on loyalty to the nation, the law, the King, and the constitution. Not long after, this theme would have led to his summary execution, but here it raised cheers of enthusiasm and tears from the crowd. Gossec's mammoth *Te Deum* was then performed to show gratitude for the blessings bestowed on France during the past year. The rest of the service was accompanied by music, primarily drawn from previous royal celebrations, since a full revolutionary repertoire was not yet available (165, 172-175). Most surviving accounts of the Fêtes Nationales agree that they had great public impact. A contemporary unofficial account (176) of the 1794 Fête de l'Être Suprême, Robespierre's "Day forever blessed," mentioned the "beautiful music of Gossec" but commented on the lack of zeal of the populace, the dispirited crowds, and the "great enthusiasm at first but mere weariness at last."

The Revolution and its Military Bands

It has been remarked that "nothing exceeds like excess" (177). The excuses of a new regime, a recent revolution, and an enthusiasm for popular display gave rise to the short-lived phenomenon of French revolutionary music.

At one extreme, the Fêtes Nationales involved huge numbers of players, often unpaid amateurs. Massive bands and choirs of thousands of singers were considered to be an excellent idea. When Johann Christoph Vogel's overture to *Démophon* was performed in the Champ de Mars in 1791 by a reported 1,200 wind instruments, one can hardly be surprised by its "unparalleled effect" (170, 173). For once, composers could indulge in musical extremes without concern for cost. Here was an unparalleled opportunity for real originality. Sadly, this musical challenge was rarely taken up. The fact that much of the music (172-175, 178, 179) is published only in piano reduction (166) is not a real problem, since the original performances seem to have tolerated any instrument that could get round the parts. Adaptability was a sign of the times.

Continuity and Change for Players

The careers of clarinettists in France from the 1750s to the 1830s *(Weston/MCVP)* allow us to see how they met the problems of a volatile social and political scene. Some players worked entirely before the Revolution, moving when bands ceased or employers died. Flieger and G Prokosch, who were with La Pouplinière from 1750 to 1762, were employed by Prince Louis François de Conti from 1763 to 1771. Beer, with the Duc d'Orleans from 1767 to 1777, then moved to the Prince Lambesc from 1778 to 1779. Meissner moved from the Prince de Rohan's employ (1766 to 1769) to the Marquis de Brancas (1769 to 1775) combining these posts with work for the Life Guards (1767 to 1775). Solère played for the Duc d'Orléans from 1778 to 1785, and from 1785 to 1789 at court, with clarinettist Hayenschink.

The best players were in demand for the Académie Royale de Musique (Opéra) (O), the Opéra Comique (OC), and the Concerts Spirituel (CS). The leading players were these: (names in italics are those who also wrote music for winds; clarinettist Duvernoy was the brother of the composer and horn player):

1750s: Flieger (CS 1755; O), Procksch (CS 1755; O).

1760s: Reiffer (CS 1763-1785?, O), Meissner (CS 1767-1775, O).

1770s: Klein (CS 1775), *Yost* (CS 1775-1785), Wolf (CS 1778).

1780s: Rathé (CS 1780), *Solère* (CS 1782-1788, O, OC), Wachter (CS 1782-1786), Barbay (CS 1786-1787), Hostié (CS 1786; with the Duc de Montmorency post-1788).

Early 1790s: *Ernst* (CS 1785-1791; O), *J X Lefèvre* (CS 1787-1791, O), *Chélard* (CS 1790-1791, O).

Other fine players worked at the Opéra (Abrahame, Assmann, L Lefèvre, Péchignier, Scharf, Schiefer), Opèra Comique (*Bouffil*, Duvernoy, Janssen) or both (Dacosta). Such key players were also members of military bands:

French Guards: *Vanderhagen* (1783-1789), L Lefèvre (1784-1789), Méric.

National Guard (1790s phase): *Fuchs*, L Lefèvre, *J X Lefèvre*, Méric, *Solère*, *Vanderhagen* 1798-1795, Duvernoy 1790-?, Hostié ?-1794, *Blasius*, Chelard, Legendre 1793-1795.

Directoire Guard: *Vanderhagen* 1795-1799, Dacosta 1798-1799.

Consular Guard: Dacosta, *Vanderhagen*, *Walter* (1799-1804), L Lefèvre 1799-1802.

Imperial Guard: Dacosta, *Vanderhagen* (1804-1814); *Walter* 1804-?

National Guard (post-1814 phase): L Lefèvre 1814-1827; 1830-1831.

Even though the top bands were reorganized several times, there was reasonable continuity in their personnel.

The court band from 1804 onwards continued to include many of the familiar names: *Solère* (?-1816; he had also played at court before the Revolution), Duvernoy (?-1824), *J X Lefèvre* (?-1829), and Dacosta (1805-1842?).

The Statistics of Revolutionary Music

Constant Pierre (173) lists 2,337 items of Revolutionary music, many appearing in several versions. These are numbered in roughly chronological order within four main groups. Items 1-167 are hymns and songs, 1790-1802, including large works. Items 168-2142 are popular songs, 1789-1802. Items 2143-2257 are songs and political or patriotic couplets. These are mainly slight, with a simple accompaniment or only a bass line; they include the music of the revolutionary armies (the so-called people's armies, the terror machine set up in 1793 [180]).

The final items, 2258-2337, are instrumental music groups, often for wind band, though only a piano transcription may survive, if indeed the work was ever performed (for some later performances, see 181). The first group consists of choral works, about 60% with wind band accompaniment and 30% with orchestra. The accompanying wind band usually comprised pic(or fl) 2cl 2hn 2bn tp tb serp timp; oboes were omitted and horns optional. Buccinas and other exotica were included at times, for the Revolutionary regime encouraged comparisons with the ancient grandeur of Rome (182). The texts are often the predictable platitudes, a lowest common denominator of social views which, by implication, gave support to a particular political force (183). One can see parallels with some of the better revolutionary music of the present century, for example Hanns Eisler's Op 18 *Ballads* of 1932, where he chose a fairly standard European Dixieland band (2cl sax 2tp tb db banjo perc pf) as accompaniment.

The Problems of Scale

No accounts seem to exist of the technical difficulties which must have arisen with such enormous forces. We may cite Berlioz's reminiscence (184) of the outdoor première of his *Grand Symphonie Funèbre et Triomphale* on 28 July 1840, a performance involving over two hundred players: "Despite the volume of sound produced by a wind band of this size, very little was heard during the procession. The only exception was the music played as we went along the Boulevard Poissonnière, where the big trees acted as reflectors. The rest was lost. In the open spaces of the Place de la Bastille it was worse. Almost nothing could be made out more than ten yards away. To cap it all, the National Guard, growing tired of standing so long at the slope in the blazing sun, began to march off before the end, to the accompaniment of some fifty side drums maintaining a relentless barrage throughout the Apotheosis, not a note of which survived. That is how they regard the role of music on public occasions in France: by all means let it figure as an attraction - for the eye."

The Aftermath and the Restoration of the Monarchy

The large works of the 1790s for revolutionary bands had their successors. While they lie somewhat outside our field, they point to the influence of experiments in large-scale wind harmony. Their title pages are especially informative. Antonin Reicha wrote two of the works (185). There is no evidence of performances in his lifetime nor of when they were written. It is possible they were written in the late 1790s and revised in Vienna; other dates commonly given (1808, 1815) seem to be unsupported guesses. The first work is **AXR-1.1m.** *Musique pour célébrer la mémoire des grands hommes qui se sont illustrés au service de la nation française,* for a solo ensemble (3pic 2ob 2cl 6hn 2bn 3db) and a ripieno ensemble (six parts; 2(+2)ob 2(+2)cl 2(+2)bn), a total of 20 parts. Reicha's comments on the autograph are interesting: "Cette oeuvre fût composée pour célébrer (1) La mémoire de quelques grandes actions en faveur de la nation française; (2) La mort des héros et des grands hommes qui auront bien merité de la Patrie; (3) pour fêter tous grands evénéments futurs. On peut l'exécuter à Paris ou à l'armée. C'est principalement pour ce dernier cas que j'ai composé la marche funèbre, qui peut aussi s'exécuter seule." The second work is **AXR-1.2m.** *Marche funèbre* (Maestoso/un poco Adagio), written for a solo ensemble (2ob 2cl 6hn 2bn 2cbn) and a ripieno ensemble (4ob 4cl 4bn 6 side drums and 4 cannon).

Berlioz (1803-1869), a pupil of Reicha, surely knew these works. Despite his spirited denials (186), a debt to Reicha is clear in Berlioz's *Symphonie Funèbre et Triomphale.* The title pages of autograph and first edition differ in their message: *combatants* are changed into *victims.* Berlioz was born too late to experience the Terror, but was well aware of the revolution of July 1830. The title page of the autograph reads "Symphonie Funèbre et Triomphale composée Pour l'Inauguration de la Colonne de la Bastille et la translation Des Restes des Combattants de Juillet par Hector Berlioz à son altesse Royale Monseigneur Le Duc d'Orléans," whereas the first edition has: "Grande Symphonie Funèbre et Triomphale pour grande Harmonie Militaire composée pour la translation des Restes des Victimes de Juillet à l'inauguration de la colonne de la Bastille et dédiée à S A R Monseigneur Le Duc d'Orléans par Hector Berlioz." Berlioz wrote one other large band work, the *March pour la Présentation des Drapeaux,* in his *Te Deum.* This is very effective (not all the twelve harps listed are essential), but the movement seems to be left out of all current recordings.

Later large works include Messiaen's *Et Exspecto Resurrectionem Mortuorum,* of 1964, written for performance "in the open air and even on mountainsides". The work was to "to commemorate the dead of the two world wars," a motive similar to those of Reicha and Berlioz. Nor were large brass and wind bands unique to France. A band of 1200 was assembled in Berlin for the 1872 Meeting of the Three Emperors (187). The phenomenon can still be experienced to some extent in places as varied as the football stadiums of North America and the monastery in Shigatse, Tibet, where in 1982 more than 550 monks blew horns and trumpets to celebrate the return of the Panchen Lama after twenty years in exile in China (188). Possibly, like the Boston music critics at the vast Strauss concert in Boston in 1872, we must accept that it is impossible "to judge extraordinary events except by extraordinary standards and rules" (189).

THE 19TH CENTURY REVIVAL

From 1815 until 1820, France was occupied by foreign forces. Music for the small wind bands disappeared from publishers' lists, reappearing only after 1820 for the larger ensembles of the bands of the new army. The major wind music in these early years of of the new monarchy was that of Antonin Reicha, who made a serious attempt to give the wind quintet (fl ob cl hn bn) the status enjoyed by the string quartet. The full impact of Reicha's initiative came half a century later, for even his pupils (like Franck) added little to the genre of wind music. Franck's pupil d'Indy and Fauré's pupils Ibert and Florent Schmitt returned to the genre. Fauré himself wrote a *Chant Funéraire* for winds for the 5 May 1921 centenary of Napoleon's death. It was so successful that he rewrote it as the second movement of his *Cello Sonata,* Op 117.

Flautist Paul Taffanel was a key figure in the revrival. He founded the Société de Musique de Chambre pour les Instruments à Vent in 1879. For it, he commissioned new music with such success that other groups emerged, notably the Double Quintette de Paris and the Dixtuor à Vent de la Société des Concerts du Conservatoire. Taffanel's core ensemble was a wind quintet, to which other players were added; thus an octet might consist of Taffanel (flute), Boullard (oboe), Grisez and Turban (clarinets), Gavique and Brémond (horns), and Espaignet and Bourdeau (bassoons) (190, 191); a second oboe was added later, though how long this was before the 1885 premiere of Gounod's *Petite Symphonie* is unclear; by then, Gillet and Mimart were the oboists. Georges Barrère, who succeeded Taffanel, was a major influence in the United States as flautist and through his wind ensemble. Other French ensembles (192) employed a more conventional form: 2fl 2ob 2cl 2hn 2bn, showing the typical Gallic predilection for the flute. These ensembles stimulated the writing of music: Bernard's *Divertissement* (1890), d'Indy's *Chanson et Danses* (1898), Caplet's *Suite Persane* (1900), Mouquet's *Symphonietta*, Enesco's *Dixtuor* (both 1906), and Schmitt's *Lied et Scherzo* (1910). Such compositions initiated a new tradition of elegant, lightweight music which continued in the music of Arrieu, Ibert, Milhaud and Françaix. One recurring feature is neoclassicism: the conscious adoption of styles, structures or sounds of an earlier period. Whether this is "right" or "wrong" in any artistic sense need not concern us. Earlier styles can be mere nostalgia, or an easy option for unimaginative composers; for others, neoclassicism may be chosen because of a dramatic context or historical association. Milhaud's *La Cheminée du Roi René* describes scenes five hundred years earlier from the Provence of King René the Good; Hahn's *Le Bal de Béatrice d'Este* recalls the Italian Renaissance. In other works, it is the clarity and supposed delicacy and noble simplicity of the classical period, rather than the historical context, which is sought as an antidote to the vast indulgences of the more ambitious (and often less talented) late romantic composers. French composers seem to be especially sympathetic to this view: Ibert, in his *Concerto for Cello and Winds* adopts this approach, as does Gouvy, although his *Petite Suite Gauloise* has an element of nostalgia as well, with movements entitled Menuet and Tambourin which consciously suggest the Bourbon court of Louis XIV.

4

German-Speaking Countries and the Austro-Hungarian Empire

PLEASURE GARDENS AND PUBLIC PLACES

Poor scholars of the music school played in the streets of Munich, more to demonstrate that charity was well spent (*Burney* Vol 2 p 52) than to entertain. In Germany and Austria, as in London, wind music was played in public gardens. Music and performance could be outstanding. The *Musikalischer Almanach* of 1782 described a scene in Vienna: "Music at the festive midnight hour, in the month of May, under the gentle shimmer of the triste moon, enveloped by the thrilling horns of Fischer and le Brun, the singing bassoons of Schubart and Schwarzer - God! - whereto might not the soul, drunk with bliss, soar!" Concerts were frequently given in Vienna's Augarten, opened in 1775 between the Danube River and the Danube Canal (193 §123; 194). One series of serenade (or, strictly, aubade) concerts ran for many years, despite the extraordinary starting time of seven o'clock on Saturday mornings. Some gardens in Vienna had regular wind bands (195, 196), like the Volksgarten and the Caroline Gardens. The lemonade stalls in public squares, which sold many flavours of ices, followed suit. Pezzl (193 §152) observed that in the 1780s that "for the past few years, the proprietors of these lemonade stalls have provided the additional attraction of Harmoniemusik ... a most pleasant accompaniment to a soft breeze on a balmy moonlit summer night. If the weather is fine, this entertainment lasts till about midnight." In winter, Viennese wind bands could still play outdoors: in the late 1780s (193 §74), there were sleigh rides (on snow specially brought in!) led by a sled with trumpets and drums, the procession ending with a huge sleigh carrying musicians, who "added to the tumult of the horses adorned with sleigh bells by playing martial music."

The *Magazin der Musik* in 1784 noted that, in Hamburg, "in the summer the whole of Society lives in the parks" (197), a tradition that continued well into the 19th century. In 1796, Vogel arranged Kozeluch's *Parthia in F,* LAK-3.1/KXV-1a, for the local forces (fl 2cl 2hn 2bn 2vla, instead of 2fl 2cl 2hn 2bn) of the Musikgesellschaft in Braunschweig. In Hamburg, on 15 July 1837, the American musician Lowell Mason (1792-1872) "passed a very good band in the street - playing at the Doors of gentlemen's houses - there were four Clarinets - two horns - trombone and Drums" (198). Several gardens opened in Berlin in the 1820s: the Hofjaeger, the Schulgarten, Fausts Wintergarten, Teichmanns Blumengarten, and the Tivoli. In Breslau, about 1860, the city's three or four military bands gave concerts on most days in the beer gardens and milk gardens along the shady, beautiful avenues which had been constructed out of the old moat and fortifications: "To these gardens mothers would, in the afternoon, take their work and their children, and many an enjoyable afternoon I spent there, listening to selections from Haydn, Mozart, Beethoven, Auber, Bellini, Boieldieu, Donizetti, Verdi, not to forget the then-popular dance music of Lanner and Johann Strauss the Elder," reminisced Sir George Henschel in 1918 (199 p 10). Military bands had an important role in public musical education, and these bands were a major market for wind music in Europe. Public awareness was aided by the formation of amateur music societies and by music published for the amateur (200). A letter dated 16 June 1800 from J M Böheim, in Berlin, sought both "good wind band pieces" from Vienna and also "small symphonies, for these are in great demand for amateur orchestras" (201). The musical education of amateurs was assisted by other means. Mason (198 p 72) described a men's choral society at Frankfurt am Main, the chorus accompanied by 3hn tb, where many members "had bottles of wine before them."

When the Novellos visited Vienna in 1829, the wind music played in gardens was what they described as commonplace waltzes; the most demanding piece they heard was a cavatina by Rossini (202). The slow movement of Beethoven's *Pastoral Symphony* (1808) portrays an only-too-credible scene, where players in a garden doze off, "remaining entirely quiet, then awakening with a start, throwing in a few vigorous blows at a venture, but generally in the right key, and then falling asleep again" (100 p 438). Some players had an easier time: "The music in the garden is played in a kind of summer house," wrote Edward Holmes in Dresden, "and the performers do not scruple during the pauses to avail themselves of certain ham sandwiches and sundry bottles of wine, thus repairing dilapidation of the spirits and keeping up excitement" (203).

COURT AND PRIVATE BANDS

Some of the best wind harmony music was found in the principal courts: those of the Emperor of Austria and of the Electoral Princes. The Prussian Court maintained a band of oboes and horns as early as 1705 (23). The famous Imperial Harmonie in Vienna was founded in late 1781 or early 1782; it soon set the very highest standards. Though Vienna's wind octet music had enormous influence, Vienna seems to have been one of the later centers where octets took over from smaller ensembles, like sextets. The influence travelled partly through the Electoral courts. In 1784, the Elector of Cologne, Maximilian Franz, brought the octet tradition from Vienna to Bonn, where he was "entertained daily by his octet, in their red uniforms with gold trimmings" (204).

At the most modest level, *Burney* observed that "in Poland, any nobleman who had four musicians appointed a master of music over them." The small court of Oettingen-Wallerstein showed how a musical community could be integrated into a larger court community. The first records mention wind harmony for special occasions. During Emperor Franz's visit, "Waldhörner und Klarinetten" played for the third serving for the banquet of 19 March 1764 (205). The court Kapelle was dissolved in 1766, when Prince Philipp Karl died; it was then rebuilt by his son, Prince Kraft Ernst (1748-1802) in the 1770s. After another period of mourning (1776-1779) following the death of his young bride, the Prince appointed Josef Reicha as Kapellmeister. Music flourished in this period ("Blütezeit") at the court (206-208).

Reicha left in 1785, and Rosetti became Kapellmeister. The Harmonie and orchestra both achieved the highest standards. Haydn observed that no other orchestra played his symphonies with such attention to what he wanted. What makes this remarkable is that the total area of the principality was only twenty square miles; it was fourteen miles from the palace at Wallerstein to the residence at Hohenaltheim, where the court spent April to November. Kraft Ernst's limited budget forced him to organize his musical forces with care. He employed three levels of musicians: the full-time leaders of each section, drawn from the ranks of first-rate established musicians; the talented young musicians starting their professional careers, who could not yet command large salaries; and servants-in-livery, who also served as rank-and-file musicians. Hoppius is an example; starting as a servant-in-waiting (Lackei), he became an accomplished bassoonist, whom Rosetti lured from Oettingen-Wallerstein to Ludwigslust.

Kraft Ernst's love of wind harmony meant that his orchestra had a splendid wind section. Economy was practised, for the Master of the Wind Harmony was also expected to serve as "Director and Composer of the Princely Hunt and Table" (209). The Prince's "talent scout" and military adjutant was Ignaz von Beecke (1733-1803), a fine composer and later Mozart's partner in the piano duet concert in the festivities for the coronation of Emperor Leopold II in 1790. Von Beecke recruited musicians at the principal musical centers, negotiated commissions, and purchased music for the Prince. Kraft Ernst preferred original wind music to arrangements, as shown from von Beecke's letter of 3 August 1790: "Monsieur Ehrenfried ... has arranged all the music of Righini for musique d'harmonie. He has offered me all these partitas for Your Majesty. I almost hesitated to accept them, because I knew you do not like this kind of table music. You prefer the *grands passages* with passages and minuets ... However, because this is the music of Righini, I accepted these partitas for Your Highness" (210 p 210).

The French invasions in the late 1790s damaged the Prince's finances, although Wallerstein itself was not overrun. The Prince even thought of buying 50,000 acres in America and relocating the entire court there. There were many deaths among the musicians around this time, and their posts remained unfilled. The Harmonie all but disappeared in 1805 after the deaths of the Prince and of von Beecke. Wind harmony continued into the 1820s only at a lower level, and only a few printed works for 2cl 2hn 2bn or fl 2cl 2hn bn were bought. The musicians who remained at Wallerstein were treated as favored retainers; pensioned off, they lived out their lives in the principality. While this Harmonie was fading, others were getting into their stride. The Fürstenberg Harmonie at Donaueschingen continued into the late 1830s. The Harmonies of Fürsten von Löwenstein (Wertheim) and Hohenlohe-Öhrigen (with musicians who produced arrangements at an average rate of one movement every two days!) continued at least until the 1840s. The Lippe Harmonie at Detmold lasted until World War I.

Bohemia and Moravia. The deepest roots of wind harmony were in Bohemia and Moravia. The Czech language was one symbol of genuine national feeling which often clashed with Bohemia's position as a province of Austria (210); their music was one route from poverty. Many of the finest instrumentalists of the late 18th century were Bohemians, who drifted from their musical, but poor, homeland to its richer Austrian and German neighbors. Dr Burney described Bohemia, somewhat sweepingly, as "a nation of musicians" and added, "It is said by travelers, that the Bohemian nobility keep musicians in their houses; but in keeping servants it is impossible to do otherwise." Burney's claim is supported both by the many Bohemian composers and by a formidable list of Bohemian and Moravian wind bands. Some of these are described in an Appendix to this chapter. These bands were matched by a formidable amount of music for winds; typically, 10-25% of the music holdings in Bohemian and Moravian court archives are for wind band. Not all bands were court bands. The *Prague Post News* of 5 August 1721 described the miners' bands which welcomed Empress Elizabeth Christina on her way from Vienna to Karlovy Vary (Carlsbad). The procession comprised over a thousand persons in 16 sections. Near the start and end (sections 2 and 14), bands of 6 trumpeters with drums played a march; they were dressed in black miners' uniforms with silver rims and bows on their hats. In the middle (section 7) was a similarly dressed band of 12 oboists and horn players (and apparently bassonists as well), who played a specially composed march. There was a further band of guitarists and singers. Later, the three bands played in front of the Empress's residence: 6 trumpeters and a drummer played at each end; in the middle was the band of 12 oboists, bassoonists and horn players. After this, the bands played by Holy Trinity Column (at one time in the Lesser Town). A bonfire was lit, perhaps with fireworks, and songs were sung. The procession, including miners' and army bands, then moved off across the Charles Bridge.

State Occasions: The Spectacular Display.   Court wind bands were part of the entertainment for special occasions. For example, in 1754, Crown Prince Franz and Maria Theresa visited Prince Joseph Friedrich Sachsen-Hildburghausen (1702-1787) at Kroissenbrunn, near Schlosshof, not far from Bratislava. The central event was a fête on a large artificial lake, a scene described in Dittersdorf's autobiography. "From bank to bank, two galleries were thrown across in the center of the lake. On each of these were seated trumpeters and drummers, with other players of wind instruments; they were heard playing alternating strains." Then came a mock tournament: "In the lake itself, there stood eight pillars, painted to look like stone, and adorned with bronze grotesques." These were no ordinary pillars: each was topped with a live wild animal in fancy dress - bears as clowns, boars as columbines, goats as harlequins, and bulldogs apparently as themselves; the pillars also contained ducks, geese and swans which could be released by striking one of the grotesque bronze masks. Knights in the bows of gondolas proceeded to joust, and to spray each other - and the animals - from hand syringes. "The animals loudly resented the rudeness of the whole proceeding," and their natural indignation was enhanced by the musicians' studied chaos: "One trumpet blew a shrill blast in D, while another did the same in C, and another in E. Some of the drummers tuned up, others down; oboists, clarinettists, bassoon players followed suit." The entertainment continued more gently, first with a Gluck opera, followed by wind harmony. Ditters concludes, "I shall never forget the scene ... the soothing music of the wind instruments, the happy faces all round, and the graciousness and kindness of the good Prince to everyone, the humblest guest included" (212).

When the King and Queen of Naples visited Vienna in 1791, Prince Auersperg asked Lorenzo da Ponte, Mozart's librettist, and Joseph Weigl to produce an evening spectacle, *The Temple of Flora.* In the Auersperg palace was a superb rotunda, set in a large garden, with a statue of Flora at the center. The rotunda held about three hundred people, with a small space reserved for the actors. "I removed the statue of Flora," recalled da Ponte (213 p 189). "On her pedestal I put a singer who stood absolutely still, so that the spectators took her for the same marble statue. A curtain, hung behind the statue, hid an exceptionally large band of wind instruments." The rotunda was kept completely dark: when the royal party entered, their path was lit by only a single lamp. All remained dark and silent. Then "suddenly the place was flooded with light from hundreds of lamps fixed to the cornices of the temple, and the hidden orchestra filled the rotunda with a ravishing sound."

Arrangements in Austria. The first identified arrangements for wind ensemble are found in seven of Asplmayr's Parthien for Count Pachta in Bohemia. They date from between 1773 and 1777. Asplmayr may have known the French arrangements. Certainly he followed the pattern of Roeser and Vanderhagen, using single numbers from more than one opera or ballet. Probably all the works Asplmayr arranged were by himself or by Starzer. At the same time, Went first prepared a small number of arrangements for 2ob 2hn bn for the Harmonie of Count Clam Gallas. Went was a seminal figure, the first to prepare multi-movement works from a single source. He established himself as the major Austrian arranger with his move to the Schwarzenberg Harmonie around 1774. The Harmonie introduced his arrangements to Vienna. When the Imperial Harmonie was founded in 1782, Went was recognized both as oboist and as arranger. He dominated the market for arrangements in Austria for a decade, and produced many arrangements until his death in 1801. Besides his large output for 2ob 2cl 2hn 2bn, he continued to arrange for the Schwarzenberg Harmonie (2ob 2ca 2hn 2bn), with versions for the Russian Imperial Harmonie (2fl 2cl 2hn 2bn), for wind sextet (2cl 2hn 2bn), for the occasional unusual wind ensembles, string quartets, and flute duets. The arrangements for the Schwarzenberg Harmonie identify Went as the arranger. This is not available for arrangements from c.1796, when the Harmonie ceased. Certainly a number of other arrangers were active, but many of the titlepages unhelpfully omit the name of the arranger (e.g., those issued by Thaddeus Weigl for the kk Hoftheater-Musik-Verlag in 1796).

Austrian copyright applied only to the first edition, so many versions of Went's works appeared. Many of the MS arrangements offered in Traeg's 1799 catalog are surely by Went. His arrangements remained in circulation for almost two decades after his death in 1801, probably due to sales to copying houses and publishers by Josef Triebensee, his son-in-law. Certainly Went's arrangements are found in manuscripts prepared by the kk Hof-Theater-Musik-Verlag after it was reestablished in May 1812. The copies in D-Rtt (purchased c.1820 from another source) are important, since they carry prices in "W.W." *(Wiener Währung,* the Viennese banknotes from the 1813 attempt to curtail inflation during the wars). Many later versions include a contrabassoon part. Such parts are not by Went; they might have been added by Triebensee. Some octet arrangements were converted merely by adding the word "et Contra" to the title, without there being a single divisi in the bn 2 part. Especially in this later period, there are often divisi sections in the bn 2 part which are not apparent from the titlepage.

Went's arrangements suggest that he had access to scores. Heidenreich (active from 1789 to 1811 or later), Went's first serious rival, usually arranged from a published piano reduction, which was less satisfactory. Went virtually monopolized arrangements of Italian operas; Heidenreich concentrated on Singspiel, which was more accessible in print. Heidenreich's advertizement in the *Wiener Zeitung* (14 Jan 1792) offered a 6-part version of his octet *Zauberflöte* arrangement, if enough subscribers demanded it.

Druschetzky and Triebensee probably began arranging c.1795, and P Mašek (Vienna) and Vogel (Prague) arranged a few works as well. The market for arrangements was growing. Many works were issued without attribution; it is likely that there were more arrangers than believed hitherto. Although there is no direct evidence, Krommer, Süssmayr, J Weigl, and T Weigl may have made arrangements at this time.

Around 1800, three major arrangers entered the market: Sedlak, Starke, and Krechler. Krechler might have made some of the anonymous house arrangements issued in manuscript by the kk Hoftheater-Musik-Verlag, for his employer, Prince Lobkowitz, was one of the principal backers of the firm. Other possible arrangers from this period include A Wranizky, Poessinger and Seyfried. The last of the major arrangers, Nicolaus Scholl, probably began arranging c.1810, although his output peaked in the 1820s and 1830s. Further possible arrangers include Haslinger and Franz de Paula de Roser von Reiter. Both octet with contrabass (cbn, db, vlne) and sextet (2cl 2hn 2bn) configurations were standard for the first two decades of the 19th century.

From about 1800 local bandmasters were expected to prepare arrangements. Such arrangements were often used solely by the group for which they were intended. Some of the more important arrangements were made by Buchal (Láncut), Havel (Chrást, then Kroměříž), Osswald and Vojáček (the Augustinian monastery, Brno), Merklein (Kinský Harmonie), and Rieger (Haugwitz Harmonie, Náměšt nad Oslavou).

By 1820, new arrangements for 2cl 2hn 2bn had disappeared, although such bands continued to play in small towns and villages throughout the Austrian Empire until World War I. Most court wind bands disappeared during the wars or in the post-

Napoleonic economic depression. From 1820, regimental bands (often 2ob 2cl 2hn 2bn cbn 2tp) were the major market. Sedlak, Starke and Scholl dominated the arrangements market, apart possibly from Roser de Reiter. It seems that Sedlak supplied the few remaining court Harmonien. Only Scholl appears to have continued to arrange from the early 1830s to the early 1840s. The main Viennese publishers to issue arrangements were (in chronological order) Lausch (in manuscript), Traeg (in manuscript), kk Hoftheater-Musik-Verlag (mostly in manuscript), T Weigl (mostly in manuscript), Johann Cappi (in manuscript), Chemische Druckerei and Mechetti (printed and in manuscript).

Arrangements in Germany. Here, arrangements were only a small part of the published output. This was due in part to the wide variation in instrumentation from band to band. Some works by Went were acquired and printed by Nicolas Simrock in Bonn, but seem to have been sold mostly to courts with Austrian connections.

In the mid-1790s, Stumpf's set of 20 Recueils for 2cl 2hn 2bn proved to be a great success throughout Europe. Subsequently, Goepfert published arrangements in the first decade of the 19th century. The known combined output of both arrangers was modest, less than half that of works arranged by Went alone. Johann André (Offenbach am Main) was the principal publisher of these arrangements, and evidently had sufficient distribution agreements with publishers in Vienna (Traeg), Paris (?Imbault), and perhaps elsewhere, to ensure a market for works scored for a specific configuration. In the 1820s and 1830s, Les Fils de B Schott issued many arrangements for larger bands, usually preferring to buy in plates from Parisian publishers for works by Berr and later by Mohr. Their only "original" arrangements appear to be Küffner's *Pot Pourris* on operas, from the 1820s.

Works like Weller's enormous arrangement of Weber's *Oberon* were published, but were exceptional. The picture emerging is of courts with one or more prolific arrangers to provide for their own needs, with little circulation of these works to other bands. Among the most important court arrangers were Sartorius (Darmstadt); Georg Schmitt, (Fulda, then Hohenlohe-Öhringen); Kirchhoff and Scholz (Hohenlohe-Öhringen); Hermstedt (Sondershausen); Prince Carl Friedrich (Löwenstein Harmonie); Anton Schneider, (Neresheim, Thurn und Taxis regimental band); Legrand and Widder (Munich); Karl Kaiser (Detmold). Dance music grew in importance from the 1820s, some as concert repertoire and probably some to be danced to. Examples include works by Lanner, Strauss (father) and Labitzky, as well as locally-composed dances.

CHURCH AND MASONIC CONNECTIONS

The Novellos were awakened in Heilbronn in 1829 by a morning chorale "tastefully played and well in tune" by a small band of wind instruments from a neighboring monastery (202). This was not unusual; there were large libraries of wind music in monasteries in the Czech Republic (Brno, Nová Říše, Rajhrad), in Austria (Melk, where the playing of local hired musicians led to complaints of the level of musicianship [214] and Kremsmünster) and at Einsiedeln, Switzerland.

At the Augustinian monastery in Brno (215), Father Cyril Napp (1792-1867) revitalized the wind harmony around 1816. He lived until Janáček had arrived as a pupil there and until Mendel, Napp's successor as Abbot of the same Monastery, had carried out his seminal studies of genetics (216). The "blue boys" of the Brno choir school "played in the roast at refectory lunch; every day at table, and every day in praise of God" (215, 217). The Harmonie also played for occasions like name days; they could be hired for such occasions, and might even stay overnight (suitably chaperoned) if necessary. On May Day mornings, if weather permitted, the ensemble would be enlarged to a full Turkish band by musicians from the local regiments and the opera.

Religious and secular celebrations could come together on occasions like harvest festivals (218). Much of the surviving religious music is modest, limited by forces available; as in England, some bassoon parts were read from organ or choral parts. As in England too, both wind band and choir might be used. Thus Emmert's *Kirchenlieder* (AJE-1v(-5v)) were transcribed in full score for six wind instruments so "the instrumental ensemble may alternate with the choir, or both may perform together, whichever is preferred." Some of the finest church music with winds is by Michael Haydn, whose *Missa Sancti Hieronymi* (JMH-2v) is scored for solo and ripieno oboes, bassoons, trombones, organ and double bass. Other examples by better-known composers include Vanhal's *Brevis et faciles hymni* (JKV-2v), Winter's *Nun danket alle Gott* (PVW-3v) and *Veni Sancte Spiritus* (PVW-1v), and several works by Schubert and Weber, culminating in Bruckner's *E minor Mass* (ANB-2v) and Brahms's *Begräbnissgesang* (JHB-1v). A large body survives of religious choral music with wind bands, and includes works from all decades the 19th century. Typically, a few percent of music holdings in Bohemian and Moravian church archives involves a wind band. Robbins Landon (50 p 55) remarks on the many wind band arrangements of Haydn's oratorios to be found in parish church archives in Austro-Hungary.

The Czech and Austrian music includes very many funeral pieces, whereas there are hardly any in Italian church music; likewise, there are more settings of *Veni Sancte Spiritus* and the full *Pange lingua* than in Italy. The funeral pieces had several functions. In part, they assisted in the sharing of grief between the bereaved and the community. They helped to define the contribution of the deceased to their families and their community. From c.1830 one sees a characteristic shift away from the horrors of the grave to images of rest and peace. In iconography, the skulls, winged skulls, skeletons and Last Judgements largely disappear. "Ruhe sanft" becomes a popular inscription, and the funeral songs often refer to sleep ("Schlummer"; a marvellous example with full orchestra is found in Mahler's *Kindertotenlieder*). The texts of these funeral songs are by poets such as Klopstock. The songs may have been a status symbol as well. Some pieces were for the funerals of specific individuals; for many, large bands were beyond their means, and small bands of 2cl 2hn bn/b-tb/bomb sufficed.

The Corpus Christi celebration (Der Fronleichnamsfeste) became one of the most popular in the Roman church, although abandoned in Protestant countries after the Reformation. It became associated with intercession for good weather. Its processions traditionally stopped four times, once for each of the supposed corners of the earth, hence the settings entitled "4 Evangelien" or "Evangelium" (i.e. Gospel readings) or "4 Stationes pro Festo Corporis Christi." The Czech equivalent of Stationes is "Zastavení." The published sets, like Schiedemeyer's *Stationes* and Vanhal's *IV Brevis et Facilis Hymne*, are the most commonly found. Music for Corpus Christi continued to be written and played through the 19th century. Many earlier bands of 2cl 2hn bn evolved into flügelhorn althorn 2cl 2hn b-tb/bomb. Some traditions still survive. In Hallstatt, some 30 miles from Salzburg, Corpus Christi and music for the dead are linked, again with a wind band component: choirs, band, priests, and others board boats to visit charnel houses of racks of painted skulls (219).

In Vienna (193 §149) the Corpus Christi procession of the late 1780s included the Emperor and senior church dignitaries, with "a company of grenadiers playing martial music" among the vocal and instrumental music. Forty years later, the English traveler, Edward Holmes (1797-1859) found wind bands being used for Church processions in Cologne in about 1827: "One of those processions of the town inhabitants, frequent in Catholic countries, took place in Cologne on Sunday morning, during the octave from the great feast Corpus Domini, and the music which accompanied it placed the combinations and effects of the art in an entirely new position. On these occasions the streets are strewed with rushes, so that the performers glide along noiseless as ghosts, and nothing interrupts the solemnity of the harmony. The singers consisted of young girls and boys, youths and maidens, and lastly of consummate men, walking in double rows of immense length, and sometimes accompanied by bands of wind instruments. The simple hymn, sung by the girls in three parts, pitched in a low key, nicely in tune, and without any vociferation - this, replied to by the men's voices, and then in return by those of the youths, produced the most affecting appeal to the feelings of which music is capable - tears came unbidden. The pauses in the music, the large body of voices, the contrast between the trebles, tenors, and basses, the sudden breaking out in different parts of that long line, some voices from their distance merging into silence, others unexpectedly swelling out near at hand, produced an entire and delicious novelty in the art, such as might by a great master of effect be turned to infinite account.... The ear was not offended by any jarring or discordant harmony, because the signals for the different parties to begin were regulated with judgment, one not commencing until the other had stopped. The priests, however, who took upon themselves to roar the Gregorian chant, made great blunders in the harmony; their basses and appoggiature were uniformly wrong. Two horns, clarionets, bassoons, and a bass trombone played in a smooth manner and extremely subdued, supplied the place of an itinerant organ, and supported the voices in those parts where modulation was somewhat more learned than suited merely vocal music" (203). The small wind ensemble (often 2cl 2hn 1/2bn) was typical of many in southern Germany and the Austrian Empire until World War I. Mendelssohn's pieces for church processions in Düsseldorf from the 1830s (51) appear to be lost. One hopes that they avoided the unidiomatic wind writing of *Elijah*.

Masonic Connections

Modern Freemasonry can be traced to the founding of the first English Grand Lodge in 1717. Following Anderson's Constitutions of 1723, the Craft spread quickly throughout the Continent: to France with Jacobite exiles in 1725, to Austria in 1731 with Francis I, Maria Theresa's husband, and to Hamburg in 1733. It is a useful oversimplification to say that English Freemasonry was mainly charitable, conservative, and sympathetic to the established (Anglican) church, whereas continental Freemasonry was mainly radical and often opposed to Roman Catholicism. Continental Freemasonry allied itself more closely to the Enlightenment than the English form. The growing belief in the ultimate potential of science led to exploration of links between music and nature, with frequent suggestions that music might ultimately be reduced to mathematical formulas. Composers like Scheibe and Naumann (220) developed a Masonic musical language in which rhythmic and melodic figures, intervals, and harmonic progressions symbolized Masonic precepts and values (221). Their Masonic songs are well written, but it needed Mozart's genius to transform such symbols into great music. One feature of Masonic cryptography was the use of parallel thirds and sixths to symbolize shared feeling and harmonious relationships, based on the widely held idea that these intervals "reflect a state of physical harmony and peace" (222). Likewise, the three flats of E♭ major or C minor could symbolize the three trowels. Such characteristics surely encouraged the Masonic adoption of wind instruments. Purely practical matters, like portability of instruments, may have mattered more; certainly wind music was conspicuous in the larger ceremonies of the Vienna lodges.

By the mid-1780s, Vienna had become the Masonic musical center of Europe, and its lodges included many musicians (223, 224). In December 1785, Emperor Joseph II decreed that the eight Vienna lodges should be reduced to three. This forced an amalgamation of the Illuminati (largely political) and Rosicrucian (largely mystical) wings of the Craft. On 20 December 1785, the members voted to reduce membership from 600 to 360, divided between two Lodges: "Newly-crowned Hope" to which Mozart belonged, and "Truth." Mozart's *Die Maurerfreude* and *Maurerische Trauermusik*, both dating from 1785, have prominent orchestral wind parts. Anton Stadler's (lost) partitas of 1785 for wind sextet must have been among the last of an overtly Masonic nature, although the musical symbolism persisted, notably in *Die Zauberflöte*. Many pieces which seem to use Masonic symbols may do so unintentionally, the composers merely adopting what they regarded as stylistic devices; we can see this in many funeral marches which, irrespective of their origin, remain largely "Masonic" in structure.

MILITARY BANDS IN GERMANY, AUSTRIA AND THEIR NEIGHBORS

Around 1800, a united German nation did not exist. Political turmoil, war, realignments of boundaries and shifts in power were frequent. Our own lists, like Hofer's book (225), show that many hundreds of marches were written for the army bands. Major collections at D-DS and D-Bds each contain several hundreds of marches. The scorings are usually 2ob bn tp in the early 18th century, 2ob 2hn bn in mid-century, and 2ob 2cl 2hn 2bn plus sundry extras (flutes, trumpet, and so on) after that (226), trends consistent with a standardization of bands by Frederick the Great. These enlarged bands stimulated original compositions and arrangements and became a major market for journals and for wind music in general. A survey (227) of music from 1740 to 1797 for the Royal Prussian wind band (which actually includes works from as late as 1832, like waltzes by Johann Strauss the Elder) includes marches for regiments from Poland, Russia, Naples, Austria, Hungary, Scotland and England: national boundaries did not need to be musical boundaries. In time, the major states compiled sets of "official" marches. In 1817, Friedrich Wilhelm III of Prussia "commanded a collection of proven musical pieces to be prepared, and a set of them to be provided for each regiment." The 1905 Procedure for the Imperial and Royal Army provided a selection of parade marches for Austrian regiments. Recordings of German and Austrian marches include those by the Berlin Philharmonic Winds/Karajan, DG 439 346, DG 2721 077; Vienna Musica Antiqua/Clemencic, DG Archiv 2533 059; RSO Berlin/Richter, Capriccio 10186; Staatsmusikkorps des Bundeswehr, 848 128-4; Stadtmusik Wien, MLP 003; Militärmusik Salzburg, D 221 170 and D 221 696.

Traditional Marches

In Vienna, as in London, a band of the Grenadiers (the Viennese garrison had two battalions) played for the formal mounting of the guard and for religious processions. What was played by bands in the Holy Roman Empire is much less clear, even though many marches survive in archives. Several marches were famous in their time, such as the *Dessauer Marsch* (c.1705, also found under a bilingual title, "So geht es ça donc") incorporated in an overture arranged by Kirchhoff (**WZK-19.1a/19.2a**) and used by Meyerbeer in his operas *L'Étoile du Nord* and *Vielka, oder ein Feldlager in Schlesien.* The march *Der Hohenfriedberger,* attributed to Frederick the Great, celebrating his 1745 victory at Hohenfriedberg, Silesia, was still in use fifty years later. Most of the early marches are, quite frankly, fairly poor and only rarely possess interesting instrumentation or a contrasting trio section. As Burney noted (*Burney* vol 2 p 195) of Prussian marches in Potsdam, "Neither the airs that were played, nor the instruments that played them, had any particular merit: however, the old-fashioned march, of dot and go one is perhaps, best calculated to mark the time and regulate the steps of the soldiers [sic]." Such marches could almost have been written using a "Composing Game," (see part 2 under Koehler) by random selection of common phrases with military rhythms. Marches are rare among composing games, and the only examples we know are French, and probably for keyboard: de la Chevardière's 1759 catalog shows *Le Jeu de Dex Harmoniques;* the catalog for 1762/63 includes what may be the same work *Le Toton Harmonique p[ou]r faire des Marches en Trio en jouant à ce jeu.*

Late in the 19th century, some splendid marches were written for larger bands by composers like Fučik (1872-1916). The famous *Des grossen Kurfürsten Reitermarsch* always impresses, despite being based largely on the clichés of military music. It was written by Kuno, Graf von Moltke (1847-1923; not one of the famous generals) for his regiment, the Breslau 1st Regiment of Life Guards (known as Grosser Kurfürst, after Friedrich Wilhelm [1620-1688], the Great Elector of Brandenburg [228]).

Several major composers wrote marches with care and skill, like Haydn, Beethoven and Krommer. Some of the marches which set the highest standards, were arranged from operas or ballets (Mozart, J Weigl, Paer, Cherubini, Spontini, Spohr, C Kreutzer, Nicolini). In Vienna, as in London, often only a piano transcription was published. A typical set is that published by Ignaz Amon c.1794, comprising marches "der Kays: Konig: Armee für das Clavier oder Fortepiano"; nine of these marches are available in a modern reconstruction by Weinmann (**AXW-1ma**) for a band similar to that used by Beethoven. All these marches are for identifiable regiments, mostly Viennese; most are named after the honorary Colonel; most omit the name of the composer. Some composers preferred to remain anonymous, possibly for social status: Franz Benda (1709-1786) wrote for a friend's dragoon regiment on condition that the players were not told who had written it (23). The writing of marches for victories or famous events, even those of other nations was quite common (229). Goepfert arranged Steibelt's celebration of Admiral Duncan's victory (**CAG-9a**); P Mašek's **PLM-1** *The Battle of Leipzig* and **PLM-2** *The Occupation of Paris* are more substantial examples. One also finds marches written for those who might be considered an "enemy." Thus Cherubini, in Paris, wrote for the German occupying forces.

Militia and the Like

Many titles refer to militia, though fewer than in British marches of the time: Fendt's 1812 collection for the Salzburg National-Garde III Klasse; Seiff's music for the Bavarian National-Garde dritter Klasse; the Bavarian series **A-77m**, which includes details of organization and regulations for uniforms; the *Vaandelmarsch der Bürger Compagnie* by B Ruloffs, and (M?) Schwarz's *Marsch* "mit einem beliebten Posthorn Trio" for the 2nd Bürgerregiment. It is not always clear how regular or transient a militia regiment might be, but we note marches by Fuchs (**GFF-1ma** for the Landwehr de la Ville de Vienne; **GFF-2ma** for the Garde Nationale à Cheval de la Ville de Vienne), Beethoven (**LVB-1m**, for the Civil Artillery Corps of Vienna), Kozeluch (**LAK-3m** Corps des Handelstandes von Wien), Kreith (**CXK-1m**, for the Wiener Scharfschützen Korps) and Schiedemayr (**JOS-2m** for the Landwehr im Erzherzogthum Österreich ob der Enns).

Prussian Wind Music

The Prussian collections (now in D-B) include four types of music: (1) marches (2) fanfares, (3) items for fifes and drums, and (4) wind harmony. In all, there are several hundred pieces for wind band. Prussian-based composers include Felice Alessandri (1742-1798), Anton Bachman (1716-1800), Johann Christian Fischer (1733-1800), Friedrich Heinrich Himmel (1765-1814), Johann Gottlieb Naumann (1741-1801) and

Wilhelm Ferdinand Rong (1759-1842), whose 1789 marches **WFR-1m** use basset horns. Some marches were composed by members of the aristocracy, including three by Amalie, the sister of Frederick the Great; one wonders if her teacher, Georg Benda, contributed to their orchestration. Other military music includes two "masureks," a fandango, all for Turkish music, and a quadrille - adding to the range of popular dances for which wind bands played. The harmony list also includes an *Allegro molto & Andante* by Bachmann for the odd ensemble of 2ob 2cl bn tp. Many composers and arrangers are represented in the collection: seven partitas for ten winds by Carl Stamitz, partitas by Dittersdorf, an arrangement of Weber's *Preciosa,* and one by Went of Mozart's *Le nozze di Figaro.* Later music for Berlin is for large band, such as Spontini's *Grosser Siegesmarsch und Festmarsch.* Some marches are more lighthearted, such as Weller's *Ein musikalischer Spass* **FYW-3m,** with its mimicry of birdsongs.

THE CONCERT AND OPERA SCENE

Regular concerts could provide enduring pleasure. They are reported in Vienna from the 1780s, but these were not unique. One interesting series took place each Sunday in summer for Count Günther Friedrich Karl I von Schwarzburg-Sondershausen, amateur clarinettist and bass horn player. This enlightened ruler heard the Langensalza regimental band in 1800, and persuaded Johann Simon Hermstedt (1778-1846) to form a band at Sondershausen two years later. The band continued until 1835, when it was replaced by a full orchestra. Hermstedt was one of the finest clarinettists of his day (104), and he was evidently an excellent musical director. The band played music by Krommer, Romberg, Eberwein, Lindpaintner, Spohr and others. The concerts were given in the thick beech woods between the town and the Count's castle. A platform was built in a natural amphitheater, previously a shooting area, and a high-domed pavilion with a semicircular stage was erected for the band. Opposite this pavilion was a covered gallery, and a third side of the square consisted of a thick beech hedge with embrasures. When the court arrived for the concert, they were preceded by Turkish music, with cymbals, triangle, bass drum, and piccolo, and they left to similar accompaniment (104). The audience could enjoy both the music and a view over the Wipper River to the Harz Mountains. Local people were encouraged to attend, making each occasion a promenade concert in the literal sense. The players seemed to enjoy the arrangement too, since many remained at Sondershausen for long periods.

Marches from the Operas

Many Austrian and German operas contain marches for winds. Examples include that for 2cl 2hn 2bn in Haydn's 1783 *Armide* or that in Weber's 1826 *Oberon.* Sometimes there is a stage band; at other times, winds emerge as a separate body within the orchestra, as in the C major march for 2ob 2hn 2bn near the end of Haydn's *Armide.* The march which concludes Mozart's famous "Non più andrai" starts in bar 61, where only 2fl 2ob 2hn 2bn accompany Figaro.

Operatic marches by major composers are quite distinct from parade marches. They are more subtle, like the marches in Mozart's *Die Zauberflöte.* They may be technically tricky, like the C major march from Haydn's *Armide*: C alto horns are for skilled musicians, not soldiers. They often have dynamics, or ingenious imitation. The best composers produce something original, even using standard formulas. Despite passing similarities (like Haydn's march with clarinets from *Armide* and the Chorus, No 8 from Mozart's *Così fan tutte,* or like the march at bar 147 of the finale to act 2 of *Così fan tutte* and the march which ends Weber's *Abu Hassan*), resemblances quickly disappear.

Stage bands in German opera followed similar conventions to those of Italian operas, especially for "magic" music. Examples are the act 2 finale of Süssmayr's *Der Spiegel von Arkadien* (1794, a sequel to Mozart's *Die Zauberflöte)* and Johann Friedrich Reichardt's *Die Geisterinsel* (1798). Reichardt's *Brenno* (1789) includes a *Triumphal March* for 2ob cl(D) bthn 2hn bn cbn serp. Spohr has stage bands (Harmonie) in *Alruna, Macbeth, Pietro von Albano* and *Faust.* Stage bands were sometimes used for effect when they were not required by the composer, especially in Mozart's *Don Giovanni.*

WIND MUSIC AFTER THE MID-19TH CENTURY

Wind harmony showed more continuity in Austria and Germany than elsewhere. At least one important work, Franz Lachner's *Octet,* was published in 1850. Brahms, Bruckner, and even Wolf wrote works for voices and winds, setting a pattern for the 20th century, with notable examples from Krenek and Weill. Conventional wind harmony recovered its status largely through the Swiss-born Joachim Raff. His *Sinfonietta,* written in 1873, is not only a fine work, but seems to have been seminal: there are signs of its influence in works as disparate as Richard Strauss's *Serenade* and Gounod's *Petite Symphonie.* Raff was then regarded as the foremost symphonist, and any of his substantial works would have been widely performed and heard.

Composers all over Europe wrote music for small ensembles and for larger wind bands. The wind quintet progressed from undistinguished efforts, like the somewhat scrappy quintet by Klughardt and the rather turgid one by Kauffman, via Hindemith's outstanding *Kleine Kammermusik,* to works by Henze, Schoenberg and Stockhausen. There is a flourishing tradition for larger wind bands in Austria and Germany (230). Schoenberg's principal contribution to wind music is best represented by his works for symphonic band; Hindemith too wrote excellent music for concert band, and even Stockhausen exploited a wind band in Lucifer's Music from *Samstag als Licht.*

In the early 19th century the Austro-Hungarian Empire was a convenient geographical unit. Nationalism became a major political force later on, and political nationalism encouraged its musical counterpart. Wind music emerged slowly in Hungary, despite the nationalism in the works of Brahms, Liszt, and Ferenc Erkel. Mátyás Seiber's *Serenade* of 1925 remains one of the best of the many neglected works for wind ensemble. It is fitting that one of the best and most popular wind works should be by the Bohemian composer, Dvořák, reviving his country's great wind harmony tradition. Dvořák's pupils, Nováček and Fučik, also wrote for winds. Fučik, best known today for his march, *Entry of the Gladiators,* was bassoonist with the Czech Wind Trio and later a bandmaster. It is likely that his *Symphonie Scandaleuse* was composed for the Czech Wind Trio. Since World War II, Czech composers have turned again to wind music, writing many interesting works.

APPENDIX: WIND BANDS IN AUSTRO-HUNGARY AND GERMANY

The complexities of political boundaries and their frequent changes make analysis by nation a futile exercise. The basic geographical framework we shall use is this: (1) northern Germany and near the Rhine; (2) the upper Danube, including the centers like Salzburg, Munich and Wallerstein, whose nearby rivers feed the Danube; (3) near the Danube, including Vienna and other cities, and the smaller centers which looked to them, like Eisenstadt and Eszterháza, Rohrau, Klosterneuburg, and Melk; (4) Bohemia:

Prague, and the smaller towns or castles (often called *Zámek,* more like a chateau or manor house) for which it was the focus; (5) Moravia, where Brno is often the regional center, and (6) those isolated Harmonien at the periphery, such as Lancut, Grosswardein, Kolosvar and Keszthely. Within each region, lists are alphabetical.

The problem of place names plagues every writer who is concerned with central Europe. An early example (231) is Hadow's journey: "Wishing to make pilgrimages to Eisenstadt, where Haydn was Kapellmeister, and to Željez, where Schubert taught music to Countess Esterházy, I took a ticket at Vienna for the first of these places, only to find, when my watch informed me of my destination, that Eisenstadt and Željez were the same place, and that the name upon the railway-station was Kis Martom." We therefore include some geographical guidance.

We give information where we can about the dates for which bands operated. The effects of the Napoleonic Wars are very clear from three brief periods of profound change. Some changes merely moved musicians from civil to military roles; others were driven by financial problems and uncertainties, so that bands were even more vulnerable to the deaths of enthusiastic patrons. In the late 1790s, when Napoleon's armies moved into Austria, several wind bands seem to have had difficulties: Clam Gallas, Eszterháza, Grassalcovics, Nova Říše, Schwarzenberg, and perhaps Jahn and von Braun. In the early 1800s, Eszterháza and Nova Říše reemerged, and new ensembles began at Keszthely, Lancut, Náměšt nad Oslavou, and Sondershausen. Many bands ceased soon after 1815 in the aftermath of the wars: Lancut, Náměšt nad Oslavou, and the Chotek, Pachta and Lobkowitz Harmonien. Other ensembles appeared in the 1820s, but more slowly.

Wind Bands of the North German Courts and those near the Rhine

In addition to the ensembles we mention, there are known to have been town bands at Aachen and Nuremberg, military bands at Aschaffenburg, Bremen, Coburg, Detmold, Erfurt, Neu Rippin, Osnabrück and Würzburg, and wind bands, possibly Harmonien, at Bamberg and Breslau. Very many other bands will have existed (see e.g., ref (7)).

Amorbach. The Abbey dates from the 1740s, and we presume that the Harmonie played there. It seems to have begun in the 1780s. In 1806, clarinettist Neuparth began a brief stay; c.1815, Georg Schmitt moved to Hohenlohe-Öhringen (qv). The clarinettist A Bauer moved to Amorbach from Hohenlohe-Öhringen. Weston (232) suggests that there was a court; perhaps this relates to a court visit by the Archbishop of Mainz. The later part of the Fulda (qv) collection is at Amorbach (the earlier part is in Frankfurt am Main) and contains an many printed works from the French Revolution.

Bonn. The accession in 1784 of Maximilian Franz as Elector of Cologne changed the Harmonie completely (233). The existing ensemble (Meuser and Joan Baum playing oboe or clarinet, with horns Riedl and Brandt and bassoonists Meuris, Zillicken and Kuchler) expanded into an octet (oboists Georg Libisch and J Welsch, clarinets Michael Meuser and N Pachtmeyer, horns Andreas Bamberger and Nickolaus Simrock, bassoons Zillicken and Georg Welsch). Only Meuser and Zillicken remained; Libisch, Pachtmeyer and the Welsch brothers came from Vienna. The music archive appears to be lost.

The Harmonie of the minister, Count Belderbusch, c.1783, comprised clarinettists Pachmeier and Mooch, two horn players and a bassoon.

Darmstadt. The Harmonie of the Duke of Hesse-Darmstadt grew out of a small military band of the 1740s (2ob bn tp). Only after the accession of Ludwig X as Duke in 1790 (Grand Duke from 1806) did it become a full Harmonie. The Harmonie continued until the 1830s. The clarinettist Sartorius may have come to Darmstadt in the 1780s and continued to arrange works until after 1806, such as that of Danzi's *Chöre aus dem Freudenfest.* In D-DS are the fair copies of the scores which Sartorius had made for the

Duke. They are beautifully bound, with all edges gilt, and carefully lettered title pages enclosed in ornate printed borders. Hassloch, who was a singer in 1809, rose to Hofkapellmeister in 1813 and died in 1823. Mangold was probably his successor, though his works all date from 1830 to 1843. Both Hassloch and Mangold wrote Masonic works. Rinck came to Darmstadt as organist in 1805 and Kammermusicus from 1817; he wrote many choral works with winds until 1833. Weston (232) lists over 20 clarinettists employed at the Court from the 1780s to the 1850s, many staying for long periods.

Detmold. The Lippe Harmonie continued without major changes until about World War I, with a number of anonymous local arrangers. In the later years, Karl Kaiser arranged music for this band.

Frankfurt am Main. In this, the free imperial city in which the later Holy Roman Emperors were crowned, only the theater seems to have employed clarinets. This it did from the late 1780s onwards. At Frankfurt are found the early (pre-1800) items from Fulda Fürstbischöfliche Harmonie, including anonymous *Divertissements* from Bern.

Fulda. The clarinettist Rihl belonged to the Hofkapelle c.1800; it is likely that he played in the Harmonie of the Prince Bishop's court. From around 1834, clarinettists André and Hamburger also played in the military band (232).

The Hague. After the 1815 Congress of Vienna, the seat of government of the Netherlands (then including Belgium) alternated between The Hague and Brussels. King William I, who fought at Waterloo, may have heard the Viennese Hofharmonie at the Congress. The surviving music includes published works printed in Vienna; there may have been a connection with Frankfurt am Main, for there are works for 2fl 2bb 2cl 2hn 2bn cbn by Stumpf and Düring, and printed works by Goepfert from André in Offenbach.

Mainz. The clarinettists at the court of the Elector Archbishop of Mainz were Harburger, Wagner, Becker, and Scribanek (232). The Duke of Bretzenheim employed wind players at Mainz, including. Hammerl (cl), Eckhert (hn) and Suvick (bn), who later played at Mecklenburg-Schwerin (qv) (234).

Mannheim. In 1777, the orchestral winds (235) comprised 2fl 2ob 2cl 2hn 4bn; in 1782, after many players had moved to Munich, there were 4fl 3ob 3cl 4hn 4bn. The players included Wendling, Metzger, Leich, Cannabich and Haffner (fl), Ramm, A Lebrun, Ludwig Lebrun, Bleckmann, Heiber and Ritter (ob), Johannes and Thaddeus Hampel, Quallenburg, and Jakob and Franz Tausch (cl), Schindlarz and Stich (Punto) (hn), and Georg and Heinrich Ritter, Schafer, Steidel and Lederer (bn).

Mecklenburg-Schwerin (Ludwigslust). Duke Friedrich the Pious (1717-1785) expanded his court orchestra after moving his court from Schwerin to Ludwigslust in 1767. This expansion continued: Sperger and Rosetti settled in Ludwigslust in 1789, Sperger bringing music with him by Stěpán and others. The court orchestra does not seem to have played as a Harmonie. Its oboists were Johann Friedrich Braun (1758-1824, a pupil of Carlo Besozzi) and J G Andrae, and its bassoonists Franz Anton Pfeiffer (1752-1787), Christoph Ludwig Hoppius (before 1751-1824; he came from Wallerstein to replace Pfeiffer in 1790) and Johann Maximilian Kadel (bn 2 from 1790 to 1794). Wind music at Ludwigslust was played by the band attached to the Duke's Leib-Grenadier Regiment. The next Duke, Friedrich Franz (1756-1837; Grand Duke from 1815), a pianist, also encouraged music. After Harmonie concerts in 1798 and 1800 by visiting players (of whom Hammerl, Eckhert [hn] and Suvick [bn for the 1800 concert] were employed by the Duke of Bretzenheim at Mainz [234]), he decided to form his own Harmonie in 1801. Three of the visitors joined the new ensemble: clarinettists Hammerl (from 1795 to 1825) and Stüber, and horn player Brassler.

The Harmonie, which wore green hunting livery, was especially welcome at the coastal resort of Doberan, where the Duke spent part of the summer (his "Badezeit"). It was here that Mendelssohn heard them, and wrote the first version of his *Ouverture*.

The players in 1812 included Richter (fl, perhaps ob), Nicolai (ob), Hammerl and Stüber (cl), Bode and Theen (hn), Haidner and Heller (bn), Winzer (tp) and Seipoldsdorf (serp). It was disbanded in 1839 by Grand Duke Paul Friedrich soon after his 1837 accession.

    Hohenlohe–Öhringen.   August von Hohenlohe-Öhringen became Fürst in 1806. At about that time, he founded the Harmonie, and acquired Triebensee's 1802 *Harmonien Sammlung* and a few other works from Vienna, including *Parthien* by Krommer. The Harmonie seems to have been the mainstay of music at Öhringen, for there is little music for full orchestra, and only a few string quartets. The octet of these early years soon grew by the addition of fl tp b-tb vlne, a configuration which it retained for many years. Kapellmeister Georg Schmitt joined from Amorbach c.1816, and stayed until his death, probably soon after the move to Silesia c.1837. Wilhelm Kirchhoff joined in the late 1820s, and probably succeeded Schmitt as Kapellmeister. W E Scholz arrived c.1838, and may have succeeded Kirchhoff in 1842 or 1843. The court seems to have employed at least one copyist throughout the life of the Harmonie, for many of the parts are not in the hands of the composer or arranger. In this large collection (well over 500 works) probably 90% of the items are arrangements. Many manuscripts date from after the Court's move to *Schlawentzitz*, the estates in Silesia from which came the zinc and lead which provided the family fortunes. This estate came into the family when August married Louise, Duchess of Württemberg, in 1811 (which may also explain why there are several works at Neuenstein, probably arrangements, by Eugen, Duke of Württemberg). Louise's death in 1831 may have been a factor leading to the move to Silesia sometime between 1834 and 1837, where the Harmonie continued until about 1850. The collection is now at Neuenstein (236).

    Ochsenhausen.   The 14 items from the Kloster und Pfarrkirche are, with one exception (an octet for solo cl 2cl 2hn 2vl bass) church choral music with winds. The wind groups are varied, e.g., 2cl 2hn 2bn, or 2fl 2hn b-tb. There is a *Messe* by Ignaz Lachner (1807-1895) brother of Franz Lachner (see Part 2).

    Potsdam.   We have already described the royal music collection of arrangements, marches, and original music, especially by Prussian composers. Among the clarinet players were Johann Joseph Beer (18 May 1744-1812, once at Wallerstein), at the Royal Military School from 1792 to 1811, and K J Krause (15 Jul 1775, Forsta-1838 Potsdam), conductor from 1810 to 1814 and arranger for the 1st Regt Prussian Guard military band, with whom he went to war in 1814.

    Sachsen-Meiningen.   The Ducal court musicians included Schilling (fl), Firkenstedt and Haak (ob), Goepfert (cl, ob, and composer; see part 2), Härtel (cl) and Kleinenhargen (hn). No wind harmony music survives in the Landesbibliothek.

    Sondershausen.   The clarinettist Hermstedt formed the Harmonie in 1802, with Lundershause and Himmelstosse (ob), Simon Hermstedt and Georg Friedrich Henrici (cl), Hartung and Seebach (hn), and Friedrich Hermstedt and Siegfried Friedrich Bendleb (bn), plus Hühne and Bartel (tp), Herrmann (b-hn) and Georg Henrici (tb).

    Wertheim (Löwenstein).   The musical initiative of Erbprinz Carl Friedrich von Löwenstein (see part 2) ensured a Harmonie with excellent players and a large and enterprising repertoire, many written or arranged by the Prince himself. There is music for the standard small military band (tp 3hn tb), some music for smaller ensembles, more than 40 opera arrangements by Sedlak, Stumpf, Widder, Witt and others, and a substantial collection for fl(E♭) cl(E♭) 2cl(B♭) 2hn 2bn tp b-tb cbn or similar ensembles. There are some remarkable works, such as the transcription of Witt's *Requiem*, and of Mozart's songs (by Goepfert) and quartets (by Hermstedt). There are versions of Beethoven's *Adelaide,* and a copy of his *Septet* arranged by Crusell. This collection contains many of the "dubious" works attributed to Weber, like the *Oboe Concertino,* and the dubious *Oboe Concertino* attributed to Hummel.

Zeist, Netherlands (East of Utrecht). The Netherlands were part of the Holy Roman Empire only from 1566-1648; they were annexed by France from 1789 to 1791, and were part of the French Empire from 1810 to 1815. Apart from the Royal Harmonie, there seems to have been little Harmoniemusik. The Moravian Brethren at Zeist were an exception; presumably their interest in wind music developed from their contact with the main location of the Brethren at Herrnhut. We are not aware of any direct links to the Moravian Brethren in Pennsylvania. The Zeist Harmonie seems to have lasted from the 1790s until the 1820s. Some of the music is incomplete, and much may have been lost. That which survives includes 9 works by Mankell (5 *Divertimentos*, 3 *Parthias* and a *Suite*), 6 *Parthias* by Hoffmeister (including one attributed elsewhere to Haydn), a *Serenade* by Gyrowetz, and several opera arrangements. The scorings are very varied, but the core ensemble seems to be 2fl(E♭) 2cl 2hn 2bn. Other works include smaller ensembles (e.g. 3 pieces for cl 2hn) and a body of music for three trombones.

German Courts near the Upper Danube

Bad Buchau, Swabia. The Bad Buchau archive is now in Tübingen. Some of the wind music (primarily 35 pieces for 2cl[E♭] 2cl[B♭] 2hn bn and 87 pieces for 2cl 2hn bn, both in MS c.1810) was sold by "Rath und Oberförster Haeckel" to the Thurn und Taxis regimental band in 1821 (see below under Regensburg). What remains is primarily marches or operatic arrangements, some from Vienna. Some items are early pieces from between 1805 and 1810; among the later pieces is an interesting 1828 arrangement by Richter of Beethoven's *Todten Marsch,* here for H[err] General von Bennendorf. It was from Kapellmeister Richter in Stuttgart that the Taxis regimental band bought music in 1821. Richter was the dedicatee of Walch's *Pièces d'Harmonie, Liv 14.*

Donaueschingen (Fürstenberg). The wind ensemble seems to date from the 1760s, with oboes, horns and bassoons forming a Jagdmusik and Tafelmusik. Some early music for 2cl 2hn bn may have been copied from the Pachta Harmonie in Prague. The octets of Mysliveček suggest there was a full octet by the late 1770s. Developements in the reigns of Prince Joseph Benedikt Maria (1783-1796) and Prince Carl Joachim (1796-1804) can be followed from the catalogs (1799, opera; 1804, pianoforte, vocal, Harmonie; 1816, music, instruments, desks [Pulte]; 1823-26, music), and from Karl von Hampeln's regular statements of spending on music from 1802 onwards. Fiala may have brought some of his own works with him from Salzburg on his move to Donaueschingen in 1792. The collection includes 164 works; 19 have voices, including later works by Kalliwoda. Most of the collection's 48 arrangements for 2ob 2cl 2hn 2bn date from the 1790s. They seem to have been in use from the 1790s to the 1820s. Some of them were copied (with added dynamics) rather than arranged by Franz Rosinack who, with Jos. Jäckle, played oboe. The *Kalendar* c.1792 shows that Rosinack was *Kammermusikus.* One major item (see part 2) is **WAM-3a**, perhaps Mozart's own wind version of *Die Entführung aus dem Serail* (237). There is a note (dated 23 Oct 1823) that, in 1820, arrangements of four Mozart operas were lent to Rosinack. The ensemble was active until the late 1830s, when French music was bought, though only two works survive.

Gutenzell, Swabia; Parish (Pfarramt) Church Band. There is a substantial collection of church music with winds (such as several *Masses* and a number of works for Corpus Christi) and a few operatic arrangements, mainly for 2cl 2hn 2bn, sometimes with added instruments. Given the amount of secular music, we wonder if the collection includes works belonging to the town band, as well as that for church use.

Herrnberg. The church band collection comprises cantatas from the 1820s by Wilhelm Adolph Müller, for bands such as terz-fl 2ob 2cl 2hn 2bn 2tp 3tb cbn timp.

Munich. One important phase began when the Mannheim musicians arrived in 1778.

These included clarinettists Quallenberg and Hampel, who had joined Mannheim from Regensburg in 1758 or 1759. Little wind music survives from this phase. A second phase lasted from the Napoleonic Wars until the troubles of the 1840s. Prince Elector Maximilian IV remained neutral in the wars, becoming Maximilian I Joseph, King of Bavaria in 1806. The wind band's music included Triebensee's *Miscellannées* (Oeuvres 5-8, of 1809 survive). The repertoire expanded greatly when Ludwig I succeeded in 1825, with massive collections of arrangements by Legrand (551 pieces, most unidentified) and Widder (76 pieces). Features of court music of this period are works for large wind band by Meyerbeer, Joseph Hartmann Stuntz (1793-1859) and Walther von Goethe (1817-1885, grandson of the poet). Problems of state affected the Harmonie around 1842, when the King was under the spell of Lola Montez; he was forced to abdicate because of this remarkable woman (Irish, despite her chosen Spanish name).

Regensburg (Thurn und Taxis).   The Harmonie emerged as a group of 2cl 2hn bn from the court orchestra c.1770, though wind music had been performed for two previous decades. By 1773, the Harmonie was well established, playing works in the standard format of up to six movements. In the late 1770s, there may have been a setback, for little new music remains. The period from 1780 saw remarkably continuous development. The music could be unconventional, with 2vla vlne added to the winds. An extra pair of horns or trumpets might be added, or bassethorns substituted for clarinets. Another ensemble of 2a-cl(G) 2vla/hn vlne emerged, apparently in parallel with the main Harmonie. The works were mostly original; there were few arrangements apart from some of Mozart. The original works, often by Regensburg composers like de Croes, Klob, Kolb and von Schacht, were often of seven or more movements, suitable for Tafelmusik. Clarinettists at Regensburg after 1770 (2) include: Engel (1755-1781?), Rottweil (1769-1787), Sänger (to 1806), Schierls junior (1784-1797) Schierls senior (1769-1786?), Wack (?1755-?1786), and W Wack (1784-1806).

The surviving wind music dating from c.1770-c.1806 comprises at least 218 works, including 4 with voices. Of these works, just over 40% include 2vla, and about 10% include 2a-cl(G). Many of the works contain large numbers of movements, including 40 works with 12 movements. One should not presume that all movements were played each time; such works may have been intended for large banquets.

Music at court was set back by the death of Carl Anselm (1733-1805) and the financial loss from lost postal concessions after the Holy Roman Empire was dissolved in 1806. Carl Alexander (1770-1827) disbanded the orchestra, and turned the nearby monastery of St Emmeram into a luxurious palace. Wind music remained at a low ebb until c.1820, when the Prince's wished to set up a private army, against the wishes of the King of Württemberg. Such an army needed a band, at least for show. We are indebted to Herr Angerer for informing us that the band was set up at Schloss Taxis, near Neresheim, not at Regensburg. The band may never have played in Regensburg, but it is likely that some of the earlier music - notably the larger works with 2vla vlne by Croes and Schacht - was loaned to the band. This may explain the regular use of violas and violone in so many of Schneider's works. The background may also explain why so much music was purchased from Stuttgart, Bad Buchau and Moravia. Much came from the estate of Graf Johann von Klenau of Janowitz (13 April 1758-6 October 1819), who ended a distinguished military career as Commandant in Moravia. The music may have been for his own band. 93 items were bought in 1820, 1821 and 1822, including many works by Krommer, two large works by Walch, Goepfert's arrangement of Mozart's *Turkish March (Allegrino alla Turca)*, 11 works for 2ob 2cl 2hn 2bn, a group of 35 pieces for 2cl(E♭) 2cl(B♭) 2hn bn, and a collection of 87 pieces for 2cl 2hn bn. Probably most of the printed works were purchased at this time. Spohr's *Notturno* and Vern's *Nocturne* were added in a different hand on blank sheets at the backs of volumes in 1822. Over the next year or two, the Gardemusik evolved into a Harmonie, typically fl 2ob 2/4cl 2/4hn 2bn tp tb 2vla vlne (and/or serp). Since there were relatively few marches, the band may have played more for civil than for military activities. This trend was to continue. About 1822, Anton Schneider arrived, an extremely energetic Kappelmeister. He arranged or adapted many works for local forces. In 1822-1823 he seems to have produced 2 works per week, on average, so that the Harmonie had available most of the popular operas. Many arrangements appeared, often of older, well-loved, works; dances, especially waltzes, appeared as well. Generally, much care was taken with the music, which was added into already-bound volumes. Over the next 3 to 4 years, Schneider was less active, but filled gaps in the repertoire, or arranged suitable new works, especially by Auber, Spohr and Weber. From 1822 to c.1827, well over 300 works were added (some 900 movements). From 1828, following Carl Alexander's death, there seems to have been no further repertoire. Yet it was still possible to put together large wind ensembles for special occasions, at least until the band was dissolved in 1831.

Stuttgart. The Hoftheater fire of 1902 destroyed much of the music listed in the 1834 *Inventorium*, which notes wind music by Beethoven, Krommer, Legrand, Mozart, Pleyel, Rummel, Schwegler and Stumpf, and arrangements by Krechler. Surviving music with winds includes Danzi's *Herr Gott, Dich loben wir*, vocal works and a *Quadrille zum Königlichen Carossel* by Lindpaintner, Schwegler's two *Märsche zur Braut von Messina*, and a number of small items associated with dramas.

Wallerstein. In the archive of this ensemble are 98 works, plus 7 quintets for solo winds and 2 large works (Kinsky's arrangement of *Die Zauberflöte,* dedicated to Prince Carl Kraft, 12 July 1818, and Zwing's *3 Grandes Pièces, Op XI,* c.1800). The collection has some striking features. First, many of the works are by the court's own composers, especially Feldmayr, Hiebesch, Josef Reicha, Rosetti and Wineberger. Such works taper off around 1795, after which there was a move to printed editions. Secondly, there are only five arrangements, consistent with the known preferences of Prince Kraft Ernst. The first dates from 1788, when von Beecke bought Ehrenfried's arrangement of Grétry's *Richard, Coeur de Lion.* One *Parthia* by a local composer, Feldmayr, was partly based on *Die Zauberflöte.* Went's arrangement of Thaddeus Weigl's ballet *Die Vermählung im Keller* is simply entitled "Harmonie ... vom Weigl," perhaps to hide its origins. Thirdly, the scorings vary widely in detail, perhaps because Prince Kraft Ernst was liberal in letting his musicians go on tours. The ensemble fluctuated in constitution, and this is reflected in the scorings. Flutes are included more than in most ensembles of the 1780s and 1790s: over half the works include 2 flutes, and nearly two-thirds use at least one flute. Fourthly, about half the works are in sharp keys (D, G) and few in Eb or Bb, consistent with the presence of flutes.

The wind band is shown in a famous silhouette on a gold background, said to date from 1791 (238). The identity of the musicians has been the subject of educated guesses (239, 240). The flutes could be Alois and Wilhem Ernst (or Feldmayer?), the oboes Gliere and Weinhoeppel (or Fiala?), the clarinets Josef Beer and Michel Fürst, the bassoons Christoph Ludwig Hoppius and Franz Xaver Meisrimle, and the horn players Josef Nagel, Franz Zwirzina (or Nisle and Thürrschmidt?). The violone player could be Franz Anton Rosetti. Yet there is no evidence that these players were at Wallerstein at the same time. Nor is the image consistent: the perspective suggests that the background was created independently. The images of the players are all of much the same size, giving an illusion (241) that the distant players are unduly tall. The music stands were clearly made from a single mask, for their images are merely translated or reversed, those on the right being strict mirror images of those on the left. The image of the bassoonist may be reversed, but it was only when the fourth (G#) key was

added that it became the norm to rest the bassoon on the right thigh. We suspect that the silhouette is a montage, put together from portraits compiled over several years. This would explain the differences in uniforms and wig styles.

The Danube Cities and Adjacent Areas

Bratislava (Pressburg). Here there were at least three Harmonien, plus the short-lived Harmonie of Count Franz Esterházy at nearby Čeklis (see under Eisenstadt and Eszterháza). That of Prince Joseph von Batthyáni, Cardinal of Hungary (242), led by clarinettist Theodor Lotz, lasted from about 1776 to 1784. Other players were the brothers Johann and Philip Teimer (ob), Michael Bum (cl), Karl Franz and Anton Bock (hn) and Franz Czerwenka and Josef Padney (bn). The Teimer brothers later joined the Schwarzenberg Harmonie; Czerwenka eventually joined the Imperial Harmonie. The Batthyáni archives are lost. The Cardinal employed Druschetzky around 1790. The Harmonie of the Counts of Erdödy (243), based near Pressburg, came mainly from the Pressburg infantry. This family supported Vanhal, Pleyel and Beethoven at various times. Count Ladislaw Erdödy died in 1786. It would seem from paper types and calligraphy that, when he left, double-bass player Sperger took with him his own music and some by Štěpán and Pichl; this music ended up in Ludwigslust (see Mecklenburg-Schwerin). Finally, Prince Grassalkovics (244) maintained a wind band; from 1796, his orchestra was reduced to a Harmonie, whose archives are now lost. Druschetzky was associated with this Harmonie (245), but his octets were written for the 50th Galizische-Linien Infantry Regiment in Linz, comprising players Valentine Kolbe and Franz Melchior (ob), Joseph and Johann Chorus (cl), Georg and Ludwig Spallek (hn) and Franz Bodany and Franz Mohr (bn). The Grassalkovic band was led by the clarinettist Reimund Griesbach (1752-1818) (232, 244), a member of the Eszterháza orchestra from 1776 to 1778, later becoming an instrument maker and extra clarinet at the Viennese court; it was to him that Hummel's *Clarinet Concerto* was dedicated. Prince Grassalkovics tried to induce Haydn to become his Master of Music in the 1790s.

Buda. The Harmonie of Josef Anton, Palatine of Hungary, was probably part of the Kapelle at the palace in Buda (which was joined with Pest only in 1873). It appears to date from c.1796, although the earlier works in H-Bn, notably octets by Went, may have belonged to this Harmonie. Druschetzky was appointed its Composer and Kapellmeister in 1802. His varied works for it were generally scored for 2ob 2cl 2hn 2bn (with a cbn from c.1805), and include 5 settings of Schiller, with an additional chorus.

Eisenstadt (Željev; Kis Martom) and Eszterháza (Fertöd). The Princes Esterházy had wind bands in their service from the 1750s until 1813, although they varied significantly in status (246; *HCRL,* passim). In the 1750s, the Eisenstadt schoolmaster and tenor Joseph Dietzl arranged for the Feldmusik; this music seems not to survive. When Haydn arrived, the band combined local schoolmasters and perhaps Grenadiers. New players were recruited, and the standards for the next thirty years or so were presumably very high. Unlike most court musical directors, Haydn does not seem to have had to compose or arrange for the wind band. His early wind music appears to have been written for Count Morzin, though perhaps it was for Count Franz Anton von Harrach (247), on whose Rohrau estates Haydn was born. The 1790s saw major changes under the new Prince Esterházy. Most musicians were dismissed or moved, some to the

---

Figure (facing page). The Oettingen-Wallerstein Harmonie. This silhouette may be a montage of portraits from the 1780s and early 1790s. Reproduced by permission of the Fürstlich Oettingen-Wallerstein'sche Sammlungen, Schloss Harburg.

Grenadier band in 1795; the Grenadier Company was itself dismissed in 1797. In April 1800, Count Franz Esterházy de Frakno formed a Harmonie at Čeklis (now Bernolákovo, near Bratislava); it lasted only one summer, for many players moved to the main Eszterháza Harmonie in November 1800. The main Harmonie may have been disbanded in 1809, although some music was bought at later dates; the last payment for music (arrangements of Spontini, J Weigl and Isouard) was authorized on 12 September 1811.

All Eszterháza wind music known from this time seems to have been purchased from Vienna, apart from some Haydn marches and *Parthia No 8* by Vice-Kapellmeister Fuchs (JAF-1). The collection comprises arrangements (57 items, with those in Triebensee's *Harmonien Sammlung*), 31 Parthias (4 by Krommer, and arrangements of Mozart's K.361 and K.407), a *Serenata* and 2 sets of variations by Starke, marches (1 by Purebl, plus a later, uncut, set of 12 by Müller), and two collections. These are a set of twelve pieces by Starke *en Musique Turque*, dated March 1807, and Triebensee's *Miscellannées* Jg I, Oe 1-12. Thirty arrangements were acquired between 1791 and 1798; 1 more item was acquired in 1801 (Paer's *Achille*, very soon after the first Vienna performance of the opera on 6 June 1801) and then nearly 30 more arrangements from 1802-1810 (247). Prince Nicolaus Esterházy's interest is shown in his 9 June 1802 letter from Kitsee, near Bratislava, summoning his Harmonie, who are to bring "a supply of quite popular music and pieces from good operas transcribed for Harmonie." From much later, c.1822, there are several religious choral works with winds by Johann Nepomuk Fuchs.

The Eszterháza wind players had links with other ensembles. Some had relatives (clarinettist Werlen was probably the son of Verlen at Oettingen-Wallerstein); others came from known ensembles (Oliver, Pauer and Pohl from that of Bishop Patatisch at Grosswardein, Michl from the Batthyáni Musikkapelle in Pressburg); others moved to known ensembles (the Czerwenkas to the Hofharmonie). Many played for theaters in Vienna (Baumgartner, the Czerwenkas, Elssler, Hyrtl, Lendway, Sommer, Zachmann). Some moved from Grenadiers to Harmonie, demoted to string players in the Chormusique (Oliver, Pauer, Peczival) or were dismissed. Flute players associated with the Harmonie had other main instruments (Schiringer, Siegel). Here we list players for each instrument alphabetically, and give the dates for which they were at Eszterháza.

Oboists at Eszterháza.   Carl Braun (Eisenstadt, 1750s); Carl Chorus (oboe 1 from 15 July 1771); Franz Colombazzo (12 Oct 1779-15 March 1780). Joseph Czerwenka *(b 6 September 1759 Benadek, Bohemia; d 23 June 1835 Vienna)* played from 1775-1783 for Count Schafgotsch at Johannisberg before moving to Eszterháza as oboe I; he was dismissed in 1790 but reappointed until 1794. He then moved to Vienna, first to play in theaters, (from 1 May 1794 at the Kärntnertortheater), later joining the Hofharmonie on 1 October 1801, possibly as Went's replacement. Joseph Elssler *(baptised 7 August 1767 Eisenstadt, d 6 October 1843 Vienna)* was oboist from 1 November 1800 (possibly starting in the Grenadier band in 1794). From 1814 he played at the Burgtheater. His father Joseph and brother Johann were both Haydn's copyists. Zacharias Hirsch was dismissed in 1790. Joseph (Jacbo) Hyrtl (Hrtl) *(b 30 September 1768 Krems, d after 1844)* joined the Harmonie on 1 November 1800 (possibly starting in the Grenadier band in 1794). In April 1800 he moved to the short-lived Harmonie of Count Franz Esterházy. He too played in theaters. His son, Johann Hirtl, was a famous anatomist. Others included: Johann Michael Kapfer (1 April 1761 - after 4 March 1769); Johann Georg Kapfer (1 April 1761 - winter 1770-71); Anton Kreibich (Eisenstadt, 1750s); Anton Mayer (dismissed 1790, reappointed perhaps until 1794); Wilhelm Merkopf (leader of Count Franz Esterházy's Harmonie from April 1800); Zacharias Pohl (replacing J M Kapfer from 1769; previously with Bishop Patatisch at Grosswardein]; Franz Siegel (1 April 1761; he also played flute).

Clarinettists at Eszterháza.   Joseph Baumgartner (c.1792; also at the Kärntnertor

Theater); Franz Finger (14? April 1802 - late 1808); Anton Griessbacher (late 1775 - February 1778); Raimund Griessbacher, (late 1775 - February 1778); Johann Hornik (from 14? April 1802); Ignaz Skrabel (who replaced Finger c.1809). Georg Werlen joined Count Franz Esterházy's Harmonie in April 1800 moving on 1 November to Eszterháza. He joined the Liechtenstein Harmonie on 1 March 1802 to replace Ferdinand Schliess (deceased). Dionysius Zachmann (c.1792), was associated with the Kärtnertortheater.

Horn Players at Eszterháza. Joseph Wolfgang Dietzl (the son of Joseph Dietzl, mentioned above), from 15 May 1765; he was senior to Steinmetz. Johann Knoblauch (from 1 June 1761 till his death on 22 January 1765); Knopf (with the Grenadiers 23 July 1779); L Gabriel Lendway *(b 10 June 1760 Rechnitz, d 6 June 1806)* was horn 1; dismissed in 1790, then reappointed until 1794, he may have played clarinet 2 from 1800. Lendway played for the Wiener Tonkünstler Societät in 1793, and deputized in theaters before playing for the Vienna Hoftheater from 1802. Matthias Nickl (horn 2; dismissed in 1790 but reappointed until 1794) also deputized in Vienna theaters; he was considered for the Hofharmonie and Hofmusikkapelle to replace Eisen. Joseph Oliva and Franz Pauer both came from the Bishop Patatisch's ensemble at Grosswardein; they were horn players from 1769-1790, being demoted in 1790 to play violin in the Chor-musique. Anton Prinster *(b 11 March 1777 Vienna, d 21 August 1862)* may have played for the Grenadier band from 1794, moving in April 1800 to Count Franz Esterházy's new Harmonie, then to the Eszterháza Harmonie on 1 November 1800. He prepared the 1811 music catalog. He was the son of a mason in Tirol; his sister married Johann Elssler, Haydn's copyist and valet; his daughters Therese and Fanny were famous dancers. Michael Prinster *(b 9 September 1783, Vienna, d 5 August 1869)*, was the source of Pohl's information and anecdotes about the Harmonie. He played with Count Franz Esterházy's Harmonie from April 1800, and moved to the Eszterháza Harmonie on 1 November 1800. Schitzenhofer (with the Grenadiers from 23 July 1784); Franz Steinmetz (from early 1765); Thaddeus Steinmuller (from 1 June 1761).

Bassoonists at Eszterháza. In the 1750s, the bassoonists were schoolmasters (names unknown, one from Gross-Hoefflein, the other from Klein-Hoefflein). They may have played for the Grenadiers; but were made redundant on 21 May 1761. Franz Czerwenka *(b 14 October 1745, Benadek, Bohemia, d 27 April 1801, Vienna)* played for the Batthyáni Harmonie in Pressburg until 1783. He became bassoon 1; dismissed in 1790, he experienced hardship; he was reappointed until 1794. In 1793 he played for the Wiener Tonkünstler Societät, for the Hofmusikkapelle and Burgtheater from 2 June 1793, and with the Hofharmonie from 20 June 1793 until his death. Ignaz Drobney (late 1775 to April 1778, with the Hofharmonie from 1782); Johann Hinterberger (from 1 April 1761); Joseph Kugler (from 1805, allowing Michl to play the contrabassoon; Kugler also played clarinet); Lattesperger (with the Banda from 30 April 1784); Johann Michl (Rigl?) (with the Grenadiers, then with the Batthyáni Musikkapelle, then the Eszterháza Harmonie from 1 November 1800; he also played cbn from 1805). Caspar Peczival (who died "of suffocation" on 1 April 1802) was dismissed in 1790, then reappointed until 1794, and later reduced to playing violin for the Chor-musique. He deputized in Viennese theaters, returning to the Harmonie in late 1800. Johann Georg Schwenda (from 1 April 1761 to c.30 September 1765); Carl Joseph Schiringer (1 March 1767; previously with Count Csaky, Pressburg; he played double-bass and, from 1788, flute; dismissed in 1790); Johann Sommer *(26 January 1772-5 May 1843)* replaced Peczival on 1 May 1802; he played in court theaters and deputized for Drobney in the Hofkapelle; Joseph Steiner was dismissed in 1790.

Trumpet Players and Others. Those for 15 March 1780 until later in that year were Lorenz Markl and Johann Peschko. Those c.1808 were Sebastian Binder, Ignatz Goth, Joseph Greiner, and Anton Khayl. The timpanist at this time was Martin Csech.

Feldsberg (Valtice).   In 1782, Mozart was hoping to write for a planned Harmonie of Prince Johann Liechtenstein (248). It was not until July 1789, a wind band was formed for the Prince's hunting lodge, close to the borders of Moravia. The players included Josef Triebensee and Friedrich Zinke (oboes), Ferdinand Schliess and Georg Klein (clarinets), Anton Hollmayer (who was Musikdirektor) and Georg Eisner (horns), and Johann Harnisch and Franz Steiner (bassoons). Its initial season was a success, and contracts were renewed for at least two more years; in 1791, a note from the Prince to his secretary states his plans to go to Vienna without his Harmonie, despite the wishes of his wife. The band's position was formalized in 1794. Josef Triebensee became fürstlichen Kammer- und Theater Kapellmeister from 1 May 1794, a position which made him and the band major influences on the development of wind music. The ensemble continued for over 40 years, with a brief gap from 1809-1812. It was led by players and arrangers like Triebensee from 1794 and Sedlak from 1812; it survived until 1835 and perhaps later. There were two bands at times, the second being Turkish music for hunt, dance, theater, and even church. The Harmonie gave concerts; thus, in May 1807, it performed in the Gartenpalais in Vienna at 6 pm each Tuesday, Thursday and Sunday. The Harmonie was based for some of the year at Feldsberg, and from here the first of Triebensee's journals were published. The Feldsberg archive has been missing since the last years of World War II.

Vienna.   The Hofharmonie, or Kaiserlich-Königlich (Imperial & Royal) Harmonie (239 p 146 citing Christopher Raeburn; 249) comprised the best of Viennese virtuosos from late 1781 or early 1782: oboists Georg Triebensee (father) and Johann Went, the brothers Anton and Johann Stadler as clarinets, horn players Martin Rupp and Jacob Eisen, and bassoonists Wenzel Kauzner and Ignaz Drobney (Trobney). Other members joining later included Sebastian Grehman, Josef Khayll, Ernest Kräner, Franz Josef Czerwenka and Josef Sellner (ob), Josef Purebl, Thomas Klein, Georg Klein (not related) and Josef Friedlowsky (cl), Willibald Lotter, Johann Härmann and Friedrich Hradetzky (hn) and Franz Czerwenka, Matthieu Sedlacek, Franz Hollmayr, Wenzel Mattuschek and August Mittag (bn). There seems to have been no contrabassoon until 1802, after Went's death. Many of the players wrote wind music, including Went, the Stadlers, Czerwenka, Purebl, Sellner and Klein. We emphasize that this band was special because of its quality, not because it was an early example of an octet. Its skill and musicianship encouraged the development of the octet medium and the increasingly popular emphasis on opera arrangements. In 1783, two members of the Batthyányi Harmonie reported in Cramer's *Magasin der Musik* on the ensemble as "a society of virtuosi containing only wind instrumentalists who have reached a high degree of perfection." The English traveller John Scott heard what must have been this Harmonie ("the band of the Emperor of Austria") during his tour of Waterloo and Paris in 1815, remarking that it "surpassed ... any military orchestra I ever heard" (250).

The music for the Hofharmonie is dispersed within A-Wn and, because of transfers to and from the Conservatorium, much is lost. it is impossible to describe the full repertoire. There seem to be no original works written earlier than 1795, not even by Mozart. Most original works were written later by members of the ensemble. Almost all the works were arrangements, and most seem to have been purchased. Contrary to common belief, Went's music appears to have been prepared for the commercial market (Lausch, Traeg, Hoftheater-Musik-Verlag and others) from which the Hofharmonie bought copies. After Went's death, arrangements were bought from Triebensee, from the anonymous arrangers of the Hoftheater-Musik-Verlag, T Weigl, and Sedlak, many probably via publishers Johann Cappi and, later, Carlo Mechetti. There are no works arranged by Starke: Sedlak may have had a near monopoly for arrangements from the time of his appointment as Kapellmeister to the Liechtenstein Harmonie.

The Harmonie of Count Karl von Palm was the short-lived, if ever fully established. It is known solely from a Tonkünstler Societät concert on 12 March 1780, when Starzer directed an ensemble including Anton and Johann Stadler, horn players Nagel and Zwirzina, and bassoonist Jacob Griessbacher.

There must have been many ensembles put together for a few special performances. Schönfeld's 1796 *Jahrbuch der Tonkunst für Wien und Prag* mentions the Harmonie of Herr von Braun. Presumably it was this ensemble for whom Salieri wrote his *Armonia per un tempio della notte* in 1794; Herr von Braun is surely Baron von Braun, for whom Cherubini wrote a march in 1805. Schönfeld also records that the Harmonie of Hoftracteur (court supplier) Jahn played in the Augarten in summer months.

Some ensembles are associated more with other residences outside Vienna, mainly in Bohemia, and will be noted separately: the Kinský Harmonie with Budyně, the Liechtenstein Harmonie with Feldsberg (Valtice), the Lobkowitz Harmonie with Roudnice, and the Schwarzenberg Harmonie with Český Krumlov and Třeboň.

Wind Bands in Bohemia

Prague is the center of Bohemia, geographically and musically. We shall relate smaller towns to four larger ones: Český Krumlov to the south; Hradec Králové (Königgrätz, where the Austrian army was defeated in 1866) to the east; Plzeň to the west, and Roudnice to the north; still further north lie Frýdlant and Liblice. In addition to the bands listed here, there were church bands such as those at Blovice (Blowitz, south east of Plzeň), Bohdaneč (south of Kutná Hora, south east of Prague), Cheb (west of Plzeň, with a church and a Dominican monastery), Chroustovice (south east of Hradec Králové; the church is associated with a castle), Kasejovice (Kassejowitz, south east of Plzeň), Krašnovice (north of Plzeň), Kunvald (Kunnwald, east of Hradec Králové and east of Rychnov nad Kněžnou), Ledce (north west of Plzeň), Mladá Boleslav (north east of Prague), Nepomuk (south south east of Plzeň). and Starý Plzenec (Alte Pilzen, south east of Plzeň).

Bakov nad Jizerou (near Frýdlant). Here many items - largely church music - were copied by Jan Augustin Fibiger.

Březnice and Kasejovice (Bresnitz, south east of Plzeň).   The collections, now in Plzeň, are largely in the hands of the brothers Vaněček (Waniček). František (Franz) Vaněček styled himself Chorrector in Březnice in 1838; he seems to have composed too, mainly funeral hymns. Ladislav Vaněček was a teacher ("učitel"); he was succeeded by Josef Floriána c.1860. The collection from Kasejovice mainly comprises funeral songs or marches. There are 9 *Funeral songs* and three *Stationes* by Ryba and a *Prelude* for cl(Eb) cl(Bb) 2hn 2tp flug a-hn basso by Vaněček. There are several works by Vaněček in the music of the band of the church of St Ignatius, alongside a work for 2fl hn (c.1765), a Gyrowetz *Parthia*, Volánek's (pre-1817) *Pange lingua* and many funeral songs by Ryba. This collection includes music from the 1840s and even some dated as late as 1869. Most is choral music with a core wind ensemble of 2cl 2hn 2bn, with varying extra instruments such as trumpets, trombones and percussion.

Broumov. This Baroque monastery, near the Polish border NW of Prague, has a few religious works with winds and a copy of V V Mašek's Concertino for 2pf, 2cl 2hn 2bn.

Budyně nad Ohří (Budin) (Zámek Budenicky; Budin Castle; also probably at Prague and Vienna). The Kinský Harmonie seems to have been formed in the late 1780s, presumably by Prince Joseph Kinský (d 1798), father of Ferdinand Johann Nepomuk Kinský, patron of Beethoven. It survived at least until c.1815; the few later works suggest that it declined in importance thereafter. The Harmonie was basically an octet drawn from the court orchestra. Of the 39 surviving works, 25 are for 2ob 2cl 2hn 2bn, of which 13 have an added cbn. There are a few larger works, including Neukomm's late *Messe St Louis Philippe,* a handful for octet with extra instruments (fl, tp) or voices, and a few smaller works for 2cl 2hn 2bn or cl 2bthn. Most of the compositions are original parthias (9 by Krommer, 4 by V V Mašek, 2 by Gyrowetz). Arrangements include six operas and the first issue of Triebensee's *Miscellannées* (a local version lacking trumpet parts). Budyně nad Ohři is 3 miles west of Roudnice, so it is possible that music was exchanged with the Lobkowitz ensemble.

Český Krumlov. The Harmonie was associated with Princes Joseph Adam and Johann Joseph Schwarzenberg (251), and was active from the 1770s until at least 1796. The fortress itself contains a complete 18th century theater, with music stands, candle holders and other equipment. The Schwarzenberg archives are now in CZ-K and A-Wgm; the material was probably moved regularly as need arose. The music is distinctive in its use of cors anglais, in later years played by musicians previously in the Batthyáni Harmonie. The Schwarzenberg collection in A-Wgm comprises 80 works (only 2 are arrangements, these being of Mozart's K.388 and a *Serenata,* retitled *Cassation,* by Salieri), with a further group possibly from this archive, mainly 24 pieces by Druschetzky for 2ob 2hn bn. Of the 80 works, the largest group of 36 items is for 2ob 2ca 2hn 2bn (17 by Druschetzky, 12 by Went); there are 2 more for 2ob 2taille 2hn 2bn. Carlo Besozzi is strongly represented, with 7 pieces for 2ob 2ca 2hn bn and 17 works for 2ob 2hn bn. The obvious link is that Schwarzenberg oboists Georg Triebensee (later with the Imperial Harmonie) and Jan Šlechta were sent by the Prince to improve their technique with Besozzi in Dresden. There are 8 of Rosetti's *Parthien,* transcribed for ob(concertante) 2cl 2hn 2bn. In CZ-K there are nearly 100 works, 38 original and 60 arrangements. The commonest scoring is 2ob 2ca 2hn 2bn (72 cases, with three sets of *Pièces* by Went), with a further 8 works for 2ca 2hn bn. The original works include many by Went, probably from before his joining the Imperial Harmonie in 1782. There is also a copy of Mozart's *Gran Partita,* K.361, one of a few items from the first years of the 19th century. The arrangements are by Went, and include one of the slow movement of Haydn's *Symphony No 94* (Surprise). The 15 ballet arrangements (one is just a single movement) are primarily of works from the 1770s by Asplmayr and Starzer, apparently arranged from orchestral parts also at CZ-K. There are 44 operatic arrangements, 1 being a collection and 6 others single movements from Gluck. Went's links with Schwarzenberg music continued after 1782, and this family influence may show in the inclusion in the collection of the two issues of the first journal series by his son-in-law, Triebensee. The CZ-K material and that of the Clam Gallas Harmonie, suggests links, possibly through Went and Besozzi. The Schwarzenberg castle of Hluboká nad Vltavou, north of Český Krumlov, also contains church music with winds.

Music owned by the Schimežek family, also from Česky Krumlov, dates from the 1820s to perhaps 1850. It comprises small pieces, marches and a suite of movements.

Česká Třebová. The first works associated with church and town band date from 1818, so it may have been formed by bandsmen returning from the wars. The early pieces are mainly for 2cl 2hn 1/2bn, sometimes with 2bthn replacing 2cl. There are seven arrangements dating from the 1830s. With time, the band grew larger, and brass instruments began to dominate. The band continued at least until the late 1850s. Of the 53 items, 25 are funeral songs and 11 funeral marches. The 4 *Cantilena pro Sepeliendis parvulos baptizatos* make this one of the few places where baptismal pieces are found.

Dlouhý Most (Langenbruck). This town lies in the spa region of the far north, not far from Frýdlant, where the music found is that of the local Musical Society. The wind band was most active from 1799 until 1808, with some activity even after 1822. The manuscripts mainly identify copyists, rather than composers: Ignaz Hübner (the earliest works), Augustin Erasmus Hübner (school assistant, styled Schulfach, or Schulgeheilf, or Preceptor, who copied 49 works between 1799 and 1822), Dominik Hübner (teacher, who copied 24 works from 1800 to after 1812), and Anton Zasche, who copied 2 works, and composed several Parthias and arranged works by Pleyel and possibly V V Mašek. The works are varied. There are two versions of *Stationes* by Süssmayr; apart from this choral music, all is instrumental. The standard ensemble seems to have been 2cl 2hn 2bn, with 2fl tp timp as frequent additions. Oboes are used only in the *Stationes* and in one other *Divertimento*. Many items are small pieces, marches or dance movements. There are also six brass works, and nearly fifty pieces for three horns.

Frýdlant (also probably Prague and possibly Vienna).   Th Clam Gallas Harmonie dates from the early 1770s, and may have survived until 1806-1810 or even later. It was formed at much the same time as the Pachta Harmonie. The two ensembles have many works in common, some being printed music from distant centers like Paris, Amsterdam and Berlin. In later years, especially after 1790, the Pachta Harmonie is referred to more often than that of Clam Gallas; perhaps, by that stage, the Clam Gallas ensemble was performing less often. Speer was Master of Music to Count Christian Philipp Clam Gallas (21). The archives of this ensemble are now in CZ-Pnm under shelfmark XLII.A-E. The collection contains 138 original works, 17 arrangements, and 16 marches, most for 2ob/cl 2hn (2)bn. The scorings are interestingly varied. Some works use flutes; others experiment with bthns or ca/taille.

Jestřebi (near Česká Lípa).   The music comprises 17 funeral songs, usually to German texts, and church choral music with winds, some dated from the late 1860s.

Kačina and Veltrusy.   Zámek Kačina was built between 1802 and 1822 for the Counts Chotek; the grounds were planted 15 years before construction began. The Counts also owned the hunting lodge at Zámek Veltrusy (north north east of Prague), and it was probably here that the Harmonie was formed. The archive of the Harmonie of Count Jan R Chotek contains 88 items, 81 being for 2cl 2hn 2bn. There are 32 original works (1 march, 31 parthias), the others being arrangements which date mainly from the 1790s-1810. Of the 88 items, 61 are in manuscript (many copied by Joseph Johann Pražák). There are some early works (like Haydn parthias, here for 2cl 2hn 2bn), but it is probable that these were copied after 1800.

Klášterec nad Ohří (50 km north east of Karlovy Vary).   Here the archive has 16 original works, now in CZ-Pnm, XL.A.

"Lukavec," meaning Dolní Lukavice.   It is believed that Haydn's early wind works for 2ob 2hn 2bn were written for performance at Count Morzin's summer residence, near Přeštice, south of Plzeň (Pilsen).

Opočno (east of Hradec Králové). Here, the castle collection includes the music for the 1810 Carousel at Laxenburg, for which Beethoven and others provided music.

Osecky Kláster (Osek Monastery).   This monastery, of a Cistercian community, was founded in the 12th century. It is roughly midway between Prague and Dresden, with a splendid church begun in 1712. The Harmonie was formed early, and its music dates from 1762 until c.1835, although most is pre-1800. Of the 71 works in CZ-Pnm, 32 are for 2ob 2hn bn and 11 for 2ob 2hn 2bn, mainly earlier works. These were clearly for players from the orchestra's wind section. There are no arrangements. Of the 59 instrumental works, 53 are parthias (often written "Barthia"); 8 of the 12 vocal works are funeral pieces, 2 being by a local composer, Jakob Trautzl. There are 8 items by Dittersdorf, 7 by V V Mašek, and three sets of 6 *Parthien* by Strouhal (*Strauhal* on all MSS; like Trautzl, he is styled "Pater" on the MSS). The music of Strouhal is a delight, whimsical as well as talented. One of the sets comprises titled pieces, often with musical jokes: an unexpected ending, cuckoos, bassoon quail calls, cackling hens, bagpipe imitations, and chromatic mimicry of the opening and shutting of a parasol.

The Harmonie seems to have declined from the 1780s, and had largely disappeared by 1805. There are isolated later works, like Haslinger's *Europas Sieges Feyer* of 1815-16.

Prague.   The Pachta Harmonie (also at Liblice) regarded as one of the best in Prague, was active from 1767 or earlier. It survived for half a century, remaining small, essentially the winds of the Pachta orchestra (2 oboes, 2 horns and 1 or 2 bassoons until the 1790s, when the manuscripts seem to indicate clarinets replacing oboes and alto clarinets replacing cors anglais or tailles) since the family, while prestigious, was not wealthy. Weston (232) notes that Farník played clarinet for the Counts Pachta in Prague from 1799-1838; he also played for the National Theater, Conservatory, and Blind School. We are grateful to Dr Markétá Kabelková for emphasizing the doubts as to which Count Pachta was its patron: the most likely is Jan Josef Pachta (1723-1822), another possibility being his nephew, of the same name. Some manuscripts (such as those by V V Mašek) were for the Harmonie of Count Ernst Pachta of Rayhoven (based at Cítoliby) a collateral branch of the family (251). The large Pachta archives, now in CZ-Pnm at XXII.A-E, contain over 300 original works. The very few arrangements are within Asplmayr's *Partittas,* and there is just a single march.

Prague: Břevnov.   At this church (possibly part of a monastery), just south west of Hradčany Castle, there are two masses with winds.

Prague: Strahovsky Klášter.   At this Praemonstratensian monastery, most of the works for winds are for funerals, with two religious works by Pařízek and Vitásek.

Prague?   Count Hartig may have maintained a Harmonie in Prague before 1778, including Grimm (cl); the Count's son also played clarinet (232). Hartig was in the same Masonic lodge as Counts Sporck and Pachta (252); he was also able to help Fiala at a critical time.

Roudnice nad Labem.   The Lobkowitz castle dominates this village where Dvořák was born. Prince Franz Joseph Maximilian Lobkowitz (253, 254; we shall use the contemporary spelling *Lobkowitz*; the Czech form *Lobkovic* is used for the collection in Prague; the modern family uses the form *Lobkowicz*) had charge of Viennese theaters from 1807. His Harmonie probably dates from the 1790s and seems to have ended with his death in 1816. Its archives are currently (1996) in CZ-Pnm. Cartellieri, who became Musical Director for Prince Lobkowitz in 1796, also wrote works for winds, but these works are in Vienna; perhaps the archive was divided between Vienna and Prague. At its peak (1800-1816) the Harmonie may have been directed by Faknrich (officer cadet) Krechler, who certainly made many arrangements for it. The Harmonie comprised 2ob 2cl 2hn 2bn, often with cbn and perhaps tp.   Anton Wranizky also had links with Roudnice, leading the Schlosskapelle from 1794 until 1806. There was a larger Turkish band too from c.1810, led by Joaues Prachenski. The Lobkowitz collection includes 20 original works, 32 arrangements, 60 marches and 1 *Todtenmarsch.* There are also 2 military journals, 18 collections compiled and arranged by Krechler, and 21 Oeuvres of Triebensee's *Miscellannées* (the copyright slip of Jahrgang II, Oeuvres 1 & 2 has the name Esterházy overwritten by Lobkowitz, so presumably the order was first prepared for the Esterházy Harmonie, but altered when it was dissolved). There is evidence that the Harmonie made efforts to fill gaps, given its relatively late start, since it bought copies of arrangements like *Don Giovanni* and *La Clemenza di Tito* as late as 1807.

Rychnov nad Kněžnou.   In this small town west of Hradec Králové, the castle was built for Karel Kolowrat in 1676 and remodelled with the adjacent church in 1722. The church Harmonie was drawn from an orchestra (perhaps that of the castle). The 37 works are all vocal, most for 4-part chorus with winds. Often there is an organ part, but it is not clear whether this was used merely by the musical director, or for variety, or to fill in for missing musicians. This ensemble is unusual in two ways. First, the instruments used differ from work to work, with little consistency, though there are a few with scoring close to 2cl 2hn bn. Secondly, the ensemble was fairly late, with 26 printed works, dating from 1826 to 1920, so that instruments like saxophone, helikon, "Bassorka [bass] in B[b]" and flugelhorn are included.

Svojšín Castle. The band here seems to have been drawn from the orchestra, and 18 of the 31 items are for 2cl 2hn 2bn. Around 1810 it was expanded to play Turkish music. There are 19 works described as parthias, including Lickl's *Cassation* once mistaken for a work by Mozart (ob/cl cl hn bn) and three parthias by Beda Müch (Mück) whose music we find in other sources. There are 8 marches, including Purebl's *VI* [sic, = 4] *Märsche* of 1812 and MS copies of ones by Starke. The collection includes three opera arrangements.

Uterý. Here is a puzzling collection and location, for Uterý is very isolated. It is in the middle of what was a silver-mining district, not far from Plzeň, Teplá (Tepl) and Mariánské Lázné (Marienbad, whose springs were owned by the abbots of Teplá). Its music (54 items, mainly 19th century) is almost all for chorus (usually CATB) and winds. The core ensemble is fl 2cl 2hn bn, but extra parts are common. The 2 instrumental pieces are an anonymous *Divertimento* (for solo cl, solo bn, 2hn 2vla basso) and a funeral march. 31 of the items are funeral pieces, all anonymously composed, though one is for a named person (Julie Wurda, described as "Jungfer" (maiden) dated 17 March 1837) and others are for specific types of person (adult, child, small child, one who was holy [Vereheiligte], a person of substance [grosse], and so on). Yet there are no pieces for Corpus Christi, the usual festival for outdoor wind music in rural Bohemia.

Wind Bands in Moravia

In addition to the Harmonien noted here, there were many others. We know of eight regimental bands (based in Brno, Jihlava (there was a band too at Kamenice, near Jihlava), Kroměříž, Nový Jičín, Olomouc, Prostějov, Uničov, and Znojmo) and five town bands (Brno, Kroměříž, Olomouc, Vyškov and Znojmo). Graf Franz Josef Silva-Tarouca maintained a Turkish band at Český pod Kosířem. Graf Johann von Klenau, Freiherr von Janowitz, was Commandierender General in Moravia and Silesia; and the music of his wind ensemble moved to the Regensburg ensembles after his death.

There are at least 2 works from the castle at *Stražnice* (Strassnitz, south south east of Brno). Church bands include those at Břeclav (Lundenburg, close to Stražnice; 1 of the 2 works is Michael Haydn's *Deutsche Messe* in an 1849 MS), *Býstřice pod Hostynem* (south of Hranice; 11 works, now CZ-Bm[bh]), *Čehovice u Prostějova* (8 works, mainly funeral pieces; CZ-Bm[cp]), Česke Křídlovice (2 works; CZ-Bm[ck]), Hranice (W of Olomouc; two works, again Michael Haydn's *Deutsche Messe* (but here in Czech) now in CZ-Bm[bh]), Júr u Bratislavy, Svätý Júr, Lukov and the nearby Horní Břečkov, Nové Město na Moravě (north west of Brno, not to be confused with its Bohemian namesake; 5 masses, mainly c.1870; CZ-Bm[nm]), Ostrava, Rešov, Rozstání, Telč (Teltsch, west of Brno; CZ-Bm[te]; the Haugwitz Harmonie is nearby, at Náměšt nad Oslavou), and Třebeč. At Karlovice u Bruntálou (in the far north) the Aloys Englisch(e) collection includes much funeral music. Lomnice u Rymařova Monastery (north north west of Brno) also had a wind band.

Not surprisingly, the music collections of all these churches are dominated by religious music. The Harmonien we list here include one (Kroměříž) associated with a bishopric, and three associated (Brno, Nová Říše, and Rajhrad) with monasteries.

Brno. The Harmonie of the Augustinian monastery lasted from 1741 until c.1865. The monastery was a major cultural center, whose collections include 283 works for winds, 15 being vocal works. The commonest of the 117 different scorings are 70 works for 2ob 2cl 2hn 2bn cbn 2tp, 15 for 2ob 2cl 2hn 2bn cbn tp, 21 for 2ob 2cl 2hn 2bn cbn, and 13 items for 2ob 2cl 2hn 2bn 2tp. The smaller works and octets are mainly early items, before 1816 when Napp became involved. The collections differ from most that we describe, in that the ensemble was in its prime through the mid-19th century. Thus bass trombone sometimes replaces second bassoon, and high clarinets (C, D, F) are used in 49 of the works. The largest works (which include a Neukomm mass and Krommer's Op 96 *Marches*) might have been for the May Day occasions when the Harmonie was augmented by town and regimental bands.

Kroměříž (Kremsier; Olomouc, Olmütz). The Court of the Archbishop of Olomouc (255) at Kroměříž maintained a Harmonie from 1759 until 1822 or later. Its important music archives, now in CZ-KRa, were built up by Anton Theodor Colloredo Waldsee (25) and his two predecessors, Leopold Egk and Maximilian Hamilton. Under Egk (1758-1760), the players were Franz Fogenauer and Anton Fernier (cl or ca), Johann Carl Franz and Johann Michael Pumm (hn), and Ignáz Špalek (bn). Under Hamilton (1761-1776), they were Josef Premoti, Franz Heinitz and Conrad (ob), Fogenauer, Franz Mellan and Franz Hickler (cl), Jan Blecha and Antonín Havel (hn), and unidentified bassoons. Under Colloredo Waldsee (1777-1811), Melan, Blecha and Havel continued, with Josef Bassanini (ob), Franz Lössel (ob, hn) and Keller (hn); again the names of the bassoons are not known. Maria Thaddäus Trauttmanndorf, enthroned at Olomouc on 26 November 1811, founded a Tafel-Harmonie at Chrást u Chrudimi (south south east of Hradek Králově) c.1803. His Private Secretary was Václav Havel (see Part 2; we note that the second horn player of the Olomouc Harmonie from c.1772 was one Antonín Havel, possibly related). Trautmannsdorf's smaller Harmonie (2cl 2hn 2bn) replaced his predecessor's octet. A total of 389 items survive. The two largest groups being 2cl 2hn 2bn (197 items) and 2cl 2hn bn (46 items); there are a dozen or so further items adding a single instrument (tp, fl or - in two cases - alphorn). Octets are plentiful (22 items for 2ob 2cl 2hn 2bn; 21 with added cbn, and a few with tp or other extra instruments; a few works substitute flutes for oboes). Works for ensembles lacking clarinets include 24 items for 2ob 2hn 2bn, 28 for 2ob 2hn bn, and 10 for 2ca 2hn bn.

Náměšt nad Oslavou. The Harmonie of Count Karel Josef Villém (Heinrich Wilhelm) Haugwitz appears to have been formed in the 1790s from players (basically 2ob 2cl 2hn 2bn, plus cbn and tp) from the Court orchestra. From about 1804 to 1808, it was directed by Gottfried Rieger, whose 11 compositions and arrangements indicate a smaller ensemble of 2cl 2hn 2bn. Of the 57 items, 36 are original works (29 parthias, with 10 works by Krommer and 6 by Hoffmeister), 14 are opera arrangements, 5 ballet arrangements, and there is an arrangement of Haydn's *Symphony* Hob I/82. After 1808, there were few new works. It is possible that some music was borrowed from the Augustinians in Brno.

Nová Říše. The Harmonie of the Premonstratensian monastery existed from the 1770s to the early 1790s. The surviving collection comprises 4 vocal works, 20 parthias (7 for 2ob 2hn bn, 5 for 2cl 2hn 2bn and 6 for 2cl 2hn bn; there is also a work for 2vl 2cl vc) and a single arrangement.

Rajhrad (Gross Reigern). This Benedictine monastery was the oldest foundation in Moravia. Its Baroque church was begun in 1722. From about 1800 until 1830, it maintained a Harmonie, drawn from a larger body of musicians. Pater Gregorius Wolney seems to have been the guiding force. Much of the music dates from the time that Napp took over in Brno, with many works having an acquisition date of 1819. The Brno Augustinians complained that Rajhrad did not return borrowed music, nor did it buy many works to exchange. The 29 works examined comprise 12 parthias, 2 opera and 2 ballet arrangements and 1 small work. The 12 vocal works with winds include 4 funeral pieces, 2 masses, 2 settings of the *Pange lingua,* and 4 other religious pieces.

Wind Bands Far from the Center

Keszthely (Kesthely) (46.46N, 17.16E; at the south end of Lake Balaton).   Count Georg Festetics was confined to his estates here in the 1790s as a suspected Jacobin. In the fall of 1799 he asked Anton Stadler to plan his Music School, which included a Harmonie. Much of the wind music was obtained in 1802 from Johann Gallyus, an advocat in Zagreb, from whom the music by Druschetzky was acquired. The collection was saved in 1945 by being walled up by a Russian officer.

Lancut: Lubomirska Palace.   The Harmonie was drawn from the musicians brought together by Princess Elzbiety (Isabella) z Czartory Lubomirska (1733-1816). The Harmonie dates from after 1795. Its main burst of activity was in 1803, when many opera and ballet transcriptions were prepared in Lancut, and also during the Harmonie's sojourn in Vienna. Copies are dated 16-28 April 1803, Vienna; 11 May 1803, Eisenstadt; 4-7 June 1803, Vienna. Its director, Johann Anton Buchal prepared six cycles of arrangements for 2cl 2hn bn ("No 1 z cyclu Harmony Stücke" and so on) in the summer of 1804. Of the 43 items, 16 are original works, 14 being parthias (mainly for 2cl 2hn 2bn, but with a Hoffmeister work for 2bthn 2hn bn and with 5 works for 2bthn 2hn by Hoffmeister and V V Mašek). The two sets of marches (16 marches in all) are all for larger ensembles (2ob 2cl 2hn 2bn, some with added tp cbn). There are 20 sets of opera arrangements and 6 of ballets (in some cases there is more than one opera or ballet in the item). Among these are Sedlak's 1816 version for 2cl 2hn 2bn of Rossini's *Il Barbiere di Siviglia* and 1822 version of *Zelmira,* suggesting that the ensemble lasted a further two decades at least, under Count Jan Potocki, who wrote the classic gothic novel *The Saragossa Manuscript* (published in St Petersburg in 1804, 1805).

Plogwitz, near Löwenburg, Silesia.   Baron Hochberg's Harmonie dated from about 1780 until the Baron's death in 1787. The ensemble included members of the Krause family: the father, who played horn and bassoon, and clarinettist sons Johann Gottlieb Krause (b 1777) and Karl Joseph Krause (1775 - after 1838). Both sons learned horn in their early years. The clarinettists and basset horn players David and Springer were in Plogwitz in the late 1780s.

Tulchin, Ukraine.   We presume that the Potocki Harmonie was linked to that at Lancut, since Sophie Potocka's name appears on the music, and the family inherited Lancut on the death of Princess Lubomirska. The Harmonie was probably directed by Franz Ludwig Michel, and active in the 1780s and perhaps the 1790s; it adopted the Russian Imperial (so-called French) configuration of flutes, clarinets, horns and bassoons. The family fought strongly for Polish independence. Count Ignatius Potocki (1751-1809) had lands in the Ukraine.

5
Italy

Italy was not a united nation in the 18th and early 19th centuries, but was divided into Hapsburg, Bourbon, Papal, and other smaller states. The Italian love of vocal music ignored their boundaries. Italian enthusiasm for wind bands is also widespread, but far less familiar. Wind music flourished in Bergamo, Bologna, Florence, Genoa, Milan, Modena, and in many small towns and villages. Some of this enthusiasm arose from Napoleonic or Austrian influence. In the Austrian dominions, like Lombardy and Tuscany, the enjoyment of wind music was perhaps grafted on at first. Collections in Bergamo show that wind music was well established in what is now northern Italy, with works by the Bavarian, Mayr, by Mayr's pupil Donizetti, by Mozart (a supposed autograph of K.388), arrangements (in score) by Krechler, Sedlak, Triebensee and Went, and 47 items of church music accompanied by winds. In Genoa, there were six civic bands immediately before the Napoleonic invasion. One notices that some Italian composers, like Righini, wrote their wind music when they moved to Austria or Germany, whereas it was Austrians like Mozart and Bohemians like Mysliveček who provided wind music for Milan. This is somewhat too simple, for there were Italian composers for winds, like Ercolani, Fetter, Galotti, Magnelli and Mosell. Yet the Austrian influence was strong culturally, as well as politically. Its bands played in St Mark's Square, Venice, from 1814-1866, apart from the difficult years of 1848-49 (257) when revolution affected most major European centers.

Bologna had a reputation for its love of massed wind instruments from as early as the 13th century (256). *Burney* noted on August 24/25, 1770: "After dinner an itinerant band stopt under my window who executed several sinfonies and single movements extremely well - 'twas the best I have heard here." Half a century later, Bologna bands had available works by Krommer and arrangements of Haydn's music and works by local composers. The two *Sextets* (1817) and *16 kleinen Quintetten* (1817) by clarinettist Petronio Avoni appear lost, but his opera arrangements of 1826 survive. His fellow Bolognese, Benedetto Donelli, left a manuscript *Armonia in F per soli strumenti da fiato,* composed in 1821. These works were intended for the Conservatorio. Whether the wind band interjections in Donizetti's *Concertino* for cor anglais (Bologna, 1817) stem from the same influence remains uncertain.

The Napoleonic occupation was another powerful influence (257). Many small towns created their own wind bands, a change which had lasting effects on opera. Music schools on French guidelines were set up in cities like Naples, Milan, Parma and Turin, emphasising the training of military and municipal bandsmen and of opera chorus singers. This common training may account in part for the close affinity between opera and band in Italy.

WIND BANDS AND ITALIAN OPERA

Stage bands ("banda sul paco") and religious processional bands link Italian wind music to that of the rest of Europe. Neither category is dominated by Italian music. Czechs and Austrians had more ambitious church music; German stage bands were more enterprising. The British stage band tradition of Arne and Shield was long established, and its bands were to be both seen and heard. How stage bands were used in Italy was often left to local initiative. The composer usually provided only a reduced score for the stage band, and the local maestro was required to devise parts as needed (25 p 222).

Experienced composers like Rossini, Donizetti, and Verdi knew the potential of the wind section, not least from Mozart's marvellous examples. They found in wind harmony a wide range of sound effects and a new approach to characterization. Rossini used a stage band in *Ricciardo e Zoraide;* Spontini's *La vestale* includes a stage band for the procession of victorious Roman soldiers; Donizetti uses stage bands (often with some care) in *Maria Padilla, Maria de Rudenz, Anna Bolena* and *Alfredo il grande.*

Stage bands do not only represent military bands. There can be special effects where the winds might mimic a church organ or heighten drama by suggesting the magical motion of a fairy coach or the appearance of a ghost. Wind bands could be used subtly too, to point to differences of personalities (e.g., Doctor Dulcamara and Sergeant Belcore in Donizetti's *L'Elisir d'Amore)* or classes (e.g., to contrast rough camp life with an artificial upper-class milieu in *La Fille du Régiment).* The effect can be achieved merely by use of winds as accompaniment: Rossini uses winds to suggest an organ for the prayer "Deh! calma, o ciel" in his *Otello* (259); in act 1 of his *L'Italiana in Algeri,* a Corsairs' chorus with winds alone contrasts strongly with interludes for strings. He has complete numbers for winds alone in *Tell* and in *Mathilde di Shabran.*

The stylized effects lasted well into the 19th century, not just in Italian operas. In Massenet's *Manon* (1884), the offstage music in the Cours-la-Reine pleasure garden in act 3 scene 3 is for strings alone, followed by a shift to the winds alone; in act 3, scene 2, (the seminary of Saint-Sulpice), a similar shift occurs from church organ to the winds. Verdi's use of winds explores the darker, more sinister side of music. The winds appear in the ghost scene in *Macbeth.* In the *Libera Me* of his *Requiem,* four bassoons respond to the fire of judgment and hint at the despair and trembling it will produce. At the start of act 4 of *Il Trovatore,* outside the Aliaferia Palace in which Manrico is confined, pairs of clarinets and bassoons provide not an evening serenade, but an evocation of what is (literally, according to the stage directions) the darkest night.

COURT BANDS

The Renaissance in Italy produced many innovations in the arts. One idea was that of artistic patronage by enlightened rulers; another idea was that of large-scale displays of an artistic, rather than a bellicose, nature. Such displays were not disinterested love of art. The development from church festivals into court festivities involved a show of power, either in support of authority or an attempt at political reconciliation; in short, a transformation which might adapt ritual to secular forms (260). Sponsorship we shall not discuss, except to mention the Este family at Ferrara, and especially Beatrice d'Este (1475-1497). Hahn's *Le Bal de Béatrice d'Este* celebrates a parallel rather than a relative, for it expresses his appreciation of Princess Edmonde de Polignac (1865-1943, the daughter of the sewing machine magnate, Singer), whose salon in Paris was open to the leading French composers. Beatrice d'Este's later namesake, the wife of Ferdinand of Austria, Duke of Milan, was the one for whom Haydn's musicians played wind music in a splendid outdoor setting at Eszterháza in 1775.

The collection of wind music in Florence (Tuscany) is exceptional. In Napoleon's reorganisation of northern Italy, Archduke Ferdinand III was given Salzburg, and he may have taken the collection of wind music back to Florence on his return. In Milan (Lombardy) Pichl, who composed much music for winds, was an agent for Eszterháza as well, ensuring that suitable music was passed on to other parts of Austro-Hungary (8). The Hapsburg Duke of Modena's wind band, the Reale Armonia, had music by Krechler and Scholl, which must have been imported from Vienna.

WIND BANDS AND THE CHURCH

Many church and monastic archives contain wind music, and many of these are settings of religious texts. Such settings are not confined to Italian music, but the strength of the church in Italy, the influence of the Roman church throughout the world, and its long-standing links between music and ritual help to clarify the relationships of wind bands to religious music and ceremony.

Music for the great festivals

These festivals inspired use of wind bands, notably at Christmas, Easter (including Holy Week; the carnival weeks before Lent also kept bands busy), Pentecost, the Feasts of the Virgin Mary and, above all, the Feast of Corpus Christi (the Thursday after Trinity, usually in June). The Feast of Corpus Christi was instituted by Pope Urban IV in the 13th century; for it was written St Thomas Aquinas's hymns *Lauda Sion* and *Pange lingua*, and the commonest settings are of *Pange lingua* or of its last two verses, *Tantum ergo*. Corpus Christi celebrations thrived in Italy (261, 262) and Catholic areas of Germany and Austro-Hungary (261, 203).

The wind band had a clear advantage over a fixed organ (however grand) for major processions. Processional bands did not restrict themselves to a religious role. Reports early in the 19th century (203) note bands playing "not particularly appropriate music", bands which simply "wandered off" when the procession reached the church, or where the inhabitants were roused at dawn "by the band marching round the village." In 1825, Sebastiani (263; see also Holmes (203 p 49)) observed a band which "provided amusement for the people from time to time, and I enjoyed Rossini's symphony in *Tancred* [sic]." The disconcerting mix of religious and secular persists to this day (264).

Mass Settings

High Mass, the sung form of the principal service of the Roman Catholic Church (261), comprises the "Proper," the "Common," and the "Ordinary." The Proper traditionally uses plainsong; it is only for the Requiem Mass that choral settings are common, notably the Introit (Requiem Aeternam), the Offertory (Domine Jesu Christe), the Communion (Lux Aeterna), and the Responsory (Libera Me).

Settings with winds of the Common (Kyrie; Gloria; Credo; Sanctus; Agnus Dei) or its subsections (the Benedictus [from the Sanctus], Qui Tollis and Dona nobis pacem [from the Agnus Dei] and Quoniam [from the Gloria]) appear in various languages, including Czech and German. The Ordinary is normally spoken or intoned; choral settings are largely confined to the Pater Noster (in English, The Lord's Prayer; in German, Vater unser, or Das Gebet des Herrn).

Settings for Other Offices

These include psalms, hymns, and antiphons. The texts can form part of the Proper of the Mass, but most come from the offices of Vespers or Compline, the last two of the canonical hours of the Divine Office. Texts set range from the Te Deum (the hymn of thanksgiving) to many settings of individual psalms. In alphabetical order, wind settings include these psalms (with Vulgate numbering): Beatus vir (No 1); Confiteor (Nos 110, 137, 138); De Profundis (No 129); Dixit Dominus (No 109); Dominus ad adjuvandum (No 69); Laetatus sum (No 121); Laudate Dominum (No 116); Laudate Pueri (No 112); Libera Me (No 108); and Miserere (No 50). Many hymns are associated with local saints, with dedications, or with funerals.

Statistics of Church Vocal Music with Winds

We have analysed 1477 surviving church works with winds to build a picture of the major forms. The data include all of Europe. There are strong regional variations. The many funeral songs, some 45% of the total, all come from Austro-Hungary. The major categories are these:

Masses	87 (including 35 Deutsche, 31 Latin, 11 Requiem, 10 Czech).
Single Mass movements	97 (29 Gloria, 26 Kyrie, 21 Credo, 14 Songs (Messlied), and other pieces.
Funeral pieces	654 (592 Songs, 50 Marches, 9 Harmonien, 3 Trauermusik).
Corpus Christi music	96 (57 sets of 4 Stationes, 39 Pange lingua).
Other Choral	36 Tantum ergo, 34 Salve Regina (often associated with funerals), 25 cantatas, 11 Libera me, 10 Graduale, 10 Stabat Mater, 9 Veni Sancte Spiritus, 9 Miserere, 8 Dixit Dominus.
Instrumental music	44 Marches, 40 Intrada, 39 Aufzug.

If we turn to Italy, we find significant differences even in small regions. As an example, we can look at the wind music for bands near Bergamo during the 19th century. The individual collections vary greatly. In Bergamo itself, the 47 works (4 instrumental) are primarily mass movements or relate to the Virgin Mary (4 Ave maris stella, 3 Stabat Mater, 3 Qui tollis, 3 O salutaris hostia); most of these works are from before 1850. The 61 works at Gandino (5 instrumental) mostly relate to Corpus Christi (14 Tantum ergo, 7 Pange lingua); 20 works are explicitly for processions. There are no instrumental items in the 33 works at Vertova, and most are mass movements. The 20 works at Leffe show no special features, but include 3 settings of the Stabat Mater.

ITALY UNIFIED: MILITARY AND CIVIC BANDS

Band music of some sort continued to be played on special occasions, especially during the unification of Italy. The London *Times* correspondent covering Garibaldi's insurrection in Sicily, describing the entry to Alis on June 29, 1860, observed "detachments of people nearer the town came out on foot, shouting and cheering. At the ascent to the town, we were received by a band of music at the entrance. The municipality and clergy were waiting to welcome us. Bonfires were lit on the heights, the town was illuminated." A note on the score of Girolamo Forini's *Inno a Garibaldi* describes how this cantata was sung to great effect by "100 coristi" accompanied by the military band in Bergamo on 22 January 1861. Brancaccio (265 p 144) remarks on the "mystic mournful yet harmonious" sound of the Neapolitan military band playing the Ave at sunset, heard from the Vicaria prison. He compares this with the Austrian band in Milan where the Italian poet Giuseppe Giusti (1809-1850) described their playing in San Ambrosio Church in a poem beginning, "Gently, gently, a German song/ Through the sacred air took flight..." Just as it was an alien (Austrian) band playing in Milan, so it was an alien Neapolitan (Bourbon) band playing in Sicily. Italian wind bands revived, as in other countries, later in the 19th century. There were reputedly over 6000 civic bands in the 1880s, many presumably very modest. Florence and Bologna retained their enthusiasm for wind harmony: in 1868, Emilio Cianchi's *Nonetto* and Teodulo Mabellini's *Sinfonia,* both for winds, were published in Florence. Works of the revival from outside Italy, like Raff's *Sinfonietta*, are also found in Bologna, and were for use in the Conservatorio.

6

The Periphery: Russia, Scandinavia, Iberia, and Distant Empires

RUSSIA AND THE EASTERN FRINGE

Russia was host to many visiting virtuosos. Tbe clarinettists in St Petersburg were exclusively of Western origin, though there were native virtuosos. *Sainsbury* mentions Sila Dementiewitsch Karelin, considered the finest performer on the cor de chasse in Russia, who was director of the musique de chasse for a St Petersburg nobleman in 1796. Pleasure gardens developed late in Russia. Only in 1854, as London's Vauxhall was nearing its end, did a Vauxhall appear near St Petersburg. The Tsarko-Selo Railway Company hired Johann Strauss the Younger to give concerts in a pavilion at Pavlovsk. Success gave an entirely new meaning to the name, for "Voksal" became the Russian word for railway terminus (there is even a "Foksal" in Warsaw, in the gardens of the Zamoyski residence, but we do not know how it got its name). The connection between music and Russian railways began earlier still: in 1836, the Czar supplied a band of 11 trumpets and a trombone to give warning of the approach of the first trains.

One remarkable form of wind harmony in Russia resembled the conventional form in the broadest sense only. This specialty was the horn band: from twenty-four to three hundred serfs, each playing a horn which produced a single note. Horn bands were collected and trained by itinerant conductors, and they could play works as complex as symphonies by Haydn and Mozart. The serfs and their families were often sold en bloc, and well-trained horn bands could command high prices (266). In 1821 the Grand Duke Constantine presented a band of three hundred to the Duke of Saxe-Coburg-Gotha.

Deciding how much conventional wind harmony there was in Imperial Russia is hampered by inaccessible material and lack of published catalogs, as well as by the destruction of primary sources during the Napoleonic invasion, the Revolution and Hitler's 1942 campaign. Isolated works have survived, including a quintet by Alyabyev and polonaises by Kozlowski, which are discussed in Part 2. The Imperial Harmonie, based in St Petersburg, appears to have consisted of 2fl 2cl 2hn 2bn, though the Masonic wind music of Boieldieu and Cavos adopted oboe and cor anglais instead of flutes. There are at least 51 parthias and arrangements in the Imperial Harmonie collection, including 2 by Went and 2 by Kozeluch.

Paisiello, in his 4 July 1783 letter to Ferdinando Galiani in Naples, states that he is sending 24 divertimentos for 2fl 2cl 2hn 2bn, presented [previously] to Catherine the Great "for use as Tafelmusik, or for dinners at Posilipo [near Naples] or as hunting music" (267). The ensemble 2fl 2cl 2hn 2bn is sometimes referred to as the "French" configuration, but its use by the Russian Imperial Harmonie predates French practice by nearly two decades. The earliest example we know is the *March,* Act I, No 9 from

Paisiello's *Achille in Sciro,* first performed in St Petersburg in 1778. There are arrangements by Went in which flutes replace oboes. Perhaps this music was played on the June 1785 boat trip with the Empress Catherine (268) where "At Borowitz we embarked in handsome galleys. That destined for Count Cobenzl [Austrian ambassador], Mr Fitz-Herbert [the English ambassador] and myself [French ambassador] contained three rooms, elegantly furnished, and had a band of musicians, who awoke us and lulled us to sleep, with the sound of pleasing harmony."

Wind music was certainly played outside the major cities, e.g., by the Potocki and Rasumovsky ensembles in the Ukraine. Glinka (269) recalled how his uncle hired a band: "During supper they usually played Russian songs arranged for two flutes, two clarinets, two horns and two bassoons." This ensemble, an octet with flutes instead of oboes, is the same as that of the Russian Imperial Harmonie, for which Paisiello, Went and others wrote. Glinka continued "I loved exceedingly these sadly gentle, but to me completely acceptable sounds (I found it difficult to bear harsh sounds - even the low notes of horns when they were played loudly), and perhaps the songs which I heard in my childhood were the prime reason why I later began to cultivate mainly Russian music". Perhaps similar sounds are recalled in the wind passage opening the Canzonetta of Tchaikovsky's *Violin Concerto.* At Kiev, also in the Ukraine, was the Razumovsky Harmonie. The music of this early band (2ob 2hn bn) included 6 parthias (5 surviving) by Kozeluch. The two Razumovsky brothers (b 1709, 1728) were singers at the Russian court who prospered by attending to the needs of the Empresses Elizabeth Petrovna and Catherine II. The Razumovsky (b 1752) who was Beethoven's patron was the fourth son of the younger Prince.

Church and Masonic Music

Visitors to Moscow included Boieldieu (1775-1834), who conducted the Russian Imperial Opera from 1803-1811, and Catterino Cavos (1775-1840), musical director, then managing director, of the Imperial theaters. Their *Hymnes et Cantiques* (1 Boieldieu/Pushkin; 2 Cavos/Dalmas; 3 Anon/Pushkin; 4 Cavos/Pushkin) are settings for chorus and winds (ob ca 2cl[C] 2bn 2hn) of Masonic texts in French. In Russia, wind bands were used in masonic ceremonies early in the 19th century.

Military Music

Early Russian military bands were used in diplomacy: in 1717, Peter the Great's mission to Khiva included a band. Grand Duke Constantine was a ruler who combined culture with barbarity: infamous as the oppressor of the Poles, he was the dedicatee of a march by Chopin in 1817 - scored by an unknown arranger and played in front of the Saxon Palace in Warsaw (271) - and commissioned marches by Hummel. The Grand Duke Constantine also introduced the keyed bugle to Russian bands.

Concert Music

The Russian nationalist composers used winds extensively, but wrote little for wind ensembles. In the 1860s, Tchaikovsky wrote a student work for a strange ensemble in which cor anglais and bass clarinet share the melodic interest, accompanied from above by 2fl 2ob 2cl (a device typical of Raff, whom Tchaikovsky admired). Yet parts of

Tchaikovsky's other works, such as the Trio of the *Fourth Symphony,* or *Romeo and Juliet,* could easily have formed part of a serenade. Rimsky-Korsakov's interest in orchestration did not lead to any serious wind harmony, and only a small number of his works exploit woodwinds: the *Quintet* for flute, clarinet, horn, bassoon and piano, and the three concertos with military band. Even his *Principles of Orchestration* (271) lacks a serious discussion of wind harmony; the few illustrations of winds playing in ensemble, e.g., his illustrations No 215 (*The Golden Cockerel*) and No 216 (*The Snow Maiden*) have pizzicato string or harp accompaniment. As for stage bands, these are dismissed as "dramatically clumsy," with the comment that "choice must be regulated by esthetic considerations of greater importance than those governing the selection of a military band" - which tells us much about contemporary production standards.

Rimsky-Korsakov's omissions did not prevent his pupil, Alexander Sergeyevich Taneyev (1850-1918) from writing an *Andante* for double wind quintet, although this may have been written through the influence of Balakirev. It is regrettable that Balakirev, with his ingenious innovations in orchestral tone color, did not compose more wind harmony: his "English Song" in *King Lear* (actually based on the Welsh tune, "The Men of Davey's Delight") exploits the special sound of the cor anglais; this small gem is scored for fl ca 2cl 2bn harp. Stravinsky, a pupil of Rimsky-Korsakov, proved to be one of the major innovators in wind writing in the 20th century. Shostakovich's music for winds includes two somewhat Stravinskian arrangements of pieces by Domenico Scarlatti. He wrote the march for winds in the music for *The Bedbug* because its author, Mayakovsky, enjoyed the music of firemen's bands.

SCANDINAVIA

Sweden was a major military power in Europe under Charles XII, later subsiding to a more modest role. Wind music in the University Library at Uppsala includes French printed music for 2cl 2hn 2bn, for the band of Fredrik Adolf, younger brother of Gustaf III; Fredrik Adolf died in 1803 in Montpellier after a period of illness (272). Manuscripts for octet by Kapellmeister J C F Haeffner were used by a band at the university. The Danish Royal Kapelle also had a Harmonie, and a few printed works survive. In addition, there is the 1791 *Carasel Musique* [sic] for the Royal Riding School, by Claus Nielsen Schall and Skalle. A recording (Caprice CAP 1074) of six anonymous marches for the Royal Sodermannland Regiment shows enterprising use of the 2ob 2cl 2hn 2bn s-dr. The marches of many Finnish units date back to the 1700s (273), when Finland was under Swedish domination. Good bands survived into the 19th century when Finland became an autonomous grand duchy under Russian rule. In 1874, thanks to the efforts of the Army Bandmaster, Adolf Leander, all Finnish batallions adopted as standard for their bands the ensemble (*Torviseitsikolle* (Finnish) *Hornseptett* (Swedish)) of Eb soprano cornet, 2 Bb cornets, Eb althorn, Bb tenorhorn, Bb baritonhorn (euphonium), Eb bass and percussion. This format was soon adopted by other bands, such as those of working men's clubs and of fire brigades. It resembles closely the German and Eastern European bands, and even resembles the somewhat different bands found in the West, which were based on Sax's instruments. These bands were associated with mainstream classical music, not least through the bandmasters. Gustav Levander, one of Sibelius's first violin teachers, was bandmaster at Hämeenlinna. Christian Haupt, Prussian horn player with the Swedish Theater Orchestra, later a founder member of what became the Helsinki Philharmonic, directed the Fire Brigade Band at Loviisa as part of his duties as town *kapellmästar*; this band played early works by Sibelius. The Czar's Russification plans around 1900 disbanded the Finnish army in the fullest sense.

DISTANT EMPIRES: SOUTH AFRICA

Wind bands in India and other parts of Asia were largely associated with the British military, and have been discussed accordingly. However, the serf bands (we do not know whether they were slaves or indentured servants) in South Africa, early in the 19th century - rather like those which Glinka described - were associated with German settlers (274-276). The Dutch East India Company (Vereenigde Oostindische Compagnie) brought a growing German influence. Some 2000 mercenaries from Württemberg came to the Cape in 1787-1788, remaining for about 20 years. They brought with them 12 Hautboisten, presumably trained musicians, for their pay was higher than that of the fifers and drummers. The influence lasted until the company's bankruptcy in 1794 and subsequent British takeover, when the Dutch Governor of the Cape capitulated in April 1795. The surrender ceremony was accompanied by a German-style fife and drum band. The musical influence of German musicians and teachers lasted well into the period of British government; certainly the Württemberg soldiers attended performances by slave bands. When Heinrich Lichtenstein travelled through South Africa in 1803-1806, he encountered slave bands playing wind music, and was impressed to hear a chorale, several marches, and dances played by clarinets, horns and bassoons at the farm of Jacob van Reenen.

SPAIN, PORTUGAL AND THEIR EMPIRES

There is strikingly little information on wind band music from Spain and Portugal. William Beckford's evocative descriptions in his letters (277) range from the "whizzing of fireworks, blazing of bonfires, and flourishing of French horns" on St Anthony's Eve (Letter XII, 12 June 1787) to his fascination with the sound of "this wonderful band of performers," the wind players of the Queen of Portugal's chapel. In the morning of 26 August 1787, "All my faculties were absorbed by the harmony of the wind instruments, stationed at a distance in a thicket of orange and bay trees" (Letter XXI). On 10 Septemeber 1787, "It was after 10 when we got back to the Marialva villa, and long before we reached it, we heard the plaintive tones of voices and wind instruments issuing from the thickets. On the margin of the principal basin sat the Marchioness and Donna Henriquetta, and numerous groups of their female attendants, many of them most graceful, and listening with all their hearts to the rehearsal of some very delightful music with which her majesty is to be serenaded a few evenings hence" (Letter XXVI). We do not know what the music was, or its scoring. Beckford mentions that the Queen's oboe and flute players were unrivalled (Letter XXI), and horns are mentioned elsewhere in his letters. *Weston/MCVP* mentions one clarinet player in that region of Portugal in the 1780s, the Spaniard, Ignacio Canongia.

There is a small collection of wind music in Madrid. It includes some of Krommer's marches in the Chemische Druckerei (Vienna) editions. One fascinating work bears the name J C Bach, but has every appearance of an octet by Mysliveček. We know only of piano arrangements or isolated works for winds elsewhere. Yet records suggest a significant level of activity, especially during and after the Peninsular War. Several early marches relate to Gibraltar (Shield's 1780 march, celebrating the temporary relief of the siege, and Coleman's set, c.1790, for the Gibraltar garrison). Surprisingly few marches can be linked to the Peninsular War, an exception being the *Marche pour les armées anglaises-espagnoles dans les Pyrénées* by Berger, pupil of Clementi and teacher of Mendelssohn. A French title is odd for a march by a Berlin musician for the English and Spanish. Similarly international is *Buonaparte's Grand March* "composed for him when in Spain" by Paisiello; this survives in a version for piano, "compressed from an original MSS score" by James Salmon [GB-Lbl, g.433.1.(18)]. Farmer (13) cited reports of British Army bands at the battles of Talavera (1809), Busaco (1810) and Ciudad Rodrigo (1811). Rifleman Harris (278) relates the chequered tale of a British bandmaster of the 95th Regiment who deserted after Vimiera (1808) and played in a French band; he later found a position in another British regiment. Major-General Dickson's accounts (279) for December 1809 mention the band of the Portuguese army's 3rd Regiment of Caçadores. The French bands in Portugal provided entertainment in testing circumstances (280). After the battle of Fuentes de Oñoro in 1811, when the wounded had been carried from the battlefield, "The French brought down a number of bands of music to a level piece of ground, about ninety or a hundred yards broad, that lay between us [the British and French armies]. They continued to play until sunset, whilst the men were dancing and diverting themselves at football." One wonders if the bands played opera arrangements.

In the years from 1816 Portugal had problems both internally and in its relations with Brazil. Some of Neukomm's marches appear to date from his 1816-1821 stay in Rio de Janeiro, such as the *Trauermarsch* SVN-1t for Comte da Barca. Further links to South America show in the lives of two clarinettists (*Weston/MCVP*). The career of Eduard Neuparth (6 Jan 1784, Poetwitz-23 June 1871, Lisbon) was very cosmopolitan. He began at the Löwenstein court, then moved to Freiburg, becoming director of the miltary band. From 1808 he belonged to French bands; after the 1815 peace, he moved to Lisbon, joining a Portuguese band. He went with Princess Leopoldina to Rio de Janeiro, returning in 1821. Pedro Broca y Casanova (26 June 1794, Barcelona-22 September 1836, Havana), son of the military bandmaster in Cuencal, played in the Zafra Regt of Caçadores, the 2nd Badajoz Regiment, and in Valencia before an uprising forced him to move to Havana. There he combined work at the Opera with the direction of an artillery regimental band. Even Juan Chrisóstomo de Arriaga (1806-1826), the prodigy who died tragically young, wrote a *Marcha Militar*, but only a 1901 version for large band appears to survive (281). In all, there is circumstantial evidence that there were bands in Spain and Portugal, just like those elsewhere. But where is their music?

Part 1: References and Notes

1. B Boydell 1988 *A Dublin Musical Calendar 1700-1760;* Dublin: Irish Academic Press. Faulkner's *Dublin Journal* records that on 29 September 1755 the oysters were preceded by "Trumpets, French Horns, and other Wind Music."

2. See *Mozart Letters* for 3 November 1781 (letter 638/ii).

3. F H Shera 1939 *The Amateur in Music;* London: Oxford University Press. See also p 80 of *Weston/CVP.* For a royal amateur bassoonist and flautist, although not in wind harmony, see Nancy Mitford 1954 *Madame de Pompadour;* London: Hamish Hamilton, p 101; 1970 *Frederick the Great;* London: Hamish Hamilton.

4. D N Leeson and D Whitwell 1972 Music and Letters **53** 377.

5. "Pastoral" does not always imply "outdoors". Pastoral masses are those with well-defined traits, e.g. in overall sound (homophonic, use of folk instruments, emphasis on winds), harmony (drones, use of thirds and sixths), melody (lyrical, herding horn-calls, chirping birds), and rhythm (lilting). Bruce MacIntyre 1996 *Johann Baptist Vanhall and the pastoral mass tradition*, p112 et seq of *Music in eighteenth century Austria* (editied David Wyn Jones); Cambridge: Cambridge University Press.

6. Anrik Decriès and François Lesure 1979 *Dictionaire des Éditeurs de musique français. Vol I Des origines à environ 1820;* Geneva: Éditions Minkoff, pp 113-114.

7. Carl Fischer's list of 41 subscribers includes 34 identified as Musikdirektor, including 25 from the military sector. Of the others, there are two from the music trade, two Town Musicians, and three from associations (one a shooting club) in Eberfeld.

8. *HCRL/2* p 46.

9. H G Farmer 1912 *The Rise and Development of Military Music;* London: William Reeves; reprinted 1970, New York: Books for Libraries Press.

10. H G Farmer 1950 *Military Music;* London: Max Parrish.

11. H G Farmer 1904 *Memoires of the Royal Artillery Band;* London; updated in 1954 as *History of the Royal Artillery Band;* London: Royal Artillery Institution.

12. H G Farmer 1965 *Handel's Kettledrums and Other Papers on Military Music;* London: Hinrichsen H-164.

13. H G Farmer (sd) *British Bands in Battle;* London: Hinrichsen H-1482.

14. R F Camus 1976 *Military Music of the American Revolution;* Chapel Hill: University of North Carolina Press.

15. A Carse 1925 *The History of Orchestration;* London: Kegan Paul.

16. A Carse 1940 *The Orchestra in the Eighteenth Century;* Cambridge: Cambridge. University Press; reprinted 1969, New York: Broude Brothers.

17. N Zaslaw 1976-1977 Proc Royal Mus Assoc **103** 158.

18. C S Terry 1932 Bach's Orchestra; London: Oxford University Press, Chapter 1.

19. A Einstein 1936 *A Short History of Music;* London: Cassell.

20. A Myslík 1967 *Introduction* to Druschetzky's arrangement for winds of Mozart's K.455; Basel: Kneusslin (für Kenner und Liebhaber 50).

21. P M Young 1965 *The Concert Tradition;* London: Dobson.

22. A Yorke-Long 1954 *Music at Court;* London: Weidenfeld and Nicolson. Yorke-Long's source is François Louis, Baron Wimpffen de Broneborg, whose *Mémoires du général Baron de Wimpffen, écrits par lui-même* (Paris, 1788) comment on Württemburg after 1763 but before the financial reforms of Duke Charles Eugène in 1769.

23. H von Flemming 1726 *Der vollkommene Soldat;* Leipzig. Cited in *Salmen* p 143.

24. For a vivid description of pipe bands at dawn, see G M Fraser 1974 *Johnny Cope in the Morning,* in *McAuslan in the Rough*: London: Barrie and Jenkins.

25. R F Goldman 1974 *The Wind Band: Its Literature and Technique;* Westport, CT: Greenwood Press.

26. Georges Kastner 1848 *Manuel Général de Musique Militaire;* Paris.

27. E. Croft-Murray 1980 British Museum Yearbook 4. *The Wind Band in England 1540-1840;* pages 135 et seq. show contemporary illustrations by Wenceslaus Hollar.

28. L Winstock 1970 *Songs and Music of the Redcoats;* Harrisburg, PA: Stackpole Books.

29. R Palmer (editor) 1977 *The Rambling Soldier;* London: Penguin Books.

30. This could be a serious matter. In the Hapsburg monarchy, the Schwarzenbergs held 99 castles, one less than the number which would oblige them to send an army to war at the Emperor's behest. The Schwarzenbergs won special privileges after the 1813 Battle of Leipzig, and so were allowed a private army of twelve soldiers at Česky Krumlov. These soldiers, dressed in Napoleonic uniforms, doubled as the court orchestra; one of them would sound the bugle from the tower each morning.

31. J A Read 1981 *Music from the Court of the Sun King;* Nova NM174 (2ob taille bn).

32. This Bach march is cited by P M Young 1970 *The Bachs, 1500-1850;* London: Dent, p 266, and is recorded by Karl Haas/London Baroque Ensemble. We have been unable to trace it. Krieger's *Lustigen Feldmusik* (Nürnberg, 1704, and various modern editions) is an example of early German band music for a similar ensemble.

33. Cited H G Farmer (9). While the statement is entirely plausible, extensive searches (*Hellyer* and others) failed to locate the order. We are grateful to Mr Christopher Duffy, the author of a major study (38), for confirmation that the order is not among surviving material and for the suggestion that the order may have been destroyed in the late 19th century. The Berlin Allerhöchste Kabinetts-Ordnung of 13 March 1816 specifies Prussian bands comprising pic 2cl(F) 2cl(C) 2hn 2bn tp b-tb. Many German court Harmonien had similar configurations.

34. A Palmer 1972 *The Life and Times of George IV;* London: Weidenfeld and Nicolson, p 26.

35. W T Parke 1830 *Musical Memoirs;* London.

36. H G Farmer 1950 *Foreign Army Bandmasters: Their Rise and Fall;* in reference 12.

37. F J Cipolla and D Hunsberger 1994 *The Wind Ensemble and its Repertoire;* Rochester, NY: University of Rochester Press.

38. C Duffy 1974 *The Army of Frederick the Great;* Newton Abbott: David & Charles.

39. J Cassin-Scott and J Fabb 1978 *Military Bands and Their Uniforms;* Poole, UK: Blandford Press. Fig 12 shows an illustration of the incident. Likewise, the Japanese warrior Minamoto-no-Yoshitsuné (1159-1189) fought off an attacker with his flute (*Who's Who of Japan;* 1989 Japan Travel Bureau, p 45).

40. *Grove V,* under "Military Signals".

41. *Burney* vol II pps 30, 52-53. Many have remarked on the wonders a band can do for morale, not least Rudyard Kipling (*The Times,* 28 January 1915).

102 *The Phenomenon of Wind Harmony*

42. W Braun p 123 of *Salmen*. Modern bands may be exposed to new dangers: in October 1991, the Prague Castle Guards band had severe problems in the new Czechoslovakia because both the band and the secret police were administered by the same ministry during the Communist regime.

43. *HCRL/1* p 269 et seq. Note the anonymous French marches A–47m(–53m) "detachées et mises dans une form portative" (namely thick sheets about 10cm by 12cm) and similar publications of Gossec's *Hymne à l'Égalité*. A number of French publications from c.1800 onwards were printed 4 parts to the page, in folio or oblong folio.

44. G Scharf's Sketchbook, showing the Royal Marine Band c.1826, reproduced in E. Croft Murray, *British Museum Yearbook* Vol 4.

45. J R Western 1965 *English Militia in the Eighteenth Century;* London: Routledge and Kegan Paul, p 142. Note that musicians appear in its index as "drummers."

46. *Weinmann.* The relevant volumes by (Reihe/Folge) are: Cappi (1/11 and 2/23); Chemische Druckerei (2/19i); Eder (2/12), Haslinger (2/19ii); Leidersdorf (2/15); Steiner (2/19i); Traeg (2/16 and 2/17); Weigl (2/22).

47. *Whistling.* This important series is a systematic compilation (as Orchestral, Harmonien, and so on) of music then believed to be available, often from current catalogs. The year a work first appears is an unreliable date for its date of publication or composition. Not all wind music is classified as "Harmonie"; Beethoven's Op 16 and Paul Wranitzky's *La Chasse* are in other sections; wind quintets are listed as Harmonie at first, then moved to section XVII (Sextets and Quintets for the Flute) in 1824.

48. A Weinmann 1973 *Verlagverzeichnis Johann Traeg und Sohn;* Vienna: Universal Edition. See also A Weinmann 1956 Studien zur Musikwissenschaft 23 135ff; 1962 Haydn Yearbook 1 132.

49. F Blume, in H C R Landon and D Mitchell (editors) 1956 *The Mozart Companion,* London: Rockliff, reissued 1965 London: Faber, p 232.

50. *HCRL/5* p 139.

51. J Rietz *Catalogue of Mendelssohn Works,* appendix to Lady Wallace (translator) 1863 *Letters of Felix Mendelssohn Bartholdy from 1833 to 1847;* London: Longman, Roberts and Green.

52. Theodor Grawert and Oskar Hackenberger sd *Ausgewählte Königlich Preussische Armeemärsche;* Berlin: Bote und Bock.

53. We have encountered several hundred misidentified works. Error cannot be not in doubt when the same work is found to be listed under several different composers.

54. Indeed, many opera arrangements carry no indication of their origin at all.

55. See (47). At least one author has mistaken "Ebend" (ebenda, and so on, i.e. ditto, meaning the same publisher as on the previous line) for a real publisher's name.

56. A W G Ord-Hume 1982 *Joseph Haydn and the Mechanical Organ;* Cardiff: University College of Cardiff Press.

57. Else Radant 1980 Haydn Yearbook 11 5.

58. Haydn wrote accompaniments for Bertie's catches and glees. One striking sequence of modulations is found later in *The Creation:* compare bars 9 et seq of "Where Shall a Hapless Lover Find" with bars 32 et seq of Uriel's "Nun scheint in vollem Glanze."

59. A contemporary description is given in pp 33-60 of J Dietz (1665-1738) 1987 *Memoirs of a Mercenary, Being the Memoirs of Master Johann Dietz, Surgeon in the Army of the Great Elector and Barber to the Royal Court;* London: Folio Society.

60. L M Fox 1967 *Instruments of Processional Music;* London: Lutterworth Press.

61. See Vehbi's *Surname* (Chronicles of the Festivals of Sultan Ahmet III, c.1720; Topkapi Sarayi Müsezi, Istanbul A.3593), reproduced in part in Metin And 1987 *Turkish Miniature Painting: The Ottoman Period;* Istanbul: Dost.

62. Peter Stadlen 1963 Musical Times **104**(1739) 33.

63. *HCRL/2* p 217.
64. W Nixon's original is dated 15 July 1789. King George III's first visit was from 30 June to September 1789. P A Scholes 1942 *God Save the King*; Oxford: Oxford University Press, or p 69 of M Boddy and J West 1963 *Weymouth: An Illustrated History;* Wimbourne, UK: Dovecote.
65. E Hobsbawm and T Ranger (editors) 1983, *The Invention of Tradition;* Cambridge: Cambridge University Press; R Fiske 1983 *Scotland in Music;* Cambridge: Cambridge University Press.
66. *Scholes* p 855.
67. Bálint Sárosi 1978 *Gypsy Music;* Budapest: Corvina Press, pp 108, 213.
68. Anthony Donato 1963 *Preparing Music Manuscript;* New York: Amsco Music Publishing Company (Everybody's Favorite Series, No 130); London: Boosey & Hawkes.
69. Your nearest music information center should have up-to-date information on computer music printing systems. For a discussion of the possibilities of fax machines, see: Thomas Heck 1986 Fontes Artis Musicae 33(1) 77.
70. We note, in passing, the excellent manuscript parts prepared by anonymous Viennese copyists c.1800. The parts are laid out with the performer in mind; often as much as half a page or more is left blank to permit a page turn during rests.
71. O E Deutsch 1955 *Handel: A Documentary Biography;* London: A and C Black.
72. *Scholes,* entries under "Waits or Waytes," "Inns and Taverns," "Mealtime Music," "Street Music." See also *Oxford Companion to Music,* 21st edition, revised Judith Nagley, under "Waits" and "Street Music."
73. Typical music of the waits is recorded on Argo ZRG 646. *New Grove* (vol.19, p 155) has a picture c.1670 of a waits band.
74. W L Woodfill 1953 *Musicians in English Society from Elizabeth to Charles I;* Princeton: Princeton University Press, Appendix D, reprinted 1969 New York: Da Capo Press.
75. C Weir 1981 *Village and Town Bands;* Princes Risborough: UK Shire Publications.
76. Charles Babbage 1864 *A Chapter on Street Nuisances;* London: Longman. This paper, by the computer pioneer, says most of what might be said against street bands.
77. The *Bath Journal,* 1 December 1774 printed the following notice, dated 19 November 1774: "Orders have been sent by Authority to the Musicians & City Waits to desist from playing at Lodging houses, to the great disturbance of the sick and others who visit this place. - And this order having been disobey'd Notice is hereby given that information against them either as vagrants or entertainers will be received of the Magistrates at the Town Hall any Monday morning at eleven-o-clock."
78. Emily Brontë 1847 *Wuthering Heights,* chapter 7. The passage appears in a diary dated 1801, and records events dating from about 30 years earlier. The band is identified with that of Southowram in the late 1770s.
79. P Bate 1971 *The Oboe;* London: Benn.
80. J Harley 1968 *Music in Purcell's London;* London: Dennis Dobson, p 107.
81. The *Gentleman's Journal.* London, January 1692, p 117.
82. D'Urfey's *Wit & Mirth, or Pills to Purge Melancholy* of 1719, vol 4, pp 40 et seq, describes thus the scene after the Lord Mayor is sworn in: "And when that is ended, home again he comes/ With joyful Noise upon the Thames of Trumpets and Drums;/ His Lordship lands at Pauls-Wharf, and on along he jogs/ Attended by his Companies, as Hungry as any Dogs./ Then they go to Greenwich all in the City Barge,/ And there they have a Noble Treat all at the City Charge;/ And when they come to Cuckold's-Point, they make a Gallant Show,/ Their Wives bid the Musick play Cuckolds-all-in-a-row."
83. H C Robbins Landon 1959 *Collected Correspondence and London Notebooks of Joseph Haydn;* London: Barrie and Rockliff.

84. That the wind serenade was familiar in London in 1801 can be deduced from the cover of Nicola Sampieri's *Serenata* (GB-Lbl, h.61.h.[15]), which shows a guitarist serenading and, in the background, a wind band, and a clock showing 3:13 am!

85. Fanny Burney 1778 *Evelina;* London; Letter XLII.

86. Leopold Mozart, letter of 28 June 1764, in *Mozart Letters.*

87. Warwick Wroth and A E Wroth 1896 *The London Pleasure Gardens of the Eighteenth Century;* London: Macmillan. Reprinted 1979. Whether there were any links to Turkish gardens and entertainments (61) is not clear.

88. Mollie Sands 1946 *Invitation to Ranelagh;* London: John Westhouse.

89. Mollie Sands 1987 *The Eighteenth-Century Pleasure Gardens of Marylebone, 1737-1777;* London: The Society for Theatre Research.

90. C Cudworth 1967 Galpin Soc Journal **20** 24-42 *The Vauxhall Lists.*

91. The Dublin musical scene was active, with visitors such as Handel. Mr Charles gave early performances on horn and clarinet in 1742. The Great Brittain-Street [sic] Gardens held "Grand Concerts of Wind Instruments, weather permitting, at 12.00 to 3.00pm and 6.30 to 9.30pm in summers from 1755"; regular water concerts at the Bason were held in the late 1750s. Handel's *Fireworks Music* was a popular event (1); see B Boydell 1979 *Four Centuries of Music in Ireland;* London: BBC.

92. Over 50 years later, Vauxhall's closure is shown poignantly in J Findlay's painting of 1859 (now in the Museum of London) reproduced in *Rococo Art and Design in Hogarth's England,* Catalogue, Victoria and Albert Museum, London, 1984, exhibit F41.

93. H Harington 1800 *Songs, Duetts, and other Compositions by Doctor Harington of Bath never before published. ... Printed for the Author & Sold by the Engraver, E. Riley, etc;* London, (preface dated 20 March 1800), p 42.

94. M Searle 1977 *Spas and Watering Places;* Tunbridge Wells: Midas, p 51.

95. Letter of 3 September 1873 from Henry B Falconar to Mrs Jane Falconar, Bath Reference Library ALb. 1736. Text given in: J A Gillaspie (compiler & editor) 1986 *The Catalogue of Music in the Bath Reference Library to 1985;* London: K G Saur, p 233.

96. K Young 1968 *Music's Great Days in the Spas and Watering Places;* London: Macmillan. See also W Addison 1951 *English Spas;* London: Batsford. P J N Havins 1976 *The Spas of England;* London: Hale.

97. J Stevens 1961 *Music and Poetry in the Early Tudor Court;* Cambridge: Cambridge University Press.

98. Reginald Nettel 1946 *The Orchestra in England;* London: Jonathan Cape, p 47.

99. Theodore Bridault's *Characteristic Sonata for the Piano Forte* (London: Cahusac & Sons, 1797) has a *Grand Salutation of Cannon and Music, on His Majesty's Embarking on Board the Royal Barge,* and later *Music heard from several Boats on the River.*

100. *Thayer.*

101. P J Willetts 1970 *Beethoven in England: An Account of the Sources in the British Museum;* London: British Library.

102. A Carse, 1946 Music and Letters **27** 147-155 *The Prince Regent's Band.*

103. *The Times* 19 February 1812.

104. *Weston/CVP* (plate 14).

105. *Weston/MCVP.*

106. A Einstein 1946 Musical Review **7** 154.

107. T L Peacock 1831 *Crotchet Castle;* London; Chapter IX.

108. *HCRL/3;* see also (83).

109. John Hampden (compiler) 1940 *An Eighteenth Century Journal, 1774-1776;* London: Macmillan, pp 71-74.

110. The Hon Roger North, edited by J Wilson 1959 *Roger North on Music c.1695-1728;*

London: Novello. See also: F H Shera, reference 4, p 55.

111. K H MacDermott 1948 *The Old Church Gallery Minstrels;* London: SPCK.

112. N Temperley 1979 *The Music of the English Parish Church;* Cambridge: Cambridge University Press.

113. Quoted without source in *Radio Times;* London: BBC, 20 August 1979.

114. R Nettel 1951 *The Englishman Makes Music;* London: Dennis Dobson, p 108.

115. James Boswell 1791 *Life of Johnson;* London: MacMillan, 1893, p 534.

116. Francis Grose 1783 *Advice to the Officers of the British Army* (reprinted 1867 New York Agathynian Club); cited in H G Farmer, reference 36.

117. F Willan 1900 *History of the Oxford Regiment of Militia 1778-1900;* Oxford: Horace Hart. See E E Thoyt 1897 *History of the Royal Berkshire Regiment;* Reading, UK: privately printed. Both volumes are in the Oxford Central Reference Library, section 356. See also C Oman 1943 *Britain against Napoleon;* London: Faber and Faber.

118. *The Times* 27 March 1843. In 1827, in the early stages of building the tunnel, Brunel hired a Guards' Band to play while visitors watched the work in progress.

119. M Kelly 1826 *Reminiscences* Vol 2 pp 148-149; p 248 of the 1975 edition (Oxford: Oxford University Press, edited Roger Fiske). The circumstances led to accusations of plagiarism, but Eley wrote to clarify what happened "concerning the march in Blue Beard, of which you [Kelly] gave to me the melody, to put parts for the orchestral wind instruments ... I wrote this score in the music room, at Covent Garden Theatre, during the acts of the play, which several of the orchestra did see, and concluded it was my melody; though I assured them it was not; from whence this error has arose."

120. J Trendall 1978 *Operation Music-Maker: The Story of the Royal Marine Bands;* Southampton, UK: John Trendall, West End.

121. Joseph Doane 1794 *A Musical Directory for the Year 1794;* London: Printed for the Editor (available as a bound photocopy from the Royal College of Music).

122. *The Times* 28 Feb 1797. Five years later the band of the Royal Pembroke Militia played patriotic airs as Lord Nelson received the Freedom of the Town and County of Haverfordwest. The military plans for this invasion by "La Seconde Légion des Francs" were drawn up shortly before his death by no less than Général Hoche (*The Times,* 13 February 1798) for whom Cherubini, Paisiello and others wrote funeral marches. Hoche had planned to be a musician; his fine voice earned him a place in the choir of St Germaine-en-Laye. Thomas Busby *(Concert Room and Orchestra Anecdotes of Music and Musicians Ancient and Modern,* 1825, p 104) notes "To the state and perfection of his military bands he was ever attentive. His partiality to martial music marked his attachment to both harmony and arms."

123. Fanny Burney 1961 (reprint) *Diary;* London: The Folio Society; p 282. Her observation contrasts with that of Henry Redhead York, who saw Napoleon's review of the French Consular Guard in 1802, and noted that "only one batallion seemed to pay attention to distance or time" (reprint edited J A C Sykes, London: Heinemann, 1906).

124. *Sainsbury.*

125. *Grove V* vol 6 p 1023.

126. *Sainsbury* describes the adventurous lives of the Petrides brothers.

127. Samuel Hale's *A Select Collection of Martial Music* SYH-1m Vol 1 contains a *Quickstep by Mozart,* loosely based on K.388.

128. G Hogarth 1862 *The Philharmonic Society of London from its Foundation, 1813, to Its Fiftieth year, 1862;* London.

129. A Carse 1951 *The Life of Jullien;* Cambridge: Heffer.

130. Fritz Spiegl 1984 *Music Through the Looking Glass;* London: Routledge and Kegan Paul, p 231. A different set of forenames is given in *New Grove.*

131. D Cox 1980 *The Henry Wood Proms;* London: BBC Enterprises.

132. Sir Henry Wood 1938 *My Life of Music;* London: Gollancz (reprinted 1946).

133. Gerard Hoffnung (1925-1959) founded the Hoffnung Music Festivals in London as successors to Liverpool's April Fools' Concerts. Hoffnung's success came partly from his special style of humor and partly from his skill in persuading the best British composers to write original works for the festivals.

134. Theon Wilkinson 1967, 1987 *Two Monsoons: The Life and Death of Europeans in India;* London: Duckworth.

135. M Hardwick 1970 *Discovery of Japan;* London: Hamlyn.

136. Charles Allen and Sharada Dwivedi 1984 *Lives of the Indian Princes;* London: Century Publishing, p 16.

137. Emily Eden (edited E Thompson) 1930 *Up the Country;* Oxford: Oxford University Press, p 293 (also pps 78, 83, 138, 141 of this collection of letters from India, 1838-39).

138. P Hopkirk 1982 *Trespassers on the Roof of the World;* Oxford University Press.

139. A David-Neel 1927 *My Journey to Lhasa;* (reprinted 1969 London: Virago Press).

140. *The Times,* 9 May 1989.

141. Patrick Leigh Fermor 1959 *The Traveller's Tree;* London: John Murray, p 354.

142. L E R Rees 1858 *A Personal Narrative of the Siege of Lucknow* p 343; quoted in Winstock (ref 28) p 173.

143. Toshio Akiyama 1994 p 201 et seq of Cipolla and Hunsberger (37).

144. The *American Musical Journal,* New York, **1** pp 231-232, September 1835. This is an extract from the *Sydney Monitor* of 20 December 1834.

145. R Camus 1994 p 57 et seq of Cipolla and Hunsberger (37).

146. C S Shire 1986-1987 J Band Res **22** 1-8.

147. G Chase 1966 *America's Music from the Pilgrims to the Present;* New York: McGraw-Hill, pp 141, 144-146.

148. J Mates 1962 *The American Stage before 1800;* New Brunswick, NJ: Rutgers Univeristy Press. Mates cites J F Watson 1846 *Annals and Occurrences of New York City and State* and G C D Odell 1927 *Annals of the New York Stage.*

149. O G Sonneck 1907 *Early Concert Life in America;* Leipzig: Breitkopf und Härtel, reprinted 1978 New York: Da Capo Press.

150. P L Ford (editor) 1892-99 *The Writings of Thomas Jefferson;* New York, vol 2, p 159; quoted in Mates (148) p 87.

151. H H Hall 1967 *The Moravian Wind Ensemble: A Distinctive Chapter in America's Music.* Ph D Thesis, George Peabody College of Teachers.

152. H H Hall J Band Res **1**(2) 27; H H Hall 1985 Moravian Music Journal **29** 98.

153. David Moritz Michael *Lebenslauf;* manuscript in the Archiv der Brüder-Unität, Herrnhut, Germany (R22 No.4029).

154. R A Grider 1873 *Historical Notes on Music in Bethlehem, Pa. (1741-1871),* reprinted 1957 Winston-Salem, NC: The Moravian Music Foundation.

155. K van W Keller 1981 *Popular Secular Music in America through 1800: A Preliminary Checklist of Manuscripts in North American Collections;* Philadelphia: Music Library Association; MLA Index and Bibliography Series No 21.

156. Other works on US bands include: F M Marciniak 1977 J Band Res **13** 7 *(American Band of Providence);* G Carroll 1966 J Band Res **2** 16 *(Band of Musick of the Second Virginal Regt, 1779-1783);* H H Hall 1984 Moravian Music Journal **29** 98 *The Columbian Band: Bethlehem Moravians in the Early 19th Century Militia;* see also H H Hall 1965 J Band Research **1**(2) 27 on the Moravian Bands and H H Hall 1982 J Band Res **17**(2) on the Salem band; J Cermek 1889 *History of the Civil War;* Chicago: Geringer *(Czech Musicians in the American Civil War);* Barry H Kolman 1985 *Origins of American Wind Music,* Thesis, N Colorado.

157. *American Musical Journal* 1835 **1**(11) 251; New York: James Dunn.

158. James R Heintze 1990 *Early American Music;* New York: Garland Publishing. See also S E Jones 1959 National Geographic Magazine **116**(6) 252; K W Carpenter 1971 J Band Res **7**(2) 23-29. Francis N Mayer 1966 J Band Res **3**(1) 24-28 discusses the scoring of the Marine Band music c.1850, from the Scala Library of MSS; that quoted for c.1845 is fl cl(?E♭) 2cl 2hn serp 2tp tb, slightly larger than indicated by Scala.

159. H Kallmann 1981 *A History of Music in Canada*, in Kallmann, Potvin and Winters 1981 *Encyclopedia of Music in Canada;* Toronto: University of Toronto Press, p 53 et seq. Camus (ref 14) quotes the band as present in America only from 1779-1782 (so Canada in 1814 must have been a later trip, after the regiment's involvement in the Peninsular War. In 1777 it had "A handsome Band of Music, genteely dressed". See also S T Moloney 1988 J Band Res **23**(2) 10 *A History of the Wind Band in Canada.*

160. For a broad-ranging discussion, see R M Isherwood 1986 *Farce and Fantasy: Popular Entertainment in 18th Century Paris;* New York: Oxford University Press. He cites Mercier's *Tableau No 12* (sd, probably from the 1770s).

161. Henry Redhead Yorke, 1802 letters, edited 1906 by Lady J A C Sykes as *France in 1802;* London: Heinemann.

162. C Hogwood 1980 *Music at Court;* London: Gollancz, p 59.

163. L Norton 1982 *The Sun King and His Loves;* London: Folio Society.

164. G Pillement 1972 *Paris en Fête;* Paris: Grasset.

165. R M Isherwood 1973 *Music in the Service of the King: France in the Seventeenth Century;* Ithaca: Cornell University Press.

166. C Pierre 1975 *Histoire du Concert Spirituel 1725-1790;* Paris: Heugel.

167. M Brenet, (pseudonym of Marie Bobillier) 1900 *Les Concerts en France sous l'Ancien Régime;* Paris: Fischbacher; reprinted 1970 New York: Da Capo.

168. Rameau's *Acante et Céphise* contains two items **(JPR-1e)** for 2cl 2hn in act 2.

169. This can be dated approximately by the publication of Valentin Roeser's 1764 *Essai d'Instruction à l'usage de ceux qui composent pour la clarinette et le cor avec des remarques sur l'harmonie à deux clarinettes, deux cors et deux bassons;* Paris; reprinted 1972 Geneva: G Minkoff.

170. J H Elliot, in A Jacobs (editor) 1963 *Choral Music;* London: Penguin Books.

171. For another fine work, see D Swanzy 1969 J Band Res **6**(1), who discusses Gossec's *Symphonie Militaire,* and whether his *Choeur Patriotique* could have been used as a fourth movement to make a *Choral Wind Symphony* ("Le triomph de la Loi" would replace "Simoneau maire d'Étampes").

172. *Pierre/MF.*

173. *Pierre/HC.* This describes all the major occasions and such music as is extant.

174. P Landormy 1944 *La Musique Française de la Marseillaise à la mort de Berlioz;* Paris: Gallimard.

175. D Whitwell 1979 *Band Music of the French Revolution;* Tutzing: Hans Schneider.

176. R Hesdin (anonymous translation 1895) *The Journal of a Spy in Paris during the Reign of Terror. January-July, 1794;* London: John Murray.

177. L Durrell 1958 *Stiff Upper Lip;* London: Faber, p 27.

178. C Pierre (unpublished?) *La Musique aux Fêtes et Cérémonies de la Révolution française* (we have not traced a copy; it may not have been issued).

179. D P Swanzy 1966 *The Wind Ensemble and its Music during the French Revolution;* Ph D Thesis, Michigan State University.

180. R Cobb 1987 (translated M Elliott) *The People's Armies;* New Haven: Yale University Press. See also S Schama 1989 *Citizens;* New York: Viking.

181. A Guellette 1962 *L'Opéra au Palais Garnier 1875-1962;* Paris: Slatkine.

182. S Schama 1989 *Citizens;* New York: Viking, p 562. The French revolutionaries

wished to mimic Rome. An earlier 18th-century view of Roman military music (also illustrated) is B Kennett 1746 *Romae Antiquae Notitia, or, The Antiquities of Rome;* London: W Innys et al. On p 208 the discussion begins: "The Romans us'd only Wind-Musick in their Army; the Instruments, which serv'd for that Purpose, may be distinguish'd into the Tubae, the Cornua, the Buccinae, and the Litui."

183. That some conventional musical standards survived is shown by a memorandum by Cherubini to Méhul (*Pierre/HC* p 860), where the score of a *Marche des Français sur les bords de la Grande-Bretagne,* by one Horix, is found to be full of errors in harmony and instrumentation, suitable neither for military use nor for the Fête.

184. *The Memoirs of Hector Berlioz 1803-1865,* translated D Cairns 1975 London: Gollancz, p 254.

185. M Emmanuel 1937 *Antonin Reicha;* Paris: H Laurens. This contains facsimiles of part of the autograph of both works.

186. H MacDonald (editor) 1967 *Berlioz Complete Edition;* Kassel: Bärenreiter, Vol 19. This contains facsimiles of parts of the autograph.

187. Heinrich Saro (1827-1891) conducted; the Emperors were Wilhelm I, Franz Joseph and Alexander II. The Dreikaiserbund was set up by Bismarck to prevent the French seeking revenge on Prussia; its 1873 accords were soon superseded.

188. *The Times,* 27 July 1982.

189. Joseph Wechsberg 1973 *The Waltz Emperors: The Life and Times and Music of the Strauss Family;* London: Weidenfeld and Nicolson, pps 177-179. This quotes Johann Strauss the Younger's description of his concert at the Boston World Peace Jubilee in July, 1872: "In order to conduct the giant assembly of singers and orchestra members I had assigned one hundred sub-conductors. I could see only those who stood closest to me. In spite of our previous rehearsal it was impossible to think of giving an artistic performance... Imagine my situation, in front of one hundred thousand wildly enthusiastic Americans. There I stood on the highest platform. How would this thing begin, how would it end? Suddenly there is a cannon shot - a subtle hint to us twenty thousand to begin The Blue Danube. I give a sign. My hundred sub-conductors follow me as fast and well as they can. And now there begins a terrific racket which I won't forget as long as I live. Since we all had started at approximately the same time, I did all I could so we would all finish at approximately the same time. Somehow I managed to do it - it was really the only thing I could do. The audience cheered. The noise was fantastic. I took a deep breath when I was outside again in the fresh air and felt firm ground under my feet. The following morning I tried to avoid a number of impresarios who promised me the whole of California for a tour of America."

190. *Cobbett;* see the article "Taffanel."

191. Frédéric Robert, sleeve notes for Calliope CAL 1827, 1975.

192. For members of the Société Moderne in 1906, see the dedication of Albert Roussel's *Divertissement.* For other ensembles, see (190) and *Grove V* under "Paris."

193. Johann Pezzl 1786-1790 *Skizze von Wien;* reprinted Graz 1923; see H C Robbins Landon 1991 *Mozart and Vienna;* London: Thames and Hudson.

194. E Wangermann 1973 *The Austrian Achievement 1700-1800;* London: Thames and Hudson.

195. *HCRL/4.*

196. An unidentified illustration of a typical setting of wind harmony at the Sperlbauer Inn in 1807 is reproduced on the cover of the London Wind Soloists' 1976 recording of Sedlak's arrangement of Beethoven's *Fidelio* (Decca SDD485).

197. H E Reeser 1949 *The Sons of Bach;* Stockholm: Continental Book Co, pp 28-29.

198. Lowell Mason 1837 *Journals;* published (edited N Broyles, 1990) as *A Yankee Musician in Europe;* Ann Arbor, MI: UMI Press.

199. Sir George Henschel 1918 *Musings and Memories of a Musician;* London: Macmillan; reprinted 1970, New York: Da Capo.

200. M Beaufils 1983 *Comment l'Allemagne est devenue musicienne;* Paris: Laffont.

201. *HCRL/4* p 553

202. V Novello and M Novello 1955 *A Mozart Pilgrimage, Being the Travel Diaries of Vincent and Mary Novello in the Year 1829;* London: Allen and Unwin; reprinted 1975 London: Eulenburg.

203. E Holmes 1828 *A Ramble among the Musicians of Germany;* London, 2nd Edition; reprinted 1969 New York: Da Capo.

204. M M Scott 1934 *Beethoven;* London: J M Dent (reprinted 1965) p 231.

205. A Diemand 1899 *Anwesenheit des Kaisers Franz I ... zu Wallerstein im Jahre 1764; Unterhaltungsblatt der Augsburg Postzeitung No 100.*

206. L Schiedermair: 1907-1908 Sammelbände der internationalen Musikgesellschaft 9, *Die Blütezeit der Öttingen-Wallerstein'schen Hofkapelle.*

207. J R Piersol 1972 *The Oettingen-Wallerstein Hofkapelle and its Wind Music;* PhD diss., University of Iowa (Ann Arbor, MI: University Microfilms: 73-13,583).

208. G Haberkamp 1976 *Thematischer Katalog der Musikhandschriften der Fürstlich Oettingen-Wallerstein'schen Bibliothek Schloss Harburg. Mit einer Geschichte des Musikalienbestandes von Volker von Volckamer.* Katalog Bayerischer Musiksammlungen. G Henle: Munich. Microfiches of the music manuscripts and music prints from Schloss Harburg (Augsburg University since 1980) were published in 1985 Munich: K G Saur.

209. J R Piersol (207) citing the article, *Nachricht von der fürstl. Wallersteinischen Hofkapelle,* Die musikalische Realzeitung, 1(7) p 33 (13 August 1788).

210. Letter from I von Beecke, Aschaffenburg, 3 August 1790, to Prince Kraft Ernst, Wallerstein (Fürstlich Oettingen-Wallerstein Archiv), quoted by Friedrich Munter 1921 *Ignaz von Beecke und seine Instrumentalkompositionen.* PhD diss. Ludwig-Maximilians-Universität: Munich, p 16 (translated by J R Piersol, [207] p 258).

211. A Robertson 1964 *Dvořák;* London: Dent, pp 1-9.

212. C Ditters von Dittersdorf 1801 *Lebenschreibung;* translated A D Coleridge 1896 as: *The Autobiography of Karl von Dittersdorf, dictated to his Son;* London; 1967 edition edited by N Miller, reprinted by Da Capo Press: New York, 1970.

213. L da Ponte *Memoirs of Lorenzo da Ponte;* Elisabeth Abbott (translator), 1929; reprinted 1967 New York: Dover.

214. R N Freeman 1971 *The Practice of Music at Melk Monastery in the Eighteenth Century.* PhD thesis, University of California, Los Angeles, pp 135 et seq.

215. J Senhal, J Band Research 12(2) 12; 1983 Časopis Moravského Muzea (Acta Musei Moraviae) 118 117-148 *Harmonie na Moravě 1750-1840.*

216. V Orel 1984 *Mendel;* Oxford: Oxford University Press, for Abbot Napp's support for the scientific breeding of apples and vines, for experimental gardens and other encouragement of Mendel, and for his opposition to Bishop Schaffgotsch's conservatism.

217. J Vogel 1962 *Leoš Janáček, His Life and Works;* London: Paul Hamlyn, p 37.

218. The *Prager Neue Zeitung* of 17 August 1794 describes a procession in Roudnice comprising harvesters with scythes, shepherds and sheep farmers, and a chosen "Harvest Maiden, a poor orphan girl whose brothers were serving soldiers." Music came from eight musicians playing wind instruments (presumably the Lobkowitz Harmonie, based at Roudnice), bagpipers and fiddlers, and from four boys and four girls who had learned harvest songs. The procession moved to the castle, where it was received with trumpets and drums. The Harvesters' Wreath was presented from a silver salver carried by the Harvest Maiden; the singers sang, accompanied by the instruments. Finally, the instrumentalists provided a musical entertainment in the castle hall.

219. Peter Fairley *Daily Telegraph* 30 April 1994.

220. J A Scheibe 1776 *Vollständiges Liederbuch für Freymaurer;* Copenhagen, Leipzig. J G Naumann 1782 *Vierzig Freymaurer-Lieder;* Berlin; 2nd edition, 1784.

221. Masonic cryptography is outside our scope; see Paul Nettl 1970 *Mozart and Masonry;* New York: Philosphical Library; See also the bibliography in (222).

222. K Thomson 1977 *The Masonic Thread in Mozart;* London: Lawrence and Wishart; p 43. This book has a useful bibliography on the relationship of Freemasonry to music.

223. J Chailly 1970 *Haydn and the Freemasons,* in H C Robbins Landon (editor) *Studies in Eighteenth Century Music - A Tribute to Karl Geiringer on his Seventieth Birthday;* London: George Allen and Unwin, pp 117 et seq.

224. H C Robbins Landon 1982 *Mozart and the Masons: New Light on the Lodge "Crowned Hope";* London: Thames and Hudson.

225. A Hofer 1988 *Studien zur Geschichte des Militärmarsches;* Tutzing: Schneider.

226. An early example for 2ob 2hn bn is given in facsimile in *Die Infanterie-Märsche der vormaligen Churfürstlich-Sächsischen Armee 1729;* Freiburg: Fritz Schultz, 1981.

227. E W Steinquest 1971 *Royal Prussian Wind Band Music, 1740-1797;* PhD thesis, George Peabody College for Teachers, NY; E E Helm 1960 *Music at the Court of Frederick the Great;* Norman: University of Oklahoma Press. Other general references include: A Haberling 1967 J Band Res **4** 17 *Die Blasmusik in der Schweiz;* W Stephan 1972 J Band Res **9** 10 *German Military Music;* W Smialek 1984 J Band Res **20** 2 *Jozef Elsner and Military Band Music in 19th Century Poland;* E Brixel G Martin and G Pils 1982 *Das ist Oesterreichs Militärmusik;* Graz: Verlag Styria.

228. Friedrich Wilhelm (1620-1688) was "der Grosse Kurfürst" (the Great Elector of Brandenburg), not to be confused with Frederick the Great (1712-1788).

229. See, e.g. Druschetzky *Marche du Coronnement de l'Empereur Napoléon à Paris.*

230. Wolfgang Suppan 1983 *Blasmusik in Baden; Freiburg im Breisgau:* Musikverlag Fritz Schulz. For a discussion of many of the composers, see also W Suppan 1995 *Lexikon des Blasmusikwesens* (4th edition); Freiburg im Breisgau: Musikverlag Fritz Schulz.

231. W H Hadow 1897 *A Croatian Composer: Notes toward the Study of Joseph Haydn;* London: Seeley & Co Ltd.

232. *Weston/MCVP.*

233. *Thayer.*

234. D J Rhodes 1995 IDRS Journal 21-34; D J Rhodes 1994 IDRS Journal 7-29, citing J N Forkel 1782 *Musikalischer Almanach für Deutschland auf das Jahr 1782;* Leipzig. C Meyer 1913 *Geschichte der Mecklenburg-Schweriner Hofkapelle;* Schwerin, and C F Cramer 1783 *Magazin der Musik,* vol 1 part 2; Hamburg.

235. J P Newhill 1979 Musical Review **40**(2) 90.

236. Personal communication of Herr Beutter, Archivist, to Dr B Blomhert, 1996.

237. Bastiaan Blomhert 1987 *The Harmonie of Die Entführung aus dem Serail by Wolfgang Amadeus Mozart: Study about its Authenticity and Critical Edition;* PhD thesis, Den Haag: Rijksuniversiteit Utrecht.

238. 1791 is the date given in *New Grove.*

239. H Fitzpatrick 1962 Music and Letters **43** 234

240. *Hellyer.*

241. R Gregory 1970 *The Intelligent Eye;* London: Weidenfeld & Nicholson.

242. A Meier 1978 Haydn Yearbook **10** 81 *Die Presssburger Hofkapelle 1776 bis 1784.*

243. H Seiffert 1978 Haydn Yearbook **10** 154 *Der Verbindungen der Familie Erdödy zur Musik.*

244. *HCRL/2* p 539. See also the other volumes passim, including *HCRL/1* errata.

245. Musicalia Danubiana 4, quoting from A Weidemann, in *Festschrift Joseph Schmidt-Görg zum 70. Geburtstag;* Bonn 1967, p 445.

246. R Hellyer 1984 Haydn Yearbook **15** 5 *The Wind Ensembles of the Esterházy Princes, 1761-1813.*

247. O Biba 1978 Haydn Yearbook **10** 39 *Nachrichten zur Musikpflege in der gräflichen Familie Harrach.*

248. H Stekl 1978 Haydn Yearbook **10** 173 *Harmoniemusik und "türkische Banda" des Fürstenhauses Liechtenstein.*

249. A-Wn, Katalog sämtlicher in dem kk Hofmusikarchiv vorhandener Bücher und Musikalien 1856.

250. H G Farmer (sd) *British Bands in Battle;* London: Hinrichsen Edition 1482, p 16.

251. A Myslík 1978 Haydn Yearbook **10** 110. *Repertoire und Besetzung der Harmoniemusik an den Höfen Schwarzenberg, Pachta und Clam-Gallas.*

252. H C Robbins Landon 1988 *1791, Mozart's Last Year;* London: Thames and Hudson, p 100.

253. V Schwarz 1978 Haydn Yearbook **10** 121 *Fürst Joseph Lobkowitz und die Musikpflege auf Raudnitz und Eisenberg.*

254. State regional archives, Litoměřice, branch Žitenice: Lobkovic Central Accounts Office 1807/229, reproduced in T Volek and I Bittner (editors) 1991 *The Mozartiana of Czech and Moravian Archives;* Prague: Archives of the Czech Ministry of Interior [sic].

255. J Senhal 1978 Haydn Yearbook **10** 132 *Die Musikkapelle des Olmützer Erzbischofs Anton Theodor Colleredo-Waldsee (1777-1811).* Also J Senhal 1983 Časopis Moravského Muzea (Acta Musei Moraviae) **117** 117 *Harmonie na Moravě* and 1977 J Band Res **12** 12 *The Harmonie (Wind Band) of the Augustinian Monastery at Staré Brno (Old Brno).*

256. John Rosselli 1991 *Music and Musicians in 19th Century Italy;* London: Batsford.

257. H Acton 1979 *The Pazzi Conspiracy: The Plot against the Medici;* London: Thames and Hudson, pps 63-64.

258. Marino Anesa 1988 *Musica in Piazza. Contributi per una storia della bande musicale Bergamasche;* Bergamo: Sistema Bibliotecario Urbano di Bergamo.

259. R M Longyear 1978 J Band Res **13**(2) 25 *The Banda sul Paco: Wind Bands in 19th Century Opera.*

260. Roy Strong 1984 *Art and Power: Renaissance Festivals 1450-1650;* London: Boydell.

261. Appendix I, in A Jacobs (editor) 1963 *Choral Music;* Harmondsworth: Penguin Books. *New Catholic Encyclopaedia,* 1967, New York: McGraw-Hill, vol 4 p 347.

262. Thomas Ashby 1929 *Some Italian Scenes and Festivals;* London: Methuen. This includes illustrations of bands in processions from A J B Thomas's 1823 *Un An à Rome;* Paris: L'Imprimerie de Firmin Didot (see plates XXVIII and XLII of Thomas's book).

263. Alessandro Sebastiani 1828 *Viaggio a Tivoli;* Fuligno: Tipografia Tomassini.

264. The *Sunday Times* of 22 September 1991 described a traditional Holy Week band in Bilbao, Spain, where modern political graffiti covered their bandstand. Drew Launay (BBC Radio 4, 25 July 1993) remarked on a religious fiesta at which the village band "played a pasa doblé more suitable for a bullfight." J Milsom (*BBC Music Magazine,* February 1996 p 18) reports far better quality from Maundy Thursday at Avila.

265. F Brancaccio di Carpino 1860 *Tre Mesi nella Vicaria di Palermo nel 1860* (translated J Parris 1968 as *The Fight for Freedom, Palermo 1860);* London: Folio Society. Alvise Zorzi 1985 *Venezia Austriaca;* Rome-Bari: Editori Laterza, describes how, at 9 pm on 21 July 1856, 90 singers and winds provided a serenade from on board the Galeggiante, moored at the Pier Piazetta on the Grand Canal, Venice. Italian composers could take a pragmatic view. Thus Teodulo Mabellini wrote a cantata in 1847 to celebrate moves to a constitution for Tuscany, and in 1849 a further cantata to welcome the Grand Duke and the Austrian army which supported him (256 p 94).

266. R Ricks 1969 The Musical Quarterly Vol 55(3) 364, *Russian Horn Bands.* Such bands are illustrated under *Horn band* Vol 8 of *New Grove;* London: Macmillan, p 716; T Volek

and S Jareš 1977 *Dějiny České Hudby v Obrazech;* Prague: Supraphon, plates 282-284.
267. M F Robinson with U Hofman 1989, 1994 *Giovanni Paisiello. A Thematic Catalogue of his works;* Stuyvesant, NY: Pendragon Press.
268. Eveline Cruikshanks (editor) 1960 *Memoirs of Louis Philippe, Comte de Ségur;* London: Folio Society, p 272.
269. D Brown 1974 *Mikhail Glinka: A Biographical and Critical Study;* London: Oxford University Press.
270. A Hedley 1947 *Chopin;* London: Dent; K Kobylanska 1955 *Chopin In His Own Land;* Cracow: Polish Music Publications. The march is now lost. Could it have been arranged for Chopin by Jozef Elsner? W Smialek 1985 J Band Res **20** 2 discusses Elsner.
271. N Rimsky-Korsakov 1964 *Principles of Orchestration;* New York: Dover. This is the corrected version of a translation by E Agate of the 1922 publication by Édition Russe de Musique; the original was published in 1891.
272. Anders Edling 1995 *Between Düben and Haeffner: A survey of the 18th Century Music at Uppsala University Library;* BIBLID 91-554-3448-7 (1995) p 251-258.
273. V Helasvuo 1952 *Sibelius and the Music of Finland;* Helsinki: Otava.
274. Fanie Jooste 1991 J Band Res **26**(2) *The Primary Influences on South African Wind music of the Seventeenth and Eighteenth Centuries;* p 54.
275. M C H Lichtenstein 1812 *Reisen in Südlichen Africa in den Jahren 1803, 1804, 1805 und 1806;* Berlin (especially p 44).
276. J H Verduyn den Boer 1929 *Schetsen uit het Kaapse Leven van de Agtiende en Negentiende Eeuw;* Cape Town (especially p 1).
277. William Beckford 1834 *Italy, with Sketches of Portugal and Spain;* Paris: Baudry's European Library. Beckford's revisions do not affect the letters which we quote (William Beckford 1840 *Italy, Spain and Portugal, with an Excursion to the Monasteries of Alcobaça and Batalha;* London: Richard Bentley).
278. Christopher Hibbert (editor) 1970 *The Recollections of Rifleman Harris;* London: The Military Book Society.
279. J H Leslie (editor) 1905 *The Dickson Manuscripts;* Woolwich, UK: Royal Artillery Institution Publishing House.
280. Anon (Thomas Howell?) 1819 (edited Christopher Hibbert 1996) *A Soldier of the Seventy-First. The Journal of a Soldier in the Peninsular War;* Moreton-in-Marsh, UK: Windrush Press. References to French bands are found on pp 62, 96.
281. We are indebted to Señor Jon Bagüés, of the Archivo de Compositores Vascos, Renteria, Guipuzcoa, for making it possible for us to study Arriaga's *Marcha militar.*

Part 2

COMPOSERS AND ARRANGERS: BIOGRAPHICAL INFORMATION

Introduction

This part provides historical and biographical information on wind harmony and those who created it. One aim is to give such social and historical information as might be helpful for concert program notes. Another aim is to guide players to a broader repertoire. We have become suspicious of judgments made without either hearing or performing works; it is too easy to underestimate the effectiveness of a piece because of apparent lack of sophistication, and even easier to be uncritical when a famous name appears on the title page. We therefore identify good works wherever possible, usually from examination of the scores, from performing the works ourselves, or from views of ensembles who have played them. The historical information will not replace standard sources, though we shall correct obvious mistakes, usually without comment.

The entries which follow cover a significant fraction of the works and composers listed in our second volume, *Wind Ensemble Catalog*. When composers and works appear in the *Catalog* but not in this part, it is often because we have no reliable information, or because of the losses of archives over the years. Please tell us if you know something useful and verifiable (secondary sources are notoriously unreliable). We have normally followed *New Grove* in spellings of composers' names. We have avoided eccentric (if arguably logical) rules which lead to confusing variants like "Chaikovsky." One controversial area concerns Czech versus German alternatives. Normally we shall give both forms. If in doubt, we tend to use the spelling which the person concerned used in his lifetime (Went, not Wendt or Vent, and so on). For the names of rulers and the like, we have used R F Tapsell 1983 *Monarchs, Rulers, Dynasties and Kingdoms of the World;* London: Thames and Hudson. Where this is not sufficient, we have usually followed *HCRL/1-5*.

Composers and arrangers are listed alphabetically. By "composer" we mean the person who provided the first wind version. Thus arrangements of Mozart by Went are found in our composer list under Went, referenced to Mozart, and in the arrangements list of the *Catalog* under Mozart. Where available, we provide information on dates and places of birth and death. If a composer's date of birth is unknown, we provide an "effective date." This is done as follows: Subtract 25 years from the earliest date at which the composer was active or his work was published; then round down the date to the start of that particular decade. Thus a composer writing in the early 1760s (Haydn) will be listed as born in (1730), for 1762 - 25 = 1737 rounds down to 1730. Clearly, such estimates are merely an indicator, but they are an aid in relating the work of a little-known composer to that of major figures. The "effective date of birth" is always shown in parentheses (1730) to distinguish it from known dates. For each composer, the works are presented in a standard order and are given a systematic reference number. The lists in the *Catalog* use these same reference numbers. A typical reference number has the form **ABC-1**, where C is the first letter of the composer's family name, A is usually the first letter of the composer's given name, and B may or may not be the first letter of the composer's middle name.

We separate works into wind harmony, vocal music with winds, and military music; in appropriate cases, we treat funeral music as a further class. These classes are indicated by an extra letter in the reference number (so **ABC-1v** would be vocal music with winds, **ABC-1m** military wind music, and so on). Within each division, we list works in decreasing order of size, to help readers find works for a chosen ensemble. In very rare cases (such as Krommer's published works) we ignore minor differences in scoring and follow chronological order instead; major differences are still retained, e.g., sextets after octets. If any further organization is needed, we use some explicit scheme, like shelf marks, to make sense of a long list of works. No ordering will satisfy all users, but our approach is one which we know works well in practice. Our scheme cannot do anything to help Anonymous, that great enricher of all forms of art, for whom we can only offer a place in the later tables. Since these reference numbers will be of value outside these volumes, we remark that we do plan to keep our full lists up to date, as new works become known. However, we do not plan to revise the numbers of works in our lists at the time of printing: Krommer's **FVK-1** will stay **FVK-1**, even if larger works appear. A stable numbering scheme is essential if music publishers and recording companies are to be able to tell their customers what they are selling.

Those familiar with other substantial lists, like *Whitwell* will note some major differences. One is organizational: we have made a special effort to give a tested structure which works well. A second difference is that we list very many works and locations which were not available previously. Thirdly, we have resolved a large number of anomalies (such as duplications and problems with secondary sources) inevitable in previous pioneering studies. Finally, we omit certain classes of wind works which are included in *Whitwell*, because they are too big, too small, of the wrong character (e.g. brass ensemble), or appear to be lost (in a very few cases we give works where we believe copies survive but for which we have no location). We have extensive lists (not given here) of works which we have decided lie outside the scope of our book.

Suspicions and Deceptions: Dubious and Spurious Works

A sure sign of a composer's success is seen when publishers issue large numbers of his works. A still better sign is that works by other composers are published under his or her name. While good music librarians will create a section "Dubious and Supposititious," record companies usually lack inhibitions on record sleeves, so the more popular composer gains a "new work." The demand for recorded music makes "just one more work by Mozart" tempting, even when much of the authentic music of great composers is still not available.

Sometimes, at least, these deceptions can be self-deception rather than malpractice, and need not be harmful. Listeners can be very conservative, and some admirable works have been revived solely because they were believed to be by one of the select "great composers." Nor is the distinction between genuine and spurious clear. Consider these possibilities: (a) entirely genuine work by X; (b) poor work by X that X would like to disown (Picasso is said to have remarked, "Sometimes I paint fake Picassos"); (c) poor edition, perhaps a work by X written down from memory or an incomplete text; (d) transcription by Y of a work by X; (e) work by Y on themes by X; (f) a work by Y trying to mimic X's style; (g) a work by Y labelled wrongly because of scholarly ignorance, commercial greed, or error. We shall list cases (a,b and c) as genuine X, cases (d and e) as arrangements or original works to be listed under Y but cross-referenced under X, and (f and g) as spurious X, to be listed under Y if Y is known. In our lists, we add a qualifier "d" for works which we do not believe to be correctly attributed (so **WAM-1d** is highly unlikely to be by Mozart). We use another qualifier "c" to identify conjectures based largely on circumstantial evidence. Thus, no one but Went is known to have arranged for the Schwarzenberg Harmonie; a work **JNW-1c** could be for that ensemble, and credibly by Went, but with only inconclusive evidence for the attribution.

Since we accept that we ourselves could be guilty of scholarly fallibility, we state here the criteria we use in cases of doubt. Key criteria are provenance and style. Provenance includes the nature of early copies (copyist; internal dates; watermarks; publisher; locations of libraries which hold copies), the background (which players, what occasion), and historical references (if X is known to have composed an octet, we may be more easily persuaded that some unidentified octet is that one). Style, a well-known deceiver, includes factors such as the level of technical correctness (so Mozart would not have written parallel fifths, except for effect), relation to other works by that composer, and the more subjective "sound" to the listener and "feel" to the player. None of these guides is decisive and, even taken together, they can only ensure that one's judgment is better informed.

Coverage

For larger works, our general rule is to omit those with more than 18 players, which allows us the big Strauss works (16 players) and the wind ensemble of a standard classical orchestra (2fl 2ob 2cl 2bn 2tp 4hn 3tb tu). For smaller works, we exclude those without pairs of instruments, so wind quintets are usually omitted. We usually ignore works for fewer than 4 players. We break these rules in two ways. We shall mention within the biographies some works for winds outside our scope (and hence not in the *Catalog*), if they provide a context for the central repertory. We shall also use our privileges as authors to include a few works we feel are relevant. These might be half-harmony (typically ob cl hn bn) or a special large-scale work. Usually these are pieces of a sort which a regular wind ensemble might wish to keep in its repertory.

References and Recordings

Our references to other sources of information are not exhaustive. The references are either necessary, when material is not easily found, or else they offer useful further information or background. Information on recordings presents a challenge to even the most diligent. The same performance may be available in one month in two countries on two labels with two numbers, and available in neither country the following month. It may then be reissued in combination with different works a year later, and broadcast by a foreign radio station without identification. We take the view that it is better to know some facts than none; we give numbers where available, we give basic details where available, and we mention the existence of recordings for which we have little more than an announcer's introduction. There are experts in most countries who can help the reader who needs to investigate further. These include the major retailers, and also the national branches of the International Association of Sound Archives.

Biographical Information

ABEL, Carl (Karl) Friedrich *22 Dec 1723, Cöthen-20 June 1787, London* Composer of symphonies and other music, Abel was viola da gamba player and chamber musician to Queen Charlotte, wife of King George III. He organized concert series in London from 1765 with his friend, J C Bach, whose name appears on some copies of Abel's *Due Marce di Cavalleria e d'Infanteria le Prince Wallis de la Gran Bretagna d'un Regimento di Dragoni* (the Prince of Wales's 3rd Regiment of Dragoon Guards). We cannot rule out the possibility that the *Buckingham March*, by "Able," is actually by C F Abel.

ABINGTON, William *(1765)* Lieutenant in the 1st Regiment of Royal East India Volunteers. His *Royal East India Slow March* is dedicated to Col Inglis, and the corresponding *Quick March* to Col Scott, both belonging to the Regiment.

ACERBI, Domenico *(1830-active 1859-1870s)* Composer of church music with winds. I-Vsmc has many fragmentary sets of parts by Acerbi; some may be for winds.

ADAM, Adolphe Charles *24 Jun 1803, Paris-3 May 1856, Paris* Composer influenced by Boieldieu, writing successful ballets like *Giselle* and opéras-comiques. His 1841 *Marche* was for the "translation des cendres de Napoleon" (see also Auber). The names of the players are written on the F-Pn parts. They show that a large band was used, with 8 first clarinets; 12 ophycleides [sic] played one part. The ink on some parts has run, suggesting the weather was poor for that early performance. Napoleon's remains were moved from St Helena and received at the Hôtel des Invalides on 15 December 1840. The final transfer was not until 1861, as the tomb remained to be built.

ADAMS, Thomas *(1775)* Organist of St George's, Camberwell.

ADDISON, John *b 16 Mar 1920, Chobham, Surrey, UK* Professor of Composition from 1951 at the Royal College of Music, where his studies were interrupted for six years by war. His teachers included Gordon Jacob (qv), Leon Goossens (for oboe) and Frederick Thurston (for clarinet). His 1949 *Sextet for Woodwind* was performed at the 1951 Frankfurt festival of the International Society for Contemporary Music.

ADOLPH I.K.H.P. We do not know if "Adolph" is a forename or surname; the letters may be a motto. He composed a *Quadrille ex Ex* (E♭) for the Clam-Gallas Harmonie.

AGRELL (Agrelli), Johann Joachim (Giovanni) *1 Feb 1701, Löth, East Gotland-19 Jan 1765, Nuremburg* After studies at Linköping and at Uppsala University, he became court musician in Kassel in 1723, then conductor to the city of Nuremberg in 1746.

AHL, C. (le cadet) *(1780)* Arranger of operas by Paer and Weigl for 2cl 2hn 2bn.

AHLBERG, Gunnar *b 29 Mar 1942, Mora, Sweden* His 1984 *Fluente* is for 2fl 2cl b-cl bn; he has also written a wind quintet, *Impulse*.

AIBLINGER, Johann Caspar *23 Feb 1779, Wasserburg, Bavaria-6 May 1867, Munich*

Conductor and composer, holding posts at Vicenza, Venice and Munich, where he was Kapellmeister for the Italian opera from 1819 and court conductor from 1823. During a period at Bergamo from 1833, he developed his interest in early music. Apart from parts of his one opera, *Rodrigo und Zemene* (1821) his music for winds was primarily for the church or for state occasions, e.g. welcome songs and military hymns.

ALBINONI, Tomaso   *14 June 1671, Venice-17 Jan 1751, Venice*   Financially independent, the self-styled "dilettante Veneto" was wholly professional in the art of composition. Three of the works for winds under his name (*Whitwell/7* p 192, 1, 2) may all be spurious (1), but have merit and are recognizably precursors of wind harmony. The *Concerto à cinque:* **TXA-5** (in F) has been recorded by Karl Haas and the London Baroque Ensemble (two oboes d'amore, two horns and bassoon) on Vanguard SRV 192 SD, reissued on Ricordi OCL 16007.

1. Michael Talbot 1990 *Tomaso Albinoni;* Oxford: Oxford University Press.
2. Bruce Haynes 1992 *Music for Oboe 1650-1800;* Berkeley, CA: Fallen Leaf Press.

ALBRECHTSBERGER, Johann Georg *3 Feb 1736, Klosterneuburg-7 Mar 1809, Vienna* Famous for his contrapuntal skill, he taught Beethoven, Weigl, Eybler, Seyfried and others. His one wind work, *Serenata,* **JGA-1,** was written late in his career (1806).

ALCOCK, John *11 Apr 1715, London-23 Feb 1806, Lichfield*   Distinguished as an organist, Alcock was a pupil of the famous blind organist, John Stanley. As a young chorister, he sang for Handel, and his choral training shows in some excellent works, including ones with church wind bands. Alcock's 1771 *Six and Twenty Anthems in Score* includes a list of works, biographical details, and a Preface asserting that, while some people have said Alcock's music resembled that of Maurice Greene and others, it was his (Alcock's) which came first. The splendid small work **JYA-1** *Let chearful Smiles in ev'ry Face. A favourite hymn for Christmas Day, 1779,* has an introduction and coda for two oboes and bassoon in the best tradition of Boyce. His instrumentation, though not his style, resembles that of the small church bands in Bohemia and Moravia. The anthem *Behold how Good* also has an opening symphony scored for two oboes and bassoon, though just what these winds play later is less clear, apart from specific instrumental sections, especially those in the third verse. The plates of the *Six New Anthems for Two, Three and Four Voices, with Two Hautboys and a Bassoon, and figured for the Organ,* indicate dates 1778 (Nos 1-4) and 1779 (Nos 5, 6). The first three are by John Alcock, the Younger (1740-1791); they have only organ accompaniment, although No 3 includes a section for "Bass Solo with Accompanyments for 2 Bassoons."

ALEXIUS (Alessio), František (Francesco) *1717-1780*   A prolific composer of nearly 50 parthias; the little that is known suggests that he was musician and composer for Count Pachta. The wind works by Alexius date from 1768 to c.1780, and are pleasantly typical of early wind harmony. They fall into three groups: those for 2ob 2hn (2)bn, those for 2taille 2hn 2bn, and those for 2cl 2hn (2)bn. The works with taille are unusual, for there are later alternative parts for alto clarinets in E♭. Clarinets are suggested as alternatives to oboes in later comments on the title pages; similar comments are found on other works for the Pachta Harmonie. Some of the parthias by Alexius appear too at Donaueschingen (D-DO). We believe these to be copies of the Pachta parthias, along with other works for winds by Asplmayr and Pichl.

ALKAN, Charles Henri Valentin (pseudonym of C H V MORHANGE) *30 Nov 1813, Paris-29 Mar 1888, Paris*   A composer and recluse, who was deeply interested in the occult, Alkan had perhaps the most formidable piano technique of his time, certainly in the same class as Liszt. The inevitably enormous demands of his finest piano works have led to their neglect today, although this has been remedied by excellent recordings. Many of Alkan's works show a trace of black humor, and a funeral march on the death of a parrot is no exception. **CHA-1v** *Marcia funebre sulla morte d'un pappagallo* was composed in 1859. The text is the composer's own, comprising just eight words: in the first section, the singers repeat "As-tu déjeuné, Jaco?" (the French version of "Polly want a cracker?"); in the second section, "Et de quoi?" ("And what?"); in the last, realizing the bird is dead, "Ah". We do not know which was the parrot that died, but when Alkan's illegitimate son, pianist Élie Delaborde, took refuge from the Franco-Prussian War, he brought 121 cockatoos and parrots to London in 1870. French literary life was somewhat preoccupied with parrots at the time (see, e.g., J Barnes 1984 *Flaubert's Parrot;* London: Jonathan Cape). Raymond Lewenthal (whose recording of **CHA-1v** is on CBS Classics CBS 61117), mentions that Delaborde later kept two pet apes, Sara and Isidor; what might Alkan have written for their funerals?

ALPAERTS, Flor *12 Sept 1876, Antwerp-5 Oct 1954, Antwerp*   Professor at Antwerp Conservatoire from 1903, and Director from 1934 until his retirement in 1941. He is well known for his impressionistic music, and for his skill as conductor and teacher.

ALYABYEV, Aleksander Alexandrovich *15 Aug 1787 Tobolsk, Siberia-6 Mar 1851 Moscow*   One of the earliest Russian composers to be noticed outside his own country. His song, *The Nightingale* was often used in the singing lesson in Rossini's *Il Barbiere di Siviglia.* After his discharge from a chequered army career, he was accused of murder and exiled to Siberia. Most of his music dates from after his return to Moscow in the 1830s. There is said to be a *Symphony for Winds* c.1830 (1), but we have not traced a copy. The modern edition of **AAA-1** *Quintet in E♭* is for 2tp 2hn tb (there is a much less satisfactory version for fl ob cl hn bn), though we think it probable that the original used woodwinds. Keyed bugles and trombones might have managed the parts, but the writing suits clarinets and bassoon far better. This aside, it is an original work, at times reminiscent of Weber. The rich, dark-colored introduction in E♭ minor leads to a fast main section mixing the romantic with somewhat academic fugal passages. At the end, the slow and sombre music of the introduction reappears.
1. Gottfried Veit 1972 *Die Blasmusik;* Innsbruck, p 60.

AMALIE, *Princess of Prussia* *1723-1787*   Her marches raise the question: Did she score them herself? Or was this done by another, like her teacher, Franz Benda? The marches are for the regiments of General F de Millendorf [Moellendorf], Comte Lottum (dated 29 March 1767), General Bülow (14 August 1767) and General Saldern (16 May 1769).

AMANTINO, ( ) *(c.1730)*   His name may be Italianized from a Czech or German original. He was probably employed by Count Pachta, since his attractive, if unexciting, *Divertimentos* for 2ob 2hn 1(2)bn survive only in the Pachta collection. A later addition "ò Clarinetti" dates from when the Pachta Harmonie changed instrumentation.

AMBROZ, Anton   Kapellmeister, kk Österreich 57. Linien-Infanterie Regiment, Grossherzog von Mecklenburg-Schwerin.

AMON, Johann Andreas (André) *1763, Bamberg-29 Mar 1825 Wallerstein?*   Amon was Musical Director at Heilbronn from 1789 until his move to Paris c.1790. At first he was a horn player, a pupil of Punto (Stich); after a serious illness, he became a violinist and pianist. From 1817 he was Musical Director at Oettingen-Wallerstein. He may be related to Ignaz Amon, a music publisher at Heilbronn, who issued a set of marches including the *Coloredo March* sometimes attributed to Haydn (see under Weinmann, **AXW-1ma**).

AMOS, Keith *b 1939*   Amos has written a *Concertino for Two Clarinets* with winds, as well as a number of both larger and smaller works for wind ensembles.

ANDRÉ, Johann Anton *6 Oct 1775, Offenbach am Main-6 Apr 1842, Offenbach am Main* Member of a German musical family and a successful publisher who allied himself with Senefelder, the inventor of lithography.

ANDREOZZI, Gaetano *22 May 1775, Aversa-21 Dec 1826, Paris*   Pupil of Jommelli; Master of the Royal Chapel, Naples. One of his marches was printed in London.

ANDRIESSEN, Jurriaan *b 15 Nov 1925 Haarlem*   Dutch composer active as a music consultant to Dutch National Radio and Television. He studied under van Otterloo (qv) at Utrecht Conservatory, graduating in 1947. While a student, he wrote a *Hommage à Milhaud* for fl ob cl bn sax hn tpt tbn vn va vc. He then went to Paris, studying film composition and also with Messiaen, returning to Holland in 1948, where his *Het wonderlijk uur* for wind band won the 1948 J Wagenaar Prize at Utrecht. Andriessen spent part of 1949-1950 at Tanglewood, working under Copland and Koussevitsky. His wind music is wide-ranging, also including works with electronics (his 1976 *The Cave* is for 12 woodwinds, 4 keyboards and electronics) and smaller works (the wind quintet *Sciarada spagnuola* of 1962). There are several works which use small numbers of strings, as found too in the 18th century. Examples include his 1971 *Ars antiqua musicae* (fl ob 2hn tp gtr vla perc) and his 1967 *Les bransles éxotiques, pantomime musicale au XVIième siècle* (3ob ca 2vla hpcd perc). He has written much music for The Hague Theatre Company as their resident composer. The *Concertino for solo bassoon and winds* (a rare combination) is recorded by Robert Thompson with the English Chamber Orchestra under Geoffrey Simon on Chandos CHAN 9278. The *Respiration Suite* (1962, JZA-3) was commissioned by the 22nd International Congress of Physiological Sciences, and is dedicated to Dr Wallace O Fenn, a physiologist. Its structure reflects its origin: a Blood-Air dialogue; a Deep Sea Sarabande; a menuet at High Altitude; and Flowing Air, a tarantella reminiscent of the sarabande, and giving a dynamic impression of air moving into and out of lungs. It is recorded by the Amsterdam Wind Ensemble/Blomhert on STH-CD 19053. **Hendrik A Andriessen** (1892-1981) and **Louis A Andriessen** (b 6 June 1939, Utrecht), of the same family, have also written wind works.

ANGERER, Paul *b 16 May 1927, Vienna*   From 1972, Angerer was the Director of the South German Orchestra, Pforzheim.

APEL, ( ) ?David Aaron Apell *Kassel, 1754-after 1806*   Counsellor of War, and composer of the *Kronprinz Marsch.*

ARENSKY, Anton Stepanovich *11 Aug 1861, Novgorod-25 Feb 1906, Terijoki, Finland* Pupil of Rimsky-Korsakov; from 1882 Professor at the Moscow Conservatoire, and from 1894, Director of the Imperial Chapel at St Petersburg. Composer of much church music and of three operas, one using folk tunes.

ARICI, Marco *1778, Foresto, Italy-1827, Chiari*   Organist at Palazzola, Rovato, Martinengo and Maestro di Capella at Chiari. Many of his works are in Brescia.

ᐢ **ARNE, Thomas Augustine** *12 Mar 1710, London-5 Mar 1778, London* Success in writing for the London public demanded that Arne know what appealed on stage and in pleasure gardens and how to write effectively for winds. Winds dominate in "Rule Britannia" from Arne's masque *Alfred*, so much so that, with minimal changes, it can be performed with only voices and winds (for *authentic* performance, note the text reads "Britons never will [not *shall*] be slaves," which does not imply complacent expectation).

Artaxerxes contains Arne's finest wind writing, remarkably advanced for 1762, and admired by Haydn. The full score is one of the few of 18th century English operas to survive; publishing economics meant that, after 1770, vocal scores were the norm, and disastrous fires at Covent Garden (1808) and Drury Lane (1809) destroyed unique scores and parts. In several numbers, the string parts are almost superfluous: "In infancy, our hopes and fears" (pp 86-89; clarinets, horns, bassoons), "Fair Aurora" (pp 16-19; oboes, horns and bassoons) and "Water parted from the Sea" (pp 134-137; clarinets, horns, bassoons). In *Thomas and Sally,* stage instructions read "Half the following symphony is played behind the scenes at the further end. Then the Horns and Clarinets come on sounding the rest of the symphony, several huntsmen follow, and last of all the Squire." This chorus, with tenor solo, neither indicates nor needs a bass, but a bassoon may have helped to keep the chorus in tune. Arne's hunters are much livelier than those in Beethoven's comparable *Jagdlied* in the *Musik zum Ritterballet,* WoO 1, No 3.

Arne's horn writing in his operas and masques presents problems as regards the correct octave. Arne, like Dibdin but few others, shifts clef, rather than telling the player which crook to use. The horns in *Thomas and Sally,* act 1 scene 1 are surely not in C alto, as a modern score has them: the engraver has merely economized so both clarinet and horn parts are on one stave. Similarly, the score of "Fair Aurora, prithee stay" in *Artaxerxes* indicates G basso, which should be perfectly manageable.

ARNELL, Richard (Anthony Sayer) *b 15 September 1917, London* Composer of highly effective music appreciated by such discerning musicians as Beecham and Karl Haas; he is also the composer of a wind quintet. The four movements of the *Serenade* Op 57, **RAA-1,** are a serious-minded Prelude, a witty and brief Scherzo, a Canzona, and an exhilarating dance-like finale entitled "Ballet." It was recorded in 1949 by the London Baroque Ensemble/Haas on CCL 30120 (also Collection ZCGC 7054).

ARNOLD, (Sir) Malcolm Henry *b 21 October 1921 Northampton* Once the principal trumpet of the London Philharmonic Orchestra, he has been outstandingly versatile, and has written some of this century's wittiest music. This includes music for the Hoffnung Festivals, and the *Three Sea Shanties* for wind quintet. The *Trevelyan Suite, Op 96,* **MHA-1,** was written for the opening of Trevelyan College, University of Durham. It is in three movements: the first is Palindrome: Allegro spiritoso and, true to its title, does play the same backwards. The second, Nocturne, uses the cello (or 2bn) as soloist(s). The final movement is Apotheosis: Maestoso.

ARRIEU, Claude *30 November 1903, Paris-7 Mar 1990, Paris* One of France's most eminent women composers, she has written much for smaller wind ensembles, including a *Wind Quintet in C* and a *Concertino* for wind quintet and orchestra (or piano). A pupil of Dukas, she wrote inventively and with a light touch. Nor was she afraid of C major; indeed, her 1967 *Dixtuor pour Instruments à Vent,* **CLA-1,** ends in that key. It is a fine work, lasting only about 11 minutes, in five movements, each with subsections. The instruments are best placed in two groups (2fl ob 2cl 2bn) (tb hn tp).

ASCHE, W *(1840)* Kapellmeister, 1st Hanseatic Regiment, Hamburg.

ASHLEY, Josiah *1780, Bath-1830, Bath* Oboist and flautist; elder brother of bassoonist John Ashley of Bath. His *Royal Dorsetshire March,* "as Repeatedly Perform'd before their Majesties at Weymouth," was "Composed expressly for that occasion."

ASIOLI, Bonifacio *30 Aug 1769, Correggio-18 May 1832, Correggio*   Maestro di Cappella first in Correggio, then in Turin from 1787, in Venice from 1796 to 1799, and in Milan as Director of Music to the Viceroy, Eugène Beauharnais (Eugène Napoleon; see also under Bitterman and Pfeilstücker). When the Austrians regained Milan in 1814, Asioli lost his position and returned to his birthplace. We have no locations for Asioli's *2 Sextets* of 1817 (cl 2hn bn va pf; Milan c.1820), or his *16 kleine Quartetten* (also 1817) for cl 2hn bn. Asioli's orchestral works in I-Vsmc have a bassoon part; we believe that the bassoonist read off the organ bass for other works listed. I-Vsmc also has many fragmentary sets of parts, of which some may have been for winds alone. He was the teacher of Mozart's son Carl, and also of Pugni (qv) and Soliva (qv).

ASPLMAYR (Aspelmayr, Asplmaÿr, Aspelmayer), Franz (Francesco) D? *(baptized) 4 Apr 1728, Linz-29 July 1786, Vienna* Like his near contemporary Starzer, Asplmayr wrote extensively for the choreographer Noverre at the Kärntnertor Theater in Vienna. Asplmayr was Secretarius to Count Morzin from 1759 to 1760, at much the same time as Haydn, though we know of no direct links. Leopold Mozart believed Asplmayr to be one of the schemers who prevented production of Mozart's *La finta semplice* in Vienna in 1767-1768. Asplmayr's wind music is conventional, though with interesting features. There is, for example, the *Partitta a 2 chori* **FDA-1,** for two wind bands. As in Handel's far greater works, each band consists of 2ob 2hn bn. Some parthias have distinctive names: *Partitta di Campagnia,* presumably outdoor music, and *Partitta da Camera,* probably for use indoors. Six of Asplmayr's partitas provide an interesting snapshot of the diffusion of early wind harmony. These works were published prior to 1778 in versions for 2fl/vl 2hn violone/cello bn(doubling) in a printed version by Guera in Lyons (as Op I) and in manuscript by Breitkopf in Leipzig (listed in their catalog, Supplement XII, 1778), scored for 2fl 2hn bn. Five of the six works appear in the Pachta collection in CZ-Pnm for 2ob 2hn (2)bn, with the second (XXII.A.195) being in autograph dated 1769. Four of the Breitkopf & Härtel MSS (Nos 2-4, 6) remain in the Clam Gallas collection. Several of Asplmayr's partitas were acquired by the Donaueschingen Harmonie, probably around 1775-1780 and probably copied from the Pachta copies (as were many works by Alexius and Pichl). There are at least 66 original partitas.

FDA-5 *Concertino à 7 Strumenti* (2ob 2talia 2hn bn). Of interest for the markings on its parts: the Talia Primo part has a pencil doodle enclosing the name Went, in line with the view that Went was the principal cor anglais player in the Schwarzenberg Harmonie. The suggestion of flutes instead of oboes is a later addition.

FDA-11 *Partitta di Campagnia in D,* 1768. This work may be an arrangement of a ballet. The opening Andante bears the secondary title "Morgen Segen" (morning blessing).

FDA-14 *Partitta in F,* 1769. An attractive, if simple, three-movement work. After the opening Andante, the Minuet has three trios (the first for 2ob bn; the second for 2hn bn, with oboes from bar 5; the third for 2ob bn, with horns entering in bar 5). The final Presto begins with a typical hunting flourish from the horns and bassoon.

FDA-30 *Partitta in C,* for 2cl/ob 2hn bn. The MS, dated c.1790, appears to be a copy of a work c.1770. The work may be an arrangement of a ballet, rather than a compilation of several partitas; there are 14 movements.

FDA-36 *Parthia ex D à 5 Strumenti,* c.1770. This *Parthia* has 6 movements, starting with a Marche and ending with a typical hunting movement. One trio is for 2ob bn only.

FDA-38 *Partitta, in D* The 9 movements of this *Partitta* constitute a suite whose length could be adjusted to need. It begins with a Marche.

FDA-39 *Partitta, in G* The 7 movements include an "Allegro staccato".

FDA-1a (-7a) These works, dating from c.1770-1774, are among the earliest Austro-Bohemian arrangements for winds. They are similar to works by J C Bach (**JCB-3**) and Mozart (**WAM-2**) in that the arrangements are contained within "original" partitas. Apart from two movements from Salieri's opera *La fiera di Venezia* and one from Gluck's *Paride,* the works arranged are all ballets by Asplmayr and Starzer.

FDA-1ad, -2ad *Alexandre et Campaspe de Larisse; Die kleine Weinlese* These arrangements, found in the Clam-Gallas archives in CZ-Pnm, may be by Asplmayr himself. *Die kleine Weinlese* was previously believed to be lost in any version.

ASSMAYER, Ignaz *11 Feb 1790, Salzburg-31 Aug 1862, Vienna* A pupil of Salieri, and a member of the Imperial Harmonie in Vienna. In his early career, Assmayer was encouraged by Salzburg musicians like Michael Haydn, Brunnmayr, and Gerl. His Eb *Octet* is recorded by the Consortium Classicum/Klöcker on Koch Schwann 110002.

ATTERBERG, Kurt *12 Dec 1887, Göteborg-15 Feb 1974, Stockholm* Cellist, Royal Dramatic Theater conductor (1913-1922) and engineer, from 1912 to 1940 in the Swedish Royal Patent Office. A composer of colorful romantic music, often using folk melodies.

ATTWOOD, Thomas *23 Nov 1765, London-24 Mar 1838, London* One of Mozart's favourite pupils (for his minuets, corrected by Mozart, see Musical Review 1946 7 166), friend of Mendelssohn, and later composer to the Chapel Royal. Attwood is buried under the organ of St Paul's Cathedral. His *Royal Exchange March* was "Composed and

Inscribed to Lieut Colonel Birch and the Rest of the Officers of the Royal Exchange, or First Regiment of Loyal London Volunteers."

AUBER, Daniel François Esprit *29 Jan 1782-12 May 1871, Paris*   A successful opera composer, whose wind music includes an *Andantino*, a setting of *O Dieu puissant, Dieu créator* for SATB 2cl 2bn, and several marches. His 1841 *Marche*, like that of Adam (qv) relates to the translation of Napoleon's remains to Les Invalides.

AUBÉRY du BOULLEY, Prudent Louis *9 Dec 1796, Verneuil-28 Jan 1870, Verneuil*   His *Cantate pour les réunions de Ste Cécile*, to a text by M. Darde de Longuy, is dedicated to "Monsieurs les Membres de la Société Philharmonique de l'Eure, de l'Orne et Loir." One assumes that in 1836, when it was published, the Société was all male.

d'AUBIGNY, L *(1830)*   Organist at Poitiers Cathedral. His *Prière* for solo oboe 2cl 2hn 2bn 2vla was first performed on 1 Nov 1867 by members of the Société des Concerts et de l'Opéra at the Société académique des Enfants d'Apolon (MM. Berthélemy, Leroy, Jancourt, Schlottmann, Dupont, Duprez, Villaufraut, Adams, Millaus).

AVONI, Petronino *(1770; Bolognese)*   Composer of *Armonia* for 2fl 2ob 2cl 2hn 2bn, sometimes with 2tp b-tb, based on themes of Paisiello, Cimarosa and Paer. Avoni was first clarinet at the Teatro Communale, Bologna, from 1797-1826. He is styled "Il S[ignore] Prof Avoni" on **PYA-1**, which comprises variations on a theme of Paisiello. Avoni was the first professor of clarinet at the Bologna Conservatoire from 1812 (prior to 1812, the oboist Giuseppe Casa taught both oboe and clarinet).

AVSHALOMOV, Jacob *b 28 Mar 1919, Tsingtao, China (US citizen from 1944)*   His large-scale and impressive *Inscriptions at the City of Brass*, an Oriental fantasy based on the Arabian Nights, was first performed in New York in 1958, conducted by the composer.

BACH, Carl (Karl) Philipp Emanuel *8 Mar 1714, Weimar-15 Dec 1788, Hamburg*
J S Bach's second son, famous as a virtuoso keyboard player and as a composer who catalyzed the change from the baroque to the classical. For most of his career, he was domestic musician and principal harpsichord player to Frederick the Great, a cultured musician of distinction whose armies destroyed in the Seven Years' War much of a civilized way of life sympathetic to music. Despite Frederick's interest in military music, all Bach's wind music dates from after 1767, when he succeeded Telemann in Hamburg. There Bach wrote for the five main churches, but he was able to compose for others too (1). Some of the wind works might have been for performance in the parks in Hamburg (see part 1), presumably after 1773, since they are not mentioned in his autobiography (2). Most of the wind harmony works also exist in smaller forms (e.g. cl bn hpcd). Burney described Bach in Hamburg as "rather short in stature, with black hair and eyes and brown complexion; and has a very animated countenance" (3).
CPB-1 (-6) *6 Piccole Sonate* (Wq184; H629-H634) (4).   These six Sonatas date from about 1775, and are works of great originality. Flutes are not mere oboe substitutes, but have idiomatic parts. Both in style (with typical C P E Bach idiosyncrasies) and keys (D, F, G, E♭, A, C) these lovely and imaginative works lie outside the fashion of the time. They are recorded by Karl Haas with the London Baroque Ensemble (PMB 1004) and with oboes instead of flutes (and with a few phrases discreetly lowered an octave) by Melbourne Windpower/Richard Runnels on Move MD 3082.
CPB-7, 8 *2 Kleine Stücke* (Wq186; H620).   Headed "Langsam und traurig" (slow and sad; in C) and "Sanft und etwas langsam" (softly, somewhat slow; in F). c.1767.
CPB-1m (-6m) *6 Kleine Stücke oder Märsche* (Wq185; H614-H619).   These short works are recorded by the Netherlands Wind Ensemble on Philips 6599 172 (now 652 7117).
CPB-7m, 8m *2 Märsche* (Wq187; H637).   These two marches, for an ensemble similar to that Telemann used in Hamburg, are recorded on Philips 6599 172 (now 652 7117).

1. E Reeser, p 30 of *The Sons of Bach,* Continental Book Co, Stockholm.
2. C P E Bach's autobiographical sketch (1773) is translated by William S Newman 1965 as *Emanuel Bach's Autobiography* in Musical Quarterly 15 363-372.
3. *Burney* (or p 28 of Reeser [1]).
4. *Wq* numbers refer to: A Wotquenne 1905 *C Ph Em Bach Thematisches Verzeichnis seiner Werke;* Breitkopf & Härtel, Leipzig. *H* numbers refer to: E Helm 1989 *Thematic Catalogue of the Works of C P E Bach;* New Haven, CT: Yale University Press.

BACH, Johann (John) Christian *5 Sept 1735, Leipzig-1 Jan 1782, London*   J S Bach had eleven sons by his two wives. The youngest, and half-brother to Carl Philipp Emanuel, was Johann Christian Bach (1). He came to England in 1762 and, apart from brief visits to the Continent, remained in and around London until his death. "You have probably heard the English Bach is dead," wrote Mozart (2), "What a loss to the musical world." Mozart was particularly indebted to the "English" Bach. The two first met during Mozart's childhood visit to London. Mutual respect lasted much longer. In Mozart's A major *Piano Concerto* K.414, written soon after Bach's death, the elegiac slow movement is based on Bach's Overture *La calamita de cuori.* Bach had composed the overture to an opera by Galuppi twenty years earlier, a few months before Mozart arrived in London. Mozart may have recalled the piece in a trio for basset horns (the fourth movement of No 4 of K.439b). Alfred Einstein remarks on the similarity of style of Mozart and Bach (3); one might say that the differences between Haydn and Mozart arise because one knew C P E Bach, the other J C Bach.

JCB-1-6 *Sei Sinfonia pour deux Clarinettes, deux Cors de Chasse et Basson*   In fact, numbers 2, 3, 4 and 6 need two bassoons; even numbers 1 and 5 can benefit from doubling. The arrangements within them suggest that they were written in 1778 or later, perhaps for performance at Vauxhall Gardens. They may well be the *Musique Militaire* by J C Bach announced in *The Public Advertiser* of 3 March 1780 by Longman and Broderip, who published the set in 1782. The *Symphonies* are typical of the best pleasure garden music, showing not only an elegant style and grace of melody, but a natural understanding of the clarinet, and a depth of feeling and a sense of structure beyond that of most of his contemporaries. Those who visited the pleasure gardens were privileged indeed. The *Symphonies* are recorded by the London Wind Soloists/Brymer (Decca LXT6337), by the Camden Wind Ensemble (Pye GSGC 15029, reissued as ZCGC 2033; it is not clear why they use B♭ alto horns in No 2 [3rd movement] and No 4 [1st movement]) and by Consortium Classicum/Klöcker (Harmonia Mundi MDG 3434).

JCB-1 *Symphony No 1 in E♭*   Only one bassoon is needed. The March (the third movement) also exists in keyboard form. There is some attractive horn writing.

JCB-2 *Symphony No 2 in B♭*   The final Rondeau is based on the Larghetto first movement of Boccherini's 1773 *Ballet Espagnol* (G.526/i), also used by Françaix in his *Scuola di Ballo.* The March (third movement) has no trio.

JCB-3 *Symphony No 3 in E♭*   The Andante is based on the act 2 ballet of Gluck's *Armide,* which means this symphony must date from after 1777. Since Bach probably first heard the opera in Paris in 1778, this *Symphony* is likely to date from that year. This is the best of the set, with a strong symphonic first movement containing an example - rare in wind music - of a Mannheim crescendo. The excellent Minuet and Trio is related to that in an orchestral *Concerted Symphony* (1 p 288).

JCB-4 *Symphony No 4 in B♭*   The work ends with a Cotillion. The march is very brief.

JCB-6 *Symphony No 6 in B♭*   This work was surely not designed as a whole, but is just a set of pleasant, unrelated movements available when delivery was demanded.

JCB-7(-10) *Four Military Pieces* (4 Quintets; 2cl 2hn bn). Published in 1794 by B Cooke, Dublin, they are dedicated to the "Right Honorable Lord O'Neill, Colonel of the Antrim Militia"(4). Only one copy remains, not an uncommon state of affairs. These shorter works have some fine movements, exploiting imitation in the clarinet and bassoon parts. Not all movements are so successful; Robert Eccles has aptly described the finale of No 2 as a "yard and a half of rondo." Several movements are reminiscent of the Op 3 orchestral *Symphonies* of 1765. All four have been recorded by the French Wind Ensemble (Oiseaux- Lyre OL 50135), and recordings of transcriptions exist.

JCB-1m, 2m *Märsche Nr 1 vom ersten und Nr 2 von zweiten Bataillon Garde-Regiment Hannover* The link with Hanover presumably comes through the extended royal family, the House of Hanover. Bassoons double or double at the octave. The marches have been recorded by the London Military Ensemble on CFP CFP40230.

JCB-3m, 4m *Due Marce di Cavalleria e d'Infanteria della Maestà Regina della Gran Bretagna d'un Regimento di Dragoni*   One march is marked "Marcia zu Fuss," for infantry, the other "Marcia zu Pferde," for cavalry. Only one bassoon is listed, but it may be doubled. There are keyboard versions of both in GB-Lbl.

JCB-5m, 6m, 7m *Marche du Regiment de Prince Ernst; Marche du [Infanterie] Regiment de Braun[schweig]; Marche du [Husaren] Regiment de Wu[e]r[te]mb[erg]* These three *Marche Ex Es di Bach a London*, c.1780, and all for 2ob/fl 2hn basso, survive in Schwerin, close to the original homeland of George III's wife, Sofia Charlotte.

JCB-1d In Madrid (personal communication, Ernest Warburton) is a *Sujto, in Dis No 1* for 2ob/fl 2cl 2hn 2bn under J C Bach's name. The music is not typical of Bach, but strongly resembles that of Mysliveček. "Dis" for E♭ is an Austrian usage (see Part 3).

JCB-1md, 2md Two marches, now believed to be by Abel (qv).

1. C Terry 1967 *John Christian Bach;* London: Oxford University Press.
2. W A Mozart, letter of 10 April 1783 to his father.
3. A Einstein 1936 *A Short History of Music;* London: Cassell.
4. S Sadie 1956 Music and Letters 37 107.

BACH, Johann Christoph Friedrich *21 June 1732, Leipzig-26 Jan 1795, Bückeburg* The eldest surviving son of Anna Magdalena and J S Bach, J C F Bach was the father of W F E Bach. A visit to his brother (J C Bach) in London in 1778 may have stimulated his interest in writing for winds. Rumors that his one wind work is lost are wrong.

BACH, Johann Sebastian *21 March 1685 Eisenach-28 July 1750 Leipzig* J S Bach was a man whose energy was as formidable as his genius. It would take a copyist a whole lifetime, it is said, to copy all his music, let alone compose it. His music for winds, usually with voices, is often outside our main interests. The *Quoniam* of the *B minor Mass* uses with subtlety the unique combination of horn, two bassoons and continuo to accompany the bass (1). The second trio in the *First Brandenburg Concerto* combines adventurous writing for two horns accompanied by three oboes in unison (in the Minuet, the winds double all the strings parts, and at least one recording uses winds alone in a repeat for variety). The instrumental scoring of Cantata 118, *O Jesu Christ, mein's Lebens Licht,* presumably intended for outdoor performance, is so unusual (2 Lituus, cornetto, 3 trombones) that there is doubt about how to perform it. The little *Marche pour la Première Garde du Roy* (2) is not in Schmieder's catalogue, but was recorded by Haas and the London Baroque Ensemble. Bach's use of instruments is highly idiomatic, and shows a wealth of experience. Changes in instruments and technique are especially clear when comparing Haydn's wind writing with Bach's: both used oboes, horns and bassoons; both could rely on virtuoso performers; yet the differences are profound.

Bach's main contribution to wind music was through his sons. J S Bach had two wives: Maria Barbara (1684-1720, mother of W F Bach [qv] and of C P E Bach [qv]) and Anna Magdelena (1701-1760, mother of J C F Bach [qv] and J C Bach [qv]). J C F Bach was the father of W F E Bach (qv), who (not his uncle, W F Bach) who wrote wind music.

1. C S Terry 1932 *Bach's Orchestra;* Oxford: Oxford University Press.

2. P M Young 1970 *The Bachs 1500-1850;* London: J M Dent, p 266.

BACH, Otto *9 Feb 1833, Vienna-3 July 1893, Unterwaltersdorf* The autograph of his large *Trauer Marsch* is dated 1861. His setting for male voices of a poem by Chamisso, based on Beringer uses a typical 19th century ensemble, 2fl 2ob 2cl 4hn 2bn.

BACH, Wilhelm Friedrich Ernst *baptized 24 May 1759, Bückeburg - 25 Dec 1845, Berlin* Two Bachs wrote wind music in London in the years around 1780: J C Bach (the "London" Bach) and his nephew, W F E Bach (not to be confused with W F Bach, his half-uncle). W F E Bach came to London in 1778 with his father and first teacher, J C F Bach. He was just 19 when he arrived, but stayed as a pupil of his uncle until J C Bach's death in 1782. W F E Bach returned to Germany, and was Kapellmeister to the Queens of Frederick William II and III in Berlin from 1789, retiring from court when only 51. He attended the inauguration of J S Bach's statue in Leipzig (23 April 1843), surprising Mendelssohn, who had not expected to see a surviving grandson of J S Bach.

WFB-1 *Parthia in E♭* (2ob/fl 2cl 2hn 2bn). This is clearly by W F E Bach from the autograph in GB-Lbl, where he signs himself W Bach (W F Bach uses both initials). There are six movements. The flute parts are puzzling; as *Hellyer* notes, the flute parts omit sections of the oboe parts, yet cannot double because of internal conflicts.

WFB-2 *Parthia in B♭* The manuscript contains a note by Carl Zoeller, the composer and violist (1840-1889; he would not have known W F E Bach personally) verifying that W F E Bach was the composer.

WFB-3 *5 Konzertstücke (Five Parade Pieces)* The pieces are an Andante with an echo, another Andante, an Allegretto, two Minuets and a Quadrille.

WFB-1m, 2m *Two Marches* The modern edition (edited by D Townsend) suggests that these marches (now in D-Bds) were written for London. We cannot rule out their use in Bückeburg, where *Weston/MCVP* mentions that there were clarinets too. The *Marches* are recorded by Banda Classica/Siegmann on Koch Schwann SCHW 310110.

BACHMANN, (?G ?Anton) *1716, Berlin-8 Mar 1800, Berlin* One of the Berlin-based family of musicians, probably Anton, the inventor of machine screw heads for cellos.

BÄRR, Anton Two sets of Bärr's variations for 2cl 2hn 2bn are now in CZ-KRa.

BAILLIE, R., Miss, (of Mellerstane) *(1760)* Her *Favourite Quick March* dates from 1794, and was written for the Edinburgh Volunteers. We doubt that she was related to the Scottish fiddler, Pate Baillie (1774-1841).

BAINES, Anthony Cuthbert *6 Oct 1912, London-3 Feb 1997, London* Author of major books on the history and development of woodwind and brass instruments.

BAKER, Lance *b 24 May 1947, Birmingham, UK* Son of Ruth Gipps (qv) and of Robert Baker, once principal clarinet with the City of Birmingham Symphony Orchestra. He has arranged Berlioz's *Nuits d'Été* and music by Ravel and Mozart for winds, the first movement of Janáček's *Sinfonietta* for 8hn, and Mozart's *Gigue* K.574 for wind quintet.

BALADA, Leonardo *b 2 Sep 1933, Barcelona* Balada has written a *Concerto for piano, winds and percussion,* as well as his *Sonata* for 10 Winds.

BALL, S. *(1780)* Composer who wrote for the Ipswich Volunteers a *Slow & Quick Marche, with a Funeral March.*

BANNER, John *(1780)* His *March* is for the Loyal London Volunteers (8th Regiment).

BARRÈRE, Georges *31 Oct 1876, Bordeaux-14 June 1944, Kingston, New York* Flautist and pupil of Taffanel who formed the Société Moderne d'Instruments à Vent in 1895, two years after Taffanel's ensemble was disbanded. He was principal flute with the New York Symphony Orchestra from 1905 until his death. He did much to popularize wind music in America, forming the Barrère Ensemble of Wind Instruments, with which he recorded his own arrangement of Elgar's *Salut d'amour.* See also under Griffes.

BARTH, Wilhelm Leberecht *10 May 1774, Grimma-22 Aug 1829, Leipzig*   Arranger of works by Marschner, Paer and Weigl. A fine clarinettist who moved from the Prince of Dessau's employment to play with the Leipzig Gewandhaus Orchestra until 1829.

BARTHÉLÉMON, François-Hippolyte *27 July 1741, Bordeaux-20 July 1808, London* Barthélémon came to England in 1765; he collaborated with Garrick for theater music, and also wrote for pleasure gardens.

BARTÓK, Béla *25 Mar 1881, Nagyszentmiklós, Hungary, now Sînnicolau Mare, Romania- 26 Sept 1945, New York*   Bartók, born in the same year as Enesco, and indeed in what is now the same country, also became a soloist of international calibre as well as a composer. He too was influenced by the folk music of Romania as well as of Hungary, and he too moved to another country later in his life. Bartók, however, did not write any wind music, nor did he use winds as strikingly as he used strings, piano, or percussion. Yet the opening movement of his *Second Piano Concerto* shows many parallels with other works of its day (1931-1932) in using winds alone with the soloist, and Bartók's influence on Hungarian music - including wind music, like that of Seiber - is significant.

BARTOŠ, Jan Zdeněk *4 June 1908, Dvůr Králové-nad-Labem-1 June 1981, Prague* Violinist, later composer who combined modern techniques with romantic and Slavonic traditions; his compositions include operas and symphonic works, one for wind band (the *Promenade Prelude* of 1956). The *Divertimento for Winds*, Op 14, JZB-1, was written for the Chamber Music Association of Professors of the Prague Conservatoire, and was first performed by them on 1 May 1957 at the International Music Festival. Its six movements balance lyricism and wit within a neoclassical structure; it is highly recommended.

BASSI, Luigi *(1800)*   Arranger of Donizetti's music in 1832, and so not the baritone of the same name (1766-1825) who sang in *Don Giovanni*.

BASSUS, (Baron) Jean Marie *(1770)*   Clarinets in D are used in his music, which mainly comprises works "in uso di Offertorio." One was written "per la Chiesa di Sollern."

BATISTE, Antoine-Edouard *28 Mar 1820, Paris-9 Nov 1876, Paris*   The *Symphonie Militaire* for "douze instruments solos" (fl 2ob 2cl 2hn 2bn tp tb oph) dates from 1845. Batiste, a pupil of Halévy, was an organist and the winner of the second Prix de Rome.

BAYER, ( ) *(1780)*   His dance music for winds, probably c.1810, is now in CZ-Pnm.

BAŽANT, Jaromír *b 8 Aug 1926, Krásný Dvůr*   Oboist and composer, best known for pioneering compositions for the accordion. His *Parthia* Op 18 was written in 1960, the same year as his *Divertimento* Op 14.

BAZIN, François-Emmanuel Joseph *4 Sep 1816, Marseille-2 Jul 1878, Paris*   His *Mélodie* includes parts for two solo horns, with fl 2ob 2cl 2bn.

BECHLER, Johann Christian *7 June 1784, Oesel-15 Apr 1857, Herrnhut*   Music by this composer was played by the Moravian wind ensemble at Bethlehem, Pennsylvania.

BECKER, Günther *b 1 Apr 1924, Forbach*   Becker's *Quasi una fantasmagoria*, for 2cl 2hn 2bn, is described as "Scenes from Schumann's *Sphinxes.*"

BECKFORD, William *1759-1844*   One marche is attributed to the author of *Vathek* and of reminiscences of travels in Portugal. The date is acceptable (1) and no other suggestion seems more convincing for this "Mons de Beckford." A man of considerable fortune (2), in Portugal he borrowed musicians from the Queen's chapel to play among orange and bay trees. In 1793, when staying near Evian, he wrote that he had "the first artists of Paris, who are all here in my suite, with the addition of the best clarionets, oboes, drums major and minor, of the ci-devant Gardes du Roy des Françaises [sic]". Later on his travels, he mentions a "reduced band of seven musicians" with him in Italy.

1. C B Oldham 1966 Music and Letters 47 110.

2. See Rose Macaulay 1946 *They went to Portugal*; London: Jonathan Cape.

BÉDARD, Jean Baptiste *c.1765, Rennes-c.1815, Paris*   Violinist and conductor at Rennes till his move to Paris in 1796. He wrote or arranged a number of wind works after 1799, including a *Pot-pourri d'airs connus,* as well as marches for the "demis-brigades de la République française," the military groupings which lasted from late 1793 until around 1803. Bédard's *Hymne à Voltaire* has been recorded.

BEDFORD, David *b Aug 4 1937 London*   Bedford studied with Lennox Berkeley in London, Luigi Nono in Venice, and at the Studio for Electronic Music in Milan. He has written music for large wind bands (*Sea and Sky and Golden Hill,* for the Avon Schools' Wind Band, first performed 1985; *Sun Paints Rainbows on the Vast Waves,* for the Huddersfield Festival of Contemporary Music, 1984), brass quintet (*Pancakes with Butter, Maple Syrup and Bacon and the TV Weatherman,* 1973), and *With 100 Kazoos,* in which members of the audience play the 100 kazoos. His *Susato Variations,* a showpiece for the winds of an orchestra, was premiered recently at the 1993 Leeds Centenary Festival of Wind Music. DXB–1v *When I Heard the Learn'd Astronomer* (1972) comprises settings of texts by Walt Whitman and Camille Flammarion.

BEECKE, Ignaz von *28 Oct 1733 Wimpfen in Tal-3 Jan 1803 Wallerstein*   Von Beecke, military adjutant to Prince Kraft Ernst at Oettingen-Wallerstein, was both virtuoso pianist and composer. His military duties were light, so von Beecke could travel widely to recruit musicians and acquire new music. It was on such travels that he joined with Mozart for a piano-duet concert during coronation festivities for Leopold II at Frankfurt in 1790. He was promoted from Captain to Major in 1791 or 1792, retiring from military duties in 1792 to devote his remaining years to composition.

IVB–1   This *Parthia in Dis* (E♭, c.1780) "Del Sigr. Capitano de Beecke" is attractive and unusually scored for fl ob 2cl 2hn bn. It dates from around 1780, at the beginning of the great period of the Oettingen-Wallerstein Harmonie when wind musicians were still being recruited. Surprisingly, it appears to be his only work for Harmoniemusik.

IVB–2ad *Parthia Das Waldmädchen*   The 13 movements, arranged from the ballet by Paul Wranizky and Joseph Kinsky, are attributed to von Beecke, but could well be by Went; the name Beecke on the trumpet part may indicate no more than that he brought the music back from one of his trips. The Oettingen-Wallerstein catalog suggests a date of 1800; the copyist was Franz Xaver Linx (1759-1825). Given that Prince Kraft Ernst did not normally like arrangements, one must assume that the ballet had special appeal.

BEETHOVEN, Ludwig van *15/16 Dec 1770, Bonn-26 Mar 1827, Vienna*   Given his other achievements and the high opus numbers of his wind works, one might expect major works of exceptional originality and power. To be sure, these works are good, better than those of some major contemporaries, but one is still disappointed. The high opus numbers attest to the invention of his publishers, to temporary financial embarrassment, or both. Beethoven is uncertain at times whether to entertain listeners, to stretch players, or (rarely) to reflect what he achieved in other fields. His wind works do not approach comparison with the richness of invention and design of Mozart's or the assured innovation of Haydn's smaller, simpler parthias. Krommer, a good but not great composer, succeeded just because of a sureness of aim which Beethoven does not always show. Beethoven's finest wind writing is in his major works, as in the superb Poco Andante section in the finale of his *Eroica* Symphony. Near the end of his life, he sketched a *Kyrie* with winds and organ (*Thayer* pp 793, 814), a fascinating idea.

Beethoven needs no detailed biography. His piano playing was legendary, recognized in Bonn and in Vienna, where he received instruction from both Mozart and Haydn, and where he was acquainted with many of the wind players and composers discussed in this book. At Bonn he played viola in the court orchestra, where his colleagues included Nicolaus Simrock, horn player and future publisher, and Anton Reicha (qv) flautist, composer of wind quintets, and future teacher of Berlioz, Franck, Gounod and Liszt.

Beethoven also wrote wind works which we shall not discuss here: the *Quintet* for ob cl bn hn pf, Op 16, is a delight, and other smaller pieces include his two trios for 2ob ca, namely the *Trio in F,* WoO 28 (Variations on "Là ci darem") and the Op 87 *Trio in C,* probably written for the Teimer brothers, Johann, Franz and Philipp, for whom Went wrote a similar Terzetto (*Thayer* p 19). The solemn *Equali* for 4tb, WoO 30 (*Thayer* pp 541, 1054) were written for Glöggl, of Linz Cathedral, in 1812; Nos 1 and 3 were arranged by Seyfried (qv) as a *Miserere* for Beethoven's funeral.

The many recordings all include most of the "standard" works (**LVB–1, 2, 4**). Two use "authentic" instruments: Classical Winds (referred to below as CW) on Amon Ra CDSAR26 and Mozzafiato/Naidich on Sony Vivarte SK 53367. Modern instruments are used by Haas/London Baroque Ensemble, Pye GSGC 14038 (the Marches are especially well done) and some works on CDM7 64135; London Wind Soloists, Decca SDD 383; Netherlands Wind Ensemble, Philips 9500087; Wind Soloists of the Chamber Orchestra of Europe, ASV CDCOE807; Czech Philharmonic Winds, Supraphon, SUA 111 0703 (a related unnamed Czech ensemble has **LVB–4** and **LVB–5** on Supraphon 11 1445-2); Melos Ensemble, HMV ASD 2671; Melbourne Windpower, on Move MD 3082 (**LVB–2**); Ricercar Academy, Ricercar RIC 092078; Philharmoniker Oktetts Berlin, Deutscher Gramophon 439852-2; Bratislavská kamorná harmoniá/Pavlík, Opus 9111 1219 (**LVB–2** only), and by an unknown ensemble, Murray Hill S-41838. Recordings vary as to which works are included; no so-called "complete" recording of the wind music contains **LVB–3**.

LVB–1 *Rondino,* WoO 25.   An extended Andante of particular charm, first published by Diabelli in 1830. Several sketches exist (labelled "Rondo" rather than the published title "Rondino"), and these led CW to suggest that it was conceived as a fourth movement to the Parthia **LVB–2**; in particular, sketches of the Rondino and of the Menuetto appear in the Fischof miscellany, and the opening horn theme of the Rondino is found on the page following the Menuetto in the autograph of the Parthia. The idea that the Parthia really is a five-movement work is interesting but not wholly convincing; it is recorded by CW in this form. The notes to CW also discuss the nature of chromatic mutes to play the unusual passage near the end of the work on natural horns, and the CW performance does show that a practical solution can be achieved.

LVB–2 *Parthia in Es*   This work (also known as *Octet in Eb,* Op 103) seems to have been written in Bonn (1). Yet both an autograph (2 p 72) and sketches (the Fischof miscellany) are on paper with a Viennese watermark, and seem to date from after his arrival in 1792, rather than during his earlier stay (CW). Since the autograph contains changes, the final version must date from Beethoven's Vienna days, even if the original was written in Bonn. The work was first published by Artaria in 1830. Only in 1851 did it get its "Op 103" label; much more logical is the Op 4 number of its arrangement for string quintet. It is in four movements (see **LVB–1** for the suggestion of a fifth), with a finale which is a tour de force, for players at least. Yet one feels that it never quite fulfils the composer's intentions, and one's attention is held by virtuoso playing, rather than musical invention; the slow movement, which lacks such display, is rather dull.

LVB–3 *Harmonie auf dem Theater* from *Die Ruinen von Athen* (Beethoven's own title is often replaced by *Musik hinter der Scene)* was written in 1811 for the 1812 opening of a theater in Pest (now part of Budapest). This quiet interlude is delicately written, and the instruction "dolce" appears frequently. Much of *The Ruins of Athens* is rich in its use of winds, and other numbers use Turkish instruments to good effect. The autograph of **LVB–3** is more legible than most Beethoven scores, and one of his changes of mind makes it very clear the horns are in C basso, not alto. No recording is known to us: this item is missing from those we have heard of the incidental music.

LVB–4 *Sextet in Eb,* Op 71.   Although the *Sextet* dates from 1796 (*Thayer* p 197; 3) it was not performed until April 1805, at the benefit concert for the violinist

Schuppanzigh. Bähr's clarinet playing at the first performance was especially praised. The review by the *Allgemeine musikalische Zeitung* of 15 May 1805 remarked on the pleasure the work gave through "its lively melodies" and its "wealth of novel and surprising ideas." Certainly the lovely bassoon solo in the slow movement and the marchlike finale work very well; the main part of the opening movement and the quirky Minuet and Trio are perhaps less effective. Publication was delayed until April 1810. Beethoven, offering the work to Breitkopf und Härtel in August 1809, claimed that the "work was written in a single night," a thin excuse to make it clear that he was "one who had written a few better works at least."

LVB-5 *"Quintet" in E♭*   This work probably dates from 1798-1802 (4), and was left incomplete. Movement 1 is only a fragment and lacks the start, although it can be reconstructed from the second half; Movement 3 has only the first 19 bars. Movement 2 is complete. Beethoven's manuscript has an extra stave for a clarinet, but it is blank. The slow movement, Adagio maestoso, is attractive solemn *Nachtmusik,* and exploits the three horns (a rare number, also used in the *Eroica* Symphony and in a small trio in E). The Adagio could have been written earlier than the outer-movement fragments. The completion of the outer movements often used is that by Leopold Zellner (qv). The third movement, not a success, sounds as if it is based on sketches of the *Sextet* **LVB-4.**

LVB-1v *Bundeslied,* Op 122.   A setting of Goethe's "In allen guten Stunden erhört von Lieb und Wein", a somewhat formal drinking song in four verses, and revised many times before publication in 1822, when Beethoven was working on his major achievements. Thayer (1 p 793) discusses Beethoven's problems in publishing this work. It is recorded by Tilson Thomas/London Symphony Orchestra/Ambrosian Singers CBS 76404 and by the Berlin Radio Symphony Orchestra and Chorus/Rickenbacher on Koch Schwann 31485-2.

LVB-1m *March in D* WoO 24   This is for a large band of 33 parts, commissioned for the Civil Artillery Corps of Vienna by Lt Commander Franz Xaver Embal, who asked for a "march for Turkish Music." Embal was a Magistratsrat (that is, a Councillor) as well as Honorary Colonel. This big work has some unusual modulations, but is not one of Beethoven's more inspired efforts. The autograph is dated 3 June 1816. The march is recorded by the Berlin Philharmonic Wind Ensemble/Priem-Bergrath on DG 419 624-2.

LVB-2m *Zapfenstreich No 1 in F,* WoO 18.   One of the very best classical marches - a splendid slow march in which the tempo is fast - one pace per bar - and the rhythm is memorable. Hindemith rewrote it (also for winds and percussion only) as the second movement of his 1946 *Symphonia Serena.* Beethoven himself prepared several versions, and the connections between them and the recordings are not easily unravelled. The final versions of this work and its companion pieces (**LVB-3m, 4m**) were written not long before the *Choral Symphony,* and indeed their scoring matches precisely that of the Turkish March section of the finale ("Froh, wie seine Sonnen") of the symphony. We describe the several versions of **LVB-2m** chronologically:

1809 versions   One copy is inscribed to His Royal Highness Archduke Franz Anton (1 p 475) who was the elder brother of Beethoven's patron, Archduke Rudolph. Anton was also Grand Master of the Teutonic Order, and this 1809 version was inscribed to them. The autograph survives in the Order's Central Archives in Vienna. This version has no trio, and omits triangle and cymbals. A second 1809 version exists as "Marsch für die boehmische Landwehr" (for the Bohemian Militia), still lacking a trio, but now with triangle and cymbals. This seems to be Artaria 144 in D-Bds (5, 6).

1810 version   This version was chosen for the Carrousel (8) at Laxenburg, near Vienna, on 25 August 1810; again there is no trio. The Chemische Druckerei edition (pn 1620, so 1810/1811) bears the title "CARROUSEL MUSIK aufgeführt an dem Glorreichen Nahmens Feste Ihrer Kais: Kön: Majestät MARIA LUDOVKA in dem K:K:

Schloß Garten zu Laxenberg arrangirt für die TÜRKISCHE MUSIK." There are twelve movements, all in the keys of C or F: Marsch la Familie Suiße (from J Weigl's opera) zum Iten Einzug; Marsch de L: v: Beethoven [**LVB–2m**] zum Iten Abzug; La Chasse, wo Sr Majestät der Kaiser der Kronprintz Erzherzog Karl u: Anton ritten; Ecoaise [sic]; Allemande; Allemande; Marsch zum IIten Einzug; Allemande; Ecossaise; Polonaise; Allemande Saxone; Marcia Abzug des Carrousels. Del Sig Beethven [**LVB–3m**]. Only the two items with Beethoven's name are by him. Apart from the Beethoven marches, La Chasse, and the Marsch zum IIten Einzug, all movements have trios.

Two versions pre-1816 are found in in the Lobkovic Collection in CZ-Pnm. One (at X.H.a.77) is for a full band (pic 2ob 2cl 2hn 2bn cbn tp tri cym "Tamburo" "Gran Tamburo"); the other (at X.H.a.76) is for a smaller band (2ob 2cl[F] 2hn 2bn cbn tp).

1819 version The early Schlesinger edition (as No 37 in a collection of marches) is an arrangement. There is no hint that Beethoven knew of the edition. It may be this version which is used in the Berlin Philharmonic Winds recording, which does seem to differ from the earlier versions in minor ways and is the only recorded version without a trio. Notes with the recording say that the march's Yorck'scher title comes from the name of Graf Yorck von Wartenburg (the Prussian general who broke away from alliance with France in 1812) given on the front of an unspecified early edition, presumably this one. There are no verifiable links with the Duke of York or with Yorkshire, England.

1822/1823 versions Offered by Beethoven for publication by Peters in a letter which mentions trios. In 1823 he decided to give WoO 18, 19, 20 each the title *Zapfenstreich* (*Thayer* p 502, 793). Peters was not keen. On the autograph version with the Trio is Beethoven's comment "Ein Schritt auf jeden Takt" (5), i.e. one pace per bar, a slow march to rapid music.

LVB–3m *Zapfenstreich No 3 in F,* WoO 19. Again an impressive march, and again a slow march to rapid music. Several versions exist, one autograph dated "1810, Baden, 3 June," and dedicated to the Archduke Franz Anton. The versions in the Vienna Archives of the Teutonic Order indicate it was paired with **LVB–2m**; again, like **LVB–2m**, it was also used for the Carousel at Laxenburg. In offering the marches **LVB–2m, 3m** for the Carousel, Beethoven wrote to the Archduke "I see that your Imperial Highness wishes to test the effect of my music on horses. All right, I will be interested to find out whether it will lead the riders to a skilful somersault or two... The horse music you want will arrive at the fastest possible gallop." There are at least five earlier sources, namely those (a) in the archives of the Teutonic Order, (b) in A-Wgm, in the Haslinger-Rudolphinische collection, Vol 19, (c) a further version in A-Wgm, and (d, e) two MS scores owned by Archduke Rudolph, also in A-Wgm. Only versions (d, e) seem to have triangle and cymbals. The later version, which gave the work its title, dates from 1822/3, and adds the Trio for the first time (this is also in the Berlin manuscript).

LVB–4m *Zapfenstreich No 2, in C,* WoO 20. Another excellent march, probably dating from 1809/1810. The autograph, now in private hands, was inspected in 1977; it seems (6) to be on paper from 1806, but the date and reason for composition are not known. The Trio is present in all versions, even published ones.

LVB–5m *Polonaise in D,* WoO 21. A good movement. In at least one source, the Trio is marked ad lib; to omit it weakens the scale and effect of the music.

LVB–6m *Écossaise in D,* WoO 22. In the same source, the Coda is ad lib, again not a good idea. This MS is in Archduke Rudolph's collection (Sig XV 17234, cited (6)) which has **LVB–4m, 5m** together; Baden is given as the place and 1810 as the date of composition; *Thayer* p 502 agrees with the 1810 date. Another autograph exists in the Bodleian (GB-Ob, c21 fol 19). The wind version of the second Écossaise, **LVB–7m**, seems lost, although it may match the piano version WoO 23 (*Thayer* p 503).

LVB-8m *March in Bb, WoO 29.* A small, slight march without a trio, possibly linked with the Eszterháza Grenadiers (*Thayer* p 429) because of Beethoven's September 1807 visit to Eszterháza. Notes (by Roger Cotte?) to the recording on Arion ARN 90806 suggest instead that the music was for Masonic ceremonies, just long enough for those officiating to cross the temple as far as the throne of the Grand Master.

We note the following recordings of arrangements of Beethoven's music:

Fidelio (arranged Sedlak): recorded complete by the London Wind Soloists, Decca SDD 485; and by Melbourne Windpower on Move MD 3110. The overture only is recorded by Octophorus on original instruments, Accord ACC 48434 D.

Symphony No 7 Anonymously arranged, (not by Beethoven, though he would have known of it), it is transposed from A to G. It is recorded on original instruments by Octophoros, Accord ACC 48434 D (the Netherlands Wind Ensemble recording, Chandos CHAN 9470, is a modern arrangement). Detailed analysis (9) notes that the arrangement is based on a MS by Anton Diabelli. The arranger was clearly experienced in writing for wind ensemble, for there are some neat solutions to problem passages. The arrangements for 6-part and 9-part Harmonie were advertized in the *Wiener Zeitung* of 24 December 1817. No copies survive of the 6-part version, nor are there copies of arrangements of *Symphony No 8* which, like *Symphony No 7* and *Wellingtons Sieg,* was among the music which Steiner purchased in August 1815 from Beethoven. As to the arranger, possibles include Sedlak, Starke, Scholl, and the anonymous arranger (perhaps Haslinger?) for the early Chemische Druckerei journals; less likely are composers like Druschetzky, Czerny, and Poessinger. Sedlak's name usually appears prominently on his arrangements, which argues against it being his work.

Wellingtons Sieg This anonymous arrangement is attributed to Beethoven, surely wrongly (arrangement for this large wind band by someone such as P Mašek would be more likely). The arrangement is recorded by Octophoros on original instruments on Accord ACC 8860 D. The arrangement was advertized in the *Wiener Zeitung* of 6 March 1818 as Heft 1 of the *Neue Journal für türkische Musik,* some five years after the Battle of Vittoria (10). The use of the five clarinets (cl[Eb] 2cl[C] 2cl[Bb] is interesting; Kinsky (11) wrongly identifies a D clarino (trumpet) part as clarinet). The Eb clarinet plays for a mere 13 bars in part 2. In part 1, the C clarinets play only in the French band's "Marlborough" *(Malbrouk s'en va t'en guerre,* known as "For he's a jolly good fellow") and the Bb clarinets only in the British army's "Rule Brittania" [sic].

Pathétique Sonata An anonymous arrangement, attributed to Druschetzky (we consider this unlikely); recorded by the Österreichische Kammerharmonie/Prammer.

Septet, Op 20. An intriguing anonymous arrangement is **LVB-1a(d)**, in which the start of the Andante con Variazione and the Finale are scored for 11 winds. In 1952, prior to auction, unidentified handwriting experts suggested that it was in Beethoven's own handwriting. There is some similarity, but Schweger (12) gives good reasons for doubt; he is supported by our comparison of the facsimile in the auction catalogue with a facsimile of the corresponding page of the autograph of the original *Septet* (2 p 80). While the manuscript (now in the Beethovenhaus, Bonn) is not an autograph, Schweger does sympathize with the view that Beethoven was involved in the arrangement. We doubt it. The instrumentation is not clearly given; indeed, the 1952 sale description incorrectly gave 9 winds and 10 winds for the two respective movements. The scoring seems to be fl(Eb) cl(Eb) 2cl(Bb) 2hn(Eb) [tp or hn](Bb) 2bn[or other bass instruments]. This was a common German band configuration in the first part of the 19th century. The arranger may well have been a clarinettist, for the Finale follows Beethoven's own Op 38 version for (cl vc pf), rather than the original Op 20 *Septet,* and the Trio version would be well known to clarinettists (like Crusell or Mejo) and far less so to others.

Schweger notes that the arrangement is close to that by Crusell (qv), another clarinettist. Arrangements of the *Septet* by identified composers are the following:
Czerny: 2cl 2bn 2hn. The manuscript is dated 12/7-17/8 1805. Czerny was a pupil of Beethoven's from c.1800-1803, the period during which the *Septet* was published. Czerny's *Autobiography* (quoted in *Grove V)* mentions his arrangement of the *Leonore* overture for piano, saying "It is to Beethoven's remarks on this work that I owe the facility in arranging which has been so useful to me in later life."
Druschetzky: 2ob 2cl 2hn 2bn cbn (Vienna, c.1812); recorded by the Collegium Musicum   Pragense   on   Supraphon   SUA   111   2180   and   by   Österreichische Kammerharmonie/Prammer.
Crusell: terz-fl cl(E♭) 2cl(B♭) 2hn 2bn tp b-tb serp (Leipzig, c 1825). The scoring is almost that of the so-called autograph sketches. We have confirmed the "Beethoven" manuscript is not in Crusell's hand, but it could be a copy of Crusell's version.
1. Haydn, reporting on Beethoven's progress in Vienna, sent samples to the Elector in Bonn, mentioned specifically an eight-voice Parthie (*Thayer* pp 144, 145). The Elector's reply asserted that all the music sent (with the exception of a fugue) "was composed and performed here in Bonn before he departed on his second journey to Vienna." Two copies may have existed, namely the one sent and the one which remained in Vienna.
2. J Schmidt-Görg, H Schmidt (editors) 1969 *Ludwig van Beethoven;* Hamburg: Polydor.
3. The autograph of the Minuet and Trio are in GB-Lbl, as are some sketches; the first page is reproduced on the sleeve of the Classical Winds recording.
4. D W MacArdle 1946 Music and Letters 27 15.
5. W Hess 1953/1954 Beethoven Jahrbuch p 251.
6. O Biba, Introduction to Doblinger Edition No 698.
7. Illustrations of carrousels (events in which horsemen tilted at targets) are given for 1719 in R Hatton 1969 *Europe in the Age of Louis XIV;* London: Thames and Hudson, and for 1814 and 1843 in National Geographic Magazine 1958 114 406-7; see also our discussion of music for the Carrousel by Anton Wranizky.
8. H-G Klein, notes for DG 419 624 (Berlin Philharmonic Winds/Hans Priem-Bergrath).
9. Bastiaan Blomhert 1995, private communication to Jon Gillaspie.
10. The first performance of the original *Wellingtons Sieg* in Vienna in December 1813 included Moscheles, Meyerbeer and Hummel in the large percussion section.
11. G Kinsky and H Halm 1955 *Das Werke Beethovens: thematisch-bibliographisches Verzeichnis;* Munich.
12. Myron Schweger 1970 Music Quarterly 56 p 727.
BEINET (Bienet), ( ) *(1760)* His *Amusemens militaires* **XJB-1** and *Recueil de pot poury [sic] d'airs connus* are scored - unusually for France - for 2ob 2cl 2hn 2bn. The title page of his *Suite d'airs arrangées pour harmonie* for 2cl 2hn 2bn styles him "Musicien au Régiment des Gardes Suisses."
BELLI-SANDRE, P M M *(active 1869)*   Composer of church music with winds, in Venice.
BELLOLI, Agostino *(1800)* Arranger for winds of the quintet from Donnizetti's *L'Elisir d'Amore.* Possibly related to the family of distinguished horn players.
BELOTTI, Guiseppe *(1820)-active until 1898* After studies at the Instituto "Donizetti" in Bergamo, he held posts as organist in the Bergamo region (Gorno, Nossa, Abbazia), and was known as a pianist. He, with his father and brothers, constituted "Contrapunto Belotti", composing liturgical music between 1872 and 1898. Apart from a *Suonata con variazione* for bassoon and winds, his output is mainly church music with wind bands.
BÉM (Behm), Václav *(1740)* His Parthia is in the Pachta collection, CZ-Pnm, probably c.1770. His oboe concerto at Oettingen-Wallerstein is believed to date from 1770.
BENDA, Franz (František) [not Georg Benda nor Jan Jiří Benda] *baptized 25 Nov 1709,*

Staré Benátky, Bohemia-7 Mar 1786, Nowawes, near Potsdam Son of Jan Jiří Benda and Dorota Brixi, both from families of Bohemian musicians. Franz Benda is known to have written marches anonymously (part 1). He was Konzertmeister to Frederick the Great, and wrote many sonatas and concertos for violin. His daughter, a singer at Gotha, married Dismas Hataš, the brother of Jan Václav Hataš (qv).

BENDA, Georg *baptized 30 June 1722, Stáre Benátky-6 Nov 1795, Köstritz, Thuringia* Violinist in Berlin, Kapellmeister at Gotha from 1750, and an innovator in opera from the mid-1760s. The melodrama *Medea* (Leipzig, 1775) uses winds sparingly. Benda may have scored marches by his pupils, Princesses Amalie and Philippa Charlotte of Prussia.

BENNETT, William *b 7 Feb 1936, London* English flautist, playing for the English Chamber Orchestra, for whose wind ensemble he arranged Theobald Boehm's *Grande Polonaise* **WXB-1a**. Boehm (1794-1881) revolutionized flute design and wrote a number of showpieces to demonstrate its capabilities. There is the usual slow introduction, with a vigorous polonaise to follow. In arranging the original piano part, Bennett gives the first horn a formidable challenge, and uses a C clarinet to give a brighter wind sound. The work needs a flautist capable of both virtuosity and fine ensemble playing; it is recorded on EMI Eminence 41 2053 4 by Bennett with the ECO winds.

BENTZON, Niels Viggo *b 24 Aug 1919, Copenhagen* In addition to his *Concertino for Piano and Winds,* Bentzon has written a wind quintet, a quintet for fl ob cl bn pf, and a *Chamber Concert* for cl bn 2tp 3perc 3pf db.

BENZ, Johann Baptist *(19th century)* Composer, active in Český Krumlov, who wrote an *Offertorium* with winds. J B Benz is not D Benz.

BERERA, Francesco Antonio *24 Aug 1737, Trento-8 Apr 1811, Trento* Berera was both organist of S Maria Maggiore and composer for religious functions of Trento's confraternities (which ended in 1810). His *Messa in F,* **FNB-1v,** may be a rescoring for voices and "strumenti di fiato per la Banda della Guardia Civica" of his *Missa S Rocca,* completed on S Rocco's Day (16 Aug 1801); it was performed on 16 March 1802 for a band festival. Gerolamo Pietrapiana (Vice-Podesta of the Bishop of Trento, who wrote eyewitness accounts of Trento in the Napoleonic period) is quoted as describing the Mass as a "messe solenne con musica strepitosa [strident, clamorous]."

BERG, Alban *9 February 1885, Vienna-24 December 1935, Vienna* A pioneer of twelve-tone music who kept links with Viennese traditions. His new musical language did not force him to reject musical expression. He appreciated the Viennese wind sound, which he used in the chorale (3cl b-cl) in his *Violin Concerto* and elsewhere. His *Chamber Concerto* **AYB-1** for solo violin and piano with winds was written in 1925 as a birthday present to his friend and teacher, Arnold Schoenberg, to whom it is dedicated. The same year saw the first performance (in Berlin, after 137 rehearsals) of *Wozzeck* and the start of Alban Berg's affair with Hanna Fuchs-Robettin, sister of Franz Werfel (who later married Alma Mahler; see [1] for connections between these members of European intellectual society). A key to the *Chamber Concerto* is the number 3, the number of movements, of instrumental groups (two soloists and the wind band), and of many of the rhythmic and harmonic details (2). The work opens with an Epigraphe, which follows the crossword principles beloved of twelve-tone writers; here the names of Berg, Schoenberg and Webern are transcribed to make three key themes. There are three movements, and the magic number occurs in each. In the Tema Scherzoso con variazioni for piano and winds, there are six uses of the same idea, then a 30-bar variation in three sections. This movement and the second movement are issued for separate performance. The Adagio (for violin and winds) is palindromic, and apparently represents Schoenberg's wife, Mathilde (who left Schoenberg for an artist, whose suicide led her to return). The Adagio is in three parts. The final Rondo ritmico con introduzione combines material from the other movements in three ways. The work was first performed in public on 2 July 1927 (a date weak in the number 3; the day before [1/7/1927] would have been far better [1+7+1+9+2+7 = 3x3x3 = 3³]) at the Frankfurt Music Festival. Recordings include those by the London Sinfonietta/Atherton (Argo ZRG 937); the Norwegian Wind Ensemble/Ruud (Simax PSC 1090); the Ensemble Intercontemporain/Boulez (DG 2531 007 and DG 447 405-2GOR); the Budapest Chamber Ensemble/Mihály (Hungaroton SPLX 11807); and the Prague Chamber Ensemble/Pešek (Supraphon SUA ST50679).

1. K Monson 1984 *Alma Mahler;* London: Collins.

2. N Del Mar 1981 *Orchestral Variations;* London: Eulenberg.

BERGER, Ludwig *18 Apr 1777, Berlin-18 Feb 1839, Berlin*   Piano pupil of Clementi and teacher of Mendelssohn. His march "pour les armées anglaises-espagnoles dans les Pyrénées" is one of the few surviving marches identified with the Peninsular War.

BERKES, Kálmán *b 1952*   Clarinettist, prime mover of the Budapest Wind Ensemble, and arranger of *Weiner: Two Hungarian Dances.* This is based on movements of the Op 20 *Divertimento No 1 on Old Hungarian Dances* (for strings) by Leó Weiner (1885-1960).

BERLIOZ, Louis Hector *11 Dec 1803, La Côte-Saint-André-8 Mar 1869, Paris*   See part 1 pps 57, 58 concerning his *Grande symphonie funèbre et triomphale.*

BERNARD, (Jean Auguste) Émile *11 Nov 1843, Marseilles-11 Sept 1902, Paris* Winner of the Prix Chartier for chamber music. His *Divertissement in F,* Op 36 (**EMB-1**) for 2fl 2ob 2cl 2hn 2bn, is a major work in three movements. It was published in 1890, and was played at Taffanel's Société des Instruments à Vent. It is recorded by Sylvan Winds (Koch International 3-7081-2HI) and by the Triebensee Ensemble (Astoria 90029).

BERNER, Friedrich Wilhelm *16 May 1780, Breslau-9 May 1827, Breslau*   Composer, valued by Weber as pianist and clarinettist; pupil of Reichardt. He was involved from 1811 in the setting up of a Singakademie in Breslau, along the lines of that in Berlin.

BERNHARD, M *(1810)*   Teacher in Donauwörth; possibly the composer of a *Leichenlied* for CATB terz-fl 2cl 2hn bomb.

BERR, Friedrich (Frédéric) *17 Apr 1794, Mannheim-24 Sept 1838, Paris*   Originally a bassonist, who played in a French infantry regiment during the Peninsular War. Composer, arranger for winds, and a clarinettist who changed the French style of playing. He wrote for a *Journal d'Harmonie* with the Chevalier Louis and C Münchs; at this time (1821-1825) he was styled Chef de Musique au 2e Régiment Suisse de la Garde Royale and (from 1825) Artiste du Théâtre Royal Italien. He became professor at the Conservatoire in 1831, and took charge of the Gymnase de Musique Militaire in 1836. He became Chevalier de la Légion d'Honneur in 1833. The *Journal* includes his *Walz [sic] de la Duchesse de Berry;* she was a Royalist whose scandals gave her great social visibility. Berr made the well-known arrangements of Rossini's *String Sonatas* 1-5 for fl cl hn bn. Most of his opera arrangements for band date from the late 1820s-1830s, when pic cl(Eb) and optional 2cl tp 2/3tb db were added to the earlier core of 2cl 2hn 2bn (serp). His arrangements of Rossini's overtures (*Tancredi* **FXB-21a**, *Il Turco in Italia* **FXB-22a**, *Mathilda di Shabran* **FXB-23a**, *La siège de Corinthe* **FXB-24a**) have been recorded (as by "Beer") by the Ottetto Italiano on Arts 47162-2.

BERTIE, Willoughby, Fourth Earl of Abingdon *16 Jan 1740, Gainsborough, UK-26 Sep 1799, Rycote, near Oxford, UK*   Friend and patron of J C Bach and of Haydn, radical politician, and composer of some attractive music for winds or now arranged for winds.

BERTON, Henri Montan *17 Sept 1767, Paris-22 Apr 1844, Paris*   Member of a French musical family, pupil of Sacchini, and violinist in the Paris Opéra from an early age. Opera composer, later angered by Rossini's success. Professor of harmony at the Conservatoire from 1795, where he replaced Méhul as Professor of composition in 1818.

BERTONI, Ferdinando Gasparo *15 Aug 1725, Salò, Venice-1 Dec 1813, Dessenzano* Composer of church music with winds, as well as many works with organ.

BERTUZZI, A M Composer of church music with winds, now in Venice (I-Vsmc).

BERWALD, Franz *23 July 1796, Stockholm-3 Apr 1868, Stockholm* His 1845 *Cantata* **FYB-1v** is for solo voices, fl 2cl 2hn, and celebrates the victory of Carl II over the Russians at Narva in 1700; it carries the subtitle "Schwedisches Soldatenlied." **FYB-2v** is the *Nordiske fantasibilder* of 1846, for male chorus, winds and organ. The 1845 Cantata *Gustav Adolph the Great's victories and death at Lötzen* is for chorus, brass and organ. Berwald's *Marsch, Hymne & Jubelchor* is a cantata with large wind band, written for what appears to have been a trade fair; it dates from 15 June 1866.

BESOZZI, Carlo *c.1738, Naples (Dresden, in some sources)-22 March 1791* Oboist, son of Antonio Besozzi (1714-1781) with whom he played duets in the Concerts Spirituels, Paris. He was a member of an extensive family of musicians, some of the other oboist members being Carlo's grandfather Giuseppe (Naples), uncle Gaetano (London), cousin Girolamo (Paris) and son Francesco (Dresden). Carlo's playing was admired by Burney and by Leopold Mozart. He had many pupils, including Jan Šlechta (Schwarzenberg Harmonie) and Georg Triebensee (Schwarzenberg Harmonie, then the Hofharmonie; the father of Josef Triebensee, qv), and is said to have taught Druschetzky in Dresden (Damien Frame 1995, broadcast on BBC Radio 3). He wrote 15 surviving *Sonatas* for 2ob 2hn bn, apparently from a set of at least 20 (the numbering to XX was added at a later date to what are professional copies). There are 9 *Parthias* (the title *Sonata* is used interchangeably) for 2ob 2ca 2hn bn, apparently arranged for the Schwarzenberg ensemble; all but one of these are based on one for the smaller ensemble. The works are all in the standard four movement form. Their Minuets are interesting, for example with a "Minore" instead of a trio; trios often omit the horns. **CXB-25, 26** in the Clam Gallas collection are cataloged under "Mateo" Besozzi, but appear to be by Carlo.

BETTINELLI, Bruno *b 4 June 1913, Milan* Music critic, composer, and teacher at the Milan Conservatario, where he had studied. His *Otetto* was written in 1975.

BEUTEL VON LATTENBURG, Felix Valerian *(1780)* The MS score of his *Marsch in C* for octet dates from 1815. He also wrote a *Jägermarsch* for brass, now in CZ-Pu.

BIALAS, Günter *19 Sept 1907, Bielschowitz, Upper Silesia-19 July 1992* Bialas wrote a *Partita* for winds, a *Romanza e Danza* based on Meyerbeer's *L'Africaine,* and also *Six Bagatelles for Four Saxophones,* as well as much music for the theater.

BIBER, Heinrich Ignaz Franz von *12 Aug 1644, Wartenberg, Bohemia-3 May 1704, Salzburg* *In Festo Regnum Mottetum Natale à 6* **HIB-1v** is an early example of a Christmas work for voices, winds and organ.

BIBL, Rudolf *6 Jan 1832, Vienna-2 Aug 1902, Vienna* **RXB-1v** celebrates Emperor Franz Josef's Golden Jubilee in 1898. Its old-fashioned scoring (SATB chorus, 2ob 2hn 2tp a-tb t-tb b-tb timp) may have been dictated by its intended church performance.

BIGGS, Edward Smith *c.1765-c.1820* Possibly resident in or near Norwich, he is best known as a glee composer. He set poems by the poetess Mrs [Amelia] Opie (1769-1853), whom he taught piano. She was a friend of Sheridan and of Mme de Staël.

BINDER, ( ) *(1770), active 1802* He was a composer at Langenbruck. "Author Mozart" is on the cl 1 and bn parts of **QXB-2**, which is neither by nor based on Mozart.

BIRD, Arthur H *23 Sept 1856, Belmont, Mass-22 Dec 1923, Berlin* His *Serenade* Op 40 **AHB-1** won the 1901 Paderewski Prize for the best American chamber work. The *Suite in D* **AHB-2** was written for Taffanel in Paris; it was first performed in the United States in 1908. Bird's works are attractive, and deserve a wider appreciation.

BIRTWISTLE, Sir Harrison *b 15 July 1934 Accrington, England* His initial training as a clarinettist can be seen in his works, rich in their use of the clarinet and other winds. They include a wind quintet (*Refrains and Choruses,* 1957), a work for brass band (*Grimethorpe Arias,* 1973), and a major opera, *The Mask of Orpheus* (written in the 1970s, completed in 1986) for winds, percussion and electronics, with voice, mime and scenic effects. He has been Musical Director of the National Theatre since its inception in 1976. He has criticized "the way music has become a sort of secondary pollution"; his objection to the "pop-rhythm pacifiers" of many radio stations could apply to some beer garden music but not, we hope, to most of the serenade music we discuss.

HXB-1 *The World Is Discovered* comprises six movements (three verses and three choruses) for double wind quintet, after Heinrich Isaac (c.1450-1517). Commissioned by Anthony Friese-Green's Tonus Musical Promotions and dedicated to Peter Maxwell Davies, it was first performed on 6 March 1961 under James Verity by the women musicians of the Portia Wind Ensemble with Marie Goossens (harp) and John Williams (guitar). Rhythmic monody is enriched by contrary motion, just as the *vox organalis* was added to the *vox principalis* in the early form of harmonized singing known as *organum*.

HXB-2 *Verses for Ensembles* was commissioned by the London Sinfonietta, which performed it under David Atherton on 12 February 1969, and recorded the work on Decca HEAD 7. It makes use of Christian chant, the 26 sections grouped to exploit one or other of the chants. The use of antiphony and of responses between the three choirs, plus the use of soloists and single choirs, provides the effect of ritual. The ritual is, nevertheless, early Christian at first (rather than the pagan one of the *Rite of Spring*, with which it has been compared) but later there is a parallel mood of desecration. The work is dedicated to Bill Colleran, of Universal Edition.

BISCH (Bische), Johann *(1760)*   Arranger of Pleyel, publishing in Paris.

BISCHOFF, Ernst Ferdinand *(?1800)*   His *Introduction and Variations on a theme by Weber* is dedicated to Countess Emile von der Lippe, Detmold.

BITSCH, Marcel *b 29 Dec 1921, Paris*   Composer of a *Concerto* for piano and winds.

BITTERMAN, Carl Friedrich *(1780?)*   His march "pour le corps de Janitscharen" is dedicated to "Prince Eugèn Napoléon Archi-Chancelier d'État Français, Vice-Roi de Italia" [sic], presumably Eugène Beauharnais, son of Napoleon's wife, Josephine, and son-in-law of Maximilian Joseph, Elector (later King) of Bavaria (see also Pfeilstücker, Asioli). Does this point again to confused loyalties between Napoleon and his opponents?

BLACHER, Boris *19 Jan 1903, Niu-chang, China-30 Jan 1975, Berlin*   Comments on Blacher's music stress his un-German lightness of touch, his use of flexible rhythms (including both bar-to-bar variations and organized rhythms), and hints of oriental influence apparently unrelated to his birthplace. His *Virtuose Musik* for solo violin and winds was first performed on 24 February 1967 as part of the Dartmouth Festival. The *Sonata* **BZB-2** (1972) is for two solo cellos, with 11 wind instruments ad lib. His *Estnische Tänze* Op 9 **BZB-3** (1936) may have been destroyed in World War II.

BLAKE, David Leonard *b 2 September 1936, London*   After studies at Cambridge University, Blake won a Mendelssohn scholarship to study with Eisler in Berlin. He was Granada Arts Fellow in the University of York for 1963-64. Blake's **DZB-1** *Nonet* was commissioned by the Northern Sinfonia Wind Ensemble, who first performed it in the Purcell Room, London, on 21 June 1971. It is in four movements: Chorale; Andante sostenuto, including canons for cl, b-cl and later fl, bn; Scherzo; Chorale, with an interrupted quick march. His *Cassation* **DZB-2** was written in 1979. It is in five movements: March; Scherzino; Ebb and Flow; Alla Tanza; Finale.

BLAKE, Howard *b 1938, London*   Blake's *Serenade* (2ob 2cl 2hn 2bn) dates from 1990.

BLASIUS, Mathieu Frédéric *23 Apr 1758, Lauterbach (now Alsace)-1829, Versailles*
A clarinet and violin virtuoso and a good player of flute and bassoon, Blasius (like Vanderhagen) had a career which spanned the Ancien Régime and the aftermath of the Revolution. He joined the Garde Nationale in 1793, and his *Ouverture* **MFB-1.1** was published in 1794; it was republished with modest changes **MFB-1.2** in the *Journal d'Harmonie*. In 1795, he became Professor of Wind Instruments of the First Class in the Paris Conservatoire. He directed the band of Napoleon's Consular Guard. After the

restoration of 1815, Blasius became a member of Louis XVIII's private orchestra and, later, the conductor of the band of the 5th Regiment of the Imperial Guard. Usually Blasius arranged for the smaller ensemble of 2cl 2hn 2bn, and wrote for half-harmony. His *Harmonie Militaire* (1815-16) is for fl(D) cl(F) 2cl(C) 2hn 2bn tp b-tb serp b-dr.

BLATTNER, Orrin Composer of *American Sketches* for double wind quintet.

BLAYNEY, James *(1770)* Master of the Band, 1st Regiment of Foot Guards; several of his substantial marches are dedicated to the Officers of the Brigade of Foot Guards. An interesting inscription on his *Three Grand Military Pieces* states that they are "from the 49th Demi Brigade in the French Service." The link to this French unit (which was so named from about 1794 till 1803) is not clear; it may mean merely that he took themes from the French. Blayney's marches were probably published in the temporary peace between England and France from about 1801 to 1803.

BLECHA, Oldřich *(1910)* Active in Plzeň shortly after World War II. Blecha wrote works for many types of band; **OZB-1a, -2.1a, -2.2** are for 2cl 2hn tp tb (tu), **OZB-3a** for cl(Eb) cl(Bb) 2tp flug b-flug tu drums. Such bands are common in Bohemia, and are close to ones known to Sibelius, Joplin and many others around the world. Blecha wrote for wind quintet and for large bands, often reusing older works.

BLOCKX, Jan *25 Jan 1851, Antwerp-26 May 1912, Antwerp* Flemish composer who trained in Antwerp (where he was later to direct the Conservatoire Royale) and with Reinecke (qv) in Leipzig. His works range from opera to the small folk-song setting accompanied by 2ob 2bn, *Het looze visschertje* (the artful fisherman).

BLOMBERG, Erik *b 6 May 1922, Järnskog, Sweden* His three short works for winds, *Blåsklang I, II, III* date from 1981-82; his *Debatt* (1969-70) is for large wind band.

BLOMHERT, Bastiaan *b 1944, Groningen* Arranger, conductor, and scholar, especially of music for winds. Educated at the Rijksuniversiteit Utrecht, where he studied viola and conducting, and at the Koninklijk Conservatorium, The Hague. He was Musical Director of the Oktopus Wind Ensemble. He has recorded his arrangement **BQB-6a** of Poulenc's *L'histoire de Babar* with Jane Asher and the Amsterdam Wind Ensemble on STH Favourites CD 19245. His arrangements of Mozart's music for mechanical organ (K.594, K.608, K.616; **BQB-3a,-4a, -5a**) were presented to H C Robbins Landon on his 75th birthday. He is currently advisor to the Royal Dutch Military Band, and has prepared arrangements for them, including one of Debussy's *La Mer*. Blomhert's analysis of the Donaueschingen version of *Die Entführung* suggests it as the most likely of surviving arrangements to be that which Mozart himself began (see **WAM-3a**).

BLUMENTHAL, Casimir von *d 1849, Lausanne* Blumenthal succeeded Triebensee as conductor of the opera in Brno; occasionally he directed the Augustinian Harmonie, for whom he wrote a *Harmonie*. He later became Music Director in Zurich.

BLUMENTHAL, Leopold von *(1780?)* His two marches, now in Madrid, may well be among the few surviving works associated with the Peninsular War. He may be related to Josef (Jacques) von Blumenthal (1 Nov 1782, Brussels-9 May 1850, Vienna).

BN. (B., Bnn.), E S T M, Mons *(1720)* The *Ouvertures* for oboes, horns and bassoons, probably date from the mid-18th century. The initials may be a motto.

BOARA, Giovanni "del fu Gio Veneziano" (active 1833-1860) Composer of church music with winds, now in Venice. There are many fragmentary sets of parts of his works; some may have been scored for winds.

BOCHMANN, ( ) *(?1800)* Associated with the Lippe Kapelle, Detmold.

BOCHSA, Carl (Karl) *c.1760-1821, Paris* Oboist who arranged works for winds, such as Haydn symphonies for 2fl 2cl 2hn 2bn tp tb serp (note that his version of No 102 substitutes the slow movement of No 104). In 1811/1812 he published his *Ouverture Militaire* and his *Trois Pot-pourris* for 2cl 2hn 2bn. The *Pot-pourris* are dedicated to "M.M. les Amatuers de la Société Harmonique De la Rue Mêlée [sic] à Paris." Dufaut

& Dubois may have reissued some of these "self-published" works c.1824.

BOCHSA, Robert Nicolas Charles *9 Aug 1789 Montmédy-6 Jan 1856 Sydney, Australia* The son of Karl Bochsa, R N C Bochsa was a celebrated harpist and oboist, who had to flee France after legal problems (1). His *Requiem* for Louis XVI (1815) is in 15 movements, with a solo cor anglais in the *Christe eleison* and *Recordare,* and a solo horn in the *Pie Jesu;* a tam-tam is used in the *Marche funèbre* (cf. Gossec). Only 2cl 2hn 2bn are needed in the *Liber scriptus.*
1. A Pougin 1907 Le Ménestral *Un musicien voleur, faussaire et bigame.*

BODE, (possibly Johann Joachim Christoph) *1730-1793*   Composer of three early marches for Ludwigslust.

BODINUS (BODINI), Sebastian *c.1700-c.1760, Durlach*   Concert master at Baden-Durlach, 1756.

BÖHNER, Johann Ludwig (Louis) *7 Jan 1787, Töttelstadt-28 Mar 1860, Gotha* His Motet *Preise Jerusalem den Herrn,* has wind accompaniment; we have not located his *3 grosse Märsche und Trios* for 3cl 2hn bn cbn 2tp (Augsburg: Gombart, 1817).

BOIELDIEU, (François) Adrien *16 Dec 1775, Rouen-8 Oct 1834, Jarcy* Best known as the composer of *Le calife de Bagdad.* His wind music includes marches and Masonic music to Pushkin's texts for St Petersburg, part of a set with works by Cavos (qv).

BONASEGLA, Carl Philipp *b 1779*   Probably associated with the Kapelle of Fürst Bentheim-Bentheim at Burgsteinfurt.

BONDON, Jacques *b 6 Dec 1927, Boulbon, France*   His 1978 *Symphonie Concertante* is scored for solo piano with double wind quintet.

BONNO (Bono), Joseph (Guiseppe) *29 Jan 1711, Vienna-15 Apr 1788, Vienna*   Court musician in Vienna, who wrote 11 *Parthias* in the 1780s for the Clam Gallas and Schwarzenberg Harmonies. Bonno may have written some of the anonymous works associated with the Schwarzenberg Harmonie.

BOOREN, Jo van den *14 Mar 1935, Maastricht*   Composer of a *Sextet* Op 60 (1980) for 2cl 2hn 2bn, and of the larger wind work, *Rofena,* Op 79 (1990).

BORDES, Charles *12 May 1863, La Roche-Corbon-8 Nov 1909, Toulon*   A pupil of Franck, Bordes was organist at Saint-Gervais, Paris. He collaborated with d'Indy (qv) in concerts of early choral music, and was a scholar of Basque music. His *Divertissement (Fantaisie)* for trumpet and orchestra uses winds only.

BOROVY, Antonín *12 June 1755, Sedlak-29 Mar 1832, Zlatá Karona* His *Offertorium pastorale* was written for Christmas Eve 1789 at the parish church, Zlatá Koruna.

BOSER, ( ) *(1730)-1790s*   Possibly Carlo di Bose, composer of instrumental music at Dresden (cited by *Sainsbury).*

BOST (?Rost), ( )   His *2 Harmonien* (early 19th century) were Gutenzeil band.

BOUFFIL (Boufil), Jacques Jules *14 May 1783, Muret-1868 ?Paris*   French clarinettist, pupil of Lefèvre, who played in the distinguished wind quintet for which Antonin Reicha wrote his wind quintets; this same ensemble played for Spohr. Bouffil arranged for winds music by Boieldieu. Our spelling of his name follows the title page of **JJB-1,** which was published in Bouffil's lifetime.

BOYLE, Rory *11 Mar 1951*   Boyle's *Ayr Sorceries, Charms and Spells* was written for the Bournemouth Wind Quire. The first three movements match the sections of the title, each having a pair of spellcasters: 2bn, then 2hn, then 2cl. The pairs go their own ways in the last movement, until brought together by the clarinets.

BOZZA, Eugène *4 Apr 1905, Nice-28 Sept 1991, Valenciennes* Well known for his large output of work for smaller combinations of winds, intelligently and attractively written. In particular, his 1972 *Octanphonie* **EUB-1** with its lively rhythms, is a colorful and well laid-out octet. It opens with an ominous Molto moderato, leading to an Allegro; the central Andantino includes rubato solos for oboe and clarinet, and the perpetuum mobile finale, Allegro vivo, ends with a short quotation from Schoenberg. It is recorded by Melbourne Windpower on Move MD 3082. Bozza has also written a number of larger works with winds, such as his *Messe de Ste Cécile* and *Children's Overture*.

BRÄUTIGAM, Helmut *16 Feb 1914, Crimmitschau-17 Jan 1942, Ilmensee* German composer and poet, collector of Schwabian and central German folk songs.

BRAHMS, Johannes *7 May 1833, Hamburg-3 Apr 1897, Vienna* Brahms was familiar with Mozart's great serenades, having been given scores of K.375 (by Th. Avé Lallemant, on 5 June 1859) and K.388 (by Clara Schumann, in 1861). The opening of the *St Antony Variations* is remarkably faithful to the wind divertimento from which it derives; indeed, A-Wgm has a copy by Brahms of the slow movement of that divertimento **FJH-1d** made from Pohl's score (Konvolut A 130, f.44v). The start of the slow movement of the *Violin Concerto* could have been taken from a wind serenade, as could the Trio in his first orchestral *Serenade* of 1857-1858. Soon after, probably in 1859, he wrote his Op 13 **JHB-1v** *Begräbnissgesang*. This early predecessor of the *German Requiem* is a richly scored and effective choral funeral march, recorded by the Schütz Choir of London and the London Classical Players under Roger Norrington on EMI Reflexe CDC7 54658. **JHB-1va** *Ellens zweiter Gesang*, Op 52 No 2, is arranged from Schubert's setting of Storck's translation of the song from Sir Walter Scott's *The Lady of the Lake;* it dates from 1873, the year of the *St Antony Variations*.

BRAKKEE, Stefan *(1960)* Dutch pianist and horn player, who has arranged Debussy's *Petite Suite* for winds (2ob 2cl 2hn 2bn, and also for 2ob 2ca 2hn 2bn).

BRAUER, Max *1855, Mannheim-2 Jan 1918, Karlsruhe* A pupil of Franz Lachner (qv) Brauer composed a *Pan Suite* for 2fl 2ob 2cl 2hn 2bn db.

BRAUN, C A P *(1790)* Composer of a *Quatuor* in D, for 2fl 2hn, published in 1812.

BRDIČKA, František (Franz) *(1770, active 1805)* Local composer at Langenbruck (Dlouhý Most), northern Bohemia.

BREITENBACH, Joseph Heinrich *1809-1886* One funeral march survives at Einsiedeln.

BRENDLER, ( ) Only the first of the *6 Märsche* in the Clam Gallas collection in CZ-Pnm is actually credited to Brendler.

BRESCIANI, Bartolomeo Antonio *(1790)* Maestro di Capella at the Cathedral, Brescia, who wrote a *Miserere* for male voices and winds.

BRESCIANI, Giovanni Battista *(1770)* Father of B A Bresciani (qv) and Maestro Concertatore at the Teatro Grande, Brescia. He wrote church choral music with winds, including a *Messa Breve* and a *Pange lingua* for SATB, 2ob 2hn bn "per la Processione del Corpus Domini a Quingano."

BRESGEN, Cesar *16 Oct 1913, Florence-7 Apr 1988, Salzburg* His *Jagdkonzert* is for solo horn and winds.

BRIDGEMAN, Charles *20 Aug 1778, Hertford-3 Aug 1873, Hertford* "Organist of Hertford and one of the Hertfordshire Volunteers" who wrote an "Ode on the Royal Review of the Hertfordshire Volunteers in Hatfield Park June 13 1800." Perhaps his marches were for the same occasion. They are for the Hertford Volunteers, St Albans Volunteers, Royston and Barkway Volunteers, Bishop Hatfield/Ware Volunteers, Hitchin Volunteers, Bishop Stortford/Wormley Volunteers and Hunsden Volunteers.

BRINER, Beat *(1960)* Arranger for octet of Stravinsky's *Four Norwegian Moods* and of Arvo Pärt's *Fratres* (see under Pärt).

BRISCOLI, Domenico *(1770); flourished 1800-1815, Dublin* The *Conversation of the Five Nations* comprises three Grand Overtures: The Italian; The German and French; Grand Medley of Five Nations (Spanish, Italian, English, German, French). Briscoli was Professor at the Conservatorio della Pietí de'Turchini, Naples, and was Director of Music to the Louth Regiment, Louth being a county a few miles north of Dublin.

BRIXI, František *2 Jan 1732 Prague-14 Oct 1771 Prague* Prolific composer in a family of composers and musicians, now perhaps best known for his concertos for organ. Most of his wind works are for 2ob (or tailles or cors anglais) 2hn 2bn, but he has also written a fine *Ritornello* for soprano 2cl bn, recorded by Eva Charvátová and the Prague Mozart Trio on Multisonic 31 0250-2.

BROOKS, James *(1760)-(pre-1813, Bath)* Violinist, active in Bath in the 1790s, whose **JRB-1m** "Thirty Six Select Pieces for a Military Band consisting of Marches, Quicksteps, Minuets & Rondos" was "Printed for Culliford, Rolfe, & Barrow, 112 Cheapside." This address indicates publication between 1795 and 1797. Composers are named only on the clarinet 1 part. The works are divertimentos, rather than marches. There are original works by Brooks and also arrangements. No 1 is unidentified Dibdin; Nos 9-13 are by Pleyel (**IJP-12.6**; they include movements found elsewhere under Mozart's name (**IJP-12.3**, K.C17.10)). No 19 is not identified, and may be by Brooks.

BRUCHSCHLÖGL (Bruchschloegl) ( ) *(1810)*   In a MS from the Collegium Mariano Rupertinum, Salzburg, are his six *National Stey'er*, c.1844, possibly arrangements.

BRUCKNER, Anton *4 Sept 1824, Ansfelden, Austria-11 Oct 1896, Vienna* Bruckner the symphonist is well known; Bruckner the organist was famous in his day; as a composer of wind music he may be known by two somewhat disappointing marches for large bands. Yet his achievement is also clear from his choral works (1), with many works using brass ensemble or just trombones; *Das deutsche Lied* needs 4hn 3tp 3tb b-tb.

ANB-1v *Dom-Kantate: Festkantate, Preiset den Herrn*   Bruckner was organist at the old Cathedral in Linz from 1856-1868. The town was growing rapidly, and a new Cathedral was built, the Maria-Empfängis-Dom. The cantata was performed on 1 May 1862, directed by Engelbert Lanz, when the new Cathedral's foundation stone was laid. Lanz himself was the composer of two works for voices and winds.

ANB-2v *Mass in E minor*   One of Bruckner's finest works, for a double chorus without soloists, and with a wind band (no fl or timp; the clarinets are mostly in C). It is austere in places, such as the opening Kyrie, which uses only the horns and trombones, and the pianissimo ending of the whole work. The mass was written in 1866, and revised before its first performance on 29 September 1869 for the dedication of the Votive Chapel of Linz Cathedral. The performance took place outside the building, for there was not enough room inside. The choice of winds was not dictated by outdoor performance, but did make the change of venue an advantage. Subsequent versions were made in 1876, 1882 (the main second version, edited by Nowak 1959 [2]), 1885 and 1896 (in preparation for the first printing by Doblinger). Recordings (3) include ones by Martin Best/Corydon Singers/English Chamber Orchestra, Hyperion A 66177 (1985); Mehta/Vienna State Opera Chorus/Vienna Philharmonic Orchestra, Decca SXL 6837 (1977); Simon Halsey/CBSO Chorus/City of Birmingham Symphony Orchestra Wind Ensemble, Conifer CDCF 192 (1990); Stuttgart Chamber Choir/German Philharmonic Wind Ensemble/Bernius, Sony Classical CD48037; Chapelle Royale and Ghent Collegium Musicum/Musique Oblique Ensemble/Herreweghe, Harmonia Mundi HMC90 1322.

ANB-3v *Cantata, Auf, Brüder! auf, und die Saiten zur Hand*   The *Cantata* was written for St Florian Monastery, near Linz, where Bruckner was organist; his grave is beneath the present organ. Enterprising tourists can reach St Florian by an antiquated tram.

1. Thematic catalog (referred to as WAB): Renate Grasberger 1977 *Werkverzeichnis Anton Bruckner;* Tutzing: Schneider, vol 5, Bläsermusik; the marches are WAB 115 (the *Apollo-Marsch* of 1862) and WAB 116 (the Eb *March* of 1865).

2. Collected Edition, Vienna: Musikwissenschaftlicher Verlag der Internationalen Bruckner-Gesellschaft.

3. Lee T Lovallo 1991 *Anton Bruckner: A Discography;* Berkeley, CA: Fallen Leaf Press.

BRUN, Georges *1878-(1918?)*   Composer of a *Passacaille* (1908) for 2fl ob 2cl 2hn bn, with an optional db.

BUCHAL (Bouchal, ?Buchnal), Johann Anton *(1770)* Principal arranger and copyist for the Lubomirska Harmonie at Lańcut, and possibly leader and clarinettist for that ensemble. He arranged operas by Mayr, Paer, J Weigl and Winter.

BÜHLER (Bihler), Franz (Gregor) *12 Apr 1760, Nördlingen-4 Feb 1824, Augsburg* His choral works with winds include a *Messe in Eb*, a *Deutscher Gesang* (in fact, a full German Mass) and several choral works for processional use at Corpus Christi. He wrote a *Nacht Musique* for ob 2hn 2vla b, and may well be the composer of an anonymous *Divertimento* for oboe solo 2cl 2hn bn/vc 2vla. Many were written when he was Maestro di Capella in Bolzano, where he had the support of Anton Melchior von Menz (1757-1801). Bühler moved to Augsburg as Kapellmeister in 1801.

BUHL, Joseph David *1781, Amboise-after 1829* Trumpeter in the Garde Parisienne 1792, then in the Consul's Grenadiers de la Garde; Professor of the Cavalry's School of Trumpeters at Versailles from 1805. His *Marches* survive only in a trumpet part.

BURRELL, Diana *25 Oct 1948, Norwich, UK* Her **DIB-1** *Archangel* is scored for the same 23 winds as Stravinsky's *Symphonies of Wind Instruments*. This 20-minute dramatic work opposes the earthly (most of the players) and the angelic (trumpets, oboes and cor anglais). *Archangel* was premiered as a commission for the Greenwich Festival, London, by the English Chamber Orchestra Winds under David Parry.

BUSBY, Thomas *Dec 1755, Westminster-28 May 1838, London* Organist, composer of sacred music and three stage works for Covent Garden, and the author of a dictionary and a grammar of music; D Mus, Cambridge, 1801. **TZB-1e** *Mrs Wybrow's Pas Seul* is from act 2, scene 1 in *A Tale of Mystery* from Thomas Holcroft's "Melo-drame," first performed on 13 Nov 1802. Busby provided an early example (1798-1801) of a band journal (see part 1).

BUSCHMANN *c.1760* Not the Buschmann who invented the terpodion, London, 1820.

BUSHELL, Geoffrey Clifford *b 7 Feb 1958, Croydon* Horn and double-bass player; conductor of the St Giles Orchestra, Oxford; he composes in a late romantic style.

BUTLER, Martin (Claines) *b 1 Mar 1960, Romsey, UK* His "operatic adventure story," *Craig's progress* **MAB-1v** (1994) uses 2fl 2ob 2cl 2hn 2bn pf(4 hands) perc.

C, I H *(1770)* Possibly "G.H.C.," who copied Reid's *Parthia* for the Kinský Harmonie.

C, J *(1790)* Arranger of operas by Rossini and Weber for the Lobkowitz Kapelle in the 1820s. The Weber horn parts are unusual: "Corno Soprano in Es [Eb], Corno Alto in Es, Corno Tenore in B[b] alto, and Corno Basso in Es."

CADOW, Paul *b 19 June 1908, Lübeck* Choir director, Darmstadt and Bremerhaven.

CAGLIERO, Giovanni, "di Torino" *1838-1926* His works for TTB, fl 2cl 2hn tp tb, timp, organ, now in I-Vsmc, are *Credo, Dominum ad adjuvandum, Gloria, Kyrie, Dixit*.

CALIFF, Pietro His *Sanctus* and *Agnus Dei* for chorus, winds and organ are in I-Vsmc.

CALVI, Girolamo *?, Piazza Brembara, Italy-1848; active in Bergamo* Composer, author of a biography of J S Mayr (qv), and patriot. His music (both for winds alone and for voices with winds) often uses flutes, rather than oboes, as the upper instrument.

CAMBINI, Giuseppe Maria Gioacchino (Giovanni) *13 Feb 1746, Leghorn, Italy-29 Dec 1825, near Paris* Cambini and his fiancée were captured by corsairs and sold as slaves on the Barbary coast in the late 1760s; he was bought and released by a rich Venetian. Her fate is unknown. He was a violinist who wrote many string quartets and some early wind quintets. In Paris in the 1770s, realizing that Mozart was a far better composer, Cambini is said to have helped to lose the manuscript of the K.297b *Sinfonia Concertante*. He wrote *Marches* and *Hymns* for the bands of the French Revolution.

CAMPBELL, Arthur *d Apr 1996* Arranger of music for winds, including works by Albeniz, Bach, Fauré's *Dolly*, Handel's *Music for the Royal Fireworks* and *Arrival of the Queen of Sheba*, Quilter, Sullivan, Warlock's *Capriol Suite* and works by Weber.

CANNABICH, Carl (August) *baptized 11 Oct 1771, Mannheim-1 May 1806, Munich* Member of a distinguished musical family. His work in memory of Mozart, *Mozarts Gedächtnis Feyer* (1797), uses an ensemble of 2cl 2hn 2bn as an echo.

CAPLET, André *23 Nov 1878, Le Havre-22 Apr 1925, Neuilly-sur-Seine* Violinist in the Grand Théâtre, Le Havre, at age 14; timpanist, winner of the 1901 Prix de Rome for composition, and conductor of the Boston Opera 1910-1914. His *Suite Persan* (which he renounced as an early work) is recorded by the Triebensee Ensemble on Astoria 90029.

CARAFA DI COLOBRANO, Prince Michele Enrico (Francesco Vincenzo Aloisio Paolo) *17 Nov 1787, Naples-26 Jul 1872, Paris* Composer of works for military band (*Les souvenirs de Naples* **MCC-1**), an *Allegretto* (19 September 1845) for fl(F) 2ob 3cl 2hn 2bn crt, and several works for solo instrument (horn, cornet, clarinet) with 2cl bn oph. That with solo horn is for the same ensemble as was adopted by Dauprat.

CARPENTER, Gary *b 13 Jan 1951, Hackney, UK* **GQC-1** *Pantomime*, based on music for an earlier children's pantomime, is scored for the same 13 instruments as Mozart's *Gran Partita*. Carpenter's ingenious octet *Ein musikalisches Snookerspiel*, following Mozart's *Composing Game,* is discussed under Koehler (qv).

CARRARA, Vittorio *(1890)* His *Pange lingua*, for large wind band and "coro di populo all'unisono," is a late example (published 1920) of music for Corpus Christi.

CARTELLIERI (Cartellier) Casimiro Antonio *27 Sept 1772, Danzig-2 Sept 1807, Liebeshausen, Bohemia* A composer of much early promise: his oratorio *Gioas, Re di Giuda* was played in Vienna in 1795 at the same concert as the first performance of Beethoven's *Piano Concerto No 2;* his *Concerto* for two clarinets was played by the Stadler brothers in 1797; however, his operas, which made much use of winds, were said to "try too hard to imitate Dittersdorf." Cartellieri's wind music has been recorded by Klöcker/Consortium Classicum on COP CPO999 140 and appears strongly influenced by Beethoven's early works (like the *Octet* **LVB-2** and the *Sextet* for two horns and strings, Op 81b, c.1795?). This suggests a date in the second half of the 1790s (Klöcker suggests earlier, 1792-1794), perhaps after Cartellieri became Musical Director for Prince Lobkowitz. Oddly, there are no copies in the corresponding archive from Roudnice in CZ-Pnm (although the works by "Kathaliery" in CZ-KRa could well be by Cartellieri). The works are all in F (rather than the commoner Eb) and clearly written for a virtuoso ensemble; the horn writing is especially demanding. While the music does not seriously look forward to Krommer, there are enterprising passages, especially in the Alla cosacca [Cossack dance] which ends the *Divertimento No 2*, **CAC-3.**

CARULLI, Benedetto *3 Apr 1797, Olginate-8 Apr 1877, Milan* His *Divertimento* for solo trombone and winds is an unusual and attractive bravura piece in three movements.

CASADESUS, François (Francis) Louis *2 Dec 1870, Paris-27 June 1954, Paris* Casadesus was a pupil of Franck and a composer and violinist. For a time during World War I he was director of the American Military Band School at Chaumont. He was often inspired by popular song, hence his effective, direct, and clear writing. His *London sketches. Petite suite humoristique* (said to date from 1916, though copies in F-Pn are dated 1925) is in three movements: The Policeman at the Zoo; Trafalgar Square Idyll; Hyde Park. Children Play. The suite was arranged for piano by his brother, **Robert Marcel Casadesus** *(7 Apr 1899, Paris-19 Sep 1972, Paris).*

CASKEN, John *15 Aug 1949, Barnsley, UK* Casken studied in Poland; he has been influenced by Lutosławski (qv). His 1973 *Kagura* was written for the St Paul's Orchestra, Birmingham, who gave its first performance under James Young in 1973.

CASTIL-BLAZE (Blaze), François Henri Joseph *1 Dec 1784, Cavaillon-11 Dec 1857, Paris* Castil-Blaze is known as a victim of masterful, stylish and effective damnation in Berlioz's writings. These comments offer a relatively correct assessment of Castil-Blaze's reworking of Weber, Beethoven and others, but do him some injustice as regards his original work outside the field of opera. Castil-Blaze added the first part (Castil) to his name to avoid confusion with his father, also a musician and friend of Grétry and Méhul, though a lawyer by profession. Castil-Blaze himself also studied law and indeed became sous-préfet of Vaucluse before changing to a musical career in 1820. In addition to his operatic ventures, both with operas of his own and modifications of others, he made a collection of songs from Provence (none of which, to our knowledge, actually appear in his works) and wrote copiously on musical matters.

FHC-1 *Sextet in Eb, Op 18 No 1*. The *Sextet* is more interesting than one might expect from Berlioz's comments. Dedicated "à son ami Weichenheim," it was published around 1832; the florid clarinet parts are perhaps the most obvious signs of its period. The use of the word "chalumeau" (cf. Part 3) to indicate a passage to be played an octave lower (clarinet 2, first movement) appears old-fashioned. The final "Bolero" is a lively triple-time movement which other composers might have called a polonaise.

1. H Berlioz 1852 *Evenings in the Orchestra* (translated C R Fortescue 1963; London: Penguin). See especially the Eighteenth Evening. Several wind arrangements use the titles of Castil-Blaze's adaptations, e.g. *Robin des Bois* for *Der Freischütz*.

CATEL, Charles Simon *10 June 1773, L'Aigle, Orne, France-9 Nov 1830, Paris* Catel wrote some of the finest band music of the Revolutionary period. Some celebrated specific events, like the 1794 *Battle of Fleurus* (**CSC-1m, 4mv, 5mv**). His *Ouverture in C* is recorded by Banda Cittadina di Brescia/Ligasacci on Concerto GSCR 00105.

CAVOS, Catterino *30 Oct 1775, Venice-10 May 1840, St Petersburg* Contributor to a set of Masonic works to Pushkin's texts; No 4 is scored for winds, and Nos 2, 3 hint at similar scoring. No 3 is probably by Boieldieu. Cavos went to Russia c.1800, being associated with the Imperial Opera at St Petersburg from c.1805.

ČEJKA (Czeyka), Valentin, *Conte b c.1769, Prague* All of the three manuscripts in the CZ-Pnm Pachta collection style him as "Illustrissimo Sig. il Conte Di Czeyka in Praga."

CELESTINO, Eligio *20 March 1739, Pisa-24 Jun 1812, Ludwigslust* Regarded by Burney as Rome's best violinist c.1770. Celestino moved to Stuttgart in 1776 but, by 1780, was Konzertmeister to the Mecklenburg-Schwerin court at Ludwigslust.

CERHA, Friedrich *17 Feb 1926, Vienna* Cerha studied with Alfred Uhl at the Vienna Conservatory, subsequently becoming professor of composition, and interpretation of new music at the Hochschule für Musik in Vienna. Cerha is also a conductor, and is known for his successful completion of Berg's *Lulu*. **FYC-1** is a *Divertimento: Hommage à Stravinsky*, and his *Curriculum*, **FYC-2**, includes quotations from Charles Ives. He has also written a work for large wind band, his 1964 *Symphonien für Bläser und Pauken*.

CHANDLER, Mary *b 16 May 1911, London* Mary Chandler played oboe and cor anglais with the City of Birmingham Symphony Orchestra from 1944 to 1958. Her music for winds includes her *Octet* of 1957 and the *Cassation* for octet. Her 1975 *Badinages* for double wind quintet is subtitled "Pictures from the life of a Music Centre."

CHÉLARD, Hippolyte André Jean Baptiste *2 Jan 1789, Paris-12 Feb 1861, Weimar* Composer of a *Hymne à Orphée* **HAC-1** for winds, as well as works for large wind band and the *Fantaisie militaire: Le Camp* for two large wind orchestras.

CHERUBINI, Maria Luigi Carlo Zenobio Salvatore *14 Sept 1760, Florence-15 Mar 1842, Paris* Cherubini, Director of the Paris Conservatoire in its formative years, studied with Sarti in Bologna and Milan before settling in Paris in 1788. His was no feeble talent. "Who is the greatest living composer, yourself apart?" asked Cipriani Potter. Beethoven replied "Cherubini" (*Thayer* p 683). Cherubini's operas and C minor *Requiem* are major achievements. The commonest criticism is that they are as uncompromising as the composer himself. This rigidity showed often. Sometimes it was comic, as when he chased Berlioz around the Conservatoire library for entering through the wrong door. His impassivity could be cruel: the death of Henri Brod, oboist and composer, moved

him only to say "Ah, weak tone." Yet it could be impressive. "You are undoubtedly a
fine composer, but your music is so noisy and complicated I can't make anything of it"
observed Napoleon. "You are most certainly a great general" replied Cherubini "but you
must excuse me if I do not compose to your understanding." This independent attitude
is evident from his wind music, both in its high quality and its inspiration. There are the
standard Hymnes for the symbols of the Revolution (for revolutionaries like Marat as
well as for generals like Hoche and Joubert; for fraternity as well as for victory).
However, Cherubini was happy to take advantage of Napoleon's exile (May 1814 to
March 1815) to write marches for Colonel von Witzleben's Prussian Rifle Regiment.

GMC-1mv *Hymne funèbre sur la mort du général Hoche*   One of the masterpieces of
the period, large in conception: Lent; Marche - Lent; Verse sung by young girls; Verse
sung by Les Vieillards (these Elders are clearly men; the French Revolution, like many
others, had little regard for older women); Verse sung by warriors. The state funeral
was on 1 October 1797 (for details of Hoche, see part 1). The music was performed
again at the Grand Opéra on 11 October 1797. Recorded by the Banda Cittadina di
Brescia/ Giovanni Ligasacchi on Concerto GSCR 00105, and possibly by Cologne Chorus
Musicus/ Das Neue Orchester/Spering on Opus OPS30-116. Adapted by Cherubini in
1799 as *Hymne funèbre sur la mort de général Joubert.*

GMC-2mv *Chant Républicain*   Written for the Fête of 10 August 1795. *Pierre/HC* p 111
reproduces a facsimile of a part of the autograph.

GMC-3mv *L'Hymne du Panthéon*   Written for the transfer of Marat's remains to the
Panthéon, and played a week later by a large band at the Fête of 21 September 1794.

GMC-4mv *Hymne à la Fraternité*   First performed at the Tuileries on 22 September
1794, and later at the Grand Opéra.

GMC-6mv *Hymne à la Victoire*   A celebration of the fall of Milan (1796); the work is
recorded by the Wallace Collection on Nimbus NI 5175.

GMC-7mv *Le Saltpêtre républicain*   Based on a song from 1794, it was apparently
intended for the opening of a gunpowder factory, and was not associated with the 1792
massacre of women prisoners in the Salpêtrière.

GMC-2m *Marcia für Baron von Braun*   In 1805, the year this march was written, the
Baron (for whom Salieri also wrote music) was Intendant of the Oper an der Wien and
in charge of both Vienna Court Theaters; Cherubini was in Vienna too, to supervise a
production of *Lodoïska*. The *March* might be a commission, or perhaps a gift. There are
prominent horn parts. It is recorded by the Garde Républicain on SERP MC 7033, and
perhaps by Banda Classica on Koch Schwann SCHW 310110. We remark that *Lodoïska*
contains in the finale to act 2 **GMC-1ve** *Amis que ce divin breuvage*, which could be
used separately in concerts; the opera is rich in its use of winds.

GMC-4m, 5m *Marches written for the Princess of Chimay* (12 July 1809, 22 September
1810). The Prince was an enthusiastic amateur; he and his wife invited Cherubini to
convalesce at their country house in Belgium. Cherubini's *Mass in F* is from this period.

GMC-7m *Six Pas Redoublés and Two Marches, for Col Witzleben*   These date from the
May 1814 (the Pas Redoublés from 24, 27, 28, 30 and 31 May, the Marches both 31
May). Witzleben was the brother of the director of the Berlin Opera. The scoring (tp
3hn tb) is typical of Jäger battalions before the reforms of J G Rode (1797-1851). These
works are recorded by the Ars Nova Ensemble on Erato STW 71265, the London Baroque
Ensemble on R 20613, and the London Gabrieli Brass Ensemble on Hyperion CDA66470.

CHRISTIANSEN, Asger Lund *23 May 1927, Copenhagen*   His *Octet for Winds* is
recorded by the Danish Wind Octet on Da Capo 8224002.

CHRISTIANSEN, Carl *1890-7 Dec 1947*   Only Pacific 123 of the five movements of his
1938 *Toybox* (*Leksaksasken Svit: Spielkasten*; Humoresque, Menuett, Pacific 123,
Pastoral, Tennsoldaternas Marsch) uses the full ensemble of 2fl ob 2cl 2hn 2bn tp tb.

CIANCHI, Emilio *1833-1890* His attractive *Nonetto* **EZC-1** is dedicated to the Società Artistico-Musicale in Florence. It dates from 1868, just before the works by Raff and Dvořák; at this time, there was a demand for wind music in Italian conservatories.

CIGLER, ( ) *(1730?)* His *Barthia* [sic] for 2ob 2hn bn, is in manuscript in CZ-Pnm.

CIMAROSA, Domenico *17 Dec 1749, Aversa, near Naples-11 Jan 1801, Venice* The Tree of Liberty was a symbol of the Republican ideals of the Parthenopean Republic, founded in Piedmont in 1799, the year in which Cimarosa joined an Italian Revolutionary party. This led to his imprisonment and risk of execution. Cimarosa wrote his one work for winds, a product of the French invasion of Italy, for the 19 May 1799 Feast of the Tree of Liberty, held in the square in front of the palace in Naples.

CIMOSO, Domenico *1780-1850* Composer of church works for choir, winds and organ. S Joseph Calasanz, for whose festival the *Tantum ergo* **DXC-1v** was written, founded the Piarists, an order which included vocal and instrumental music in its school curricula. Its members were a powerful force in music in places like Litomyšl.

CLEMENTI, Aldo *b 25 May 1925, Catania* Pianist and composer of serial and electronic music. He studied with Sangiorgi (a pupil of Schoenberg) and Petrassi, and won the 1963 composition prize of the International Society for Contemporary Music.

COCCON (Cocconi), Nicolò *1826, Venice-1903, Venice* Coccon was associated with the Venetian church of Santa Maria della Consolazione, where his name appeared on many MSS, possibly either as copyist or approving the copyist's work. Many of his works include parts (possibly later additions) not found in the autograph scores.

COLE, Hugo *6 Aug 1917, London-March 1995* Composer and critic; biographer of Malcolm Arnold. His *Serenade* **HYC-1,** written in 1965, is a series of short movements, imaginatively and entertainingly written: Intrada; Cantilena; Burleska (horns tacet); Scherzo; Aria; Intermezzo; Pasamezzo; Finale. The Scherzo and Finale have tricky moments for inexperienced ensembles. Alternative scorings are given.

COLEMAN, James *(1760)* Composer of *12 Quick Marches* and *12 Slow Marches.* The title page describes them "as now in use in the ... garrison of Gibraltar."

COLLAUF, ( ) *(1770?)* His music is found among the Moravian Brethren collections.

CONNOLLY, Justin *11 Aug 1933, London* **JUC-1a** *Brahms: Variations* Op 23 (1961) Connolly notes that he has "preserved the sequence and substance of the original," a set of variations for piano duet on a theme by Schumann, dedicated to Julie Schumann.

CONSTANT, Marius *b 7 Feb 1925, Bucharest* Composer of a *Symphony* for winds.

COOKE, Thomas Simpson *1782, Dublin-26 Feb 1847, London* Singer; also a violinist who made his solo debut at the age of seven.

CORNECK, (Mrs) F *(1770)* Her *Royal Highness the Duchess of York's March* is so elegantly engraved that the composer's real name could be Morneck or Horneck.

CORRI, Montague P *1784, Edinburgh-19 Sept 1849, London* See part 1 for some of his biography. Of particular interest is his work **MPC-1m** from c.1835 *A Complete Course of Instructions on the most efficient system of Arranging Music in Score for Voices, Orchestras, Military Bands, Brass Bands &c. with a Description of the Power and Compass of All the Wind Instruments in General Use.* This includes a number of small military pieces as examples.

COSSART, Leland A *1877, Madeira?-1956* His *Suite in F* is recorded by the Triebensee Ensemble on Astoria 90029.

COURTIN, Henri *(1770)* Arranger and compiler of arrangements for winds. The title page of his arrangement of a march by Lesueur states that the work was performed by the "Musiciens des chasseurs à Pieds de la Garde Impériale" at the Battle of Austerlitz. Courtin is styled as "Sergent retraité des Chasseurs à Pied, Professeur d'Harmonie, Membre de la Société des Concerts du Conservatoire."

CROES, Henri-Joseph de *16 Aug 1758, Brussels-6 Jan 1842, Brussels* Violinist son of composer, conductor, and violinist Henri-Jacques de Croes (1705-1786). In the service of the Prince of Thurn and Taxis at Regensburg in 1775 (Maître de Chapelle from 1776 to 1783), he composed a large amount of music, much in large groups of movements for 2cl 2hn 2bn 2vla vlne. Some are unusually scored, using alto clarinets in G.

CROSS, William *d 1826, Oxford*   His *March for the Oxford Loyal Volunteers* is dedicated to Sir Digby Mackworth, who was also the dedicatee of John Mahon's *Oxford Association Marches.* Cross held organist's posts in Oxford.

CROSSE Gordon *b 1 Dec 1937, Bury, Lancashire, UK*   His *Concerto da camera* for violin and winds is recorded on HMV ASD 2333 and Argo ZRG 759.

CRUSELL, Bernhard (Henrik) *15 Oct 1775, Nystad, Sweden-28 July 1838 Stockholm* Clarinettist and composer; arranger for winds of Krommer's *Concerto for 2 Clarinets,* and of one of the arrangements for winds of Beethoven's *Septet* (see under Beethoven).

CURSCHMANN, Karl Friedrich *21 June 1805, Berlin-24 Aug 1841, Langfuhr, near Danzig*   A pupil of Spohr and Hauptmann at Kassel, and a composer of attractive if unexciting songs who was well known for his choral music. His early death was the result of tuberculosis.

CUTLER, William Henry *14 Jan 1792, London-after 1824*   Organist, composer, child prodigy as violinist and pianist, and successful singer, performing at state funerals for Lord Nelson and for statesmen such as Pitt. His career ended when in 1821 "want of nerve prevented his giving full power to his voice." His *March for the 6th Regt Loyal London Volunteers,* dedicated to Lady Blizard, was his first published work (at age 13).

CZERNY, Carl *20 Feb 1791, Vienna-15 July 1857, Vienna*   Pianist known to many for his studies; Czerny also arranged music for winds, including Beethoven's *Septet*; the arrangement of Winter's *Das unterbrochene Opferfest* could, in fact, be by Went.

CZŮBEK, ( ) *(1770)*   Active in Langenbruck, northern Bohemia, in 1802.

DALE, Joseph *1750-21 Aug 1821, Edinburgh*   London publisher and composer of a *March* "for the Gentlemen Volunteers of England."

DANZI, Franz *15 May 1763, Mannheim-13 April 1826, Karlsruhe*   The son of Mannheim cellist, Innocenz Danzi, Franz joined the the Mannheim orchestra as cellist at age 15 in 1778, the year it moved to Munich with the Elector Karl Theodor. Franz Danzi remained with the reduced establishment in Mannheim until 1783, when he succeeded his father as principal cellist. Danzi's earlier wind music may well have been written for the Munich players: a *Sinfonia Concertante* for flute, oboe, horn and bassoon soloists, and possibly the *Eb Sestetto* FAD-2. From 1790 to 1798 he toured Europe with his wife, Marguerite Marchand, a singer and former pupil of Leopold Mozart; he was profoundly affected by her death in 1800. His period as Vice-Kapellmeister in Munich from 1798 was unhappy also because of disagreements with the Kapellmeister, Winter.

The slow movement of his *Symphony in C* (Op 20, Breitkopf & Härtel, February 1804; Op 25 in other editions) is almost entirely for winds, all but 16 of its 84 bars being for fl 2ob 2hn 2bn. John Humphries has shown that the string parts can be successfully transcribed for 3cl b-cl. Danzi's other wind works are the later quintets: those for wind and piano (Op 41, 53, 54) and those for fl ob cl hn bn (Op 56: Bb, G minor, F; Op 67: G, E minor, Eb; Op 68: A, F, D minor). Danzi conducted the Württemberg Orchestra in Stuttgart from 1807. The Stuttgart Opera archives are said to contain more of Danzi's wind music, but we could not find any. Danzi was Kapellmeister in Karlsruhe from 1812; here he corresponded with his friend Weber, who knew just how much he owed to Danzi's help. As Spohr observed more simply, "Danzi was a most amiable artiste."

FAD-2 *Sestetto in Eb*   The opening Allegro is followed by a charming Andante, with two Alternativo sections, a fast Minuet and a splendid "hunting" Finale. Presumably it was written for the Munich winds in the late 1790s. It is the sort of work one might expect from a man described by Max Maria von Weber as "a plump little chap, with a round head and sharp, intelligent eyes that seem good-humoured all the time" (1, p 68). The work shows Danzi's strengths and weaknesses. There are no sophisticated technical devices nor counterpoint; instead, there are catchy rhythms and an individual style of melody looking forward to Weber and Bellini. It is recorded by the Michael Thompson Wind Quintet [sic] on Naxos 8.553352 and Consortium Classicum on BASF KBF-21107. The septet version for cl hn bn and strings appears to be an arrangement to meet the demand generated by Beethoven's *Septet;* likewise, the 1802 publication (as Op 10) for oboe or violin, two violas and cello is surely an arrangement.

1. John Warrack 1976 *Carl Maria von Weber;* Cambridge: Cambridge University Press.

DASSEL, Johann Anton *(1800)* Arranger of two *Galops* by Johann Strauus the Elder.

DAUNEY, ( ) Dr *(1770)* Composer of a *March for the Aberdeen Fencibles.* Not the composer Dr William Dauney (1800-1843), also of Aberdeen.

DAUPRAT, Louis François *24 May 1781, Paris-16 July 1868, Paris* Horn player in the quintet for which Antonin Reicha wrote. Note that the unusual scoring of his *Solo de Cor* (solo horn, 2cl bn ophicleide) was also used by Carafa (qv).

DAVIDE DA BERGAMO, Felice Moretti, Pater *1791-1863* The autograph title page of his one (untitled) work for winds describes him as "Min[ore] Rif[ormato]".

DAVIES, Sir Peter Maxwell *b 8 Sep 1934, Salford, UK* Davies's original path has been associated with The Fires of London, and later with the St Magnus Festival in the Orkney Islands, north of Scotland. Much of his other music uses winds extensively, including his instrumental motet *Eram quasi Agnus* and his *St Thomas Wake: Foxtrot for Orchestra on a Pavan by John Bull.* His 1963 *St Michael Sonata,* **PMD-1,** was a "succès de scandale" at its first performance at the Cheltenham Festival.

DAVIS, Carl *b 1936, New York* Resident in England since 1960, Davis writes with fluency in a variety of styles. He studied under Paul Nordhoff at Bard College. Much of his work (like **CAD-1**) has been for television (including music for Dame Edna Everage) and for revivals of major silent films. In 1991, he collaborated with Sir Paul McCartney in the *Liverpool Oratorio.* **CAD-2** *The Searle Suite* Based on incidental music for a BBC TV documentary on Ronald Searle, whose schoolgirls of St Trinians have become legendary. The suite was then scored for cl vl vc pf. A concert suite for octet was commissioned by Alan Hacker's Whispering Wind Band with funds from the North West Arts Association. The first movement (which is the only one to use b-cl) is the St Trinian's March, characterizing the ingeniously scandalous young ladies. The Hamburg Blues uses a sultry clarinet to hint at the temptations available; the third movement, Snails, uses it quite differently in an indolent waltz. The finale, Toulouse-Lautrec Revisited, is what should be described as a Montmartre ragtime. The work is recorded on MFY HAC 811 (through Banks and Son Music, York).

DAVY, John *23 Dec 1763, Crediton-22 Feb 1824, London* Violinist, cellist and organist, he also composed for Sadler's Wells. **JHD-1mv** sets "To Arms: To Arms! - or - John Bull's Charge to his Country," words by James Fisher, "a member of the Honourable Society of the Inner Temple." The work is dedicated to the Duke of York.

DELLO JOIO, Norman *b 24 Jan 1913, New York* Composer, influenced by Hindemith to some degree, and a pianist; he has ranged from touring with his own jazz band to writing a ballet for Martha Graham. He has written music for small wind ensembles, as well as his *Satiric Dances for a Comedy by Aristophanes* **NJD-1.**

DEOLA, Paolo *(1800; active 1845-1856)* Composer of much music for choir and winds. Many of Deola's works include additional parts not on the autograph scores. I-Vsmc also holds many fragmentary sets of parts by Deola, some of which may be for voices and winds; there are also a number of choral works with two horns and organ.

DERENZIS, Rafaelo *17 Feb 1879, Casacalenda, Campobasso-3 Nov 1970, Rome* Music critic, and editor of a collected edition of Palestrina's works.

DESHAYES, Prosper Didier *1751-1815, Paris*   Composer of oratorios and operas for Paris, of whom little is known. For a time, he was a member of the Garde Nationale.

DESIRO, ( )   His works for voices, winds and organ are now in Venice (I-Vsmc).

DESVIGNES, Pierre (Louis Augustin) *27 Sep 1764, Vélars-21 Jan 1827, Paris*
His *Deprofundis [sic]* for voices and winds was performed at Notre Dame Cathedral to celebrate the Battle of Austerlitz (1805). There are two autograph scores in Paris, dated 1806. One styles him "Maitre [sic] de Musique de la Métropole de Paris" and notes that the mass was performed in March 1806 "à la Métropole ... Pour la Service de la Bataille." Desvignes wrote several other *Masses* accompanied by small wind groups.

DEVASINI, Giuseppe *20 Mar 1822, Milan-21 Jun 1878, Cairo*   Devasini's *Sestetto* was composed and published (by Ricordi) while he was a student at the Milan Conservatorio, and is dedicated to its Director, Count Renato Borromeo.

DEVIENNE, François *31 Jan 1759, Joinville-5 Sept 1803, Charenton*   Bassoonist, who wrote music for bands of the French Revolution, and arranged operas by Gaveaux.

DIBDIN, Charles *baptized 4 Mar 1745, Southampton-25 July 1814, London*   Dibdin's enormously popular songs (such as "Tom Bowling") continued to appear in collections for decades after his death. His sympathetic understanding of naval life earned him the name "the Tyrtaeus of the British Navy" (the martial songs of Tyrtaeus inspired the Spartans at the siege of Ithome; Dibdin inspired the British Navy in the Napoleonic Wars shortly before Trafalgar). Largely self-taught, Dibdin had been a chorister at Winchester Cathedral, but soon entered the London theatrical scene, where his "Entertainments" were far more successful than his financial affairs. His songs show originality and a general freedom from the uninspired musical formulas found in the work of some of his contemporaries. Little of Dibdin's instrumental music survives. His wind music consists largely of his own arrangements of the so-called *War Songs* and similar works from their fuller orchestral versions. Dibdin's other songs often mention music, musicians, and bands; more novel are his songs relating to army camps or to special occasions, like Royal weddings or the Lord Mayor's Day: "And now, while trumpets rend the air, / And sweet musicians sing / Haste to the feast, where, while the band / The social hour prolong." **CXD-1**, *Lancachire [sic] Witches* (who bewitch by charm, not by potion), is an original movement from the opera of that title produced at The Circus in 1782. This deftly written short allegro for 2cl 2hn basso (normally Dibdin's "basso" means bassoon) appears in the autograph of the opera immediately after a full air with orchestra. "Peotr[?] at dinner" is partly crossed out above it.

The *War Songs* date from the middle of 1803, when the brief peace from 1801 was ending. It appears that Dibdin was granted a government pension of £200 per annum (1) which lapsed with the next change of ministry. The standard source (2) asserts: "In 1803, Didbin was engaged by the government (3) to write a series of songs, to keep up the national feeling against the French. He sang them in turns in the entertainment called *Britons! Strike Home* and published them under the title *British War Songs*. The series consisted of but five [actually nine, see below], his engagement ceasing with the war he thus assisted in bringing to a glorious close." *Britons! Strike Home* (named after Purcell's song, still popular, cf. Steibelt's *Naval Battle* music arranged by Goepfert, **CAG-9a**) has an interesting introduction by Dibdin (ref 2 p 228): "This piece was written, as its title imports, to keep up the enthusiasm against our Gallic neighbours, that had been in part excited by the previous publication of our author's *British War Songs*." In the preface to the book of the songs in this entertainment he says "I have introduced characters of every country appertaining to Britain, and have made the drift of my doctrine union and conciliation." He knew well that war meant death, as well as glory (4). *The Manes of the Brave* (on remembering the dead of war in peace) reads:

"Now that bands of musicians so gayly advance / In the concert to join, or enliven the dance, / At one grateful idea the tumult shall end; / The soft flute the sad cadence alone shall suspend." Most of the texts are by Dibdin himself (except where stated below) and are given by Davidson (2) who omits *War Songs* 1, 6, 7, 9, and the *Ode in Honour of His Majesty's Birthday).* The *War Songs* are all numbered, and mostly dated. **CXD–4.1m.** *No 1 Fall and Conquer;* 2cl 2hn 2bn bassi 2tp; no date (probably June 1803?). The text is not by Dibdin, but is a parody on "Bruce's Address to the Scots." **CXD–4.2m.** *No 2 British Heroines;* 2cl 2hn 2bn bassi; 4 July 1803 (the title does *not* refer to Heroes, as commonly given, erroneously, including [2]). The autographs of *War Songs 1, 2* carry the "Directions for Bands" which we quote in part 3. **CXD–4.5m.** *No 5 The Song of Acre;* 2cl 2hn bassi; 4 October 1803. The title refers to the defence of Acre against Napoleonic besiegers from 16 March to 20 May 1799 by the Turks and British forces under Sir Sidney Smith, and not to the siege during the Third Crusade. The cigarette is said to have been invented by the Turks during the later siege. There is no wind band version of *No 7, The Lion in his Den,* 4 December 1803.

There are five further songs with band arrangements of the original orchestral versions. Three are from Dibdin's *Britons! Strike Home*: **CXD–5.1m** *The Auld Pibrough;* **CXD–5.2m** *Subscription at Lloyds;* presumably it was written soon after 20 July 1803, and refers to the voluntary contributions to the war effort by the Exchange; **CXD–5.3m** *Victory and George III.* A march **CXD–1mf** for 2cl bn (with empty staves for horns and trumpets) is in GB-Lbl; its start is very similar to that of *Subscription at Lloyds,* but develops differently. The other two songs with band refer to events in the life of King George III: **CXD–1m** *Ode in Honour of His Majesty's Birthday,* and **CXD–2m** *Ode to Gratitude;* presumably composed soon after 15 May 1800, the date of the attempt on King George III's life by the lunatic, Hatfield, at Drury Lane Theatre.

1. *Grove V* entry on Dibdin by Alfred Loewenberg.
2. G H Davidson 1844 *The Songs of Charles Dibdin chronologically arranged...to which is prefixed a Memoir...by George Hogarth, Esq.*; London: Davidson.
3. Elsewhere, the commission is said to be an Admiralty one (L Winstock 1970 *Songs of the Redcoats;* Harrisburg, PA: Stackpole Books p 276, citing Evett *Our Songless Army).* The regularity of the songs (almost a monthly series) and the print quality suggest a subsidy. The format makes the series an example of a periodical music journal.
4. Most of Dibdin's songs about naval life come after the naval mutinies at the Nore and at Spithead in 1797. The mutinies do not seem to be referred to, yet their origins may have encouraged his sympathy. See G E Manwaring and B Dobrée 1937 *The Floating Republic;* London: Penguin Books, which notes several occasions on which ships' bands played, especially "God Save the King" and "Rule Britannia."

DIETHE, Johann Friedrich *1810-1891* Known as an oboist.

DIJKSTRA, Lowell *b 1952* Composer of *Fantasia* (1988) and *Peccadillos* (1991).

DIMITRAKOPOULOS, Apostolos *b 4 Jan 1955, Greece* His works for winds (*Void, Impexus, Lux prima*) include one with tape, entitled *5.1.8.*

DISCHER, J D See under **Fischer, J**

DITTERSDORF, Carl Ditters von *2 Nov 1739, Vienna-24 Oct 1799, Zámek Červená Lhota (between Soběslav and Jindřichův Hradec, Trěbonško), Bohemia* Born the son of a theatrical costumier, Dittersdorf's stage works had more than passing fame. They include a *Marriage of Figaro,* earlier than Mozart's, and a *Merry Wives of Windsor* much earlier than Nicolai's. Ditters (as he then was) took over Michael Haydn's position with the Bishop of Grosswardein, Adam Patátisch, leaving when the Bishop, rebuked by the Empress for his laxity, dismissed his musicians (1). Presumably Dittersdorf's wind music for Grosswardein is lost with the rest of the archives (2). After a period with another Bishop in disgrace (Count Schaffgotsch, Prince Bishop of Breslau, based at

Johannisberg), Dittersdorf prospered, and was ennobled in 1773 at least as much for his skill in forestry as in music. A stage wind band (2ob 2hn 2bn) is used to good effect in act 2 of his 1794 komisches Singspiel *Das Gespenst mit der Trommel* for the ducal theater at Oels, Prussian Silesia (3). In this fascinating work, the Graf, supposedly killed in the wars, carries out military exercises in a melodrama with the stage band.

Dittersdorf's large set of parthias for 2ob 2hn bn includes both works in the multi-movement form of a suite and in the format of a symphony. Thus **CDD-1** has seven movements, with three minuets and two polonaises (one Larghetto, the other Allegro). Twelve are in four movements, though dance movements are common (so **CDD-28**, comprises an Andante, a Minuet, a Polonaise, and a Finale: Tempo di Contradanza, with three trios and a coda). The main set is from the Pachta collection. The second, fourth and twentieth of this set were numbered 2, 4 and 20 in the version published by Breitkopf & Härtel, Wiesbaden. These three (**CDD-9, 11, 26**) have been recorded by the French Wind Quintet on Oiseau Lyre OL-50014; an unidentified Partita in F recorded by Hickel *et al* on Musica Rara MUS-16 may be from this set. The Partita **CDD-15**, edited by Haas from a manuscript in the Royal Music, has been recorded by the London Baroque Ensemble (on PMB 1008 and HQM 1083). This divertimento contains a difficult horn parts; Dennis Brain demonstrates in the recording how well it can sound. Yet the Polone in **CDD-9** has an unconvincing high horn part, perhaps erroneously reconstructed from an alternative version. Some movements have quite complex structures, with several tempo changes. Examples include the third movement of **CDD-32**, the Contradanza of **CDD-28**, and some of the movements of **CDD-35**. Dittersdorf seems to want to experiment, rather than to accept conventional formats.

CDD-1d is not by Dittersdorf, but is a copy by Druschetzky of Rosetti's **FAR-9.1**.
1. *Dittersdorf's Autobiography;* translated A D Coleridge 1896 London: Bentley & Son; reprinted Da Capo Press.
2. K Krebs 1900 *Dittersdorfiana*, Berlin. The only wind work listed is K 136 (**CDD-38**).
3. Thomas Bauman 1985 *North German Opera in the Age of Goethe;* Cambridge: Cambridge University Press; pp 304-307.
DITTRICH, Francis *(1770)*   His *Collection of Military Music* is dedicated to the Earl of Dalkeith, 4th Regiment North Berwick Militia. It comprises marches and dances.
DIXON, William *(c.1760)*   Composer of works for church choirs, with flutes or oboes and bassoon; he also wrote glees and songs.
DOBIHAL, Josef (Joseph) *1779-1824*   Clarinettist, arranger (possibly one of the unnamed publishing house arrangers in Vienna during the period 1800-1820), compiler, and "Capellmeister des k k E H Maxm 2ter Feld Artillerie Regiments." Dobihal's *Marsch* **JUD-1m**, originally in common time, was included in Romani's *Die Fee und der Ritter*, ending up in 2/4 in Sedlak's arrangement. We suspect that the farce *Larighetto* **JUD-1a** may be based on a work by Dobihal, not merely an arrangement by him.
DOMAŽLICKY, František *b 13 May 1913, Prague*   His initial success as amateur composer, band leader and instrumentalist was followed by wartime experiences in concentration camps and on death marches. Only later did Domažlicky complete formal studies, then playing violin and viola in the Film Symphony Orchestra and other ensembles. He has written two wind quintets, a brass quintet, a saxophone quartet, and a *Concerto for Wind Octet, Op 45* (1973).
DONATONI, Franco *b 9 Jun 1927, Verona*   Donatoni rescored his *Movimento* **FCD-1** of 1959 for full orchestra in 1962.
DONIZETTI (Domenico) Gaetano (Maria) *29 Nov 1797, Bergamo-8 Apr 1848, Bergamo*   Donizetti received free tuition from Mayr (qv) for about a decade; their lifelong friendship is one reason Mayr is remembered. It was for Mayr's funeral in S Maria Maggiore, Bergamo, that Donizetti arranged Mayr's *Miserere* for six solo voices, chorus

and winds (**DGD-1va**, 1822). Donizetti concentrated on opera after his *Enrico di Borgogna* was produced in Venice in 1818 (in fact it was his fourth opera, the earlier ones being unperformed). His few works with winds date from about this time, and include church music as well as his *Sinfonia* for winds and his *Concertino* for cor anglais, with its wind interjections. His operas use stage bands in *Maria Padilla* (1841), *Maria di Rudenz* (1837) and *Alfredo il Grande* (1823) (1, 2). Even Donizetti's popular *La figlia del reggimento,* is redolent of contemporary military wind harmony music.

The *Sinfonia in G* of 1817, **DGD-1**, is a single-movement overture, with a short opening flourish. It is operatic in style, with flute, oboe 1 and bassoon 1 as principals. One does not look to the average Italian opera for subtle wind writing, and there is little here to show Mayr's tuition. There are many ill-judged doublings, which increase whenever a *piano* instruction appears and disappear when *forte* is demanded; however, judicious editing and a hefty dose of melodrama can make this work a pleasure.

DGD-1m *Marcia in F* may be the march recorded on Frequenz Conifer 011 008. There is also a *Gran Marcia Militaire Imperiale* (1840) for the Sultan Abdul Medjid Khan, and another march, for his brother, from 1840.

1. W Ashbrook 1965 *Donizetti;* London: Cassell.

2. W Ashbrook 1982 *Donizetti and His Operas;* Cambridge: Cambridge University Press.

DONNINGER, Ferdinand *1716-1781* Oboist at Regensburg, and also the composer of *See Schlacht* (a battle at sea) for orchestra with cannon and muskets.

DOUBRAVSKY (Dobrawský, Däubrawsky), František *7 Feb 1790, Lomnice-28 Apr 1867, Lomnice* Among his religious music with winds (including *Stationes* and a *Stabat Mater)* is a funeral piece "for a husband."

DOUW, André *1951* Douw's 1990 *Octet* is unusually scored, for 2fl 2ob 2cl hn bn.

DOVE, Jonathan *b 1959* **JQD-1** *Figures in a Garden* was written to precede Mozart's *Le nozze di Figaro* at Glyndebourne, 1991. It uses period instruments, and was recorded by the Orchestra of the Age of Enlightenment, directed by the composer, on EMI CDC 7 54424. The seven short movements hint at the events of the summer day and night of the opera: Dancing in the dark; Susanna in the rain; A conversation; Barbarina alone; The Countess interrupts a quarrel; Voices in the Garden; Nocturne: Figaro and Susanna.

DOWNEY, John W(ilham) *b 5 Oct 1927, Chicago* Professor and composer in residence at the University of Wisconsin, Milwaukee. His *Octet* is for fl ob 2cl hn 2bn tp; he has written *Agort* for wind quintet and *Almost Twelve* for fl ob cl hn bn cbn vl vl vc perc.

DRAHLOVSKY, Josef C His *4 Stationes* for Corpus Christi (Op 92) are from the church archives in Břeclav, and are now in CZ-Bm.

DRANREL, ( ) *(1790)* Active c.1810, in Langenbruck, Northern Bohemia.

DREHER, Josef Anton Composer of a *Harmonie* for fl 2cl 2hn bn b-tb from Gutenzell.

DROBISCH, Carl (Karl) Ludwig (Carlo Luigi) *1803-1854* Active in the 1830s, composing church music for the Frauenkirche in Munich.

DROBISCH, Johann Gottfried Trautgott *d 1807, St Petersburg* Violinist and composer.

DRÖSLER, ( ) **YXD-1** is possibly an arrangement of a work by Josef Dreschler.

DROSTE-HÜLSHOFF, Maximilian Friedrich, Freiherr von Vischering *22 Oct 1764, Hülshoff, Münster-8 Mar 1840, Alst Hülshoff bei Münster* Uncle of Germany's most famous woman writer, Annette von Droste-Hülshoff. He also wrote a *Grand Quatuor Concertante* for fl ob hn bn and orchestra. The title of **MDV-1v** *Das Hallelujah von Pfeffel* indicates the author of the text, Johannes Würmchen von Pfeffel.

DRUOT, ( ) *(1770)* Active at Regensburg c.1800.

DRUSCHETZKY (Družecký), Georg (Jiří) *7 Apr 1745, Jemníky (near Kladno) Bohemia-6 Sept 1819, Buda (now Budapest, Hungary)* Druschetzky was a prolific and able (rather than great) composer of wind harmony. His wide-ranging output suggests that he was a composer people turned to for some special occasion, for his music often has unusual or nonmusical aspects: folk instruments are used (**GYD-3, GYD-6**), the metronome (or its precursor) is celebrated **GYD-20**, and so on.

Druschetzky was known in his time as one of the last of the virtuosi of the heroic full timpanist's art, presumably the style matching the high trumpet or horn parts in Bach cantatas or the flamboyant military style (the *Concerto for Solo Timpani*, said to be with wind octet, is actually with orchestra; it is recorded by the Bournemouth Sinfonietta on CRD 3449). He is said to have studied oboe with the oboist Besozzi (qv) in Dresden. Druschetzky joined the 50th Regt Grenadiers at Eger (Cheb) in 1768, becoming Kapellmeister. He was discharged in 1775, and moved to the Linz Cuirassiers, whose Honorary Colonel, Count Harsch, encouraged him. In 1783, Druschetzky moved to Vienna, publishing his first octets, **GYD-7(-12)**, in 1784. They were dedicated to Count Jean Esterházy, either Johann Baptist (1748-1800) or János Nepomuk (1754-1840) for whom Paul Wranizky was Musical Director. Druschetzky moved to Pressburg where, from 1787, he was employed by Anton, Prince Grassalkovics, an enthusiast for wind harmony. The Prince, who had gained his wealth in the Seven Years' War, married into the princely Esterházy family; his father-in-law was Haydn's employer. Grassalkovics was later to employ Krommer and to attempt to persuade Haydn to join him.

The Grassalkovics collection of wind music is lost, though some of Druschetzky's extant works may date from this period. One special piece was written first for the 15 November 1790 Pressburg coronation of Leopold as Emperor of Austria and King of Hungary (it was for this Prague coronation that Mozart wrote *La clemenza di Tito)*. For Pressburg, the Esterházy and Grassalkovics wind bands combined to play a (now-lost) 21-part Harmonie of Druschetzky's with such success that Salieri conducted a second performance of the work for the Tonkünstlerverein in April 1791. Grassalkovics died in 1794. For a time, Druschetzky was associated with Prince Archbishop Josef Batthyáni; in 1796, he moved to Buda, where his next major appointment was as Master of Music to Josef Anton, Palatine of Hungary, from 1813. We presume that, in the interim, Druschetzky supported himself by his arrangements and occasional pieces.

Larger works. Two of the examples here are religious works, with titles which might suggest vocal works, but which inspection shows are purely instrumental. The first, **GYD-1** *Messlied und Heilig: Wir werfen uns darmieder* is stated to be "accomodato del Sig: Druschetzkÿ," which suggests an arrangement of another work. The *Messlied* is in three main sections, one broken up into a series of cadences ending with a fermata. The *Heilig* comprises four sets of four bars, ending with a fermata. The scoring is for 2ob 2cl(C) 2hn 2bn cbn, with optional cl(F; it plays only in the Heilig) 2tp b-tb. There are two earlier horn parts for the *Heilig* only. **GYD-2** *Adagio con un Imatazione [sic]* is also complicated. There is an organ part (which bears the title Offertorium de S^{cto} Stephan), and there are some parts (2tp timp organ) which may have been added later to the 2ob 2cl 2hn 2bn scoring. The Adagio is labelled N° 3; there are also two other title pages (N° 2, and what may also be N° 3) for movements with full orchestra and voices. There is little doubt, however, that this movement is an Offertorium for winds alone. Likewise, **GYD-19** is a *Mottetto* [sic] for 2ob 2cl 2hn 2bn and **GYD-161** a *Miserere* for 2bthn/cl 2hn 2bn; no voices are intended. **GYD-4** is scored for 2ob cl bthn 2hn 2bn cbn, and appears alongside arrangements bearing the same title: the arrangement **GYD-9a** of Bohr's *Rondo: Fresco Ungaria* is followed by Druschetzky's **GYD-4** *Rondo Fresco ungaria*. Similarly, the arrangement **GYD-12a** of Hassler's (untitled) *Rondo in F* is followed by **GYD-5**, a *Rondo in C minor*.

Regular Octets for 2 oboes 2 clarinets 2 horns and 2 bassoons.

The *6 Parthias* **GYD-7(-12)** were advertized in the *Prager interessante Nachtrichten* of 10 January 1784; a printed edition of unspecified octets (probably these) was advertized by Christoph Torricella, Vienna in the *Wiener Zeitung* of 7 July 1784. They are among the best of Druschetzky's works, with some interesting instrumental writing, such as the horn and bassoon coloring in No 4, or the interaction of the second clarinet, first horn and bassoons in the trio of No 5. No 2 has a Polonaise instead of the usual slow movement. No 3 is recorded by Collegium Musicum Pragense/Vajnár on Supraphon SUA 111 1839 and No 4 on SUA 59704F, 11 0097-1 031G and Opus 9111 9419.

GYD-22 *Variazioni in Bb*   These "Variationen" were advertized by Torricella in the *Wiener Zeitung* of 1784. They are sometimes confused with the different set, *Variations on a March Theme by Count Louis de Széchény,* which dates from July 1805.

GYD-23 *Zrini Ungaria: Entre Act [sic]. adagiosissima [sic] dopoi And^{te}*   The title must refer to Miklós Zrinyi (1620-1664), Hungarian statesman, military leader, and author of the epic *Szigeti Veszedelem* describing the 1566 defense of the Szigetuar fortress against the Turks. Kodály has set the poetry of Zrinyi in his *Zrinyi's Appeal.* We suspect Druschetzky wrote this interlude for Theodor Körner's *Zriny,* produced at the Vienna Burgtheater in 1812. It is unclear whether the topic relates only to the Turks, in view of their invasions of central Europe and their continuing presence in Greece (cf Beethoven's *Ruins of Athens),* or to the control of Hungary by Austria, or perhaps to suggest an analogy between the Turkish and Napoleonic invasions. There is no sign of a tune associated with Zrinyi, though the autograph note "acomodato in Harmoni di Druschetzki" suggests it is an arrangement. All that survives of the first oboe part is five bars (two solo) written on the back of the first bassoon part.

Special Octets, all with some unusual effect, like folk or toy instrumentation.

GYD-3 *Partitta Berdlersgarn*   The players include a "damborino" (tambourine) and a "violono pigola" ("piculino" on the part) tuned to a D g G; it always plays 2, 3 or 4 notes together, except for single-note tremolos in the third movement. The wind players double on toy instruments, five playing Schelerl (bells, probably sleigh bells, perhaps [headless] tambourines; oboes 1, 2; clarinets 1, 2; bassoon 2). Other instruments are: Oboe 1: Wachtel weibl (female quail) and Trompett; Clarinet 2: the cuckoo, either as a "C gugu" (notes G, E) or as a "D gugu" (notes A, F). Horns 1, 2: "Trompetta" in the trio of the minuet. Bassoon 1: Ratschen (cog-rattle); Bassoon 2: Rohlerl (again bells, but here probably tubular bells), Wachtel mannl (or Mañ, male quail). Presumably the title *Berdlersgarn* (like that of Leopold Mozart's *Sinfonia Berchtoldsgardensis)* comes from Berchtesgaden, whose factories supplied the Nuremberg toy trade. The work is recorded by Collegium Musicum Pragense/Vajnár on Supraphon 1 11 1156 and 10 1156-1 111G.

GYD-6 *Parthia auf Bauerninstrumenten*   This *Parthia* has been recorded by Capella Savaria on SLPD 12874. The players double on various folk instruments: Oboe 1: Leyer, a hurdy-gurdy, with its usual drones; Oboe 2: Span Fidl, a slim, small folk fiddle; Clarinet 1: Klachter, a xylophone of tuned wooden bars on straw rolls (the part is in Bb); Clarinet 2: Bruma [tromba] marina, a single-string instrument with rasping tone; Bassoon 1: Tudlsak, a single-drone bagpipe (Dudelsack) with a Bb fundamental; Bassoon 2: Citer, a flat-bodied instrument, not unlike a guitar, wire strung and here tuned to B d f a' c'; Horns: Trombi a Tiroli, alphorns in two sizes. The instruments themselves are listed in a 1798 inventory for the Batthyáni Harmonie, valued in all at a mere one and a half Forints. A later autograph cimbalon part has been added, inserting 7 movements after the original first movement. The cimbalon part has 8 bars rest at the start of three of the new movements, for which no other parts exist.

GYD-13 *Echo Partita*   Using opposing wind bands is an old idea, well known to Venetian composers like Giovanni Gabrieli and exploited by Handel in his *Concerti a due cori.* Classical wind band composers used the same idea (qv Asplmayr, d'Ordoñez, Seyfried, Hoffmeister and Triebensee) but also aimed at the effect of distance rather than stereophony, so that the echo band's parts may consist mainly of rests.

GYD-19 *Des Herrn V. Zmeskal. Tact Messer Wiener Zoll des Herrn Mälzels Bestimmung*

des Tempo durch das Metronom   These five short items "acomodato Di Druschetzky"
use a theme from a sonata by Anton Halm, once a Lieutenant in the Imperial and Royal
Army. They demonstrate early devices for setting tempos; each item has two markings,
one for the "Takt Messer" (or Vienna Standard Timing Device, effectively a pendulum,
a lead bullet with a string knotted at critical points) and the other for the metronome.
This work allows a direct check of how accurate (or inaccurate) metronome marks can
be (see part 3). Most of the public discussion of such devices was in 1817 (2), so perhaps
this work was written then. Nikolaus Zmeskall von Domanovec was a cellist and an old
friend of Beethoven's, whom he addressed as "clarissime amice." Both played wearing
spectacles, so Beethoven's WoO 32, composed for them to play together, was for viola,
cello and "zwei obligaten Augengläsern" (two obbligato eyeglasses) (*Thayer* p 686).
GYD–40(–45)   Druschetzky wrote quite extensively for the basset horn, including an
unusual set of works (*Partittas 25-28* and *Partittas à la Camera Nos 22, 23*). These
include three basset horn parts, written for a transposing instrument in F basso, even
though the home key is G. In **GYD–45**, bthn 1 and 2 lead, and bthn 3 accompanies with
typical arpeggio "woodles." The oboe generally doubles bthn 1, so the omission of the
oboe in one work is not especially significant. For **GYD–43**, the oboe and bassoon parts
are marked "CONC^(TINO)"[sic] and certainly the oboe leads in several movements.
   Works for Seven Instruments.   The modest *Parthias* **GYD–23(–39)**, written for the
Schwarzenberg Harmonie, are all in four movements except for the fifth (which lacks
a slow movement) and five others, which have an extra Minuet and Trio.
   Sextets for 2 clarinets, 2 horns and 2 bassoons.   The two *Concertos* **GYD–57, 58** are
for Solo clarinet, cl 2hn 2bn (six instruments, not seven, contrary to *MGG*). Wind works
with a soloist like this are not uncommon, though they rarely bear the title "Concerto."
GYD–55, 63, 67 *Parthia Concertand* or *Concertante*   These works are not really
concertos. **GYD–55** is available in a modern edition; it has a good slow movement, but
the trio reminds one only too much of what Mozart parodied in *A Musical Joke*. They
are among the *Parthien* purchased for Count Festetics's Harmonie at the spa resort of
Keszthely on the shores of Lake Balaton. The Count was confined to his estates in the
1790s as a suspected Jacobin. He commissioned Anton Stadler to prepare a plan for a
music school in 1799. All the very many MSS at Keszthely were purchased as a single
lot in 1802 from Johann Gallyus, Advocat, Zagreb. The Festetics collection in the
Helikon Library was saved after World War II by a far-sighted Russian officer, who
walled up the entrance (*HCRL/1 p240*). Several works (**GYD–68, 73**) are *Echo Partittas;*
others are the *Partittas Concertante*. **GYD–59**, *Ronde Nationale,* ends with a medley
of national dances, with the structure ABACADAEA. The A section (2/4) leads to an
Andantino alla francese (6/8), Polonese (3/4), Tedesco (3/8) and Inglese (2/4).
GYD–123 *Partitta La Fantasia*   An unusually ambitious and eccentric work, opening
with a 5-bar cadenza for horn. The fifth movement opens with hunting fanfares, and
has frequent dynamic contrasts; the first movement returns as finale.
GYD–125   A set of 88 dances, of which 2 carry titles: 40 Pastorella; 41 Thema. The
item preceding the collection is a Ländler from Süssmayr's *Spiegel in Arkadien*.
   Sextets for flute, two oboes, two horns and bassoon.   Four of the set **GYD–47(–53)**
from the Clam Gallas archive are labelled "Parthia" and three "Partitta." **GYD–47** is
a rarity, both as a wind work in a minor key and as a concertino for flute with winds.
   Works for 2 oboes 2 horns and 1 or 2 bassoons.   All those we have checked exist in
more convincing scorings with a single bassoon, so we shall treat them as quintets.
There is also a set of six quintets with clarinets, rather than oboes, in Regensburg, of
which one is found in a version with oboes in Vienna.
GYD 128(–151) *24 Partiten*   This collection in A-Wgm has *Partitas* grouped by key: Nos
1-6 in C, 7-11 in F, 12-14 in B♭, 15-17 in E♭, 18-21 in G and 22-24 in D (No 22 in D

minor); the *Parthia* listed by Traeg in his 1799 catalog may be one of this set. Four (Nos 9, 10, 13, 21) are published in a modern edition, which states that the works have been recorded (not verified by us). One has a pencil marking "Wagenseil," but there is nothing to suggest he wrote it; another (**GYD-148**) is marked "Favorito" in another hand. No 21 alone rises above the mundane. As its title ("Al valet") implies, it is a "Farewell" partita, similar to Haydn's *Farewell Symphony* (Hob.I:45 of 1772). The last movement starts with a march, followed by five variations. After the first variation, horn 1 leaves, followed by horn 2 after the second; oboe 2 departs after variation 3, soon to be joined by oboe 1. This leaves the bassoon to play a plaintive solo in G minor before taking leave. This work is recorded by the Ensemble Philidor on Supraphon CD 11 2182-2 131. Other works in this group have bravura parts, labelled solo: the oboe in **GYD-132, 136,** the bassoon in **GYD-133, 138,** and the *second* horn in **GYD-144.** In the third movement of **GYD-135,** every one of the parts is marked *con sordini.*

Arrangements of works by others.   Druschetzky probably wrote many more arrangements than we can identify, and others may survive among the anonymous versions in European libraries (*HCRL/5 p 139*). Some are substantial, like his versions of Haydn's *The Creation* **GYD-13a** and *The Seasons* **GYD-14a.** The copy of **GYD-13a** in A-Wgm calls for contrabassoon, but there is no extra part; some of the parts have been transposed, and there are many markings by performers. The A-Wgm copy of **GYD-14a** includes a piccolo part which does not belong to the arrangement: the bar counts are wrong as well as the paper being different in type and size. His set of opera arrangements **GYD-7a** has a title page stating "Von Herrn Georg Druschetzky Compositeur bey deiner Eminentz und Primas in Ungarn Graff Joseph Battiany." The set confirms that the Batthyáni Harmonie comprised 2cl 2hn 2bn.

GYD-8a *Beethoven: Septet, Op 20*   The *Septet,* published in 1802, was arranged for winds by several composers (see under Beethoven); Druschetzky's version for 2ob 2cl 2hn 2bn cbn/vlne was published in 1812 in Vienna, and is recorded by Collegium Musicum Pragense/Vajnar on Supraphon SUA 111 2180, by Bratislavská komorná harmoniá/Pavlík on Opus 9111 0583, and Oesterreichischer Kammerharmonie/Prammer.

GYD-10a Arranged from Josef Drechsler's *Nelsons Trauermarsch* for piano, published in Vienna by Artaria (pn 1849) in 1807. Nelson died at Trafalgar on 21 October 1805. Performances listed on the horn 2 part are 29 May 1807, 9 June 1807, 1 Feb 1810, and 2 Aug 1812. Artaria published an anonymous *Nelson-Trauermarsch* (pn 1746) in 1805.

Sets of variations are a feature of Druschetzky's music. Thirteen works end in a set (**GYD-49, 68, 70, 80, 85, 93, 99, 102-104, 110, 111, 118**), five more appear as interior movements in **GYD-60, 71, 76, 93, 116,** and there are six sets within the 62 movements of **GYD-164** (movements 15, 25, 28, 39, 52 and 60).

GYD-1a *Six Thema con Variazioni "Acomodato [sic] Nel Harmonie Di Giorgio Drushetzký [sic]*   The themes are identifiable, the original composers of the variations less so. Thus one finds **GYD-1.1a:** 5 variations "Sur le Menuetto Danse [sic] par Mademoisell [sic] Venturini"; **GYD-1.3a:** 2 variations on the Andante from Haydn's *Symphony No 81*; **GYD-1.4a:** 6 variations on Haydn's "The Heavens Are Telling" (*The Creation*); and **GYD-1.6a:** 6 variations on Sesto's aria (No 19, from bar 53) in Mozart's *La clemenza di Tito.* The other two sets of variations are based on Mozart's piano variations; neither title nor composer is indicated on the MSS. **GYD-1.2a** comprises 6 of the 12 variations Mozart wrote on "Ah, vous dirai-je, Maman" (K.300e/265). **GYD-1.5a** contains 6 of the variations Mozart wrote on "Unser dummer Pöbel meint" from Gluck's *La rencontre imprévu.* Druschetzky's set differs from Artaria's 1786 publication of the Mozart: the first and second variations (plus some bars at the end) appear new to the wind version; perhaps (8) Druschetzky's arrangement is based on the now-lost first edition of Mozart's variations, published by Torricella in Vienna in 1785.

Vocal works with winds. Around 1811-1812, Druschetzky set a number of Schiller verses (**GYD–1v to GYD–5v**); only the wind parts are autograph. There seem to be no religious settings accompanied by winds. The sections for winds within religious works do not use voices either. Druschetzky made two arrangements **GYD–1.1va, 1.2va** of Haydn's "Gott erhalte [Franz] den Kaiser," the first for SATB 2ob 2cl 2hn 2bn, the second for TTBB ob cl hn bn.

Military Music. Both the *Französischer Zapfenstreich* (Tattoo) and *Marsch* **GYD–1m** were for General Gudin's French Division. Composed in April 1806 (the wrapper records later performances on 6 December 1807 and 29 March 1808), they are examples of an Austro-Bohemian writing for a foreign army when the threat to his own country was real. The same point applies to **GYD–2m**, *Marche du Couronnement de l'Empereur Napoléon à Paris.* The performance dates on the bn 2/cbn part (21 June, 10 July, 13 July, 14 August 1805) are soon after the date of the coronation on 2 December 1804. **GYD–3m** "Regimentsoboisten" Marsch is an archaic title; one version describes it as the *Regiments Marsch* of the Palatine Hussars, 1818.

1. For folk instruments, see Sybil Marcuse 1966 *Musical Instruments: A Comprehensive Dictionary;* London: Country Life, and Bálint Sárosi 1986 *Folk Music: Hungarian National Idiom;* Budapest: Corvina.

2. R E M Harding 1983 *The Metronome and Its Precursors;* Henley on Thames UK: Gresham Books. See especially p 25.

DUBOIS, Pierre-Max *1 Mar 1930, Graulhet, France-1995* Professor of analysis at the Paris Conservatoire where, as a first-year student in 1949, he had his first commission from French Radio, RTF. Winner of the 1955 Prix de Rome and the 1964 Grand Prix of the City of Paris; he has also worked in Quebec. His writing shows a light touch and discreet wit, influenced by Milhaud, Françaix and Prokofiev, with a fine feeling for instrumental color. Dubois has written a *Scherzo* for 4bn and an especially fine saxophone quartet.

DU BOIS, Rob *b 28 May 1934, Amsterdam.* Self-taught composer, who has specialized in writing for woodwinds, as in his *Iguanadon* for 3cl 6b-cl db.

DUBOIS, (Clement François) Théodore *24 Aug 1837, Rosnay-11 June 1924, Paris* Dubois's career was what most French musicians would wish for: every possible distinction at the Paris Conservatoire, Prix de Rome 1861, Maître de Chapelle at Sainte Clothilde, organist at the Madeleine, where he followed Saint-Saëns; elected to the Institut in 1894, he succeeded Ambroise Thomas as Director of the Conservatoire. For such success, conservatism is essential, and in France at that time a glutinous chromatic style could hide aridity of thought. Dubois was forced to resign as Director of the Conservatoire in 1905, as a result of his conservatism, and especially opposition to Ravel, whom the Conservatoire rejected several times for the Prix de Rome.

Dubois's wind works were all written late in his career, and happily avoid the inflated harmonium sound of some of his organ works; nevertheless, they are of no great distinction. His *Première Suite* (1898) uses only a single oboe, as so often in works for Taffanel's ensemble. The five short movements of the *Deuxième Suite* (1898) have some intriguing titles, like Ronde des Archers; Chanson Lesbienne; Stella Matutina (i.e. morning star). The three-movement *Au Jardin: Petite Suite* (1908) has fascinating comments as well. (1) "Les Oiseaux ... Ils sautillent de branche en branche ... et gazouillent." (2) "Les Petites Visites ... Voulant imiter les manières des grandes personnes." The oboe has a recitative "Bonjour, ma chère, comment vous portez-vous? Vous voici, quel bonheur! Bien de vous voir ... Asseyez vous!" Later, the oboe has "imagant le caquetage des petites filles," and the clarinet, "avec un point de sentiment" says "Adieu." (3) "Gouttes de Pluie. Tranquille. Pendant l'accalmie, un petit tour de valse." The solo flute has "Elles tombent ... et ... ne ... mouillent guère."

DUREY, Louis-Edmond *27 May 1888, Paris-3 July 1979, St Tropez*   One of "Les Six," but one whose direction changed towards a "sober gravity." He began his musical training late, entering the Schola Cantorum in 1907. His interest in winds took several forms, including composing a wind quintet (*Les Soirées de Valfère,* Op 96, 1970) and being co-author with Désiré Dondeyne (well known for an especially enterprising series of recordings of wind band music) of *Nouveau traité d'orchestration à l'usage des harmonies, fanfares et musiques militaires* (Paris 1968). Durey's *Le Printemps au fond de la Mer, Op 24* **LED-2v** was first performed on 31 January 1920 by Jane Bathori and an ensemble directed by Vladimir Golschmann, and has been recorded by Denise Duval, Paris Conservatoire, under Georges Tzipine, on Columbia FCX 264 or Angel 35158 (ANG 35117-35118). The work is said to be pantheistic.

DURKŐ, Zsolt *b 10 April 1934, Szeged, Hungary*   After studies with Farkas in Budapest, Durkó attended Petrassi's master classes in Rome. He writes precise, small-scale, but colorful twelve-tone music.

DUŠEK (Dussek, Duscheck, Dusik, Tuschek), František Xaver *8 Dec 1731, Chotěborky, Bohemia-12 Feb 1799, Prague 1799*   A pupil of Wagenseil, the teacher of Leopold Kozeluch and Vincenc Mašek, Dušek was highly regarded as a pianist and composer. He and his wife, the singer Josepha (née Hambacher), were friends of Mozart of long standing. When Mozart was finishing *Don Giovanni,* it was with the Dušeks that he stayed, in the Villa Bertramka, at Smíchov, near Prague. This friendship left another legacy. Josepha Dušek decided to lock Mozart in a summerhouse until he completed the concert aria he had promised. Mozart, in revenge, made her sing the aria (K.528) at sight in public. She seems to have been able to deal with the technical traps set.

   Dušek's wind music is soundly written and pleasant, but unremarkable. There are about 50 works, mainly in Prague, and these are almost exclusively for 2ob 2hn 2bn, with titles "Parthia," "Partia" or "Partitta." Of these 44 cases, 18 are in F, 7 in D, 6 in B♭, 6 in A, 4 in C and 3 in G. Two copies of several exist, occasionally (**FXD-14, 15**) with different titles. One parthia dates from 1762, so the obvious comparisons are with Haydn's more imaginative works of the same period. One of the quintets (2ob 2hn bn, **FXD-26,** in F) has been recorded on Supraphon SUA 19665.

   A *Parthia* **FXD-32.2** under F X Dušek's name broadcast by the Bournemouth Wind Quire causes some problems. It is for 2cl 2bn 2hn, an ensemble not used by Dušek elsewhere, and its style suggests a later composer. We are indebted to Mr Ian Lowe for telling us that the manuscript has on its title page "František Xaver Dušek Parthia in Dis." We have checked many other Dušeks (and Dusseks and similar spellings), Dušek's pupils, and other possible composers, but we are still unsure who wrote it.

DUVERNOY, Frédéric Nicolas *16 Oct 1765, Montbéliard-19 Sept 1838, Paris*   Horn virtuoso, whose technique covered the full range of the instrument; he played the famous solos in Spontini's *La vestale.* He composed a number of quartets and sextets for horns. Like his brother, clarinettist Charles Duvernoy (1766-1845, father of horn player Antoine Duvernoy), he played in the band of the Garde Nationale.

DUYN, Wilhelm *b 1922*   Composer of *Rhapsody* (1990) for double wind quintet.

DVOŘÁK, Antonín Leopold *8 Sept 1841, Nelahozeves, near Prague-1 May 1904, Prague*   Dvořák, one of the first to adopt unmistakably Czech idioms, was also one of the earliest to revive the special Bohemian talent for the wind serenade. His music was a practical matter, with skills achieved by playing in churches and in popular bands (1, 2). Dvořák's early career was beset by the usual financial problems, though his fortunes changed dramatically in the late 1870s as his music matured into a more personal and national style. Here he was helped by Louis Ehlert and Brahms. Indeed, the (wind) *Serenade* was dedicated to Ehlert, music critic of the *Berliner Nationalzeitung,* in gratitude for his enthusiastic support. Brahms recognized Dvořák's promise especially early. The Austrian state awarded prizes to young, poor, and deserving artists and composers. Brahms was a member of the panel, and Dvořák's successful entries in 1875 and 1876 made a strong impression. Perhaps more important, Brahms wrote to the publisher Simrock in 1877 "For several years I have been delighted by the works of Antonín Dvořák," and he strongly recommended that Simrock publish Dvořák's *Moravian Duets*. These were the success Brahms predicted. Simrock, in turn, suggested that Dvořák write what became his *Slavonic Dances*. The *Serenade* dates from this period, as do the *Symphonic Variations* and the 5th and 6th *Symphonies*.

AZD-1 *Serenade in D minor* Op 44   The *"Serenada"* (as it is named on the autograph title page [2]), written in 1878, was performed by the orchestra of the Provisional Theatre in Prague on 17 November 1878. Dvořák himself conducted the concert, which consisted entirely of his own compositions, notably the first two *Slavonic Rhapsodies*.

The *Serenade* is unusually scored. In addition to the standard octet and contrabassoon (not optional according to the autograph, contrary to what other sources say), there are a third horn (always in a different crook from the others), a cello and a double bass. Several of the earlier serenade conventions are found. Just as Spohr's *Notturno* contained special movements for the entry and departure of the court party, so the first and last movements of Dvořák's work contain the same march. The opening movement is less substantial than that of a symphony. Yearning passages, rather than a formal trio, contrast with the march, and it is this lyrical section which ends the movement quietly. The second movement is a first cousin of the *Slavonic Dances;* this so-called Minuetto (with its Trio) has so much of a Bohemian accent that one should talk of *sousedská* and *furiant*. The third movement, Andante con moto, is the high spot: it would do credit to a symphony and even shows parallels with Mozart's *Gran Partita*. The main melody moves slowly (with typical Czech ornaments written in) over a continuous and subtle syncopated background, this time from the three horns; the cello and bass move in steady quarter notes below them, as do the lowest parts in the Mozart. The different tone colors of widely spaced notes are exploited too, here by the third horn. The result is typical Dvořák, an exceptionally lovely movement. The last movement opens with a vigorous Allegro molto. This leads into a slower passage, a somewhat nostalgic Molto tranquillo, from which the march of the first movement emerges; the Allegro molto takes over again, with increased vigor, and the movement ends with farewell fanfares.

Recordings include: London Baroque Ensemble/Haas, HMV XLP 30011; Chamber Orchestra of Europe/Schneider, ASV COE801; London Symphony Orchestra/Kertesz, Decca Jubilee JB87; English Chamber Orchestra/Mackerras, EMI EMX2031 and CFP 4597; Academy of St Martin in the Fields/Marriner, Philips 6514 145; Netherlands Wind Ensemble/de Waart, Philips 6570 205; St Paul Chamber Orchestra Winds/Wolff, Teldec 2292-46315; New York Harmonie Ensemble/Richman, Music & Arts CD691; New York Chamber Music Society/Shifrin, Delos DE3512; Sabine Meyer Wind Ensemble, EMI CDC555 2722. Czech recordings include those by the Czech Philharmonic Harmonie on Panton 11 0693; Prague Conservatory Chamber Ensemble, Supraphon SUA 10326, Prague Chamber Harmony/Turnovský (1967) on Supraphon SU 8389; Virtuosi di Praga on Discover DICD 920135; and Collegium Musicum Pragense on Supraphon 1111 3373.

1. A Robertson 1964 *Dvořák;* London: Dent.
2. Antonín Horejs 1955 *Antonin Dvořák: The Composer's Life and Work in Pictures;* Prague: Artia. This contains a facsimile of the title page of **AZD-1**.

EASTLAND, Edwin *(1760)* Composer of a set of marches to be played in different keys.
EBDON, Thomas *1738, Durham-23 Sept 1811, Durham* Organist of Durham Cathedral from 1763 until 1811; teacher of Thomas Wright (qv); also conductor of Newcastle-on-

Tyne subscription concerts. Composer of a *March for the Installation of W[illia]m: Hen[ry]: Lambton Esqr., Grand Provincial Master of Free and Accepted Masons for the County of Durham.* English Masonic music for winds is rare.

EBERWEIN, Trautgott Maximilian *27 Oct 1775, Weimar-2 Dec 1831, Rudolstadt*   For a time, Eberwein was a violinist in the Weimar court orchestra. He visited Italy and, after touring Germany, settled in Leipzig.

EDELING, Johann *(1770?)*   In his *Concerto in E♭* JXE-1 the bassoon part is marked "Fagotti" but does not divide. Both JXE-1 and the *Parthia* JXE-2 have a part for "violon," here meaning violone.

EDENHOFER, F H *(1780)*   His *Türkische Musique Militair* [sic] comprises three groups of four movements, called *Simphonia* [sic]. The last group is "orango" [sic] F.H.E.

EDER, Helmut *b 26 Dec 1916, Linz*   HYE-1 *Suite mit Intermezzi, Op 71* (1981). The last of its four movements is entitled Rondo: Hommage à W.A. Mozart; between each movement is an Intermezzo. The *Suite* was written for the Wind Ensemble of the Berlin Philharmonic Orchestra. The scoring matches that of Mozart's *Gran Partita,* K.361, except that there are no basset horns. HYE-2 is subtitled *Hommage to Johannes Kepler.*

EGK, Werner (pseudonym for Mayer) *17 May 1901 Auchsesheim, near Donauwörth-10 July 1983, Inning*   Primarily an opera composer, Egk was director of the Berliner Hochschule für Musik from 1950 to 1953. It is said (probably incorrectly) that he chose his name Egk as the initials of "Ein guter Komponist." His style is largely diatonic, freshly-coloured, and practical both in his approach to the theater and use of available instrumental groups, rather than the bizarre scorings of some of his contemporaries. Five pieces for wind quintet date from 1975. The works listed are recorded by the Mainz Wind Ensemble under Klaus Reiner Schöll (Wergo WER 60179-50).

WXE-1 *Divertimento für 11 Bläser*   Commissioned in 1973 by the Mainz Wind Ensemble for the Schwetzingen Festival, it was first performed on 8 May 1974. The three movements (Contredanse, Allegro molto; Air, lento; Rondeau, Molto allegro) form what he describes as a "ballet without scenario." The liveliness and the features like the juxtaposition of rapid and slower motifs in the finale give hints of Raff's *Sinfonietta.*

WXE-1a *Ouverture, Die Zaubergeige*   Arranged by the composer from his 1935 opera, at the request of the Mainz Wind Ensemble to celebrate Egk's 80th birthday. It was first performed on 14 June 1981 at Kloster Eberbach, Wiesbaden. The opera is based on a story by the Bavarian Count Pocci, in which poor Kaspar is led on adventures by a magic fiddle, but ultimately chooses humble happiness instead of fame. Musically it is an attractive mix of Bavarian band sounds and touches of Stravinsky.

WXE-2a *Sinfonia Concertante K.297b, attributed to Mozart*   After the premiere of **WXE-1a** in 1981, the composer expressed a wish to arrange this work for winds. He (like Tovey; see under Paul Wranizky) felt unhappy about the flute supposedly used in the original, so the arrangement is for standard octet and double bass. It was finished shortly before Egk died, and first performed at Donauwörth on 8 October 1986. The effect is less of a concerto than a substantial and fascinating new serenade, which would fit without incongruity alongside Mozart's own wind music.

EHRENFRIED, Franz Heinrich *(c.1750)*   The scoring of his opera arrangements for Oettingen-Wallerstein has unexpected features. In **FHE-1a** (Dalayrac: *Nina*) the "basso" part (which is divisi in several movements) is marked *pizzicato* and *arco* in one movement, so that a db/vlne is needed. A string bass is also needed in **FHE-2a.**

EICHHORN, Johann (Paul) *b 22 Feb 1787, Coburg*   Trombone and basset horn player; he wrote a set of variations for solo bassoon with 2cl 2hn.

EICHNER, Ernst Dietrich Adolf *9 Feb 1740, Arolsen, near Mannheim-before 10 Oct 1777, Potsdam*   Eichner, a bassoonist and organist, spent much of his composing career in Zweibrücken. He made one brief trip to England in the first half of 1773, on a tour prior to his joining the orchestra of Prince Frederick William at Potsdam. Eichner's English visit coincided with the later years of Johann Christian Bach and was not long before the 1778 visit of W F E Bach and J C F Bach: English wind music at this time may have been richer than previously thought. How much wind music Eichner wrote is not clear; Cramer's *Magasin der Musik* of 1783 lists 4 octets; *MGG* notes a 1780 octet *Divertissement* and a work for 2cl 2hn bn. The *Divertissement in E♭* **EXE-1** appears to date from Eichner's London visit. This early octet (but not, as too often claimed, the earliest work for octet) has interesting features. It is relatively advanced in texture for its time, yet its form is that of a seven-movement suite, not that of a lightweight symphony. The movements include a March, a Siciliano, and an Allemande, in addition to the usual Allegro, Minuet and Trio, a short Amoroso, and a closing Allegro, which is based on the same motif of falling fourths as in Pachelbel's famous *Canon in D*.

EILHARDT, Friedrich Christian Carl *(1830)* His large *Sieges Triumph Festmarsch* is contrasts two different bands. That for the cavalry is smaller, and it omits most of the woodwinds and percussion included in the infantry band.

EINEM, Gottfried von *24 Jan 1918, Berne-14 July 1996, Oberdürchbach* Swiss-born of Austrian parents, Einem studied with Blacher, and was influenced by Hindemith, Stravinsky, Milhaud and Prokofiev. He took a keen interest in light music.

EK, Gunnar *26 June 1900, Åsarum-21 Jun 1981, Lund* Stockholm-trained organist and cellist; his 1970 *Octet* is for 2fl 2ob 2cl 2bn.

EK, Hans *b 31 Jan 1964, Sweden?* His 1991 *CNN* [sic] is for fl cl 2bn 2tp 2tb.

EKSTRÖM, Lars *b 1956, Sweden?*   Scored for 2cl 2bn, his *Teroni* has the subtitle *Brondläppens erogena zon.*

ÉLER, André Frédéric *1764, Alsace-21 April 1821, Paris* Professor and librarian at the Paris Conservatoire from 1795 to 1816, who wrote many accompaniments to verses of Rouget de Lisle. *Pierre/HC* wonders what pressures led him to set Lebrun's *Ode sur les dangers de la patrie* as *Ode sur la situation de la République*, **AFE-1mv**, and observes that the result "n'est pas heureux."

ELEY, Charles Frederick (Francis) *July 1756, Hanover-1832, London?* Clarinettist, composer and arranger, recruited from Hanover to improve British military bands, later playing in Salomon's Haydn concerts. Bandmaster of the East India Company's Volunteer Band, and later of the 2nd Regt of Guards (Coldstreams) until 1816.

ELGAR, Sir Edward William, Bart *2 June 1857, Broadheath, near Worcester-23 Feb 1934, Worcester* Elgar's *The Dream of Gerontius* and two symphonies demonstrated that English music needed to be taken seriously outside England. His *Pomp and Circumstance Marches* founded a new genre of symphonic march (and the so-called God-is-an-Englishman musical style). Elgar's wind music comprises his late *Severn Suite* (Op 87, 1930) for brass band and the early quintets which we describe here. Interestingly, they have a movement in common, for Elgar reused material from the quintets late in his life (see **EWE-2.2, 4.1**). Despite our general exclusion of wind quintets, we include these partly because they show that wind music was still played at a time when little of it was published, and partly because Elgar actually uses the title "Harmony Music" for five individual movements; indeed, the way Elgar uses an extra flute, not a horn, means that his writing is often in the wind harmony tradition.

Elgar wrote these works in 1878-1879 for domestic performance with his friends: an experienced flautist (Hubert Exton) and an equally competent oboist (Elgar's younger brother, Frank), and another flautist (Frank Exton) and clarinettist (William Leicester) who were clearly less skilled. The fifth instrument was either a cello (the autograph copies show double-stopping, and *pizzicato* and *arco* markings), or a bassoon played by Elgar himself. The ranges of the clarinet and second flute parts are fairly restricted, although the frequent low Cs of the second flute part are a good test of the player and his instrument's efficiency. The works were played in Worcester (perhaps in concerts at the county's Powick Asylum), then lost, and later rediscovered by the enthusiast John Parr, who performed some of them in Sheffield. The Sheffield copies, now in the British Library (with some arrangements for the same ensemble, including partsongs), were rediscovered once more, broadcast in 1976, and published soon afterwards. All these works are for 2fl ob cl bn, and all are recorded by the Athena Ensemble on Chandos CBR 1014/1015 and RCA RL24144. Parr's ensemble often re-ordered the movements. The groupings given here correspond to the modern published edition.

EWE-1 *Six Promenades* 1878: No 1 Moderato e molto maestoso; No 2 Moderato: Madame Taussaud's [sic; after Madame Tussaud's London wax museum]; No 3 Presto; No 4 Andante "Somniferous," which does have hints of approaching sleep; No 5 Allegro molto; No 6 Allegro maestoso "Hell and Tommy." To play hell and Tommy is obsolete English slang, meaning to play havoc (from "hell and torment" or from "Hal and Tommy," King Henry and Thomas Cromwell, the destroyers of the monasteries). The title is written over a cartoon (by Elgar?) of two men fighting. The relation to the music is unclear.

EWE-2.1 (-2.5) *Harmony Music 1-5:* Nos 1-4 (1878) are single movements only and not ordered as a suite (so No 1 sounds like an end, rather than a beginning, and No 3 is incomplete). They have the alternative name "Shed," e.g., Harmony No 5 is Shed No 5, but why is another of Elgar's enigmas. No 5 (1879) is in four movements: 1 The Mission, 2 Menuetto and Trio, 3 Noahs's Ark, 4 Finale. Its Menuetto was used again in 1930 as the fourth movement of his *Severn Suite*. There is a separate *Allegro Molto* (4/4, in C) labelled Shed No 4 and also *The Farmyard*; it is distinct from the *Intermezzo* (2/4, in G) with the same title.

EWE-3 *Five Intermezzos* 1879: No 1 The Farmyard: Allegro moderato; No 2 Adagio; No 3 Nancy (Allegretto); No 4 Andante con moto; No 5 Allegretto. The Farmyard (Shed No 4) contains some splendid imitations, notably the clarinet-rooster.

EWE-4 *Four Dances:* 1 Menuetto; 2 Gavotte "The Alphonsa"; 3 Sarabande; 4 Gigue. All have 18th-century titles. The Minuet was used in his *Serenade for Strings* (1892); the Sarabande was to have been used in his planned opera, *The Spanish Lady*.

EWE-5 *Adagio cantabile. "Mrs Winslow's Soothing Syrup"* (1878). The syrup of the title was a proprietary medicine for soothing babies with wind, including rhubarb, caraway, and opium in a special mix with a sugar base; it even inspired popular songs.

EWE-6 *Andante con Variazione, Evesham Andante* (1878), six variations. Evesham is a small town not far from Worcester. The title of **EWE-6** is not on Parr's MS parts.

ELLIOTT, Willard Somers *b 18 July 1926, Fort Worth* **WSE-1** *Five Impressions for Wind Octet* was completed in January 1982 for the Chicago Symphony Winds, and was first performed at Ravinia later in 1982. Neoclassicism is consciously avoided, with impressionism exploiting two motives based on half the chromatic scale: C, B, B♭, A, F#, G, A♭ and C, E, F#, E♭, D, F, D♭. The movements are 1: Autumn Haze, with a cold quietness and solitude, a nostalgic oboe theme over a clarinet ostinato; 2: Dust Devils, a scherzo and trio hinting at miniature desert whirlwinds; 3: Enchanted Forest, with horn and echo horn; 4: Foxfire, night sounds associated with eerie phosphorescence; 5: Helios, the radiance of the sun and the cooling and refreshing rain.

EMERSON, Geoffrey *b 30 Jan 1938, Ramsgate, England* Arranger for winds, and author of *Ideas for Wind Orchestras* (1972) and *More Ideas for Wind Orchestras* (1975). His wife, June Emerson, founded Emerson Edition, which specialises in wind music.

EMMERT, Adam Joseph *24 December 1765, Würzburg-16 Sept 1812, Vienna* Keeper of the archives for the Salzburg Privy Council, son of composer Johann Joseph Emmert (1732-1809), and amateur composer. His works, some using unusual combinations of instruments (not in our lists), date mainly from 1797 to 1807. Many of his works were published in Salzburg by Franz Xaver Duyle, and indeed **AJE-3v** is explicitly for "die Duylesche Hauskapelle an 3ten May 1801". This work is the *Kirchen und Danklied auf den Frieden*, presumably referring to the Peace of Lunéville (9 Feb 1801) which had effectively brought the Holy Roman Empire to its end. **AJE-4, 5** are for only 2hn bn, but are called *Harmonie*. As the Notice in **AJE-4** observes "Our local horn-players Herr Mayer and Herr Gutscher and the Court bassoonist Herr Weiss have often shown, to the delight of the local public, what an ensemble of two horns and bassoon is capable of in skilled hands." **AJE-1** is in 7 movements, in between suite and partita. His *Kirchenlieder* were arranged in score for wind sextet for use with (or even without) choir. Some are identified with specific occasions: **AJE-1v** with "das Fest des h. Kreuzes", **AJE-2v** with "des Fest Maria Himmelfahrt," **AJE-4v** with "des Kirchweihfest," and **AJE-5v** for the "Durlachtigsten Landesherrn." Duyle published the texts of **AJE-1v(-4v)** in 1802. Emmert's own 21-movement arrangement for winds of his opera *Don Sylvio von Rosalva* was done at the request of Freiherr von Bolza, Colonel of the kk Regt of Cuirassiers.

ENESCO (Enescu), Georges *19 Aug 1881, Leveni-Vîrnav (Dorohoiu), Romania-4 May 1955, Paris* An infant prodigy, Enesco began composing when studying at the Vienna Conservatory at the age of seven. The cultural links between France and Romania led him to Paris, to study composition with Fauré and Massenet and to continue a career as virtuoso violinist, Enesco conducted the first concert of his own music at age 16. He wrote his *Dixtuor,* Op 14 **GYE-1** in 1906, presumably for the Dixtuor des Concerts du Conservatoire. His national pride shows in his use of folk idioms; these sound especially natural played by Romanian ensembles. The main theme of the first movement is based on a folk carol which Enesco heard played by a small wind band at his home in Romania. The Dixtuor's movements are Doucement; Modérément (which has a central Vivement section); Allégrement mais pas trop vite. The *Dixtuor* is recorded by the Lausanne Chamber Orchestra/Foster (Claves-Pinnacle CD50-8803) and untitled groups on Electrocord ST ECE 01751 and on Olympia OCD 445 (directed by Horia Andreescu).

ENGLEMANN, C *(1790)* Arranger of Boieldieu's *La Dame blanche*; associated with the Lippe Kapelle, Detmold.

ENGSTRÖM, Torbjörn *b 11 Oct 1963, ?Sweden* Composer of *Musik för bläsorkester*.

ERCOLINI, Giuseppe *(1780) active in Naples, 1810s* A collaborator with Fetter, qv.

ERNST, Franz (François) Anton *21 Feb 1745, Georgenthal, Bohemia-13 Jan 1805, Gotha* On Ernst's arrangement of Haydn's *Symphony No 82*, he is said to belong to the "Accademia Royale" at Paris. In 1785 he was first clarinet of the Concerts Spirituels.

ESCH, Louis von *(1760?)* His *Airs champêtres* **LVE-1** for solo harp cl 2hn bn db are dedicated to Madame Comtesse de Brionne, and are pre-1789. See also under Jouve.

ESCHLER, J *(1810)* Active with the Löwenstein Kapelle. His *Larghetto* uses terz-fl cl(E♭) as the upper instruments, rather than the more common 2fl or 2ob.

ESSEX, Timothy *1764, Coventry-27 Sep 1847, London* Dr Essex of Coventry received his bachelor's degree in 1806 and doctorate in 1812 from Oxford. He was a flautist and violinist. Several of his band works listed by *Sainsbury* are lost; surviving marches include those **TYE-1m, -2m** for the Royal Westminster Volunteers, **TYE-3m** for the Angus Fencibles, and **TYE-4m, TYE-6m** for the Hampstead Loyal Association.

ETT, Caspar *5 Jan 1788, Eresing-16 May 1847, Munich* Notes on the score of Ett's *Grablied* **CXE-1** show that it was used for the funeral or memorial services of musicians in Munich from 1819 until 1861, including the composer's own service on 29 May 1847.

EVANS, Charles *(1780)* "Organist of St Lawrence, Ludlow, late of St Pauls [sic] Covent Garden London and one of the State Musicians to His Excellency the Lord Lieutt. of Ireland" and composer of a march for the Loyal Ludlow Volunteer Infantry.

EYBLER, Johann Leopold [Edler von] *8 Feb 1765, Schwechat, near Vienna-24 July 1846, Vienna* Eybler, a pupil of Albrechtsberger, was held in high regard as a composer by both Mozart and Haydn. He remained a close friend of Mozart throughout his final illness, and it was to Eybler that Mozart's *Requiem* was first entrusted for completion. He succeeded Salieri as principal Kapellmeister to the Emperor in 1824 and was ennobled for his services when he retired ten years later. The autograph of the *5 Minuetti mit Trios*, often said to be for winds, shows that they are for full orchestra.

EYSER, Eberhard *b 1 Aug 1932, Kwidzym*   Now a violinist in Sweden, his *Circus Overture (Cirkus-Uvertyr: Clownernas upptåg)* is "Omaggio a Alfred Schnittge."

FAHRBACH, Joseph (Giuseppe)   Composer, and arranger of two *Fantasies* from *Aida.*

FANE, John, Earl of Westmorland (Lord Burghersh) *3 Feb 1784, London-16 Oct 1859, Althorpe House, Northants, UK*   Friend of Prince Albert, diplomat in Berlin (1841-1851) and Vienna (1851-1855); violin pupil of Mayseder, Portogallo and Bianchi, and a founder of the Royal Academy of Music in 1822. He wrote seven operas and much church music. When he died, military bands assembled in Berlin in the presence of the Prince Regent to play Beethoven's funeral march (perhaps Walch **JHW-1tm**).

FANTINI, I *(1760)*   Composer of a march for Archduke Charles's Austrian Band. The English publication by Longman and Broderip must date from before their closure in 1798. The Archduke was the commander of all Austrian forces on the Rhine in 1796.

FARKAS, Ferenc *b 15 Dec 1905, Nagykanizsa, Hungary*   Farkas has written several works for winds which ingeniously exploit early Hungarian music.

FARQUHAR, David Andross *b 5 Apr 1928, Cambridge, New Zealand*   The scoring of **DYF-1** is similar to that of the Stravinsky octet, though not identical: the Stravinsky has fl cl, the Farquhar 2ob. Farquhar has also written a wind quintet.

FELDMAYR, Georg (Johann) *1757, Pfaffenhofen/Ilm-after 1831, Hamburg?*   Trained in music and Latin at the Indersdorf monastery, Feldmayr was hired by von Beecke for the Wallerstein orchestra around 1781 to play violin and flute, and also to sing tenor. In 1785, on the departure of J Reicha (qv), he became Rosetti's assistant; in 1789, he succeeded Rosetti as orchestral director. Rosetti tried to persuade him to leave too, so as to join him at Ludwigslust, just as the bassoonist, Christoph Ludwig Hoppius, had been lured. Rosetti's letter fell into the hands of Prince Kraft Ernst, who protested to the Duke of Mecklenburg-Schwerin. Feldmayr seems to have been constantly in debt at Wallerstein and ultimately moved to a more highly paid position at Donauwörth, only to run up further debts. He is styled "Hof Musicus" on an opérette *Sultan Wampun oder die Wünsche*, c.1797. He returned to Wallerstein in 1798, leaving for good in 1800. On his departure, he tried to find a position at Ludwigslust. Yet, although he remained at the court of Mecklenburg-Schwerin for nearly two years, and although he received payments and gifts for his compositions, he failed to obtain a permanent job. He moved to Hamburg, where he was still living in 1831. He wrote over 20 parthias.

Feldmayr often chose the term "Fresco" (fresh, brisk) for marches and minuets, local to Wallerstein. The term is also found in music of Hiebesch, Rosetti, Wineberger and Witt. Usually only one minuet will be "fresco," if there are two in a work. Trios are indeed trios in many cases, for cl 2bn and for 2bn vlne in **GJF-1**, or ob bn vlne in **GJF-6**. Small groups like ob 2cl bn (**GJF-7**) are also deployed. Clarinets generally have weak parts, likewise his horn 3 parts, which are often in a different key from the other horns, e.g. two horns in G and a sparse part for horn 3 in D. In several works there are signs that Feldmayr changed his mind: in **GJF-5** he clearly did so (writing a more elaborate Minuetto and Trio) after the copying of the parts had begun. **GJF-21** may have been intended as three Parthien. Of its 18 short movements, items 6 and 12 are labelled Finale. There are dance movements (Deutsche Walzer, Poloneso, Allemande), a Marche à la Chinoise, and the last movement, in 6/8, is marked "Fanfarre."

FELSHUT, C *(1780) active in Tischingen, 1819*   **CPF-1,** *Twelve Dances,* is dedicated to Her Royal Highness the Princess of Thurn und Taxis, the former Princess Royal of Mecklinburg-Strelitz, for her name day and for the ceremony of homage. Beneath the dedication, which is dated 12 October 1819, is the note "Felshut Vater und Sohn Franz." The scoring is for the unusual small ensemble of 2vl fl 2hn bn.

FENDT, A *(1780)* Lieutenant and Music Inspector in Salzburg, who put together five collections of wind music, which he presented to "der K. National-Garde Klasse III" on 2 June 1812. The music is in various hands and on different papers. In one case, marbled paper is pasted over Edenhofer's (qv) title page and Fendt's printed title sheet has been put in on the clarinet 1 part. Another set is clearly by von Kriset.

FERGUS, John *1767, Huntley, Aberdeenshire-10 June 1825* His self-published march (c.1795) for the Royal Glasgow Volunteers **JNF-1m** bears the note "N.B. This is the March Appointed by the Committee."

FESCA, Friedrich Ernst *15 Feb 1789, Magdeburg-24 May 1826, Karlsruhe* After his debut as violinist at age 16, Fesca studied composition with A E Müller at Leipzig. Fesca was employed at the courts of Oldenburg and Westphalia before settling in Karlsruhe as solo violinist to the Archduke of Baden.

FETTER, Giuseppe *(1780?)* Arranger with Ercolani of works by Paisiello, and possibly other arrangements in I-Fc.

FEUCH, ( ) *(?1780)* Local composer in Langenbruck, northern Bohemia.

FIALA, Joseph (Josef) *3 Feb 1748, Lochovice, near Příbram, Bohemia-31 July 1816 Donaueschingen* Fiala's career shows some of the realities of musical life: the problems of moving from one job to another, the lack of freedom to move, the time needed to travel and become known, and the need to move on when an employer died. As the son of a serf (serfdom was abolished in 1780 in Bohemia and in Hungary, and in 1781 in Austria), Fiala both gained and lost from his position. When, on the estate of Countess von Netolitz, he showed early musical talent, he was taken to Prague, where he played in the Netolitzky court orchestra and in local churches. In Prague he was taught oboe by Johann Stastný and cello by Franz Joseph Werner, who also taught Joseph Reicha. These benefits of servitude made Fiala aware of opportunities beyond those in his Netolitz employment. As a serf, leaving his employment was not allowed in law and not simple in practice. He escaped and went with other Bohemian musicians to Regensburg, where he came under the protection of the imperial envoy, Count von Hartig (presumably the Count Hartig who kept a Harmonie in Prague). Discovered, Fiala was lured back to Prague and imprisoned. There are unverified stories of escaped musicians having teeth pulled or fingers crushed on recapture, so that they lost their profession as well as their freedom (1). Fiala could consider himself lucky merely to be imprisoned for a short time, for he was able to travel to Vienna in 1774, where he published his first work. The title page of this work, which appeared in Paris soon after, shows that he had met and studied with Vanhal (qv). Perhaps more important was his meeting with Ignaz von Beecke who was recruiting players for Oettingen-Wallerstein; in 1774, Fiala's Op 1 described him as "Musicien chez Monseigneur le Prince de Wallerstein." The Wallerstein orchestra broke up after the death of Kraft Ernst's wife in 1776; Fiala stayed on until he performed before Maximilian Joseph, Elector of Bavaria, in 1777, which led to a request to the Prince to permit Fiala to leave Wallerstein for Munich. There, he married the daughter of the horn player Prohaska.

Mozart wrote from Munich to his father in Salzburg on 3 October 1777 of a band of two clarinets, two horns and bassoon, hired for the Schwarzer Adler (Black Eagle Inn, where the band often played) for the name day of its landlord, Herr Abert. Mozart observed (2) that they "played not at all badly together ... one knows at once Fiala trained them." They played some of Fiala's music, which Mozart found very attractive, with some very good ideas. The letter shows that Fiala, a member of a court orchestra, could train and write music for a band to play in an inn. No music of Fiala's for 2cl 2hn bn survives. Letters like this told one court of fine musicians in another. Perhaps as a result, Leopold Mozart tried to recruit Fiala for the Salzburg orchestra. His letter to Wolfgang (then in Paris) on 10 September 1778, reports that he had written for Fiala, who was coming that day from Munich on the mail-coach, and returning "on Sunday, so that no-one in Munich will know that he has gone away. If he can come to terms with the Prince [Archbishop of Salzburg] then he will come here as first oboe." Such negotiations needed care; it was a mere four years since Fiala had been imprisoned for an ill-considered move. Maximilian Joseph, Elector of Bavaria, died on 30 December 1777, being succeeded by Carl Theodore, previously Elector Palatine, who brought with him his own Mannheim players. The Munich band was redundant, and Leopold Mozart's approach to Fiala was timely. In the event, Fiala moved to Salzburg in November 1778.

The Mozarts and Fialas became close friends, both professionally (for Fiala was a link to the court at Munich) and personally. Fiala played too much for the good of his health, reputedly playing as many as 12 oboe concertos in one evening (3); this caused him to vomit blood, so he concentrated more on cello and viola d'amore (hence references to him as "viola" in the Wallerstein records). Fiala left Salzburg in 1785 for Vienna, where he lived for a time with the Mozarts. In 1787-1789 he made a successful Russian tour, including St Petersburg. The years 1790-1791 brought more tours, this time to Bohemia and to Prague. On 1 January 1792, Fiala settled in Donaueschingen as cellist, later composer and chamber musician, remaining there until his death in 1816.

JSF-1 *Divertimento "No 1"* (D-DO, Mus Ms 427)   Recorded on Supraphon 1111 1854 H, where it is presumed without clear reason that three horns make a "hunting" piece.

JSF-11 *Divertimento in E♭* (D-DO, Mus Ms 431)   Recorded on Supraphon 1111 2973. There is a single bassoon part, with a later alteration from "Fagotto" to "Due fagotti."

JSF-13 *Divertimento VI Pastorale; in B♭* (D-DO, Mus Ms 439)   The title fits the pastoral yodels in the finale and the pipings in the first movement. The work makes it easy to understand Mozart's pleasure at the Schwarzer Adler. Again the problem of 1 or 2 bassoons arises. Moreover, two oboes are listed while the parts call for two cors anglais; nevertheless, the parts are untransposed oboe parts. Recorded on Supraphon SUA 1111 2616 by the Collegium Musicum Pragense, where the work is described as "Divertimento Pastorale."

JSF-21 *Divertimento in F*   Recorded by Ensemble Philidor on Supraphon 11 2182-2 131.

JSF-28 *Parthia in E♭*   Recorded by members of the Prague Chamber Harmony on Supraphon SUA 19665.

1. The 1769 Penal Code of Maria Theresa (Constitutio Criminalis Theresiana; see also E Wangermann 1973 *The Austrian Achievement* London: Thames and Hudson pps 132-3) allowed both torture and the death penalty. Fiala's offence was civil, rather than criminal, but severe punishment was doubtless permitted.

2. *Mozart Letters:* Letter to Leopold Mozart, 3 October 1777.

3. J R Piersol 1972 *The Oettingen-Wallerstein Hofkapelle and its Wind Music;* Ph D Dissertation, University of Iowa (University Microfilm: Ann Arbor, Mich 73-13, 583).

FIALA, Petr *b 25 Mar 1943, Pelhřimov*   Composer and choral conductor who also studied piano and oboe in Brno. He combines mainstream modern classical approaches with new techniques like aleatorics, jazz and extramusical elements. He has composed a *Wind Quintet*, a *Concerto for Wind Quintet and Chamber Orchestra* (1987), and a *Rondo-Concerto* for piano, winds and percussion (1986).

FINNISSY, Michael (Peter) *b 17 Mar 1946, London*   *Obrecht Motet V* is the last of a series of pieces based on Obrecht's *Salve Regina* and *Ave Regina Coelorum,* commissioned for the tenth anniversary of the Dutch ensemble Die Volharding. Motets I, II and IV also involve winds or brass extensively.

FISCHER, ( )   One (or two) Fischers wrote nine *Ländlerische* and a *Todten Marsch*, the former copied in 1808 by Augustin Erasmus Hübner in Langenbruck, northern Bohemia.

FISCHER, Carl *(1800)*   Director of Music of the 17th Royal Prussian Infantry Regiment. His 1834 *Marches* are dedicated to Prince Alexander of Prussia. His four sets of operatic arrangements are dedicated thus: **CFY-1a** (1826) to Monsieur de Dresky, Commandeur du 2me Bataillon 17me; **CFY-2a** (1827) to "Prinz Frédéric de Prusse"; **CFY-3a** (c.1827, based on Boieldieu's *La Dame Blanche*), and **CYF-4a** (1832, an *Introduction and Polonaise* based on Kalkbrenner and Kalliwoda, "à son Ami Charles Klotz", Master of Music of the 16th Regiment of the Prussian Infantry. Arrangements of Mozart and Tausch by "Fischer" for the Lippe Kapelle, Detmold, may be by him.

FISCHER, Heinrich Wilhelm *(1790)*   On the MS of his 14 December 1814 *Trauer-Musick* for Duke Friedrich Wilhelm of Braunschweig, Fischer is described as private teacher (Privatlehrer) of music and composition from Braunschweig.

FISCHER, I G C *(1810)*   I G C Fischer, who styled himself a student of Walch (qv), published his set of *Militair Musik* in Hanover, c.1835.

FISCHER (Tischer, Ticher, Ficher; in CZ-KRa as "J Discher"), J *(1750)*   These names are found on nine early works for 2cl 2hn bn in Kroměříž and Regensburg. The larger work (**JYF-10**, 2cl 2hn 2bn 2va vlne) under the name Fischer at Regensburg may be an anonymous local arrangement: movement 1 is movement 1 of **JYF-1**; movements 5-7 and 11 are movements 1-3 and 7 of **JYF-3**. The remaining movements do not match other surviving *Parthias*.

FISCHER, Johann Christian *1733 Freiburg im Breisgau-29 April 1800, London*   His early career had links with the Besozzi family. In Dresden from 1760 to 1764, he then visited Italy to learn from singers and players; in 1767, he succeeded C P E Bach in the service of Frederick the Great. Presumably his *Triumphmarsch* **JCF-1** for octet and percussion, was for one of these courts. Fischer next moved to London, where he delighted audiences until his playing and his life ended dramatically when he collapsed in mid-performance at the Queen's house (1). He left his music to King George III.

1. *Sainsbury.* There were many oboists with names like Fischer: John Abraham Fisher/ Fischer (1744-1806), husband of Nancy Storace, wrote four concertos for oboe; W Fish (b 1775) wrote an oboe concerto. Oboist J Tischer (b 1707; apparently distinct from Johann Nikolaus Tischer, 1706-1770, pupil of J S Bach) wrote a *Parthia in Eb*. J Fischer, probably the same person as J Discher, wrote parthias now in D-Rtt. Further Fischers include Anton (1778-1808), Matthäus (1763-1840) and Michael Gotthard (1773-1829).

FISCHER, Thoma *(1740)*   Unidentified except for his description *Functionaire*. His work "Il Coraggio" for solo oboe ca 2cl 2hn 2bn is an attractive puzzle, written for the Schwarzenberg ensemble. There is nothing to reflect the title, apart from a first movement "Risoluto," and the oboe part is not seriously concertante.

FIŠER, Luboš *b 30 Sept 1935, Prague*   Composer of many television and film scores, whose classical works tend to the compact forms of Webern. He trained in Prague with Emil Hlobil (qv). His *Chamber Concerto* (1970) is rescored from a 1964 orchestral work.

FLACHS, Karl *(1790)*   His arrangement of Weber's *Der Freischütz* is recorded by Consortium Classicum on Telefunken 6.35366 FK, omitting the overture.

FLACK, (John) Caspar *(1750?)*   Horn player with the 1st Regt of Guards (Grenadiers).

FLOSMAN, Oldřich *b 5 Apr 1925, Plzeň*   Flosman's music is grounded in the Slavonic folk tradition and the music of Prokofiev and Shostakovich. His *Overture* for winds is recorded by Supraphon, as is his *Sonata* for wind quintet and piano.

FOERSTER, Christoph (Heinrich) *30 Nov 1693, Bibra bei Laucha, Thuringia-6 Dec 1745, Rudolstadt*   Composer of instrumental and church music. His *Concerto à 6 in C*, **CFF-1**, is typical music for oboe band; his lost *Partita* for 2fl 2hn bn (advertized after his death in the 1765 Breitkopf catalog) seems to be an early example of wind harmony.

FOJTÍK, Bohumil *b 1927* His *Impressioni* (1983) are scored for fl 2ob 2cl 2hn 2bn.

FORSTMAYER, Ehrenfried Andreas *1730-1787* Chamber musician at Karlsruhe c.1780.

FORSYTH, Malcolm *b 8 Dec 1936, Pietermaritzberg, South Africa (Canadian citizen, 1974)* A pupil of Mátyás Seiber who makes use of African folk tunes and rhythms in colorful, rhythmic music. A trombonist, he has also written chamber music for brass.

FOWLER, Jennifer Joan *b 14 April 1939, Bunbury, Western Australia* She studied first at the University of Perth, Australia, then at the Utrecht Electronic Studio. She was a prizewinner at the International Composers' Competition, Berlin 1970. Her *Chimes, Fractured* **JJF-1** is recorded Festival Records, Vol 10, Australian Festival of Music.

FOX, Christopher *b 10 Mar 1955, York* **CZF-1** *Some Creation Myths* (see under Koehler on composing games). This work is for the same ensemble as Janáček's *Mládí*).

FRACKENPOHL, Arthur Roland *b 23 April 1924, Irvington, New Jersey, United States* After studies at the Eastman School of Music and with Milhaud and Boulanger, he then joined the staff of the Crane School of Music, Potsdam, New York. His work includes many pieces for concert band, a wind quintet, and *Meet Job*, for chorus and winds.

FRÄNZEL, Ferdinand *24 May 1770, Schwetzingen-Nov 1833, Mannheim* Composer of two *Echos* for wind harmony.

FRÄNZL, Ignaz *3 June 1736, Mannheim-3 Sept 1811, Mannheim* Joined the Mannheim orchestra at age 11, moving with it to Munich in 1778; he became its conductor in 1790.

FRANÇAIX, Jean *b 23 May 1912, Le Mans* The son of the Director of the Le Mans Conservatoire, and a pupil of Nadia Boulanger. His music has wit and an unforced yet polished sound, always inventive. Many of his works are linked with the Schwetzingen Festival, and with the Mainz Wind Ensemble (MWE) and its conductor, Klaus Rainer Schöll. With the recording Wergo WER 60 143-50 (aptly titled *Musique pour faire plaisir*, after one of the items), Françaix gives a delightful note on his association with the Mainz Wind Ensemble, which has led to at least 14 works. The wind version of Françaix's *L'heure du berger* is cataloged under its arranger, Wanek (qv) as **FKW-3a**.

JEF-3 *8 Danses exotiques* Originally (1957) for two pianos (4 hands), the *Danses* were often played by Françaix and his daughter Claude. This 1981 version was made at the request of Schöll. The dances are Pambiche, Baiao, Nube gris, Merengue, Mambo, Samba lento, Malambeando, and Rock'n'Roll. Recorded by the MWE on Wergo 60143.

JEF-4 *Petite valse européenne* Written for the 1980 Schwetzingen Festival, the *Valse* has a solo tuba; "Pour mon petit-fils Eric".

JEF-6 *Quasi improvvisando* First performed on 25 November 1975 at the Braunschweig Festival Day of New Music; it is recorded on Wergo SM1017 and Wergo 60143-50. Here, as Françaix remarks, he "rediscovers" Paul Lincke's march *Berliner Luft*, and embellishes it with a rumba rhythm. The music recalls how Françaix himself tried to remember the theme, with excursions via Bach *(Well-tempered Clavier)*, Beethoven *(Für Elise)* and Weber *(Invitation to the Dance)*.

JEF-7 *Variations sur un thème plaisant* (1976) Recorded with the composer as piano soloist, with the MWE under Schöll, on Wergo 60087 and WER 6087.

JEF-8 *Mozart-new-look: petite fantasie pour contrebasse et instruments à vent sur la sérénade de Don Giovanni* First performed 5 June 1983 at Kloster Eberbach by the MWE, under Schöll, and recorded on Wergo 60143-50, it includes an juxtaposition from *Carmen* while the double bass plays other delights, including *Don Giovanni*.

JEF-9 *Hommage à l'ami Papageno* (1984) Recorded by the MWE/Françaix on Wergo 60143-50, and dedicated to Kurt Breuer, as the Chairman of Wiesbaden's "Mozart-Gesellschaft." The work evokes various Papageno themes from all parts of *Die Zauberflöte*. Françaix claims that here he is "disguised as a pianist," invoking "Mozart's "spirit" accompanied by an English horn... and once *Die Zauberflöte* is heard, "an ideal dialogue begins between the greatest composer of all times and your humble servant."

JEF-10 *7 Danses après le ballet Les Malheurs de Sophie*   A suite of seven dance movements after the ballet, which received its first performance in a concert on R-T Zagreb on Mainz Day in Zagreb, 22 May 1970. The original ballet, based on a scenario of G Flevitsky, dates from 25 February 1948 and it, in turn, is based on the 1935 novel of the Comtesse de Ségur. Recorded on Wergo SM 1017, and also by the Amsterdam Wind Ensemble/Blomhert on STH Favorites CD 19245.

JEF-11 *Neuf Pièces caractéristiques pour instruments à vent*   First performed on 8 May 1974 at the Schwetzingen Festival, the pieces (Presto, Amoroso, Notturno, Subito vivo, Allegro, Andantino, Leggerissimo, Moderato, Finale) are on Wergo SM 1017.

JEF-12 *Le gai Paris* (1974).   First performed on 6 April 1975 at the Wiesbaden Internationaler Internisten-Kongress, with Carole Dawn Reinhart as the trumpet soloist. This straightforwardly neo-classical work is recorded on Wergo SM 1017.

JEF-13 *11 variations on a theme of Haydn* (1982).   The theme is that of the slow movement of Haydn's *Symphony No 94*, with many extra surprises, not just the trumpet which replaces Haydn's timpani, or the double bass which mimics a Valkyrie. Recorded by the MWE on Wergo 60143-50, where Françaix remarks "I would like to be Gran' Pappy Haydn's spiritual grandson. His art's clarity, serenity and humour represent, in my opinion (but don't tell anyone I said so) the antidote to contemporary art."

JEF-4a *Musique pour faire plaisir* (1984).   Recorded by the MWE on Wergo 60143-50. This comprises arrangements for winds of Poulenc's collection of piano pieces of the same title, made at the request of Schöll. Included are "Valse" from the *Album des Six,* "Elégie" to the memory of La Comtesse Jean de Polignac (related to the husband of Reynaldo Hahn's "Beatrice d'Este"), and "L'Embarquement pour Cythère," an allusion to Watteau's painting which Poulenc transfers to the Marne where (says Françaix) the nymphs have "even looser morals than their mythological ancestors."

FRANKE-BLON, Lars-Åke *b 1941, ?Sweden*   Composer of three fantasy pieces for winds, entitled *Ekon från svunnen tid* (1978).

FRANTZL, Jacopo, Pater See TRAUTZL

FRANZEN, Olov *b 22 Jan 1946, Umeå, Sweden*   His *In memoriam 1791 sopra Requiem di W. A. Mozart* was written in 1991 as a tribute to the finest composer for winds.

FREEMAN, Thomas Augustine *(1750)*   Composer of *The Earl of Carlisle's March and Quickstep,* published c.1780.

FREUNDTHALER, Cajetan *(1760), active in Austria before 1799*   A prolific composer of wind music (Traeg lists 4 items in 1799), often including a part for basset horn. None of these works seem to survive apart from one choral work with winds, **CQF-1v.**

FRICKE, Elias Christian *(1750, editor)*   **ECF-1,** a collection of "englische Tänze" for the year 1776, is unusual in being scored for wind ensemble. Such collections were common, however, to help dancing masters, to ensure that dancers would find the same tunes at fashionable assemblies, and also as a souvenir of the season.

FRICKER, Peter Racine *5 Sep 1920, London-1 Feb 1990, Santa Barbara, California*   Fricker's early Op 5 *Wind Quintet* won the Clements Memorial Prize. Since his *2 Canons* for 2ob 2fl of 1966 **(PRF-2)** his only wind work appears to have been that in memory of Britten of 1976-7. He contributed to the Hoffnung Festivals.

PRF-1 *Sinfonia in Memoriam Benjamin Britten, Op 76*   First performed in Europe at Aldeburgh by the English Chamber Orchestra winds soon after the death of Britten.

FRID, Géza   *25 January 1904, Máramarossziget, Hungary-13 Sept 1989, Beverwijk*   Hungarian-born and a student of piano with Bartók and of Kodály, Frid became a Dutch citizen in 1948 and Professor of ensemble playing at Utrecht. His *Serenade* Op 4 **GXF-2** dates from 1928, not long after Seiber's.

FRIEDRICH II (called "the Great"), King of Prussia *24 Jan 1712-17 Aug 1786*   A reformer of military music, and a composer of talent. Several marches are attributed to him; there are also autograph marches for fife and drums, together with other sketches, at D-Bds.

FRIEND, John *(1780)* Composer of a *March for the Durham City Loyal Volunteers.*

FUCHS, Georg Friedrich *3 Dec 1752, Mainz-9 Oct 1821, Paris* Best known as a clarinettist, Fuchs seems to have played horn and bassoon well too. He studied at Mannheim under Cannabich (and reputedly later under Haydn), with clarinet tuition from Quallenberg or Hampel. Fuchs served in several military bands, becoming bandmaster to one from Zweibrücken, with which he travelled to Paris in 1784. There he joined the Garde Nationale after the Revolution, rising to its highest rank in 1793. Five *Harmonie* from 1792-93 describe French victories at the sieges of Thionville (GFF-2) and Mons (GFF-3) in 1792. He also celebrated the Battle of Marengo on 14 June 1800 (GFF-1; its sections are: La Généralle; Pas de charge; Mort de Général Desaix; La victoire à nous). In 1795, he became one of the first professors of clarinet at the Conservatoire, but was relieved of his duties during the reforms of 1800. The title page of his Op 37 *Duos* for horn and clarinet describe him as "Membre du Conservatoire et chef de Musique de la 33me 1/2 Brigade" (this demi-brigade existed from about 1795 to 1803). From the early 1800s, he supported himself mainly by arranging for publishers, including Imbault, Sieber and Nadermann. His marches for the Landwehr and for the National Guard in Vienna are probably arrangements from periods when Austria and Napoleon were in alliance. Sadly, little of his own music survives, since what there is (such as that fine half-harmony, his Op 1 for cl hn bn) confirms the understanding of winds evident from his arrangements. Fuchs's many excellent arrangements are often for 4cl 2hn 2bn or 2cl 2hn 2bn, with flutes and oboes omitted or optional. Some, like his arrangement of Lesueur's *Ossian* GFF-23.1a have virtuoso parts. Fuchs wrote quartets for cl 2hn bn.

FUCHS, Johann Nepomuk *1766-29 Oct 1839, Eisenstadt* Vice-Kapellmeister at Eszterháza from 1802, later Kapellmeister until at least 1835. His *Nro 8 Parthia* JAF-1 is amiable but of no special distinction. The (9) *Messlieder* JAF-2 are puzzling; they start with the same opening, but have increasingly complicated conclusions; it is hard to see how they fitted into the Mass. The choral works with winds JAF-1v (-3v) indicate that a wind ensemble was available at Eszterháza at least until 1822.

FÜHRER, Robert (Johann Nepomuk) *2 Jun 1807, Prague-28 Nov 1861, Vienna* Pupil of Vitásek, whom he succeeded as choirmaster of St Vitus, Prague in 1839. Führer held the post only until 1845 because of his tempestuous lifestyle. Many of his compositions (over 400) remain in the repertoire in Bavaria and Eastern Europe; they show a transition in style from classical to romantic.

FUSCO, Michele Fusco's wind music from a *Cantata* MZF-1 is for the Reale Armonia, wind band of Francesco IV, Archduke of Austria and Duke of Modena from 1814-1846.

FUX (Fuchs), ( ) *(1770)* Active at Březnice, near Plzeň, c.1800, composing religious works for CATB, 2cl 2hn 2bn (the MS parts are by Horetsky and by František Vaněček).

GÄNSBACHER, Johann *8 May 1778, Sterzing, Tyrol-13 July 1844, Vienna* Conductor and composer, pupil of Vogler (qv) and Albrechtsberger (qv), and friend of Weber; Gänsbacher was appointed Kapellmeister of the Cathedral in Vienna in 1823. He wrote several marches, found in the Lobkowitz Harmonie collection. His *Alpenlied*, for SSAATTBB, 2fl 2cl 2hn 2bn cbn, is dated "Innsbruck, Oct. 5, 1822."

GAILLARD, Marius François *13 Oct 1900, Paris-23 July 1973, Évèquemont, Yvelines* *Guyanes* (the Guianas), a colorful work written in 1925 by one who has written many film scores, is for voice (optional; the autograph indicates how it can be replaced), winds and percussion (two players; some novel instruments). The 18 movements have some interesting titles, such as Quinine; Femmes de couleur; Rocking Chair; Virginie

sans Paul (relating to the 1787 romance by Bernardin de St Pierre); Tam-tam funèbre.
GAL, Hans *5 Aug 1890, Brunn, near Vienna-3 Oct 1987, Edinburgh*   A composer of successful operas, and a musical scholar and lecturer in musical theory in the University of Vienna from 1919 to 1929. He left Vienna at the time of the Anschluss in Austria and came to Edinburgh at Tovey's invitation. After a period of internment during the war, Gál was appointed lecturer at the University of Edinburgh.
GALOTTI, All[esandr]o *(1790)*   Arranger for winds of music from Rossini's *Semiramide*, probably for the wind band of the Duke of Verona. The copy seen by us bears the stamps of the Duke and of Picinelli, the Veronese music seller.
GAMBARO, Giovanni Battista (J-B) *baptized 1785, Genoa-1828, Paris;* also **GAMBARO, Vincenzo** All the wind works in Paris appear under the name Vincent (VN^T, V^t). There is little doubt that one person wrote all the music, probably J-B Gambaro (1, 2). A distinguished clarinet virtuoso, he settled in Paris after serving in an Italian regiment of the French army. From March 1814, he published music and sold musical instruments to the French army. His arrangements include the *Suites de Musique Militaire* which included parts usually printed 4-to-a-folio. These date from 1814-1815, the time of the restoration of the monarchy. Some sets have no separate bassoon parts. The trombone parts and serpent parts are sometimes in C, sometimes in Bb. On **VXG-3a** Gambaro is styled "Première clarinette du Théâtre Royale Italienne." His playing influenced many clarinet players, as did his advocacy of Müller clarinets and the music he sold. Some of his works were dedicated to well-known players, like Klosé. His *Ouverture de Tivoli* **VXG-1** was written for the Fête of 10 August 1815, and is dedicated to "leurs Majestés Les Souverains Alliés." One wonders if this was the occasion on which the Viennese Imperial Harmonie performed. Gambaro was also an early user of metronome marks (c.1818). His arrangements of Rossini overtures (*L'Italiana in Algeria* **VXB-5a**, *Il barbiere di Siviglia* **VXB-6a**, *Otello* **VXB-7a**, *Ricciardo e Zoraide* **VXB-10a**) are recorded by the Ottetto Italiano on Arts 47162-2. Gambaro's music for smaller ensembles (1) includes two sets of *3 Quatuors Concertans* for fl cl hn bn (Op 4, based on Beethoven's works, and Op 5, c.1815, dedicated to "son ami Xavier Lefèvre"), which we class as half-harmony. Some are recorded by the Rossini Quartet on Dynamic CDS107.
1. *Weston/MCVP* p 107; this book gives sources for Gambaro's smaller works.
2. Gian Enrico Cortese (sleeve notes to Arts 41762) suggests there were two clarinettists and composers, both dying in 1828. We know of no evidence for this.
GAMSTORP, Göran *b 17 May 1957, Stockholm*   His 1984 work for solo flute and winds bears the novel title *Caccia per flauto e fiati da camera.*
GAN, Nikolay Karlovich *b 28 Apr 1908, Tbilisi*   Gan's *Children's pictures*, published in 1955, is scored for 2fl ob 2cl hn bn.
GANZ, Rudolf *24 Feb 1877, Zurich-2 Aug 1972, Chicago*   Cellist, conductor, teacher, and composer who introduced many modern classics to the United States. In 1946, when he wrote *Woody Scherzo,* he was Vice-President of Chicago Music College.
GASSMANN (Gassman), Florian Leopold *3 May 1729, Most, Bohemia-20 Jan 1774, Vienna*   Gassmann's life parallels that of Gluck; both were educated at the Jesuit seminary at Komotau. After a period in Italy, Gassmann succeeded Gluck as composer for the Vienna ballet, and was later director of the opera buffa at the Burgtheater. Perhaps Gassmann is best remembered for his indirect contributions to music as the founder of the Tonkünstler-Societät, and as the teacher of Salieri. Four of his *Parthien* for 2cl 2hn bn are listed as string quintets in the 1773 Breitkopf catalog.
GAZZANIGA, Giuseppe *5 Oct 1743, Verona-1 Feb 1818, Cremona*   Gazzaniga wrote a successful *Don Giovanni* opera just before Mozart's version. He spent much of his life in Venice (where his choral music with winds survives); from 1791, he was Maestro di Cappella at Cremona cathedral, where he wrote much church music.

GEBAUER, Étienne François *1777, Versailles-1823, Paris* Arranger of operas by Spontini and Dalayrac, a flautist, and brother of M J and F R Gebauer. All of his arrangements appear to have been for the publishing firm of Mlles Erard.

GEBAUER, François Réné *15 Mar 1773, Versailles-28 Jul 1845, Paris* Bassoonist member of this musical family who arranged music by Haydn (*Symphony 73*) and Isouard. He collaborated with J Frey in publishing three *Marches* **FFG-1m** for the entry of King Louis XVIII into Paris; the date of the event is conspicuously left blank, so the music must date from between Napoleon's abdication (11 April 1814) and the actual entry on 5 May, a fine example of opportunism. Both Gebauer and Frey are styled as "Artistes de l'Academie Royale"; Frey is otherwise known only as a publisher.

GEBAUER, Franz Xaver *1784, Eckersdorf, Prussian Silesia-13 Dec 1822, Vienna* Not one of the Parisian Gebauers, Franz Xaver knew Beethoven well enough to inspire bad puns like "Geh' Bauer" (Bauer means peasant, so "Go, clod"). He played the Jew's harp, and was an early member of the Gesellschaft der Musikfreunde. As choirmaster of St Augustine, Vienna, he directed early performances of major choral works.

GEBAUER, Michel Joseph *1763, La Fère, Aisne, France-1812, Russia?* Whereas the violin earned Gebauer his living at the start of his career, he joined the Garde Nationale as oboist, becoming Professor at the Paris Conservatoire from 1794 to 1802, and later a member of the Imperial band. His suites of Mozart arrangements must date from this period. Published c.1802, they are dedicated to the Demi-Brigade d'Infanterie; demi-brigades were units of the French army between 1793 and 1803. He became bandmaster of the Consular Guard and, probably from 1807, produced a substantial wind music journal. Probably some, at least, of the original works and arrangements are his own. Gebauer perished on Napoleon's Russian campaign.

GEBHARD, Johann Gottfried *(1780)* Moravian Brethren composer.

GEHOT, (Jean) Joseph *8 Apr 1756, Brussels (?Liège)-c.1820, United States* Violinist and author; Gehot's music was also published in Paris and Berlin.

GELLERT, Josef *1787-17 Nov 1842, Chomutov, Bohemia* Composer of much church music with winds (such as a set of *Stationes* and a *Mass in D* probably played at Osek), and especially of a large number of funeral songs for varied types of person.

GEMROT, Jiří *b 15 Apr 1957, Prague* From a family of musicians, he studied composition in Prague, initially with J Z Bartoš (qv). He emphasizes the use of melody, drawing on the Czech tradition. His *Returns and Metamorphoses* **JZG-1** is the largest of his works for winds, lasting about 21 minutes.

GENERALI, Pietro *23 Oct 1773, Masserano, Vercelli-3 Nov 1832, Novara* His most successful work was the 1804 opera *Pamela nubile,* based on Samuel Richardson's novel. From 1827, Generali was Maestro di Capella at the cathedral in Novara.

GENZMER, Harald *b 2 Feb 1909, Blumenthal, near Bremen* Genzmer, who studied in Berlin and in Freiburg im Breisgau, has been influenced by Hindemith.

HZG-1 *Divertimento for Symphonic Winds* The *Divertimento* is in three movements, with a stately introduction and an effective and imaginative finale.

HZG-2 *Sextet* Written in 1966, it provides a valuable foil to the standard classical repertoire. The four movements are subdivided. The first is a Largo, alternating with Allegro; then comes an Andante molto tranquillo, with a central Allegretto, followed by a striking Intermezzo, with hints of the Chinese sections of Hindemith's *Symphonic Metamorphoses.* The Finale starts Lento, proceeding via Allegro molto to Presto.

GERHARD, Roberto *25 Sept 1896, Valls, Catalonia-5 Jan 1970, Cambridge* A pupil of Granados and of Schoenberg, he edited much music by Catalan composers (who doubtless were an influence for his *Sardana* **RUG-1**). His national influences and originality combine with 12-tone disciplines to produce striking music.

GERKE, August *1790, Lüneburg-1847* Violin virtuoso and composer.

GEROLD, J *(?1820)*   The 1877 copy by Karl Kaiser of his arrangement of the Adagio from Beethoven's *Sonata Pathétique* may be rescored for the Lippe Kapelle, Detmold.
GERSHWIN, (Jacob) George *25 Sept 1898, Brooklyn-11 July 1937, Hollywood*   His one original work for winds is the *Figured Chorale* from his music for George White's *Scandals.* It dates from 1921, the period of his opera *Blue Monday.*
GIANELLA, Luigi *1788-1817, Paris*   Flautist and composer.
GIESLER, D Victor *(1790)*   In his funeral music *Ecco quomodo moritur justus* for CATB fl 2cl 2hn 2bn 2tp, the trumpets (marked *clar*) are muted.
GILLASPIE, Jon Alan *b June 16 1950 Potsdam, New York, USA*   Gillaspie studied piano and composition with Leah Haywood Haynes and bassoon with Harry I Phillips and Robert Reinert at the Crane School of Music. While taking degrees in anthropology and folklore studies at the University of Pennsylvania, he performed regularly with the Philadelphia Baroque Ensemble. Since 1973, he has lived in England, dividing his time between the music business (as performer, producer and arranger) and musicology. He cataloged the music collection in the Bath Reference Library and is involved in other cataloging projects. Gillaspie's arrangements of opera accompaniments for wind harmony are especially useful for the small orchestra pits of many theaters. His compositions are generally neo-romantic in style, often using folk modalities.
JAG-1 *In Memoriam: Francis Poulenc* (1981)   Neoclassical, with tongue firmly in cheek, its movements are: Ouverture; Gioacchino, écrasez donc cette mouche (referring to the adopted Parisian, Rossini); Luxembourg: un point (poking fun at the banality of the Eurovision Song Contest); Nocturne d'un certain âge; Les Bassons vindicatifs (their revenge for years of oom-pah); Prélude et Grande Valse Brillante des Lapins.
JAG-2 *Wolf Song* (1985) for winds and tape (or sampler with a keyboard trigger).
The result of a lifelong love affair with wolves. This piece derives its structure from "group howls." The tape includes electronically-processed field recordings of wolves.
JAG-3 *Une Nuit dans le Palais de Tango*   Although looking back to the many styles of tango popular in Paris in the 1920s, this commission by the Ensemble Philidor uses the double reeds and horns (2ob 2ca 2hn 2bn cbn) to suggest the Argentinian "big bands," which featured a front line of four bandoneons.
JAG-1a *Berlioz: Three Pieces for Harmonium (1845); fl/pic ob 2cl 2hn 2bn cbn*   The *Pieces,* Hymne pour l'élévation (a part of the Mass), Sérénade agreste à la Madone (Rustic Serenade to the Virgin, on the theme of the Roman Pifferari), and Toccata, were composed by Berlioz in Paris in 1845. Their character suggests that he wrote them with the varied color of orchestral winds in mind.
JAG-6a to 22a: Joplin arrangements   The dates are those of Joplin's originals (1). Many have been recorded by the London Wind Soloists (not yet issued).
Arrangements for fl ob 2cl 2hn 2bn cbn (ob may replace fl with some minor changes)
JAG-6a *Cleopha,* March and Two-Step (1902)   Once a favourite of Sousa's band.
JAG-7a *The Entertainer* (1902)   Marked "not fast," like many of Joplin's works.
JAG-8a *Bethena, A Concert Waltz* (1905)   Like *Cleopha* and *Antoinette,* named after an unidentified woman; one of Joplin's most attractive works, a gentle, tender, waltz.
JAG-10a *Stoptime Rag* ("Fast or Slow"; 1910)   "Stamp the heel of one foot heavily where marked." This is obviously not effective on a carpeted floor.
JAG-11a *The Cascades;* (1904)   Named after the Cascade Gardens at the 1904 St Louis World Fair, which had a huge watercourse of falls, ponds and fountains.
JAG-12a *Solace - A Mexican Serenade* (1909)   A Ragtime Habanera ("very slow march time") with Mexican color.
Arrangements for 2ob 2cl 2hn 2bn cbn (a flute may often be used instead of oboe 1).
JAG-13a *Great Crush Collision March* (1896)   Joplin's first work with ragtime elements. Named after William George Crush, of the Kansas and Texas Railroad, who

staged a spectacular railroad crash on 15 September 1896 at the (temporary) site of Crush, between Waco and Dallas, Texas. The crash was seen by as many as 50,000 people. A recent article (2) reproduces original photos of the occasion and speculates that the Joplin work may have been a commission by William Crush before the event.
JAG-14a *Maple Leaf Rag* (1898-1899) Not a Canadian inspiration, but named after the "Maple Leaf Route" of the Chicago Great Western Railroad. Scott Joplin wanted this rag to be played at his own funeral.
JAG-16a *Ragtime Dance* (1899)   This went through various stages, including one as a folk ballet. There is also a stamp section (as in the much later Stoptime Rag, **JAG-10a**).
JAG-17a *Scott Joplin's New Rag* (1912)   Written soon after the opera *Treemonisha.*
JAG-18a *Pine Apple Rag* (1908)   Not fast, but the quarter note is 100, nevertheless!
JAG-19a *Magnetic Rag* (1914)   Joplin's very last rag; with *Maple Leaf Rag,* recorded (badly and perhaps not really authentically) by the composer on pianola.
Arrangements for 2ob 2ca 2hn 2bn db/cbn   These versions have been prepared for the Ensemble Philidor. **JAG-22a** is a new version of *The Entertainer*, distinct from **JAG-7a**.
JAG-20a *A Breeze from Alabama - A Ragtime Two Step* (1902)   Dedicated to "P. G. Lowery, World's Challenging Colored Cornetist and Band Master."
JAG-21a *Pleasant Moments - A Ragtime Waltz* (1909)   A gentle, rather tender, waltz; Joplin wrote it while he was in New York.
JAG-23a, 24a Mozart: *Marriage of Figaro*   The orchestral music, (a) Overture plus full opera: 2fl ob 2cl 2hn 2bn vc/db/cbn; (b) Overture: fl ob cl bn hn hpscd. These arrangements are for use in small theaters, where space is insufficient even for Mozart's orchestra. Much of Mozart's own wind writing is incorporated, so that the power and variety of the original is always evident.
JAG-28a Johann Strauss the Younger: *Tales from the Vienna Woods*   Arranged for the same ensemble as Mozart's *Gran Partita*, K.361; the basset horns mimic the zither.
JAG-29a, 30a Sullivan: *Yeomen of the Guard*   These are arrangements for wind band of the orchestral accompaniment of Sullivan's most substantial score for the Savoy operas. They retain the color of the original, and have the advantage of being practical in orchestral pits too small for Sullivan's orchestra.
JAG-33a *Tango paraphrase* on the Miserere scene from Verdi's *Il Trovatore;* an encore lollipop for the Triebensee Ensemble, which grew out of **JAG-3**.
1. James Hawkins with Kathleen Benson 1979 *Scott Joplin*; London: Robson Books.
2. Kent Biffle, in the *Dallas Morning News* of 15 September 1985. We are indebted to Professor Samuel Trickey for this reference.
GIORGI, Andrea di *1836, Bergamo-1900, Gandino*   Organist and Maestro di Banda at Gandino from 1859-1899, and composer of 40 works for voices with winds and a few pieces for winds alone. Many of his works are explicitly "per processione," and others are for occasions like Corpus Christi, for which processions were common. Some are dedicated to senior clergy; some carry personal notes, e.g. **AUG-12v** refers to the anniversary "della morte dell'Esimio Professore Lorenzo De Giorgi." Giorgi wrote many other works, some for brass and organ. There is a *Lungo inno a quatro voci per processione* jointly by Andrea di Giorgi and Frederico di Giorgi (presumably a relative).
GIPPS, Ruth *20 Feb, 1921, Bexhill, UK*   Pianist; pupil of Jacob and of Vaughan Williams. Her *Wind Sinfonietta* Op 73 **RZG-2** was written for the Rondel Ensemble in 1989. It includes an optional tam-tam, played by horn 1. Her *Octet* Op 65 **RZG-3**, for the Janus Ensemble, includes a section which can be repeated ad lib if the music is used as an entr'acte, rather than for concert performance.
GLASER, Werner Wolf *b 14 Apr 1910, Germany (active in Sweden)*   The three works for winds by Glaser are a *Capriccio e canzone* for 2cl 2bn, a short *Marsch* for double wind quintet and percussion, and his 1966 *Konsert* for wind band.

GLASS, Philip *b 31 Jan 1937, Baltimore* One of the seminal figures of the Minimalist movement, where music is structured mainly by rhythm. He studied at the Juilliard under Bergsma and Persichetti; since 1985, his works have moved closer to the mainstream. *Glassworks,* **PYG-1,** has been recorded by the Philip Glass Ensemble on FM 37265. Glass has also written a Brass Sextet (1966) for 2tp 2hn tb tu.

GLEISSNER, Franz Johann *6 Apr 1761, Neustadt an der Waldnab-18 Sept 1818, Munich* Advisor to the publisher André, Offenbach am Main, for whom he prepared a Sinfonia Concertante version of Mozart's *Gran Partita,* K.361. André also published his *6 Pièces d'Harmonie,* **FOG-2.** He was editor of a *Journal de musique militaire,* **FOG-1.**

GLUCK, Christoph Willibald, Ritter von *2 Jul 1714, Erasbach-15 Nov 1787, Vienna* Gluck used winds sparingly in his operas. Yet, late in his life, he wrote a *De Profundis* for four-part chorus, sombrely accompanied by ob hn bn 3tb and lower strings.

GNOCCI, Pietro *(?1690)-1775, Brescia* Chorister at the cathedral, Brescia, in 1712 and 1713, who became Maestro di Capella on 16 June 1723.

GODDARD, Mark Timothy Robert *b 28 June 1960, Aylesbury, UK* Goddard studied composition at the Royal Academy of Music in London, where he won prizes (including one named after Charles Lucas (qv) and wrote several works for winds: a *Wind Quintet, Colloquy* for clarinet and guitar (Battison Haynes Prize winner) and *Retrospection* for clarinet and bassoon (William Elkin Prize winner). In 1986, he was commissioned to write a piece for massed woodwinds for children in Oxfordshire Schools. Goddard's works for conventional wind ensemble successfully fill gaps in the standard repertoire, and range from music for a wedding (**MAG-1**) to a set of variations for the Dorchester Wind Players to play during a Sunday afternoon communal picnic in September 1985 in the Oxfordshire village of Cuddesdon. As a bassoon player who married another one, he has composed and arranged much music for bassoon quartet. His Sextet **MAG-1** *Fanfare, Romance and Jig* was written in January 1986 for a wedding (at which it was played) but had its premiere at (unrelated) christening celebrations. The syncopated rhythmical drive of the opening Fanfare is contrasted with the timeless, steamy, central slow movement; the work concludes with a somewhat bumptious and cheeky jig. **MAG-2** *Marshall's Diversion* (published as *Freestyle* with alternative instrumental combinations) was commissioned by Marshall Stoneham in 1995 on his move to University College London. It is an attractive work for 2cl 2hn 2bn, whose somewhat jazzy style makes it an ideal foil to classical serenades. The movements carry descriptive subtitles: Vivo: Latin-American feel; Gently unrelenting: Monsoon quality; Andante: a lament for Sarah Moore, an oboist friend; Relaxed: Modern jazz idiom. This last movement has ingenious rhythmic twists. **MAG-2a** *Washington Post* (Sousa 1854-1932) was written as a "lollipop" for an Oxford charity concert in July 1986. Goddard and Marshall Stoneham (qv) reconstructed Weber's *Trauermusik* **MAG-1va** from sketches and from the other works which Weber was reusing in this choral work with bass soloist and winds.

GODFREY, Charles, the Elder *22 Nov 1790, Kingston, Surrey, UK-12 Dec 1863, London* At first a drummer with the 1st Royal Surrey Militia, he moved to the Coldstream Guards as bassoonist, becoming bandmaster in 1825; he continued his ties with the regiment after his discharge in 1834. Godfrey edited *Jullien's Military Journal* (a continuation of Boosé's *Supplemental Military Journal*), producing 160 numbers between 1847 and 1857. All of his sons were famous military bandmasters.

GODFREY, William *(1780)* We know of no link to the family of Charles Godfrey.

GOEHR, Alexander *b 10 Aug 1932, Berlin* Goehr studied with Messiaen and Yvonne Loriod in Paris. He joined the staff of the BBC before taking academic positions in the America, then at Leeds and at Cambridge in England. His *Chaconne* Op 35 was written as a commission from Leeds University, and combines professional skills with humor.

GÖLLER, ( ) This name has been added (in another hand) at the start of the clarinet 1 part of a parthia in Donaueschingen; at the end, in the copyist's hand, is "Dell: S Forstmeyero" (sic), perhaps E A Forstmayer, Hofmusiker at Karlsruhe c.1782.

GOEPFERT, Carl (Karl, Charles) Andreas (André) *16 January 1768, Rampad, near Würzburg-11 April 1818, Meiningen* The son of Würzburg's official surgeon, Goepfert studied clarinet with Meissner (qv) before moving to Vienna. In 1793, he became first clarinet in the Meiningen Court Orchestra, and later took charge of court military music. He left Meiningen in 1798 to establish himself as soloist in Vienna, but his leave of absence was cancelled; the apparent offer of the post of Kapellmeister never materialized, and Goepfert became, according to *Sainsbury*, a "disillusioned man." The head-title of **CAG-2** (c.1800-1804) describes him as "Première Clarinette de la Chapelle et Directeur de la Musique du Corps de Chasseurs de S A Le Duc de Saxe Meiningen." The *Harmonie* **CAG-1** comprises 8 multi-movement works: *10 Marches*; *15 Dances*; six *Parthias*. The dedication to Napoleon allows us to date them from soon after the Battle of Marengo (1800). There is excellent music, some very demanding for the serpent.

When first in Vienna, Goepfert was a pupil of Mozart for about eighteen months (1). In a letter of 25 February 1817 Goepfert, writing to apply for a post at Oettingen-Wallerstein, claimed (2): "As I have been studying music with the greatest fervor for some twenty years, and also for a year and a half enjoyed instruction from the immortal Mozart in the more advanced science of music theory, I have always felt a great preference for those instruments which are used in a wind ensemble, and therefore my great teacher, Mozart, handed to me the scores of all his operas, charging me to arrange them for wind band." We presume that Mozart sanctioned arrangements, rather than required them, and we are given no reason for Goepfert's delay of twenty years, until 1802-1806, in publishing the works which are now known.

The extant Goepfert arrangements are good, so his claims could be true. Certainly, his arrangement **CAG-8a** of *6 Marches* by Mozart carried the assertion "edition faite d'après le manuscrit original de l'auteur" (André, Offenbach s/M, pn 1511 [1801] and pn 1661 [1803]). If so, then which works were arranged? Those arrangements which survive are not the obvious choices: the *Paris Symphony* K.297, the *Rondo alla turca* from the K.331 Piano Sonata, plus marches and songs. Meysel's 1817 *Handbuch* names Goepfert as the arranger for Simrock c.1812 of the *Gran Partita* K.361; Goepfert may have been "house arranger" for Simrock (3). Even his arrangement of Steibelt's *Combat Naval*, truly a "pièce d'occasion" to celebrate a British victory, has virtues (4). We might also ask if the D-DO version of *Die Entführung aus dem Serail,* the only version with any serious claim to be Mozart's own, could be a completion of Mozart's arrangement by a pupil such as Goepfert, a possibility consistent with Goepfert's claim. Some of Goepfert's later arrangements are known only from advertizements, such as the *4 grosse Parthien* of 1815, and an 1817 arrangement of Haydn's *Creation*.

1. *Deutsch* p 516.

2. L Schiedmair 1907-1908 Sammelbänden der internationalen Musikgesellschaft 9 16 *Die Blütezeit der Öttingen-Wallerstein'schen Hofkapelle.*

3. B Blomhert 1991 *Mozart Jahrbuch* p 206.

4. Steibelt's original piano piece, published in 1797 by Longman & Broderip, London, was called *Britannia: An Allegorical Overture in commemoration of the signal victory obtained by Admiral Duncan over the Dutch Fleet on the 11th October 1797.* The event was the defeat of de Winter's Dutch fleet off Camperduin by Adam, Viscount Duncan. The work quotes "God Save the King," "Rule Britannia," and Purcell's "Britons! Strike Home." Surprisingly, Goepfert's "Combat Naval" was published in Paris when that city can hardly have been pro-British. Goepfert's political stance might also be shown by **CAG-1,** dedicated "aux Armées françoises particulièrement [sic] à la Garde du premier Consul Bonaparte"; Napoleon became Consul only in 1802, after the brief period in

1800-1801 in which Prussia might have become part of the "Northern Coalition."

GOŁĄBEK, Jakub *1739, Silesia-30 March 1789, Krakow* Gołąbek was a member of the Kraków Cathedral choir as singer and composer from c.1774 until his death.

GOLLER, Martin, OSB *1764-1836, Innsbruck* Composer of a *Tantum ergo* for choir, winds and organ, Innsbruck 1829. He was probably not the composer Göller listed above, nor the V Goller who wrote a *Zweite Messe* Op 63 with organ or Harmonie.

GOOSSENS, Sir (Aynsley) Eugène *26 May 1893, London-13 June 1962, Hillingdon* Written in 1924, his *Fantasy for 9 Wind Instruments*, Op 36, is a delightfully colourful and somewhat Gallic work. It is recorded by the winds of the Sydney Symphony Orchestra/Vernon Handley on ABC Classics 8.770013.

GOSSEC, François Joseph *17 Jan 1734 Vergnies, Hainault, Belgium-16 Feb 1829 Passy, near Paris* In the mid-18th century, Paris was the musical center of Europe. This was not due to French composers, for most of those active, like Johann Stamitz and Gossec, were aliens, nor because Parisian audiences were discriminating, for Mozart's letters and many other sources demonstrate the contrary. Music was encouraged, especially when squabbles between rival operatic factions added spice to the scene, and the potential rewards tempted many musicians.

Gossec, the son of a poor Belgian peasant farmer, made the major change from cowherd to chorister. Gossec remained at Antwerp Cathedral until 1749. Two years later, armed with a letter of introduction to Rameau, he moved to France. His first position was with the private orchestra of the Fermier-Général Jean de la Pouplinière. A Fermier-Général (and there were perhaps fifty such in France) was contracted to collect taxes on behalf of the Monarch; the system, open to much abuse, was suppressed in 1790. La Pouplinière seems to have been a discriminating person, who appreciated the music of Rameau. His orchestra had directors as fine as Stamitz from 1744 to 1745 and Gossec from 1754 to 1762. Gossec and Stamitz pioneered the use of the clarinet in France, and their enthusiasm led to the rapid acceptance of this relatively new instrument. The orchestra's clarinettists were Gaspard, Proksch, and Flieger; its horn players were Schencker (who also played harp) and Louis (who also played double bass). Gossec wrote much of his music for the orchestra, although it is not clear whether it played in the remarkable *Messe des Morts* of 1760, in which the *Tuba Mirum* includes a separate wind band. La Pouplinière died in 1762. Gossec and some of the other musicians moved to the service of the Prince de Conti. Around 1769 came a further move, this time to the Prince de Condé. Gossec founded the Concerts des Amateurs and revived the Concerts Spirituels. His influence survived the dangers of the French Revolution, for he was one of the founders of the Paris Conservatoire and was an Inspector there from its foundation in 1795 until 1816.

Gossec's works for small wind band are for pairs of clarinets, horns and bassoons. **FJG-1, 2** *Pièces pour deux clarinettes, deux cors et deux bassons pour SAS Mr le Prince de Condé* The second item is entitled "La grande chasse de Chantilli," Chantilly being the seat of the Prince de Condé. The Rondo **FJG-4** *Chasse d'Hylas et Silvie faite par Gossec à Chantilli* was written for a Pastorale by Rochon de Chabanne, and performed on 7 November 1768 at Chantilly and on 10 December in Paris. The dramatic repertoire at Chantilly is discussed by Isherwood (1). The four-movement suite **FJG-5** *La Bataille* was played for "Meur. le Prince de Condé à Chantilli et executée chaque jour par les musiciens pendant son souper devant Mgr le Duc d'Orléans et le Roi Louis V [strictly XV] pendant leur séjour à le [sic] Chateau." It has colorful features, using horns to mimic trumpets: Largo: L'appel des trouppes (E♭); Marche fièrement et marqué (E♭); Allegro molto: la mêlée ou l'attaque (C minor); Gaîment: La victoire (E♭).

Gossec's music for the large military bands of the revolutionary period are among the best of their genre. His *Te Deum* (which has been recorded by the Banda Cittadina di Brescia/Ligasacchi on Concerto GSCR 00105) was played at the Fête de la Fédération. The *Marche lugubre* **FJG-2m** (recorded by the Wallace Collection on Nimbus NI 5175) includes dramatic use of the tam-tam, and both his Marches and Hymnes show an imaginative response to the needs of large outdoor performances. The titles are standard for their time, with a *Hymne* and a *Choeur* to Liberty, and *Hymnes* to Humanity, to "L'Être suprême", or for specific occasions. His *O Salutaris* (for Rousseau; note also the 1794 *Hymne à la Liberté*) exists in several early wind versions; that apparently for 2ca bthn (*Weston/MCVP* p 51) in Gossec's *Saul* was arranged by Betz.

1. R M Isherwood 1986 *Farce and Fantasy: Popular Entertainment in 18th Century Paris;* New York: Oxford University Press; pp 34-37.

GOULD, Morton *b 10 Dec 1913, Richmond Hill, New York-21 Feb 1996* Gould wrote a number of works for concert band, including a suite from his music for the television series *Holocaust.* His work is grounded in jazz (his own "folk music"), and many of his works are on patriotic and holiday subjects.

GOUNOD, Charles François *18 June 1818, Paris-18 Oct 1893, St Cloud* Gounod's *Faust* has enjoyed lasting success, but his church music, by which he set so much store, is now largely ignored. "Had my father lived, I have no doubt I should have wanted to be a painter rather than a musician, but my mother's profession and the education she gave me when I was young turned the scale to music." Yet another possibility was the church, and indeed Gounod studied theology seriously for several years.

CFG-1 *Hymne à Sainte Cécile* Published in 1866, this sparsely scored Andante sostenuto assai is dedicated "à mon ami Alard." Jean Delphin Alard (1815-1888), violinist and composer, was professor at the Paris Conservatoire from 1843 until 1875. He taught Sarasate and other eminent violinists. One presumes that the solo violin part was intended for Alard himself.

CFG-2 *Petite Symphonie* Almost all writers on Gounod have grounds for shame. After *Faust,* the *Petite Symphonie* must be the work of Gounod's most often played and recorded. Yet, of the major biographies and encyclopedias we have consulted (about 15) only one gets the date of composition right, and only three give the correct scoring; several fail to mention the work at all. Since we have said (or thought) hard things about record sleeve writers on occasion, we can make partial amends here: the most reliable and detailed source readily available is the sleeve note by Frédéric Robert on Calliope CAL 1827 (a fine recording too). *Cobbett* provides a standard reference which does get both date and scoring right; he may even have been present at the first performance. We can usefully ignore all writers except Robert and Cobbett.

The *Petite Symphonie* came at the end of Gounod's life. Apart from a few bars of a march for the 119th Régiment, it was the last instrumental piece he composed. It was written for the Société de Musique de Chambre pour Instruments à Vent in 1885, and is dedicated to the Société's founder, Paul Taffanel. The first performance was on 30 April 1885, with the composer present. This performance had been advertized in *Le Ménestral* of 26 April 1885 as "une symphonie inédite, spécialement écrite" by Gounod. It is scored for flute plus an octet of 2ob 2cl 2hn 2bn. However, the second oboe part is exceptionally unimportant and can easily be taken over by the others (mainly the first bassoon) in the rare places where it matters. This may be intentional. When the Société was founded, no second oboe was named, and many works, including Taffanel's own arrangement of Saint-Saëns *Feuillet d'Album,* omit a second oboe too.

The *Petite Symphonie* is in four movements. The serious slow introduction leads into a delicate Allegretto. An Andante cantabile follows, in the best traditions of songs without words, with lovely flute writing. The Scherzo is a vigorous 6/8, and the Finale a masterly demonstration of the subtle use of syncopation. The work shows the composer at his best throughout and is free from the hints of indulgence and sentimentality common in French music of this time. Gounod was a lover of Mozart, whose influence is present, if not explicit. Some twenty years before the Symphonie was written, Saint-Saëns had said of Gounod that "his aim was to achieve the maximum effect with a minimum of apparent effort...to concentrate all the interest on the expression of feelings...expressiveness was his ideal...each note sings." If we add "wit" and "vitality" to expressiveness, we have precisely the ingredients of the Symphonie. It has been recorded by the London Baroque Ensemble/Haas, HMV XLP 30011; Maurice Bourgue Ensemble, Calliope CAL 1827; Münchener Blasakademie, Orfeo C 051 831A; Netherlands Wind Ensemble/de Waart, Philips 6570 205; Collegium Musicum Pragense, Supraphon 1411 2844; Ensemble Fidelio, Gallo CD 674; Amsterdam Wind Ensemble/Blomhert, STH Favorites CD 19245.

GOUVY, Louis Théodore *2 July 1819 Goffontaine, Saarbrücken-21 April 1898 Leipzig* Gouvy was a late developer. Indeed, he may have heard classical music for the first time as a law student in Paris in 1840. Yet he followed a musical career with determination and (unlike many others) with the consent of his parents. He was, like many, influenced by Mendelssohn, but teachers like Adam and contacts such as Chopin, Berlioz and others broadened his outlook. After periods in Berlin and in Italy, he settled in Paris in 1846, making only occasional visits to Germany. He was made a member of the Berlin Academy in 1895 and a Chevalier of the Légion d'Honneur in 1896.

Gouvy seems to have favored instrumental music at a time when it was out of fashion and to have preferred abstract music to program music. The French public did not share his views. After the mid 1870s, he responded with works like the *Petite Suite Gauloise,* rather than a direct successor to the Op 71 *Otteto.* These two works raise again the issue of the scoring of Gounod's **CFG-1**: the earlier Gouvy work includes one flute and one oboe, whereas the later one has flute and two oboes.

LTG-1 *Petite Suite Gauloise Op 90* Written c.1898 for Taffanel's Société de Musique de Chambre pour Instruments à Vent, the suite was one of Gouvy's last works. This attractive neoclassical work harks back to France before the Revolution and to idealized notions of rural life. The morning and evening movements involve much less activity than does Starzer's musical representation from a hundred years earlier. It is recorded on Supraphon SUA 1411 2844 QG.

LTG-2 *Ottetto Op 71* Written after 1873, and published in 1882, the *Otteto* is a stylish and enjoyable work which exploits well the characters of the winds.

GOW, Nathaniel *28 May 1763, Inver, near Dunkeld-19 Jan 1831, Edinburgh* One of His Majesty's Trumpeters for Scotland from 1779, famous as a violinist and for his dance music. His *March* and *Quickstep* are named for the Hon. Mr Ramsay Maule of Panmure.

GRAESCHI, ( ) (possibly Franz Joseph Graetzl, 1770-1824) Manuscript parts c.1820 by Joseph Spät survive of his *Komm heiliger Geist,* for choir and winds.

GRAF, Christian Ernst *30 Jun 1723, Rudolstadt-17 July 1804, The Hague* The Battle of Austerlitz took place on 2 December 1805, when Graf had been dead for 18 months, so there is an inconsistency which may simply indicate an imaginative re-titling by others of **CEG-1** as *Die Schlacht bei Austerlitz.*

GRAUGAARD, Lars *1957, Denmark)* His *Seven Summerscapes* are recorded by the Danish Wind Octet on Da Capo 8.22.4002.

GRAUN, Carl Heinrich *7 May 1703, Wahrenbrück, near Dresden-8 Aug 1759, Berlin* Composer of opera and church music, later Kapellmeister to Frederick the Great and Konzertmeister to the Berlin Opera.

GRECO, José-Luis *b 1953* His *Swallows* (1992) is for piano with wind octet.

GRELL, (August) Eduard *6 Nov 1800, Berlin-10 Aug 1886, Berlin* His *Waisen Musik* **EXG-1v** was written for the centenary of the Schindler Orphanages in Berlin. Others who wrote for charity performances, especially orphans, included Handel and Sauer.

GRENSER, (Grenzer), Johann Friedrich *1758, Dresden-17 Mar 1794, Stockholm* Oboist to the King of Sweden, c.1780.

GRETSCH, Johann Konrad *1710-1784, Regensberg* Whereas his *Parthia XV* **JKG-2** seems to be in seven movements, movement 6 has the note "Fine del Sig. Gretsch," and the subsequent movement is by Anton Rudolph. Above the start of the second movement in the first horn part is the pencil note "Madame la Princesse Regnat."

GRIESBACH, Charles *(1770)* We have not linked him to the other musicians named Griesbach. He wrote *12 Military Divertimentos,* c.1800.

GRIESBACH (Griesbacher), Reimund (Raymund) *1752, Vienna-1818, Vienna* Clarinettist and bassoonist: at Eszterháza from 1776 to 1778; basset horn player to Count Pálffy until 1781, and associated with the Imperial Harmonie in Vienna c.1795. He was clarinettist and Kapellmeister to Prince Grassalkovics in Pressburg from 1796.

GRIFFES, Charles Tomlinson *17 Sept 1884, Elmira, New York-8 April 1920, New York City* Berlin-trained composer and schoolmaster, whose music included influences as wide as Javanese and other oriental music. His wind music (1) owed much to friendship with Barrère (qv; Barrère was a pallbearer at Griffes's funeral) and to links to theaters. *The Kairn of Koridwen* (a dance drama, first performed 10 February 1917) and the incomplete *Salut au Monde* (1919) were for the Neighborhood Theater; the *Three Tone Pictures* (The Lake at Evening; The Vale of Dreams; The Night Winds; for fl 2ob 2cl 2hn 2bn harp) were first performed on 19 December 1915 at the Court Theater, New York. All the music was played by the Georges Barrère Ensemble; Griffes rescored the *Tone Pictures* so as to omit the harp, so that Barrère could play the music on tour.

1. Donna K Anderson 1983 *The Works of Charles T Griffes: A Descriptive Catalog;* Ann Arbor: UMI Research Press.

GROH, Josef *(1830) active in Velenice, 1864* Composer of several sets of funeral songs using voices and winds. Some have parts for instruments missed out on their title pages, such as the *Grab-Candate [sic] in Ass [sic; A♭]* **JSG-3tv**. The 1864 date of his *Grab-Arien* **JSG-1tv** is given on the manuscript parts, prepared by Konrad Zimmer.

GROSS, Johann Gottlieb *c.1748-8 June 1820* His "Echo" uses an oboe to echo two oboes, two bassoons and trumpet, a rather old-fashioned ensemble for 1770.

GROVLEZ, Gabriel (Marie) *4 Apr 1879, Lille-20 Oct 1944, Paris* Composer, pianist music critic, conductor of the Paris Opéra from 1914-33, and Professor of chamber music at the Paris Conservatoire from 1939. His arrangement of Fauré's *Nocturne* was published in 1925, when his conducting took him to Chicago and to Lisbon.

GRUBER, Johann Georg *18 Apr 1855, Wöserdorf, Lower Austria-2 Dec 1933, Linz* A composer who continued the Corpus Christi music tradition in the late 19th century.

GRUSS, Anton Josef *(?1840) Lehrer (teacher) at Holtschitz (near Česká Lípa)* Gruss arranged one (perhaps two) of the funeral pieces **JXG-6tv** by Gellert (qv).

GÜNTHER, Carl Friedrich Possibly the bass Friedrich Günther who sang at the Weimar and Gotha theaters between 1770 and 1780.

GUERINGE (Guering), ( ) "Directeur de Musique de la Princesse de Bade Bade."

GUEST, George *1 May 1771, Bury St Edmunds-10? Sep 1831, Wisbech* Chorister with the Chapel Royal, from 1789 organist at St Peter's, Wisbech, Guest wrote marches for the Wisbech Volunteer Band (which he directed), the First Regiment of Norfolk Volunteer Infantry, the Third Regiment of Cambridgeshire Volunteer Infantry, and the Isle of Ely Regiment of Local Militia.

GÜTTLER, Josef *(1840); active 1870-1900* Composer and arranger of church music with winds, and especially funeral music.

GWILT, David William *b 3 Nov 1932, Edinburgh* Gwilt studied music in Cambridge, with Robin Orr as his tutor for composition. He teaches at the Chinese University of Hong Kong, where he has been Professor since 1981. His *Suite* **DWG-1** is in four movements (Prelude; Dance; Melody; Badinerie), and is part of a series intended for amateur instrumentalists, so that there are alternative parts (clarinet 3 for bassoon, with cues for horn 1) and optional percussion. Gwilt has also written a wind quintet.

GYROWETZ (Jírovec) Adalbert (Mathias) (Vojtěch Matyás JÍROVEC) *19 Feb 1763, České Budějovice (Budweis)-19 Mar 1850, Vienna* Gyrowetz was a prolific and celebrated composer who lived long enough to see his once-fashionable works pass out of favor; he was also almost certainly the author of anonymous memoirs which give an informal view of the musical life of his time. His early musical education was from his father, a choirmaster. Gyrowetz first moved to Prague to study law. After a long illness, he spent several years in the early 1780s with Count Franz von Fünfkirchen as private secretary; the Count expected and encouraged his staff to be active musicians, and Gyrowetz had ample opportunity to write music and to have it performed. The early part of the *Memoirs* shows more than a touch of the incipient romanticism of Goethe's *Young Werther*, whose *Sorrows* were then fashionable. As the autobiography recalls (1), he was often "carried away by his feelings so that he began to weep and sob openly." This attracted attention, of course. "I began composing small ensemble pieces for wind instruments, and having seen that they managed to win favour and were excellently suited for outdoors in the summertime, I wrote twelve and was stimulated thereby to compose works of larger scope and to devote myself to musical creation with increasing love and joy." These twelve pieces were written in Chlumec in 1783; like many of his early works and some in Traeg's catalogue, they appear to be lost.

Gyrowetz made extensive travels: to Naples, where he strolled beside the harbor with Goethe; to Paris, where he arrived soon after the Revolution and found one of his symphonies issued as Haydn's; and to London, where Salomon engaged him to write for his concerts in 1791 and 1792. On his return to Vienna in 1793, Gyrowetz secured a post in the Imperial War Department. In 1804, Baron von Braun (qv Cherubini, Salieri), the Intendant of the two Viennese Court theaters, offered him the post of Kapellmeister, a position he held until 1831. He produced an enormous amount of music, including symphonies, operas and chamber works. Yet, after retirement, he was reduced to poverty, for his pension no longer sufficed. His friends arranged a benefit concert for him, and its success led to other performances of his music in his later years.

His *Aria Russe,* arranged Havel, uses the same Russian tune ("Schöne Minka") as does Beethoven's Op 107 No 7; the source was presumably the *Sammlung russischer Volkslieder,* published by Ivan Pratsch in St Petersburg in 1790.

ADG-1 *Parthia in Dis (Eb)* The first horn part is difficult. Recorded by Collegium Musicum Pragense on Supraphon 1 11 1839 and Supraphon C0-2060.

ADG-2 *Parthia in Bb* Recorded on Panton 11 0522 G, and also under Carl Stamitz's name by the Consortium Classicum on CPO 999 081, apparently from parts in Schwerin.

ADG-6,7 *Serenades Op 3 Nos 1 in Eb and 2 in Bb* These appear to date from 1790, when Gyrowetz was in Paris (see *MGG*). This being so, we use the opus numbers of the editions of Imbault (Paris) and André (Offenbach s/M, pn 315; see *RISM* [G 5337]). There are conflicts in the numbering of his works, with Op 3 also assigned to a Sinfonia Concertante (*RISM* [G 5279]) published in Amsterdam; in the Amsterdam sequence, the same Serenades are Op 5 (published by J J Hummel, Berlin and Amsterdam, pl 819; *RISM* [G 5338]). Occasional claims that the Op 3 serenades are in C and F are errors in the reading of Bb clarinet parts. Likewise, we believe that the lost André Op 32 serenades are simply a misprinted Op 3 set.

ADG-1e *Incidental Music for Grillparzer's Der Traum ein Leben* This incidental music was specially written in 1834. There are references to "Telegraphenzeichen" as cues or prompts. The "telegraph" known at this time was the system of semaphore towers initiated in France during the Napoleonic Wars, and the Berlin-Cologne semaphore link was built in 1832-1834, just before the music was written and played.

ADG-1v *Lasst Fenisens Lob* Composed for act 3, scene 3 of Gaston's *Randgesang,* it is sometimes incorrectly attributed to Weber, even though Jähns's catalog (2) of Weber's music gives it as "probably Gyrowetz."

1. Adalbert Gyrowetz 1848 *Biographie des Adalbert Gyrowetz;* Vienna: Mechitharisten Buchdruckerei. Reprinted (1915), edited by Alfred Einstein; Leipzig: C F W Siegel.

2. F W Jähns 1871 (reprinted 1967) *Carl Maria von Weber in seinen Werken: Chronologisch-thematisch Verzeichnis seiner sämtlichen Compositionen;* Berlin.

HAAN, Stefan de *b 25 Jan 1921, Darmstadt* Bassoonist, now resident in the England.

HABERHAUER, Maurus (Mauro, Mauritius) *1749-1799* Haberhauer studied in Brno. He composed a concerto for cor anglais. His *Missa Adventalis* is a "pastoral" Mass.

HABERT, Johannes Evangelista *18 Oct 1833, Oberplan, now Horní Planá-1 Sept 1896, Gmunden, Upper Austria* The piano version of his *Scherzo,* Op 107 No 1b, is dedicated to his teacher Fräulein Maria Haas.

HABERT, M (M may simply mean "Monsieur") *(?1780)* Habert styled himself "Musicien de M: le Duc de Deuxponts." The Duc is none other than Maximilian Joseph (1756-1825), Elector (from 1806, King) of Bavaria, Count of Zweibrücken (Deuxponts), son of Carl Theodore. A previous Duc was a friend of Louis XV and acquaintance of Casanova.

HAEFFNER, Johann Christian Friedrich *2 Mar 1759, Oberschönau-28 May 1833* Leader of the Swedish Court Chapel from 1795-1808 but, dismissed because of quarrels, he became Director Musices at Uppsala University. There he developed the orchestra and contributed to other facets of Swedish music. All his wind music was written after 1808 and is for 2ob 2cl 2hn 2bn. It includes a 3-movement *Partie,* various dances, and an arrangement of four movements from Mozart's *Figaro.*

HAERING, Joseph *(1780)* Composer of many short pieces now in CH-E, including 18 items "dédié à l'usage aux Élèves de l'École de Notre Dame des Hermites." Haering referred to himself as "Directeur de la Musique Militaire du Canton de Schwytz." The ensemble he uses (2fl 4cl 2hn 2bn) is typical of French bands of the time.

HAGMANN, L "Chef de Musique des Pionniers," whose music is dedicated to the Garde Nationale de France.

HAHN, Reynaldo *9 Aug 1875, Caracas, Venezuela-28 Jan 1947, Paris* Oddly, Hahn's birth certificate records his year of birth as 1874, but he always claimed 1875. His fame rests mainly on his operettas, such as *Ciboulette* (1) and songs. **RXH-1** *Le Bal de Béatrice d'Este* (1905), dedicated to Saint-Saëns, attempts to reproduce the atmosphere of the Milanese court which vanished four centuries earlier. Beatrice d'Este (1475-1497), raised at the court of Ferrara and wife of Lodovico Sforza (Il Moro), helped to make the court at Milan a showplace for the best in art and literature (2). Hahn's title draws attention to another patron of the arts, Princess Edmonde de Polignac (1865-1943, née Winnaretta Singer, daughter of the sewing-machine magnate). *Le Bal* was an especial success with Queen Alexandra, who heard it during Hahn's visit to England and who, once King Edward VII had gone to play bridge, asked for it to be repeated. The seven short movements are Entrée de Lodovic le More; Lesquercade; Romanesque; Ibérienne; Leda et l'Oiseau (a bird, not the usual swan); Courante-gai, sans vitesse (with a trio section); and Salut final au Duc de Milan, which includes material from the first and sixth movements. Recordings include: New London Orchestra/Ronald Corp; Hyperion CDA 66347; Hahn/chamber orchestra HMV 1990-1 (on 78s); New York Harmonie Ensemble/Richman, Music & Arts CD 649; Paris Orchestra/Jacquillat.

1. James Harding 1979 *Folies de Paris;* London: Chappell/Elm Tree, p 159 and passim.

2. J R Hale 1981 *Concise Encyclopaedia of the Italian Renaissance;* London: Thames & Hudson. The Beatrice d'Este who heard wind music during her visit to Eszterháza in

1775 was of the same lineage, but not the one of Hahn's title.

HAJEK, Aleš *1937*   Composer of an *Octet* (2ob 2cl 2hn 2bn) published in 1982.

HÀJEK, Jan (Johann)   Hàjek was "Rector chori zu Teschen" (now Česky Těšín, on the route between Brno and Kraków), and composed a German requiem with winds.

HALE, Samuel *(1770)*   Hale's *Select Book of Martial Music,* **SYH-1m,** contains a movement attributed to Mozart, possibly loosely based on the finale to K.388.

HALLAGER, A   His tone poem for band, *Reminiscences of the last days at St Helena,* presumably relates to Napoleon's exile. A march by Salner also refers to the island.

HALLAM, Norman *(1960)*   Composer of *Seven Variations for Six* for the Bournemouth Wind Quire.

HALLBERG, Bengt *b 13 Sept 1932, Götenborg   Hällristningar,* a 15 minute tone-poem, is one of the rare works combining wind ensemble with jazz soloists.

HAMBRAEUS, Bengt *b 19 Jan 1928, Stockholm   Strata* (1979-80) is scored for the same ensemble as Mozart's *Gran Partita, K.361.*

HAMILTON, Iain (Ellis) *b 6 June 1922, Glasgow   Antigone* was written for the Paragon Ensemble, and first performed in Glasgow in 1992; it is scored for fl cl 2bn 2tp 2tb.

HAMMER, August   "1st Hautbois chez le 7 Reg. s. Hollande," who wrote a *Fantasie* for solo oboe and winds.

HAMMERL, Carl Anton *(1770)*   Hammerl's *Partita,* c.1800, is his only surviving work. One movement bears the note "da Haydn." We cannot relate him to P C Hammerl (qv).

HAMMERL, Paul Cornelius *13 Dec 1769, Munich-27 April 1839, Ludwigslust*   Clarinet player with the Duke of Bretzenheim then, from 1795 to c.1825, first clarinet for the Duke of Mecklenburg-Schwerin at Ludwigslust. His *3 Parties* **PCH-1(-3)** are partly original, partly arrangements of Haydn and others. His other works for Ludwigslust include arrangements of Mozart and partly original works. Hammerl died of typhus.

HANDEL, George Frideric (Georg Friederich) *23 February 1685, Halle-14 April 1759, London*   Handel is the first grand master of wind music. His work spans ensembles from giant outdoor bands (1, 2) to small military bands. Some of these works anticipate wind harmony; others, like fife music and recorder music, lie outside our scope.

GFH-1 *Music for the Royal Fireworks (HH351)*   The first movement was originally for winds alone, with strings added later. For the other movements, strings were in from the start, but then struck out in the struggle between Handel (who wanted strings) and the King who "hoped there would be no fidles" (1). The numbers of instruments varied too. Handel wanted 16 trumpets and 16 horns, but then agreed to 12 of each, noted the Duke of Montague in March 1749; the number had fallen to 9 of each by the time of the autograph score, and this is the size of the largest bands in "authentic" recordings.

Part of the autograph of the Fireworks music (3), shows the instruction "The second time by ye french Horns and Hautbois & Bassons without Trumpets without violins and kettledrums the third time all together." This may or may not correspond to what was performed. The engraving (4) "A View of the Public Fireworks to be exhibited on the occasion of the GENERAL PEACE concluded at Aix la Chappelle, Octr.7.1748" indicates "The Steps wch. go up to a grand Area before the Middle Arch, where a band of a Hundred Musicians are to play before ye Fireworks begin, the Musick for wch. is to be compos'd by Mr. Handel." This suggests that the music was to start proceedings, not accompany the fireworks; this is consistent with the fact that, as the same source shows, the events were to last at least three hours.

Most of Handel's works for 2ob 2hn bn date from the 1740s (5, 6). Such bands, typical of military bands of the 1740s, are used on a larger scale in Handel's second and third *Concerti a due cori,* where the pieces are technically demanding. Many of these works are based on Handel's larger works. Thus the first of the *Arias in F,* **GFH-2** (HH410, 411; c.1725) is arranged from "Benche Tuoni" (*Teseo,* 1713). The *Arias* are recorded by the London Baroque Ensemble (Parlophone R20581) and on authentic instruments by the Academy of Ancient Music (Oiseau-Lyre DSLO548).

GFH-3   A version of this *Minuet in G* (HH422, 1746-7) is found in **GFH-1**.

GFH-6   There is a version of this *March in G* in *Judas Maccabaeus*, c.1745.

GFH-7   The *March in D, HH365*, is related to a chorus in *Alexander Balus*, c.1746.

The pieces for 2ob bn tp (5, 6) correspond to the earlier military bands, before horns were standard. **GFH-8** *March in D*, HH416, also found in *Trio Sonata* Op 5 No 2. The still smaller ensembles of three instruments are also typical of early military bands; two such small bands (2ob bn) are used in the *Concerto a due cori* No 1.

GFH-11 *Rigaudon & Bourée*   The Rigaudon is a version of a dance in *Almira*.

GFH-12 *March in G*   The scoring is uncertain; it is known as the *Grenadiers' March*. A version is found in the Trio Sonata Op 5 No 2.

More interesting is **GFH-10** *Overture: Suite in D*. Part of the autograph is illustrated in the Haas edition. This fine work is important, since it is one of the earliest for clarinets (in D in the original). The material was used again by Handel, notably in *The Arrival of the Queen of Sheba*. It is recorded by the London Baroque Ensemble on Parlophone R20617, and on authentic instruments by Keith Puddy, Gary Brodie and Susan Dent on Clarinet Classics CC0004 and L'École d'Orphée on Caedmon CRD 10812.

1. O E Deutsch 1955 *Handel: A Documentary Biography;* London: A and C Black.

2. C Hogwood 1984 *Handel;* London: Thames and Hudson.

3. A Hyatt King 1967 *Handel and His Autographs;* London: British Museum. See also D Burrows & M J Ronish 1994 *A Catalogue of Handel's Musical Autographs;* Oxford: Oxford University Press.

4. The structure built for the band and the fireworks is very similar to those used elsewhere in Europe (see G Sievernich 1987 *Das Buch der Feuerwerkskunst;* Nördlingen: Delphi/Greno Verlagsges.). An early print is in the possession of one of us (AMS).

5. *Händel Handbuch* vol 3, 1986; Kassel-Basel-London: Bärenreiter.

6. *New Grove;* reprinted as a separate volume by Winton Dean with work list by Anthony Hicks; London: Macmillan 1982. Dates given in (5, 6) do not always agree.

HANDL, Johann *(?1780)*   Primarily a copyist; he copied many works now in A-Wn, and these have inscriptions "pro me" or "ex rebus." Some of the copies are of otherwise unknown composers like Eremitasch, Grot and Lutter. While he may have adapted works for local forces, all attributions to him as composer are suspect.

HANMER, Ronald (Charles Douglas) *b 1917, Reigate, UK*   In addition to his *Serenade* and his *Suite for 7*, Hanmer has written quartets for fl fl/ob 2cl and trios for fl 2cl.

HANSCHKE (Handscke, Hanisch), Anton *(1770)-active c.1801*   His surviving music is associated with the collections from the Chotek Harmonie.

HARKE, Friedrich *(1770)*   Kapellmeister of the 2nd Infantry Regiment E H Ferdinand; his set of marches was written c.1800 and dedicated to Generalissimus E H Carl, of the Royal and Imperial Austrian army.

HARPER, Edward *b 17 Mar 1941, Taunton, Devon, UK*   Harper scored his *Double Variations* for solo oboe and solo bassoon with an orchestral wind section.

HARREX, Patrick *b 26 Sept 1946, London*   Violinist and composer, who studied with Messiaen at the Paris Conservatoire. He won the BBC Composers' Competition and a French Government scholarship in 1968 prior to studying with Gilbert Amy in Paris.

HARRINGTON (Harington), Thomas *(1760)*   Possibly the "celebrated oboist" mentioned in *Sainsbury*, who was born in Sicily, was a pupil of Lebrun, and played for Salomon. He wrote *Lord Broome's March*; another *Grand March in Honor of Admiral Nelson's Victory* is attributed to Harrington, but apparently on the basis of a signature which is actually on the copy of *Lord Broome's March*.

HARTMANN, Emil *21 Feb 1836, Copenhagen-8 Aug 1898, Copenhagen*   A composer influenced by his brother-in-law Gade and by Mendelssohn. Hartmann often chose Scandinavian subjects for his music. His *Serenade* Op 43, published in 1890, is recorded by the Triebensee Ensemble on Contrapunctus Musicus VC 2447 and by Consortium Classicum (number untraced).

HARTMANN, Erich *1920, Germany*   The *Nachtstück* of 1992, for 3ob ca 3bn cbn, was composed for the Netherlands Double-Reed Ensemble.

HARVEY, Jonathan (Dean) *b 3 May 1939, Sutton Coldfield*   **JIH-1** *Serenade in Homage to Mozart*. Written to be played in the gardens at Glyndebourne before performances of *Die Zauberflöte* in 1991. The two movements each exploit a chain of 7 melodies, with complex textures influenced by Mozart's own wind writing. The piccolo represents Papageno's pipes; E♭ chords point to the Masonic links of the opera. The first movement quotes from Harvey's opera *Inquest of love,* itself inspired by *Die Zauberflöte.* The work is recorded on EMI CDC 7 54424 by the London Philharmonic Winds (who gave the first performances at Glyndebourne)/Parrott. For other Glyndebourne commissions in this series, see Dove, Oliver, Osborne and Saxton.

HASLINGER, Tobias *1 March 1787, Zell, Upper Austria-18 June 1842, Zell*   Publisher and composer whose music to celebrate victory in Europe was published in Vienna before 1816; it clearly refers to Napoleon's defeat: **TZH-1.** *Europas Sieges Feyer* "A grand musical portrayal for military band [türkische Musik]. Dedicated to the most exalted victorious allied Emperors and Kings, and to the brave commanders and heroes of the hard-won victories." The movements are *Triumph Marsch* of the infantry to the victory celebrations; Hymn of thanksgiving to Omnipotence [der Allmacht, rather than the expected dem Allmächtigen, the Almighty] (Andante; Marsch & Trio); Rejoicing at the Victory. Rondo militar (Allegro). In 1814 Haslinger became Anton Steiner's partner in the Chemische Druckerei, and then sole proprietor from 1826.

HASSE, ( )   Composer of music for the "Volhynischen Leib-Garde Regiments" and the "Polnischen Leib-Garde-Grenadier-Regiments," based on Auber's *La muette de Portici.*

HASSLOCH, Carl *1769-1829*   His works include both marches and choruses with winds. **CYH-1v** *Hexen Chöre zu Mekbet* [sic] is the witches' chorus from *Macbeth,* with three choral sections and a march. **CYH-2v** is a cantata "von Br: Cer: Mstr Hassloch" for the inauguration of the Masonic Lodge of Johannes der Evangelist, Darmstadt.

HATAŠ (Hattasch, Hattisch), Jan Václav (Ivan Wenzel) *3 Sep 1727-after 1752*   Not the same person as Hotiš. Jan Václav Hataš, Cantor at Rožmitál, was the brother of Dismas Hataš, a violinist in the service of the Duke of Gotha from 1751. Several of his parthias are labelled *Pastoritia* [sic], possibly for use during Advent. He also wrote a cantata and Turkish music for the Prince Carl [Anselm] of Thurn und Taxis.

HAUFF, Wilhelm (probably Wilhelm Gottlieb) *(1740-d ?1777)*   A singer in the Saxe-Gotha regiment in the service of Holland. *Sainsbury* states that he published six wind sextets (and other works not for winds) in Paris in 1776 and 1777.

HAUSLER (Häusler, Haussler, Hausser), ?Ernst *1760/1761-1837*   His largest work is his *Parthia National Marche & Aria François Saira [sic]* (c.1792), for which pic 2fl 2tp b-dr are added to octet. His smaller works include six *Notturni* for 2hn 2bn. Since the autograph parts are at Regensburg, he may have been associated with that court.

HAUSSER, Joseph *(1800) active 1837*   Kapellmeister of the 14th Linien Infanterie Regiment Richter von Bienenthal; arranger of an aria from Donizetti's *Marino Faliero.*

HAVEL, Václav *c.1778, Prague-after 1826*   Personal secretary to Maria Thaddäus Trautmannsdorf, Bishop of Königgrätz (Hradec Králové) from 1794-1811 and then Archbishop of Olomouc at Kroměříž from 1811-1817. When Trautmansdorf added a Harmonie to his Kapelle in 1803, Havel became its director. Trautmannsdorf moved his Harmonie (2cl 2hn 2bn) to Kroměříž in 1811, displacing the resident octet. Havel and horn player Josef Čuda were the Harmonie's main copyists. Havel made many arrangements, including excellent reductions of Krommer parthias; he also made adaptations, such as an extra bassoon part for Lickl's Op 21 *Quintetto*. Havel's **VXH-1** (dated 21 January 1806), recorded on Supraphon 1111 2616 G, exploits a tuba pastoralis. The horn player named Havel at Kroměříž in the 1770s may have been a relative.

HAYDN, Franz Josef *31 March 1732, Rohrau, Lower Austria-31 May 1809, Vienna* Haydn was born of poor parents in an isolated village in the Hungarian marches of Austria (1). Through luck and his own ability he was able to train as a chorister at St Stephen's, Vienna, and to survive privation after his voice broke. The same combination of fortune and talent led to his becoming Kapellmeister to Count von Morzin in 1759. When the Count's financial difficulties made another move necessary two years later, Haydn's appointment at Eszterháza was crucial for him and for the development of music. Both Eszterháza and the Morzin palace (which is more country house than palace) at Lukavec (Dolní Lukavice) remain. Eszterháza has been splendidly restored; Lukavec awaits its turn, in overgrown gardens, the place where one of the greatest composers wrote his earliest symphonies and where he began to establish his fame.

The early wind music Almost all of Haydn's wind music dates from his years at Lukavec or his first years at Eszterháza. These works are for two oboes, two horns and two bassoons, and are called "Parthia" or "Feld Parthie" (the titles vary from source to source). They are constructed more as suites than as symphonies of the type Haydn was writing at that time, being in five movements in most cases: a fast movement, Allegro or Presto; a Minuet and Trio; a slow movement; an Adagio or Andante; another Minuet and Trio; a fast finale, Allegro or Presto. The form is standard, but the music is impressively fresh and imaginative, never archaic. The manuscripts were found mainly at the courts of the Counts of Clam Gallas at Frydlánt, Count Harrach at Rohrau, and of Archbishop Egk in Kroměříž.

These early sextets are remarkably effective, despite their small scale and simplicity. Haydn exploits the different characters of the instruments, with novel timbres yet completely idiomatic writing. Another strength is the originality and variety of the individual movements. The fast movements, notably the finales, have a momentum few composers could maintain. The slow movements and some of the trios (like that of **FJH-4**, headed "Incipit lamentatio [Jeremiae Prophetae]," pointing to a plainsong reference) have an exceptional poignancy, sometimes from the nostalgic quality of the oboes, as in the *Polonese* of **FJH-9**, which appears in place of both the slow movement and the second minuet and trio. Elsewhere, as in the slow movement of **FJH-3**, horns and bassoons achieve this by themselves. Further special features include the way in which the first movement of **FJH-4** builds up as simple phrases are echoed by oboes and horns, and the especially beautiful theme of the slow movement of **FJH-5**. The Eszterháza players would have appreciated such writing.

Most of these works are recorded as a set, including Wiener Volksoper/Sommer (Amadeo AVRS 6208); London Wind Soloists/Brymer (Decca SXL 6338, later SDD 450); Consortium Classicum/Klöcker (Telefunken 6.35473 and 6.35550; Teldec 8.35814; 2292 42740-2XC); an un-named Hungarian ensemble (Hungaroton HRC 155); London Baroque Ensemble/Haas (PMA 1013 [Divertimento in C], SW 8118, 8119 [Divertimento in G] and R 20578, R20579 [Divertimento in F]); Münchener Bläser und Motettenchor/Zobeley (Caliope CAL 30844, CD version 50844). **FJH-2** is not recorded, to our knowledge.

FJH-2 *Feld-Parthie in F*. The autograph of this work was one of the few which Haydn kept all his life (*HCRL/1* p 273) It confirms that cors anglais were available at Lukavec, and shows signs of the symphonic handling Haydn was to develop later. The melancholy yet pungent sound of the cor anglais seems to have had a special appeal to Haydn at that time: two are used in the Philosopher Symphony (Hob I:22) and in the lost Hob II:12. Unusually, the octet includes two violins as well as two cors anglais. The violins fulfil both accompanying and more assertive roles.

FJH-4 *Parthia in F, Hob II:23.* The inscription "Incipit lamentatio" is on the oboe part, just prior to the plainsong theme noted earlier. The same theme is used in Haydn's Symphonies 26 and 45. A copy in the Clam Gallas archives (actually in the key of G, rather than F) contains an extra movement, probably not by Haydn, but reproduced as an appendix to the modern edition (*HCRL/1* p 270). An extra movement is found too in **FJH-6** *Parthia in D, Hob II:D18,* this time in the Kroměříž source (*HCRL/1* p 270).

FJH-11 *Parthia in C, Hob II:14.* The one work of Haydn's using clarinets (2cl 2hn) which survives in full (*HCRL/1* p 538). It is strangely tentative, as if oboists were trying out a new toy. The C basso horns give a rather soggy sound. There is no evidence that bassoons were used, although a bassoon in place of horn 2 works well. Other clarinet pieces are lost, although one has been reconstructed by Hellyer from an arrangement for baryton, two horns, viola and bass **(FJH-10).** This shows much more enterprising writing for clarinets and horns than does **FJH-11.**

The middle period   The period from the late 1760s until Haydn's first visit to London in 1791 is notable for its lack of wind music. Certainly the wind band at Eszterháza was used (see part 1 and *HCRL/2* p 223), and it is hard to believe that no locally-written music was played. Possibly such music was destroyed in the several fires at the palace. The operas contain some enticing fragments. In *Il Mondo della luna* (1777), the opening of act 2 (No 25) divides the orchestra into two parts, one of strings, the other (offstage) comprising two horns and two bassoons. These two groups play alternate four-bar phrases to set the mysterious atmosphere of the (supposed) moon.

Little other wind music survives except for a few marches and for those works discussed later as "dubious or spurious." The three marches are the following:

FJH-6m *Marche Regimento de Marshall*   Dating from 1772, the band parts were found in the archives of Count Clam Gallas at Frydlánt in a form modern bandsmen would recognize, namely small cards to be clipped to an instrument for outdoor performance (*HCRL/2* p 576). We assume "Marshall" was an honorary Colonel, not yet identified.

FJH-7m *Marcia in Eb*   Believed to date from the 1780s (*HCRL/2*; Larsen [3] favors 1792), the march was later arranged for musical clock.

FJH-8me *Marcia,* from act 1 of *Armide* (1783). Like **FJH-7m**, this march is for clarinets rather than oboes; another march (not an isolated movement) for oboes, horns and bassoons occurs later in the opera. In the Dorati recording (Philips 6769 025) a separate march (actually **FJH-6m**) is interpolated just before the final scene.

London and after   If Haydn abandoned the wind band in the middle of his career, his interest revived later, as with Richard Strauss a century and a half on. "I have only just learned how to use wind instruments in my old age and, now that I do understand them, I must leave the world," Haydn observed to Kalkbrenner. It is fitting that the last major work he completed, the *Harmoniemesse*, should affirm his mastery of the wind enemble. He had shown similar mastery and invention in his symphonies, like the flute and oboes at the start of his *Symphony 100*. Wind instruments and players had changed, and Mozart's influence was felt. No longer was the clarinet ignored, but used in new ways. "He [Josef Haydn] surprised me most pleasantly with wind band music quite unknown to me then" wrote Michael Haydn after a lunch in Vienna with his brother in 1799, "and even his parrot cried out `What's that?' when he heard it" (*HCRL/4* p 330).

The Eszterháza wind ensemble continued throughout most of Haydn's career (see part 1; 4; *HCRL/4* p 314), with an important interruption from 1797 until September 1800. Prince Anton Esterházy, who had succeeded Prince Nicolaus Esterházy (Haydn's main patron) in 1790, had little enthusiasm for music. The wind band, with its outdoor functions, survived longer than any other part of the musical establishment. It was also needed, combined with the band of Prince Grassalkovics, for Leopold II's coronation celebrations at Pressburg; Druschetzky wrote a 21-part Harmonie for this performance on 15 November 1790. In due course, even the wind band disappeared for a period.

FJH-1 *Introduzione.* This solemn A minor interlude was composed for the choral version of the *Seven Last Words.* In 1785, Cadiz Cathedral commissioned seven extended adagios for orchestra for its sombre Good Friday services. The challenge led Haydn to write what he considered the finest of all his works to that date. Its success encouraged arrangements, that for string quartet being prepared by Haydn himself. When Josef Frieberth produced a choral version in the 1790s, Haydn decided to do the job better himself, adding choral parts to largely unaltered orchestral parts. The new *Introduzione,* a stark and intense piece, opens the second half.

FJH-1v *Arie des Schutzgeistes* This Guardian Spirit's aria is from the incidental music to *Alfred,* a play by John Bicknell, given at Eisenstadt in 1796 in a German translation by Johann Wilhelm Cowmeadow (*HCRL/4* p 183). It was a convention, used by Shield, Kelly, Mozart, Weber and others, to associate spirits and other supernaturals with wind music. Haydn's aria is exceptional, not least as a precursor to "On Thee each living soul awaits", the central part of "Achieved Is the Glorious Work," in *The Creation* (*HCRL/4* p 412). It is an example of melodrama: the Guardian Spirit sings, but Evida speaks against a musical background. Melodrama, in this sense (like "melos" in the orchestral parts of many modern musicals), is quite distinct from the highly sensational spoken plays described by the same word. Another example of melodrama accompanied by winds is found in Schubert's *Die Zauberharfe* (**FPS-2ve**). Benda's *Medea* is melodrama on a large scale, but uses a wind band only in the scene with Jason and Kreusa.

The later works for military band Haydn was deeply involved with his symphonies and his opera *Orfeo* during his second visit to London. Not surprisingly, he was reluctant to write small pieces such as marches. One persistent patron - an anonymous naval officer - only succeeded by an offer of 50 guineas for two marches to be composed in two weeks. After two weeks the patron returned. A man of few words, he listened in silence as Haydn played the first march. Haydn finished. The patron asked him to play it again, and again listened in silence. Haydn, worried that there might be something wrong, asked if he should play the other march? No, replied the silent one, it could not be better than the first. Who he was and which marches were offered is not clear; there seems no reason to believe the officer was the one who commissioned the only pair of marches to survive, **FJH-2m.** Robbins Landon has conjectured the sea captain may have been Captain Blount, who subscribed to *The Creation* (3). Since the fragment (**FJH-5m,** Hob VII:7) later completed by Robbins Landon, is on British paper, perhaps it was a sketch for the sea-captain's marches (see *HCRL/3* p 207 and p 488).

FJH-1m(a) *March in C, from Symphony No 100* The "Military" Symphony was written in 1794 for the Salomon concerts in London. The second movement, arranged for wind and Turkish instruments, exists in a contemporary manuscript *(HCRL/3* p 561).

FJH-2m *Marches for the Derbyshire Volunteer Cavalry (Hob VIII:1, 2)* The British militia were reorganized in the 1790s and many marches written for their bands. The Sheriff of Derbyshire, Sir Henry Harpur, Bart., did the best for the Volunteer Cavalry of Derbyshire, for he persuaded Haydn to write these two excellent marches (*HCRL/3* p 488). Probably the slower second march is for unmounted troops. Autographs, original plates, original prints and much extra material are in the Derbyshire Records Office.

FJH-3m *Ungarischer National-Marsch, (Hob VIII/4)* One of Haydn's last completed works, dating from 1802, it is neither specially national nor Hungarian (*HCRL/5* p 241). The autograph is reproduced by Vécsey [4].

FJH-4m *March for the Prince of Wales, (Hob VIII/3)* This march differs from the Derbyshire marches in having a trio. Haydn seems to have taken some trouble over it, for he exploits the trumpet in ingenious imitation, and contrasts triplet and dotted rhythms effectively (*HCRL/3* p 488). During Haydn's first visit to London (1791-1792) he wrote that the Prince of Wales "is the handsomest man on God's earth, is extraordinarily fond of music, has a great deal of feeling but little money."

Most of these marches have been recorded: Netherlands Wind Ensemble (Philips 652 7117); Wiener Volksoper/Sommer (Amadeo AVRS 6208); Chateauroux Philharmonic (ARN 336030); London Military Ensemble (CFP 40230); Grenadier Guards/Parkes (Decca SB706); London Baroque Ensemble/Haas (SW 8119, R20579).

"Haydn?" Dubious and spurious works   Haydn achieved financial security and international recognition in his lifetime. His music was played, and published widely. Commercially minded publishers exploited this popularity, providing a wealth of wind music with Haydn's name on it. In some cases, other composers, arrangers and copyists were the malefactors, but publishers rarely rejected or questioned works with Haydn's name attached. There is an accepted core of authentic works, for which issues of provenance and of style are discussed in *HCRL/2* and by Hellyer (2). Hoboken's catalogue lists many dubious works, and some of the best have been recorded by Klöcker's Consortium Classicum. There are four groups of works with features which make Haydn's authorship questionable. These are (1) the works with clarinets, both octets (2ob 2cl 2hn 2hn) and sextets (2cl 2hn 2bn); (2) the set of six works containing the famous *Chorale St Antoni;* (3) some sextets for two oboes, two horns and one or two bassoons; (4) certain smaller works, like those for two flutes and two horns. There are also many wrongly described arrangements of Haydn's music, including marches, church music and accompaniments to his three- and four-part songs.

Haydn's authentic wind music has distinctive features which can be an aid (although never a decisive one) in questions of authenticity. First, Haydn's wind works show a clear relationship to his other works of the same period. His early sextets have parallels with his early symphonies; his late aria from *Alfred* is recognizably from the same composer as *The Creation*. Secondly, Haydn avoids conspicuous display; even though first-rate wind players are needed: he shuns mini-concertos. Thirdly, he uses full forces sparingly. Even in small ensembles, he often deploys one or two instruments alone: a solo bassoon in the trio of **FJH-6** or just two horns at the start of the slow movement of **FJH-3**. Fourthly, Haydn often exploits poignancy, rather than luxuriant sounds, especially in early works. Finally, Haydn's fast movements have a sense of purpose, and maintain their momentum. Many dubious works miss these features.

Octets and sextets with clarinets   These illustrate an important point: spurious works need not be feeble or dull. Nevertheless, these divertimentos fail all the stylistic criteria just mentioned. They bear no real relationship to Haydn's genuine works of the period, apart, for example, from the use of a Haydn theme. Thus the Rondo of **FJH-14d** is said to be based on a theme (not traced by us) from *Die Feuersbrunst (Das abgebrannte Haus)*. They are often fairly fully scored throughout, and very relaxed in mood. Slow movements are amiable, rather than poignant, fast movements active and vigorous rather than purposeful. There is often a fair amount of display, especially in the virtuoso clarinet parts. A secondary factor is that Haydn appears never to have used the standard octet (2ob 2cl 2hn 2bn) in any of his authentic works. Nor (apart from marches) did he ever use E♭ or B♭ for any of his accepted wind works, yet all these dubious ones are in just these two keys. Further, while there were occasions at Eszterháza at which wind music was played in this period (1770-1780), there is no record in Haydn's catalogs or elsewhere that he wrote these works.

Some inauthentic works can be attributed to other composers. **FJH-11d** is regarded as by P Wranizky (**PYW-2**) and is discussed later under his name (the Consortium Classicum has recorded this work under both names: as Wranizky on Telefunken 6.35334 and as Haydn on Telefunken 6.35473). Another work appears as Haydn (**FJH-17d**, Hob

II:B7) and as Mozart (**WAM-18d,** K.C17.09) and is by neither. The octet Hob II:Es13, (**FJH-8d**), can be found under the name of Hoffmeister, albeit in D rather than E♭, and could well be by this fluent minor composer (**FAH-10**).

The St Antoni Chorale and its companions   For at least a century musicians, including Brahms and Tovey, had no doubt that the works **FJH-1d** (**-6d**) were what they claimed, namely original compositions by Haydn. For the last few decades all have been equally confident that Haydn had no part in them. Robbins Landon, noting that the Zittau source of these works is "notoriously unreliable" (Zittau presumably got their copies from Breitkopf, in whose 1782-84 catalogue the works are announced), comments that their "stylistic content ... is totally foreign to Haydn's wind band writing" (*HCRL/2* p 271). In preparing this book, we fully expected to repeat this view. While we have no doubt that these works are not by Haydn, actually hearing these works (instead of merely hearing about them) made us reluctant to rule out a Haydn link. A common claim (10) is that Pleyel wrote the set. *This suggestion does not stand even the most superficial scrutiny.* In particular, there is not the remotest stylistic similarity to Pleyel's contemporary authentic divertimento (**IJP-16**).

Against Haydn's authorship, one cannot ignore the extraordinary scoring of three of these works (**FJH-1d,-4d,-6d**), for two oboes, two horns (in B♭ basso at times), three bassoons (two obbligato, one ripieno) and serpent ("ô Quart Fagott" on No 4 only). The serpent was not common in Austria at that time, though it was used in German bands. Trost's *Parthia,* at Zwickau, uses a quart-fagott. The sound is bottom-heavy and congested, even played expertly in a recording studio. Five of the six works remain in the same key throughout (**FJH-4d** is the exception) and most end with a march, neither typical of Haydn's parthias. Moreover, the movements are short and relatively crude. The failure to exploit the novel and interesting moments in the "Aria à la Vierge Marie" (**FJH-4d**) contrasts with the much stronger slow movements of Haydn's own sextets **FJH-4** or **FJH-5**; this supports the emphatic rejections of Haydn's authorship. At times, the works look back to Haydn's parthias of the 1760s. There is some technical ingenuity, as in the thematic links throughout the parthia with the St Antoni Chorale. The repeated chords, a special feature of Haydn's first trio in **FJH-4**, have parallels in the austere repetitions found in this set. The odd numbers of bars, the unconventional sound, all hint at some connection with Haydn. Other features are closer to Haydn in the 1770s, with marches not unlike the authentic ones, **FJH-6m(-8m)**. Perhaps too there is similarity between the mood of "Dolcema l'amour" (possibly "Dolceamaro") (**FJH-2d/ii**) and Haydn's own "Schoolmaster in love" *(Symphony No 55/ii).*

What makes this set so special is, as Tovey observed (6), "one of the greatest melodies in the world." The St Antoni theme, like the trio of Beethoven's *Seventh Symphony,* is reputed to be an Austrian pilgrims' hymn. If so, the pilgrims had a truly remarkable heritage (7). Presumably titles like "Aria à la Vierge Marie" needed no explanation; they may have referred to familiar religious songs (cf. Haydn's use of church melodies in **FJH-5**; see also Pichl). Our guess - no more - is that some of these works are based on genuine Haydn material (not necessarily wind music; perhaps organ improvisations, for Haydn is known to have conducted works from the organ [*HCRL/2*]). The religious titles do suggest music for church use, and it is hard to think of any other setting for which the deep turgid sound would be accepted. Not all movements are serious, but they are rarely, if ever, too frivolous for a church band.

We suspect that the composer was a competent musician who knew Haydn's style of the 1760s, perhaps a player at Eszterháza or in the Sopron town band (*HCRL/2* p 342) and who tried to imitate Haydn's style. The Eszterháza lists (4; *HCRL/2* pp 70-82) include several musicians present in the 1760s when Haydn's own wind music was played, present twenty years later when this set was published, and known as competent composers. Perhaps one of them wrote this puzzling set: Franz Novotny (organist); Joseph Wolfgang Dietzl (violinist, horn player); Joseph Purksteiner (violinist and violist); Carl Schiringer (double bass player, bassoonist, flautist).

Works for oboes, horns and bassoons   The dubious works in this category can be attractive, but are slight and conventional. For some movements, especially minuets and trios, there is a hint of Haydn; others (here **FJH-21d**) are what Robbins Landon describes as "obviously apocryphal" (*HCRL/1* p 271).

Recordings from "the Old Spuriosity Shop" include these: Zurich Tonhalle (Jecklin Disco 534); Consortium Classicum/Klöcker (Telefunken 6.35473; Telefunken 6.35550; Telefunken 6.35334; Teldec 8.35814 ["complete" works]; Claves CD 50-9515); Vienna Bella Musica Ensemble (Harmonia Mundi HM 1057, **FJH-25d**); London Bach Ensemble/ Sharpe, **FJH-1d** (Pan SPAN 6209; Saga 5417); London Baroque Ensemble/Haas, **FJH-1d** (SW 8120/SW8121); Soloists Ensemble/Lev Markiz, **FJH-1d** (Melodia 33C10-08505-06[a]); Melbourne Windpower, **FJH-5d** (Move MD 3082); Bratislavská komorná harmoniá/ Pavlík, **FJH-11d** (Opus 9111 1219); Albert Schweizer Oktett, **FJH-11d** (CPO 999 314-2); Cracow Wind Ensemble, **FJH-1d** (Golden Touch Classics 820088).

1. W H Hadow 1897 *A Croatian Composer;* London: Seeley and Co, pps 96-98, lists 16 variants of the spelling of his name "within the limits of the composer's family."

2. R Hellyer 1984 Haydn Yearbook **15** 5-180.

3. H C Robbins Landon 1959 *The Collected Correspondence and London Notebooks of Joseph Haydn.* London: Barrie and Rockliff.

4. J Vécsey (editor) 1960 *Haydn Compositions in the Music Collection of the National Széchényi Library, Budapest;* Budapest: Hungarian Academy of Sciences.

5. Marion M Scott 1954, in her article on Haydn in *Grove 5.* Many others have repeated her hypothesis uncritically on radio and on sleeve notes for recordings.

6. Donald F Tovey 1949 *Essays and Lectures on Music;* Oxford: Oxford University Press, p 23.

7. C F Eley refers to a Voluntary comprising a March and Choral St Antoni in 1801, with no mention of Haydn (*British Museum Yearbook* **4** p 146), although Eley also used Mozart's and Pleyel's music without mention of their names).

HAYDN, Johann Michael *14 Sept 1737, Rohrau, Austria-10 Aug 1806, Salzburg*   Joseph Haydn's importance has overshadowed the music of his younger brother, Michael Haydn. Only recently have critics stopped quoting earlier superficial dismissals of Michael's work and begun to assess it on its own considerable merits. He was a prolific composer, widely respected for his church music for the Archbishop of Salzburg. It was Michael who first obtained a permanent position, as Master of Music to the Bishop of Grosswardein in 1757, before his brother was settled (*HCRL/1* pp 78-80). Michael Haydn's works, if not his private life, were appreciated by such critical musicians as Leopold and Wolfgang Mozart; indeed, several of his compositions have been attributed to Mozart, and vice versa. Michael seems to have lacked ambition, content to stay isolated and little known beyond Salzburg. Leopold Mozart suggested, uncharitably, an immoral streak: Michael was "lazy" and "drinking himself into a dropsy" (1). Yet, as one of Weber's teachers, admired by E T A Hoffmann and others, he deserves attention.

Michael Haydn's wind music is remarkably varied, and several of his works lie at the fringes of our field. Some are basically wind harmony with one or two strings added, while others combine winds and strings differently, with the winds largely optional. Likewise, his choral works are often scored for organ and a handful of winds (2). Many are worth revival, as are his orchestral works. Michael Haydn's style is distinctive, with a characteristic vulnerability instead of the poignance his brother emphasized. A few works are lost; Perger's catalog (3) lists two items, namely P97, an *Allegro molto in C* for 2bthn 2hn bn, and P107, a *Partita* in F for 2cl 2hn bn, written in Pressburg in 1762;

an Allegro molto incipit is all that survives. Perhaps Haydn wrote the *Partita* on his journey from Grosswardein to take up his post at Salzburg. The Grosswardein archives are lost, and may have contained still more wind works. Another lost work is the *National Marsch (P 67)*, whose incipit suggests that it is an arrangement of the classic *Coburger Josias Marsch,* the original of which first appeared c.1750 (4).

JMH-1 *Turkish March* Completed in Salzburg, and dated 6 August 1795, this is one of the better Turkish marches of its time. It is recorded by the Netherlands Wind Ensemble on Philips 7311 117 and by the Collegium Aureum on Harmonia Mundi 1C 065 99897. Note that all other marches listed in Perger are for full orchestra.

JMH-3 *Divertimento in D, P95* Composed in Salzburg, and dated 9 March 1786, this interesting work is in five movements, and recorded on Koch Schwann Musica Mundi 310002. Michael Haydn's strengths are evident: the opening Allegro is bright and well written, making skilful use of all the instruments; the two Minuets and Trios and the central Andante grazioso have unconventional touches (for example, the way the horns are used in the first Trio, where they superimpose an independent unison fanfare on the elegant woodwind music, or the onward movement of the Andante, which is not a standard slow movement). The Finale is an extended hunting rondo, and shows touches of disquiet amid the chase. In all, it is a work very well worth performing.

JMH-4 *Divertimento in G, P96* Composed in Salzburg, dated 4 September 1790. The work uses both winds and strings, yet stylistically it follows the pattern of wind harmony; contrast the quintet, P94 (fl hn bn vl va) which is clearly not wind music, with a largely optional horn part added to a fairly conventional quartet.

JMH-7 *Divertimento in D, P100* A good example of half-harmony (fl ob hn bn), scored to produce the characteristic sound of wind serenade music.

JMH-1v *Deutsche Messe* The Mass in German is normally a less formal setting, cf Schubert's *Deutsche Messe,* also with wind accompaniment. Haydn's *Messe* had long-lasting popularity, and was regularly adapted for local forces. It is recorded by the Münster Cathedral Choir/Münster Wind Ensemble/Freimuth on Calliope CAL 50824.

JMH-2v *Missa Sancti Hieronymi, Kll:11* Like his brother, Michael Haydn believed that worship was an occasion for joy. Completed on 14 September 1777, the work was presumably written for the same Salzburg musicians as Mozart's sextets, such as K.270. Leopold Mozart praised this "Hautboisten" Mass for the vocal way in which oboes and bassoons were used. Neukomm, a pupil of both Haydn brothers, arranged it for a different wind ensemble soon after Michael Haydn's death. Haydn's smaller choral works use winds to some degree, such as **JMH-4v**, and others (4) use oboe and 2 horns, such as Kl.II:41 Juravit Dominus, 1784, Kl.III:3 Ad Te Dominum, 1792, Kl.III:6 In adoratione, Kl.III:14 Timete, 1784, Kl.III:19 Canta Jerusalem, Kl.III:29 Jehova Deus, Kl.III:36 Sic Pater, Kl.VI:25 Magnificat.

1. Leopold Mozart, letter of 29 June 1778, cited A Einstein 1946 *Mozart;* London: Cassell p 126.

2. A M Klafsky 1925 *Thematscher Katalog der Kirchenmusikwerke von Michael Haydn,* Denkmäler der Tonkunst in Österreich **62**, Jg 32/1. See also C H Sharman 1967 *The Masses of Johann Michael Haydn: A Critical Survey of Sources;* Ph D thesis, University of Michigan.

3. L H Perger 1907 *Thematisches Verzeichnis der Instrumentalwerke von Michael Haydn,* Denkmäler der Tonkunst in Österreich Jg 14/2 pp 25-26.

4. G Pätzig 1971 *Historische Bläsermusik;* Kassel: Bärenreiter, gives an early version of the march for 2cl 2hn 2bn tp. The date is from *Grove V,* under "March".

HEDWALL, Lennart *16 Sept 1932, Göteborg, Sweden* His two works for winds are the 1961 *Partita* and the 1975 *Danssvit och sorgmarch.*

HEIDENREICH (Haydenreich, Haydnreich), Josef (Georg) *(1760)-post 1807* From c.1789 (1), Heidenreich was the first Viennese arranger for winds to compete seriously with Went. Unlike other leading arrangers, he does not seem to have played any wind instrument. Unlike Went, who appeared to work from scores of operas, Heidenreich seems to have worked from piano reductions, even though he must have had access to scores when preparing his piano reductions of operas for Lausch, the copyist firm. Whereas Went emphasized Italian opera, Heidenreich concentrated on the German *Singspiel*, especially works by Wenzel Müller. Most of his arrangements are for octet, but the *Wiener Zeitung* of 14 January 1792 advertizing his octet arrangement of *Die Zauberflöte* also offered a sextet version, if demand was sufficient (2). Some anonymous sextet versions may indeed be his. His other early works include several arrangements of Mozart. That of the *Horn Quintet* K.407 (1794) inexplicably incorporates a minuet from K.375. His arrangement of the *String Quintet* K.614 (like that of *Die Zauberflöte*) was once attributed to Rosinack. Heidenreich is unlikely to have been responsible for the D-DO arrangement of *Don Giovanni*. The idea that he arranged the *Gran Partita* K.361 is given without evidence in the 6th edition of Köchel, and must be doubted. Heidenreich's last known arrangements were of Mayr's *Adelasia ed Aleramo* (1807) and Satzenhoven's *Der Körbenflechter* (1805), for which there is a bill and a receipt from Prince Esterházy dated 6 April 1811. He wrote a substantial body of church music, including a *Tantum ergo* for chorus and winds, and it was probably he who, in 1805, rescored Haydn's early *Missa brevis in F* to include winds.

1. It is just possible that Heidenreich's arrangement of Gerl and Schack's *Der dumme Gärtner* was the basis for Went's 2ob 2ca 2hn 2bn version for the Schwarzenberg Harmonie. We have not been able to check this because of the inaccessibility of the only surviving octet version (I-Fc).

2. Lausch announced Heidenreich's piano reduction in the *Wiener Zeitung* of 22 October and 5 November. Heidenreich, who styled himself "Publisher" in his advertizement, clearly felt he would gain by offering the wind arrangements directly, rather than via Lausch. His subscribers could collect the manuscript on 16th February, allowing a month for copies to be made. The price of the octet was 6fl.40xr (with 60xr to the florin); later that year, the monthly rent for Beethoven's small apartment was 14fl.

HEINE, Gotthelf Sigismund *(1780)*   Kapellmeister, Sebnitz in Sachen.

HEINE, Samuel Friedrich *1764-1821*   Member of the Ludwigslust Hofkapelle.

HEINRICH, ( ) *(1810)*   His one movement *Harmonie Piece*, c.1844, is in a collection for the Collegium Mariano Rupertinum, Salzburg.

HEMMERLEIN, Ignaz Carl *1773, Bamberg-24 Feb 1840, Bamberg*   Hemmerlein was Konzertmeister in Bamberg from 1798 to 1802.

HENNEBERG, Johann Baptist *6 Dec 1786, Vienna-26 Nov 1822, Vienna*   Composer who, from 1790, co-wrote some of the popular "Anton" farces for Schikaneder at the Kärntnerthor Theater. He moved to the country because of his wife's illness, becoming organist to Prince Esterházy at Eisenstadt from 1809 and Kapellmeister in 1811. When economy forced the Kapelle to close, Henneberg returned to Vienna as organist, first at the church Am Hof, later as court organist. His *Pange lingua* and *Vexilla regis* for chorus and winds are probably from this period. He died from an infection of a severe cut on the thigh, incurred while examining repairs inside the court organ.

HENNIG, T   Civic Music Director in Gustrow, whose marches were for the Gardehautboisten-Corps of the 89th Regiment. The music is now in Schwerin.

HENSHER, Ray *b 12 Nov 1934, Rotherhithe, London*   Like many composers for winds, a military band player (in his case during national service). He studied horn and piano from an early age, and continues to play around Sheffield, where he moved in 1974. His music is varied, including suites (*English Countryside Suite, North Country Suite*), works with solo wind groups (*Latin Horns*, with 4 solo horns, *Clarinet Polka*, with two solo clarinets) and dance movements with a South American connection.

HENZE, Hans Werner *b 1 July 1926, Gütersloh, Westphalia* Twelve-tone composer, pupil of Fortner, whose work includes operas, symphonies, and *Dance Marathon* for jazz band and symphony orchestra. His 1947 *Concertino* is for solo piano and winds.

HERMSTEDT, Johann Simon *29 Dec 1778, Langensalza-10 Aug 1846, Sondershausen* Outstanding clarinettist (*Weston/CVP, MCVP*) responsible for the high quality of the Sondershausen band. Hermstedt's own arrangements included those of three of Mozart's *Quartets;* only that of K.438 and the first movement of K.575 survive. The autograph of the latter (F-Pn) includes a biography (dated 11 Oct 1860) by a descendent. They were probably prepared for the Sondershausen band; their scoring is the same as for Spohr's *Notturno.* Possibly these were the works played at Nuremburg in 1823 for the relief of the sufferers by fire (Quarterly Musical Magazine & Review Vol 5 p 404).

HERTEL, Johann Wilhelm *9 Oct 1727, Eisenach-14 June 1789, Schwerin* Hertel was Konzertmeister to the Duke of Mecklenburg-Strelitz, moving later to Mecklenburg-Schwerin. He changed from violin to piano after his eyesight failed. His *Concerto à 5* JWH-1 is recorded on Desto DC 6438.

HEUSCHKEL, Johann Peter *4 Jan 1773, Harras-5 Dec 1853, Biebrich* Oboist and organist to the Duke of Hildburghausen; he arranged works by Rossini and Weber.

HEWITT, J (*?*James) *(1770-1827)* Composer of *4 Quick Marches* for the Lichfield Loyal Association.

HEYSE, Anton Gottlieb *(1770)* A flautist, active c.1800 in Halle.

HIEBESCH (Hibesch), Johann Nepomuk (Marquard) *18 May 1766, Birkhausen, near Wallerstein-1820, Wallerstein* Hiebesch, a cellist, pianist, virtuoso horn player and composer, was fortunate: he found a position at a court where he was able to stay for the rest of his life. Born a few miles from Wallerstein, Hiebesch was first engaged as a servant in livery and cellist; he is said to have studied with Rosetti. Hiebesch seems to have held a favored position as piano teacher to Prince Kraft Ernst's children, and he obtained the lucrative post of Chorregent in 1807, a position he held until his death. His *Parthia* JKH-5 includes movements arranged from *Die Zauberflöte.* Especially interesting is the full-blown title to the *Partita* JKH-4, for it shows it was written in Leipzig on 18 October 1813, near the end of the Battle of Leipzig (16-18/19 October). Evidently the Prince's military forces included his wind band and the copyist, F X Link.

HILL, Frederick *1760 Louth, Lincolnshire-? York* Organist of Loughborough, later in London, then in York. Hill's *Favourite Quick Step* is for the "Yeomanry, Cavalry, & Infantry, In the County of Leicester." It includes a "relief" (trio) for 2 fifes and drums.

HIMMEL, Friedrich Heinrich *20 Nov 1765, Treubrietzen, Brandenburg-8 June 1814 Berlin* Court conductor in Berlin from 1795; a pianist whom Beethoven respected, but with whom he had disagreements (see *Thayer* pp 185-186). He wrote a Terzetto for SST winds and glass harmonica (Leipzig: A Kühnel; untraced). Himmel's funeral cantata FHH-1tv (Potsdam, 1798) was written for Friedrich Wilhelm II, who died in 1797; it is dedicated to J G Naumann (qv). Two movements are for winds; a further movement uses two choirs, one of strings, the other of 4fl 4bn. The print includes a subscription list: the Duke and Duchess of Mecklenburg-Schwerin took two copies each.

HINDEMITH, Paul *16 Nov 1895, Hanau, Frankfurt-28 Dec 1963, Frankfurt am Main* Hindemith wrote for almost all types of ensemble. His wind quintet, the *Kleine Kammermusik* Op 24 No 2, and his *Quartet for Four Horns* are both outstanding pieces. His larger works include several at the fringe of wind harmony, like the *Symphony in B♭ for Wind Band,* an important contribution to the band repertoire.

PAH-1 *Symphonia Serena (movement 2: Paraphrase on Beethoven's March WoO18)* Just as Vaughan Williams used a march for winds alone as the *Scherzo* of his *8th Symphony,* so Hindemith used a march for wind band in place of a scherzo as the second movement of his 1946 *Symphonia Serena.* It was written for the Dallas Symphony Orchestra, which gave the work its first performance under Dorati on 1 February 1946. Hindemith's march is based on Beethoven's finest wind march (**LVB-2m,** WoO 18). Hindemith uses a large band, but provides a splendid twentieth century revival of the spirit of the original. It is recorded by the Philharmonia/Hindemith on Columbia 33CX 1676.

PAH-2 *Der Schwanendreher* Hindemith, a distinguished violist, wrote three works for solo viola with an accompanying orchestra consisting largely of winds: the *Chamber Concerto,* Op 46 No 1 for viola d'amore (1927), the *Concert Music* Op 48 (written in 1930 for Darius and Madeleine Milhaud), and this work (1935), which uses folk melodies. It was first performed on 14 November 1935 with Hindemith as soloist, by the Concertgebouw Orchestra/Mengelberg. *Der Schwanendreher* (who turns the spit as the swan is roasted) was inspired by a medieval scene in which a minstrel displays the music he has brought back from abroad: serious songs, happy songs, and a final dance, each expanded as if improvised: 1 Langsam-Mässig bewegt mit Kraft; based on the 15th century tune "Zwischen Berg und tiefen Tal" ('Twixt mountain and deep valley); 2 Sehr ruhig; fugato; based on the 15th or 16th century melodies "Nun laube, Lindlein, laube" (Give shade, dear linden tree) and "Der Gutzgauch auf dem Zaune sass" (The cuckoo sat on the fence); 3 Finale: seven variations on "Seid ihr nicht der Schwanendreher" (Aren't you the turner of the spit?). The swan, Hindemith emphasises in a sketch, is on the spit (two years before Orff incorporated the roasting swan in *Carmina Burana*). Recorded on Biddulph LAB087 (Hindemith/Arthur Fiedler Sinfonietta/ Reibold), on Schwann VMS 734 (Georg Schmid/Bavarian RSO/Kubelik), on Hungaroton-Conifer HRC148 (Bársony/ Hungarian State Orchestra/Erdélyi), on ASV CDDCA931 (Cortese/Philharmonia/ Brabbins) and DG 423 241 (Benjamini/Orchestre de Paris/Barenboim).

PAH-7 *Septet* Written in Taormina in 1948, and first performed in Milan in that year. The second and fourth movements are mirror images, so the fourth is the second played backwards. In the Finale, the trumpet plays an old Berne march while the others play a jaunty fugue around it. The New York critics displayed good musical judgment but poor sense of chronology when they named it "Best Chamber Work of 1953." It is recorded by the Czech Philharmonic Winds on Supraphon 50582, and by the Deutsche Kammerphilharmonie on Virgin Classics VCS 45056-2.

HINDMARCH (Hindmarsh), John *c.1755-1796* A violinist and pupil of Salomon, whose march for the Staffordshire Band is dedicated to the Earl of Uxbridge.

HINTZE, W *(?1820)* Composer of two marches now in Detmold, one entitled *Die 55ger,* which refers to the regiment to which Kaiser (qv) belonged.

HLADKY, ( ) *(1810)* Associated with the Augustinian monastery, Brno, c.1844.

HLAVAČ, Miroslav *b 23 Oct 1923, Protivín* His *Elegikon, Sinfonietta* of 1964 is scored for orchestral wind section with piano and percussion.

HLOBIL, Emil *11 Oct 1901, Veselí nad Lužnicí, near Tábor-25 Jan 1987* A pupil of Křička and of Foerster in Prague, he has composed works from operas to a *Marimba Concerto* and music for small wind ensembles. His *Octet* dates from 1956; in 1971 he wrote a *Concerto* Op 82 for an orchestra comprising winds and percussion.

HNOJIL (Hnogill), Jan *5 July 1795, Sloupno, near Hradec Králové-20 Nov 1852, Brno* Hnojil was as student at the Augustinian monastery in Brno from 1814-1824; from 1826 he was Kapelník of the Brno theater. Later, he moved to Bucharest. Almost all his wind music dates from between 1819 and 1824. Presumably it was for the monastery that he made his several settings of *Regina coeli.* His other works include three sets of *Deutsche* and a march for the 29th Linien Infanterie Regiment von Kurz Wahlegeborn.

HOEDL (Hödl), Al[bert?] *(1820)* Active c.1845 at the Collegium Mariano Rupertinum, Salzburg. He was the composer of several marches and a *Trauermarsch und Grabgesang,* and the arranger of a *Quodlibet* and perhaps of other works in the same collection.

HÖNIG, ( ) *(1790)* Hönig referred to himself as "Herrn Capellmeister Hönig."

HÖPPLER, ( ) Höppler [sic] might be Simon Höpler, whose religious works are in Brno.

HÖRGER, G *(?1810)* Associated with the Lippe Kapelle at Detmold.

HOFER, Frédéric "Chef de Musique au 5e Régiment d'Infanterie Légère."

HOFFMANN, Carl Heinrich, Oberaufseher *(1810)* Hoffmann's two *Feldschritt* and *Walzer* for winds date from 1840. They include three trumpets (two chromatic).

HOFFMANN, Ernst Theodor Amadeus *24 Jan 1776, Königsberg-25 June 1822, Berlin* Several of Hoffman's dramatic works contain movements for winds alone, or for chorus and winds, including the tragedy *Das Kreuz an der Ostsee* of 1805, the one-act *Wiedersehen!* of 1808, and the "grosse heroische" opera *Aurora* of 1811/1812.

HOFFMANN, Johann Georg Gottfried *1781 Lübeck-1814 Frankfurt am Main* Noted for his beautiful clarinet tone; Hoffmann wrote for unusual combinations, such as his (lost) *Symphonie Concertante* for seven clarinets and Turkish music.

HOFFMANN, Leopold *c.1730, Vienna-17 Mar 1793, Vienna* The Viennese Domkapellmeister whom Mozart hoped to succeed.

HOFFMEISTER, Franz Anton *12 May 1754, Rottenburg-9 Feb 1812, Vienna* Hoffmeister was known for the firm of music publishers he founded in Vienna c.1784. On his shopfront, he styled himself as "Master of Music and Imperial Licensed Seller of Music, Art and Books." The firm was sold in 1806; his branch in Leipzig, with A Kühnel (the Bureau de Musique) was then taken over by Peters in 1814. Hoffmeister's name is still sometimes wrongly associated with the quite distinct firm of Friedrich Hofmeister.

Hoffmeister's careers, as man of music and as man of business, were soundly based on early law studies and on several decades as a practising musician and composer. He seems to have been one of Mozart's closer friends, and his loans to Mozart were sometimes repaid with compositions. Hoffmeister's own music dates mainly from the 1780s. While relatively lightweight, some is sufficiently good to have been attributed to Haydn. The music is fluently and effectively written, and technically demanding at times. An enormous amount of flute music survives. In some of his own works for wind ensemble, he adopts the common ploy of suggesting flutes as an alternative to oboes (though it should be stressed that, like Pleyel, he printed little of his own wind music). There are isolated examples of works for unusual ensembles; thus, from Rajhrad, there is a *Setsteto* [sic] for solo cl, solo vn, 2hn vla basso (CZ-Bm, A.12.571). As so often, there are problems in identifying some of Hoffmeister's wind music, especially as little remains in autograph: we have had to take some information on trust. Four of Hoffmeister's works (**FAH-1, FAH-4, FAH-25** and **FAH-36**) are recorded by Klöcker/ Consortium Classicum on CPO 999 107.

FAH-1 *Parthie in Bb* (Zeist 1). There are 6 *Partias* for 2ob 2cl 2hn 2bn at Zeist (NL-Z); four are also found as sextets (2cl 2hn 2bn) in Kroměříž (in CZ-KRa), and others are at Donaueschingen (D-DO) listed as "6 Partitas by Rosetti." The evidence overall suggests they are by Hoffmeister, with the D-DO set based on the sextet form.

FAH-9 *Parthia in D* The three versions differ in detail. **FAH-9.1** (Kroměříž) has three movements, with a Da Capo to movement 1; **FAH-9.2** (Vienna) is a single movement in four sections, omitting the Romance (movement 2) but with the Da Capo to the first section; **FAH-9.3** (Zeist) is in two movements, lacking the Romance and the Da Capo.

FAH-10 *Parthie in D* (Zeist 4) The only one of the NL-Z set not to appear as by Hoffmeister in other sets. Hoboken attributes it to Haydn (Hob II/Es13) on the basis of an untitled copy in A-Wgm. The work is recorded in the "Haydn" Eb version on Telefunken 6.35473, and is convincing as a work by Hoffmeister.

FAH-16 This *Notturno*, originally for fl fldam 2hn 2vla vc/bn, is found in arrangements which replace the rare flauto d'amore by clarinet and (later) by oboe.

FAH-17(-19) *Three Parthias, No 1 in Eb, No 2 in Bb, No 3 in Eb* The first two are

"Echo" parthias, scored for one group (cl bn hn) and its echo (cl bn hn). They are listed in Traeg's 1799 catalog. Klöcker has recorded one (**FAH-18**) on Telefunken 6.35334.

FAH-25(-27) *Partitas in Bb, Bb, Eb*   These, with **FAH-19** in Bb as No 2, constitute a set of four partitas in D-DO (however, **FAH-26** is "Serenata V. in B" and **FAH-27** is "Serenata VI. in Eb"). Note that **FAH-19,** the second one of the set, may not be part of the set of echo works with which it is grouped.

FAH-32   This appears in a bound volume in CZ-KRa entitled "Serenate del Sig Kromer [sic] / Variazioni del Sig Mozart." Other similar volumes are compilations by Havel from a number of composers, not just those in the title.

FAH-36   A "Hello and Farewell" work, in which players join one at a time, and ultimately take their leave too (here more in spirit than in body). The last movement, which sounds as if it is based on a popular tune, has some tricky low horn writing.

FAH-40 *Parthia for 3bthn 2hn*   A set at PL-LA includes three (Nos 1-3) by Mašek **VVM-50(-52)**, three by Hoffmeister, and four by Voíánek for 3bthn. The copyist and paper are the same for all and unique to PL-LA. **FAH-50** is No 4; No 5 is **FAH-5.2,** an arrangement of the octet version in A-Wgm VIII 39983, and No 6 is **FAH-1.2,** an arrangement of *Serenade No 1,* published by Simrock in 1812/1813.

HOLLOWAY, Robin (Greville) *b 21 Oct 1943, Leamington Spa, England*   Composer, and lecturer at Cambridge. His *Concerto for Organ and Winds,* **RGH-1,** 1965-1966 is a serial work, influenced by his teacher, Alexander Goehr. Two of his other works use winds extensively: the *Concertino No 3,* Op 29 (1975) for 2 violins, 4 winds 3 brass and percussion, and the (wordless) song cycle, *Evening with Angels.*

HOLMBOE, Vagn *20 Dec 1909, Horsens, Denmark-1 Sep 1996, Ramlose*   A leading Danish composer who entered Copenhagen Conservatory at age 16, partly on the recommendation of Nielsen. As Professor at the Conservatory, his pupils included Per Nørgaard and Ib Nørholm. He has written works for brass and a *Notturno* for wind quintet, as well as his *Music* for 2fl 16bn and his *Divertimento* for 2ob 2tp 2tb.

HOLST, Gustav (Theodore) *21 Sep 1874, Cheltenham, UK-25 May 1934, London*   Holst's early music (1) includes an incomplete work for wind harmony (**GTH-1,** M10, 1896), a wind quintet (M196), and a quintet for wind and piano (M197). His music for wind band includes three masterpieces of the repertoire. Holst specifies one instrument to a part; he was scrupulous about which instruments were to be used (including advice as to alternatives should some instruments not be available), and shows a fastidiousness which is not evident in most published versions or most recordings, which introduce inauthentic doublings. One recording which correctly follows Holst's scoring is that by the Eastman Wind Ensemble/Fennell, on Philips GL5840.

GTH-1s *Suite 1 in Eb, Op 28a (M248)*   The essential core is fl pic(Db) 4cl(Bb, solo+1-3) 2hn(F) bn 2crt t-tb b-tb euph bomb cym s-dr; there are ad lib parts for 14 more instruments (including db) and timpani. The piano part on the autograph is meant solely to serve as a conductor's score. The *Suite* was written in 1909, and first performed in 1920. The score has three instructions: "As each movement is founded on the same phrase, it is requested that the suite shall be played right through without a break"; "It is requested that in the absence of a string bass the ad lib part for the instrument in the intermezzo shall be played on any brass instrument but omitted except where the notes are cued in other parts. Also in the absence of timpani the ad lib parts for the latter to be omitted entirely"; finally (crossed out) "The introduction of extra flutes, piccolos and sidedrums at the end of the march is only advised when there are sufficient brass instruments to make the countermelody that they play, stand out."

GTH-2s *Suite 2 in F, Op 28b (M249)*   The score includes ad lib parts for an extra pair of horns (Eb); a t-sax is not listed on the autograph, but emerges in the slow movement. The piano part should not be played. The *Suite* was written in 1911, and first performed in 1922. Its four movements are based on folksongs: Morris Dance ("Glorishears"), "Swansea Town," "Claudy Banks," "I'll Love My Love," "The Song of the Blacksmith," "Greensleeves," and "The Dargason"; five pages based on "Young Reilly" are crossed out. Bound with the autograph is a sheet reading: "Emma's First Beginning / for HB (and military band) from GH (and Emma Smith)." We have not identified Emma or HB.

GTH-3s *Hammersmith-Prelude and Scherzo, Op 52 (M91)*   Dedicated "To the Author of The Water Gypsies" (A P Herbert), the work was written to a BBC commission in 1930, but not performed until 1954 in this version.

Holst also made arrangements for wind band (*Fugue à la Gigue*, M85; *Three Folk Tunes*, M81; *Morris Dance* M146), and there are arrangements for wind bands of Holst's works by others (*Festival Chorus*, M75; *Moorside March*, M143; *Songs of the West*, M237; *Marching Song*, M238). Further, he used a small wind band (3 cornets or trumpets, 2 bombardons, percussion) to accompany his *Dirge for Two Veterans* (M59). 1. M Short 1974 *Gustav Holst (1874-1934): A Centenary Documentation;* London: White Lion Publishers. M numbers (M197, etc) are from this list (alphabetical by title), which gives full documentation about editions and recordings.

HOLYOKE, Samuel Adams *15 Oct 1762, Boxford, Massachusetts -7 Feb 1820, Concord, New Hampshire*   A pioneer in American music and education, Holyoke graduated from Harvard College in 1789. He taught and organized music teaching in Massachusetts; his first published compositions followed soon afterwards. A *Quintet in B♭* **SAH-1** has been recorded by the Federal Music Society. Holyoke based his *Turkish Quickstep* **SAH-1ma** on Kotzwara's famous *Battle of Prague.*

HOLZBAUER, Ignaz *17 Sept 1711, Vienna-7 April 1783, Mannheim*   Holzbauer's opera *Günther von Schwarzburg* earned Mozart's respect. His one piece of wind music appears to be the *Divertimento pro Cassatione* for the unusual ensemble of 2hn 2bn.

HOLZINGER, Peter Benedictus *(1720) Aibach, Bavaria; flourished 1747-1805*   His works for Turkish music include a 9-movement suite on the siege and capture of Mantua (which surrendered to the French in 1797), the 7th movement being the Marseillaise, and on the siege and capture of Alexandria (relating to the events of July 1798).

HONAUER, Lorenz (Leontzi, Leonz) *1728, Paris-c.1790*   In his two *Suites de Pièces* for 2cl 2hn 2bn pf, most movements include a *Variazio*, rather than a Trio.

HONEGGER, Arthur *10 Mar 1892, Le Havre-28 Nov 1955, Paris*   This French-born composer of Swiss parents, who studied both in Zurich and at the Paris Conservatoire, was one of the composers known as "Les Six." His "dramatic psalm" (later "symphonic psalm") *Le Roi David* **ARH-1v** is one of Honegger's most effective and durable works. There are three main version: (1) incidental music to René Morax's "drame biblique", first performed on 11 June 1921 at the Théâtre du Jarat in Mézières, directed by Paul Boepple; (2) an oratorio (1923), scored for the same small wind and percussion ensemble as (1) but with a narrator too, and (3) rescored (1923) with strings added. Version 2 is recorded under Baudo (Accord/Pinnacle CO-20082) and by Dutoit (Erato 2292-45800); version 3 is on Supraphon/Koch International CO-1412/3, conducted by Serge Baudo.

HORAK, Josef *23 Dec 1883, Rožďalovice-10 June 1968, Nymburk*   Czech choirmaster, and Kapellmeister of the Infanterie-Regiment Nr 69 in Pécs from 1907 to 1918. He was the arranger of a march *Michálek* by Suda (qv).

HOROVITZ, Joseph *b 26 May 1926, Vienna*   Horovitz was one of the many who left Vienna in the difficult period before World War II. He came to England in 1938; a student of Jacob (qv) and of Boulanger, he was a contributor to the Hoffnung Festivals.

HOTTETERRE, Martin *(d c.1712, Paris)*   Member of a distinguished musical family including flautists and oboists in Lully's orchestra.

HUMMEL, Berthold *b 27 Nov 1925, Hüfingen, Baden*   Composer of an octet whose scoring matches that of Stravinsky's *Octet* (fl cl 2bn 2tp 2tb).

HUMMEL, Johann Bernard *1760, Berlin-before 1806, Berlin*   Pianist and son of the famous publisher Johann Josef Hummel.

HUMMEL, Johann Nepomuk *14 Nov 1778, Pressburg-17 Oct 1837, Weimar*   Hummel's life was enormously successful. He was a child prodigy as a pianist; a pupil of Mozart, Salieri and Clementi; a friend of Beethoven; and the successor to Haydn at Eszterháza; small wonder that Hummel was regarded as musical heir of Mozart and the classical tradition. This view hardly survived his death. Bernard Shaw called Hummel's work "tastefully barren," because a less successful work convinced an acquaintance that it was in the nature of classical music to be dull (1). The writings of Berlioz and Schumann show that the early 19th century was a vintage period for the superficial and conventional. Poor Hummel attracted blame because his music was strong enough to survive beyond that period, and he had remained faithful to the classical tradition long after it had ceased to be fashionable. Hummel, through technique and business acumen, maintained a market long beyond his time. He was a very good - not great - composer. His piano concertos are thoroughly satisfying, as are many of his chamber works, and the *Bassoon Concerto* is outstanding. Should any doubt Hummel's quality at his best, we recommend both the *Octet Partita* and, on the grand scale, his Op 80 *Mass in E♭*, notably the "Et incarnatus est." Hummel's own monumental manual on the art of piano playing offers valuable insights into Mozart's piano style.

Hummel's father was Director of the Imperial School of Music at Pressburg, where he also directed the theater orchestra. When the school was dissolved, Hummel senior moved to a post at Schikaneder's theatre in Vienna. Johann Nepomuk Hummel's success as a prodigy was matched by a promising career move to Eszterháza. While there, he made a comprehensive catalog of music (2). Hummel was dismissed from Eszterháza for neglect of duties in 1811. By that stage, his career was sufficiently established for him to have few regrets. He is said to have been large and ungainly in appearance, with the air of a healthy businessman, and an abundance of common sense.

Several works fall outside our brief, but deserve mention. Two have dominant piano parts, though their use of the winds often reminds one of wind harmony. These are the Op 74 *Grand Septuor* (fl ob tp vl vc db pf) and the Op 114 *Military Septet* (fl cl tp vl vc db pf). In A-Wn (Mus.Hs.4713) there is a *Larghetto* in G for 4hn db pf. Other wind music is found within more substantial works. Autographs in GB-Lbl include a setting of "God Save the King" (2cl 2hn 2bn) within the *Overture für Frieden.* There are also large marches S83, including basset horns, quart-flutes and bass horns as well as a standard large band for its time (c.1810; we believe these are the ones for the Grand Duke Nicolas; the first is Hummel's Op 45 No 1) and the *Marsch für das löbl[iche] bürg[er]l[iche] Artillerie Corps in Wien,* S26 of 1798. Three of Hummel's large marches are recorded on Houston Educational Records Stereo 1065.

His arrangement of Cherubini's *Echo Piece for Panharmonicon* is cataloged as for winds alone (3). This is misleading. There are strings, though they only appear in the central part, and the brass and timpani are used only in the last 40 bars. The work takes us into strange byways of music: the panharmonicon was invented by Maelzel, who is remembered more for two devices he did not invent (the chess-playing automaton and the metronome). Maelzel's panharmonicon was admired: it was a mechanical device which could reproduce Turkish music, with animated figures. He encouraged the composition of Beethoven's *Wellingtons Sieg, oder: die Schlacht bey Vittoria,* and used music by composers such as Hummel, Weigl, Pleyel, Haydn, Cherubini, Krommer and others. Cherubini's piece was for the mechanical organ, and dated from 1806, the year of the first version of this early synthesizer (4).

JNH-1 *Parthia in E♭ (Octet Partita)*   Although often listed as *Parthia à 8 parties,* the title on the autograph is *Parthia in E♭ a 8 parti per 2 clarinetti 2 oboe 2 corni e 2* *fagotti con serpente ad libitum; composa del Sigre Giov. Nep. Hummel di Vienna.* It is dated 27 October 1808. This is a far better work than most of Hummel's rivals could have written. The three movements have more than a touch of individuality, with a distinctive rhythmic motto in the slow movement. It is recorded by The Music Serenade (Max Sound/Harmonia Mundi MSC B31); Wind Soloists of the Chamber Orchestra of Europe (ASV COE812); Bratislava Chamber Harmony/Pavlik (Rediffusion Opus 9111 0419); Little Orchestra of London/Jones (Peerless Oryx 1830); German-English Mozart Ensemble (Saga SAGA 5481); Consortium Classicum/Klöcker (MDG 3440). Consortium Classicum has recorded four works attributed to Hummel: an arrangement of Mozart's *Symphony K.425*, actually an anonymous wind version based on Hummel's arrangement for fl vl vc pf; a *Serenade* which is actually by Triebensee (JZT-6.1); the spurious *Concertino for Oboe* from Wertheim (which includes two works: the *Concertino* itself and a *Tempo di valse* with two alternativos; the pencilled "Hummel" is a modern addition), and an untraced *Sextet*, also from Wertheim.

JNH-2 *Statt Graduale Harmonie Stücke* This work uses a Klappentrompete in D (keyed trumpet, as in Hummel's 1803 *Concerto;* we have not been able to check the possibility that **JNH-2** is arranged from the *Concerto*) with 2cl 2hn 2bn. It is not cited in any thematic catalog; the MS is in the church archive of Kvasice, Moravia.

JNH-1tv *Leichen-Gesang, in A♭* The copy of this funeral music (text by Henneberg; MS parts by Johann Winkler) clearly names Hummel as composer. It is uncited in any thematic catalog. The title page states "für vier Männerstimmen" (ATTB, accompanied by 2cl 2hn 2bn 2tp timp) but gives alternatives for mixed chorus.
1. G Bernard Shaw *The Star* 6 December 1889.
2. Else Radant 1980 Haydn Yearbook 11 5.
3. Joel Sachs 1974 Notes: The Quarterly Journal of the Music Library Assoc 30 732 lists Hummel's works, the S-numbers labelling those without opus numbers.
4. A W Ord-Hume 1982 *Joseph Haydn and the Mechanical Organ;* Cardiff: Cardiff University Press. This gives a survey of many mechanical devices.

HURNÍK, Ilja *b 25 Nov 1922, Poruba, Ostrava, Moravia* Hurník's works for winds have wit and grace, and are influenced by Janáček and the French impressionists. Most use solo winds, like his wind quintets; others have pairs of winds too, like the pair of oboes in *Moments Musicaux,* **IYH-2.**

HUSA, Karel *b 7 Aug 1921, Prague* Husa has written many pieces for large wind band, which he regards as an ensemble capable of matching the orchestra.

HUTSCHENRUYTER (Hutschenreiyter), Wouter, the elder *28 Dec 1796, Rotterdam-18 Nov 1878, Rotterdam* Arranger for winds of Beethoven's *1st Symphony.*

IBERT, Jacques (François Antoine) *15 Aug 1890, Paris-5 Dec 1962, Paris* A pupil of Fauré, a Prix de Rome winner, and the first musician to be Director of the Académie de France in Rome. His earliest important works date from the early 1920s.

JFI-1 *Concerto for Cello and Winds* Written in 1925, just a few months after that by Martinů, the *Concerto* is a natural extension of the many wind works (like those of Rosetti, Mozart and Dvořák) which include cello or bass. It is in three movements: Pastorale, Romanze and Gigue. Happily, the neoclassicism is not overdone. It is recorded by Vectomov on Supraphon SUA 50877 and by Ralph Votapek with the New York Harmonie Ensemble on Music & Arts CD 649.

d'INDY, (Paul Marie Theodore) Vincent *27 Mar 1851, Paris-1 Dec 1931, Paris* D'Indy was a capable horn player and, like Druschetzky, was a professional timpanist at one stage of his career. He did much to encourage French music and to reform its teaching, a periodic problem in a system as centralized as that of France, and one whose reform was often entrusted to political conservatives like d'Indy. His pupils (qv) include Paz,

Poldowski, Sporck, Tomasi and Varèse. In addition to his admirable *Chanson et Danses* (for fl ob 2cl hn 2bn), d'Indy wrote *La Vengeance du Mari* for SATB with four winds (ca cl bn hn); the autograph manuscript (F-Pn) is dated 14 July 1931.

PVI-1 *Chanson et Danses, Op 50* Is this an extended quintet or wind harmony? The use of the instruments and the subtitle "Divertissement" confirm its rightful place in our volume. This short work was written in 1898 and first performed by Taffanel's Société in the Salle Pleyel on 7 March 1899; it reached England soon after at a Promenade Concert on 23 September 1899. The work is dedicated to the clarinettist Prosper Mimart who, like Taffanel himself, took part in the first performance.

The work produces its subtle effect with economy of writing. As the title suggests, the two movements comprise just one song, but two dances. The song of the first movement has a distinct resemblance to Wagner's *Siegfried Idyll* which vanishes in the animated middle section. The two dances of the last movement are an energetic but somewhat heavy-footed rural dance, enclosing a delicate one. At the end, the song of the first movement returns. It is recorded by the Maurice Bourgue Ensemble on Calliope CAL 1827; Collegium Musicum Pragense on Supraphon 1411 2844; Ensemble Fidelio on Gallo CD 674; it is (almost) recorded by Sylvan Winds on Koch International 3-7081-2HI (an editorial disaster removes the last slow section of the last movement).

ISAKSSON, Madelaine *b 3 Dec 1956, Stockholm* Her *Modell Maddes Modul Tvärskur* is very brief (about 90 sec).

IVES, Charles Edward *20 Oct 1874, Danbury, Conn-19 May 1954, New York* Not only one of America's most original composers, but also a major influence in American music. His *Overture and March 1776* is for theater orchestra. Ives also wrote two marches for small bands: *March Intercollegiate* (1892?) and *Omega Lambda Chi* (1895).

JACOB, Gordon (Percival Septimus) *5 July 1895, London-8 Jun 1984, Saffron Walden, Essex, UK* Jacob is noted especially as a fine orchestrator, and wrote many works for wind and brass ensembles of all sizes. His outstanding skill in the use of instruments has given many players pleasure. Many works are small, such as the wind quintet *Swansea Town* and the *Sextet in Memoriam Aubrey Brain;* others are large, like the *Music for a Festival,* written for the 1951 Festival of Britain, and the *Concertino for Trombone and Wind Orchestra* (1980). Jacob's *Orchestral Technique* (Oxford University Press, 1931) includes four short sections arranged for winds, namely: p 39, Grieg: *Piano Sonata,* for 2fl 2ob 2cl 2hn 2bn; p 41, Schumann: *Faschingsschwank aus Wien,* for 2 fl 2ob 2cl 2hn 2bn; p 42, Tchaikovsky, *Scherzo Op 21 No 6,* for 2fl ob cl hn 2bn; p 44, from Mussorgsky, *Pictures at an Exhibition,* for 2fl 2ob 2cl 2hn.

GPJ-1 *Old Wine in New Bottles;* **GPJ-2** *More Old Wine in New Bottles* Jacob was a pupil of Stanford and of Charles Wood, and his works based on folk songs happily contradict Constant Lambert's dictum that, once one has played a folk song, the only thing that can be done is play it again, louder. *Old Wine* has four contrasted movements laid out like a classical serenade. The first movement is based on "The Raggle-taggle Gypsies"; "The Three Ravens" is the basis of the Gothic slow movement. "Begone, Dull Care" becomes a 6/8 Scherzo, and the work ends with a Finale which brings out the pastoral in "Early One Morning" before turning it into a comic march. The four movements of *More Old Wine* are based on "Down among the Dead Men," "The Oak and the Ash," "The Lincolnshire Poacher" and "Joan to the Maypole."

GPJ-3 *Variations on Annie Laurie* Written for the 1956 Hoffnung Music Festival, it is for perhaps the oddest ensemble ever used (2pic heck 2cb-cl 2cbn serp b-serp sub-cb-tu hurdy-gurdy harm). The choice of instruments (Hoffnung's own) precludes frequent performances. There are, after all, rather few sub-contrabass instruments of any sort in any one place. The theme (Alerto, ma non troppo) and variations (numbered 1,2,3 and

5 only) have titles which are only too clear: Poco Inglesemente; Molto Zingaresemente; Alla gigolo; and Finale, assai. A photograph of the ensemble is reproduced on p 140 of Annetta Hoffnung 1988 *Gerard Hoffnung;* London: G Fraser.

GPJ-6 *Divertimento in E♭* First performed in Cambridge in 1950, this work is perhaps closest to the standard 18th century work in approach. It opens with a March and Trio, clearly 20th-century in conception, and arguably the strongest movement. This is followed by a Sarabande on a ground (i.e., there is a bass repeated throughout the movement while the other parts develop as usual). The work is rounded off by a Rondo containing a written-out cadenza for the two horns. It is recorded by the Queensland Wind Soloists on 4MBS CD 1 (4MBS denotes Brisbane Radio, Australia).

JADASSOHN, Salomon *13 Aug 1831, Breslau-1 Feb 1902, Leipzig* Known mainly as a pianist and as a contrapuntalist of skill, he dedicated his one work for winds, *Serenade Op 104c,* **SXJ-1,** to "Seinem lieben Freund Hans Sitt." The violinist Sitt (1850-1922) was a colleague at the Leipzig Conservatory. The *Serenade* is in four movements. An Allegro di Marcia opens the work, followed by a Notturno, Andante non troppo sostenuto. The Scherzo (Allegretto) which follows is a canon (mentioned on the title page of the score, but not on the parts), albeit a relatively simple one in no more than two parts at any one time; there is no trio. The finale is marked "In Tempo di Bolero," effectively a polonaise; there is a short clarinet cadenza.

JADIN, Hyacinthe *1769, Versailles-Oct 1800, Paris*   Professor of piano at the Conservatoire as well as composer. A man, not a woman, despite recent writings. His arrangement of Méhul's splendid overture to *Le jeune Henri* follows the original closely. His *Ouverture in F* is recorded by the Wallace Collection on Nimbus NI 5175.

JADIN, Louis Emmanuel *21 Sept 1768 Versailles-11 Apr 1853 Paris* Prolific composer of operas, who succeeded his brother Hyacinthe as Professor of piano at the Paris Conservatoire. Apart from his three sextets for 2cl 2hn 2bn, his output for winds is for bands of the Revolution and dates from around 1794 (see *Pierre/HC*). Pierre remarks on the novel rhythms and modulations in both the Haydnesque *Ouverture in C* and in the *Symphonie,* with its hints of Beethoven. The *Ouverture* was for the 1794 Fête de la 5me sans culottide (i.e., 21 September, the last of the revolutionary calendar's five intercalary days). There are also some marches and two works with voices: an *Ode to J J Rousseau* and the song of a slave, given her citizenship by the recent national decree, sung at the cradle of her son; unusually, this song is one to awaken the child.

JANÁČEK, Leoš *3 July 1854, Hukvaldy-12 Aug 1928, Ostrava* Janáček was born in Moravia in the same year as Humperdinck, when Spohr and Rossini were still alive. His individual style suggests later dates, partly because he developed late and achieved success later still. The wind works we consider were written at the end of his life, in the 1920s. As with Haydn and Strauss, the appeal of wind instruments grew in old age. Janáček was stimulated by hearing a concert by the Parisian Société Moderne des Instruments à Vent. The results included the *Concertino* of 1925, the *Capriccio* for piano (left hand) of 1926, and *Mládí.* We make no excuse for regarding *Mládí* (for fl/pic ob cl b-cl hn bn) as wind harmony for, in its unique way, it is in that same tradition.

LXJ-1 *Mládí (Youth)* Why Janáček wrote a work called "Youth" in his old age, and the way it links to his own youth, are partly clear. Certainly he was collecting autobiographical material for a volume to celebrate his 70th birthday; he was also working on *The Makropoulos Case*, which concerns the artificial youth of Elena Makropoulos. He wrote "I listen to the birds singing, I wonder at the manifestations of rhythm in its million different forms in the world of light, of color, of shapes, and my music remains young through the eternally young rhythm of nature" (1). *Mládí* is in four movements, complex in idiom, with subtle changes of rhythm, mood and tempo. The first movement is a free rondo, Allegro, based on the speech rhythms of the Czech phrase "Mládí, zlaté mládí" (Youth, golden youth). The second, slower movement can be considered a set of four variations on a Czech theme. One oddity is the appearance of 17/16 bars at the ends of sections, a curiously nostalgic effect. The main autobiographical moments come in the third movement, the March of the Blue Boys, which corresponds to the expected scherzo. The Blue Boys were the choristers of the Augustinian Monastery, Brno, whose company Janáček had joined at age 11. Their name came from their light blue uniforms. The choristers had formidable musical talents (see part 1), and many became famous musicians in due course. The evolution of the march is complicated, and the version for piccolo in *Mládí* represents stage four. Stage one was a small work for the odd ensemble of piccolo, bells, tambourine and piano, inscribed "The little singers of the monastery cheer as they march - blue like bluebirds." Stage two appeared only in a musical journal, in which Janáček recalled the Prussian fife and drum band, part of the force billeted in the monastery in the war of 1866. Version three was a revised form of the first, now closer to the *Mládí*. The final form in the sextet itself has a repeated trio (March-Trio-March-Trio-March). The last movement is the most nostalgic; even the most animated sections are poignant, and the effect of the rhapsodic oboe cadenza lasts through the hectic final bars.

The first performance, on 21 October 1924, in Brno, was a disaster. The players, professors of the Brno Conservatory, were capable players, but the problem of a sticking clarinet key could not be overcome. Janáček stormed onto the stage, complaining "This wasn't my composition - the clarinet pretended to play, but didn't." The first proper performance was on 23 November 1924, when seven members (with a separate piccolo player) of the Czech Philharmonic played it in the Vinohrady Theatre. Performances abroad followed quickly: in Venice in May 1925, when Hindemith's *Kleine Kammermusik Op 25 No 2* was played, and in London in 1926 (*Weston/ MCVP*, plate 11, shows the London players with Janáček). The many recordings of *Mládí* (2) include those by the London Sinfonietta (Decca D223D5), Koenig Ensemble, which plays the *March of the Blue Boys* too (Bedivere BVR 304), Vienna Wind Soloists (Decca SDD 523), Prague Wind Quintet (Supraphon 111 1177; 11 1254-2 131), Orpheus Chamber Orchestra (415 668-2), and Wind Soloists of the Chamber Orchestra of Europe (ASV COE 812).

LEJ-1v *Říkadla (Nursery Rhymes, or Nonsense Songs)* Like *Mládí*, this work developed from small beginnings. Here the original was 8 *Nursery Songs* written in 1925 for women's voices, clarinet and piano. The texts were from the children's pages of the newspaper *Lidové Noviny*. Following a successful performance in Brno in 1926, Janáček extended the series to 18 songs, with larger forces. Vogel (1) remarks that the songs "are not easy, even for grown-ups." The image of wind whistling through ragged trousers is surely unique in wind harmony. The ocarina is used to suggest a witch's spells, showing again the link of wind music and magic. The work is recorded (2) by the Czech Philharmonic Chorus and Orchestra under Veselka (Supraphon 112 1486, Supraphon 11 0768) and under Kühn (Supraphon SOMMCD201), London Sinfonietta/ Mackerras (Decca 430 375-2DH2), and Netherlands Chamber Choir/Schoenberg Ensemble/de Leeuw (Phil 442 534-2PH).

1. J Vogel 1962 *Leoš Janáček: His Life and Works;* London: Paul Hamlyn.
2. Early recordings are listed comprehensively by William D Curtis 1978 Discography Series 18: *Leoš Janáček;* Utica, NY: Discography Series (ISSN: 0095-8115).

JANSSEN, Guus *1951* **GUJ-1** *Dans van de Malic Matrijzen (Dance of the Malic Moulds)* for winds and solo piano. The "Moulds" were apparently those used in fashioning lead figures, as used in a painting "La Mariée mise à nu par les celebataires," once notorious, by Marcel Duchamp (1887-1963). Commissioned by the Johan Wagenaar Foundation, the work was written in Amsterdam, 1976-1978. It is recorded by the Hague Philharmonic Orchestra under Lucas Vis on Residentie Orkest 6812.901/906.

JAROCH, Jiří *23 Sept 1920, Smilkov, Czechoslovakia-30 Dec 1986, Prague* From 1941, he worked for many years in the music department of Czechoslovak Radio; in this time, he wrote some light classical works for programs. His music is often vigorous and rhythmically challenging. *Metamorfózi* **JXJ-1** was written in 1968 for Prague's Chamber Harmony, and is recorded by them on Panton 11 031; it offers an imaginative approach to variations and the way they relate.

JAVAULT, Alexandre *(1780)* Arranger c.1815 of music from Cherubini's *Les deux journées*, on which he is styled as Chevalier de la Légion d'Honneur, Élève du Conservatoire de Paris, et Chef de Musique du 5e Régiment de la Garde Royale.

JELL, Josef (Jean) *(1770)* The first three of his attractive *[4] Variationen* for 2cl 2hn 2bn treat players as soloists in turn (cl 1, bn 1, hn 1); the horns are tacet in Var 1, 2.

JETSCHMANN, ( ) His marches are for the I Bataillon Königlich Leib-Garde.

JEŽEK, Jaroslav *25 Sept 1906, Prague-1 Jan 1942 New York* Able to compose brilliant works in classical and popular jazz idioms, a composer of marches of the revolutionary and twenty scores for the "Liberated Theater," he is a kind of Czech Gershwin or Weill. Like Weill, he wrote a *Concerto for Violin and Wind Orchestra;* Ježek's dates from 1930. This is a splendid work in three movements, with written-out cadenzas, and lucid scoring. Ježek's *Wind Quintet,* also from 1930, is recorded on Supraphon 1 11 0481.

JIRAČKOVA, Marta *b 22 Mar 1932, Kladno* She studied first in Prague, with Hlobil and Hába, then in Brno at the Janáček Academy. Her *Center of Gravity for Humanity* (1993) is for eight double-reed instruments. Her other music includes electroacoustic music for film and radio. She has been a music editor in Prague for over thirty years.

JIRASEK, Ivo *b 16 July 1920, Prague* Conductor and composer, whose early Czech influences were later enriched by those of the music of Berg and of Les Six. In addition to his 1972 *Partita for Winds,* he has written *Musique pour le café d'après midi* (for 4cl) and a *Stabat Mater* accompanied by brass and organ, recorded on Supraphon 1 12 1537.

JIRKO, Ivan *7 Oct 1926, Prague-20 Aug 1978, Prague* His *Sonata* for winds is recorded on Panton 11 0301.

JÖRNS, Helge *b 1943, Germany* The composer of the two-movement *Dectet* for fl 2ob 2cl 2hn 2bn db for Consortium Classicum, c.1981.

JOHANSON, Sven-Eric *b 10 Dec 1919, Västerrik, Sweden* His short *Fanfar* was for the Expo Norr, 1967; his other work for winds is the 1985 *Hornpipe.*

JOHANSSON, Gunnar *b 23 Mar 1906* Arranger of the *Festpolonäs* by Yngve Skäld (qv).

JOLAS, Betsy *b 5 Aug 1926, Paris* French-born of American parents, Jolas was a student of Milhaud and of Messiaen; she has spent much of her life in the United States. Her *Points d'Aube* is for solo viola and winds. She has also written *Mots,* 7 pieces for SMATB soli, fl ob(ca) cl bn hpcd hp perc (Heugel 1969, recorded on Adès 14.1013).

JOLIVET, André *8 Aug 1905, Paris-20 Dec 1974, Paris* One who experimented with literature and the arts before turning to music. A founder, with Messiaen and Daniel-Lesur, of La Spirale, to promote chamber music. He became Director of the Comédie-Française in January 1945. His *Concerto* for trumpet and winds dates from 1954.

JOMMELLI, Niccolò *10 Sept 1714, Averso, near Naples-25 Aug 1774, Naples* Opera composer and Kapellmeister to the Duke of Württemberg in Stuttgart from 1753 to 1768. The failure of later works led to melancholy and apoplexy from which he died.

JONES, Daniel Jenkyn *7 Dec 1912, Pembroke-29 April 1993, Swansea* Welsh composer whose music has been widely recognized. His *Epicedium* (with words by Prudentius) is for soloists, chorus, and winds.

JONES, John *1728, London?-17 Feb 1796, London* His use of flutes, rather than oboes, in his *Sixteen select military pieces* **JZJ-1m,** is close to French band configurations.

JONSSON, Josef Petrus *21 Jan 1887, Enköping, Sweden-9 May 1969 Norköping* Composer, pianist and music critic, whose Op 53 *Suite* is for winds and percussion.

JORDAN, ( ) Mr *(1760)*   Composer of a *March* for the 3d Regiment [Lord Amherst's; East Kent: Buffs] and 17th Regiment [General Monckton's; Leicestershire].

JOSEPHS, Wilfred *b 24 Jul 1927, Newcastle*   The *Papageno Variations*, for the same ensemble (fl ob cl b-cl hn bn) as Janáček's *Mládí*, were commissioned by the Albion Ensemble for Mozart's bicentenary.

JOUVE, Joseph *(1766, Aix-1832, Paris*   Composer of *The Austrian Retreat* for the First Regiment of Life Guards, arranger of music by von Esch, and composer of music arranged by Samuel Hale (**SYH-1m**).

K., E., *a Lady (1770)*   She wrote a new *March* for the Regiment of Bengal Sepoys. Marches for indigenous regiments are rare; marches by women are rare too.

KAA, (Franz) Ignaz *baptized 27 Oct 1739, Offenburg, Baden-8 May 1818, Cologne*   His Motet "per la Processione della Madonna del Rosario" is for choir with winds and organ.

KABELAČ, Miroslav *1 Aug 1908, Prague-17 Sept 1979, Prague*   Conductor, composer, and a Music Director for Radio Prague, where he worked from 1932 to 1954, apart from a period during the Nazi occupation. His *Sextet* for fl ca 2cl(sax b-cl) hn bn was written in 1940, soon after the arrival of the Nazis. It is in four movements, the first and third being in ternary form with contrasting parts; the finale is in sonata form, with a folk-like theme in its development. His *Symphony No 3* is for organ, brass and timpani, and was written between 1948 and 1957; he joined the Prague Conservatory as Professor in 1958. He was a teacher of Loudová, Lukáš, Málek, Matoušek and others.

KAGEL, Mauricio Raul *b 24 Dec 1931, Buenos Aires*   He was at the Electronic Studios, Cologne, in 1956; in his music he exploits indeterminacy, the player selecting options. His *10 Marches to Miss Victory* are recorded on Preciosa Aulos PRE 66004 AUL.

KAISER, Karl *(1850)-after 1924, Detmold*   Hautboisten (even at this stage, a military musician, rather than an oboist; indeed, his works usually omit oboes) in the 6th Westfällischen Infanterie-Regiment No 55, Detmold, and arranger of music by Auber, Beethoven and others between 1878 and 1882. Some of the later arrangements at Detmold may be by him. He wrote a *Wind Quintet* as late as 1924.

KALABIS, Viktor *b 27 Feb 1923, Červený Kostelek*   Kalabis studied in Prague both at the Conservatory and at Charles University. From 1953 until 1972 he was an editor and music producer for Czechoslovak Radio, Prague. His *Jarni Pístalky* (Spring Whistles, Op 50) was written in 1979, and is recorded on Panton 111 92736.

KALACH, Jiří *b 9 Mar 1934, Prague*   Educated at the Prague Conservatory, Kalach was a freelance composer for many years. His *Octet* for wind instruments dates from 1982. Since 1990 he has been a dramatic advisor to Czech Radio.

KALICK, R D *(?1770)*   German composer based in Vienna; **RDK-1** is a 3-movement *Sinfonia* in C.

KALINSKY, Jan   His *Andante* for 2ob 2ca bn is late Romantic in style.

KALLIWODA (Kalivoda), Johann Wenzel (Johan Wenzeslaus; Jan Křtitel Václav)
21 Feb 1801, Prague-3 Dec 1866, Karlsruhe   Bohemian violinist and composer who spent most of his career at Donaueschingen as conductor of the orchestra of the Prince Karl Egon II von und zu Fürstenberg. His music shows how the use of the word "Harmonie" changed in the 19th century. Some works, presumably early ones, have conventional scoring: **JWK-3** *Harmonie* is for fl 2cl 2hn 2bn and **JWK-5** *Harmoniemusik für heil[igen] Communion* is for 2cl 2hn 2bn (ca ad lib). Other works, from just before the 1848 revolution, are quite different: the *6 Pièces d'Harmonie pour Musique militaire* **JWK-1**, c.1845, are scored for a large band, including piccolo "in Des" (actually A♭), bombardon and ophicleide. The work is divided into two books of three items, with some inconsistency in numbering. The last item in each book has two vocal parts; in the first of these, the *Marche funèbre,* the side drum is muted.

KAMMEL (Kamel, Kammell, Kamml, Khaml, Cammell), Antonín *baptized 21 Apr 1730, Běleč-early 1788, London* As a mere gamekeeper and son of a forester, Kammel had the skill and luck to be sent by Count Wallenstein to Italy to study the violin with Tartini. He came to London later, where he was involved in the Bach-Abel concerts. Contrary to myth, he was not a member of the Royal Music (certainly not its Master), he did not marry a rich wife, and **AAK-1** *Serenata in G* is indeed for ob 2hn bn.

KANNE, Friedrich August *1778-1833* His March is for "die k.k. Oester Armee."

KANTCHELI, Gia *b 1935, Tbilisi, Georgia* *Magnum Ignotum* is a single movement for tape and fl 2ob 2cl 2hn 2bn db. Composed for the Netherlands Wind Ensemble, to whom it is dedicated, its first United Kingdom performance was on 20 February 1995.

KARG-ELERT, Sigfrid *21 Nov 1877, Oberndorf am Neckar-4 Sept 1933, Leipzig* The "-Elert" part of Karg's name was added at the suggestion of his concert agent. He was a pupil at Leipzig of Reinecke (qv) and Jadassohn (qv). A virtuoso organist well known as composer for his instrument, he is also known for his Harmonium works. His Op 30 *Quintet* for ob 2cl hn bn dates from 1903, a productive period in his career.

KARKOFF, Maurice *b 17 Mar 1927, Stockholm* Caprice CAP 3009 includes a recording of **MIK-2**, *Chamber Concerto No 2 "från 803."* He has written for winds **MIK-1** *Concerto da camera*, **MIK-3** *Quasi una marcia*, and **MIK-4**, a *Divertimento* for 2cl 2bn.

KATZER, Hynek (Ignác) *30 Sept 1785, Velky Ukrinov, Bohemia-post-1820* His dances were written c.1820 for Prince Eugen von Bentheim-Bentheim.

KAUER, Ferdinand *18 Jan 1751, Klein Thaya (Tayax) near Znaim; now Dyjákovičky, near Znojmo, Moravia-13 April 1831, Vienna* Prolific composer whose 1798 opera *Das Donauweibchen* enjoyed enormous success and was the basis for several arrangements for winds. Presumably his *Partitas* for 2ob 2hn bn are early works.

KEIL, Johann *(? = Joseph Kail, early 19th century horn virtuoso from Prague)* Keil's *Parthia No 12* **JXK-1** includes a quart-bassoon.

KÉLER, Béla (pseudonym of **Adalbert Paul von Kéler**) *13 Feb 1820, Bártfa, Hungary-20 Nov 1882, Wiesbaden* Conductor, violinist and successful composer of light music. His arrangement of a scena from Lortzing's *Undine* was presumably for the infantry band which he conducted in Wiesbaden from 1856.

KELLER, Georg Friedrich *1806-1849* The autograph score of his *VI Versette* for fl 2ob 2hn 2bn is dated Würzburg, 10-17 April 1848.

KELLER, Max *7 Oct 1770, Trostberg, Bavaria-16 Sept 1855, Altötting* His *Menuett* is recorded on Musica Bavarica MB 316 (LP), MB 75103 (CD), MB 75057 (cassette).

KEMPTER, Karl *17 Jan 1819, Limpach, Bavaria-11 Mar 1871, Augsburg* Kempter's *Veni Sancte Spiritus* **KEK-3v** is for Pentecost and other occasions.

KETTING, Otto *3 Sep 1935, The Hague* **OYK-1**, *2 Canzoni* (1957) is recorded in Vol 2 of Vierhondert Jaar Nederlandse Muziek.

KEULEN, Geert van *b 1943, Holland* Composer who studied with Robert Heppener and clarinettist and bass clarinettist with the Concertgebouw Orchestra and the Netherlands Wind Ensemble, which recorded his **GVK-1** *Chords* for 15 Winds (1974) conducted by van Keulen (Composers' Voice CV7804). The five sections (lasting nearly 20 minutes), are based on a series of chords; the first is fast and aggressive, with "big-band" brass chords, while the last forms a quiet, static epilogue. These components are separated by Interludes of a few bars.

KEURIS, Tristan *3 Oct 1946, Amersfoort, Holland-14 Dec 1996* Composer who studied under Ton de Leeuw at the Utrecht Conservatory, where he won the prize for composition. He taught at the Music Lyceum in Hilversum. His work also includes *Catena*, for large wind band and percussion. **TRK-1** *Capriccio for 12 winds and double bass* (1978) is recorded on Composers' Voice CV7804 by the Netherlands Wind Ensemble/Lucas Vis for whom it was commissioned by the Johan Wagenaar Foundation.

Its scoring is much the same as that of Mozart's *Gran Partita,* with the Eb clarinet chosen to enhance the higher winds' sound. An attractive and interesting work which would be a good filler for discs of the Mozart. It lasts about 9 minutes.

KIEL, August *1813-1871* Composer of a *Walzer* and a *Fest-Marsch* for winds, and an arranger of Auber's *La Sirène* overture; associated with the Lippe Kapelle, Detmold.

KING, Matthew Peter *1733, London-Jan 1823, London* Composer of the *Mary-le-Bone March,* for the Duke of York's Band, but known more for his music for the stage and his sacred music, including the long-popular *Eve's Lament* from *The Intercession* (1816).

KIRCHHOFF, Wilhelm *(1800)* "Maitre de la chapelle de S.A. du prince August de Hoh. Öhringen" [sic], and composer or arranger of a large group of works in the Hohenlohe archives from Neuenstein. The collection includes divertimentos, individual dance movements, and many opera arrangements. His arrangement of **WZK-21a,** Adam's *Le postillon de Longjumeau,* is dedicated to Louise, Duchess of Württemberg (1791-1831); that of Bellini's *I Capuleti,* **WZK-28a** c.1830, was for the birthday celebrations of her husband, August (1784-1853). Many of Kirchhoff's works are dated. Kirchhoff probably succeeded Georg Schmitt as Maitre de la chapelle c.1837, after the ensemble moved to Schlawentzitz, Silesia; Scholz may have succeeded Kirchhoff c.1842 or 1843.

KIRSTEN (Kirstin), (Friedrich?) *(1750), flourished 1770-1797* Organist in Dresden.

KLAUS (Klauss), Josef *(?1840)* Composer of a number of funeral cantatas, mostly scored for CATB, 2cl 2hn 2bn 2tp.

KLECZINSKY (Kletzinsky), Jan (Johann Baptist) *14 June 1756-6 Aug 1828, Berlin* After seven years at the Paris Conservatoire, he returned to Poland and gave up composition for writings on music. His *Partie* (lost?) may date from his time in Paris.

KLEIN, Bernhard *6 Mar 1793, Cologne-9 Sep 1832, Berlin* The son of a double-bass player, Klein managed to study with Cherubini in Paris. He wrote much church music on his return to Germany, but his two *Divertimentos* appear to be lost.

KLEIN, Gideon *6 Dec 1919, Plerov-Jan 1945, Fürstengrube concentration camp, Silesia* His *Divertimento for Eight Wind Instruments* was written in 1940, just before he was sent to Terezin; he was transferred to Auschwitz in 1944, then to Fürstengrube. He continued to compose under terrible conditions. He was trained in Prague, and was inspired by the music of Janáček, Novák, and Schoenberg, and by Moravian folklore.

KLEINPETER (Kleinpetter), Joseph *(1770)* Probably a local musician in Langenbruck (Dlouhý Most, northern Bohemia). His five *Parthias* for 2cl 2hn bn are in copies by Augustin Erasmus Hübner, and date from 1799 to 1809.

KLEITZ, F *(1770)* Kleitz arranged music by Dalayrac and, with Faltzann (on whom we have no further information), produced *Six Harmonies Extraites des Compositions de Mozart Arrangés.* The first Livre proves to be movements 1, 2, 3 and 7 of the *Gran Partita* in what is essentially the Breitkopf & Härtel reduction for 8 winds, largely unaltered apart from the remark "o flautino" on the oboe parts. Livre 2 is K.C.17.01.

KLIEBENSCHÄDL, Johann Joseph *(1800)* Composer of "Die Nachtigal" and "Schön wie der Mond", two *Marienlieder* for mixed chorus and winds to texts by Guido Görres.

KLOB, Stephan *(1750), active 1770s-1790s* Not to be confused with Kolb, a contemporary composer at Regensburg. Klob's works form three groups: two early four-movement *Parthias* for 2cl 2hn bn (c.1770), two five-movement *Parthias* from about a decade later for 2cl(G) 2vla basso, and seven *Divertimentos* for larger ensembles, also with 2vla, c.1790, in 8-14 movements; these were probably for Tafelmusik. He also arranged 12 movements from Haydn symphonies for 2cl 2hn bn 2vla vlne.

KLOS, ( ) His *Parthia* ZYK-1 for octet (early, c.1780?) is in the Lobkovic archive.

KLUSAK, Jan-Filip *b 18 Apr 1934, Prague* Founder of the Prague Chamber Wind Ensemble, formed to introduce new music. He has written two wind quintets (*Inventions* and *Music for a Fountain*), and has composed for the theater and films, in addition to his orchestral music. His *Obrazy* (Pictures; **JAK-1**) was first performed at the Troisième Biennale, Paris. Three of his other works for winds use soloists: a soprano in *Studies after Kafka* (**JAK-1v**) and low voice in *Dämmerklarheit* (settings of Rückert, **JAK-2v**), and a violin in his *Sonata* (**JAK-2**).

KNECHT (Kneht), (?Juntin Heinrich) *(1810)* Arranger in 1841 of Neubauer's *Quatuor Stationes* (**FCN-1v**) with new texts, for Gutenzell, Swabia.

KNĚŽEK (Knieschek, Knischek), Václav *1745, Prague-1806, Regensburg* Second bassoon at Regensburg from 1769. Note his use of clarinets d'amour in **VZK-3**.

KNORR, Bernhard, Baron von *18th century, Vienna* The dedicatee of a *Flute Concerto* by Krommer and the composer of works for 2fl and fl pf, so presumably an amateur flautist; there was also someone of this name in the Masonic lodge to which Haydn belonged. Knorr's lightweight but attractive *Quintetto* is for fl ca 2hn bn.

KOCH, Heinrich Christoph *10 Oct 1749, Rudolstadt-12 Mar 1816, Rudolstadt* The son of a member of the Rudolstadt court orchestra, and a violinist, who studied with Goepfert (qv). His known wind music consists of three *Pas Redoublés*.

KOECHLIN, Charles *27 Nov 1867, Paris-31 Dec 1950, Le Canaden, France* Koechlin wrote extensively for wind, though mainly for small ensembles, for solo instruments, and original band music, notably the four-movement suite *Quelques Chorales*. He was the author of a small book, *Les Instruments à Vent*. His *Septet* Op 165, **CHK-1**, dates from when he was 70. It is an extended wind quintet (fl ob ca cl sax bn hn) in the same sense as d'Indy's *Chanson et Danses*. The six movements are: Monodie (cl solo); Pastorale (fl cl bn); Intermezzo Allegretto con moto; Fugue; Serenite (Calme, très doux, with a note to the saxophone to play it *cool*); Fugue (sur un thème de mon fils Yves). It is recorded on Accord ACC 140056.

KOEHLER, Benjamin Frédéric *1 Oct 1773, Leignitz, Silesia-after 1818, Guhrau* **BFK-1** *Jeu de dez [sic] d'écossaises à composer; 2cl 2hn bn tp* This rarity is a composing game, where pieces are constructed by the throw of a dice. Published by Leuckart in 1803, it would have been a boon to the overworked bandmaster. Some of these composing games are both complex and rewarding in their results. We have no locations for this work of Koehler, and would be keen to learn of any surviving copies.

The *Musikalisches Würfelspiel*, K.516f, attributed to Mozart, was used at a 1991 concert by the Composers' Ensemble as the basis of three wind works. The first is a short *Minuet* by Nicholas Maw for fl cl 2bn 2tp 2tb, the same combination as Stravinsky's *Octet*. The second, called *To Compose Without the Least Knowledge of Music...* was written by Colin Matthews for fl ob cl b-cl hn bn, the ensemble Janáček used in *Mládí*. The third was by Gary Carpenter, *Ein Musikalisches Snookerspiel*, a suite of five waltzes for 2ob 2cl 2hn 2bn, each conceived as a snooker frame, and incorporating as "fouls" chords from Mozart's Musical Joke, K.522. For each frame, the first 16 bars followed the letter of the Musical Dice Game, with dice thrown by Carpenter's wife. After these bars, "snooker rules" were imposed, based on what happened in an actual snooker game between Carpenter and Peter Leighton-Jones.

KÖHLER, Ernst *28 May 1799, Langenbielau, Silesia-26 June (May?) 1847, Breslau* We have no locations for his 1835 *Septet* for fl ob cl 2hn 2bn. His 1831 *Chor* is for soloists with male-voice choirs and optional 4hn 2bn; the autograph was in the collection of Aloys Fuchs. Köhler was Oberorganist at the church of St Elisabeth in Breslau.

KÖHLER, Nicolaus *(1800)* In his Latin Mass for Advent, the organ and violone are obbligato, and the winds (2cl 2hn) are explicitly not obbligato.

KÖNIG, M Composer of marches for the Prussian court.

KOETSIER, Jan *b 14 Aug 1911, Amsterdam* In 1966, Koetsier became Professor at the Munich Hochschule, where his Octet **JNK-1** was written. His *Baroque Suite* **JNK-2** is another example (see also Ibert, Martinû) of a work for solo cello and winds.

KOHN, Karl Georg *b 1 Aug 1926, Vienna*   Kohn left Vienna because of the turmoil in Europe, moving to the United States in 1939, and might be regarded as an American composer. He studied under Walter Piston. In his *Concert Music for 12 Winds,* **KGK-1,** the first movement is a Passacaglia on a 12-note theme; the last movement pits woodwind against the brass.

KOLB, Johann Baptist *31 Aug 1743, Fürth, near Nuremburg-1st decade, 19th century, Neudetreithau, Franconia*   Not to be confused with Klob, a contemporary of his at Regensburg. His parthias, probably written in the 1780s, comprise large groups of movements. There are many movements in D-Rtt for 2cl 2hn and 2bthn 2hn.

KOLBE, Oscar *10 Aug 1838, Berlin-2 Jan 1878, Berlin*   His *Overture* to celebrate the coronation of Her Majesty Carolina, Kaiserin von Oesterreich, as Queen of Hungary, would have been written for the 8 June 1867 coronation, following the division of the Austrian Empire to allow greater independence for Hungary.

KOLLESCHOWSKY, Zigmund Michael *2 May 1817, Prague-22 July 1868, Prague*   The *Adagio religioso* **ZMK-1** is dedicated to Franz Reis, "Med Doctor" [sic] and to Fraulein Theresia Tittel. The set of published parts in GB-Lbl has with them a manuscript score in the hand of John Parr, the pioneer and enthusiast for wind music.

KOLLMANN, August Friedrich Christoph *c.1756-1829*   Organist of His Majesty's German Chapel at St James, he wrote for the Corps of the Light Horse Volunteers of the Cities of London and Westminster. His *Characteristic March,* "as performed by the 3rd Regiment of Guards," has "Sentiments" appended, identified by letters above each passage: 1st Part. (A) Boldly we march, and fear no danger. (B) Our Loved-ones we must leave, but we shall again see them. 2nd Part. (C) Fear shall precede us, and Victory shall follow us; (D) As it is for our Friends and Liberty! (E) That we now boldly march and shall victoriously return. 3rd Part. (F) But the Defenceless we must treat with Tenderness, (G) For we have Friends who are also defenceless. 4th Part. (H) And who knows how great their Anxiety for us will be! (I) Therefore the Defenceless we will treat with Tenderness.

KOLOVRATEK (Kollovrátek), Tomaš (?Johann/Jan) *(1780); active 1812*   His works include a *Cassation,* religious vocal works and funeral hymns, all from Choceň, Bohemia. On one of the funeral hymns he styles himself "Decani Chorenensium Zelozissimi." **TXK-1,** a *Parthia pastoralis,* uses a solo flute with 2cl 2hn 2bn.

KONTZVINDT (Ganswind), ( ) *b 1775, Čechách*   His *Notturno* and two *Parthias* for 2 violas d'amore, 2a-cl, 2bn basso use alto clarinets described as "tous clarinets."

KOPPEL, Hermann David *b 1908*   His music for wind octet, Op 123, is recorded by the Danish Wind Octet on Da Capo 8.22 4002.

KOPPRASCH, Wenzel *c.1750-after 1844*   Kopprasch's *Serenata* includes a quart-fagott.

KORN, Peter Jona *b 30 Mar 1922, Berlin*   His *Variations and Fugue on a Theme of Carrie Jacobs-Bond* **PJK-2** is based on the popular song "I Love You Truly."

KORTE, Oldřich František *b 26 Apr 1926, Šala*   Composer and pianist whose career has ranged from film actor to fireman, from forester to trade-union official. His music is likewise diverse. *Retrospects* (1971) is for wind ensemble, harp, and percussion. His *The Wonderful Circus* is for large orchestra and a separate wind orchestra.

KOSPOTH, Otto Carl Erdmann, Baron von *1753, Mültroff, Saxony-23 Jun 1817, Berlin*   The André print of **OCK-2** offers 2bthn or 2vla as alternatives, confirming violas as common members of wind bands at that time.

KOTTERZ, ( )   Probably a musician associated with Osek monastery.

KOWANDO, ( ) *(1770)*   Probably a local musician associated with Langenbruck (Dlouhý Most), northern Bohemia. His *Parthia* dates from 1801.

KOZELUCH (Koželuh; CZ-KRa, "Gosheloch"), (Johann Evangelista) Jan Antonín Tomáš *14 Dec 1738, Velvary-3 Feb 1814, Prague*   It is often unclear whether Jan or Leopold

Kozeluch wrote a particular work. Our *Catalog* lists details under Leopold's name, with only doubtful cases listed as Jan's. Jan was a pupil of Josef Seger in Prague and, after a period in Vienna, returned to Prague. From 1784 until his death, he was Choirmaster at the Cathedral. He wrote much church music. The *Parthia alla Camera No 1* JTK-1d is recorded by members of the State Philharmonic of Brno/Drápela on Pronto 0 014.

KOZELUCH, Leopold Anton (Antonín) *9 Dec 1747, Velvary-7 May 1818, Vienna* Kozeluch is remembered without sympathy. Beethoven called him "miserabilis"; Alexander Straton, of the British Embassy in Vienna observed "All that can be said of Kozeluch is that he is a Biped without feathers" (*HCRL/4* p 493). Kozeluch alone seems to have had an unfailingly high opinion of himself. Talent he had, with a fluent style matching popular taste. A composition pupil of his uncle (J A Kozeluch) and a piano pupil of F X Dušek (qv), he had all the political skills. Yet he turned down Mozart's Salzburg post in a rare moment of modesty: if the Archbishop would let Mozart go, what could such as he hope for? Kozeluch was created Imperial Court Composer in 1792, after Mozart's death; Krommer succeeded in 1818 after the death of Kozeluch. It is hard to be sure whether Jan or Leopold Kozeluch wrote any particular work. The Soloists of the State Philharmonic, Brno/Emil Drápela, have recorded **LAK-1d** as by J A Kozeluch on Pronto 0 014. The *Marsch für das Corps der Freywilligen des Handelstandes von Wien (Tradesmen's Volunteers)*, **LAK-3m**, was for an Austrian volunteer unit; it was probably written soon after the invasion of Styria in 1797. Kozeluch also wrote pieces for 3hn. A thematic catalog is given by Milan Poštolka 1964 *Leopold Koželuh. Život a dílo;* Prague: Stání hudební vydavatelství, pps 159-170.

KOZLOWSKI, Josef Anton (Józef Ossip Antonowitsch) *1757, Warsaw-27 Feb 1831, St Petersburg* In 1775 Kozlowski became a tutor to Count Ogiński's children at Troki. Count Michael Casimir Ogiński (1731-1803, uncle of Kozlowski's pupil Michael Kleofas Ogiński, composer of marches and other works) was a skilled clarinettist (*Weston/ MCVP*), and there are reports of his "astonishing virtuosity" in performances in Moscow; Hellyer (1) mentions performances in Vienna, and these may have been occasions for performances of Haydn's clarinet music. Kozlowski joined the Russian army, rising to the rank of major in 1790, when he came to the attention of Prince Potemkin, who took him to St Petersburg as conductor of the Prince's band. It was probably during this period that Kozlowski wrote his 60 or so military marches. He was appointed Inspector of Music at the Imperial Theater and, in 1799, Director of the Court dance music. All his wind harmony seems to date from this period (c 1800-1810). He pioneered the use of the polonaise, and indeed one of his polonaises was used in Tchaikovsky's *Queen of Spades.* Kozlowski retired in 1821, after an attack of paralysis.

We have not been able to determine whether the works for 2fl 2cl 2hn 2bn JOK-1(-3) (all found in the Potocki Harmonie collection in PL-LA) are original works for winds or arrangements by F L Michel. The cl 1 part of JOK-1 is headed "Stucke [sic] in B," and possibly the 8 movements which follow (A-14.1a-A-14.2a) are also by Kozlowski. The use of flutes is typical of Russian wind music of this period.

JOK-1e, 2e These are choruses with winds from the tragedy *Fingal*, and are yet another sign of the impact and popularity of Ossian and the associated legends.

1. R Hellyer, Introduction to *Haydn: Hob.II.5,* citing Count Zinzendorf's memoirs.

KRAL, Johann Nepomuk His two marches (*Hoch-Hapsburg* and *Donaugruss*) are for the 49th kk Inf[ante]r[ie]. Reg[i]m[en]t v[on]. Hess.

KRASA, ( ) *(1760?) (Not Joseph Martin Kraus; probably one of the Chotek Harmonie)* The Missa in B♭ is a substantial work, probably dating from the 1790s.

KRECHLER (Krechter), F, Faknrich *(1780)* "Officer-cadet" Krechler, so far as one can deduce from surviving collections, was attached to the Fürstlich-Lobkowitz Corps. He may have led the Harmonie of Prince Joseph Franz Maximilian von Lobkowitz from c.1807, when Anton Wranizky moved to Vienna. Apart from five military pieces **FFK-1m,** Krechler's entire output appears to be arrangements and appropriations for winds. The influence of Triebensee's *Miscellannées de Musique* is strong. For several of his own collections, Krechler chose the same title and scoring (2ob 2cl 2hn 2bn, with ad lib cbn, tp), and he compiled two sets of pieces for the Lobkowitz Harmonie from the first five Oeuvres of Jahrgang I and Oeuvres 5, 6 of Jahrgang II. Krechler's collections *Auszug der besten Stücke aus verschiedene Opern* may have been intended for sale in manuscript, although the only known copies are in the Lobkovic archive. His arrangements in the Lobkovic collection show many pieces reused in different combinations. Krechler seems to have arranged regularly for the kk Hoftheater-Musik-Verlag from 1806 to 1816, and his works are found as far afield as Italy and Swabia. The Prince was a major investor in the firm, and Krechler may have made some of its anonymous arrangements. When the Prince died in 1816, and the Lobkowitz Harmonie closed, Krechler dropped out of sight. His own arrangements show flair, and exploit wide dynamic contrasts; often the forces drop to mere pairs of clarinets and bassoons.

FFK-2a *Harmonie, Oeuvre 1* Copies of this compilation from works by Haydn, Mayr and Paer are found in the Lobkovic collection in Prague and in the Haugewitz archives.

FFK-16a *Miscellannées [sic] pour Harmonie* The clarinet primo part bears Krechler's stamp. The parts bear many cuts and interpretation marks.

FFK-22a *Spontini: Fernand Cortez;* **FFK-23a** *Vogler: Samori* These are among the rare cases where a MS score (rather than just copies in parts) survives for Harmoniemusik. **FFK-22a** has piccolo and percussion parts added to the score, perhaps for use by the Prince's Turkische Musik.

FFK-1ad *Miselln [sic]* The majority of these arrangements of Gluck and I Umlauf may be drawn from Went's earlier arrangements.

KREITH, Carl (Carlo, Karl) *1748-1807* Remarkably little is known about this productive composer; he seems to have been a flautist. Some of his wind music was published by Eder, Vienna, between 1799 and 1806, including *Partitas* (Op 57, 58, 59, 60, 63, all 1802) and *Marches* (1799, without Opus number, and Op 95, c.1804). Eder's agents were Halm in Munich, Gayl & Hedler in Frankfurt, and Nägeli in Zurich. Kreith's March **CXK-1m** for the Wiener Scharfschützen Korps has two bars in which the oboe II part divides, so that the band would have been larger than first suggested. This march carries the dedication: "Seiner Durlaucht dem in Nieder ... u[nd] Vorder ... Oesterreich Commandierenden Herrn Generalen F: Z: M: Herzog Ferdinand von Württemberg." Kreith is easily underestimated; his works are good, without reaching great heights.

Other works of interest include *III Quatuors* Op 66 for fl cl hn bn, *Tre Terzetti* (2cl bn/vc; *Wiener Zeitung* [WZ 4 July 1801], and *12 Originalaufzüge für die kk Regimenter zu Pferd* (5tp, WZ 1 September 1802). Others, now lost, were advertized by Eder in the *Wiener Zeitung,* such as the *Partita in B[b]* for 2ob 2cl 2hn 2bn *(WZ 2 July 1806,* possibly **CXK-1** or **CXK-6**). *Der Trompetenstoss Andantino (The Trumpet sounding),* Op 51 (WZ 17 October 1801) is lost in the version for solo tp, 2ob 2cl 2hn 2bn, although there is a piano version (Eder, pn 176 c.1800). Likewise missing are the *Journal de musique militaire für Harmonie* (WZ 24 July 1805) and the *Regimentsmarsch für Harmonie* (WZ 1 September 1802) in 9 parts. The *Quintetto del'Opera Il Rè Theodoro (Paisiello)* (pn 267, 1803; WZ 7 September 1803) for 2fldam 2hn bn is his only wind harmony including flutes. He also wrote a *Marcia i morti,* Op 52 for 2ob 2cl 2hn 2bn db.

KREJČÍ, Iša *10 July 1904, Prague-6 March 1968, Prague* Conductor, music producer for Czechoslovak Radio from 1934 to 1945, and the composer of two *Concertinos* with winds, one for solo piano (1935), the other for solo violin (1936).

KREJČÍ, Miroslav *4 Nov 1891, Rychnov-1964, Prague* His *Sextet* Op 79 is scored for the unusual ensemble of 2cl bthn 2hn bn.

KRENEK (Křenek), Ernst *23 Aug 1900, Vienna-23 Dec 1991, Palm Springs, California* Krenek began his formal studies with Franz Schreker in Vienna in 1916 and, after his military service and completing a degree in philosophy, continued with Schreker in Berlin. At this time he was married to Anna Maria, daughter of Gustav and Alma Mahler. He held musical positions with the Kassel and Wiesbaden operas, and was music correspondent for the *Frankfurter Zeitung*. Krenek emigrated to America in 1938, where he has been increasingly recognized as a major composer. His *Deutsche Messe,* written in 1968 for SATB choir, unison congregation, cl(Bb) 2tb timp perc, was praised for its austerity, breadth of vision and stark beauty and drama. Apart from winning a number of musical prizes, Krenek was elected to the National Academy and Institute of Arts and Letters, New York, and received a number of Austrian distinctions.

Initially Krenek's reputation was determined largely by his jazz opera *Jonny spielt auf,* neither his best work nor his most typical. Krenek's writing for winds includes works for both smaller and larger ensembles. The smaller ensembles include the 1962 *Alpbach Quintett* (Op 180 is the quintet; for the ballet score Op 180a the quintet is joined by percussion). His works for wind orchestra deserve mention: the *Dream Sequence* Op 224 (1975-6) (Nightmare; Pleasant Dreams; Puzzle; Dream about Flying); *Sinfonie für Blasinstrumente und Schlagwerk* Op 34 (1926, Leipzig); *Drei lustige Märsche* (Three Merry Marches) Op 44 (1929, Baden-Baden) and *Kleine Blasmusik* Op 70a (1932, Frankfurt). The *Marches* and *Kleine Blasmusik* are recorded by the Louisville Orchestra on LS756 and Crest CB DNA77-4; the *Sinfonie* is on Thorofon MTH 341.

KREUTZER, Conradin (Konradin) *22 Nov 1780, Messkirch, Badenia-14 Dec 1849, Riga* He is best known for his operas like *Das Nachtlager von Granada,* from which famous marches were adapted, but he also wrote instrumental music (like the *VI Walzer und VI Trio* for winds) and his *Offertorium in Eb,* "Venite exultamus," for chorus and winds.

KREUTZER, Rudolphe *16 Nov 1766, Versailles-6 Jan 1831, Geneva* Violinist after whom Beethoven's sonata was named, and a member of a musical family. It is not clear whether or not he arranged his own *Ouverture de la journée de Marathon* for winds.

KRICKEL, ( ) The title of his *No 2 Missa Bohemica* implies there was another wind work, No 1. Krickel was associated with the small town of Kratochvilka in Moravia.

KRIEGER, Johann Philipp *26 Feb 1649, Nuremberg-6 Feb 1725, Weissenfels* Member of a family of German musicians. His *Lustige Feld-Musik* comprises well-written suites for oboes and bassoons.

KRISET, ( ) von *(1780)* Composer of *Harmonie Stück* [sic] in four movements, in the collection put together by Fendt (qv).

KRISTINUS, Carl Raimund *(1870)* Composer of published music for Corpus Christi c.1900-1910, long after the apparent peak in popularity for this music.

KROL, Bernhard *b 24 June 1920, Berlin* Horn player, educated in Berlin; a member of the Berlin Staatskapelle from 1945 to 1961, then of the South German Radio Orchestra from 1962. Krol's many works for winds include his *Konzertante Musik* for solo viola and octet, the *Linzer Harmoniemusik* for octet, and a *Missa brevis* for chorus and four horns. His *Kantate nach alten Weinachtslieder* is scored for soprano and baritone, 2ca 2bthn b-cl bn. Some of his works for winds and for organ are recorded on Audite 95 453.

KROMMER (KRAMÁŘ, Krommer-Kramář), Franz Vincent (František Vincenc) *27 Nov 1759, Kamenice, near Třebíč-8 Jan 1831 Vienna* A composer of major importance for his music for winds, and one who wrote some of the most idiomatic and original wind harmony in the late classical and early romantic periods.

Krommer's father, Jiří Kramář was an innkeeper, later Bürgermeister, in Kamenice, near Třebíč in southern Moravia. Franz Krommer showed early musical talent, though he was not especially precocious. This was reflected in his career, for he held only modest posts for long periods. Krommer moved to Turany in his midteens. It was here that his uncle, Antonín Mátyás Kramář (1742-1804), himself an experienced composer and an organist, gave Franz much of his formal musical training. A year spent in Vienna around 1785 must have given him ample time to take note of the way Mozart and others wrote for wind instruments. From Vienna, Krommer moved to Simontornya (about 50 miles south south west of Budapest) to direct the orchestra of Count Styrum-Limburg. It is often suggested that Krommer wrote his earliest wind works at this time, but his published wind works were certainly written later. After a few years, Krommer moved to Pécs (about 100 miles south south west of Budapest) as organist and choirmaster in the cathedral. He moved again in the early 1790s, first as conductor of Count Antal Károlyi's regimental band, then to Prince Anton Grassalkovics, presumably at Pressburg. The Prince was an enthusiast for wind harmony: he had employed Druschetzky (it is just possible that the terms of Druschetzky and Krommer with Grassalkovics overlapped) and he had made a serious effort to persuade Haydn to join him in 1790. Krommer wrote at least one work for winds at this time, for the A-Ee copy of **FVK-14.1** is dated "7ten May scripsit" and "Finis um 1794." His position with Grassalkovics must have been rewarding, and Krommer would have learned much from the experienced players. Unfortunately, the Prince died; from 1795, Krommer was without a settled position for about a decade.

Most of these difficult years seem to have been spent in Vienna, interrupted by journeys, including ones to his former home. In Vienna, he was known and respected. In a letter of 1798 (*HCRL/4* p 332) P Wranizky noted that Krommer played "oboe, fortepiano and cimbalon with great dexterity" as well as acknowledging his skill on the violin. At about this time, Krommer served briefly as Kapellmeister to Count Ignaz Fuchs, but his misfortunes continued (1, 2). Economies forced on the Vienna court by the Napoleonic Wars and their consequences led to his being refused a post as violinist in 1806. The modest post of Musical Director of the ballet at the Royal and Imperial Palace Theater (kk Hoftheater) in 1810 brought some relief but, after a second refusal of a position, Krommer took the position of Chamberlain (Kammertürhüter) at court (whereas the contemporary English court orchestra consisted of non-musicians in sinecures, the Viennese court had extra musicians in sinecures).

In his new position, Krommer toured with Emperor Franz I, visiting Paris and Padua in 1815 and Verona, Venice and Milan (where he became an Honorary Member of the Milan Conservatorio) in 1816. The visit to Paris had consequences: in 1818 he became an Honorary Member of the Paris Conservatoire, with the support of Antonin Reicha, and his major wind works were introduced, and later published again, in another major capital. It was also in 1818 that Krommer finally became Court Composer and Master of the Imperial Chamber Music in Vienna, a post he held until his death. The position did not prevent Krommer visiting his home again in 1827. It was in 1818 that Krommer became a member of the Vienna Gesellschaft der Musikfreunde, the society largely responsible for founding the Conservatorium a decade earlier. Krommer died aged 71. Early in the 19th century, the chances of a patient benefiting from a visit to a doctor were still limited. Krommer, it is said, died more from the cure than the illness.

Recent recordings of some of his orchestral and chamber music reinforce the high reputation of his wind music; his excellent masses have still to be revived. One might compare him with present-day composers like Malcolm Arnold: both produced wide ranges of orchestral, band and other music; they share great wit and professional skill; and they tend to be undervalued because their music is such a pleasure to play and hear. Krommer's wind music falls into four main groups. The unpublished octets (only one calling for a contrabassoon) appear to be early works, preceding the splendid series (13 works, starting with Op 45, all including contrabassoon) on which Krommer's reputation rests. A third group comprises smaller works, like the *C Minor Partita* (but not the spurious sextet published under his name). Finally there are the many works for military band, all marches apart from the arrangement of Haydn's *Volkslied*.

Krommer's major Harmonie series was first published in Vienna early in the 19th century, and appeared in Paris after his 1815 visit. Presumably they were written shortly before publication in Vienna. Style is an unreliable criterion for dating compositions, yet the operatic style of the slow movement of Op 67, hinting at the cavatinas of Bellini, can hardly have appeared before 1800. An important group (Op 57, 67, 69, 71, 73 and 76) are dedicated to Archduke Josef, Palatin of Hungary; the next, Op 77, is dedicated to the Emperor, Franz I, and was published close to the time when Krommer took up his position with the Imperial ballet (a later Italian edition is dedicated "Al celebre Maestro Rossini"). Nothing is certain about the band for which these pieces were written, but it was probably the Imperial Harmonie, rather than the wind bands of Károlyi or Grassalkovics, neither of which employed a contrabassoon.

FVK 1-13: The mature wind music, published in Krommer's lifetime The Viennese editions of Krommer's works can cause confusion because of mergers of the several publishers, namely (1) Bureau des Arts et d'Industrie (2) Chemische Druckerei or Magasin de l'Imprimerie Chimique, founded by Alois Senefelder in 1804, and (3) A Steiner. All are linked to some degree: Bureau des Arts et d'Industrie became Riedl in 1811; it was taken over by the successors of the Chemische Druckerei (where Siegmund Anton Steiner and Rochus Kranitzky became partners); Steiner became the sole owner in 1812. Tobias Haslinger (qv) joined Steiner as partner in 1814, becoming sole owner in 1826 and remaining so till his death in 1842. The same plate numbers are used for several editions (so one can spot an error in RISM, where I-Mc has switched Op 78 (K 2548) for Op 69 (K 2540). The plate numbers suggest that the Op 45 set is from around 1803 and the later ones from 1808 to 1810; this is supported by the existence of both Chemische Druckerei and Steiner editions, since the changeover occurred in 1809. Earlier dates seem most unlikely. Prior to the establishment of Bureau des Arts et d'Industrie, Krommer's music was published mainly outside Vienna, notably by André. Krommer gave opus numbers only to published works; confusions here arose occasionally when one opus number was given to different works published in different cities.

The autograph of Op 73 is in Paris, possibly a sample Krommer brought with him on his first visit to persuade Bochsa (who issued Op 73, Op 76 and Op 45 Nos 1, 2) to print the set. The Paris editions of Dufaut & Dubois (later, as it uses the address to which they moved in 1826) is of interest for its title pages. That for the oboe mainly gives publishing details, but notes the option of clarinets instead of oboes. The clarinet 1 title page has more revolutionary ideas, suggesting not only "...deux Bassons Trombone ou Contrabasse" but continuing "Il y a une partie de grande Flûte pour plusieurs des suites de/ cette collection et de grande Flûte en mi Bémol [Eb] pour les autres/ Arrangée par Mr MOUDRUX pour remplacer le 1er haut-Bois ou clarinette/ 2°. dans le 1ère 3ème et 13me suite il se trouve une partie de Trompette ad libitum/ ... 3°. Il sera préférable d'éxécuter la Partie de Trombone avec le Serpent, en Transposant." Another part reads "Serpent, Trombone ou Contrebasse"). Given Krommer's splendid use of the oboe, the substitution of flute or clarinet is sad. The idea of any but the very best trombonists negotiating the contrabassoon part is heart-rending, and the idea of an average trombonist doing so is mind-bending. It is hard to see how some passages could be played on trombone (e.g., the slurred chromatic passage in bars 39-41 of Op 77). Perhaps the French edition assumed that distance could heal the worst consequences.

The 13 published wind works contain splendid music, imaginative in rhythm and structure. Particularly memorable are the driving rhythms, the dramatic changes of key and sonority, and the vivacity and wit in these compositions. Even the newer dances sound completely natural; the polka which ends Op 69 (wrongly labelled "Rondo") is an early example, yet fully assimilated in its new setting. The magnificent Polonaise which ends Op 57 is surely one of the most exciting pieces for winds. Stylistically, Krommer can sound like a precursor of later opera composers, and the *scenas* of the Op 57 and Op 67 slow movements suggest Bellini and even Verdi; however, the Trio of Op 79 serves as a reminder that Schubert and Krommer were contemporaries.

Krommer's writing for the instruments is highly idiomatic, showing his experience as oboist and band director. He exploits technical developments too, as seen from the confident clarinet writing of Op 45 No 1, Op 71 and Op 78, and also in his use of the contrabassoon. Even the second horn has its solos, notably in Op 69, a useful reminder to composers that every player likes relief from accompanying parts.

FVK-1, -2, -3 *Partitas Op 45, No 1 in Bb, No 2 in Eb, No 3 in Bb*   All the Op 45 *Partitas* are recorded on Etcetera KTC1141. **FVK-1**, which contains some individual clarinet writing, is recorded on Supraphon SUA 59764 F and Supraphon 11 0097-1. The trumpet parts in this set are minimal, although that in **FVK-3** adds just the right touch as a surprise in the second half of the Trio. The so-called Op 45 *Parthia* recorded on Music & Arts CD691 is not, in fact, from this set, but is **FVK-2d**. The *Partitas* Nos 1 and 3 were arranged by Václav Havel in 1808 for 2cl 2hn 2bn and ad lib tp.

FVK-4 *Harmonie in F, Op 57*   Probably Krommer's finest wind composition, the final Polonaise bearing comparison with the very best wind music written. That great music is based on tension and release is simple to assert but very hard to put into practice. This work shows Krommer's clear grasp of the principle in a work bursting with wit and invention. The opening Allegro is full of boisterous good will as instruments toss phrases to and fro, and as sections dovetail through striking harmonic progressions. Krommer introduces the short rising and falling chromatic figures which reappear in the Minuet (descending only) and in the Polonaise (ascending only). The Minuet and Trio present an extended musical joke on the interplay of rhythm and pulse: having established an almost ponderous triple time in the Minuet, Krommer gradually shifts rhythmic units of the Trio to duple time (1-2, 3-1, 2-3) while keeping the original single pulse per bar (perhaps to tease "toetappers" in the audience); the Trio creeps back hesitantly to triple time for the reprise of the Minuet (it should be impossible for performers to miss the point here, yet, sadly, at least two recordings by distinguished ensembles miss it completely by pulling the tempo around). We have mentioned the operatic nature of the slow movement, a tour de force for the first oboe. What is so extraordinary is that, while looking forward to the long romantic melodies of Bellini, Krommer hints at that profundity which raises Mozart so much above other composers. The dark and sombre scoring of the opening has the seriousness of some of Mozart's Masonic works (not that the Krommer has any known Masonic links); tension builds through the minor-key cavatina until, after a series of pianissimo two-note figures, the accompaniment erupts into a fortissimo cadence, both a musical "surprise" and a comment on the emotional melodrama. The pianissimo repetitions which follow set the scene for a masterstroke, for the listener is led back to a final major-key reprise of the melody, with delicate exchanges between first oboe and first clarinet leading to the final cadence. The final Polonaise projects relentless energy, yet it is still a dance. All instruments display their virtuosity; false fugues appear and disappear, and tension is increased by ascending chromatic passages which hark back to the first movement. Especially notable is the sudden shift to the subdominant in a section dominated by the clarinets. This finale is hard to follow, so concert programs should be planned accordingly. Few works in the wind repertoire have this unity and consistent originality and quality. The work has been arranged extremely well by Havel for 2cl 2hn 2bn and ad lib tp.

Op 57 has been recorded well several times, in very different performances. The Prague Chamber Ensemble (Supraphon SUA 59703) has a very Czech style and sound, and a stupendous finale; the Nash Ensemble (CRD 1110) catches beautifully the operatic feel of the slow movement; there are fine performances by the Wind Soloists of the Chamber Orchestra of Europe (ASV COE812) and the Budapest Wind Ensemble on Naxos 8.553498; the Netherlands Wind Ensemble (Philips 9500 437, reissued as 412 362) give an immaculate, high-precision virtuoso reading, and the Sabine Meyer Ensemble's disc EMI CDC 7 54383 puts the work in focus alongside three other mature parthias.

FVK-5 *Harmonie in Bb Op 67*   Many Krommer works start dramatically, or even deceptively, and the false start of Op 67 is a good example: Krommer, like Haydn, was a skilled musical joker. Op 67 is recorded by the Nash Ensemble on CRD 3410. Havel arranged the work for 2cl 2hn 2bn and ad lib tp.

FVK-6 *Harmonie in Eb Op 69*   As with Op 45 No 2, it is the second horn who has most of the fun, indeed starting the work with a solo. The lyrical second movement is followed by a Menuetto exploiting wide leaps and a Trio whose rhythm, as so often in Krommer, is designed to trick the ear. It is recorded on Philips 9500 437. Havel arranged the work as for 2cl 2hn 2bn and ad lib tp.

FVK-7 *Partia in Dis (Eb) "La Chasse," Op 71*   The Finale has an Adagio introduction to "La Chasse", the movement which gives the work its name. Note the striking clarinet writing again, this time in the third (Andante Allegretto) movement. The Menuetto shows signs of being a furiant. It is recorded on Panton 11 0522 G, on Eurosound ES 46.442 and on EMI CDC 7 54383 and by the Budapest Wind Ensemble on Naxos 8.553498.

FVK-8 *Harmonie in Eb Op 73*   The autograph is in Paris in the Conservatoire collection of the Bibliothèque Nationale. Like Op 57, it ends with an excellent Polacca. There is a copy in Regensburg comprising the last two movements and an unidentified Andante; in this composite work, each movement is in a different key (Bb, F, C).

FVK-9 *Harmonie in C, Op 76*   A relatively straightforward work, but well worth playing; recorded by the Sabine Meyer Ensemble on EMI CDC 7 54383.

FVK-11 *Harmonie in Bb, Op 78*   Recorded by the Sabine Meyer Ensemble on EMI CDC 7 54383, and by the Budapest Wind Ensemble on Naxos 8.553498. There is virtuosic clarinet writing in the finale.

FVK-12 *Harmonie in Eb, Op 79*   Note the Schubertian character of the Trio, and the way (typical for Krommer) in which the slow movement takes unexpected turns. Recorded on Panton 110693 (Czech Philharmonic Winds), Philips 9500 437, reissued as 412362 (Netherlands Wind Ensemble) and CRD 3410 (Nash Ensemble).

FVK-13 *Harmonie in F, Op 83*   The first movement is in Krommer's more operatic style; the finale is worth waiting for.

FVK-14 to 27: Octets   These octets, unpublished in Krommer's lifetime, are to be found mainly in Donaueschingen, Regensburg and Prague. There are versions by Václav Havel for 2cl 2bn 2hn tp (his versions of **FVK-16, 17** date from c.1808) and Rosinack for 2ob cl bn (**FVK-14, 18, 20**). Rosinack often added articulation and phrasing to the D-DO copies. Dr Bastiaan Blomhert (personal communication 1995) notes that the D-Rtt MSS (**FVK-15, 17, 20.1, 21.2**) were either prepared or altered by Rosinack; these D-Rtt copies were purchased c.1820 (**FVK-14, 22** from Graf von Klenau; **FVK-15, 17, 20.1, 20.2, 23** from Scheffauer in Stuttgart, June 1820). There is strong circumstantial evidence that the 2cl 2hn 2bn versions of **FVK-19.1, 20.1** are the original form.

FVK-14 *Partita in Eb*   The MS parts in A-Ee have "7ten May scripsit" and "Finis um 1794" on the horn 1 part, so this may have been for the Károlyi or Grassalkovics bands.

FVK-18 *Partita in Eb*   The cbn part in the I-Mc copy of **FVK-18.1** (for 2ob 2cl 2bn 2hn cbn) seems to be a local addition; it merely doubles bn 2 when not resting. A note says "Manca la parte del Fagotto grande," later altered to "Fagottone." **FVK-18.2**, for 2cl 2hn 2bn, is one of the "lost Partittas" cited by Jerkowitz (3).

FVK-19 *Partita in Eb*   **FVK-19.1** 2ob 2cl 2hn 2bn; **FVK-19.2** 2cl 2hn 2bn. There is an arrangement by Rosinack (No 2 for 2cl hn bn) in D-DO. **FVK-19.2** is one of a set of four recorded by Consortium Classicum on Claves CD 50-9004, the others being **FVK-20.2**, **FVK-28** and **FVK-3d**. The work demands real virtuosity from all six players. The writing is so idiomatic in **FVK-19.2** that surely the sextet form is the original, with **FVK-19.1** an arrangement. The finale, a fast dance-like movement, includes a highly original passage using horns and bassoons to mimic bagpipe drones, while the clarinets mimic the chanters in unison, except that clarinet 1 has grace notes which simulate the yelps common in folk bagpipe playing. This passage seems to look forward even as far as Janáček. The MS of **FVK-19.1** in Brno is a copy by "George Bouraiche, ex Hautbois au premier Régement de Ligne, Abbaye à St Thomas le 5 Octobre 1817."

FVK-20 *Partita in Bb* **FVK-20.1** 2ob 2cl 2bn 2hn; **FVK-20.2** 2cl 2bn 2hn. **FVK-20.2** has been recorded by the Consortium Classicum on Claves CD 50-9004. As with **FVK-19.1**, **FVK-20.1** it is probable that the sextet version is the original form.

FVK-23 *Partita in Eb, "La Chasse"* 2ob 2cl 2bn 2hn. *La Chasse* is recorded on Supraphon SUA 1 11 0614. A broadcast by the Bournemouth Wind Quire included an extra Polonaise as finale; we are indebted to Mr Ian Lowe for identifying the source as a transcription made by Bohumír Koukal around 1972 from the CZ-Bm archive of the Haugwitz Harmonie. It appears that this polonaise is found in copies in D-DO and D-Rtt too, but not in that of the Kinský Harmonie in CZ-Pnm.

FVK-24 *Partita in Bb* 2ob 2cl 2bn 2hn. Recorded by the Collegium Musicum Pragense on Supraphon SUA 1111 2973 G. There is a 1799 string quintet version in A-Wn.

FVK-26 *Harmonie in Eb* The copy for 2ob 2cl 2hn 2bn from the Augustinian monastery in Brno is dated 5 October 1817, but the work is probably much earlier.

FVK-28 *Partita in C minor* Published by Supraphon from a manuscript dating from 1800, the Partita has been recorded by the Consortium Classicum on Telefunken EK6 35334, and again on Claves CD 50-9004. The C minor opening section is original; the rest of the work, though good, is much more conventional.

FVK-29 *Parthia, in Eb* This is one of the "lost" works cited (in this case wrongly, as Partitta in C minor) by Jerkowitz (3). Movements 1, 4 survive in parts by Havel c.1808. The titlepage lists cl I as "Clarinet Primo Concertanto."

FVK-31 *Parthia in Ab* 2cl(one marked clarinet concertanto) 2bn 2hn. It has been recorded by the Soloists of the the Brno Philharmonic/Drápela on Pronto 0 014.

FVK-34 *Parthia in Eb* J A Buchal's manuscript copy in PL-LA is dated "Wien den 1 May [1]803."

FVK-1c *Harmoniestücke für des Fronleichnams Umgänge* These four anonymous marches for 2ob 2cl 2hn 2bn cbn do not have an opus number. They are characteristic of Krommer, and were written for the 1829 Corpus Christi (Fronleichnamfeste) procession at Melk Abbey.

Krommer: Military Music Krommer's surviving military music consists of published works for octet plus trumpet, contrabassoon and sometimes Turkish percussion instruments. Parts even reached the Pennsylvania Moravians, though only isolated (and unidentifiable) individual band parts survive at US-BETm. Two items are arrangements.

FVK-1ma *Volkslied als Marsch für türkische Musik eingerichtet* (1827). A large-scale arrangement of Haydn's Austrian national anthem, "Gott erhalte Franz den Kaiser."

FVK-2ma *12 Märsche* The MS parts, probably issued by Traeg in 1804/1805, are of arrangements of marches by various composers (one is from Mozart's *La clemenza di Tito*). Krommer's name has been added to the title page at a later date, but the attribution is surely correct. One of the marches is possibly by Krommer. Four of the marches are recorded by Soloists of the Brno Philharmonic/Drápela on Pronto 0 014.

FVK-1m *Six Marches (F, Eb, C, Eb, F, Eb) Op 31* Nos 3, 4, 5 are recorded by the Budapest Wind Ensemble on Naxos 8.553498.

FVK-2m *Trois marches (F, E♭, E♭) Op 60*   We note that the Marches "Op 6" are this set, Op 60, with a (probably modern) typographical mishap.

FVK-6m *VI neue Regiments Harmonie Märsche nach dem geschwinderen Tempo*   These marches in faster tempo carry the note "Componirt und gewidmet den Löbl K auch K.K. 49e Linien-Infanterie-Regiment Baron v. Kerpen." The set dates from around 1807.

FVK-7.1m (-7.3m)   The set of *VI Märsche* in D-Rtt was purchased in 1820 from the estate of Graf von Klenau. Nos 1, 3 and 4 are Nos 6, 5 and 3, respectively, of Krommer's Op 31 set (**FVK-1m**), without a contrabassoon part; Nos 2, 5 and 6 do not match any known marches by Krommer, but are almost certainly authentic.

FVK-1mc   This march from the Lobkowitz Harmonie is found on the verso of the manuscript parts of Krommer's Op 82 march (**FVK-3m**). The scoring is the same.

FVK-1d *Partita in E♭*   One sextet published in editions both ancient and modern is spurious: Krommer himself felt it necessary to disown it in the press (4). The original was published by Peters (pn 1341); the error was compounded by Havel's arrangement of it as *Parthia No 6*.

FVK-2d *Partita in Dis (E♭)* 2ob 2cl 2hn 2bn. A two-horn concerto with formidable parts; the work is in three movements. The title page in D-Rtt states "Del Sig Schoen"; "Krommer" is added in pencil, and Krommer's name is given in the Gardemusik Katalog (Nr 34). However, the known wind music of Schoen dates from 1778-82, and only includes small oboe-led works. This work sounds more typical of the late 1780s or 1790s (indeed, if it is not by Krommer, one might have guessed either Cartellieri or Pleyel). The watermark shows the paper comes from North Italy and dates from 1775-1798. The work is recorded by the Triebensee Ensemble on Etcetera KTC1141 and the New York Harmonie Ensemble on Music & Arts CD 691.

FVK-3d *Sestetto Pastorale in E♭*   Recorded by the Consortium Classicum on Claves CD 50-9004, this work is notable for its use of a theme best known from the finale of Beethoven's *Pastoral Symphony* (1807-1808). The work is, in fact, Lickl's *Quintetto* **JGL-3,** though someone, perhaps Krommer, has added a second bassoon part (apparently different from the bassoon part added by Havel to the CZ-KRa version) and made minor changes to stress the resemblance to Beethoven. All these works may be based on a traditional tune; it was used by other composers, as in Lefèvre's **JXL-1mv;** and the same motif is cited by Szadrowsky in the 1868 *Jahrbuch des Schweizer Alpenclubs*.

FVK-4d(-11d) *Unpublished Mixed Octets*   A set of partittas for 2cl 2bthn 2hn 2bn 2vla is held at Regensburg (D-Rtt), the last bearing the title "De Lucile," perhaps implying that movements are taken from Grétry's opera. Given the existence of scores, and that the paper of the parts (from Joseph Anton Unold [Vnold]) dates from before 1785, it seems likely that the Thurn und Taxis regimental band acquired the works from the earlier Harmonie; they could be by someone like Croes or Schacht.

There are many further works dubiously attributed to Krommer. The anonymous works in the bound volumes at Kroměříž (CZ-KRa, A4451/R.I.21, Nos 9-14) are undoubtedly spurious, and may be by Hoffmeister.

1. See also *Hellyer* p 280, Othmar Wessely's article in *MGG*, J Raček's notes for Supraphon and John Warrack's notes on the recording IC-065-03-429Q.

2. Z Zouhar 1959 *František Vincenc Kramář: Vyberova Bibliographie;* Brno Univ Press.

3. *Thematische Verzeichnis* bey Jos Jerkowitz / Schasslowitz / den 1 July 1832. The MS, a catalog of works by many composers, is now in D-Mbs, Mus.Ms.6330.

4. Othmar Wessely, Die Musikforschung **13** 194. Krommer's notice is in *AMZ* of 1817.

KUBAT, Norbert *7 July 1881, Kolín-20 March 1966, Prague*   Czech violinist and pedagogue. **NYK-1** is in four movements, the first a *Fanfára*, dated 19 July 1931, for the dedication of the bells and organ at the church in Doubravka, in the suburbs of Plzeň. It is scored for the typical modern Czech band of 2cl 2tp 2flug 2tb. His *Kantáta* to a text by Jitty Zdeňka Honzíková (dated 25 October 1931) is for four-part chorus and winds, and was for the dedication of bells at the archdeaconal cathedral in Plzeň. It seems that the bells had names: Bartoloměje, Marie, Anny.

KUBÍČEK (Kubitschek), Adalbert *1776, Hodětín, near Tábor-26 Jan 1838, Brno* His works for the Augustinian monastery at Brno may be drawn from his own dance collections, possibly arranged by himself.

KUČERA, ( ) *(1820?)* His *5 Ländler für Musica Turca* include a *cimbasso*, a valved bass trombone sometimes employed in mid-19th century operas, such as Verdi's *Aida*.

KÜFFNER, Joseph (Josef) *31 Mar 1776, Würzburg-9 Sept 1856, Würzburg* A performer on clarinet, basset horn and violin, Küffner was Chamber Musician to the Würzburg court until 1802, when the bishopric was secularized and the state annexed to Bavaria. Between 1802 and 1805 he was a military bandmaster, composing much music for his band. When Würzburg became a grand duchy in 1805, Küffner returned to his previous post, but was pensioned off when the state was handed to Bavaria in 1815. His 15 Recueils of *Musique Turque* series for Les Fils de B Schott date from 1812-1818; most of his various *Pot-Pourris* are from 1822-26 or later. **JYK-5,** issued in 1828, includes four original movements and two arrangements (one of Weber's *Invitation to the Dance,* the other of Schubert, wrongly attributed to Beethoven). His Op 163 (**JYK-11**) is an arrangement of his own *Symphony No 4, Op 141.*

KULAK, J *(1770)* Kulak's name or initials as copyist are found on parts at Lancut, Poland, where he was a member of the Harmonie under Buchal. The arrangement of the ballet *Die Athenienische Tänzerin* by J Weigl, wrongly cataloged as Sedlak, has "Acomodato J Kulak Wien den Mai...[1]804" [sic] on the MS. His claim must be treated caution, for this version closely resembles anonymous ones in CZ-KRa, CZ-Pnm.

KULKA, Ignác (Ignaz) *(?1800)* Composer of pieces for fl 2cl 2hn bn; possibly composer (or arranger or copyist) of anonymous works over his signature.

KUNERTH, Johann (Jan) Leopold *27 Dec 1784, Huzová-8 Aug 1865, Kroměříž* His religious compositions are in the archive of the Collegiate Church of St Maurice (Chrám Sv Mořice), Kroměříž, and now in CZ-KRa.

KUNTZEN, Adolph Karl *22 Sept 1720, Wittenberg-1781, Lübeck* Harpsichordist, mainly based at the court of Mecklenburg-Schwerin.

KURKA, Robert *22 Dec 1921, Cicero, Illinois-12 Dec 1957, New York* His suite *The Good Soldier Schweik* is based on his opera, itself based on Hašek's classic character.

KURZWEIL (Kurtzweil), Franz *(1770)-1806 (?Vienna)* Two of his seven *Partitas* are sufficiently good to have been attributed to Rosetti and to Hoffmeister.

KUTTICH, Franz *(1800)* Possibly associated with the Augustinian monastery, Brno.

KVANDAL, Johann *b 8 Sept 1919, Oslo, Norway* Kvandal's two *Nonets* are recorded on Simax PSC 1037. The first was revised in 1990 from the 1946 *Octet in G, Dorian Mode* (for which the db was optional). The second, *Night Music,* written in 1981, is also recorded by the Queensland Wind Soloists on Brisbane Radio 4MBS-CD1.

KYPTA, Jan *30 Nov 1813, Borotín, near Tábor-5 Apr 1868, Telč* There are some fragmentary sets of parts from Telč, some of which may have been for winds alone.

L, Sig[nor] Composer of *6 Variations* for solo cl, 3bthn for the Clam Gallas Harmonie.

LABLER, František Xaver Martin *11 Nov 1805, Unhošť-15 Nov 1851, Prague* Labler's *IV Stationen,* **FML-1v,** were very popular in Bohemia, with known performances as late as 1872. The set was published, unlike most such music, though it was adapted locally.

LABURA, Jiří *b 3 April 1931, Soběslav* In his early career, Labura concentrated on choral music. One example is his 1964 cantata *Glagolitica,* based on Slavonic texts, for which the voices are accompanied by brass, percussion and organ. He later favored aleatoric and dodecaphonic techniques. His *Ottetto* **JRL-1** dates from 1987.

LACHNER, Franz *2 Apr 1803, Rain am Lech-29 Jan 1890, Munich* Bavarian pianist and conductor, contemporary of Schumann, friend of Schubert, and a composer who narrowly missed real distinction. His work ranged from a Bavarian National Anthem (since replaced) to symphonies. The autographs of three of Lachner's wind quintets are in D-Mbs. "Lachner's *Third Symphony* shows his combination of qualities with all its strengths and weaknesses" wrote Robert Schumann, "Great breadth, Italian cantilena, German detail, brilliant orchestration, commonplace rhythm" (1).

His *Octet,* Op 156 **FXL-1,** dates from 1850, a decade after Schumann's comments. The German detail and craftsmanship are still there; the songlike slow sections remain; the scale is large: it is a long work. Happily, the rhythms are more subtle; the Scherzo, in particular, is deftly handled. Lachner was one of the first to pair a single flute and a single oboe in wind harmony, a scoring later adopted by Nováček and Reinecke; Gounod does essentially the same. Probably Lachner wrote for the musicians he knew in the Munich Opera orchestra. The work opens with an Allegro moderato, rather like Schumann in style. The second movement, Adagio, is slow and sonorous, and can outstay its welcome, despite some splendid moments, like the brief excursion to F flat major. The Scherzo has a Krommer-like trio, ripe for use as a school song, and the finale, Allegro non troppo, is a rondo based on what sounds like a German folk song (which we have not been able to identify). Recorded by the Consortium Classicum/Klöcker on EMI I C 065 46310 and by the German Wind Soloists on Marco Polo 8.223356.

1. Robert Schumann (translated by F R Ritter) 1877 *Music and Musicians;* New York: Edward Schuberth and Co, p 55.

LACHNER, Ignaz *11 Sept 1807, Rain am Lech-24 Feb 1895, Hanover* Brother of Franz Lachner (qv) who held musical appointments in Vienna, Stuttgart (where he was Court Music Director), Munich, Hamburg, Stockholm and Frankfurt. His 1844 *Messe* was published in Stuttgart two years after he had moved to Munich.

LAHOTKA, Gábor *(1960)* His 5-movement *Suite Hongroise,* scored for 2ob ca 2hn, was written for the Ensemble Philidor; it includes an excellent Lamento.

LAMAN, Wim (Willem Fredrik) *b 1946* Laman studied philosophy and music history at Leiden, then musicology at Utrecht, but has had no formal composition training.

WIL-1 *Musica subtilior* for viola, 16 winds and bass drum (1976). Recorded by the Netherlands Wind Ensemble on Composers' Voice CV7804 (conducted Arie van Beek). The title comes from a comment in Jacob of Liège's *Speculum Musicae,* on strained relations between the ars nova and ars antiqua in the 14th century. Laman uses woodwinds and brass to point to similar contemporary strains, with the viola as a catalyst. Initial security passes to anxiety, then escape, then a "danse macabre," then weariness, but not resignation to "deafness of the mind." It lasts about 12 minutes.

LAMPE, Walther *28 April 1872, Leipzig-23 Jan 1964, Munich* The Op 7 *Serenade,* by this pupil of Humperdinck, is a symphonic, richly romantic work, well worth revival.

LANGE, Gustav Friedrich *22 Feb 1861, Fredrikshald-1889* The *Nonetto* is a pleasant early work of a composer better known for operettas and salon music.

LANGLÉ, Honoré François Marie *1741, Monaco-20 Sep 1807, Villiers le Bel, near Paris* A teacher in the École de Chant, in the section of the Gardes Françaises, his enthusiasm for the Revolution led him to dedicate a work to all the *sans-culottes* in France. *Pierre/HC* dismisses several of his works as mediocre.

LARSSON, Håken *b 7 Nov 1959, ?Sweden* His 1993 *Oktett* is for fl cl 2bn 2tp 2tb.

LAUBE, Antonín *13 Nov 1718, Most-24 Feb 1784, Hradčany, Prague* Choirmaster of St Vitus's Cathedral, Prague, from 1771, after Brixi. His *Parthien* seem to be earlier works for the Pachta Harmonie. Horns or oboes are tacet in all the Trios.

LAWTON, D *(1760)* Composer of a *March* for the Leeds Volunteers.

LAZZARI, Joseph Sylvio *30 Dec 1857, Bozen-18 June 1944, Surennes, Paris.* One of the first composers to exploit cinema effects in opera (1928). His *Octuor,* Op 20 (for fl ob 2cl 2hn 2bn; 1920) is dedicated to Taffanel and, as so often in works for that ensemble, Lazzari's work uses just one oboe.

LEACH, Thomas *(1770)*   Organist of Cheshunt, Herts, whose *Full Military Piece* was written for the Hatfield Royal Review, for which there was other music by Bridgeman.

LEFÈVRE, Jean Xavier *6 Mar 1763, Lausanne-9 Nov 1829, Paris*   Clarinettist, pupil of Michel Yost (qv), and Professor at the Paris Conservatoire from 1795 to 1825. His clarinet tutor dates from 1802.

LE FLEMING, Christopher *26 Feb 1908, Wimborne, Dorset, UK-19 June 1985, Woodbury, Devon, UK*   *Homage to Beatrix Potter* **CLF-1** was composed for a school piano pupil; in this version, Beatrix Potter's introduction wished "Good luck ... to those lucky little people who will play them some day." Le Fleming arranged the second book of the set for fl ob 2cl bn as a charming suite, dedicating it to "Peter Corlett and the five windplayers at St Edward's School, Oxford, who first performed these pieces." The movements are Mr Jeremy Fisher; The Flopsy Bunnies; Two Bad Mice; Mr Jackson calls on Mrs Tittlemouse; The Puddle-Ducks take a Walk; Samuel Whiskers and Anna Maria.

LEGRAND (Le Grand), Wilhelm (Guillaume) *5 Mar 1770, Zweibrücken-1845*   Composer or arranger of very many pieces now in D-Mbs. Thus the part-books **WYL-1** comprise 549 items for 2ob 2cl 2hn 2bn; after No 70, the ensemble changes to fl ob 2cl 2hn 2bn, sometimes with an extra fl, ob or bn. We believe that Legrand was the leader of the Harmonie for Maximilian I and Ludwig I in Munich; he probably joined the Harmonie c.1814. Many of his arrangements were what would then have been the older favorites.

LEHMANN, Friedrich Adolphe von *(1770)*   Counsellor of the Legation at Dessau, and previously in the Elector's infantry. His *6 Marches* are for use with full orchestra as entr'actes or for winds.

LEIBL, Carl *3 Sept 1784, Fussgonheim, Pfalz-4 Oct 1870, Cologne*   His cantata with winds was for the 1842 laying of a foundation stone for Cologne Cathedral, to start the project to link the chancel to the south front tower, filling a centuries-old gap.

LEITERMEYER, Fritz *b 4 Apr 1925, Vienna*   His Op 21 *Concerto for Violin and 21 Winds* won the 1963 *Österreichischen Staatspris.*

LENOT, Jacques *b 29 Aug 1945, St Jean-d'Angély, France*   Lenot's *Comme un loin* is for three groups of winds: fl ob bn; ca cl hn bn; a-fl(G) b-cl hn. It is dedicated to Sandro and Paulo Gorli, and was written for the Divertimento Ensemble.

LENZI, Carlo *1735, Azzone-1805, Bergamo*   Lenzi's choral music with winds (usually CATB 2ob 2hn bn) are primarily of texts for Corpus Christi; some of the parts have the mounting holes needed for outdoor performance. From 1767 to 1802 he was Maestro di Capella of the Basilica di S. Maria Maggiore, Bergamo.

LERCH, Vendelín *(1810) (attributed)*   The parts of this *Graduale Pastoralis* are dated 23 December 1844, and include keyed trumpets.

LEROY, Pierre *(1770)*   Lyons-based composer and publisher, who wrote 35 of the 74 items in the *Journal de Musique Militaire* published by him, and later by Leduc.

LESSARD, John Ayres *b 3 July 1920, San Francisco*   A pupil of Nadia Boulanger, often favoring a neoclassical approach. His *Octet* (fl cl 2hn bn 2tp b-tb) dates from 1952.

LESSEL, Franciszek (Franz) *(1780), Puławy, Warsaw-26 Dec 1838, Piotrków*   Lessel moved to Vienna in 1797 (about the same time as Neukomm), becoming Haydn's favorite pupil; his counterpoint exercises, with Haydn's corrections, are in the archives of the Warsaw Music Society. Lessel returned to Poland in 1810, and was employed by Prince Czartoryski until the Prince was forced to flee after the 1830-1831 uprising against the Czar. Lessel is said to have died of a broken heart soon after writing a *Requiem.* Consortium Classicum has recorded an attractive 5-movement work for 2cl 2hn 2bn db (perhaps **FYL-1** or **FLY-2**?) on EMI IC 185-30 663/67.

LESUEUR (Le Sueur), Jean François *15 Feb 1760, near Abbeville-6 Oct 1837, Paris* Composer, initially of choral music, later of opera (e.g., *Ossian ou les Bardes*); from 1786 Director of Music at Notre-Dame; later Professor at the École de la Garde Nationale and Inspector at the Conservatoire.

LEWIS, James *b 1938* **JML-1** *You Must Remember This* is one of the rare works which combines a jazz ensemble (solo a-sax vib e-bass drums) and wind ensemble. The wind ensemble uses E♭ clarinet, which is now rarely used outside symphonic bands.

LIBER, Anton Joseph *1732, Sulzbach, near Regensburg-1809, Regensburg* Probably a member of the Kapelle at Regensberg during its first period.

LICHTENTHAL, Peter *10 May 1780, Pressburg-18 Aug 1853, Milan* While Lichtenthal appears to have written just one work, he did prepare the scores of some of Krommer's works now in I-Mc; these have been misattributed as Krommer autographs.

LICKL (Lickel), Johann Georg *11 Apr 1769, Korneuburg, Austria-12 May 1843, Pécs, Hungary* Lickl studied with the organist Witzig at Korneuburg, then with Haydn and Albrechtsberger in Vienna. He became organist of the Leopoldstadt Carmelite Church. From 1789 to 1802, Lickl wrote music for plays and operas at Schikaneder's Theater auf der Weiden, Vienna. Presumably Lickl knew Mozart; his 1798 quartet for winds is wrongly attributed to Mozart (**WAM-20d**; qv for recordings). Lickl's *Trio* for cl hn bn was published by Eder in 1803. Around 1805 Lickl became Regenschor at Pécs, although he continued to write secular music, including an opera performed at the Leopoldstadt Theater, Vienna, in 1810. His *Quintetto* **JGL-3**, published in Vienna c.1808 with a single bassoon part, has had a second part added by at least two composers. Havel's extra part lies above the original bassoon part, indeed often above the rumblings of the second clarinet. The other version is recorded by Klöcker as Krommer's *Sestetto Pastorale* (Claves CD 50-9004), "Pastorale" because the theme of the opening movement's Allegretto is so close to that of the finale of Beethoven's *Pastoral Symphony,* first performed in Vienna in 1808. Both works might be based on Lefèvre's earlier *Hymne à l'Agriculture.* The version attributed to Krommer alters Lickl's original so as to enhance the resemblance. This is an attractive work, with some hints of Krommer's influence in the later movements. Horn 2 has an unusual written E below middle C.

LIEBERMANN, Rolf *b 14 Sept 1910, Zurich* Liebermann, later Director of the Paris Opéra, studied music under J Berr, Scherchen and V Vogel. His use of the twelve-tone system is sensuous, rather than austere. His *Capriccio* (Variations on a theme from the opera *Leonore 40/45*) for winds and percussion is dedicated to the Fondation Lamoureux and its Director, Igor Markevitch. The soprano part is wordless.

LIEBERSON, Peter *b 25 Oct 1946, New York* *Wind Messengers* **PXL-1** is scored unusually for 3fl 2ob 2cl 2b-cl 2hn 2bn. Its three movements are Breeze of Delight; Dragon's Thunder; Memory's Luminous Wind.

LILIEN, Ignacy *29 May 1897, L'vov-10 May 1964, The Hague* In addition to his *Sonatine apollinique,* there is an oratorio *Nyuk-Tsin* (The Perfect Jade) for soloists, male chorus, woodwinds, brass and percussion; it dates from 1961.

LILJEFORS, Ruben *30 Sept 1871, Uppsala-4 Mar 1936, Gävle, Sweden* His *Marionett-Ouverture* is scored for 2fl 2ob 2cl 2bn glock.

LINDPAINTNER, Peter Joseph *9 Dec 1791, Coblenz-21 Aug 1856, Constance* He was Kapellmeister in Stuttgart from 1819 until his death, gaining an outstanding reputation for his conducting. His music shows skill, rather than originality. His psalm setting with winds for the Confirmation of the Princesses Marie and Sophie von Württemberg in 1832 was also used for royal confirmations in 1837, and again in 1839.

LIQUORISH, William *(1770)* Composer who wrote for the Loyal Hampstead Association and for the First Regiment of Royal Tower Hamlets Militia. Today, these two parts of London are of strikingly different social character.

LISZT, Franz *22 Oct 1811, Raiding, Hungary-31 July 1886, Bayreuth* (See also under Raff). Apart from works for voices with winds, he wrote three marches, scored by others: the *Goethe March* (Raabe 433, transcribed by Ludwig for the Mollinary Infantry Regiment of Kecskemét) and two marches transcribed c.1870 by Strobl for his Budapest band (*Hungarian Coronation March*, Raabe 438; *Magyar gyors induló* [Hungarian quick march], Raabe 56). Strobl's band was based at the Üllöi Avenue barracks, Pest.

LIVERATI, Giovanni *27 March 1772, Bologna-18 Feb 1846, Florence* His setting of the *Seven Last Words* with winds was written c.1790 for San Francesco, Florence.

LÖWENSTEIN-WERTHEIM-FREUDENBERG, Carl (Ludwig) Friedrich, Erbprinz von *1783 -1849* Hereditary Prince at Wertheim, and composer and arranger of a large amount of wind music, mainly for 2cl 2hn 2bn or for tp 3hn tb, the typical small military band of the time. Much of his time must have been spent with the court Harmonie, for he built up a substantial and unique collection of wind music, some of which has been published wrongly as by Weber. For them, he transcribed the accompanying parts of concertante wind works. His collection includes a score, apparently in the Prince's hand, of a *Theme and 17 Variations* on *Don Giovanni's Menuetto*. This work shows its composer (whether the Prince or not) to be in complete command of writing for the capabilities of the varied wind instruments. The *Variations* show as well the virtuosity of the Wertheim players. There are solos for most instruments, including those for horn 2, for basset horn, and for two bassoons.

LOLLI, Antonio *c.1730, Bergamo-10 Aug 1802, Palermo* *Grove V* (Vol V p 368) suggests that Lolli wrote only a violin part for some works, and this was then corrected and the accompaniments added by another, unidentified, person.

LORENTZ, ( ) *(1740; active 1772)* Early works, comprising short, pleasant movements.

LORENTZEN, Bent *11 Feb 1935, Stenvad-1987* BZL-1 is a *Concerto* for alto saxophone with winds.

LORENZINI, Danilo *1952* His *Serenata in Forma di Variazioni su un Tema di Scriabin*, was written for I Fiati Italiana to mark the centenary of Stravinsky's birth. They first performed it in Turin in September 1982. It is dedicated to Paolo Castaldi.

LORENZITI, Bernardo *(1730)-after 1813 Paris* Violinist, active in 1764 at Kircheim.

LORTZING, Gustav Albert *23 Oct 1801, Berlin-21 Jan 1851, Berlin* Lortzing, who wrote some of the most popular German light operas, was also an actor and singer. His appointments included those at Detmold court theater (1826 to 1832), Leipzig (1833 to 1846), the Theater an der Wien (1846 to 1851; here he was co-conductor with Suppé) and finally in Berlin. Most of his wind music consists of choruses from stage works. For Detmold, these were for plays: GAL-1v for Schiller's *Wallersteins Lager*, and a *Tafelmusik* GAL-1e for Grabbe's *Don Juan und Faust* (analogous to that in Mozart's *Don Giovanni*). It is possible that the Detmold Harmonie played this music. He wrote more substantial works in Leipzig, such as *Undine*, an opera intended for Hamburg. The fascinating *Szenen auf Mozarts Leben* includes a quartet with 2cl 2hn 2bn GAL-3ve, for Constanza Mozart, Aloisia Lange, Valentin Adamberger, and Albrechtsberger; Mozart himself was a mere speaking role. GAL-2.1e was later expanded as GAL-2.2e to celebrate 50 years of the Berlin Urania theater company; this version includes the Marseillaise. His music for Vienna was again for stage plays (GAL-2v, GAL-5ve).

LOUDOVA, Ivana *b 8 Mar 1941, Chlumec nad Cidlinou* She studied composition with Kabaláč (qv) and Hlobil (qv) in Prague, then with Messiaen and Jolivet in Paris. Her work combines both traditional and New Music techniques. She has written concertos with wind orchestra, one for xylophone, marimba and vibraphone, the other for percussion. Her *Don Giovanni's Dream* IZL-1 was conceived to complement and extend Triebensee's octet arrangement of Mozart's *Don Giovanni*. In it, dreamlike solos alternate with more classical tuttis.

LOUEL, Jean Hippolyte Oscar *b 3 Jan 1914, Ostend* Winner of the 1943 Belgian Prix de Rome, and influenced by Ravel. From 1948, professor at the Brussels Conservatoire.

LOUIS, F, Chevalier *(1760) active c.1794-1835 (Paris)* "Chef de Musique au 1er Régiment de la Garde Royale", Louis was responsible for a number of works for winds, including a *Journal d'Harmonie* (1821-1823) in collaboration with Marchal, Münchs and Berr, and a *Journal de Musique Militaire* (1832-1835). As late as 1872, a march "par Louis et Münchs" (or, probably, simply from their journal) was published in what is clearly an arrangement for larger military band. In 1803, Louis arranged for winds Leseuer's *Marche séraphique*, which had been prepared for Napoleon's coronation.

LOWES, Ian *b 1947, Bishop Auckland, County Durham, UK* Horn player with the Bournemouth Sinfonietta; founder of the Bournemouth Wind Quire ("quire" is the old Dorsetshire name for a church wind band).

LUCAS, Charles *28 July 1808, Salisbury-30 Mar 1869, London* Lucas, composer, organist and cellist, was one of the very first pupils of the Royal Academy of Music, which he later headed. He was associated with the Royal Music for many years, first as a member of the band of Queen Adelaide (wife of William IV), then as Music Preceptor to the Duke of Cambridge, Prince George, and the Princess of Saxe-Weimar. The dedicatee of his *Septet* was Charles Nicholson, composer and flautist, who died in 1837, aged only 42. Presumably the *Septet* dates from between 1830, when Lucas joined Queen Adelaide's band, and 1837. If Nicholson had lived longer, perhaps his playing would have encouraged English wind music at a time when its popularity was waning.

CHL-1 *Septet* A single movement: an extended introduction in E♭ minor and an Allegretto in E♭ major. The manuscript shows clear signs of use: corrections and notes in pencil, and some altered horn flourishes. The work, for "flauto, oboe, due clarinetti, corno e due fagotti, Composed and Dedicated by C Lucas to C Nicholson, Esqre," is given with title and dedication in Italian on the flute part and in English on the others.

LUCKY, Štěpán *b 20 Jan 1919, Žilina* A member of an anti-fascist organization in 1939, he was arrested by the Nazis and sent to concentration camps. A serious injury in Buchenwald ended his promising career as a pianist. He studied in Prague, later becoming a music director for Czech Television. His music includes many scores for films and for radio and the theater, also three wind quintets and the 1980 *Musica collegialis* for 2ob 2cl 2hn 2bn tp db.

LUKÁŠ, Zdeněk *b 21 Aug 1928, Prague* Trained as a teacher, Lukáš founded a mixed choir in Plzeň, where he worked in the Czech Radio Studio. A powerful influence came from tutorials led by Kabaláč (qv), and Lukáš became a full-time composer from 1964. Influenced too by folk music, he makes imaginative use of modal ideas. *Musica ritmica* Op 51 is a concerto for percussion and 8 winds, dating from 1966. *Musica Boema* Op 137 (1978) comprises two symphonic movements for wind and percussion.

LULLY (Lulli), Jean Baptiste (Giovanni Battista) *28 Nov 1632, Florence-22 Mar 1687, Paris* (See also under Hotteterre) Lully rose from scullion to power in the French court, and especially to power over its opera and ballet, for which he wrote extensively. His death followed from an injury to his foot, stabbed with his own conductor's staff (which should encourage other conductors to show self-control). Lully's 1686 *Le Caroussel du Roy* would have been for one of the royal festivities noted in part 1. Music from his *Le mariage forcé* is recorded by the New York Kammermusiker Double Reed Ensemble/Illona Pederson on Dorian Recordings DOR-90189.

LUNDQUIST, Torbjörn Iwan *1920, ?Sweden* The symphonic sketch *Vindkraft (Wind power)* is an extended work for large wind ensemble. His *Arktis* is for symphonic band.

LUTOSLAWSKI, Witold *25 Jan 1913, Warsaw-7 Feb 1994, Warsaw* One of the major figures in Polish music, often using aleatoric techniques. His music with winds includes two *Fanfares* for winds and percussion, one for Louisville (1986), the other for the

University of Lancaster (1989), and his earlier (1962-63) *Trois Poèmes d'Henri Michaux* for 20-part mixed chorus, 16 winds, celesta, harp, 2 pianos and percussion.

LUTYENS, (Agnes) Elisabeth *9 July 1906, London-14 April 1983, London* Elisabeth Lutyens helped to introduce serial composition to England and, like the best twelve-tone composers (and unlike many others) she showed expressiveness and imagination, rather than the techniques used. In 1969, she was awarded the City of London Midsummer Prize and made a Dame Commander of the British Empire. She wrote much for wind, some outside our scope: the chamber opera *Isis and Osiris* (an extract is recorded by Jane Manning and Jane's Minstrels/Roger Montgomery on NMC NMCD011), vocal works with brass, works for four or fewer winds, and the 1960 *Wind Quintet*. Other works seem to be lost. The *Ballet for 9 Woodwind Instruments* was scrapped "as it was written when I was v[ery] ill & it is v[ery] bad!" (1). The *Suite Gauloise* was described as published many years ago, but probably not issued because of the publisher's concern for its possible use as background music (1). The publisher, Wolfe, tells us the music is out of print; whether it was ever issued or simply withheld is not clear. No copyright copy is deposited in the British Library.

EAL-1 *Symphonies, Op 46* Commissioned by the BBC for the 1961 Promenade Concerts. The scoring is similar to that of Hahn's *Le Bal de Béatrice d'Este*.

EAL-3 *Music for Wind, Op 60* Written in 1964. A divertissement made up of small-scale pieces, light in texture.

EAL-4 *The Rape of the Moone* Written in 1973. In eleven sections, mostly headed by literary references to the moon, starting and ending in a quiet stillness. It is one of the most impressive modern octets.

1. Letter from Elisabeth Lutyens to Marshall Stoneham, 1 December 1977.

LYADOV (Liadow, Lyadow), Anatoly Konstantinovich *11 May 1855, St Petersburg-28 Aug 1914, Novgorod* From a family of musicians, with whom he began studies; he then studied composition with Rimsky-Korsakov. With Balakirev and Liapunov, Lyadov did research on folksong for the Imperial Geographical Society. The *Musical Snuff-box (Une tabatière à musique)* is the composer's own arrangement of his piano pieces.

LYON, (Samuel) Thomas *1776-after 1824* *Sainsbury* notes he was "a very excellent performer on various instruments, and especially eminent on the bassoon." His early fame was as violist, and earned support from Attwood (himself a pupil of Mozart). Lyon was in great demand for chamber music. His published music is primarily for piano, but what he wrote ranged more widely, from opera to music for "juvenile performers."

MABELLINI, Teodulo *2 Apr 1817, Pistoia-10 Mar 1897, Florence* The son of a wind instrument maker, he studied in Florence, and later with Mercadante. He directed the Società Filarmonica in Florence from 1843 to 1880, and was *Maestro di Cappella* at the Arciducal court from 1847. From 1859 to 1887 he was Professor of composition at the Florence Conservatorio; he composed the *Lux Aeterna* for the collective requiem for Rossini organized by Verdi in 1869. Mabellini's *Sinfonia* **TEM-1** is attractive, with dramatic modulations and evident deep knowledge of counterpoint. Dating from the start of the revival of wind music, it is dedicated to the musical conservatories of Italy. *New Grove* mentions his marches and 6 waltzes for winds; these remain untraced.

McCABE, John *b 21 Apr 1939, Huyton, Lancs, UK* Distinguished pianist and composer of much orchestral and chamber music, and a *Concerto* for piano and wind quintet.

McGUIRE, Edward *b 15 Feb 1948, Glasgow* **EXM-1** *Wind Octet,* (1980). A University of Glasgow commission through the McEwan Bequest, it was first performed at the Festival of Scottish Chamber Music in 1980. It is a continuous movement, with Scottish musical elements, like Scotch snap rhythms and pibroch (a series of variations, possibly complex, often for bagpipe). The work grows from and returns to one sustained note.

MACKINTOSH (Macintosh), Robert *1745-1807* Composer of a *New March* for the Edinburgh Volunteers, c.1794.

McLEAN (MacLean), J M Composer "of the 29th [1st Worcestershire] Regiment." His works **JMM-1m, 2m** (Brighton Camp) are dedicated to the Prince of Wales; **JMM-3m, 4m** (Bagshot) are dedicated to the Earl of Harrington.

McPHEE, Colin *15 Mar 1901, Montreal-7 Jan 1964, Los Angeles* McPhee became a US citizen in 1939; he wrote varied music for winds, including a concerto for wind orchestra (1959). His 1928 *Concerto for Piano* **COM-1** is scored for pf solo, fl 2ob cl bn hn tpt tbn 2timp. It was recorded in 1973 by Grant Johannesen, with an ensemble conducted by Carlos Surinach (Composers' Recordings, Inc, CRI S-315).

MAGNALLI (Magnelli), Giuseppe *(active 1787-1845, Florence)* Most of Magnalli's works for winds are from 1792 to 1799. He accepted political changes, for his cantata *Gli Omaggi* is dedicated to Napoleon (dated 25 August 1809, Palazzo Pitti, Florence). In 1838 he was associated with the Cappella della Villa di Castello in Florence.

MAHLER, Gustav *7 July 1860, Kalist (Kaliště), Bohemia-18 May 1911, Vienna* Mahler's music shows his profound understanding of winds and their evocative power. In several works, notably the Rückert songs, there are long passages, indeed whole movements, for winds. His *Kindertotenlieder* shares the sentiments of the commonly-heard funeral songs with winds, and Mahler may well have been influenced by them.

MAHON, John *1746, Oxford?-1834, Dublin* Clarinettist (also playing violin and viola) and member (later bandmaster, c.1780) of the 3rd Regiment (Scots Guards). He was a member of a family of fine musicians associated with Salisbury. John Mahon played in Oxford in 1791 when Haydn received his doctorate. His *Slow and Quick Marches for The Oxford Association* were "approved by the Committee."

MAIER, L *(1750)* A flautist, active c.1782, whose *Parthia* **LXM-1** adds quart-fagott, 2tp timp to the standard octet. **LXM-2** *Parthia à 8 in C* (2 clarini 2ob 2hn 2bn) is the work cited in Hüschen's edition of Altenburg's *Trumpeters' and Kettledrummers' Art*, and here "clarini" surely means clarinets, not trumpets (see part 3).

MALEK, Jan *b 18 May 1938, Prague* Málek studied with Kabaláč in Prague, and then joined Czech Radio. He has had a long interest in folk music, and his music includes a *Concerto for Bagpipes*, a *Cantata potatorum (Drinkers' cantata)* for men's voices, brass and timpani, and *Tribute to Michelangelo's Hammer* for 5tp 5tb 5timp 5tam-tam, which won a 1975 UNESCO prize. His music for winds includes a cycle of four wind quintets *The Seasons of the Year* and *7 Studies* for wind and percussion (1964).

MALIPIERO, Gian Francesco *18 March 1882, Venice-1 Aug 1973, Treviso* Writer (of *The Orchestra* 1921), scholar (who has made editions of Monteverdi) and composer, whose output includes several wind quartets, like the *Sonata a Quattro* (1954, for fl ob cl bn) and the *Dialogo* (1956, also fl ob cl bn). His *Dialogo No 4* for wind quintet has been recorded by the Dennis Brain Wind Quintet (BBC REB 175). He wrote his *Serenata Mattutina à 10* (for fl ob cl 2bn 2hn 2va celesta; as in some 18th century works, violas are included too) in Asolo in September 1959. The composer's own comments emphasize the atmosphere of evening in the cloisters of St Francis at Sorrento on the Gulf of Naples, with the phosphorescent glow of the sea. Serenades, Malipiero says, are to be heard, not seen, and represent a world of secret sounds.

MANGOLD, Johann Wilhelm *19 Nov 1796, Darmstadt-23 May 1875, Darmstadt* It is likely that Mangold was a member of the Darmstadt Harmonie from 1830 to 1861. His wind music includes divertimentos, marches and works with voices.

MANKELL (Mankol(l), Mankol; formerly Mangold), Johann Hermann (Giovanni) *19 Nov 1763, Assia-4 Nov 1835, Karlskrona, Sweden* Mankell's music (much with the title *Divertissement*) is found in Zeist (where other, anonymous, music may be by him) and also in the archive of the Philharmonic Society, Bethlehem (US-BETm; "imported and sold G Willig, No 185 Market St. Philadelphia"). Both at Zeist and Bethlehem were communities of Moravian Brethren. The Zeist Harmonie seems to have had the "French" configuration 2fl 2cl 2hn 2bn, sometimes omitting the flutes.

MARCHAL, François *(1790)* "Chef de Musique de la 20e Légion" on the 1821 *Journal* with Louis and Münchs; elsewhere he is linked to the 13e Régiment d'Infanterie Légère. His absence from later journal collaborations suggests he died c.1821.

MAROS, Miklós *b 14 Nov 1943, ?Hungary (now resident in Sweden)* Most of his wind works for winds are for large bands; *Aurora* is for double wind quintet and wind band.

MARPURG, Wilhelm *(1790)-6 Aug 1836, Detmold* Active with the Lippe Kapelle from 1826, for whom he made arrangements of Küffner, Bellini, Auber and others.

MARSH, Roger Michael *b 10 Dec 1949, Bournemouth* *Point-to-Point* (1979) is for standard octet; *Jesters for Sicks* [sic] (1972) omits the horns. Marsh has also written *Music for Piano and Winds* (pf, fl/pic cl cl/b-cl hn bn tp tb tu 2perc).

MARTEAU, Henri *31 March 1874, Rheims-3 Oct 1934, Lichtenberg* Violinist who premiered Reger's *Violin Concerto;* he succeeded Joachim at the Berlin Hochschule.

MARTIN, Frank *15 Sept 1890, Geneva-21 Nov 1974, Naarden, Holland* A resident in Paris for many years. His other works involving winds include a *Concerto for seven winds* (fl ob cl hn bn tp tb) and orchestra. *La ballade pour alto,* **FYM-1** is one of Martin's last works, commissioned in 1972 by the Salzburg Mozarteum, which wanted a work for a Mozart Week. The title "ballade" was used by Martin for previous works for saxophone, for flute, for trombone, for piano, and for cello. That for viola had its first performance was on 20 January 1973 with Ron Golan as soloist; its success was such that the whole piece was encored. The *Wiener Zeitung* critic described it as "a masterpiece in its very conception," remarking that "this truly beautiful music" had "great formal purity with highly distinctive harmonies, shot through with that archaic streak so characteristic of Martin." It was recorded by Menuhin, with the Menuhin Festival Orchestra under Edmond de Stoutz (number not known).

MARTINI, Giovanni (Jean) (pseudonym of Johann Paul Aegidius SCHWARTZENDORF, also known as il Tedesco) *1 Sept 1741, Freystadt, Bavaria-10 Feb 1816, Paris* Organist and composer best known for his *Plaisir d'amour.* In the 1760s he won a prize for the best march for the Swiss Guards. He was Professor at the Paris Conservatoire from 1798 to 1802, when he was apparently expelled by Méhul and Catel.

MARTINŮ, Bohuslav *8 Dec 1890 Polička, eastern Bohemia-28 Aug 1959, Liestal, near Basle* Martinů was born in a belfry, his father being church watchman as well as a shoemaker. Although he was a precocious musician, his unwillingness to accept the discipline of a traditional musical education led him to be expelled from the Prague Conservatory twice. He lived in Paris for many years, in poverty despite occasional windfalls, such as the Coolidge Prize of 1932. Martinů eventually reached the United States in 1941, where he remained for the duration of World War II (1, 2, 3).

BXM-1. *Concertino for Cello and Winds (H143)* The *Concertino* was written in Paris in 1924 for the Dutch cellist Maurits Frank. In three movements, the slow middle movement follows directly from the first, and the work ends in an impressive cadenza before the C minor coda. Rhythmically ingenious, with jazz influence, the work is a close contemporary of Ibert's *Cello Concerto,* also with winds. Recorded by Navarra (soloist) with Turnovský on Supraphon 0(1) 40 0101, Večtomov (soloist) with Košler on Supraphon SUA 50877, with Vajnár on Supraphon 1 10 2084, and by Wallfisch/Czech Philharmonic Orchestra/Bělohlávek on Chandos CHAN 9015.

BXM-2. *Sextet (H174)* Another of Martinů's jazz-inspired works (like his 1919 *Cat's Foxtrot,* written for the band of his home town). Written rapidly in four days in 1929, it comprises a Prelude, Adagio, Scherzo, Blues, and Finale. It is recorded by Hubička with members of the Czech Nonet on Supraphon 1 10 1014 and by the Prague Wind

Quintet with Panenka, on Supraphon 110 1014 and 111 1177.

BXM-1v. *Field Mass "La messe aux champs d'honneur"* (*H279*)   The *Field Mass* was composed in Paris after the German takeover of Czechoslovakia, when the threat to France, his home for years, was becoming clear. Scored for winds, baritone solo and chorus, it is dedicated to Czech army volunteers on the French front (Československým dobrovolnikûm na francouzské frontě). There are five movements, two of them orchestral: the opening introduction and the third movement, an interlude. The text is from the psalms (the fourth movement is Psalm 44) and the poems of Jiří Mucha, not the usual Mass text. The choral writing shows Eastern European influences, enhanced by colourful use of percussion. The effect overall is both austere and dramatic, suiting either concert or open-air performance. It is recorded by Šrubař with the Czech Philharmonic/Liška (Supraphon DV 5611), Souček and the Moravian Instrumentální Soubor/Reznícek (Panton 8112 0374), Zítek and the Czech Philharmonic Chorus and Orchestra/Mackerras (Supraphon C37-7735, previously 1112 3576) and by Zítek with the Czech Philharmonic/Neumann (Supraphon [Panton] 81100124).

Soon after writing this work, Martinů planned a military march for the Czech Division in France. It does not survive, if it was ever written. We mention the unusual *Chamber Cantata: The Legend of the Smoke from the Potato Fires H360,* as it may appeal to wind ensembles. Written in Rome in 1956 to a text by Miloslav Bureš, and dedicated to Mrs Frances Ježek, it is the third of a series of cantatas which invoke the seasons in turn. All three are recorded on Supraphon 11 0767 2 231.

1. Harry Halbreich 1968 *Bohuslav Martinů: Werkverzeichnis, Dokumentation und Biographie;* Atlantis. Halbreich's H numbers (like H360) are used here.
2. Brian Large 1975 *Martinů;* London: Duckworth.
3. Blanka Červinková, Svatava Barančicová, Eva Grubauerová, Ludmilla Pažoutová and Marie Valtrová 1990 *Bohuslav Martinů: Bibliograficky Katalog;* Prague: Panton.

MARTÍN Y SOLER, Vicente *18 June 1754, Valencia, Spain-30 Jan 1856, St Petersburg* Composer of successful operas, notably *Una cosa rara.* He succeeded Sarti as court composer to Catherine the Great. The wind works under his name may be arranged.

MARTLAND, Steve *b 1958, Liverpool* Martland studied at Liverpool University, then with Louis Andriessen (brother of Jurriaan Andriessen, qv). Although he is a composer whose view of the musical establishment has given him an image as the "hard man of classical music" (*The Times,* 26 Sept 1994), his arrangements show great respect for Mozart. There are versions of K.375 and K.388 (which we gather, but have not verified, differ only modestly from the originals) and *Wolf-gang,* arrangements of six operatic arias, two each from *Don Giovanni* (one is the "Catalog" aria), *Die Zauberflöte,* and *Le Nozze di Figaro* (one is "Non più andrai"). These arrangements are in the spirit of the originals, but with greater instrumental freedom than, say, Went had. Adding soprano saxophone, cor anglais and bass clarinet to the standard 2ob 2cl 2hn 2bn allows nice touches, such as the saxophone in the "Catalog" aria. All these arrangements were recorded (Factory FACT 406c) but the recording was withdrawn after a few months.

MARX, Karl Julius *12 Nov 1897, Munich-8 May 1985, Stuttgart* From 1922, Director of the Vienna Conservatory; especially respected for his songs.

MAŠEK (Mashek, Maschek), Paul (Pavel) Lambert *14 Sept 1761, Zvíkovec-22 Nov 1826, Vienna* Younger brother of Vincenc Mašek, he was also a pupil of his father. Paul Mašek settled in Vienna in 1794, and became known as pianist and glass harmonica player. He wrote two operas, cantatas, much keyboard music, and even a collection for two flutes. Mašek's major band works celebrate the downfall of Napoleon in 1813 and 1814. Thus **PLM-1** (8 movements) describes the defeat of the French armies near Leipzig on 18 October 1813 by Austrian and Russian armies under Prince Schwarzenberg; **PLM-2** describes the approach to Paris and entry by the Austrian,

German and Russian forces in March and April 1814 (there are two distinct scorings of this work, one in 12 movements, the other in 15 movements); **PLM-3** describes the triumphant return to Vienna in June 1814, and is in 9 movements. The large band in **PLM-1** can be regarded as a Harmonie component (2ob 2cl[C] 2hn 2bn cbn tp), which sometimes plays alone, and a Turkish instruments component (pic 2fl cl[F] b-tb serp perc) which only plays with the Harmonie. **PLM-2.2** uses only the Harmonie component.

PLM-4 (-9)   A set of six *Partitte* for 2ob 2cl 2hn 2bn, originally owned by Haydn, and passing to Prince Nicolaus Esterházy on Haydn's death.

PLM-2a   Mašek's arrangement of J Weigl's *Die Athenienische Tänzerin* suggests he had trouble with the texture. The oboes are tacet in No 2, and bn 2 and cbn (which have only a handful of notes *divisi* in total) have extended rests in Nos 6, 8 and 10.

MAŠEK (Maschek, Machek), Václav Vincenc (Vincent, Winzenz) *5 April 1755 Zvíkovec, W Bohemia-15 Nov 1831 Prague*   Mašek (1) was the son of a schoolmaster and brother of Paul Lambert Mašek (qv); like his brother, he was a glass harmonica virtuoso. Vincenc Mašek's wife, Johanna was an excellent pianist; their son Kaspar conducted a military band in Russia. The family talents may be judged from Vincenc Mašek's wind music, for it is only rarely of a virtuoso type. The various concertos for keyboards and winds are also rather simple, for instance, both in the keyboard parts and in the accompanying winds, which rarely play independently. These works, which contribute more to the literature for several harpsichords than to that for winds, are in CZ-Pnm and the archives of Count Ernst Pachta of Rayhofen, at Cítoliby, northern Bohemia. We cannot but repeat the rumour that the number of players was designed to match the number of members of Mašek's expanding large family. Mašek studied composition under Josef Seger (like Pichl, Mysliveček and J Kozeluch) and piano under F X Dušek (like Kozeluch). He was then Secretary to the Count of Vtrba, and repetiteur to the Estates Theatre. Mašek and his wife travelled widely, with tours extending as far as Berlin and Copenhagen. He then returned to Prague, where he remained as choirmaster of St Nicholas, in the Lesser Town, until his death.

VVM-1 *Concerto for 3 Harpsichords in D,* 2ob 2cl 2hn bn 3hpcd   The most attractive of Mašek's concertos, advertized by Traeg in the *Wiener Zeitung,* 1796. Performances are bedevilled by the problem of bringing three harpsichords in tune together. The instruments should allow scope for a wide range of registrations, and it helps if the bassoon part is doubled. Recorded by Hala, Bilek and Kozina, with the Collegium Musicum Pragense under František Vajnár on Supraphon SUA 1 11 1839.

VVM-4(-6) *Partitas (A, Dis (Eb), D)* for 2cl 2bn 2hn hpchd.   Lightweight works, ideal if your harpsichordist feels left out. All are recorded on Supraphon SUA 1 11 2424.

VVM-7 *Serenata in Dis "a due chori"*   Recorded on Supraphon SUA 59764 and on Supraphon 11 0097-1 031. this Serenata exploits two wind choirs, the main choir comprising (2cl 2hn bn), the other (2ob 2hn bn) as echo. Perhaps the early performances combined the Clam-Gallas and Pachta Harmonies.

VVM-9.1 *Partitta*   Interesting, partly because horn 1 has to play a reasonably simple trumpet part in movements 1, 3, reverting to horn only in the central Adagio.

VVM-10, 11 *Serenades in Eb*   These form a pair. **VVM-11** is in four movements, the last a Romance with a slow introduction and two trio sections; it is recorded on Supraphon SUA 59764. In the Regensburg manuscript, purchased from the estate of Graf von Klenau, the first three movements of **VVM-10** and the last three movements of **VVM-9** constitute a single *Parthia.*

VVM-15 *Allegretto con Variazione*   Possibly composed for his concerts in Berlin in 1787 (2 p 13). The theme is that used for his variations for cembalo, 2vl basso (1785-87).

VVM-16 *Notturno in F*   This *Notturno* (not a common title) is not the *Notturno in F* advertized in Breitkopf's Supplement Catalog XVI (1785-87).

The format and handwriting of the Partitas from the Pachta Harmonie show they comprise different sets. The main groups are: (a) **VVM-20(-22), 40(-43)**; (b) **VVM-23, 24, 26, 35**; (c) **VVM-25, 28(-34), 36(-39)**. One of these works, **VVM-31** *Partita, in D*, is recorded on Supraphon SUA 1111 2616 (which calls it Partita Pastoralis); it uses the carol "Christ the Lord is Born" ("Narodil se Kristus Pán").

VVM-1v to VVM-4v *Stationes; Pange lingua; Leichlied; Adorare* Of these, **VVM-1v** is from the Klášterec collection, **VVM-1v** and **VVM-4v** may have been for St Nicholas in the Malá Strana (Lesser Town) Prague, and the *Adorare* **VVM-4v** also turns up in the Pachta collection with the text "Salve Regina."
1. A Myslík 1981 Musica Antiqua Bohemica vol 81.
2. J Mikuláš 1995 *Vincenz Maschek (1755-1831) Ausstellung zum 240 Geburtstag des bedeutenden Prager Musikers;* Prague, Národní muzeum Praha - Muzeum české hudby.

MASSIAS, Gérard *b 25 May 1933, Paris* Composer of *Concert bref* for piano and winds.

MASSIS, Amable *b 2 Jun 1893, Cambrai-10 June 1980, Troyes* His *Ballade* is for solo violin, winds and piano.

MAŠTALÍŘ, Jan *1 May 1906, Karviná-22 May 1988, Prague* His 1975 *Sonatina* is a work for fl 2ob 2cl 2hn 2bn lasting 14 minutes.

MAŤATKO (Matatko), Jan (Johann) *(1780)* Local musician and arranger at Langenbruck (now Dlouhý Most, northern Bohemia), c.1810.

MATIEGKA, Wenzel Thomas *baptized 6 July 1773 Choceň-29 Jan 1830, Vienna* Guitarist and composer who trained at Kroměříž, where he is said to have been Kapellmeister. Schubert arranged his Op 21 *Trio* as a quartet. Probably he had links with the Kapelle at Rajhrad, Moravia. He wrote a funeral song with winds.

MATOUŠ, ( ) *(1760)* His *Parthia ex Dis* **XXM-1** for 2cl 2hn bn is recorded by the Prague Mozart Trio on Multisonic 31 0250-2.

MATOUŠEK, Lukáš *b 29 May 1943, Prague* A clarinet student in Prague, later taking private lessons in composition from Kabeláč (qv). Matoušek continues to play clarinet and authentic instruments; he has a keen interest too in early music, and this is joined by improvisatory components in his music. His music for winds includes a *Concerto for Percussion and Winds* (1967), *Music for Bayreuth* (1966), an *Invention* for 10 winds, and his 1962 *Garden Music* for 12 winds. He has also written a wind quintet (1987), and *Recollections for Mr Sudek* (1979), a work for brass sextet.

MATTHEWS, Colin *b 13 Feb 1946, London* His work *To Compose Without the Least Knowledge of Music* is written for same ensemble (fl ob cl b-cl hn bn) as Janaček's *Mládí*. The work exploits Mozart's *Musical Dice Game* (discussed under KOEHLER).

MATYÁŠ (Matias, Matiaš), Mikoláš (Nikolas) *(1820)* Arranger of music by Donizetti (1851; *La fille du régiment*) and Verdi (*Nabucodonosor; Alzira*) for Česká Třebová.

MAW, (John) Nicholas *b 5 Nov 1935, Grantham, UK* Composer of another successor to Mozart's *Musical Dice Game,* here scored for the forces of Stravinsky's *Octet* (see KOEHLER regarding composing games).

MAYER (Mayer), Franz *(1750)* Clarinettist active from 1775 to 1779, and composer at Kroměříž; he wrote five *Parthien*.

MAYR (Mayer, Mair), Johann Simon (Giovanni Simone) *14 June 1763, Mendorf, Ingolstadt-2 Dec 1845, Bergamo* Mayr was respected during his lifetime both for his music and his charity. His father, Josef Mayr, was his first music teacher, but encouraged him to study canon law and theology too. Johann Simon found time to become familiar with the organ and many orchestral instruments. In 1786, the Swiss Baron von Bassus took Mayr to Italy, where he worked under Carlo Lenzi (qv) at Bergamo before his longer and more immediately profitable residence in Venice. There he studied with Ferdinando Bertoni (qv), Maestro di Cappella at St Mark's, while earning his living as a violist in the orchestra of the Teatro della Fenice. Mayr's first opera was produced in 1794. His subsequent operas won performances as far afield as London and Paris. In 1802 Mayr became Master of Music at Santa Maria Maggiore in Bergamo. Despite tempting offers, like Napoleon's invitation to take charge of the theaters and concerts in Paris, Mayr remained in Bergamo for the rest of his life (1, 2). There, he founded the Liceo Musicale in 1805, and provided two hostels for aged musicians and their families, a most practical gift in an age where even the famous could die in poverty. The best known example of Mayr's kindness is probably the free tuition he gave to Donizetti, a native of Bergamo.

Mayr was not a simple player who wrote to spin out his repertoire, nor a publisher cashing in on current demand. He was one of the best opera composers between Mozart and Rossini. He admired Haydn and Mozart, introduced Haydn's *Creation* to Italy and wrote an important memoir on Haydn. Nor was Mayr a conservative, for his operas lead towards Rossini's and Donizetti's. The operas have special features, like extensive clarinet and horn obbligatos, so one might expect significant wind music. Little is published, but the few recent recordings and broadcasts point to some excellent writing. Some of Mayr's works once listed as incomplete (1, 2) are in fact self-contained single movements. The numbers *xyzA* (e.g. *529A*) are those of Allitt (2); *F.abc* (e.g. *F.106*) is the number in the Faldone collection in I-BGc (3).

JSM-4 An untitled movement for pic pic-cl 2cbn serp 3tb b-dr. Haydn's *Creation* also exploited enterprising combinations of very high and very low-pitched instruments.

JSM-8 *(534A) Divertimento: Suite di 8 Pezzi, E♭* These are certainly not independent Septets, as listed by Allitt, nor does his scoring agree with the autograph (F.252). The work is recorded on Italia ITL 700100 (as *Divertimento*); only seven movements are listed on the sleeve notes, but eight are played. This is a serenade in the outdoor style, with some most attractive movements. The clarinet parts are in B♭, although the autograph score says E♭.

JSM-13.1 *(533A) Suonate [sic] in E♭* The viola noted in the Bergamo Catalog (3) is not found in this autograph. The *Sonate*, in five movements, is recorded on Italia ITL 700100 (where it is called *Divertimento*). An interesting outdoor type of serenade, with rich-sounding slow movements and delightful use of the basset horn. The autograph makes it clear that these are not 8 separate sonatas "a sei" as listed by Allitt.

JSM-14,-15 *(?543A) Sextuor Op 9 Nos I, II* These works for 2cl 2bn 2hn were published in Mayr's lifetime, but are not listed explicitly in Allitt. The manuscript in D-HR for 2ob 2hn 2bn is a transcription which reverses the numbers (this confusion is easy to understand because the Gombart edition used the same title page for both works, merely altering I to II and spelling his name "Mair"; the titlepage of II therefore shows pn 423, rather than the correct pn 465). No II has a somewhat conventional first movement, but shows imaginative use of the bassoons; the attractive Minuet and Trio would have been enjoyed by Haydn; the slow movement is effectively a set of variations, and the finale, an Allemande, is delightful despite its reminders of the music of the better beer gardens. We believe the octet 543A for 2ob 2cl 2bn 2tp, given by Allitt as H-Bmm [sic], is simply the H-Bn copy of Op 9 No II, since an extensive search of the catalogs in Budapest (with the help of RISM collaborator Dr Robert Murányi) failed to reveal any other Mayr wind music.

JSM-16 *(536A) Sestetto in Si Bémol* "Dono della S.a.M. Chiesa Cernvich." A theme and 12 complicated variations (and not just an "Andante"), with a final 6/8 Allegro.

JSM-1m(t) *(532A) Marcia lugubre, C minor (E♭)* The scoring given in our *Catalog* volume is taken from the autograph score, which differs from that given elsewhere (2, 3). The parts show some differences: the horns are marked "con sordini", the timpani "Coperti", and there are extra parts for pic (ottavino), 2vla 2vc vlne.

Mayr's output includes many works for wind which lie outside our present scope.

Some small works for three or four solo winds (530A *Bagatelles* "a quattro" for fl cl hn bn, I-Mc, and *Bagatelles* for fl cl bn [Kneusslin 1971]) are essentially half-harmony.

There is a collection of 19 works and 2 fragments in Bergamo by Mayr for voices and winds. The *Laudate Dominum* JSM-1v also exists in a version for orchestra. In JSM-6v, *Domine ad adjuvandum,* oboes may replace clarinets, according to a note apparently in Mayr's hand. The C minor *Miserere* JSM-9v is of interest for two reasons: it is that which Donizetti rescored in 1822, and it was probably the work performed at Mayr's funeral in 1845. Bergamo has further works outside our scope, being for brass ensemble (two settings of *O Salutaris Hostia)* or for groups of solo winds *(Alma redemptoris,* F.15; *Missa di requiem,* F.306; *Averte faciem,* F.216; *Miserere,* F.214; *Viderunt te,* F.11; *Graduale per S Luigi,* F.72; *Domine ad ad[juvandum]* and *Magnificat,* F.139; *Pange lingua,* F.16; *O Salutaris Hostia,* F.15), sometimes with lower strings or organ. Sometimes, full orchestral versions are found of the same work. There are also arrangements of a *Credo* by Haydn (F.315) and a *Libera me* by Seyfried (F.47).

1. William Ashbrook 1982 *Donizetti and His Operas;* Cambridge: Cambridge University Press. Page 674 (note 25) lists appointments Mayr refused.

2. J S Allitt 1989 *Johann Simon Mayr;* Shaftsbury, Dorset, UK: Element Books.

3. Arrigo Gazzaniga 1963 *Fondo Musicale G S Mayr;* Bergamo: Amministrazione Provinciale. Note that a particular Faldone number may relate to more than one work.

4. Marino Anesa 1988 *Musica in Piazza;* Bergamo: Sistema Bibliotecario Urbano.

MAYR, Placidus, O.S.B. (Order of St Benedict) *(1770, Switzerland)* Active from 1802 to 1813, he is styled on one MS as a famous organist, previously "Kapellmeister des Klosters Weingarten." His wind music is now at the Benedictine monastery, Engelberg.

MAZELLIER, Jules *1879-1959 Prelude and dance* is for solo bassoon and winds.

MAZZORIN (MANZORIN), Michele *(1810); active 1848 in Venice* Composer of religious works for the church of Santa Maria della Consolazione detta "della Fava".

Mc is listed as Mac. Thus names like McPHEE, etc, are listed as if MacPHEE, etc.

MEDER, Johann Gabriel *(1770)* Son of a schoolmaster at Gotha.

MEDERITSCH, Johann (known as: Georg Anton Gallus) *26 Dec 1752, Vienna-18 Dec 1835, Lemberg (now L'vov)* Mederitsch, a student of Wagenseil, was Kapellmeister of the theater at Olomouc in 1781-1782, and theater conductor in Ofen (Buda) in 1794, moving to Vienna in 1796, where he wrote for Schikaneder's theater (see *Sainsbury* and *Grove 5).* Of interest is his *Chor der Tempelherren,* with its Masonic connections (1). He wrote act 1 of *Babylons Pyramiden,* act 2 being by Winter. Schikaneder's libretto was constructed as a sequel to *Die Zauberflöte* (1).

1. E M Batley 1969 *A Preface to the Magic Flute;* London: Dennis Dobson.

MÉHUL, Étienne Nicolas *22 Jun 1763, Givet, near Mézières-18 Oct 1817, Paris* Méhul's musical maturity came at the end of the Ancien Régime, and he died just after the monarchy was restored. His writings for winds are almost exclusively for festivities of the Revolution, which he survived, unlike his teacher of composition, Edelmann, the Strasbourg-born musician and revolutionary. Méhul's vocation for opera began in the 1780s, and continued through the period when, as Cherubini's wife remarked, "in the morning the guillotine was kept busy, and in the evening one could not get a seat at the theater." Méhul's gentle disposition made him acceptable to most factions, and his talent won him appointment in 1795 as one of the first Inspectors of Instruction at the Conservatoire. In 1798, Napoleon invited Méhul to accompany him on his expedition to Egypt as official composer. Méhul's refusal, at least partly because of his health, did not prevent further commissions, nor did it prevent his becoming one of the first Chevaliers de la Légion d'Honneur. As his health declined and his operas fell from fashion, Méhul turned to horticulture, becoming an expert on tulips (just as Catel turned to roses), in correspondence with leading experts throughout France.

ENM-1 *Ouverture*   Dating from 10 December 1793, it comprises a slow introduction and a faster main movement.

ENM-1mv *Le Chant de retour, hymne pour la paix*   The peace in question was that of the Treaty of Campo Formio which (inter alia) ceded Venice to Austria. It was first performed on 10 December 1797, and is recorded (appropriately) by the Musique des Gardiens de la Paix (number untraced) and in an orchestral version under Plasson on EMI CDC 49740.

ENM-2mv *L'Hymne des Vingt-Deux (Girondins)*, described by *Pierre/HC* as superb.

ENM-5mv *Le Chant du départ*   France's second national song after *La Marseillaise*, written when France was to expand to the Rhine and Napoleon to win higher command. A good robust tune. It would not be used by a Beethoven or Weber (as was "God Save the King") nor does it show the hand of a master (like Haydn's "Gott erhalte"); neither is it the tool of a demagogue, like the Nazi "Horst Wessel Lied," though terror was known in the France of 1794. *Le Chant du départ* has been performed at the Paris Opéra at critical times, such as 29 June 1939, by which time Nazi takeovers in the Rhineland, Austria and Czechoslovakia had made war imminent. It is recorded on Chant du Monde LCD 278 963/4 by L'Orchestre Régionale de Picardie/Bardon.

MEIER, G *(?1800)*   Arranger associated with the Lippe Kapelle at Detmold, and possibly the clarinettist from that ensemble cited in *Weston/MCVP*.

MEISSNER, F W *(1790)*   Meissner's two sets of *Pièces d'Harmonie* (published in 1821) are proper four-movement Parthien, and well-written. It is not a good idea to follow the publisher's suggestion of substituting 2fl for 2ob in the octet.

MEJO (Majo), Guillaume (Wilhelm) August *1793 Nossen, Silesia-after 1846*   Mejo's first position was at Oderan, near Chemnitz; he then joined the Leipzig Gewandhaus Orchestra from 1814 until 1821, becoming Musical Director at Domanzi, Silesia, and from 1832 until 1846 Musical Director at Chemnitz. He may have been the arranger for winds of parts of Beethoven's *Septet* (see under Beethoven). His variations on "Gaudeamus Igitur" **GAM-1**, is scored for fl(E♭) cl(E♭) 2cl(B♭) 3hn 2bn b-tb, with cl(B♭) a-tb t-tb serp ad lib. Composed c.1824, these variations are dedicated to Mr Guillaume (Wilhelm) Barth (qv), principal clarinet of the Leipzig Gewandhaus Orchestra. The two E♭ parts (flute and clarinet) and the bass trombone all have demanding parts. We cannot trace surviving copies of his 1821 *Sextet* for 2hn 2bn 2serp/cbn.

MELIN, Sten *b 1957, ?Sweden*   His *Vågform 114* [sic] dates from 1980.

MELLERS, Wilfrid Howard *b 26 April 1914, Leamington Spa*   Composition student of Egon Welles, and associate of Rubbra. His penetrating comments and writings on music have had wide influence.

MENDELSSOHN, Arnold (Ludwig) *26 Dec 1855, Ratibor, Silesia-19 Feb 1933, Darmstadt*   Like Felix Mendelssohn, a grandson of philosopher Moses Mendelssohn. He was trained in law, but spent much of his life as a music teacher in universities or conservatories at Bonn, Bielefeld, Cologne, Darmstadt and Frankfurt. His Op 62 *Suite* for winds (essentially a standard orchestral wind section) was published in 1916.

MENDELSSOHN BARTHOLDY, Jacob Ludwig Felix *3 Feb 1809, Hamburg-4 Nov 1847 Leipzig.*   Two of Mendelssohn's finest works, the 1825 *Octet* for strings and the 1826 Overture to *A Midsummer Night's Dream* were written at a younger age than were any of Mozart's mature works. Mendelssohn was exceptionally popular in his time, so it is surprising that some of his music cannot be located. Several works which we cannot trace are listed by his friend Julius Rietz (1). These range from stage music to the 1833 marches for small military bands, for use in church processions in Düsseldorf. One hopes these were not in the primitive style of some of the wind writing in *Elijah* (where it is hard to believe the wind parts were written by the same person as scored *A Midsummer Night's Dream*, if indeed they were). The stage work in question is the 1834

Todeslied des Bojaren (Elegy for a Boyar), for male voices plus winds, written for Immermann's tragedy *Alexis.* Rietz implies that the music is given in Immermann's works; only the piano reduction is published. Mendelssohn also wrote choral works with winds or brass. One has been recorded, *Der Jäger Abschied* Op 50, for men's voices, 4hn tb (Leipzig Radio Chorus/Horst Neumann, on Philips 6514 362). Other works (by year of composition) are: (1827) *Festival Music;* male voices, hns tps timp vc db (1828); *Begrüssung* (for the Naturforschung-Versammlung, Berlin) TTBB 2cl 2hn 2tp celli bass (**FJM-1v,** 1840); *Festgesang;* male voices, brass (1842); *Festal song* for the unveiling of the statue of Friedrich August the Just, Dresden, 9 June 1842, 2 male choirs and brass. Mention should be made too of the touchingly original *Funeral March* for Pyramus and Thysbe, for cl bn drum, from the music to *A Midsummer Night's Dream.*

FJM-1 *Ouverture für Harmonie Op 24* This exists in two versions. **FJM-1.1** is for pic fl 2ob 2cl(F) 2cl(C) 2bthn 2bn cbn 4hn 2tp 3tb b-hn perc, and also in several modernized forms. **FJM-1.2,** for fl 2ob 2cl 2bn 2hn tp b-hn, is probably the original form, known as *Notturno.* The two versions still cause confusion, although there seems to be a simple explanation. The original work was written in the summer of 1824, when Mendelssohn, his father, and his sister Rebecka, visited the resort of Doberan, not far from the Baltic port of Rostock. The *Overture* was written for the spa band. We do not know the precise constitution of the band, but we do know from the work of Hammerl, a Ludwigslust clarinettist who played at Doberan, that the band was probably close to the smaller ensemble **FJM-1.2.** We know further that Sir George Grove (2 p 220) mentions an Andante and Allegro for the wind band of a beer garden at Doberan, dating from (he thought) c.1826, for which the manuscript was "interesting looking." This was surely **FJM-1.2.** In addition, Julius Rietz (1 p 444) asserts that the *Overture* "was first composed for the Band of the Doberan Baths, and subsequently arranged for a full Military Band". Thus we assume that **FJM-1.2** is (or is close to) Mendelssohn's first version, and **FJM-1.1** is his final, full-scale version. The *Overture* consists of a slow introduction and an extended fast section. Parts sound like mature Mendelssohn; the influence of Weber and Spohr is obvious at other times. The large band version is recorded by the Goldman Band (DEC 78633), by the Musique des Gardiens de la Paix/Dondeyne (details unknown) and by the London Symphony Orchestra/Abbado on DG 423 104. **FJM-1.2** is recorded on BASF 25 21808-2 and on Carus Car 63118 by the Detmolder Bläserkantorei.

FJM-2 *Trauermarsch für Harmonie, Op 103* Mendelssohn's other large work for winds (not to be confused with another funeral march arranged for brass from a piano work) is his A minor *Funeral March,* written in 1836 in memory of the composer Norbert Burgmüller. Burgmüller (and there were several composers so named, some related) died tragically young; both Schumann and Berlioz mention in their writings how much he had impressed his contemporaries. As in **FJM-1.1,** the bass horn doubles the cbn. The work is recorded by Dondeyne/Musique des Gardiens de la Paix on SERP MC 7034.

FJM-1v *Ave Maria (Three Motets, Op 23 No 2)* These are usually performed with the alternative organ accompaniment, but the second motet also exists in a version for clarinets, horns, cello and bass.

1. J Rietz 1863, in *Letters of Felix Mendelssohn Bartholdy from 1833 to 1847* (translated Lady Wallace) London: Longman, Green, Longman, Roberts, and Green.

2. R F Goldman 1974 *The Wind Band: Its Literature and Technique;* Westport, CT: Greenwood Press, p 221.

MENTNER, Karl (pseudonym Blasius Wind) *c.1800–1860* The title of **KZM-1** (*Sérénade amusante*) and the composer's pseudonym are both intriguing. The Opus number usually given is the extraordinary 1339; we have not been able to determine whether this is a misprint for Op 139.

MERCADANTE, (Giuseppe) Saverio (Raffaele) *?17 Sept 1795, Altamura-17 Dec 1870, Naples* Composer of several church works (*Gloria; Tantum ergo*) for Santa Maria della Consolazione detta "della Fava," Venice, perhaps c.1826 when he was associated with La Fenice. He wrote some marches as a student; perhaps these explain the extensive use of winds and timpani' in his better-known operas.

MERKLEIN, ( ) *(?1760)* Probably a member of the Chotek Harmonie, zámek Káčina.

MESSIAEN, Olivier *10 Dec 1908, Avignon-27 Apr 1992, Paris* Organist and influential composer, whose highly original music often made extensive and imaginative use of birdsong. He made equally imaginative use of wind instruments and their colors, both in self-contained works (e.g., the monumental *Et Exspecto Resurrectionem Mortuorum*) and within works (the other extreme being the movement for solo horn in *Des Canyons aux Étoiles*). A recording covering much of this range is Chandos CHAN 9301/2 by Peter Donohoe (pf) with the Netherlands Winds Ensemble/Reinbert de Leeuw.

MEYER, Karl Heinrich (Charles Henri) *1784, Buchholz bei Annaberg-1837, Leipzig* Apart from his *Partita*, c.1821, and his arrangement (1828/29) of Lindpaintner's overture *Joko*, Meyer also produced a *Journal d'Harmonie* in 1808, dedicated to W L Barth (qv) of which only one issue survives (see part 1). One surprise here is that the printed b-tb part is written a semitone below concert pitch.

MEYERBEER, Giacomo *5 Sept 1791, Berlin-2 May 1864, Paris* Meyerbeer's *Königslied* (for male voices with fl 2ob 2cl 2bn) is dated 28 December 1813; the King in question was presumably that of Württemberg. His other wind works are for large bands.

MICHAEL, David Moritz *21 October 1751, Erfurt-26 February 1827, Neuwied* The fine collections of wind music belonging to the Moravian church in Pennsylvania owe much to Michael (see also part 1). In his youth in Germany, Michael aimed to become a priest, then a pharmacist (a prospect blighted by his lack of a sense of smell), and later a musician. After experience in pit orchestras and military bands as an oboist and horn player, he planned to join the Hessians as a bugler; had he done so, he would have been in George III's army in the American Revolution. However, he became associated with the Moravians instead, joining the Barby congregation in 1781. Michael moved to Pennsylvania as a teacher, first at Nazareth in 1795, then at Bethlehem in 1808. There he organized the Collegium Musicum, and gave the first US performance of Haydn's *Creation*. He returned to Germany in 1815.

His parthias appear to have been a great success, for they exist in several copies at Bethlehem and at Winston-Salem, North Carolina. We have not traced Parthia IX (**DMM-1d**); the (bound) part books at Bethlehem continue from Parthia VIII with Parthia X beginning on the same page. It is possible, of course, that one of the named parthias (**DMM-14, -15**) was regarded as No IX. The Bethlehem Philharmonic Society copy bears a note which anyone who has played outdoors will appreciate: "That these were used for Serenading and at night may be seen & proved by the insects which fly to the light on [sic] Summer - see Parthie XII & others - some [of the insects adhering to the paper] have been broken when handling the music / Feb 28 1873 / RIG". The title of Michael's *Parthia "bestimmt zu einer Wasserfahrt auf der Lecha"* **DMM-14** and *Suiten bey einer Quelle zu blasen (to be played by a spring)* **DMM-15** show they were for outdoor performance. Contemporary accounts observe that the musicians played from a flat-bottomed boat, propelled by poles, as their audience walked along the bank. The *Suite* comprises an *Introductio,* repeated three times (first 2hn, then 2hn bn, then 2cl 2hn bn) and three suites, totalling 13 movements. There is some fascinating imagery in the *Parthia*, with anxiety when the punt poles no longer reach the bottom and a modest whirlpool is encountered. Some movements have titles: No 7 is an Echo; "Zusamenruf," the call to return, precedes No 10, "Retour Marche"; all ends with a chorale. *Die Wasserfahrt* is recorded by Pacific Classical Winds on Moramus 940101.

MICHALIČKA, František *(1780), active 1818, Kunvald, Bohemia*   The one work attributed to him **(FQM-1vd)** is, in fact, Michael Haydn's *Deutsches Hochamt Messe* JMH-1.2v. His relationship to Jan Michalička is not known.

MICHALIČKA, Jan (Johann) *(1780), active 1817-1859 Kunvald, Bohemia*   Probably Chorregent at Kunvald; composer of church music and funeral pieces; these are scored for voices and winds. **XZM-5** is a Czech-language version of the Libera me.

MICHEL, Franz Ludwig *(1750)*   Active in the Harmonie of Sophie Potocka (Tulchin, Ukraine) in the 1790s, arranging symphonies by Haydn and quartets by Pleyel. Some anonymous works in PL-LA (RM 81/1-5) may be Michel's arrangements.

MILHAUD, Darius *4 Sept 1892, Aix-en-Provence-22 June 1974, Geneva*   This prolific Provençal pupil of d'Indy wrote many works for winds. The Athena Ensemble has recorded those for small ensembles on Chandos CHAN 6536, including the wind quintets *La Cheminée du Roi René,* Op 205, the *Divertissement* and *Two Sketches.* Other works use winds extensively, such as his *Concerto d'Automne* for 2 solo pianos, fl ob 3hn 2vla vc, and *La Création du Monde.* Milhaud was one of "Les Six" who revitalized French music after the World War I. Like Reicha, Cherubini and Hummel, Milhaud was made a Chevalier de la Légion d'Honneur. His undoubted facility and ingenuity led him to be described as the most important composer since Ravel, yet the same fluency brought accusations of barrenness, modishness and superficial wit.

Milhaud wrote several works for American wind bands, such as the Op 248 *Suite française,* completed on 13 November 1944, and first performed on 13 June 1945 in Central Park, New York. The Op 260b *Marches* (In Memoriam; Gloria Victoribus) of 1945 were dedicated to the publisher, Commander Schirmer, and the Op 317 *West Point Suite,* was first performed in Paris in October 1951. Other band works include the Op 153c *Introduction et Marche funèbre,* and the Op 334b *Musique de théâtre,* first played on 28 Oct 1972, under Dondeyne, which is the 1954 music for *Saul.* The "complete" wind band music is played by the Musique des Gardiens de la Paix/Dondeyne, on MC 7024.

DYM-2 *Petite Symphonie No 5 (Dixtuor)*   The six symphonies for small orchestra, written between 1917 and 1923, are misleadingly numbered independently of his other symphonies. The fifth (Op 75) is for winds alone, and is in three short movements: Rude (i.e., rough); Lent; Violent. It is more self-consciously modern than most of his works, with striking harmonic clashes (one has the impression that only shortage of instruments prevents chords of all 12 notes at once). The *Dixtuor* is recorded by Capella Cracoviensis/Rickenbacher on Koch Schwann 311392; Orchestre de Radio Luxembourg/ Milhaud on CBS 572803 (reissued as Candide CE 31.1008 and Vox STGBY 626) and by the New York Harmonie Ensemble/Richman on Music & Arts CD 649.

MILLER (Millard), M *(1760)*   Doane's *A Musical Directory for the Year 1794* lists a bass singer, Thomas Miller, and a tenor Miller; perhaps this Miller is one of these.

MILLING, Anton *(1740)*   Composer associated with the Kroměříž Harmonie of Archbishop Hamilton in the 1770s in the 1770s. Four of his wind works are unusual in being in more than one key: **ANM-4, 5** are in three keys (G/Bb/A; C/F/G). His works are between 8 and 13 movements long, but are usually in blocks of four movements.

MINAŘEK, ( ) *(1800), active c.1824*   Associated with the Augustinian monastery, Brno.

MIŠÍK (Mischik), F A *(1730?)*   Probably associated with the Pachta Harmonie, since his works are found only in its archives. Composer of 20 attractive but undemanding parthias, 12 being for 2ob 2taille 2hn 1/2bn, similar to the Schwarzenberg Harmonie of the mid-1770s. There are much later alto clarinet parts to replace the tailles.

MOHR, J *(1810)*   Arranger of Auber's *Actéon* overture, published c.1836 (I-Mc copy from Musique du Pensionnat de Freibourg), and of the overture and five airs from Auber's *Zanetta,* c.1841. The *Zanetta* music, though published by B Schott, has plate numbers outside the main sequence; the plates came from Troupenas in Paris.

MOLTER, Johann Melchior (Giovanni Melchiore) *10 Feb 1696, Tiefenort, Werra-12 Jan 1765, Durlach* Molter enjoyed a stable and secure career. He joined the service of the Margrave of Baden around 1719 and, apart from brief periods in Italy and at Eisenach, remained in the Margrave's service at Durlach until his death. Molter wrote at least 169 symphonies, and pioneered the use of the clarinet and chalumeaux in wind ensembles. **JOM-5** uses one chalumeau in the treble and one in the bass clef. Most of his works for winds are for the then-standard ensemble of 2ob 2hn bn plus tp.

MONNIKENDAM, Marius *28 May 1896, Haarlem-22 May 1977, Amsterdam* Writer and composer who studied at the Amsterdam Conservatoire, and later in Paris with d'Indy (qv). His two works for chorus and winds date from 1967.

MONTSALVATGE, (Bassols) Xavier *b 11 Mar 1912, Gerona, Catalonia* His **XAM-2** *Peqeña suite burlesca* won the 1936 Pedrell Prize.

MORBERG, Gösta *b 29 Jun 1923, ?Sweden* *Erland von Koch* (1978), for double wind quintet, is described as a "summer tune".

MORETTI, Niccolò *(1800), Venice* Active 1823-1833, probably at Santa Maria della Consolazione detta "della Fava." He composed four Mass movements for winds.

MORGAN, David Stanley *b 18 May 1932, Ewell, Surrey, UK* He studied composition with Seiber and conducting with Walter Goehr; a cor anglais player in Sydney, 1958.

MORRIS, Joseph *(1750?)* Possibly the clarinettist and violinist from Bath, England, mentioned in Doane's *A Musical Directory for the Year 1794*. It is likely that he emigrated to Lititz, Pennsylvania, in the mid-1790s, and belonged to the Moravian Brethren. **JZM-2** is attributed to Haydn (**FJH-17d**) and Mozart (**WAM-18d**).

MORSE, Samuel *(1780)* His *Pandean Waltz,* was arranged for King George's Band (2cl 2hn bn). Pandean Bands, popular in the early 19th century, played pan pipes.

MORTELMANS, Lodewijk *5 Feb 1868, Antwerp-24 June 1952, Antwerp* His set of 11 *Old Flemish Carols* is basically for 2fl ob 2cl 2hn 2bn (this scoring varies; strings are ad lib for 8 of the carols; winds are tacet in one carol).

MOUQUET, Jules *10 July 1867, Paris-25 Oct 1946, Paris* Educated at the Paris Conservatoire, winning the 1896 Prix de Rome, the 1905 Prix Tremont and the 1907 Prix Chartier. Mouquet became Professor at the Conservatoire in 1913. His 1910 *Suite* (**JUM-2**) has the same unusual scoring (fl ob 2cl hn 2bn) as d'Indy's *Chanson et Danses.*

MOYSE, Louis *b 14 July 1912, Scheveningen* Son of flautist Marcel Moyse.

MOZART, (Joannes Chrysostomus) [Wolfgangus] Wolfgang [Theophilus] Amadeus *27 Jan 1756, Salzburg-5 Dec 1791, Vienna* Mozart's writing for winds (1-15) stands head and shoulders above that of other composers. He had an innate sympathy for the individual instruments, seeming to find no difficulty in coping with their limitations. Anyone hearing Mozart's music senses its power at once, and its quality is even more striking to the player. Moreover, he wrote four of the undisputed masterpieces of wind music: the *Gran Partita*, K.361, the two octets K.375 and K.388, and the *Quintet* for wind and piano, K.452. Wolfgang, the only surviving son of Leopold Mozart, Court Composer to the Archbishop of Salzburg, showed prodigious ability as composer, pianist and violinist. He toured Europe from an early age, adopting the now-familiar form of his name (Amadeus is the Latin form of the Greek Theophilus) when on tour in Italy. Mozart's earliest works for winds were also a result of his tours, which took him to most of the major musical centers and introduced him to many of the leading musicians. His visit to London (1764-1765) was especially important: besides writing his first symphony, he met J C Bach. The major works were written twenty years later, however, in Vienna.

We discuss first the serenades and divertimentos for winds undisputedly by Mozart. We then consider the authentic wind works in his operas or other forms. Next we turn to works for wind and voices, to arrangements by Mozart, to arrangements of Mozart's works by others, and finally to the many dubious and spurious works.

Mozart's Milan Divertimentos WAM-2 *Divertimento No 4 in B♭ K.186/K.159b* and **WAM-3** *Divertimento No 3 in E♭ K.166/K.159d* The first of Mozart's surviving works for winds alone dates from early 1773. Late in 1772, he had travelled to Milan for the production of his opera *Lucio Silla* during Carnival. Milan, like Austria, appreciated wind music. Mozart knew this, in part from his 1771 Milan success with *Ascanio in Alba,* with its repeated chorus with wind accompaniment. He may have written K.186 while there. A second *Divertimento,* K.166, may have followed when the Mozarts had returned to Salzburg. Both works add two cors anglais to the standard octet, a rare ensemble also found (with strings) in K.113, another Milan *Divertimento.* In the mid-1770s, Salzburg had cors anglais, as Michael Haydn's *Symphony No 19* shows, but lacked clarinets. The two works have a rich sound, though they are rarely in more than three parts (the bassoons usually double). The brilliant early clarinet sound seems necessary, rather than the familiar mellower tone. Probably B♭ alto horns were expected; we know Mysliveček wrote high horn parts for Milan at that time. The Andante grazioso of K.166 is transcribed from a symphony by Paisiello (16). Perhaps Mozart heard the Paisiello in Naples in 1770. Other movements match incipits in K.135a/K.Anh109, *Le gelosie del seraglio,* a ballet noted down by Mozart in Milan in 1772, in which some of the movements are by Starzer (17). In *Le gelosie,* No 30 corresponds to the slow movement of **WAM-3**; to **WAM-2** correspond No 1, from Starzer's Sinfonia to *Les Cinq Sultanes* (17) (the first movement of K.186) and No 31 (the finale of K.186).

Recordings include: Berlin Philharmonic Orchestra Winds, Orfeo C16388 1A, S152861; London Wind Soloists, Decca, SXL 6050 (K.166) and SXL 6061 (K.186); Netherlands Wind Ensemble, Philips 6747 379 and Philips Complete Mozart Edition Vol 5; Vienna Philharmonic Orchestra Winds, Deutsche Gramophon DG 429 807 (K.166) and DG 429 806 (K.186); Holliger Wind Ensemble, Philips Phil 422 505-2PME6.

Mozart's Salzburg Divertimentos **WAM-6** *Divertimento in F* K.213, July 1775; **WAM-7** *Divertimento in B♭* K.240, January 1776; **WAM-8** *Divertimento in E♭* K.252/ K.240a, January 1776; **WAM-9** *Divertimento in F* K.253, August 1776; **WAM-10** *Divertimento in B♭* K.270, January 1777. (**WAM-15d** K.289/K.271g is spurious).

These sextets for 2ob 2hn 2bn (11), apparently written for Salzburg players, may be the "whole suite of music for the Court wind instruments" to which Leopold Mozart refers at about the time they were written. The instrumental writing is far more subtle than in the Milan works, with the bassoon a tenor melodic participant, not a mere bass. These divertimentos stand at the borderline between symphony and suite, combining fewer movements and sonata form with dance movements: the second movements of K.240 and K.270 are gavottes, the finale of K.213 is a contredance, and the first movement of K.252 is a siciliana; other examples of dances are the polonaise in K.252 and the Ländler-like trios of K.213 and K.270. An Austrian popular tune "Die Katze lässt das Mausen nicht" (You can't stop a cat catching mice) forms the basis of the exciting finale of K.252; this same tune appears in Beethoven's *Piano Concerto No 1.*

There are recordings on original instruments: an unnamed ensemble/Vester, PAL 1049 (K.213/253/270/289); Octophoros, Accent ACC 8856D (K.213/240/252/253/270/ 289); Amadeus Winds, L'Oiseau-Lyre 425819-2 and CD 425 819 2; other recordings use modern instruments: Berlin Philharmonic Winds: Orfeo C152861A (K.213/240/252/253/ 270); London Wind Soloists, Decca SDDL405-9 (K.213/240/252/253/270/289) and 430 298 2DM (K.252/253/270/289); Netherlands Wind Ensemble, Philips 947379 and Philips Mozart Edition Vol 5; Holliger Wind Ensemble, Philips 422 505-2; Orpheus Chamber Winds, DG 419 192-2GH (K.252), DG 415 669-2GH (K.270); Vienna Philharmonic Winds, Deutsche Grammophon DG 2531296 (K.213/240/253/270); Zefiro Ensemble, Astrée Auvidis E8529 (K.213/240/252/253/270); Danish Wind Octet, Rondo RCD 8336 (K.213, K.252); Linos Ensemble, Capriccio 10 472 (K.252).

Mozart: The Viennese Masterpieces

WAM-1 *Gran Partita (Bb) K.361*   The autograph of K.361 (18) carries the title "Gran Partita." Whoever wrote it chose the ideal phrase for, as an early description noted, it is a "great wind piece of a very special kind by Herr Mozart" (5 p 223). There remain doubts about when and why the *Gran Partita* was written (19, 20). Some ideas are based on a date given in an unknown hand on the autograph or on arrangements for smaller groups; all these suggestions can be ruled out. Three possibilities remain: that it was written wholly or partly in Munich in 1781; that it was written in Vienna in 1782/1783 at much the same time as the two great octets; and that it was written shortly before the first known performance in 1784. The factors which are certain are these: the autograph shows no sign of being written in haste, or of having been started at one time and finished at another; the manuscript paper is typical of that Mozart used in 1781-1782; it is on an exceptionally large scale; its first known performance was not complete, with four movements being played at the Burgtheater, Vienna, for Anton Stadler's benefit on 23 March 1784; and the *Gran Partita* does not appear in Mozart's own thematic catalog, started on 9 February 1784. Other factors, hardly in dispute, are its apparent open-air character, clarinet and basset horn writing which suggest Stadler's influence, and horn parts which are far less demanding than those of the great octets.

The 1781 hypothesis. In 1781, Mozart was in Munich for the production of *Idomeneo* and vainly seeking a permanent post. He had known many of the court players at Mannheim; they had moved to Munich with their patron, Carl Theodore, when he became Elector of Bavaria in 1778. As a piece to impress a potential employer, the *Gran Partita* is splendid. Yet there is no evidence that the court boasted clarinets and basset horns to do justice to the *Gran Partita*. Indeed, when the winds are brought to the fore in *Idomeneo*, it is flute, oboe, horn and bassoon which are singled out; moreover, these same instruments are featured in Danzi's *Sinfonia Concertante* for the same band, written not long after in 1785. The 1781 Munich hypothesis is usually attributed to Alfred Einstein; in fact, his introduction to the autograph facsimile (18) makes it clear that the *Gran Partita* could not have been written in or for Munich; it could, he suggests, have been conceived there and written in Vienna in early 1781.

The 1782 hypothesis. The second possibility puts the *Gran Partita* at much the same time as the octets and other wind works. A date of 1782 would link with the supposed 1783 dates for a number of small works using basset horns, including both purely instrumental works (**WAM-3s** to **WAM-9s**) and the canzonets (**WAM-3v** to **WAM-7v**). The period 1782-1783 makes the *Gran Partita* contemporary with the series of concerts organized by Phillip Jakob Martin in 1782. Holmes (6) suggests that "To the garden concerts may be traced two serenades and a divertimento for wind instruments." Martin had obtained the Emperor's permission to give twelve concerts in the Augarten, in the suburb of Leopoldstadt, and four grand serenades in the principal squares in Vienna. The orchestra was to consist of amateurs, apart from the bassoons, trumpets and drums. Much of the *Gran Partita* could be played by experienced amateurs, and Martin's concerts could have been a convenient and economical source of such musicians. Certainly wind music was included, for Martin advertized in 1782 that the concert series would continue with a wind arrangement of *Die Entführung aus dem Serail* (see **WAM-3a**). An outdoor setting would have been ideal for the *Gran Partita* too. As Johann Risbeck described one of these 1782 concerts: "One of the finest spectacles ... during the last nights of the summer ... The excellent music, the solemn stillness, the intimacy with which night inspires a company - all this lent the scene a special charm" (5).

A further argument for suggesting 1782 comes from a note added to Mozart's letter of 7 August 1782 to his father describing his wedding to Constanze: "During supper I was surprised by a concert from sixteen wind instruments, who played my own compositions." Leeson and Whitwell (19) suggested that the insertion was by Georg Nikolaus Nissen, Constanze's second husband, who collected Mozart's correspondence and published an important biography in 1828. However, they argued against this insertion, suggesting Nissen was an unreliable scholar who exaggerated to make Mozart's importance seem greater. This is not convincing: it would be sad to suppose that Mozart's reputation was enhanced just because 16 musicians (friends, rather than nobility) chose to join the wedding festivities in a way Mozart would appreciate (we note later how musicians thanked Mozart for K.375 on his name day in 1781). The insertion is quoted as authentic by Edward Holmes (6), who toured Europe in 1827 and met many with personal knowledge of Mozart during his visit. It seems to us far more likely that the sentence records an informed comment. We cannot say that the work referred to was the *Gran Partita,* nor that it was written for the wedding. The *Gran Partita* certainly fits a special occasion, and the established facts are consistent with the possibility. There is support too from Tyson's 1987 (20) analysis of the paper type, which suggests composition in Vienna in 1781-2. Questions do remain: Was it the first performance? Who were the players, and were there 13 or 16? Why did Mozart not mention the composition in his letters to his father?

The 1784 hypothesis. The *Gran Partita* is often said to date from 1784 (21), for it is known that four movements were performed on 23 March 1784. The notice (1) states that a benefit concert was to be given by Anton Stadler in the Burgtheater and would include "among other well chosen pieces, a large wind piece of a very special kind composed by Herr Mozart." It is not asserted that the work was new, nor that it was specially composed for the occasion. Mozart was not present; he was giving a concert of his own. Clearly, Stadler's concert fixes a latest date of composition. J F Schink described the work thus (22): "I heard music for wind instruments, today, by Herr Mozart, in four movements-glorious and sublime! It consisted of thirteen instruments, viz four corni, two oboi, two fagotti, two clarinetti, two basset-corni, a contre-violon, and at each instrument sat a master-Oh, what an effect it made-glorious and grand, excellent and sublime." There are problems here too. First, the work does not appear in Mozart's own thematic catalog (2), which he began in February 1784. There are gaps in the catalog, of course, but mainly smaller pieces. The largest omission is of *Davidde penitente* (K.469), perhaps because it was a revision of the earlier Mass, K.427; the two new arias are in the catalog. It is hardly credible that Mozart forgot one of his largest instrumental works so soon after starting the catalog and before a scheduled first performance. Secondly, there are many records of Mozart writing specifically for individuals or occasions, but these make very clear the care he took to write just the right piece for the situation. Yet, if the *Gran Partita* was written for Stadler's concert, it was so misjudged in scale that almost half had to be left out. Thirdly, the horn parts are very simple and straightforward for the players Stadler would surely have chosen; a good amateur could manage them, whereas the parts in K.375, K.388 and K.452 are far more demanding. Finally, had the work been written for a benefit concert of Stadler's, it is mildly puzzling that there is not just one soloistic clarinet part, but two (or four, as Stadler specialized in the low-register second parts). There are no real arguments for 1781 or for Munich. While 1784 is the date of the first reported (if partial) performance, there are problems of unsuitability and the absence of the work from Mozart's catalog. A 1782 date has much to recommend it, whether the driving force was Martin's concerts, Mozart's wedding, or the founding of the Hofharmonie.

"Music for wind instruments ... excellent and sublime." Even the opening bars of the *Gran Partita* show it to be something out of the ordinary, with full solemn chords linked by the soft sound of a single clarinet. Mozart exploits with consummate skill this contrast between the massive effect of the full ensemble and the delicacy of small

sections. The large festive opening movement and the rumbustious closing Rondo show this well: both have passages for much smaller groups, such as the very opening of the Allegro molto in the first movement and the second section of the final Rondo. Usually the clarinets and basset horns are singled out and Mozart provides exquisite imitative writing for them; one has only to compare these passages with similar ones in J C Bach's *Quintets* to appreciate the gulf between Mozart and other composers.

Erik Smith (11) has remarked that the theme of the Allegro molto is related to an aria in Philidor's *Le maréchal ferrant* (Paris, 1761); the opening two bars of Claudine's "Je suis douce" (scene 3 of Act 1) are identical, as is the rhythm, if not the melody, of the next two bars (23). While the brief similarity could be coincidence, it does suggest a resolution of a problem not always handled well in performance. The critical phrase (the second bar of the Allegro molto in the first clarinet part) contains a note which Mozart writes as an acciaccatura. Three ways of playing it are heard on record: (1) as an appoggiatura, thus as an eighth note here; (2) short, with the emphasis on the second note, like the modern acciaccatura, and (3) short but stressed. Philidor's aria could be sung sensibly with either (1) or (3), with (3) perhaps making most sense.

The two minuets are on a large scale, stately and formal, each with two trios of contrasting character. The clarinets and basset horns play alone in the first Trio of the first minuet, whose second Trio begins wistfully in G minor, despite the horns' attempt to move it to a major key. The single reeds are to the fore again in the first Trio of the second minuet, although the mood suggests Mozart's Masonic works; the final Trio, however, is a light hearted and uncomplicated Ländler.

The remaining three movements all include slow sections of exceptional beauty. The Romanze, a characteristic slow, tranquil serenade movement, surrounds a central Allegretto whose character can vary greatly, depending on tempo. The Theme and Variations are distinguished above all by the penultimate variation; as in the Clarinet Quintet, K.581, it is slow moving and elegiac, with the oboe moving over murmurings of clarinets and basset horns. This variation severely tested the skill of arrangers. The slow movement is arguably the finest of this extraordinary work, as Peter Shaffer realized in his play *Amadeus*. This Adagio is also the most symphonic of the movements, and it alone does not exploit the contrast between large and small groups. All the eleven players (as in the Romanze, horns 3 and 4 remain silent) play for almost all the movement. Mozart uses a device later employed in wind music by composers like Dvořák and Strauss: a continuously changing and developing background against which solo instruments move. This background consists of a quarter note pulse from the two lowest instruments, harmonic filling from the horns, and a simple and subtle rhythmic figure from oboe 2, clarinet 2, basset horn 2, and bassoon 1. Against this, the three solo instruments exchange slow phrases (it is these phrases in which there are major differences between what Mozart wrote and most printed editions), the oboe with long sustained notes, and the clarinet and basset horn with long leaps to show their rich tones to greatest advantage. One can understand Schink's response in 1784.

There are numerous recordings. Some (and all of those using period instruments) use modern editions based on Mozart's autograph, rather than common and inaccurate older editions. Versions using period instruments include those by The Music Party/Hacker, Nato CD1132; Amadeus Winds/Hogwood, L'Oiseau-Lyre 421 437-2OH; Orchestra of the 18th Century/Brüggen, Philips 422 338-4PH; Octophoros/Kuijken, ACC 68642D; Collegium Aureum/Maier (modern pitch) EMI CDC 7 47818-2. Versions using modern instruments and editions based on the autograph include the English Chamber Orchestra/Barenboim, HMV ASD 3426 and EMI CZS7 67306-2; Academy of St Martin/ Marriner, Philips 412 726-2PH; London Philharmonic Winds, EMI EMX 9520; Vienna Mozart Ensemble/Harnoncourt, Teldec/Conifer AZ642981; Soloists of the Chamber

Orchestra of Europe, Teldec-Warner 2292 46471; Consortium Classicum/Klöcker, EMI EX 29 0994 3 (EMI 067 270 369-1; a later version is on Harmonia Mundi MDG 301 0494 and BR 100017). Other recordings (for which we do not have information about edition, or which use the older editions) include these: Albion Ensemble, Hyperion CDA 66285; London Mozart Players/Glover, ASV DCA 770 and CDDCS 316; Chamber Orchestra of Europe/Schneider, ASV CDCOE 804; Orpheus Chamber Orchestra, DG 423-061-2GH; Scottish National Winds/Järvi, Chandos CHAN 6575; New Philharmonia Winds/Klemperer, CMD 763349-2, Vienna Philharmonic Winds/Fürtwangler, CDH-763818-2; London Wind Soloists/Brymer, Decca 425 421-2; Berlin Philharmonic Winds, DG 2532089 and Sony Classical SK58950; London Sinfonietta Winds/Atherton, Argo ZRG 919; London Wind Quintet and Ensemble/Klemperer, Decca SXDW 3050; Netherlands Wind Ensemble/de Waart, Philips 420 711-2PSL; Toronto Chamber Winds/Webber, on Kneptune KIR 1202 and Crystal S-646, Vienna Wind Soloists, SDD 579; Chamber Music Society of the Lincoln Center/Schuller, Arabesque Z6617; Budapest Wind Ensemble/Kocsis, Quintana QU190 3051 (Harmonia Mundi HMA 1903051); Sabine Meyer Wind Ensemble, EMI CDC 7 54457; St Luke's Orchestra/Mackerras, Telarc CD80359, Maurice Bourgue Wind Ensemble, Pierre Verany PV 793031; Linos Ensemble, Capriccio 10 472. Extracts only are recorded by Czech Philharmonic Orchestra under Talich (Multisonic 310078) and under Scherchen (Multisonic 310077).

Arrangements Any reduction of the *Gran Partita* to octet (with or without double bass) has special problems when Mozart exploits the clarinets and basset horns as a solo quartet. This happens in three places. The first is in the first Trio of the first Minuet. Here both arrangers, that of K.Anh182 (whom we shall label BR after its publisher; this version omits the slow introduction to the first movement) and that of Simrock (which has an extra Trio **WAM-2s,** and which version which we shall label GP after its presumed arranger, Goepfert) adopt the same solution, with bassoons replacing basset horns. BR gives the clarinet 1 incorrect phrasing in bars 3 and 5. The second example is the end of Variation 5 in the penultimate movement. Here Mozart has the clarinets and basset horns murmuring softly. GP simply omits the basset horn parts. There is a loss, but the result does work. BR chooses a strangely obtrusive solution: oboe 2 plays the basset horn 2 part an octave up from the original. Neither arranger trusts bassoons to substitute, even though they are not seriously occupied at the time. The third example is in the Finale (bars 56 et seq). Mozart has the clarinets and basset horns moving above a unison bassoon accompaniment. BR uses oboes 1, 2 for clarinets 1, 2, and the clarinets replace basset horns; the bassoons remain as before. GP also has clarinets playing basset horn parts, with bassoon and contrabassoon playing the original bassoon parts. His solution for what were clarinet parts is to use oboe 1 and bassoon 1, not the obvious approach, but an ingenious and practical solution. Movements 5, 4, 6 of BR have been recorded by Musica Camerata Regionalis on Caprice CAP1074. Four movements (1, 2, 3, 7) of BR are recorded by the Amsterdam Wind Ensemble/Blomhert on STH-CD 19057. Blomhert (24) makes the interesting suggestion, based on early manuscript copies, that these four movements might have been a precursor to the *Gran Partita,* the other three movements being a later arrangement.

The Great Octets, K.375 and K.388 WAM-4 *Serenade in C minor K.388:* The C minor *Serenade* K.388 is wholly different in character from other serenades. Minor keys pervade, stark passages contrast with radiant ones, and the final street band sounds follow exceptional feats of counterpoint. It is the most symphonic of Mozart's wind works, with a concentration and a unity more complete than even in the *Gran Partita.* The opening movement parallels Mozart's other minor-key movements in power and urgency. While the second movement is still serious, its opening is gentler, gaining in intensity with its second theme and syncopated accompaniment and a rich and noble passage for bassoons and horns. The Minuet and Trio show a magisterial command of the composer's trade. Other composers might employ imitation (J C Bach) or canons (Haydn), yet Mozart goes further, with the tune appearing in retrograde, inverted, and even in a combination of the two. It is all so deft that one is not conscious of the exceptional technique. This is not conventional wind harmony, and parallels are rare even for Mozart (perhaps the end of the Minuet in the *Jupiter Symphony,* K.551, is close). The *Serenade* carries hints of *Don Giovanni*, both in intensity and in dramatic use of minor keys. Two features of the Finale strengthen this link. One is the marvellous horn phrase which relieves tension as the work moves from minor to major key, exactly the same phrase as appears in *Don Giovanni* at a comparable point in the drama; secondly, the Serenade ends in a street-band rout which, like the moralizing conclusion of the opera, brings a return to the reality of everyday life.

It is not known when K.388 was written. The work is often taken to be that to which Mozart referred in his letter to his father of 27 July 1782 "I have had to compose a serenade in a great hurry, but only for wind instruments," though this may well have meant other works (the *Gran Partita,* the rescoring of K.375, or perhaps the apparently abortive arrangement of *Die Entführung*). In 1787, closer to the writing of *Don Giovanni* (10) Mozart arranged K.388 for string quintet (K.406/K.516b).

WAM-5 *Serenade in E♭ K.375* **WAM-5.1:** 2ob 2cl 2hn 2bn, **WAM-5.2:** 2cl 2bn 2hn. Mozart left no doubts that he wrote the original, sextet, version to catch the attention of the influential Emperor's Chamberlain, von Strack. Some pleasant consequences followed, which Mozart described in his 3 November 1781 letter to his father (3). The letter is interesting in the way it shows the workings of patronage. The work was to be played at the house of the sister of the court painter, so that it might be heard by von Strack. The route to a commission was very indirect. Mozart wrote the work with care, so he expected attentive listeners. Success for the work meant success for the players. On that first night (St Theresa's Day) they were taken to two further venues to play the work. The players knew that their success depended on Mozart. When they serenaded him at 11 o'clock on 31 October 1781, their action was not entirely disinterested. Mozart must have realized this, though it would not have reduced his pleasure on hearing that first chord in E♭. The letter raises the question of the sense in which the players were "beggars" (or "wretches" [11]; the original has "die 6 Herrn solche exequirn sind arme Schlucker, die aber ganz hübsch zusammen blasen, besonders der erste Clarinettist und die 2 Waldhornisten"), for the music demands the very best professionals. It is possible (25) that the clarinettists were the Stadlers (only appointed to the Viennese Court on 8 February 1782), with Griessbacher as a fine horn player, all then out of work and seeking positions with the Wallerstein Harmonie via von Beecke.

The octet version shows significant changes and redistribution of parts to incorporate the oboes. One rather regrets the loss of the second Trio **WAM-2s** in the second Minuet, whoever wrote it; it makes its appearance in several places (19, 25) but not in the autograph of the original sextet. The first-movement repeat is struck out in the octet version. None of the changes affects the character of the piece. It differs from serenades by other composers simply by being better: it is always more subtle, more imaginative, and more resourceful. Even the weakest movement (and the second Minuet is modest by Mozart's standards) shows signs of his mastery. The opening Allegro begins solemnly with repeated chords, out of which emerges a distant relation of the marches which so often start serenades. The first Minuet is robust and cheerful, with an impressive and extended Trio. The Adagio is still more impressive and operatic in texture; clarinet, horn, and oboe share the opening theme and follow with echoing exchanges; it grows to a climax with second horn and clarinet weaving arpeggio accompaniments, subsiding into a gentle coda. The second Minuet is brief, and the

Finale a masterly Rondo: like many of Haydn's finales, its apparent simplicity and winning manner conceal a wide range of technical skills.

Both the octets K.375 and K.388 are recorded together in the following lists, unless stated. Period instruments are used by Collegium Aureum, VD 77576; Danzi Quintet/Vester, RCA RL30342; Amadeus Winds, L'Oiseau-Lyre 417 249-10H. Modern instruments are used by Chamber Orchestra of Europe/Schneider, ASV CDCOE802; Albion Ensemble, Mercury CDE84107; Orpheus Chamber Orchestra, DG 423 061-1GH; Netherlands Wind Ensemble (K.375 only), Philips 420 711-2; Netherlands Wind Ensemble, Philips, PME 806 907 LY and 6747379, also Chandos CHAN 9284; London Wind Soloists (K.375 only), Decca 425 421-2; London Wind Soloists (K.388 only), Decca SXL 6051 and CD 430 298-2DM; New London Wind Ensemble, CFP40211; Consortium Classicum/ Klöcker, EMI EX 29 0994 3; Toronto Chamber Winds, CBC SM-5053; Holliger plus ensemble, Philips 420 183-1 and 422505-2(6); New Philharmonia Wind Ensemble/ Klemperer, HMV SXDW3050 and CDM 763349-2 (K.375 only); Vienna Wind Soloists/ Harnancourt, Teldec AZ6 43097; Budapest Wind Soloists/Berkes, Hungaroton SLPD 12549 and (K.388 only) Quintana QU190 3051; Scottish National Orchestra/Järvi, Chandos CHAN 8407; London Sinfonietta/Pay, Argo ZRG911; Berlin Philharmonic Wind Ensemble, Orfeo S134851 A; Vienna Philharmonic Wind Ensemble (K.388 only), DG 2530 369; London Baroque Ensemble/Haas, EMI CDM 7639582, Pye GSGC 14062; Danish Wind Octet, Rondo RCD8336; Moragues Quintet, Auvidis Valois V4684; Steve Martland Band, Factory Fact 406 ("arranged Martland"); (K.388 only) Virtuosi di Praga, International Culture Net ICN 001. The K.375 sextet version is recorded by Consortium Classicum/ Klöcker, EMI EX 29 0994 3; Detmold Wind Sextet, MD GL 3245; Netherlands Wind Ensemble, Philips 420 711-2PH; Music Party/Hacker (period instruments), L'Oiseau-Lyre, DSLO 549; London Baroque Ensemble/Haas (second minuet only), Pye GSGC 14062; Vienna Philharmonic Wind Ensemble, DG 2530 369; Mozzafiato, Sony Classical SK 64306. Most sextet versions include the extra trio **WAM-2s** in the second minuet.

Autograph fragments for octet. Mozart left several fragments for octet, sadly too small for useful reconstruction: *March* **WAM-1f** K.384b, (4 bars); *Andante* **WAM-2f** K.384B, (18 bars 3/4); *Allegro* **WAM-3f** K.384c/K.Anh96, (16 bars). All these works seem to date from about the time of the great serenades.

Supplementary List. Some of Mozart's small works for wind ensemble are complete in themselves, but do not stand alone, and belong to a larger work.

WAM-1s *March of the Janissaries,* from *Die Entführung aus dem Serail.* Doubts remain as to the authenticity of this recently-rediscovered march, with its striking horn parts. It would be played in act 1, before the *Chorus of Janissaries* (27). Mozart's letter of 26 September 1781 mentioned that the drunken duet ("Vivat Bacchus") consists largely of his Turkish Zapfenstreich, so the band may have played again. The Hoftheater-Rechnungsbücher for 1782 refer to the hiring of the band of the 2nd Feld-Artillerie, under their Kapellmeister Franz Tyron, for *Die Entführung;* perhaps they played this music on stage. The work is recorded by Collegium Aureum on Harmonia Mundi 1 C065 99897 and in Hogwood's recording of the opera on L'Oiseau-Lyre 430 339-2OH2.

WAM-2s is an extra Trio, found in early sextet versions of K.375 (but not the autograph), and in several versions of K.361 (19, 26). The extra trio may have been put in first by a Traeg copyist; it may even be by Mozart. The Trio sometimes has horn parts, but these are not needed. It is recorded with sextet versions of K.375.

Smaller works with basset horns. The dates of composition of these works are uncertain: Einstein (4) suggests 1783 and *New Grove* 1785; Hacker's recording notes their solemnity and seriousness, and links them to Mozart's association with Freemasonry, which began in 1784. Possibly these works were among those used in the concert for the Three Eagles and Palm Tree Lodges on 20 October 1785 to raise funds for the itinerant basset hornists, David and Springer.

WAM-3s *Adagio in B♭* K.411/K.484a (2cl 3bthn); **WAM-4f** *Allegro assai;* K.Anh 95 (fragment for 2cl 3bthn); **WAM-9s** *Canonic Adagio in F* K.410/K.440d/K.484d (2bthn bn); **WAM-10s** *Adagio in C;* K.580a/K.Anh94 (fragment, probably for cl 3bthn). The *Adagio in B♭* is canonic for the two basset horns over the bassoon's free bass; it is unlikely that this was meant as a trio for three basset horns in disguise, although that option works well. Recordings include those by the London Wind Soloists, Decca CS 6350, CS 6349; Netherlands Wind Ensemble, Philips 6747379; Hacker and ensmble (K.411), Rediffusion Prelude PRS 2502; Berlin Soloists (K.410), Philips 6500917; Chicago Symphony Winds, CBS 12M 42144; Mannheim Ensemble, Meridian CDE 84267.

WAM-4s to 8s *Divertimentos for three basset horns* (K.Anh229/K.439b). There are five trios, perhaps from c.1787 though usually dated around 1783 (supported by the hint of J C Bach in the fourth movement of No 4, consistent with a date soon after Mozart learned of Bach's death), mainly published by Simrock around 1813 (28). All the trios are in five movements, although No 2 was published by Breitkopf & Härtel in 1803 without its Allegro and with an alternative finale not by Mozart. There are two distinct sixth trios, both spurious. Early editions were for clarinets and bassoon, sometimes with horns (probably spurious). **WAM-5s** is played by Consortium Classicum, with horns, on Dabringhaus und Grimm MDG 301 0496-2. That the works are for three basset horns was first argued by Whewell (29). Recordings include the following: Hacker (Nos 1, 5), Rediffusion Prelude: PRS 2502; Stalder (Nos 2, 4), Turnabout TV34417S; Consortium Classicum/Klöcker, EMI Electrola 29 099433; Classical Winds (2cl, bn; Nos 1-4), Amon Ra SAR25; New World Basset Horn Trio (Nos 2, 3), Harmonia Mundi HMU40 7017; Harmonie Bohemienne, Pierre Veranay PV 795021; Anches Trio, REM 311116; Ensemble Walter Boeykens, HMC 1384.

Some sources suggest that the K.487 duets are for 2bthn, mainly because of the high tesitura, but horns sound the more convincing. Recordings of both forms exist. Mozart's autograph survives only for numbers 1, 3, and 6. It adds "unterm Kegelscheiben" (while playing skittles) after the date, 27 July 1786. The duets are recorded with horns by the Netherlands Wind Ensemble (Soeteman and Peeters), Philips 6747379; Tuckwell (Nos 1, 3, 6), Decca 410 283; Czech Philharmonic Wind Ensemble, Supraphon SUP 111 671/2. Consortium Classicum play the basset horn version on EMI Electrola 1C 063-45 547.

Mozart: Vocal music with winds.   The most beautiful of serenades, "Secondare aurette amiche" **WAM-1.1ve** (act 2 No 21 of *Così fan tutte*), does not appear in the opera autograph, but in a manuscript in the Istituto Musicale, Florence. One can play this serenade with 2cl 2hn 2bn with minor rewriting. The work has been arranged with new texts as church music (one, **WAM-1.2v**, is very closely related to **WAM-1.1v**). Mozart's operas are rich sources of items for wind harmony. *Così fan tutte* has many examples, including the march in scene 16 of act 2. In *Die Zauberflöte* the examples are mainly associated with the three youths or with the priests, but include the end of the Quintet (No 5) of act 1 and the start of the Finale of act 2. In *Don Giovanni* in Act 2 (the Don's wind band) and in the Finale to act 1 (the Adagio "Proteggia il giusto cielo") where the masked trio prepare themselves for their encounter with Don Giovanni, supported by some of Mozart's most subtle and beautiful wind writing.

WAM-2ve *Ascanio in Alba*, K.111 Nos 6, 7, 10, 11, 15, 26 "Venga de'sommi eroi." This "serenata teatrale" was written for Milan in 1771. The "Coro di pastori" is for male voices and 2fl 2ob 2hn 2bn vc db, and is recorded in the complete performance on Naxos 8 660040/41 by the Choir of the Sorbonne/Concerto Academico/Grimbert.

The *Notturnos (Canzonettas)* for two sopranos and bass with three winds, are associated with Mozart's friendship with Gottfried von Jaquin. They exploit the basset horn sound in the sensuous way one associates more with *Così fan tutte*. It is just possible that von Jaquin wrote the vocal parts of these short works; he later used two of Mozart's songs (K.520, K.530) for Fräulein von Altomonte, his lady of the moment. The works are these: **WAM-4v** *Ecco quel fiero istante* K.436, for 3bthn; (Metastasio), c.1787; **WAM-5v** *Mi langnerò tacendo* K.437, for 2cl bthn; (Metastasio), c.1787; **WAM-3vf** *Se lontan, ben mio* K.438, for 2cl bthn; (Metastasio), c.1787; **WAM-2vf** *Due pupille amabili,* K.439, for 3bthn; c.1787; **WAM-6v** *Luci care, luci belle,* K.346=K.439a, for 3bthn; c.1787; **WAM-7v** *Più non si trovano* K.549, for 3bthn; (Metastasio), 10 July 1788. **WAM-1vf** *Grazie agl'inganni* K.532. A fragment, lacking vocal parts, of a setting of Metastasio, adapted from a work of Michael Kelly's; it may not be authentic. Recordings of the Notturnos include London Baroque Ensemble/Haas, EMI CDM 7 63958 2; Chicago Symphony Winds, CBS 12 M 42144; Stéphane Caillat Ensemble, Turnabout TV34275S, and the ensembles led by H-R Stalder (TFSM 1009; Turnabout TV34417S); Pieterson (Philips 6747379) and D Knothe (Philips 6500 917).

Arrangements for winds by Mozart. We discuss here the works in which Mozart appears to have used music of other composers. Some is genuine Mozart, the music for Don Giovanni's band being the best-known. Other works attributed to Mozart, and found in his autograph, are either arrangements or merely copies. Still other so-called arrangements by Mozart are merely arrangements by others. While Mozart hoped to arrange *Die Entführung aus dem Serail* in 1782, it is only too clear that most of the existing arrangements are not his. Nor is it likely that he made the octet versions of the *Gran Partita.* Yet there are some other examples of Mozart's borrowings, notably in the Milan works, **WAM-1a.** We have already remarked on the arrangement from Paisiello in the Milan divertimento, **WAM-3** (K.166), and the links via *Le gelosie del Seraglio* to Starzer's music in **WAM-2** (K.186) and **WAM-3.**

The last act of *Don Giovanni* contains the only authenticated surviving opera arrangements for winds by Mozart, **WAM-2a.** The Don's band plays three works on stage for the dinner to which the Commendatore's statue has been invited. The three works are by different composers and (rarer still) in different keys, and all are well known, even to the servant, Leporello. First comes the finale to act 1 of Vincente Martín y Soler's *Una cosa rara;* "Many of his things are very attractive" commented Mozart in 1789 "but no one will take any notice of him in ten years time". Then comes the scoffing song "Come un agnello" (like a lamb to market) from Guiseppe Sarti's Figaro-like *Fra i due litiganti il terzo gode;* finally, one has Figaro's own most famous aria "Non più andrai." Mozart's arrangements may well have been intended to show just how good a composer and arranger he was. He may well have heard all these three items in Went's arrangements. Those by Went are good, and his version of Figaro's aria is a tour de force. But there is no doubt Mozart was the master - and, since Mozart must have expected Went to play in the Vienna production, he may well have been giving Went a clear personal message. Don Giovanni's band allows some witty asides too (29): while the band plays the Sarti (itself an ironic comment on Don Giovanni's impending fate) Leporello sneaks a slice of pheasant, not realizing that he was being observed; he is then asked to sing the Figaro aria with his mouth full.

It is clear that Mozart expected the band to play from within the orchestra, not on stage. There is no time to go on and off, and the changes of horn crook and of clarinet between items would be distracting. Yet the Hoftheater-Rechnungsbüchern of 1788-89 mention a payment for what appears to be 8 musicians for *Don Giovanni,* so one assumes a stage band was an attraction, irrespective of need.

WAM-3a *Die Entführung aus dem Serail* We have remarked that most arrangements are clearly not by Mozart, despite proud claims. This D-DO version for octet (recorded by the Amadeus Winds, L'Oiseau-Lyre 425 690; Sabine Meyer Wind Ensemble, EMI 7243 5 555342) is another matter (30), and can be considered seriously as Mozart's own. The copy is not Mozart's autograph, but it is in the same hand and on the same paper as other Viennese works also in the Fürstenberg library at Donaueschingen. The seventeen numbers last over one hour, covering a large part of the opera, with many ingenious passages and inventive rewriting for the smaller ensemble, with a sense of recreation of a new wind work. True, there are weaker points, but it is outstanding in many ways. But is it largely authentic Mozart? This is less clear. We do know (*HCRL/4* p 570) of a large wind work played at Constanze Mozart's dinner on 22 January 1800, lasting over an hour. If Mozart did complete an arrangement, why did he not use the material later, or mention it later, or write again to his father about it? Why does the writing differ from his other Viennese works c.1782, as in the brilliant horn parts? Could Mozart have sketched larger parts, and then a pupil, perhaps Goepfert, completed it? Yet, if we do say "Not arranged by Mozart, even in part," we have a serious problem with who might have arranged it. There is no contrabassoon, so an early date is likely (1780s-1790s, not the early 1800s), and Sedlak and Triebensee are unlikely. Blomhert (31) rejects Went, Triebensee, Druschetzky, Rosinack, Stumpf, Heidenreich, Fiala, Ahl, von Beecke, Handl and Seyfried; he does not consider Goepfert, who must remain a possibility.

Arrangements of Mozart by others. The list is very long, and includes many operas, many instrumental works and many vocal works. Those other arrangements which take a wind work and make it choral, such as the Adagio of K.361 (K.Anh110 "Quis te comprehendat") are not considered here. Wind arrangements of K.361 have been discussed. For a version of K.388 with cors anglais instead of clarinets, see under Went. The second Minuet and Trio of K.375 is included in a wind arrangement by Heidenreich of the K.407 *Horn Quintet.*

Opera arrangements. The numbers of arrangements of the operas, in decreasing order, are: *Die Zauberflöte, La clemenza di Tito, Don Giovanni, Le nozze di Figaro* (excluding those of "Non più andrai" only), *Così fan tutte, Die Entführung, Der Schauspieldirektor, Idomeneo.* One is struck by *Figaro* lying fourth and by *La clemenza's* great popularity. Recordings of the opera arrangements are burgeoning. In addition to the recordings of early arrangements, movements from *Don Giovanni, Le nozze di Figaro,* and *Die Zauberflöte* have been recorded in enterprising modern arrangements by Steve Martland and his band (Factory Fact 406, no longer available).

Die Entfürung aus dem Serail (arranged by Went **JNW-27.1a**, with clarinets): London Wind Soloists/Brymer, Decca SDD 485; Berlin Philharmonic Winds, Orfeo C260391A. Mannheimer Bläsersolisten RBM 3057; Hungarian Wind Ensemble/Berkes, Quintana QUI 903008; (arranged Went, **JNW-27.2a**, with cors anglais) Netherlands Wind Ensemble, Philips 650 783; SDR Wind Ensemble (arranged Went?) DGG ARC 3150; Ensemble Philidor/Baude-Delhommais, Supraphon SU 3018-2 131; (arranged by Mozart? **WAM-3a**): Amadeus Winds, Oiseau-Lyre 425 690; Sabine Meyer Wind Ensemble, EMI 7234 5 555342.

Le nozze di Figaro (arranged by Went **JNW-28.1a**; versions of "Non più andrai" alone are not noted here): London Wind Soloists/Brymer, Decca SDD 280; Berlin Philharmonic Wind Ensemble, Orfeo C238911A; Mannheimer Bläsersoloisten, RBM 3057; Collegium Musicum Pragense/Vajnár; Melbourne Windpower, Move MD 3110; NY Philomusica Winds, Fono Schallplatten Münster FSM 53046; Consortium Classicum/Klöcker, Harmonia Mundi BR 100073; (arranged by Sartorius) Mozzafiato, Sony Vivarte SK 53965.

Don Giovanni (arranged by Josef Triebensee (son), **JZT-39.1a;**): Hungarian Wind Ensemble/Berkes, Quintana QUI 903008; Athena Ensemble, Chandos ABR 1015; Louvre Musicians, Erato 2292 245 473; Netherlands Wind Ensemble (attributed wrongly to Johann Triebensee [father]), Philips 6500 783; Münchener Bläserakademie, Harmonia Mundi SO 63841; Maurice Bourgue Wind Ensemble, Pierre Verany PV 787033; (arranged Went **JNW-29.2a**, with cors anglais): Ensemble Philidor, Supraphon SU 3018-2 131.

Così fan tutte (arranged by Went, **JNW-30.1a**): Berlin Philharmonic Winds, Orfeo

C260391A; Maurice Bourgue Wind Ensemble, Pierre Verany PV 787033; Hungarian Wind Ensemble (Berkes) Quintana QUI 903008; (arranged ?) Linos Ensemble, Capriccio 10 494.

Die Zauberflöte (arranged by Heidenreich, **JNH-3a**): Münchener Bläserakademie, Harmonia Mundi SO 92841 A; Melbourne Windpower, Move MD 3110; Hungarian Wind Ensemble (Berkes) Quintana QUI 903008; Maurice Bourgue Wind Ensemble (we cannot confirm this is the Heidenreich version, rather than the Went), Pierre Verany PV 787033; (arranged by Georg Schmitt, **GYS-52.2a**): Consortium Classicum, Telefunken 6 35334-00-S01; (Version unknown) Consortium Classicum/Klöcker, Harmonia Mundi BR 100003; Linos Ensemble, Capriccio 10 494.

La clemenza di Tito (usually the Triebensee version, **JZT-40.1a**, although this is not always stated): Berlin Philharmonic Orchestra Wind Ensemble, Orfeo C238911 A; Hungarian Wind Ensemble/Berkes, Quintana QUI 903008; Consortium Classicum/Klöcker Harmonia Mundi BR 100073.

Instrumental works. The authenticity of the *Sinfonia Concertante* K.297b, with wind soloists, is in doubt. It has been arranged attractively by Egk (**WXE-2a**) for 2ob 2cl 2hn 2bn db. Its concertante nature is still evident, but the effect is that of an admirable large-scale serenade. The concertante nature of Mozart's *Horn Quintet K.407*, is striking in the arrangement (K.Anh.183, K.380c) for 2cl 2hn 2bn. This is virtually a two-horn concerto; both horn parts are very soloistic. A minuet and trio are added from the *String Trio K.563*. The sextet appeared as Book 4 of "Pièces d'Harmonie par W A Mozart" in Breitkopf & Härtel's early 19th century series; the arranger is not known, though Heidenreich (qv) did make a version for octet. It is clearly not Mozart's own arrangement. The work is recorded by Mozzafiato on Sony Classical SK 64306. Triebensee's transcription of Mozart's *Symphony in E♭* K.543 is recorded by Consortium Classicum on Dabringhaus und Grimm MDG 301 0496-2.

Dubious and spurious wind works attributed to Mozart. Many of these works are sympathetically played by Consortium Classicum/Klöcker in a series beginning with Harmonia Mundi MDG 301 0494 (a previous version issued as EMI 137 EX 29 0994 3). We can start our discussion with a work still said to be Mozart's own.

The conventional wisdom is that Wolfgang Mozart wrote **WAM-1d** *Divertimento in C, K.188 (K.240b)* as an original wind work, but he merely transcribed **WAM-2d** *Divertimento in C, K.187 (K.159c/K.C17.12)*. This view has strong basic plausibility: K.188 exists in Mozart's autograph (inscribed "Del Sgr Cav Amadeo Wolfgango Mozart," apparently by Leopold Mozart [33]). One movement of K.187 is likewise in autograph, the rest being in Leopold Mozart's hand.

Even with the example of Lewis Carroll's White Queen (who, with practice, could believe up to six impossible things before breakfast) we have been wholly unable to accept K.188 as an original work, seriously composed, by Wolfgang Amadeus Mozart. It has long been known (33) that K.187 comprises arrangements of Starzer and of Gluck. Both K.187 and K.188 consist of movements which are, frankly, short and feeble. We suspect K.188 might also be by Starzer: his *Musica da Camera* for the "Regina di Moscova" is for a similar ensemble (3chalumeaux/fl 3tp(C) 2tp(D)/hn timp), with the same incipit as the first movement of K.187; his now-lost second Musica da Camera is for the same ensemble (2fl 5tp timp) as K.187 and K.188; Traeg listed two works for 2fl 5tp timp as by Starzer in 1804. The supposed dates of composition (1772-1773) are not too long after Starzer's stay in Russia. We conjecture that the lost music became K.188, and was merely copied by Mozart.

It is usually said that K.187, K.188 were written for Salzburg, though it is not clear why. Mozart would not have written them with enthusiasm: the flute was not his favourite instrument, and only a few years earlier Andreas Schachter (6), one of his Salzburg colleagues, observed "If one merely held a trumpet towards him, it was like pointing a loaded pistol at his heart." Nor is the style consistent with Mozart. One can usually compare early and late Mozart without embarrassment. One cannot do so here, if one supposes K.188 to be genuine, and compares it with the march, similarly-scored (fl 2hn 2tp 3tbn timp), in *Die Zauberflöte,* when Tamino and Pamina face their ordeal.

Among the recordings of K.187 are: Edward Tarr Brass Ensemble (as *Musica da Camera Molto Particulare in D Major),* movements 1-5 only, for 2 chalumeaux, 5tp, timp, on this untraced recording; Philip Jones Brass Ensemble (transcribed for brass), Decca SDD 274. Recordings of K.188 include those by the Czech Philharmonic Wind Ensemble, Supraphon 111 1081 2; Academy of St Martin in the Fields/Laird, Philips 422 505-2PME6; Consortium Classicum/Klöcker, EMI 137-290994. Both K.187 and K.188 are recorded by the Philharmonia/Wright on Nimbus NI5121; Clarion Consort/Ton Koopman, Philips 6769056; Virtuosi di Praga, International Culture Network ICN 001; Ensemble of Prague Trumpeters/Svejhovský, Multisonic 31-0069-2 131.

Works in the Köchel Supplement (K.C17.xx series). Several works in the supplement to the latest Köchel catalog are plausibly identified as being by others (12, 13, 33).

The so-called "Munich works." These five-movement works, it is often claimed, were written for the Munich Carnival of 1775. They were included in an early four-volume Breitkopf & Härtel edition, along with other works under Mozart's name. Book 1 is all for 2ob 2cl 2hn 2bn. No 1: movements 5, 4, 6 of the *Gran Partita* K.361, arranged; No 2: K.C17.01 (K.Anh226); No 3 Movements 1, 2, 3, 7 of the *Gran Partita* arrangement. Book 2 includes parts for 2ob 2cl 2hn 2bn, though the oboes in No 4 are redundant. No 4: K.C17.02; No.5: K.C17.03. Book 3 is for 2cl 2hn 2bn, No.6 being the sextet version of K.375. Book 4 is again for 2cl 2hn 2bn: No 7: *Horn Quintet* K.407, with the Minuet and Trio from the *Divertimento* for *String Trio* K.563.

WAM-3d *Divertimento in E♭* K.C17.01 (K.196e, K.Anh226)   This pleasant work is found in both octet form (2ob 2cl 2hn 2bn, recorded by the London Wind Soloists, Decca CS6349) and sextet form (2cl 2hn 2bn, recorded by the Consortium Classicum on BASF KBF 21107). Another MS copy appears under the name of Puschmann, who was active in the 1790s in Johannisberg in the ensemble of Count Schaffgotsch (13 p 353), and the suggestion that the work is by Puschmann is credible, if unconfirmed. There is a MS score by Alois Fuchs (c.1835) in D-B for 2ob 4cl 2hn 2bn.

WAM-4d *Divertimento in B♭* K.C17.02 (K.196f, K.Anh227)   Again, this attractive divertimento exists in both octet and sextet forms (2cl 2hn 2bn with or without 2ob); the oboes ineffectively double the clarinets. If the work was indeed written for the Munich Carnival in 1775, a more likely composer would be Mysliveček, since its style is somewhat similar to his. The sextet form is recorded by the London Wind Soloists on Decca CS 6350 and by the Netherlands Wind Ensemble on Philips PME 6747379.

WAM-5d *Divertimento in E♭* KC.17.03 (K.Anh228)   The work is by Pleyel, and found elsewhere under his name (IJP-6). It is in Pleyel's fluent, pleasing style, and is recorded in Klöcker's set of Mozart's complete wind music, EMI 137 290 994-3.

The Prague Divertimentos.   On 14 January 1792, Johann Traeg advertized music under Mozart's name in the *Wiener Zeitung,* including, inter alia, "4 Parthien à 2 Oboe 2 Clarinetti 2 Cor 2 Fag." These works are to be found in Frankfurt, and are: (Mus.Hs.221) K.361, movements 1, 2, 3, 7; (Mus.Hs.222) K.361, movements 5, 4, 6; (Mus.Hs.220) K.388 (with many errors); (Mus.Hs.223) K.Anh.226 (**WAM-3d**). Of these, Mus.Hs.221 bears Traeg's 1799 catalog number (77/25) on all parts; the others confirm their Traeg origin through similarities of paper and calligraphy. What is surely a copy (probably by Alois Fuchs, c.1836) is in Prague as *Harmonien für Blasinstrumente von W A Mozart Parthia I (II, and so on).* It may date from the setting up of *Mozarts Denkmal in seinen Werken* to commemorate 50 years since the Prague first performance of *Don Giovanni.* There can be little doubt that the Prague copy is not authentic. It has further problems, for a binder has clearly mixed up movements. Two of the *Parthias* appear to be what became an octet version of the *Gran Partita,* (BR above), and three movements are mixed with them (KV.370a Anhang B, a rondo previously not in Köchel); the other *Parthias* are KC.17.04, KC.17.05 and KC.17.07.

Leeson and Whitwell (34) suggest that these works are authentic Mozart wind music, previously lost. Their reconstruction yields the arrangement of the *Gran Partita* and what could reasonably be two serenades. These conjectures are based on two points. First, there are documentary hints that Mozart wrote more wind music than is now generally believed. Secondly, the group of movements in Prague is part of a set containing some genuine Mozart, albeit an arrangement for octet of the *Gran Partita* (**WAM-1**). Despite Leeson and Whitwell's enthusiastic advocacy, we are not persuaded that Mozart wrote these competent, pleasant, though somewhat bland, works. Style is a weak guide, but the banal Trio of KC.17.04 is just one of several un-Mozartian passages. Nor do we accept that the arrangement of the *Gran Partita* is Mozart's own; it seems to be a scissors-and-paste job by a publisher's hack, with little attempt to deal properly with Mozart's unique use of his clarinet and basset horn ensemble.

Leeson and Whitwell reassign movements of K.C17.04, K.C17.05 and KV.370a Anh B (**Serenades II, IV** are the reduction of the *Gran Partita*). They propose as **Serenade I:** Adagio and Allegro in F K.C17.05, Andante in F K.C17.05, Minuet in F KV.370a Anh B, Rondo in F KV.370a Anh B. As **Serenade III,** Leeson and Whitwell propose: Adagio in E♭ K.C17.04, Minuet and trio in E♭ No 1 K.C17.04, Adagio in E♭ K.C17.04, Minuet and trio in E♭ No 2 K.C17.04, Rondo in E♭ KV370a Anh B. The Consortium Classicum have recorded all the individual movements of Serenades I and III, and adopt a different form of **Serenade III,** namely: K.C17.07, Minuet and Trio in E♭ No 2 K.C17.04, Adagio in E♭ K.C17.04, Minuet and Trio in E♭ No 1 K.C17.04, Rondo in E♭ KV.370a Anh B. One can change the order of the tracks to compare options but, frankly, the result is inconclusive. The music has merit, but is surely by some minor composer.

WAM-8d *Divertimenti; in E♭* A set of 32 simple, short movements for 2fl 2ob 2hn 2bn found in the Oettingen-Wallerstein archives, with an added pencil note "Mozart." The music is very modest, and clearly not by W A Mozart; is is vaguely possible that Leopold Mozart was the composer, given the number of his works in D-HR.

WAM-15d *Divertimento in E♭* K.289 (K.271g), for 2ob 2hn 2bn. An attractive work, but doubts arise because of technical errors like parallel fifths (11) and other minor misjudgments. It is recorded along with many of the sets of Salzburg divertimentos. The autograph is said to have been in England, but the manuscript is now lost.

WAM-16d *Variations on a theme of Umlauf* KC17.06 (2cl 2hn 2bn). The title page of the MS in the Rudolfsarchiv, CZ-KRa, states "Serenate / del Sig Kromer [sic] / Variazioni del Sig Mozart." The variations were probably by Eberl; the arrangement for winds may be by Havel, though, contrary to his practice, it does not carry his name.

WAM-18d KC17.09 (2cl 2hn 2bn) This work is attributed to Haydn (Hob II/B7) in Prague and Brno, and by the Pennsylvania Moravians to Joseph Morris (qv), who may be the Bath clarinettist active in the 1790s (another work by Morris is listed in Bethlehem, and there is a *Military Divertimento* by Morris referred to in Pick's accounts for the Royal Music, dated 2 April 1800 (35). An amiable work, recorded by Klöcker's Consortium Classicum (EMI 137-E10 290994), it is surely neither by Mozart nor Haydn. Whether a Joseph Morris wrote it, and who he was, is uncertain.

WAM-19d *KC17.10* An arrangement of Pleyel's *Sinfonia Concertante,* which is listed by us under Pleyel, **IJP-12.3.** It is recorded by the Consortium Classicum on Telefunken 6.35334. There is only one bassoon part, not two as sometimes stated.

WAM-20d *KC17.11* This quartet (ob cl hn bn) has an attractive polonaise, but is otherwise undistinguished. The title "Cassation by Mozart" should be read in the same sense as "Ill Met by Moonlight." It is actually by Lickl (**JGL-6**; Vienna, 1798) (35). Recorded by Consortium Classicum/Klöcker, by Trio Averna on Discover International DISCD 920915/6, and by Britvík, Legát, Trnka and Secký on Multisonic 31 0348-2 (as a work by Pichl (the sleeve note writer has the good sense to say that the name on the manuscript could be Lickl, but comes to the wrong conclusion).

WAM-21d *Parthia Nr 7* Not to be confused with KC.17.06; it is recorded by the Consortium Classicum on EMI 137-E10 290994 and on Dabringhaus und Grimm MDG 301 0496-2. Klöcker's notes remark that the writing seems to be "against" the clarinet.

WAM-22d *[Untitled] in Eb* (2cl 2hn 2bn) A four-movement work from Rajhrad under the name of Mozart, found in Brno by one of us (JAG). It is unlikely to be by Mozart.

1. Ludwig von Köchel 1965 *Chronologisch-thematisches Verzeichnis sämtlicher Tonwerke Wolfgang Amade Mozarts;* 6th edition: Leipzig: Breitkopf und Härtel.

2. W A Mozart 1991 *Thematic catalogue* (Facsimile); London: British Library.

3. *Mozart Letters.*

4. A Einstein 1946 *Mozart;* London: Cassell.

5. O Deutsch 1966 *Mozart: A Documentary Biography:* 2nd Edition (translated Eric Blom, Peter Branscombe, Jeremy Noble); London: A & C Black.

6. E Holmes 1845 (reprinted 1905) *The Life of Mozart;* London: Dent.

7. E Schenk 1960 *Mozart and His Times;* London: Secker and Warburg.

8. S Sadie 1980 *The New Grove Mozart;* London: Macmillan.

9. D Mitchell 1956 (reprinted 1965) *A Mozart Companion;* London: Rockliff Corp/Faber.

10. A Hyatt King 1968 *Mozart's Chamber Music;* London: BBC Publications.

11. E Smith 1982 *Mozart's Serenades, Divertimenti and Dances;* London: BBC Publications.

12. R Hellyer 1973 Musical Review **34** 146.

13. R Hellyer 1975 Haydn Yearbook **9** 349.

14. R Hellyer 1975 Proc Royal Mus Assoc **102** 53.

15. R Hellyer 1981 Musical Times **123** p 468.

16. A M Stoneham 1984 Musical Times **125** 75.

17. W Senn 1961 Acta Musicologica **33** 169.

18. Facsimile of **WAM-1:** *Mozart: Gran Partita* 1976 Washington DC: US Library of Congress, Washington; this has an introduction by A Einstein.

19. D Leeson and D Whitwell 1976-1977 Mozart Jahrbuch p 97.

20. A Tyson 1987 *Mozart: Studies of the Autograph Scores;* Cambridge, Mass: Harvard University Press. See also Tyson's article in ref 2.

21. R Hellyer, BBC Radio 3 broadcast *New Light on Mozart's 13 Wind,* 14 July 1978.

22. J F Schink 1785 *Dramaturgische Fragmente* vol 4 part 2, pp 1001-1025; Graz, reproduced by O E Deutsch (5).

23. F A Philidor *Le maréchal ferrant,* GB-Lbl, G.397.g.

24. B Blomhert 1991 Mozart Jahrbuch (Proc Int Mozart Congress) 206.

25. P L Poulin 1988 Music and Letters **69** 49.

26. R Hellyer 1979 Musica da Camera 75; Oxford: Oxford University Press.

27. B Szabolcsi 1956 Music and Letters **37** 323.

28. M Flothius 1973/1974 Mozart Jahrbuch p 202.

29. M Whewell 1962 Musical Times **103** p19.

30. W Mann 1977 *Operas of Mozart;* London: Cassell, pp 519 et seq.

31. B Blomhert 1987 *The Harmonie of Die Entführung aus dem Serail by Wolfgang Amadeus Mozart: Study about its Authenticity and Critical Edition;* PhD thesis, Den Haag: Rijksuniversiteit Utrecht.

32. *Whitwell/8.*

33. E F Schmidt 1937 Zeitschrift für Müsik 11; see also Mozart Jahrbuch 1960/61 104.

34. D Leeson and D Whitwell 1972 Music and Letters **103** 377.

35. E Croft-Murray 1980 *British Museum Year Book* **4** 135.

MRKVIČKA, Josef *(?1800)* Composer of two funeral marches at Kunvald, Bohemia.

MÜCK (Müch), Beda *(1800)* His *Hallelujah* (the two sets of parts are dated 1833, 1836) at Kucs use flutes rather than oboes, in line with French ensembles.

MÜLLER, Adolf *(1820)* The MS score in Stuttgart for his stage *March* for scene 1 of the 1854 farce *Stadt und Land* styles him Capellm[eister].

MÜLLER, Christian Paul *(1790)* Joseph Spät, the copyist of *Danksagungslied* attributes the work to Müller. It dates from between 1815-1820; the MS bears the note "v[on] Pfarrer zu Obersirebach."

MÜLLER, Francesco Carlo *(1750)* Composer of two works entitled *Offertorium* at St Moritz (Sv Moric), Kroměříž.

MÜLLER, Friedrich (Frédéric) *10 Dec 1786, Orlamünde, near Rudolstadt-12 Dec 1871, Rudolstadt* German clarinettist and friend of Spohr. Müller served in the Rudolstadt wind band from 1811 until 1816, when he took charge of military music for the Schwarzburg-Rudolstadt court. He was the dedicatee of the 1830 *Pièces d'Harmonie* by Walch (qv). Müller became Director of Music at Rudolstadt in 1831, when Eberwein died; in 1853, his half-century of service was rewarded with the title Ducal Councillor.

MÜLLER, Jean-Marie (Johann Michael) *1683, Schmalkalden-1754 Paris* His *12 Sonatas,* dedicated to Count Philipp Reinard of Hanau, are mature examples of music for oboe band. No 1 (for "Oboe de concert" 2ob/vl taille bn basso) is recorded by Ensemble Philidor on Supraphon 11 2182-2 131. It was another, later composer named J M Müller, who wrote an *Ecce panis.*

MÜLLER, Joseph *(1760)* Linked to the Clam Gallas Harmonie; composer of one march.

MÜLLER, Wilhelm August *(1790)* His performance parts to accompany works in the printed *Sammlung verschiedener Kirchenmusiken* are from the church at Herrenberg, Swabia. The works include cantatas for Christmas, Easter and Ascension; interestingly, the bassoon, treated as an alternative to the viola, is used as a tenor instrument.

MÜLLER von KULM, Walter *31 Aug 1899 Basel-3 Oct 1967 Arlesheim* Composer of a setting of Psalm 10 with winds. Director of the Basel Conservatoire from 1947-1964.

MÜNCHS, Conrad *22 Feb 1788, Heertz, Prussia-11 Sept 1835, Paris* "Sous-chef au 6e Régiment de la Garde" and partner of with Louis from 1832-35. He, Louis, Marchal and Berr composed for their *Journal d'harmonie et de Musique Militaire* of 1821-23 (see part 1). In 1823 he published his own *Nouveau Journal,* including arrangements by Berr.

MÜNST, Matth[ias] *(?1780)* The *Mass* **MTM-1v** with winds is attributed to Münst. It was for the Primiz-Feyer (?graduation ceremony) of Matth. Münst von Huggenlaubach.

MÜNSTER, Johann Baptiste *(?1730)* Composer of a *Concertatio* for 2ob 2hn basso.

MUGNONE, Leopoldo *29 Sept 1858, Naples - 22 Dec 1941, Naples* Arranger for winds of works by "J Burgmein," the pseudonym under which Giulio (di Tito) Ricordi (1840-1912, of the family of music publishers) wrote light music.

MULDOWNEY, Dominic *b 19 July 1952, Southampton* He studied with Birtwistle, and with Rands and Blake; he was composer in Residence to Southern Arts from 1974 to 1976, when he moved to the National Theatre. His 1979 ballet *Macbeth* is for winds.

MYSLIVEČEK, Josef *9 March 1737, Prague-4 February 1781, Rome* Many composers suffered from fickle public opinion. Even the most talented could die in abject poverty: Boccherini, d'Ordoñez, Gyrowetz, Dittersdorf, Vanhal, and Mysliveček all died destitute. Mysliveček died (like other composers, including Schubert) mainly from the degeneration of the central nervous system during tertiary syphilis. Mysliveček's memorial in San Lorenzo di Lucina was put up by an English pupil, Barry (1).

Mysliveček completed his apprenticeship as a miller in Prague before turning to music. His early studies were with Josef Seger, who also taught V Mašek. Mysliveček's career in Italy began in 1763, where his fame spread after early operatic successes in Venice (2). The Italians (and others) had problems with his name, calling him "Il divino Boemo" or "Venatorini" ("little huntsman," a translation of "Mysliveček"). When poverty threatened, many composers resorted to intrigue. Mysliveček was an exception who, always spoke well of Mozart, and recommended him for important commissions. The Mozarts met him in Bologna in 1772 at the height of his fame; they saw him in 1777 near the nadir of his fortune, seriously ill. His appearance was horrifying, disfigured by the loss of his nose from bad surgery. "He'd be the man to terrify the orchestra by his very presence" wrote Mozart, when condemning the Salzburg authorities for failing to appoint such a fine musician. Mozart's comment was not in jest. Despite respect and friendship, Mozart could only bring himself to visit Mysliveček once in hospital, and could neither eat nor sleep after his visit (3).

Mysliveček's fall from fame followed the changes in fashion in the decade before Mozart's great operas. Mysliveček's more lasting influence was through his pupils, like Johann Georg (the Abbé) Vogler, himself the teacher of Weber and Meyerbeer. Probably quite a few of Mysliveček's wind works are lost. Some may be uncataloged or under another name. In particular, the three-movement **JFM-1c** *Sujto in Dis,* found in Madrid by Ernest Warburton, is typical of Mysliveček. There are no signs of his wind music in Italy, even though, as he said, "There a musician is valued and appreciated."

JFM-1. *Octet in E♭;* **JFM-2.** *Octet in E♭;* **JFM-3.** *Octet in B♭.* These octets can be dated fairly precisely. The minuet of **JFM-1** is clearly based on on "Ne' di felice quel germe altero" from his oratorio *Abramo e Isaac,* written for performance in Lent 1776 in Florence. **JFM-1** presumably dates from soon after, but before Mysliveček's final collapse in 1779. Interestingly, the Benedictus of Mozart's short *Mass* K.220, written in haste in 1775, is based on a rather similar theme; this may be coincidental. This Tempo di Menuetto has three "Alternativos," for 2cl 2bn, for 2ob 2bn, and for 2hn 2bn. The octets are advanced for their period, and written with care. The obvious comparisons are with the symphonies of the 1770s; the very best (up to Mozart's No 32 or Haydn's No 70) are, of course, more subtle and closely argued, though Mysliveček's wind writing is more mature than Mozart's in K.166 or K.186 of 1773, especially where smaller groups can show their individual colors. Clarinet 2 has characteristic broken-chord rumblings, and needs sensitivity, rather than the aggressive sound implied in some early wind works. The slow movement of **JFM-3** uses a theme from one of Mysliveček's piano concertos (Shaginyan [1]). The horn parts are sometimes formidably high.

The only known copies of the octets are in Donaueschingen, where Rosinack often "improved" such works; the dynamics and articulations may not be Mysliveček's own. Recordings by the Collegium Musicum Pragense of **JFM-1** and **JFM-2** are on Supraphon SUA 59763, with **JFM-3** on Panton 11-0229 and Supraphon 11 0097-1 031G. **JFM-2** is recorded by Queensland Wind Soloists (Brisbane Radio 4MBS CD 1) and unidentified octets are on Music & Arts CD 649 and Ex Libris CD 6010. The octets are all recorded by the Sabine Meyer Wind Ensemble (EMI CDC555 5122), the Cracow Wind Ensemble (Golden Touch Classics 820088), and the Albert Schweitzer Oktett (CPO 999 314-2).

JFM-4. *Cassation, in B♭ (Kasace; Lovecka Parthia* [Hunting Parthia] in some modern versions). This work comprises an opening March and four dances (Menuetto, Pollones, Gigue, Finale). It feels incomplete, partly because there are no slow movements. In style, there are hints of the Munich work K.C17.02 **(WAM-4d)** attributed to Mozart; one could believe that both were by Mysliveček. **JFM-4** is recorded on Panton 11-0229.

1. Barry is named in various sources without detail, sometimes as "Lord Barry" or "Sir Edward Barry". Our searches included various spellings and versions like Barrymore. Excluding musicians of the wrong age (the Earl of Barrymore and his sons) or medical men who neither visited Italy nor were musical, only James Hugh Smith Barry was in

Italy at the right age and time and interested in monuments. He (as reported in *The Times,* July 1987) ran spectacularly into debt and disease in Naples during the 1770s in pursuit of Greek and Roman marbles which were, until sold recently, at Marbury Hall, Cheshire, England. See also the text of M S Shaginyan (GB-Lbl X.439/1; in Russian).
2. Mozart's letter of 7 August 1778 to Abbé Bullinger.
3. The introduction to *Musica Antiqua Bohemica 55* is a good general source of information; see also Ludmila Vrckocová's notes to the Supraphon octet recording.

N, K Active in Elbeteinitz, Bohemia, early in the 19th century.

NÄTHER, Gilbert *b 1948* The *Two South American Songs* for soprano, ob 2bn cbn, were written for "Poetry International," Rotterdam, and published in 1994.

NANKE, Alois, the Elder *d 1834* He was active around Brno, and may be related to:

NANKE, Karel *1768, Nový Jičín-30 Dec 1831, Brno* whose *Easter Song* was acquired by Rahjrad monastery in 1829, and performed on 11 April 1830.

NARCISSE, ( ) Composer of 2 *Pas Redoublés* in a collection at Bad Buchau.

NAUMANN, Johann Gottlieb *17 Apr 1741, Blasewitz-23 Oct 1801, Dresden* Composer of opera and church music (see *Sainsbury*) and of marches for the Regiments von Kalckstein. The bassoon 2 part of his *Terzetto* **JGN-2v** may have been played from the figured bass part. There are oboe parts on the back of the clarinet parts.

NAVA, Gaetano *16 May 1802, Milan-31 Mar 1875, Milan* Composer and singing master, later Professor at the Milan Conservatorio, where he had studied with Federici.

NECCHI, Francesco Antonio *(?1770)* His church music with winds is now in CH-E.

NEITHARDT, August Heinrich *10 Aug 1793, Schleiz-18 Apr 1861, Berlin* Bandmaster whose initiatives revolutionized military music in the German states. He directed the bands of the Garde-Schützen Batallion from 1816-1822 and the Kaiser Franz Grenadier Regiment, Berlin, from 1822-1840; his 1832 *Chorgesang* was for the 40th anniversary of the Austrian Emperor coming to the throne. In 1839, Neithardt became Königlicher Musikdirektor. Many of his compositions and innovations lie outside our field.

NEJEDLY, Roman *9 Apr 1844, Dětenice u Libáně-25 Feb 1920, Manichovo Hradiště* Studied at the Prague Organists' School; from 1871 to 1901, he taught at Litomyšil, where he also was church Chorregent and conductor of the local choral society. His *12 Funeral Songs* of 1881 were a seminal contribution to this subgenre. Even at this late stage, most of the songs were for a specific social group or age group.

NELSON, Oliver E *6 April 1932, St Louis, Missouri-27 Oct 1975, Los Angeles* Any composer who studied piano, saxophone, "taxidermy, dermatology and embalming" (1) deserves notice. Nelson served in the US Marines, then studied with Elliot Carter, and worked with the Ellington and Basie Big Bands before moving to Hollywood. He has written a *Quintet* (1960), *Study in 5/4 for Wind Ensemble* (1967), *Septet for Wind Orchestra* (1968), and *Fugue and Bossa Nova for Wind Orchestra* (1973).
1. N Slominsky 1992 *Baker's Biographical Dictionary of Musicians;* New York: Schirmer.

NEUBAUER (Neubaur, Naibauer), Franz Christoph (Giovanni) *21 Mar 1750, Mělník, near Prague-11 Oct 1795, Bückeburg* Konzertmeister to the Princess of Schaumberg at Bückeburg (where J C F Bach was too). He drank heavily. *Sainsbury* notes a work for winds and violin and bass "in which all the intricacies of wind instruments, calculated for the utmost effect, are intended to be concentrated in one piece." None of the 23 extant parthias include a violin, though several have ad lib violone parts, and their flute parts might be played on a violin. **FCN-3** has a quart-fagott. The *Parthias* **FCN-2, -3** in Rudolstadt are probably the same as the set lost in World War II in Darmstadt.

NEUKOMM, Sigismond von *10 July 1778, Salzburg-3 April 1858, Paris* A student of both Michael and Joseph Haydn. In 1806 Neukomm served as court musical director and as manager of the German Theater in St Petersburg. About 1809 he returned to Vienna, thence to Paris, where he succeeded Jan Ladislav Dussek as Talleyrand's pianist. Metternich's agents believed that Neukomm's playing during the Congress of Vienna was more to hide conspiracy than to please Talleyrand (1). After the restoration, he was made Chevalier de la Légion d'Honneur by Louis XVIII, partly as a result of a *Requiem* for Louis XVI. From 1816 to 1821 he went with the Duke of Luxembourg to Rio de Janeiro, returning after the revolution in Brazil. His oratorio *David* for the 1834 Birmingham Festival was so enjoyed by the musicians that, as Mendelssohn noted (2), they called him "the King of Brummagem." The next year, alas, the organizers "neglected him shamefully," and only one short work of Neukomm's was performed.

SVN-1 *9 Marches and Dances* and **SVN-2m, 3m** *Marches (Prinz Carl von Mecklenburg, Prinz Friedrich)* These are in bound sets of parts at Regensburg purchased c.1820 from Kapellmeister Wieland (whose location is unknown). The first march of **SVN-1** has the name "Goepfert" in pencil. The *Marcia Prinz Albert* and *Marcia Prinz Heinrich* **SVN-4m, 5m** were probably rescored by Anton Schneider.

SVN-2 *Valse "La Blosseville"* One of the "morceaux" written for the military band (pic 3cl hn tp b-dr) on board the frigate Hermione en route to Rio de Janeiro in 1816 (3, 4).

SVN-4 *Serenade in Bb* Written in 1796 for Salzburg, this large-scale work is symphonic in structure, starting with a slow, serious introduction and ending with a high-spirited Rondo. It is recorded by the Consortium Classicum on Koch Schwann 310002.

SVN-1m *13 Marches à grande orchestre militaire, NV166* Written in Rio de Janeiro in February 1819. No 8, for Prinz August's Regiment, is recorded on SERP MC 7033. The sleeve refers to "onze (11, not 13) marches characteristiques" intended for Prussian regiments, some being identified in pencil on the manuscript.

Funeral Marches and Religious Instrumental Works Neukomm wrote several funeral marches for winds. **SVN-1t** *Trauermarsch in D minor, NV153* is dated June 1817, and was written in Rio "sur la mort du C[om]te da Barca." **SVN-2t** *Marche funèbre militaire, NV122*, dated 12 January 1813, was written in Paris for Count Walther, "général de division ... et exécutée à distance par l'orchestre du régiment en accompagnant le cortège jusqu'au lieu de sépulture." We believe that this is the same as the work in D minor recorded on SERP MC7033, where it is given the date 12 December 1813 and titled "Marche pour les funérailles d'un héros." **SVN-1e** *Trauermarsch NV11* was for the tragedy *Hanno* (1804, St Petersburg). **SVN-3** is the *Fantasie, in Eb NV170* on "L'Adoration du St Sépulchre" or "Fantasie pour le Vendredi- Saint: l'Adoration du Saint-Sacrement." It is dated 17 March 1819, Rio. A "Prière" for winds is mentioned on the recording SERP MC 7033.

Vocal and choral works Neukomm wrote several choral works with massive wind bands, such as the *Messe St Louis Philippe* (NV582, **SVN-1v**) of 12 December 1838 performed with 2000 voices in Mainz 24 June 1840. This seems to be the Gutenberg monument mass *"St Louis Philippi."* Other large masses with winds include the *Messe épiscopale* (NV849) or 32nd Mass *"St Cécile,"* the *Messe Solennelle, "St Joseph,"* the *Requiem 14th Mass* (NV544), and the *Requiem* and *Kyrie* (NV791).

SNV-1va *NV55 Missa St Hieronymi* A reworking of Michael Haydn's *Mass* (also for voices and winds). Neukomm had asked his teacher, Michael Haydn, for a copy, which he had partly rescored (3 pages only) for clarinets and flutes. Neukomm completed it 1809 "in the name of the widow" (the widow of Michael Haydn; Haydn had died in 1806).

1. Susan Mary Alsop 1984 *The Congress Dances: Vienna 1814-1815;* London: Weidenfeld and Nicolson; p 163.

2. Mendelssohn (letter of 4 October 1837), in Lady Wallace (translator) 1862 *Letters by Felix Mendelssohn-Bartholdy;* London: Longman, Green, Longman and Roberts.

3. Rudolph Angermüller 1977 *Neukomm, Sigismund: Werkverzeichnis, Autobiographie, Beziehung zu seinen Zeitgenossen;* Munich: Katzbichler. Angermüller's numbering (e.g.

NV170) is used, as is Neukomm's own chronological thematic list. *New Grove* lists 10 marches for wind band (1 published), 2 phantasies for winds, 6 marches for winds, and works "mostly" for winds: 1 nonet, 1 octet **(SNV-4)**, 2 septets (one is NV517, for fl 2cl hn bn tp db) and 1 sextet (NV469, for 2hn tp 3tb); we cannot identify the others. NV122, 142, 143, 153, 158, 166, 416, 445, 496, 568, 600, 623 are marches for large bands.
4. Luiz de Azevedo 1959 Musical Quarterly 45 p 475.

NEUMANN, Anton (Franz) *baptized 28 Feb 1740, Brno-Nov 1776, ?Kroměříž* Kapellmeister at Kroměříž. His *6 Parthias* are scored for 2ca 2hn bn.

NEUMANN, Heinrich *1792, Heiligenstadt-4 Apr 1861, Heiligenstadt* Clarinettist, composer and arranger, who conducted a wind band in Paderborn before moving to Detmold in 1823 as principal clarinet in the Lippe Kapelle and the band of the Leopold Corps. His brother Philipp played clarinet and flute in the band. He became conductor of the band in 1824, and left the court orchestra. He moved to Cologne 1829 to conduct another military band; in the 1840s, he moved to Antwerp, to conduct the Royal Wind Band. His arrangements for Detmold include works by Cherubini and Carafa.

NEX, Christopher Michael Martin, *10 June 1945, Capetown, S Africa,* and

NEX (née Turner), Frances Hilary *11 May 1945, Bideford, UK* Amateur bassoonist and amateur flautist, whose enjoyment of chamber music for wind and mixed ensembles has led them to research and make available practical versions of music otherwise hard to find, e.g. of Brahms/Schubert *Ellens zweiter Gesang* and the *"St Antoni" Divertimento*.

NICHOLS, Red *8 May 1905, Ogden, Utah-28 June 1965, Las Vegas* Jazz cornetist and band leader. His splendid *Holiday for Woodwinds* is a rare jazz work for wind ensemble.

NIELSEN, Carl *9 June 1865 Nørre Lyndelse, near Odense-3 Oct 1931 Copenhagen* Nielsen's achievement is dominated by his six symphonies and the opera *Maskerade.* His *Wind Quintet* (fl ob/ca cl hn bn) is perhaps the finest of the genre. Nielsen was born on Fyn, Denmark, not far from the birthplace of Hans Christian Andersen. He learned trumpet and violin as a boy, playing in several bands. With his later experience in the Royal Chapel Orchestra, he was a very practical composer as well as an original one. His 1922 *Wind Quintet,* (Op 43, FS100 [1], **CAN-2**) is a splendid work, showing many links to wind harmony, including the frequent use of instruments in pairs (e.g., bassoon and horn). Nielsen had heard the Copenhagen Wind Quintet playing at a friend's house. The *Quintet* which followed could have borne the Elgarian dedication "to my friends pictured within." The friends (Paul Hagemann, fl; Svend Felumb, ob; Aage Oxenvad, cl; Hans Sørensen, hn; Knud Lassen, bn) gave the first performance on 9 October 1922. Nielsen planned a concerto for each, a project incomplete at his death. The *Quintet* is in four movements. The fresh, clear-textured, opening Allegro ben moderato wanders between E and C, a relaxed pastoral movement. The eccentric Minuet and Trio is undoubtedly of the 20th century, but with echoes of two centuries earlier. The third movement, Praeludium, is intense and rhapsodic, the sombre cor anglais sound giving an elemental feel. This leads directly into the Finale, variations on an original gentle hymn tune ("Min Jesus, lad min Hjerte faa en saandan Smag paa dig"; roughly, "Jesus, make my heart discern Thee"). The ten variations ingeniously incorporate character sketches of the players. One is for horn alone, another for clarinet alone. There are many vivid contrasts before the 3/4 chorale reappears, now a 4/4 Andantino Festivo.

The *Quintet* provides a link to his other works for winds, both those which are arguably wind harmony and those using winds alone (like the Humoresque of his *6th Symphony;* the Intermezzo of the *4th Symphony* is also largely for winds) which are different. Most of his other works for winds were occasional pieces for festivals or plays. While they show care and often imagination, they are not easily accessible (we believe that most are in DK-Kk) and have had only rare performances. One exception is the witty *Serenata in vano* (FS68 of 1914, for cl hn bn vc db), apparently the sad story of a serenade which does not succeed. There are several occasional works for larger ensembles. The *Paraphrase for wind band on "Naermere Gud til dig"* (Nearer my God to Thee; **CAN-1**, FS63, BM50 [2]) of 1912 is recorded by the Danish National Radio Symphony Orchestra/Rozhdestvensky on Chandos CHAN9287. Choral works include occasional works like the *Hymn til Kunsten* (Hymn to Art; FS141, BM316, 1929) **CAN-1v** to a text by Sophus Michaelis, for soprano and tenor soloists, SATB chorus and wind band. Two settings of texts by Hans Hartvig Seedorff Pedersen are for narrator, male voices and winds: the *Kantate til Polyteknisk Laerean stalts 100-Aars Jubilaeum* of 1929 and *Digtning i Sang og Toner (ved Svϕmmehallens Indrielse)* or *Suommehals-Kantata* (FS153a, BM313) **CAN-3v** completed on 11 October 1930.

Other works for wind band were for the theater. The incidental music to N F S Grundtvig's *Paaske-Aften* (BM341) is for male voices and wind; the autograph is dated 4 April 1931. The plot of Harald Bergstedt's play *Ebbe Skammelsen* **CAN-2v** confirms the reputation of Scandinavian playwrights for gloom. Nielsen's incidental music (FS117, BM336; the *Suite* for winds is BM51) uses soloists, unison chorus and a standard orchestral wind section, dramatically and effectively. The autograph is dated 12 June 1925. Robert Simpson used a theme from this music for variations. The play was one of several written for Dyrehavsbakken, an open-air theater at the northern outskirts of Copenhagen. Performance outdoors favored a wind band, sometimes including exotic instruments, like the four valveless Viking bronze horns (lurs) in Oehlenschläger's *Hagbath and Signe* (BM341, written in April and May 1910). Oehlenschläger's *Sankt Hansaftenspil* (St John's Eve play, BM347) of 1913 uses winds with baritone soloist and chorus. All three works are recorded by the Odense Philharmonic Choir and Symphony orchestra/Tamas Vëto on Kontrapunkt 32188.

1. The FS numbers come from the Fog and Schousboe catalogue (see the Appendix to Robert Simpson 1979 *Carl Nielsen: Symphonist;* London: Kahn and Averill).
2. BM numbers relate to Birgit Bjørnum and Klaus Møllerhøj 1992 *Carl Nielsens Samlung;* Copenhagen: Det Kongelige Bibliotek Museum Tusculanums Forlag.

NINI, Alessandro *1805, Fano-1880, Bergamo*   Nini, a graduate of the Bologna Liceo Musicale, became the Director of the Imperial School of Singing, St Petersburg in 1830. Some of his operas were produced in Italy after his return. He was Director of the Instituto Donizetti from 1847 to 1875 and, from 1847, of the Capella Musicale at the Basilica di S Maria Maggiore, Bergamo. In this period, he wrote only church music.

NIPEL, Francesco   "Maestro della Accademia filarmonica" in Lecco, and composer of two marches, one based on Donizetti's *La gitana.*

NOACK, ( ) *(active c.1800)*   Musician at Lititz, perhaps one of the Moravian Brethren.

NOCENTINO (Nocentini), Domenico *18 Mar 1848, Laterino, Arezzo-29 Dec 1924, Florence*   Clarinettist, pianist and organist who studied with Bimboni and Mabellini (qv) at the Conservatorio in Florence, later teaching there from 1892-1921. He is said to have been the first to use a B♭ clarinet in all orchestral work, irrespective of key. His three-movement *Sinfonia* "Labor Omnia Vincit" **DXN-1** was written for a course at the Conservatorio in 1886. **DXN-1m**, *Santa Maria*, is a religious march.

NØRHOLM, Ib *b 2 Jan 1931, Copenhagen*   His *Idylles d'Apocalypse* is recorded on Erato STU 71509.

NOVAČEK, Rudolf *7 Apr 1860, Weisskirchen (Bela Crkva, Serbia)-12 Aug 1929 Prague*   Nováček was a pupil of Dvořák and, like Fučik, became a bandmaster as well as a composer. He travelled widely within Austro-Hungary. His *Sinfonietta* Op 48 in D minor was first performed on 11 November 1888 in Prague, although it was not published until 1905. Its four movements have an unmistakable Eastern European sound which makes it a clear descendant of Dvořák's *Serenade.* It is recorded by the Josef Triebensee Ensemble on Contrapunctus Musicus VC 2447.

NOVOTNÝ (Novotni), A   Late arranger of operas at the Augustinian monastery, Brno.
NOVOTNÝ (Nowotny), Johann   Teacher (Lehrer) at Rychnov nad Kněžnou, Bohemia, and composer of a set of *Stationes*.
NUDERA, Vojtěch (Adalbert Jovanne) *1748-1811*   Violinist at Prague Cathedral, and composer of works for winds including several for 3bthn (**VXN-5[-10]**) from Kolovrat, two *Parthias* for 2cl 2hn (2)bn (one of them, **VXN-2**, is recorded by the Prague Mozart Trio on Multisonic 31 0250-2, together with the *Divertimento* **VXN-8**, here for 2cl bn, and two *Parthias "la Campagna"* for 2ob 2hn bn.

OBERSTEINER, Johann   Composer of a *Harmonie Feste Messe*, Op 237, which, from its scoring, probably dates from the mid-19th century.
ODSTRČIL, Karel *b 5 Aug 1930, Valašské Meziříčí*   Odstrčil was a professor of mining technology at Příbram from 1957 to 1963. Klement Slavický, in particular, influenced his subsequent career as a composer. Odstrčil's music includes much for small wind ensembles, in particular, a wind quintet, plus a *Concerto* for percussion and 8 winds, a *Concerto* for trombone and winds, and *Moravian Archway* for 11 brass.
OESTREICH, Carl *(1800)*   A composer who chose some unusual instrumental groups, such as solo hn, fl cl 2hn bn pf, as well as writing larger military pieces. His *Sinfonia* **CXO-8** is a real symphony in size: the final Rondo is 499 bars long. The *Fantasie* **CXO-9** is also a large and complex work in many sections. Possibly Oestreich was a bandmaster in Frankfurt am Main. Most of his works date from the early 1830s.
OHNEWALD, Joseph *1781-1856*   The MS parts of his *Deutsche Messe* (CATB, 2cl 2hn basso) were copied in Gutenzell, Swabia, in 1847.
OLBRICH, Fl[orian?] *(1810)*   Composer and arranger associated with the Hohenlohe Harmonie. Some of his works use "cor chromatica," perhaps the two-valved form popular from the late 1820s, and possibly that used in Beethoven's *9th Symphony*.
OLIVER, Stephen *10 Mar 1950, Chester, England-29 Apr 1992, London*   Composer of opera and of many scores for radio and televison plays, including the BBC's *Lord of the Rings*. **SXO-2**. *Character Pieces for Wind Octet Derived from Metastasio's "La clemenza di Tito."* was written to precede the 1991 Glyndebourne production of Mozart's opera. It grew out of Oliver's experience in writing new recitatives to replace those hastily prepared by Süssmayr on the coach trip to Prague. The *Character Pieces* are recorded by the London Philharmonic Winds on EMI CDC 7 54424. Oliver remarked that the work is as much about Metastasio as Mozart, and especially about interactions and tensions between the main characters. It is a tough but impressive set of seven short movements: Rome; Vitellia and Sesto; Rome; Servilia and Annio; Rome; Tito; Presto. For other Glyndebourne commissions, see Dove, Harvey, Osborne, and Saxton.
OLSSON, Sture *3 Sept 1919-6 Jan 1987, ?Sweden*   Composer for winds of a 1974 *Divertimento* and of *Billstroem Blues* (1983).
d'ORDOÑEZ, Carlo *19 Apr 1734, Vienna-6 Sept 1786, Vienna*   Little known, he died in poverty, yet his music was mistaken for that of the finest masters (1; *HCRL/2* p 389). Apart from his octet for the Schwarzenberg Harmonie (a transcription by Went?), two lost works for winds are cited under his name. One is for two wind bands (31 players), noted in the *Wiener Diarium* of 1779 for a fireworks display in the Prater, *Das Denkmal des Friedens* (commemorating peace, rather like Handel's *Fireworks Music*). Presumably the event was the Treaty of Teschen, ending the War of the Bavarian Succession; this war had started with the death of the Elector of Bavaria, the event which also led to Mannheim players like Danzi and Fiala moving to Munich. The *Partita Turc,* listed in Traeg's 1799 catalog (long after the composer's death), may have been an arrangement.
1. A P Brown 1978 *Carlo d'Ordonnez: A Thematic Catalog;* Detroit: Michigan Information Coordinators (Detroit Studies in Musicology 39).

OSBORNE, Nigel *b 23 June 1948, Manchester* Osborne studied at Oxford with Leighton and Wellesz, then with Rodzinski; he is now Professor at Edinburgh University. *Albanian Nights* was written to precede performances of *Così fan tutte* at Glyndebourne in 1991, and is recorded by the Orchestra of the Age of Enlightenment (which gave its first performance) under Antony Pay on EMI CDC 7 54424. It exploits the sounds and demands of early instruments, such as the tuning inequalities of natural horns crooked in E and E♭. The title relates not just to the disguises in Mozart's opera, but also metaphorically to the way in which we, in the twentieth century, deceive ourselves when we attempt to respond to Mozart's day and "authentic" performances of early music. For other Glyndebourne commissions, see Dove, Harvey, Oliver, and Saxton.

OSCHMANN, ( ) *(?1800)* Composer (of *Variations on "Die Flasche"*) associated with the Lippe Kapelle, Detmold.

OSSWALD, Paul Anton *(1790)* Oboist in the Augustinian Harmonie, Brno, from 1815-1821. He made a comprehensive arrangement for winds of his own opera, *L'uomo Négro (Der schwarz Mann) [sic]*, the opera, now lost, may have been for the Brno German Opera. His cantata **PAO-1v** honors Friedrich Franz, who recommended the famous geneticist Mendel to the monastery in 1843 *(Cantate zur Namensfeyer des Hochwürdigen und Hochgelehrten Herrn Friedrich Franz verdenstvolle Professor der Physik aus Philosophischer Institute zu Brünn)*. This piece was probably borrowed for the Nová Říše Harmonie but never returned to the Augustinian monastery at Brno. Osswald describes himself as "Alumnus" in the dedication of another cantata for the monastery, so he cannot have belonged to the monastery at that time. Some of his arrangements, like the overtures to *Don Giovanni* and *Die Zauberflöte*, filled gaps in the Brno repertory.

OTTERLOO, Willem van *27 Dec 1907, Winterswijk-27 July 1978, Melbourne* Respected conductor, who has recorded his attractively-scored *Symphonietta* with the Amsterdam Concertgebouw Orchestra (Colophon/Target CVCD 9).

OZI, Étienne *9 Dec 1754, Nîmes-5 Aug 1813, Paris* Director of the Magasin de Musique des Fêtes Nationales from March 1797. Many of his arrangements were written between 1783 and 1789 (see part 1 for his journals activities). His *Hymne à l'Hymen pour la célébration des mariages* **EXO-1mv** was for the revolutionary years, when substitutes were needed for traditional church music. Ozi was famous as a bassoonist, and his 1803 *Méthode de Basson* was used for many years.

PACÁK, František *(?1800)* Composer of a set of *Stationes* used at one of the two major churches in Nový Brdžov, near Jičín, Bohemia. There are three different scorings, that for winds being first, showing the work remained popular for some time.

PAER, Ferdinando *1 June 1771, Parma-3 May 1839, Paris* Famous for his operas in his lifetime, Paer began his career in the 1790s, composing for the Italian Opera in Venice. Later he moved to Dresden, where his most famous opera, *Leonora*, was a precursor to Beethoven's *Fidelio*. Paer was Maître de Chapelle for Napoleon, travelling with him to Poland in 1806; he wrote the bridal march for Napoleon's wedding in 1810. From 1812 until 1827, Paer was associated with the Italian Opera in Paris; like many successful composers, he was known for self-interest and self-promotion, although his musicianship was not disputed; his funeral march from *Achille* impressed Beethoven. His terzetto "Sulle soglie sacrate" from this opera is scored for solo voices and a stage wind band.

PÄRT, Aavo *b 11 Sept 1935, Paide, Estonia* Pärt's early career was as a sound director for Estonian Radio. During this time, he studied with Eller in Tallin. His style developed in a distinctive way, austere and religious. This is evident in his *Fratres*, combining the hymnlike with bare fifths, and a sound which becomes deeper and richer in a series of variations. Pärt has written several versions differing in scoring and other details. These, with the arrangement for wind octet and percussion by Beat Briner (qv) are recorded on Telarc CD-80387 by I Fiaminghi/Rudolph Werthen.

PAISIELLO, Giovanni *8 May 1740, Roccaforzata-5 June 1816, Naples* The son of a veterinary surgeon, whose operas (1) brought him fame. Catherine the Great invited him to St Petersburg from 1776 to 1784. His music for winds was begun in Russia in 1777. Several items for winds appear in his 1780 *Alcide al Bivio* for the Empress's nameday; the march was used again in *Pirro* (Naples 1787). *Il mondo della luna* was written for the lavish inauguration of the Kamenny (Bolshoi) Theater in 1783, and uses two wind bands (up to 4cl 4hn 2bn "sopra il teatro" and in the orchestra, but usually both 2cl 2hn 2bn). Napoleon invited Paisiello to Paris from 1801 until 1803. The Prayer (No 14, Domine salvum fac) in his *Mass in Bb* for Napoleon's coronation (2 February 1804) includes two wind orchestras, which faced each other across Notre Dame. He wrote *Buonaparte's Grand March* for Spain; only the piano version survives. Some of Paisiello's music for Napoleon is recorded by the Prague Symphony Orchestra/Brizio on Studio SM12 2389. For Paris, he wrote a march in memory of General Hoche (this march includes strings; for details of Hoche, see part 1, ref 122).

Paisiello's *Serenata* **GXP-1** has a simple guitar part throughout, mainly consisting of Alberti patterns. Originally, it followed the Praeludio which opens his opera *Elvira* (Naples, 1794). The one-movement *Divertimentos,* including the set for Catherine the Great mentioned in part 1, have some interesting titles: **GXP-2** La Diana, **GXP-3** Il Mezzo Giorno, **GXP-4** Il Tramontar del Sole, **GXP-5** L'Andare a Letto. He included sections for winds in some of his larger works. In particular, many of his operas contain items using winds alone or with voices. *Achille in Sciro* contains a March for 2fl 2cl 2hn 2bn. His opera *Prosperine* (Paris, 1803) includes a chorus of nymphs, who sing "derrière le théâtre" with 2fl 2cl 2hn 2bn; the clarinet parts are written in the tenor clef. *Didone abbandonata* (1794) uses a wind octet as well as the orchestra in Enea's aria (No 22) and the preceding accompanied recitative.

Many of his works were arranged for winds, like the movement of a symphony which appears, unacknowledged, in Mozart's K.166 (**WAM-3**). The three marches **GXP-1m(-3m)** in M J Gebauer's *Journal de Musique Militaire* are probably arranged. Paisiello's popular opera, *La molinara* (Naples 1788), exists in at least three versions by Went alone.

1. Michael F Robinson, assisted by Ulrike Hofmann 1989 *Giovanni Paisiello. A Thematic Catalogue of his Works;* Stuyvesant, NY: Pendragon Press.

PALKOVSKY, Pavel *b 18 Dec 1939, Zlín* Composer of a work for accordion and winds.

PANIZZA, Giacomo (Jacques) *27 Mar 1803, Castellazo Bormida-1 May 1860, Milan* Pupil of Allievo in Milan; from 1839 to 1859 Maestro di Cembalo and director of the orchestra at La Scala, Milan. The Artaria title page of his attractive *Sestetto* uses the term "clarini" for the clarinets; trumpets are clearly not intended.

PANUFNIK, Sir Andrzej *24 Sept 1914, Warsaw-27 Oct 1991, London* After leaving the Warsaw Conservatory, he studied conducting with Weingartner in Vienna shortly before World War II. After the War, he conducted in Kraków, then in Warsaw; he emigrated to England in 1954, becoming a British citizen in 1961. Panufnik was one of the leaders of Polish experimental music in the 1940s, writing music which is both challenging and rewarding. His compositions won many prizes.

PARISOT, Octave *(?1790)* Composer of marches after 1823; the *Pas Redoublé Favoris de S.A.R. le Duc d'Orléans* is dedicated to the French Army in Belgium, and the *Pas de charge* dedicated "au Roi" is claimed to be a favorite of the Duc de Nemours.

PAŘÍZEK, Alexis (Alexius) Vincent *10 Sep 1748, Prague-15 Apr 1822, Prague* Composer of a 6-movement *Nocturno* for 2ob 2cl 2hn 2bn, a *Marcia militaire,* and church music for choir, winds and organ. One set of his **AVP-1v** *Messlieder* comes from the Dominican monastery in Cheb.

PARRY, Sir Charles Hubert Hastings *27 Feb 1848, Bournemouth-7 October 1918, Rustington, UK* Parry's image as a conservative landowner was deceptive. He rejected orthodox religion, and was one of the first drivers to receive a ticket for speeding. He contributed to the revival of English music, and the *Nonet in Bb Op 70*, **CHP-1**, is advanced for its time (1877). An interesting work rather than a great one, it is cyclic, involving themes common to its four movements. The opening Allegro sounds like early Strauss, but predates Strauss's earliest wind works by five years. The Scherzo, in which the cor anglais is used, is weaker. The reflective Largo also uses the cor anglais, and is more effective than the Finale, a rather pale imitation of Schumann. The work was not performed in public in his lifetime, though the MS parts in the Royal College of Music show it was rehearsed. It is recorded by Capricorn on Hyperion CDA 66291.

PARRY, John *18 Feb 1776, Denbigh-8 Apr 1851, London* A Welsh musician whose many talents showed early in his career, Parry joined the Denbigh Militia as clarinettist in 1795, when Rockeman (qv) was Bandmaster. Two years later, Parry himself became Master of Music, a position he held for 10 years. The *Royal Denbigh Militia March* is one of a series, each bearing the name of an officer of the regiment. Parry became known as "Bardd Alaw" (Master of Song) for his contributions to Eisteddfodou at Wrexham in 1820 and Brecon in 1822. His mastery of wind instruments was seen at a concert for Miss Randles in 1806 at the Hanover Square Rooms directed by the Honorable John Spencer (qv). Parry played "alternately, the flute, clarionet, and two and three flageolets" (1). He was also a harpist, as was his son, John Orlando Parry (1810-1879); John Parry (1710-1782), the blind harpist of Ruabon (2) is no relation.

Most of Parry's wind music dates from the first two decades of the 19th century. He settled in London in 1807, and was associated with Vauxhall Gardens and with James Hook. Wind arrangements **JBP-1ma** of twelve of Hook's songs are one result of this association. At that time Welsh music was becoming increasingly fashionable and, for good commercial reasons, Welsh, Scottish and Irish traditions were being invented rather than rediscovered (3). Parry did much to record surviving music from harpists of his generation. He may well have invented "traditional" penillion singing, in which the harp repeats a melody while a singer verses in descant, often improvised (3). Two sets of Welsh airs were set for military band, under the title *The Ancient Britons' Martial Music*. We have been unable to trace a surviving copy.

1. *Sainsbury* Vol 2, p 335.
2. O Ellis 1980 *The Story of the Harp in Wales;* Cardiff: University of Wales Press p 78.
3. E Hobsbawn and T Ranger (editors) 1983 *The Invention of Tradition;* Cambridge: Cambridge University Press, p 76.

PARRY-JONES, Gwyn *b 23 Oct 1946, Cardiff* Bassoonist, university lecturer, and composer and arranger for winds of Mozart works for mechanical organ: the *Fantasia* K.608 and *Adagio & Allegro* K.594. He studied with David Wynne and Alun Hoddinott.

PARSCH, Arnošt *b 12 Feb 1936, Bučovice* A faculty member, Brno Janáček Academy, which he had joined in 1963 as a pupil after an early career as an economist. His Concerto for *Winds, Percussion and Piano* dates from his student period.

PASCAL, Claude *b 19 Feb 1921, Paris* Composer and critic; winner of the Prix de Rome, 1945. Professor of reed instruments from 1951 and Deputy Director from 1966 at the Paris Conservatoire, where he studied. He writes in a classical, tonal tradition.

PASSER, Alois Wolfgang *(1790)* His *2 Prozessions-Lieder* show an enterprising range of options as regards text and instrumentation.

PAUER, Jiří *b 22 Feb 1919, Libušín* Pupil of Alois Hába, prolific composer and active in musical organization. His works for winds range from *Aurora,* a gala overture for large wind orchestra, to a *Wind Quintet* (1961) and small pieces. His *Concertante (Koncertní) Music for 13 Winds* (not the Mozart combination) dates from 1971.

PAUKERT, Stephan (J) *(1800)* His two funeral songs (dated 3 June 1831, 11 June 1840) are in the Česká Třebová archive.

PAYER, Hieronymous (Jérome) *15 Feb 1787, Meidling near Vienna-17 Aug 1845, Wiedburg* Teacher, performer and prolific composer in Vienna, in Amsterdam from 1824, in Paris, and again in Vienna. Payer studied music from age 6 and learned to play many instruments. In 1809, he became Kapellmeister at the Sommertheater, Vienna, and in 1811 organist for the kk Redouten-Saale in the Theater an der Wien. His wind music consists mainly of waltzes and marches, some including parts for keyed trumpet.

PAZ, Juan Carlos *5 Aug 1901, Buenos Aires-25 Aug 1972, Buenos Aires* A student of d'Indy (qv), Paz wrote his wind music before he adopted serial techniques in 1934. Paz founded new music concerts from 1937, and co-organized the Grupo Renovación.

PEARSALL, Robert Lucas *14 Mar 1795, Bristol-5 Aug 1856, Wartensee, Lake Constance* His output includes works for winds and organ. We have not been able to verify the following works for voices and winds, all from the last decade of his life, and all said to be in CH-E: *Introitus in D; Adeste Fidelis* (1847); *Ecce quam bonum* (1846); *Lamentatio III in Sabbato Sancto Oratio Jeremiae* (1852); *Pange Lingua* (1847); *Requiem* (1853-56); *Te Deum* (1847); *Tenebrae* (1849); *Veni Creator* (date not known).

PECHATSCHEK (Pechaczec, Pecháček, Petraczek), František (Franz) Martin *10 Nov 1763, Ustí nad Orlicí-26 Sept 1816, Vienna* Of his various works for wind harmony, one (**FMP-1,** *Variations*) has parts for oboes and trumpets which may have been added by Havel (who was also the copyist; the parts are dated 3 September 1805).

PELLARINI (Pellarin), Giuseppe *(active 1841-1850)* Composer of church choral music now in I-Vsmc.

PERCIVAL, John *(1760)* Master of the Bristol Volunteers Band.

PERSUIS, Louis Luc Loiseasu de *4 July 1769, Metz-20 Dec 1819, Paris* Composer, violinist, teacher, and successful musical administrator, whose wide-ranging career owed much to Lesueur's support; indeed, his one work for winds is a *Notturno* based on Lesueur's *Ossian*. He assisted J B Rey at the vast coronation ceremony for Napoleon and, late in life, showed his skills in opera management.

PETTER, Jan František (Johann Franz) *(1790), active Česká Třebová, Bohemia, 1818* Composer of church music (hymns, funeral songs), normally accompanied by 2cl 2hn bn. Petter may have written some of the other, anonymous, works from Česká Třebová.

PETYREK, Felix *14 May 1892, Brno-1 Dec 1951, Vienna* Composer and pianist, a pupil of Godowsky, Sauer and Schreker in Vienna, and influenced by Mahler. He taught at the Salzburg Mozarteum, then at the Berlin Hochschule from 1921 to 1923, during which period his *Divertimento for 8 Winds* (**FZP-1**) was written.

PEZZOLI, Antonio *1842, Leffe-1908, Leffe, Italy* Founder and Maestro del Corpo Musicale di Leffe; his *Duettino [Qui tollis]* with winds is dated 19 July 1898.

PEZZOLI, Giovanni *1870, Leffe-1934, Leffe, Italy* Son of Antonio Pezzoli (qv), and Maestro del Corpo Musicale di Leffe at various times between 1908 and 1929. He wrote several choral works with winds (*Domine ad adjuvandum; Kyrie*) in the 1890s.

PEZZOLI, Guiseppe *1831, Leffe-1908, Leffe, Italy* Brother of Antonio Pezzoli; organist in Bergamo and its vicinity (Bianzano, Pejz, Cazzano, Cene, Leffe); singer in theaters in Parma, Bologna and Rome, and in many churches and theaters in Bergamo and Brescia. He was involved with military bands in Cremona and Clusone in 1861 and 1862. Guiseppe Pezzoli wrote many religious choral works with wind ensemble, some whose scoring places them outside our remit. All three Pezzolis wrote secular works for the Corpo Musicale di Leffe, but we have not been able to confirm the scorings.

PFEILSTÜCKER, Nicolas *(1780)* His *3 morceaux de musique militaire* are dedicated (like a march by Bitterman, qv) to Prince Eugène Napoleon, presumably Eugène Beauharnais, son of Napoleon's wife Josephine.

PFLÜGER, Hans Georg *b 26 Aug 1944, Swabisch Gmünd* Composer of a work **HGP-2** for 2ob 2cl 2hn 2bn db whose title *Ama-Deus* points to its link to Mozart's bicentenary. He has also written *Metamorphosen* **HGP-1** for solo violin and wind ensemble.

PHILIPPA CHARLOTTE, Duchess of Brunswick *1716-1801* Sister of Frederick the Great; she wrote a march in 1751 for their brother, Prince August Wilhelm of Prussia. It is possible that it was scored by another person, perhaps Georg Benda (qv).

PHILLIPS (afterwards JAGGER), Bryony *b 10 Mar 1948, Salford, UK* *Magnifipuss* was "arranged from the Magnificat" for the Kappa Wind Ensemble in New Zealand.

PIAZZA, Felice His 12 two-movement *Quintetti* have the scoring 2ob 2hn bn/vc. The openings of Nos 5 and 9 bear the note "Con Traversia," suggesting the use of flutes.

PICCINNI, Niccolò Vincenzo *16 Jan 1728, Bari, near Naples-7 May 1800, Passy, France* Famous for his operas, Piccinni's career collapsed in the 1790s, partly through personal political links and the wars in Europe. In *Alessandro nelle Indie* (the 1774 version) the Marcia in act 2 is for 2ob 2cl 2hn 2bn (very early for an octet) with a trio for 2cl bn. Piccinni's *Hymne à Hymen* was for use at weddings in the period of the Revolution. In 1799, Napoleon paid the poverty-stricken Piccinni 25 louis for a march (now lost?).

PICHL (Pichel), Václav (Wentzel, Wenzel) *25 Sept 1741, Tábor, Bohemia-4 June 1804, Vienna* Pichl, a noted violinist as well as composer, learned counterpoint from Josef Seger, teacher of V Mašek and Myslivecek. From 1763 to 1769, Pichl played under the direction of Dittersdorf at Grosswardein. In 1775, after a period at the Burgtheater, Vienna, he became Director of Music to Archduke Ferdinand III, then Governor of Milan, for whose wedding Mozart had written *Ascanio in Alba*. Ferdinand sought music from Myslivecek, and may have persuaded Pichl (and Mozart?) to write for winds. Pichl went with the Archduke to Vienna after Milan fell to the French in 1796. Many of his works must have been lost in the wars in Lombardy in 1796 and 1799; what remains is generally good, but variable in quality. Pichl's works for winds are almost all for 2ob 2hn bn; they follow the format of earlier suites, yet are more advanced than Asplmayr or Alexius. The earliest surviving set is in the Pachta collection (CZ-Pnm); the numbering of this set shows that four ("Nro 12-15") are missing; these may match works in other collections, notably D-DO. **VXP-1(-11), 14** are definitely in the same hand. Those in D-DO, titled "12 Partien Del Sig Wenceslao Pichl" are part of a larger set which includes works by Asplmayr and Alexius. The *Quartet* for ob cl hn bn recorded on Multisonic 31 0348-2 is actually by Lickl (qv) misread as Pichl on the manuscript.

VXP-3.1 *Concertino in F con Pastorella* Apparently arranged for the winds of Count Christian Philipp Clam-Gallas from a string quintet. The first trio may be that inserted in Pichl's *Pastoral Symphony* in A. **VXP-3.4(d)** is recorded by the Collegium Musicum Pragense/Myslík, on Supraphon 1111 2616, adapted by Myslík, who added parts for db and for tambourine in the last movement, and who switched the middle two movements. Another "Tamborina/Finale" is **VXP-6.1**, and is in another hand to the Pachta MS.

VXP-8 may be related to **VXP-19**; they have similar incipits, but are not the same work.

VXP-9 Pichl uses "Tempo di Menuetto" as a tempo, rather than a description, with the last movement labelled "Scherzo pocco [sic] Andante. Finale Tempo di Menuetto."

VXP-11 is an attractive "hunting" *Partitta*. The opening movement of the Pachta copy begins with a 6/8 All° Chasse (omitted in the Osek copy, CZ-Pnm XXXII.A.302), which reappears in the coda of the Finale.

VXP-20 (-28) are eight *Parthias* for 2ob 2hn 2bn in a set in which three (II, IV, VII) match known works by Pichl. We believe that all of these works are his compositions.

PICK, Henry *(1770)* Remarkably little is known of Pick. He described himself in 1797 as "of Her Majesty's Band of Musicians." Certainly he composed, arranged and carried out various duties for the Royal Music. His 20 movement *Harmonie* mixes arrangements and original movements; he also arranged for winds J C Bach's *Lucio Silla* overture.

PIERNÉ, (Henri Constant) Gabriel *16 Aug 1863, Metz-17 July 1937, Ploujean* A pupil of Franck and Massenet, Pierné was a conductor and composer whose work showed the virtues of clarity, charm, elegance and balance. He wrote two wind quintets (the *Suite Pittoresque,* and *Pastorale* Op 14 No 1), and indeed his wind harmony can be regarded as for enhanced wind quintet. He was the cousin of composer Paul Pierné.

PINKHAM, Daniel *b 5 June 1923, Lynn, Massachusetts* Composer of a *Magnificat* for soprano solo, women's voices, 2ob 2hn hp.

PIÑOS, Alois (Simandl) *b 2 Oct 1925, Vyškov* Brno pupil of forestry as well as music, influenced both by composers like Janáček, Bartók, and Lutosławski, and by avant-garde techniques. He has written a *Wind Quintet,* as well as his 1966 *Double Concerto for solo cello (or violin) and piano, winds and percussion.*

PINSUTI, Ciro *9 May 1829, Sinalunga, Florence-10 Mar 1888, Florence* His studies were partly in London (from 1840 to 1845), with Cipriani Potter for piano and Blagrove for violin, and partly in Bologna with Rossini. He settled in London in 1848, joining the staff of the Royal Academy of Music in 1856.

PIRCH, G(eorg) von *(1760)* He was the composer of marches for 2ob 2cl 2hn 2bn (tp), now in Berlin; he was styled "Lieutenant im Regiment von Graevenitz."

PISTON, Walter *20 Jan 1894, Rockland, Maine-12 Nov 1976, Belmont, Massachusetts* Piston's musical career started in dance and theater bands. He learned the saxophone in a few days, and continued in the US Navy Band. After four years at Harvard, he went to Paris to work under Boulanger and Dukas. He returned to Harvard, where he stayed; Carter and Bernstein were his pupils. His own style emerged after early influences from Stravinsky and French neoclassical composers. He has also written a *Wind Quintet.*

PITICCHIO (Pittichio, Pitichio), Francesco *1740-1750, Palermo-after 1798* Master of Music at Palermo, having spent periods in Rome, Braunschweig and Dresden with other Italian singers. In the 1780s he published operatic and vocal works, as well as 15 quintets for 2ob 2hn bn. We lack locations for much of his wind music, including the 6 pieces for 4ob 2hn 2bn attributed to him.

PLEYEL (Plajello), Ignaz (Ignace) Joseph *1 June 1757, Ruppertsthal, Lower Austria- 14 November 1831, Paris* Pleyel's life contained periods of extreme poverty in his early years, of great controversy in his enforced competition with Haydn in London, and of high drama during the French Revolution. His wind music shows not a hint of these crises. Almost all of it consists of arrangements of his other works. Many good things can be said about it: stylish and elegant, effective and well constructed, fluent and inventive. His themes go well beyond the common, short-winded conventional formulas of his lesser contemporaries. Yet the result is rarely dramatic, distinctly original, or memorable. There are striking moments: the start of **IJP-16,** with its rapid horn call rising to the high concert G, and the subsequent harmonic moves which remind one that he was a pupil of Haydn. But then the small step to mere fluency arrives, and one can only recall the comment that the good is the enemy of the best.

It is extraordinarily hard to compile an authoritative list of Pleyel's wind music, despite an excellent catalog and thematic concordance (1). Most works exist in many forms, and it can be hard to tell which is the original. It is usually impossible to tell when the arrangement was made or by whom, even given the date of publication. The situation is aggravated by two complications: to our knowledge, none of the recorded or published works give Benton numbers or sources for identification (a situation we attempt to rectify); and some wind works exist in several versions. In addition to the works listed, Pleyel also wrote a *Nocturno* [sic] for 2 lire organizzate, 2cl 2hn 2vla bass, presumably for the King of Naples; eight of Haydn's works have similar scoring.

IJP-1 *Patita [sic] pour l'Harmonie arrangé ... par Mr: Pleyel* The Brno copy comprises parts dated December 1818, and all entitled "Serenade." The parts, for fl ob 2cl 2hn 2bn cbn, belonged to the Augustinian monastery in Brno. The work is on a large scale: the first movement has an Adagio maestoso introduction followed by an Allegro moderato section; a Menuette [sic] with two trios; an Adagio (in C, unusual for a work in D); another Menuetto, this time with three trios, and a final Rondo allegretto.

IJP-2 *Parthia in E♭*   This is based on the 1789 *String Quintet* B.285.

IJP-3 *Sérénade [F] pour deux hautbois ou flûtes, deux clarinettes, deux cors, deux bassons et contrebass ad libitum...liv 1*   The title is from the N Simrock edition of 1813, pn 980, the work being advertized in *AMZ* April 1813. The four movements are based on other Pleyel works (B.321:i/B.321:ii/B.138:iii/B.305:iii); the third movement, taken from a 1786 symphony, is also arranged as part of **IJP-21**. It is recorded by a Strasbourg ensemble on Erato STU 71278, without the double bass.

IJP-4 *Sérénade [F]*   The companion piece to **IJP-3**, also found in the *AMZ* April 1813 advertizement. It is in four movements based on other Pleyel works (B.383:i/B.383:ii/B.313:iii,iiia/B.573:ii). Since B.573 is a duo only, the wind version could be the source.

IJP-6 *6 Pieces [sic] d'Harmonie...Del Sig: Pleiel*   This work is the so-called Mozart K.C17.03 (K.Anh 228) probably following the 1801 Breitköpf & Härtel edition (pn 65; 5 movements only). It is the D-DO MS which includes the sixth movement (Adagio, E♭).

IJP-7 *Parthia in F, No 1;* B.3047   An arrangement of the 1782-1783 quartet B.302. Rosinack's arrangement for ob vl vla vc is at D-DO, Mus.Ms.1580.

IJP-8 *Parthia in B♭, No 2;* B.3546   Based on three 1791 quartets (B.353:i/B.355:ii/B.354:ii+iia/B.353:iii). It is recorded by Consortium Classicum/Klöcker on MD+G L 3460. Two smaller versions are found, perhaps reduced from the wind octet, namely the *Sextet* B.3547 (ob cl 2hn bn hpcd; A-Wgm), and the *Quintet* B.3548 (ob cl hn bn pf) based on the sextet version.

IJP-9 *Parthia in Dis [E♭] No 3;* B.3324   In only two movements, based on the first two movements of the 1786 quartet B.338.

IJP-10 *Parthia in B♭, No 4;* B.2046   Four movements, based on the 1784 *Quartets* B.311 and B.312 and on a *Minuet & Trio* not known elsewhere. The sources are B.311:i/B.X23, X24/B.311:ii/B.312:iii.

IJP-11.1 *Parthia in B♭, Nr 5;* Benton 2047   Its four movements are based on two *Quartets*: B.334:i/B.303:ii/B.303:iii/B.334:iii. A sextet version **IJP-11.2** (probably an arrangement by Havel) is the second item recorded by Klöcker on Impromptu SM92806, also on MD+G L3460. D-DO has an arrangement by Rosinack for ob vl vla vc.

IJP-12 *Parthia in E♭, No 6;* Benton 1212   This work causes quite exceptional problems, since there are many related versions, including three at D-DO, one in Vienna under the name of Mozart, and sundry English sources. These versions differ in many respects. Fortunately, Hellyer (2) has sorted out most of the problems. The largest version (D-DO Mus.Ms.1597, in E♭) has these movements: Allegro; Theme & 6 variations; Minuet and Trio; Adagio/Rondo; Adagio/Presto coda. We have listed the penultimate adagio as a separate movement but, in this version at least, where it is given a florid repeat in the middle of the finale, it would surely have formed an introduction to the finale. The Theme and Variations, the Minuet and Trio, the Adagio, and the Rondo all appear to be based on Pleyel's 1786 *Sinfonia Concertante* B.111 (and the Adagio appears in the even earlier *String Quartet* B.302, 1782-1783), so there is no serious possibility that Mozart wrote what is described as K.C17.10. How the music moved round Europe is less clear. Certainly versions of B.302 were available in London from about 1787 (indeed, Storace's 1790 *No song, no supper*, uses the Adagio (common to B.302 and B.111) and Finale (which is not the Rondo of B.111 used by Eley in 1789). The versions are these:

IJP-12.1 *Partita in E♭;* D-DO Mus.Ms.1597, as described, and **IJP-12.2** *Parthia in Dis, No 6* (B.1212, D-DO Mus.Ms.1571) are largely the same. The final Rondo of **IJP-12.2** is not linked to the preceding Adagio, and the second movement has only 5 variations, as in B.111. Rosinack's arrangement for ob vl vla vc is at D-DO, Mus.Ms.1583.

IJP-12.3 *Parthia in Dis* (E♭); Vienna (A-Wn, Ms.Hs.622); 2cl 2hn (1)bn. This version includes only the Adagio and Rondo of **IJP-12**, plus a Minuet and two Trios not in Benton; they are scored for 2cl 2hn and 1bn (not 2bn, as stated in Köchel K.C17.10). It is listed as Mozart, and recorded as Mozart on Telefunken 6.35334. The record sleeve claims two bassoons were used, but only one is audible.

IJP-12.4 Untitled, in GB-Lbl, Royal Music 21.d.2. Several Pleyel movements are to be found arranged for 2ob 2bthn 2hn 2bn; the arrangements are not especially good. Pick's accounts of 24 May 1802 refer to "6 Grand Pieces by Pleyel," which could be these plus **IJP-13**. The finale consists of the Rondo only.

IJP-12.5 *Twelve Select Military Pieces for Two Clarinets, two French Horns and a Bassoon, with a Trumpet ad Libitum. Perform'd by the Band of the Coldstream Guards. Printed for C F Eley (by Longman & Broderip): London* (1789, 1794?). The third item of the third set is the Rondo finale of **IJP-12**. Eley, like Storace, arranged a version of Pleyel's *String Quartet* B.302, which uses the same Adagio but a different Rondo; B.302 was available in London c.1787 transcribed for piano trio.

IJP-12.6 James Brooks: *Thirty six select pieces for a military band consisting of marches, quick-steps, minuets & rondos.* London: Culliford, Rolfe & Barrow, 1796. Scored for 2cl 2hn bn. In this set, No 11 is the Theme plus one Variation, based on B.111:ii, No 12 is the Minuet & Trio based on B.111:iii, No 9 is the Adagio based on B.111:iv, and No 10 is the first part of the Rondo, with the Minore section and the Da Capo based on B.111:v. The same set includes an arrangement (No 13) of the 1788 *Quartet* B.347:iii.

IJP-13 *Pieces from the Royal Music* (GB-Lbl, RM 21.d.2; B.2043) Benton (1) lists these miscellaneous pieces, with folio references: B.349:ii (note f.12b and f.14b are parts from the same work); B.321:ii (f.18); B.322:i (f.18b); B.319:ii (f.20). She overlooks the **IJP-12** items. B.322:i is of interest for the "Schwäbisch" in 3/8 as second section.

IJP-14 (-16) are a set published as *Trois harmonies pour deux clarinettes deux cors deux bassons* by the Chemische Druckerei in Vienna; all are in E♭. Their plate numbers 1557, 1558, 1559 lead RISM to give [1801], but the date of publication is, in fact, 1810/1811.

IJP-14 *Harmonie No 1 in E♭;* B.2050 Recorded by Consortium Classicum as the third item on Impromptu SM92806, it was recorded later as by "Anonymous" by the same ensemble on Koch Schwann 310 002 H1 from a Salzburg manuscript.

IJP-15 *Harmonie No 2 in E♭;* B.2608 Recorded by a Strasbourg ensemble on STU 71278 and Mozzafiato on Sony Classical SK64306. The string quintet version is B.284.

IJP-16 *Harmonie No 3 in E♭;* B.2609 The autograph manuscript, B.2610.5, dated 1780, is in the Alois Fuchs collection in D-Bds (Mus.Ms.Auto.J.Pleyel 2). This may be an original wind work by Pleyel, although a version for string quintet exists (B.384). The complete lack of resemblance to the *St Antoni Divertimento* (c.1780, attributed to Haydn, **FJH-1d**) rules out any serious possibility that Pleyel wrote the St Antoni set of parthias. Recorded by Klöcker on Impromptu SM92806, and also on MD+G L3460.

IJP-17 *Parthia in E♭* is an arrangement of B.261, a sextet (2vl 2vla vc db) first published in 1791 and advertized in the *Wiener Zeitung* of 14 May 1791.

IJP-18, 19 *Parthias in E♭* Both works open with a wind version of the first movement of B.384. Otherwise, they are distinct works. **IJP-18** is an arrangement by Havel as *Parthia No VI;* its three movements are B.384:i, B.386:ii, B.384:iii. The PL-LA copy of **IJP-19** was made (perhaps arranged) by Johann Anton Buchal in Vienna on 4 June 1803. Its movements are B384:i, B.136:iii, B.385:ii, B.380:ii.

IJP-20, 21, 22 *Drey Parthia (E♭, E♭, B♭);* Benton 2049   **IJP-20** (No 1) comprises B.575:i, B.577:i, B.577:iii, B.576:ii; **IJP-21** (No 2) incorporates B.579:i, B.X63, B.X52, B.138:iii, B.138:iv (inner section), and **IJP-22** (No 3) consists of B.547, B.573:iii,

B.578.iii. B.138 is a symphony composed c.1786 and also used in **IJP-3**. B.575, B.579 are duos for vl/fl and keyboard (1796), perhaps based on these parthias.

IJP-25 (-27) Two *Parthias* and a set of *[4] Menuetto [& Trios, [8] Salti Tedeschi et [15] Marchia [sic]* (not in Benton), but identified as by Pleyel by their Langenbruck copyists ("Ex Partibus Aug[ustin] Eras[mus] Hübner beym Schulfach Anno 1805," "Ex Partibus Ignaz Hübner," and "Pro me Augustin Hübner, beym Schulfach Anno 1804" respectively). Some marches have titles *(Französicher Marsch bei der Schlacht Genua,* presumably the 1800 battle); others are named for regiments, often for their commanders (all spellings [sic])) *(Prinz Maximilian in Gemnitz; Kuhrfürst in Zeits; General Reizenstein in Leipzig; General von Lind in Zwikau; Der Leibgarde in Dresden; Prinz Anton in Grosslager.*

IJP-1v *Hymne à la Liberté, chanté par le peuple de Strasbourg à la Fête de la publication de l'acte constitutionelle le dimanche 25 septembre 1791; B.705.* Its complex history is discussed in *Pierre/HC* (p 217) from the first concept as Rouget de Lisle's simple (indeed primitive) hymn to the more sophisticated version played at Le Champ de Mars by a huge band.

WJB-1a *Arrangements of Pleyel by Mr Bisch* as advertized in 1792 publisher's catalogs. Often listed as distinct, the two sets are the same apart from the publisher. Thus André (Offenbach) pn 470 is B.2038, RISM [P 3006], and Imbault (Paris) pl 262 is B.2040, RISM [P 3007]. The movements are as follows: B.338:ii in F, B.350:ii in D minor, B.339:iv,iva in G, B.340 in C minor, B.342:iv in D minor, B.349:ii in F, B.347:iii in F, B.X41 in F. For other arrangements, see the lists in vol 2, the *Catalog*.

IJP-1d Only the 1803/1804 D-DO catalog lists it as Pleyel, with provenance "L.v.L".

IJP-2d "Authore Vogel" suggests Vogel as composer, rather than arranger. The MS parts were made by Dominik Hübner (see **IJP-25(-27)** for other Hübners as copyists).

We have no information on some other works for winds attributed to Pleyel, namely: B.2052, B.2054, an arrangement for 2ob 2cl 2hn 2bn cbn of Pleyel by W F Happich, and other unnamed works mentioned by Robbins Landon in his review of Benton (3).
1. R Benton 1977 *Thematic Catalog of Pleyel's Works;* New York: Pendragon Press
2. *Hellyer,* also R Hellyer 1975 Haydn Yearbook **9** 349.
3. H C Robbins Landon 1980 Haydn Yearbook **11** 1980 p 212; *HCRL/2* pp 360-380.

PLIMPTON, Job *(?1760)* His *Washington's March* (recorded by the Federal Music Party on New World 276) is based on No 16 of an anonymous set **A-64m**, c.1775.

POESSINGER, Franz Alexander *c.1767, Vienna-19 Aug 1827*   Composer of a *Trio* for 2ob ca (published for 2cl bn c.1812) and an arranger in Vienna. He may have been one of the (anonymous) house arrangers for T Weigl. Certainly he made many arrangements for string quartet for him. Poessinger seems to have arranged Boieldieu's *Jean de Paris* for winds (**FAP-1ac**), and probably J Weigl's *Die Schweizerfamilie* (**FAP-2ac**) as well. He also made many small arrangements for the flute.

POISSL, Johann Nepomuk, Baron (Freiherr) von *15 Feb 1783, Haukenzell, lower Bavaria -17 Aug 1865, Munich*   His 10 pieces, written for the "Harmonie der Königl. Tafelmusik" of Ludwig I of Bavaria, include arrangements from Donizetti's *La fille du régiment.* This confirms that this Bavarian wind ensemble lasted into the 1840s.

POKORNY, Franz (František) Xaver Thomas *29 Dec 1729, Městec Králové-2 July 1794, Regensburg*   His untitled work **FTP-3** is for the unusual ensemble of 2cl 3hn. Pokorny was a member of the Regensburg Kapelle, and also wrote two clarinet concertos.

POKORNY, G J *(active 1840)*   His arrangement of Lanner's *Hoffnungs-Strahlen Walzer* uses clarinets in D and G. Other Lanner arrangements in CZ-Bm(au) may be by Pokorny.

POKORNY, Petr *16 Nov 1932, Prague*   One who met with difficulties in his career; his family background meant that he studied science, not music, at university. After the 1968 rising, his music was not performed for a time. His set of three songs *Die Reise,* to words by Günther Eiche, dates from 1990. His 1992 *Notturno* is for 2ob 2ca 4bn.

POLDOWSKI, Mme (pseudonym of Irène Regina Wieniawski, Lady Dean Paul) *16 May 1880, Brussels-28 Jan 1932, London* The daughter of Henri Wieniawski (1835-1880) who died on a tour to Moscow six weeks before Poldowski's birth. She was a pupil of d'Indy; Sir Henry Wood described her as "a composer of exceptional talent," and commissioned several works from her for his Promenade Concerts, just before the First World War.
XZP-1 *Suite Miniature de Chansons à Danser "for woodwind"* The title is similar to one used by her teacher, d'Indy. We assume this *Suite* is the unpublished octet for 2fl ob obdam ca cl bthn b-cl quoted by Rendell and by Vester. The unusual scoring is similar to that of Tchaikovsky's student work (2fl 2ob ca 2cl b-cl). It was performed under Sir Henry Wood, and "made a deep impression." It was reviewed in the *Monthly Musical Record,* 1 November 1912, p 290. We cannot trace the MS.
1. Sir Henry Wood 1938 *My Life of Music*; London: Gollancz, p 269.
2. F G Rendall 1971 *The Clarinet* (3rd ed, revised P Bate); London: Ernest Benn.
3. F Vester 1967 *Flute Repertoire Catalogue*; London: Musica Rara.
POLLAK, ( ) *(1770)* Pollak may have belonged to the Chotek Harmonie at Veltrusy and Káčina.
POML, ( ) Composer of a *Divertimento* for the same unusual ensemble (2ob 2hn 3bn serp) as the famous one containing the Chorale St Antoni (discussed under J Haydn).
PONTVIK, Peter *b 24 Apr 1963, Copenhagen* Now resident in Sweden. His 1991 *Candombe* is described as "Una danza afro-uruguaiana".
POOT, Marcel *7 May 1901, Vilvoorde, near Brussels-12 June 1988, Brussels* He studied with Gilson and Dukas; his works, at their best, are light, entertaining divertimentos. In the 1920s, he became one of the Belgian composers known as "Les Synthésistes."
MYP-2 *Mosaique pour les instruments à vent (Mozaïek),* an attractive work dating from 1969, consists of a single movement in three sections, with short passages giving a preview of the next section. The 10-bar introduction states the theme of the first section; this motto reappears in the third section and coda. The movements are Allegro grazioso (4/4); Allegro vivo e scherzando (3/4), a sprightly waltz; Alla marcia (2/4).
POPKIN, Mark *(1960)* American bassoonist and conductor, who has arranged for double wind quintet the *Sextet* Op 18 by Brahms.
PORPORA, Nicola Antonio Giantinto *17 Aug 1686, Naples-3 Mar 1766, Naples* Composer and singing teacher, who was Kapellmeister to Philip, Landgrave of Hess-Darmstadt from 1711 to 1725. Porpora's most famous pupil was Haydn.
POSSELT (BOHSELT), František (Franz) *1729-27 Jan 1801, Prague* His *No 1 Partitta* is in the Clam Gallas archives, suggesting a link with that Harmonie.
POSSIO, Gianni *(1950)* His *Serenata (Le couleurs du Son-ge),* dated 18 April 1983, Turin, includes the common modern techniques of aleatory and prepared instruments.
POULENC, Francis *7 Jan 1899, Paris-30 Jan 1963, Paris* After service in World War I, Poulenc became a composition pupil of Koechlin. He was influenced by Satie and became one of "Les Six." He wrote fine music for large wind bands and an excellent *Sextet* for wind quintet and piano. The New York Harmonie Ensemble has recorded his *Aubade* on Music & Arts CD 649. Poulenc's *Suite française d'après Claude Gervaise* **FRP-3** was dedicated to playwright Edouard Bourdet (1887-1943). This *Suite* was composed in 1935 as part of a collaboration with Auric to provide incidental music for *La Reine Margot.* It is based on Renaissance dances *(Les Danseries)* by Gervaise, ingeniously using different groups of instruments.
POWNING, Graham *b 1949, Sydney, Australia* Oboist, and composer of 45 oboe trios and 6 wind quintets. His 1984 *Wind Octet* **GRP-1** is dedicated to "Amadeus." Mozart's octets inspired its structure: five movements, as in K.375, with the second movement, a canonic Minuet with a trio canone al rovescio, as in K.388. It is recorded by Melbourne Windpower on Move MD 3082.

PRACHENSKI, Joaues (Jeau, Jounis) *(1760)*   Leader of Prince Lobkowitz's Turkish band. His *Parthias "Turcika"* were advertized as No 236 in Traeg's 1804 *Nachträge*.

PRAEGER, Heinrich Aloys *1783-1854*   His *Quintetto* (Leipzig, 1815?) for fl 2cl bn vla illustrates the way violas could be incorporated in wind ensembles.

PREISSER, M A *(1800)*   Chef de Musique of the 8e Régiment d'Infanterie Légère of the French Army. His works commemorate "les trois glorieuses," the three-day revolution of 27-29 July 1830 which removed Charles X following his repressive ordinances. The *Marche funèbre* **MAP-1mt** is "Autorisée par le Ministre de la Guerre" and dedicated "à la memoire des victims." **MAP-1m** is dedicated to S.M. Louis Phillipe I.

PROCH, Heinrich *22 Jul 1809, Česká Lipa (Böhmisch Leipa)-18 Dec 1878, Vienna*   Composer, singing master and conductor, Proch was well known for his songs. He was Kapellmeister of the Theater in der Josefstadt from 1837 to 1846, of the Court Opera from 1840 to 1870, and conducted the Comic Opera in 1874.

PROWO (Browos), Pierre *8 Apr 1697, Altona, near Hamburg-8 Nov 1757, Altona*   Organist of the Reformierten Kirche, Altona, from 1738. His attractive works include *6 Concertos à 6* for 2recorders 2ob bn, c.1735.

PUGNI, Cesare *31 May 1802, Genoa-26 Jan 1870, St Petersburg*   Known best as a ballet composer. He studied with Asioli (qv) and Rolla at the Conservatorio in Milan from 1815 to 1822; he may have written his interesting *Serenata in Eb* then. From 1832 he was Maestro di Cembalo at La Scala, moving to Paris in 1834, London in 1843, and St Petersburg in 1853, where he became Ballet Composer to the Imperial Theaters.

PUREBL (Purebel, Burebl), Josef *1768, Vienna-5 March 1833, Vienna*   From 1 February 1807, Purebl was second clarinet in the Vienna Court orchestra; later he became a Royal Chamber Musician, composing clarinet duets and other small works. At about this time, he became a member of the Imperial Harmonie. Confusion remains as to the relation between the manuscript sets of *Türkische Stücke* in CZ-Bm and in Kremsmünster and the sets printed in Vienna by Chemische Druckerei c.1810 (one set in C, pn 1006, the other in F, pn 1018; we have not located copies of either). A similar problem appears for **JSP-1a,** where Chemische Druckerei published "4 Stücke aus dem Ballete Figaro" (pn 1485, c.1810) and the "Rundtanz" from the same work (not Mozart's opera); the 3 Pieces in D-Tl are probably drawn from these publications.

PUSCHMANN, Josef (Giuseppe) *c1740? Mladá, near Bezděz, Boleslav district-3 February 1794 ?Olomouc*   From 1768, Puschmann was musician and composer to the Earl (Hrábě) Chorinsky at Slezská Rudoltke and Velké Hoštice; c.1777, he became Kapellmeister at Olomouc Cathedral (1). Hellyer (2) discusses suggestions that Puschmann was at Johannisberg, Silesia in 1796 in the service of Prince Schaffgotsch (see also under Vanhal, Dittersdorf). *New Grove* and other sources suggest that Puschmann died in 1794. There is possible confusion with composers such as Buschmann. Traeg advertised three (posthumous) partitas for 2cl 2hn 2bn and three quartets for 2cl 2hn in 1799. Puschmann's main claim to fame is as the possible composer of the octet **JEP-1** known as Mozart's K.C17.01 (K.Anh.226). The 1771 Rajhrad catalog lists a *Parthia in B à 6 Voci* (3), and he may have written much more. His *Regina Coeli* **JEP-1v** for CATB 2ob 4hn 2bn 2tp timp comes from the Minorite Church in Opava.

1. J Senhal 1983 Acta Musei Moraviae **68** p 146 *Harmonie na Moravě 1750-1840*.
2. R Hellyer 1975 Haydn Yearbook **9** p 353.
3. J Senhal 1988 *Hudba v Olomoucké Katedrále v 17 a 18 Století*; Brno : Moravské Muzeum.

QUEST, Theodor *(?1800)*   Associated with the Lippe Kapelle, Detmold.

RADAUER, Irmfried *1928, ?Germany*   *Hommage...Mozart* [sic], published in 1984, is scored for the same ensemble as Mozart's *Gran Partita*.

RAFF, Joseph Joachim *27 May 1822 Lachen, near Zurich-24/25 June 1882, Frankfurt am Main* Raff is heard most often as the ghost writer who orchestrated some of Liszt's best-known works. Yet Raff was a famous composer in his own time, and recent revivals show how good the best of his music is. Raff was largely self-taught, and it was only in the 1840s that the friendship and help of Mendelssohn and Liszt enabled him to start on a proper musical career. Even this developed slowly, coming to a peak in the 1860s and 1870s. Raff waited until he was over 40 before he wrote his first symphony in 1863. He became regarded as the major symphonist until 1876, when Brahms's first symphony appeared. Time has been unkind to Raff, so one needs reminding that in his day, his music was widely played and respected. This is especially true for Raff's *Sinfonietta* for winds, **JJR-1**, the first significant wind harmony by a composer of his stature for decades. Coming from such a composer at the peak of his powers, it had great impact. It would be illuminating to know just how many wind works were written as a consequence. One notices many parallels in Gounod's *Petite Symphonie* and Richard Strauss's early Op 4 and Op 7, so that some influence seems likely. Another work which invites comparison with the *Sinfonietta* is Dvořák's beautifully written *Serenade*, written in 1878. Raff's work compares surprisingly well. The contrast between the Czech and German idioms is clear, but the originality of both is unmistakable. Raff wrote no more wind music, but the funeral march which forms the slow movement of his *6th Symphony,* Op 189, was arranged by Heinrich Saro (1827-1891) for wind band.

The *Sinfonietta in F, Op 188* **JJR-1** was written in Wiesbaden in 1873, and first performed in November 1874. It opens with a festive Allegro, a serenade in character but symphonic in scale. The flutes, and later the clarinets and oboes celebrate in the upper register while horns and bassoons interject with a jaunty march (this technique of accompanying from above is used most effectively throughout the work). Next comes the Scherzo (the autograph shows this title was added later), a 6/8 movement which shows traces of Mendelssohn, and must have influenced the Scherzo of Gounod's *Petite Symphonie.* The third movement is an extended song without words. Reminders of Mendelssohn reappear in the Finale, where the fairies of *A Midsummer Night's Dream* seem to emerge once more. The *Sinfonietta* has been recorded by the Winds of the Swiss Radio Orchestra, conducted by Leopoldo Casella (number untraced), and by an unidentified ensemble on Tudor TUDOR787.

RAFFAEL, ( ) *(1770)* Composer of marches for Turkish music published in 1803.

RAIMONDI, Ignazio *c.1737, Naples-14 Jan 1813, London* Composer, symphonist and violinist, who came to London c.1790.

RALSTON, Alfred *c.1910-c.1985* Arranger for fl ob 2cl bn/b-cl of seven short piano pieces by Grieg.

RAMEAU, Jean Philippe *baptized 25 Sept 1683, Dijon-12 Sept 1764, Paris* Rameau's highly original operas pioneered the use of winds. He first used pairs of clarinets and horns in *Zoroastre* in 1749. These were used more extensively in the pastorale-heroique *Acante et Céphise, ou la Sympathie* written to celebrate the birth of the Duke of Burgundy, first performed on 18 November 1751. The winds play in the overture ("Feu d'artifice" and "Fanfare"), the Divertissement of act 2, the closing contredanse and chorus, and especially between acts 2 and 3, where the clarinets and horns alone (a continuo is possible but not necessary) play an attractive entr'acte. Clarinets and horns also accompany the soprano aria "L'amour est heureux."

RANDHARTINGER, Benedict *27 June 1802, Ruprechtshofen-22 Dec 1893, Vienna* Tenor and composer of works for chorus and winds, pupil of Salieri and friend of Schubert (a link later exaggerated); successor to Assmayer in the Hofkapelle.

RATHGEN, Adam *(1750)* Clarinettist, who played in the wind band at London's Marylebone Gardens (see part 1). In addition to the *6 Military Divertimentos* by

"Rathgen and other Eminent Authors residing in England," the 1777 Breitkopf catalog lists *7 Sonate, Op 1,* for 2cl 2hn bn (possibly lost). GB-Lbl has a *Divertissement* by Rathgen, Roeser and Martini, presumably an arrangement.

RATTI, Leo *(1770?)* Arranger of Mayr's 1797 *I solitari.*

RAUSCHER, J[ohann] Composer of a *March* and a *Pas redoublé;* associated with the Moravian Brethren at Zeist, Netherlands.

RAUTAVAARA, Einojuhani *b 9 Oct 1928, Helsinki* In addition to his 1964 *Octet,* he is also the composer of *Pronunciations,* 1977, and a *Concerto for Organ* with wind band. He wrote a fascinating *Cantus Arcticus* concerto for tapes of arctic birds.

RAWLINGS, Thomas A *1775, London-1850, London* Rawlings was a violinist and cellist, and composer of many works. He was the son of Robert Rawlings (1742-1814) of the King's Band, and grandson of singer Thomas Rawlings (b 1703).

RAYKI, György *b 3 Feb 1921 Budapest* Rayki studied in Budapest with Kodály, Weiner and Ferencsik. He took Swiss nationality in 1958. His *Burleske,* GXR-1, of 1953 is dedicated "A mi querido amigo Juan Astorga anta" [sic]. It is an attractive-looking single movement, lasting about 8 minutes, in sections: Allegretto; Andantino; Agitato.

REBNER, Edward Wolfgang *b 20 Dec 1910, Frankfurt* Son of Austrian violinist Adolf Rebner, he worked in South America from 1937 until 1955 before returning to teach at the Richard Strauss Conservatoire, Munich. He wrote a *Suite "1492"* for 2ob 2hn 2bn 2tp 2tb perc and a *Sextet* for fl ob cl b-cl hn bn (cf. Janáček's *Mládí*).

REEVE, William *1757, London-22 June 1815, London* Prolific composer for the stage (he completed *Oscar and Malvina,* left unfinished by Shield after a dispute with the management) as well as organist, and part-owner of Sadler's Wells from 1802. His "Minuet un Militare" [sic] was for his 1791 *Tippoo Saib.* This "Entertainment" (a popular type of evening with music) celebrated the 1791 victory of Cornwallis over "Tipu Sahib", Sultan of Mysore (1750-1799) at Seringapatam.

REGER, (Johann Baptist Joseph) Max *19 Mar 1873 Brand, Bavaria-11 May 1916, Leipzig* Apart from one movement of an unfinished 1904 Serenade (recorded by the Triebensee Ensemble on Contrapunctus Musicus VC 2447, and possibly on Eurosound ES 46.442), his only original wind music is his *Weihegesang* MXR-1v for chorus plus the same ensemble of 2fl 2ob 2cl 4hn 2bn. This Hymn of Dedication, based on a text by Otto Liebermann, celebrated the 350th anniversary of Jena University; the wind ensemble averted space limitations in the the Aula-Empore hall. The first performance was on 30/31 July 1908, with the Jenaer Akademischer Chor, mezzo-soprano soloist Maria Philippi, and conductor Fritz Stein. An occasional piece, well written but not exciting; recorded by the Bamberg Symphony Orchestra and Chorus/Horst Stein on Koch Schwann 312092.

REICHA (Rejcha), Antonin Joseph (Antoine, Antonín, Anton Josef) *26 Feb 1770, Prague -28 May 1836, Paris* Arguably the founder of the wind quintet (1), though mentioned here for three other reasons. First, his relationships with other composers: he was a colleague of Beethoven in the Bonn orchestra, a teacher of Berlioz, Gounod, Adam, Franck, Liszt and more obscure pupils like John Feltham Danneley (b 1786) who, *Sainsbury* notes, published a *Military Divertimento* (untraced by us). Some authors even claim he taught his uncle, Josef Reicha; surely the converse is true. Secondly, his innovations in wind music: he aimed to make quintets the equal of string quartets, he emphasised proper rehearsals and dynamics (see part 3), and he made striking use of large bands and spatial effects. Thirdly, he included in his textbooks some interesting musical examples, such as his *Choeur Dialogué pour les instruments à vent* (for choir, fl ob cl bn hn vc db) from the *Traité de haute composition musicale* (vol i p 74, 1824, recorded under Lubomír Mátl on Supraphon 11 0084). Reicha's larger works are discussed in part 1, p 58.

1. M Emmanuel 1937 *Antonin Reicha;* Paris: Laurens.

REICHA, Josef (Joseph, Giuseppe) *13 Mar 1746, Chudenice, near Klatovy-5 Mar 1795, Bonn* A Czech cellist and composer who studied cello with F J Werner, as did Fiala. Reicha moved to Oettingen-Wallerstein in 1774. In the early 1770s he and his Lorraine-born wife adopted his orphaned nephew, Antonin Reicha. In 1785, Josef Reicha moved to Bonn, serving first as cellist and leader of the court orchestra of Elector Maximilian Franz. The orchestra contained such players as Nicolaus Simrock (horn; later publisher), Antonin Reicha (flute) and Beethoven (viola). Josef Reicha directed the Theater orchestra from 1789, serving until the 1794 French invasion. His wind music presents minor problems. In JXR-1 the last movement bears the false headtitle "Parthia in D von J G Feldmayer" [sic]; it is definitely by Reicha. JXR-3 is also wrongly attributed to Feldmayr on the bn 1 part. The contra basso part for JXR-2 is written onto the bn 2 part, with a lot of unison writing; likewise, the violone reads off the bn 2 part of JXR-3 and probably JXR-6. The titlepage of JXR-4 carries the note "bene optime." The "flutes or no flutes" issue arises for JXR-5, 6, 9; in some cases flutes might have played from the score; for JXR-6, in particular, we believe that the (autograph) flute parts are a later addition. Some of the works have original structures. JXR-9 uses the opening Adagio at the end of the last movement; the Andantino contrasts sections for 2cl 2hn bn with ones for 2ob bn. JXR-6 opens with a hunting call from the (solo) 3rd horn.

REICHMANN, Carl *(1800)* Composer of a march for Easter Sunday 1833, Náměšt nad Oslavou, Moravia.

REID, ( ) Probably associated with the Kinský Harmonie at Budeničký.

REID, John, General *13 Feb 1721, Stralloch, Perth, Scotland-7 Feb 1807, London* Educated at Edinburgh University, where he founded the Reid Chair of Music, Reid was a professional soldier. He served mainly with the 42nd Regt against the Jacobite rebels at Culloden, then in Flanders, in Martinique, and in British North America against the Western and Ohio Indians. He rose to Lieutenant General in October 1793, and was Colonel of the 88th Foot (Connaught Rangers) from 27 November 1794 (1). A flute player (his flutes are in the Reid Library, Edinburgh), he wrote 15 marches, published in 1778 in London. These are for named regiments: 17th Regt of Foot (Lord Amherst's); 22d Regt (General Gage's); 51st Regt (Earl of Eglington's); 35th Regt (General Campbell's); 32d Regt (General Amherst's); 44th Regt (General Abercrombie's); 63rd Regt (General F Grant's); 16th Regt (General Robertson's); 1st Battalion, 60th Regt (General Haldimand's); 70th Regt (General Tryon's); 2d Battalion, 60th Regt (Colonel Christie's); 77th Regt Atholl Highlanders, Colonel Murray's Strathspey; 76th Regt (Lord Macdonald's Highlanders); Chatam [sic] Division of Marines (the first official mention of the Chatham Divisional Band of the Royal Marines was six years earlier, in divisional orders of 1772); 12th Regt of Dragoons. Suggestions that these marches are actually by James Oswald are completely without foundation. Twelve of Reid's marches were arranged for a full wind band by Winter (qv) early in the 19th century (now lost). Sir Henry Bishop (second Reid Professor) arranged music by Reid for full orchestra. Much of Reid's music was published under the pseudonym "I. R." (sometimes "J. R."). Arrangements of Reid's marches are recorded by the Royal Military School of Music, Kneller Hall (Beat Sounds: Military Music Masters MMC 0633).
1. *Dictionary of National Biography.*

REILL, Josef *1793-1865* Composer of 3 funeral songs, c.1840, for use at the parish church of St Jakob, Wasserburg am Inn, some 35 miles east of Munich.

REIMANN, Ignaz *27 Dec 1820, Albendorf, Silesia-17 Jun 1885, Rengersdorf* Reimann wrote a large number of funeral songs (Bei ein Jüngling, ... einer Mutter, ... alter Personen, and so on). His published sets of pieces aimed to meet a clear demand, with titles emphasising that collections were "für Erwachsene" (adults, **IYR-1tv**) as well as "für Kinder" (children, **IYR-2tv**).

REINAGLE, Joseph *1762, Portsmouth-12 Nov 1825, Oxford* From an English family of musicians of Austrian descent. He played horn, trumpet, cello (which he learned from his brother-in-law, Schetky [qv]), violin (playing in Salomon's concerts for Haydn) and viola. He moved to Oxford in the 1790s, playing horn in a band including John Mahon (qv). **JNR-1m** comprises a slow and a quick march for the Oxford University Volunteers

REINECKE, Carl Heinrich Carsten *23 June 1824, Altona-10 March 1910, Leipzig* Reinecke spent most of his mature years in Leipzig as Professor of composition and as conductor of the Gewandhaus Orchestra. His two wind works (the *Octet* **CAR-1** Op 216 of 1892 and the *Sextet* Op 271 **CAR-2**, 1904) were inspired and performed by Taffanel's ensemble (hence the fl ob 2cl 2hn 2bn scoring of the *Octet*), but he must have had the Gewandhaus players in mind as well. *Cobbett* remarks on the "progressive improvement in the quality of his work up to extreme old age." The *Octet* and *Sextet* are both recorded by Boston Symphony Orchestra players (Etcetera KTC1155) and by Villa Musica Ensemble (Dabringhaus & Grimm MDG 304 0478-2). The *Sextet* is recorded by the Berlin Philharmonic Wind Quintet on BIS CD-612. One movement of the *Octet* is recorded on EMI EMX 41 2053 4 by the English Chamber Orchestra Wind Ensemble.

REINER, Karel *27 June 1910, Žatec-17 Oct 1979, Prague* Reiner studied with Hába while a law student in Prague. He was interned in Terezín during the Nazi occupation. He has written a book *The Wind Orchestra* as well as works for wind ensemble, like the *Concertante Suite* of 1947, and wind quintets and works for brass ensemble.

REINISCH, Hermann *(1800)* Associated with the Lippe Kapelle, Detmold. His *Walzer Erinnrung [sic] an die Egg'stersteine [sic]* relates to the evocative Externsteine, a natural sandstone outcrop and artificial lake about 4 miles south of Detmold. This had pagan associations in early times, and attracted Christian pilgrims in the Middle Ages.

REISSIGER, Carl Gottlieb *31 Jan 1798, Wittenberg-7 Nov 1859, Dresden* Once-popular composer, now known mainly for what came to be called *Weber's Last Waltz*.

REIZENSTEIN, Franz *7 June 1911, Nuremburg-15 Oct 1968, London* Reizenstein was a composition pupil of Hindemith, and studied with Vaughan Williams. He became a naturalized Briton in 1934. He was a pianist and the composer of a wide variety of works, including a wind quintet and works for the Hoffnung Festivals.

RELLUZI, Paolo His one known *Parthia* (2ob 2hn bn) is in the Kroměříž archives.

REUTTER, (Johann Adam Karl) Georg von, the Younger *baptized 6 April 1708, Vienna-11 Mar 1772, Vienna* Organist and composer, who followed his father as Kapellmeister at St Stephen's Cathedral in 1738. In 1740 he was ennobled as Edler von Reutter, and in 1747 he became the second Kapellmeister at court; music was at its nadir for much of the time he was there. It was Reutter who brought Haydn to Vienna as a youth.

ŘEZAČ, Ivan *9 Nov 1924, Řevnice-26 Dec 1977, Prague* Director of the Prague Symphony Orchestra from 1968 to 1976 and associate professor at the Prague Academy of Arts from 1969 to 1977. He has written an *Octet* (1976) and a *Wind Quintet* (1971).

REZNIČEK, ( ) *(1790)* Kapellmeister to the kk Ignatz Graf Gyulai 60th Infantry Regt, who arranged a so-far untraced work by Krommer as a *Parthia* for large band in 1825.

ŘEZNÍČEK, Petr *18 Feb 1938, Hradec Králové* Pianist, choral conductor and composer, who worked for many years with Czech Radio, Brno. His 1965 *Prelude and Toccata for Wind and Percussion* was written soon after leaving the Brno Conservatory.

RHEINBERGER, Josef Gabriel *17 Mar 1839, Vaduz, Liechtenstein-25 Nov 1901 Munich* His *Messe in Bb* Op 172 for TTBB chorus, 2fl 2ob 2cl 2hn 2bn 2tp db timp, written in 1892, has parallels with the military masses of half a century earlier.

RHÉNE-BATON, (pseudonym of René Baton) *5 Sept 1879, Courseilles-sur-Mer, France -23 Sept 1940, Le Mans* French conductor and composer, much of whose work is influenced by Breton folklore, often colorful and vivid. His 1940 *Aubade* Op 53, **YXR-1**, is scored for the same unusual ensemble (fl ob 2cl hn 2bn) as d'Indy's *Chanson et Danses*.

RICHTER, ( ) *(1770)* The MS parts of his *Parthia* for 2cl 2hn basso/bn were copied by Dominik Hübner at Langenbruck.

RICHTER ( ) *(1780)* Kapellmeister of the Neugebauer Regiment, later (from c.1820) Kapellmeister in Stuttgart. He arranged operas by Mozart, Boieldieu and Mayr; his version of Mozart's *Don Giovanni* (cl(F) 2cl(C) 2hn 2bn serp/cbn 2tp b-tb successfully tackles the problem of the three orchestras at the end of act 1. See also Walch.

RICHTER, Anton *d 1853* Kapellmeister of Györ (Raab) Cathedral and father of the conductor Hans Richter (1843-1916). His wife was the first Venus in Wagner's *Tannhäuser* in Vienna. Richter's three substantial works date from 1827-1829.

RICHTER, Pius *11 Dec 1818, Warnsdorf-10 Dec 1893, Vienna* kk Hof-Organist, whose *4 Stationes* probably date from the 1840s, but have additional parts from c.1880.

RIEDEL, Georg *b 8 Jan 1934, Czecholovakia; resident in Sweden* Two of Riedel's works (*Intrada; Tre danser*) are for jazz group and wind ensemble, and indeed several other works combining jazz ensembles with wind quintet or wind orchestra. It is surprising how rarely this interesting cross-linking of musical genres is attempted. His 1982 *Skriket* is for the more conventional ensemble of double wind quintet.

RIEDELBAUCH, Václav *b 1 April 1947, Dyšina, near Plzeň* A student of accordion in Prague, now a teacher of composition in the Academy of Arts and Music. He has won several prizes, one in a competition associated with the 1979 International Womens' Year. His *Pastorali e Trenodi* for wind octet dates from the same year.

RIEGER, Gottfried *1764, Troplowitz, Silesia-13 Oct 1855, Brno* Leader of the Harmonie of Graf Haugwitz at Námĕšt nad Oslavou, probably mostly in the 1790s, where he composed and arranged music for 2cl 2hn 2bn. He returned to Brno when the Harmonie was disbanded, there writing **GYR-1** for a larger ensemble, 2ob 2cl 2hn 2bn cbn 2tp. His variations are from *Das Labyrinth* ("Der zweyter Theil der Zauberflöte").

RIEGGER, Wallingford *29 Apr 1885, Albany, Georgia-2 Jun 1961, New York* Composer of several works for single winds: the 1951 *Wind Quintet*, the 1952 *Concerto for Wind Quintet and Piano*, the 1931 *Canons for Winds*, and the 1941 *Duos for 3 Winds*. He studied with Max Bruch in Berlin and later promulgated ultra-modern music.

RIEPEL, Josef (Guiseppe) *22 Jan 1709, Horschlag-23 Oct 1782, Regensburg* Thurn und Taxis Kapellmeister, Regensburg. His three multi-movement works were probably intended as background music for banquets.

RIES, Ferdinand *baptized 28 Nov 1784, Godesburg-13 Jan 1838, Frankfurt* Ries wrote two *Nocturnes* for fl 2cl hn 2bn, remarkably the same scoring as D'Indy used later. Only the 1817 piano version survives of Ries's *Introduction and Grand March*, "as performed by the Band of his Royal Highness, the Prince Regent, at Brighton."

RIESS, (?Johann Heinrich) Associated with the Moravian Brethren community at Zeist.

RIETI, Vittorio *28 Jan 1898, Alexandria, Egypt-19 Feb 1994, New York* Rieti's musical career began after he had taken a degree in economics. He was a composition pupil of Respighi, and achieved early success with his *Concerto for Wind and Orchestra*. He moved to Paris in 1925, where he was associated with Les Six; in 1940 he moved to the United States. He also wrote two *Wind Quintets*, that of 1957 and the 1967 *Silographie*.

RIGEL, Henri Joseph, père *9 Feb 1741, Wertheim, Franconia-May 1799, Paris* Pupil of F X Richter at Mannheim and of Jommelli; conductor of the Concerts Spirituels and at some of the concerts of the Loge Olympique. He wrote a *Hymne à la Liberté* in 1795. It is possible that the *Parthia* **HJR-1** in CZ-Pnm and the arrangement of *Das Schlagenfest in Sangora* by W Müller **HJR-1a** in CZ-Bm may be by another Riegel.

RIGHINI, Vincenzo *22 Jan 1756, Bologna-19 Aug 1812, Bologna* In some ways, Righini's career was the reverse of the standard pattern. He moved from Italy early on, going still further afield as his career developed. While his singing career received little encouragement in Prague, his compositions flourished, and his opera *Don Juan* was performed in Vienna at the Kärntnertortheater in 1777, ten years before Mozart's opera of the same name. Righini settled in Vienna in 1780 to conduct the Italian opera; while there, he collaborated on an opera *Armide* with da Ponte, who was at the height of his collaboration with Mozart. Righini then served the Elector of Mainz from 1788 to 1792, also composing for the Elector of Trier in 1790 (see part 1 for comments by von Beecke in his 3 Aug 1790 letter). He moved to Berlin, directing the Italian opera from 1793 until it was discontinued in 1806; it was in Berlin that most of his wind music was written. Only in 1812 did Righini return to Bologna, and then because of failing health. **VYR-1** *Armonia in F* Written in 1797 for the wedding on 13 February of Crown Prince Friederich Wilhelm of Hesse-Kassel and Princess Augusta. A large and difficult but rewarding original work. There are several printed editions with the title *Serenata*, which treat the two sections of the 1st movement as separate movements and omit movements 2, 3 and 6. Also substantial is the octet *Serenata in Eb*, **VYR-2**. What may be an autograph MS (*Sonata*, for 2cl 2hn 2bn) has just 3 movements; the octet has an extra third movement. **VYR-3** is the *Armonia con Capricio* [sic] for vl hn 2bn vc.

RINCK, Johann Christian Heinrich *18 Feb 1770, Elgersburg-7 Aug 1846, Darmstadt* Rinck studied at Erfurt under Kittel, a pupil of J S Bach. He moved to Göttingen, thence to Darmstadt in 1805 as municipal organist, cantor, and music teacher in the ducal school. From 1817, he was Court Musician to Grand Duke Ludwig I. The success of Rinck's 1829 *Cantata* for the 200th anniversary of the founding of the Grand Duke's Gymnasium clearly encouraged him, and he wrote large-scale choral works, some apparently for the Easter and autumn examination periods (the title *Prüfungsleid* suggests a test piece, but this is not consistent with the works themselves).

RINDL, Hermann, P[ater?] *(1770)* "Catecheten an der Saazer Stadtschule." His two choral works with winds bear the title *Prüfungslied,* for use during the late July examination periods in 1799 and 1800. The MSS are from the Strahov Premonstratensian monastery, Prague.

RINSLER, ( ) *(1790)* Possibly a musician at Donaueschingen from c.1822-1848. He arranged a *Messe* by Kalliwoda (qv) for winds.

RITTER, (?Georg Wenzel) *7 Apr 1748, Mannheim-16 June 1808, Berlin* Bassoonist with the Mannheim orchestra. The solo part in Mozart's *Sinfonia Concertante* was intended for him. Later, in Berlin, he taught Carl Bärmann.

RIVIER, Jean *1896-1987* His 1985 *Concerto* with winds has trumpet and alto saxophone soloists; its mix of brashness and sentimental sweetness works well.

ROCKEMAN (Rakeman), ( ) For Rockeman's problems with drink, see part 3. John Parry (qv) succeeded him as bandmaster of the Denbigh militia in 1797.

RÖDER, Georg Vincent *1780, Rammungen-30 Dec 1848, Altötting* His *Deutsche Messe* was written for Palm Sunday 1835, apparently for performance in the Stiftskirche, Altötting, center for pilgrimages to the Black Madonna.

ROENTGEN, Julius *9 May 1855, Leipzig-13 Sept 1932, Utrecht* A German pianist, conductor and composer of Dutch descent, Director of the Amsterdam Conservatory from 1914 till 1924. His *Serenade für Blasinstrumente in A, Op 14* **JUR-1** is dedicated to Julius and Elisabeth Klengel, Julius being a cellist. The last of its four movements is in several sections: Allegro comodo, Andante; Allegro molto vivace.

ROESER (Röser), Valentin *1735? Monaco? Germany?-1782? Paris?* A founder of wind harmony, whose manual gives real insight into the methods of the time. This *Essai d'instruction* (**VAR-1**) was probably first printed around 1764 (1); the manuscript is in Tours (2). Roeser was a follower of Johann Stamitz (qv), and indeed remarks on the blow to the musical world of Stamitz's death in 1757. Roeser ran the wind band of the Prince of Monaco from 1763 until about 1769. The records of the Concerts Spirituels (see part 1) show the ensemble consisted of the clarinettists Klynn (Klein) and Reysser

(Reiffer, or Roeser), the bassoons Richard and Petit, and the horns Paisa (Johann Palsa? b 1754) and Tiersmith (Carl Thürrschmidt? b 1753). Roeser himself appeared in 1774 as a basset horn player, named as "M. Valentin." Most of Roeser's own compositions were destroyed in World War II, though fragments appear in his Essai and others can be inferred from a card index which survived hostilities (*Hellyer*). His only surviving original works are for 2cl 2hn 2bn. The joint *Divertissement* in GB-Lbl (Royal Music) by Roeser, Rathgen and Martini, for 2fl 2bthn 2hn 2bn is surely an arrangement. Roeser arranged at least 46 issues of a journal for wind ensembles, mainly in the 1770s. He may have been the originator of this genre (see part 1). It is possible that Nos 29-82 of **A-1a**, the anonymous bound part books in Regensburg, are drawn from this journal.
1. Valentin Roeser: *Essai d'Instruction à l'Usage de ceux qui composent pour la Clarinette et le Cor, avec des Remarques sur l'Harmonie et des exemples à 2 Clarinettes, 2 Cors et 2 Bassons;* facsimile reproduction 1972; Geneva: Minkoff.

ROETH (RÖTH), Philipp Jakob *1779-1850* His fairly late works for choir and winds (1835-1840) come from the archive of the Lateinische Kongregation, Munich.

ROETSCHE (Roetscher), ( ), Senior *(1770) - after 1806* Roetsche's marches were for the Prussian Royal Harmonie, 1799-1806. His *Lied* **ZYR-1v** was sung by orphans during Friedrich Wilhelm's birthday celebrations in 1806; its melody is drawn from **ZYR-4m**.

RÓHLÍK, Antonín *(active 1871-1877, Nové Město na Moravě)* Composer of three masses (two in Czech, one in Latin), each including the Graduale, Offertorium, and Pange lingua. The Latin mass **ANR-3v**, dated 10 June 1870, was performed on 17 June 1871 to celebrate the engagement of P T Koutesky of Clam Gallas.

ROLLER, (Samuel Andreas) *(1730) (active 1758-1773)* His 13 *Parthien* are associated with the Harmonie at Kroměříž, and date from the 1760s or 1770s.

RONG, Wilhelm Ferdinand *5 Aug 1759, Niedertrübenwasser, Bohemia-13 Nov 1842, Bützow* We are aware that *Grove V* gives a birth date of 1720, possibly through misidentification with W F Rong's father, Joseph Rong, Kammermusiker in Rheinsberg. Rong composed marches for the Royal Prussian Wind Band.

ROPARTZ, (Joseph) Guy (Marie) *15 June 1864, Guingamp, Côtes du Nord-22 Nov 1955, Lanloup* **JMR-1** *Lamento* is for solo oboe and winds.

ROREM, Ned *b 23 Oct 1923, Richmond, Indiana* Composer, diarist, and essayist, who studied with Honegger in Paris while on a Fulbright Fellowship. The first and fourth movements of his *Sinfonia* **NXR-1** are based on the first and third movements of his own *Piano Sonata III*. The work was commissioned by the American Wind Ensemble of Duquesne University, Pittsburg, and is dedicated to Mr & Mrs Henry J Heinz and the Heinz Endowment. Its large percussion section is optional.

ROSE, J H *(1760)* Rose, a member of the 1st Battalion Breadalbane Fencibles, wrote marches for that batallion, the Tay Side Fencibles and the Glasgow Volunteers. Conceivably, he could be Johann Heinrich Rose (c.1750 Trassdorf-3 Aug 1844) or Johann Daniel Rose (30 July 1784-14 Mar 1852), both from Quedlinberg.

ROSENBERG, Hilding Constantin *21 June 1892, Bosjökloster, Ringsjön, Skåne-19 May 1985, Stockholm* The *Symphonie für Bläser und Schlagzeug* is based on a 1966 Swedish Television ballet *Babels Torn*. It calls for a huge percussion section.

ROSENGART (Rosengarth), Aemilian, R.P. *(1760)* Composer of two *Ave Maria pro Adventu*, both dated 1795.

ROSER von REITER, Franz de Paula *17 Aug 1779, Naarn-12 Aug 1830 Budapest* A pupil of Mozart in 1789. He worked in Freiburg, in the service of Count von Vegh at Vereb, and in Linz. In Vienna, he may have arranged music for winds for T Weigl and for the Hoftheater-Musik-Verlag. His final post was as Kapellmeister at the German Theater in Pest. He was the son of Johann Georg Roser (1740-1797), organist at Naarn; there is some doubt which one wrote the *Tantum ergo*, the MS of which is in Budapest.

ROSETTI (Roessler, Rössler), Franz Anton *c.1750 Litoměřice, Bohemia-30 June 1792, Ludwigslust*   Rosetti first trained for the priesthood in seminaries at Kuttenberg (Znaim, now Znojmo) and Olomouc, and was tonsured as canon in Prague Cathedral in 1769. He moved to Wallerstein in 1773, remaining in the orchestra of Prince Kraft Ernst until 1789, first as violone player, then as deputy to Kapellmeister Josef Reicha (qv) from 1780; he succeeded Reicha in 1785. The orchestra had high standards and contained players such as Fiala. The ensemble introduced clarinets at about the time of Rosetti's arrival. Rosetti's sixteen years of association with Wallerstein had interruptions, notably in 1782, when he was granted permission to visit Paris, a trip which stimulated and matured his music; most of his wind works date from soon after his return. In 1789 Rosetti left to become Master of Music to the Duke of Mecklenburg-Schwerin at Ludwigslust. He came into conflict with his former employer, Prince Kraft Ernst, over attempts to lure former colleagues to Ludwigslust (2). Financially the gain from his move was substantial, but Rosetti's health suffered. He considered further moves, especially after a trip to Berlin when the visiting Duke of York heard some of Rosetti's music and arrangements (one wonders how the course of wind harmony would have altered had Rosetti, rather than Eley, come to England). There is no evidence that Rosetti was expected to write for the wind band at Schwerin, so it is possible that the Duke of York heard earlier works. The *Requiem* for Mozart played in Prague shortly after Mozart's death appears to have been Rosetti's 1776 setting, neither specially written nor a foreboding of Rosetti's own death six months later. Rosetti's style is elegant; individual, without striving for effect, skilful but without display. He wanted to entertain his audience with good music, not to disturb their composure (as did Krommer) or demand their concentration (as did Mozart). Yet his players too would have been content, and the unassuming and attractive writing must have been a consistent source of enjoyment to musicians and listeners alike.

FAR-1 *Parthia in F "pour la Chasse"* K.II, 13 (3)   Rosetti's largest wind work, written at Wallerstein in September 1785 (autograph score; a set of autograph parts date from c.1789). While the score requests "Fagotto solo e Violone," the parts require a second bassoon. Recorded on Supraphon SUA 1111 1854 H and on original instruments by Octophorus on Accent/Harmonia Mundi ACC 8860 D. There is a useful critical commentary in Hellyer's edition (Oxford University Press, Musica da Camera 14).

FAR-6 This *Divertimento* is found in two forms. **FAR-6.1** in the Royal Music in GB-Lbl, probably an arrangement by Henry Pick, is for 11 instruments (2ob 2bthn 2hn 2bn 2vla db); **FAR-6.2**, in US-BETm, is for 2cl 2hn bn. Neither this nor **FAR-20,** also at Bethlehem, has precisely the scoring of the work by "Rosetta" played in Boston in 1801.

FAR-8 We believe that the D-HR version of **FAR-8** for 3ob 2hn bn vlne is the original of the three extant scorings, and that the other five of the set are now lost. The Schwarzenberg versions (ob concertante, 2ca 2hn 2bn) are probably transcriptions by Went; those at Donaueschingen (ob 2cl 2hn 2bn) probably transcriptions by Rosinack.

FAR-18 *Partita in B♭*   The Largo opening alone is recorded by the Netherlands Wind Ensemble on Philips 7311 117. This Partita exists in two versions, one with 2 clarinets, the other with 2 cors anglais. This may be another of the set of **FAR-8(-13)**. The cor anglais version, for the Schwarzenberg Harmonie, is probably a transcription by Went.

1. Confusingly, there are at least four musicians known as Rosetti. See H Fitzpatrick 1962 Music and Letters 43 234; E M Murray 1976 Music and Letters 57 130.

2. The bassoonist Hoppius came; a critical letter to recruit Feldmayr was intercepted.

3. K numbers relate to Kaul, 1968 Denkmäler der Tonkunst in Bayern Jg XII/1:22.

ROSINACK (ROSINIACK), Franz Joseph *before 1763-1823*   Rosinack was primarily an oboist who transcribed many works by Krommer and others. He sold copies to other ensembles, often with his own added dynamics and phrasings. Bastiaan Blomhert's 1987

Thesis: *The Harmoniemusik of Die Entführung aus dem Serail* (Rijksuniversiteit Utrecht, 1987) points out that in many cases Rosinack merely copied the arrangements by others, and that these were misattributed by catalogers at D-DO after Rosinack's death. Rosinack's own arrangements are pleasant but feeble affairs. His is the one known arrangement of a Haydn opera *(Orlando Paladino,* as *Ritter Roland).*

ROSSINI, Gioacchino Antonio *29 Feb 1792, Pesaro-13 Nov 1868, Passy, near Paris* The various fragments and attributions may well be arrangements. The *Parthia* GAR-1d attributed to Rossini (and recorded by Mozzafiato on Sony Classical SK 53965) is unlikely to be by him; some sections sound much more like Mayr. The first 5 of Rossini's *"Wind Quartets"* are Berr's arrangements of Rossini's early string sonatas.

ROTH (Rothe, Rode), Johann Traugott *23 Feb 1768, Zwickau-5 May 1847, Dresden* J T Roth and his brother (Karl) Gottlieb Roth (1774-1828) were both clarinettists, first in a military band, later in the Dresden Court Orchestra while it was directed by Weber. Dresden, which had employed chalumeaux in the 1730s, took to clarinets again in 1794 largely because of the Roth brothers' playing. Wind harmony certainly featured in the Dresden concerts; in 1789, the Roths played in an octet version of *Don Giovanni,* perhaps the Went arrangement *(Weston/MCVP* p 211).

ROTH, Sinforiano *(1720)* The march "della Guardia Reale Svizzera del Rè di Napoli" (c.1750) is an isolated example from Naples. Its scoring, the composer's name, and present location in D-Rtt suggest North German influence.

ROVA, Giovanni Battista *"di Venezia" (active 1830 - 1846)* Rova's works are in Santa Maria della Consolazione detta "della Fava," Venice.

RUDOLPH, Anton *1742-after 1784* Active in Regensburg from 1773 to the mid-1780s; his name appears as the principal horn player on a part for von Schacht's *Prologue pour L'anèe* [sic] *1783.* The other horn players named were Spilhofer, Stumm and Miny.

RUDOLPH (Johann Joseph Rainer), Archduke *8 Jan 1788, Florence-24 July 1831, Baden, Vienna* Archduke Rudolph, Cardinal and Prince Archbishop of Olomouc, was pupil and patron of Beethoven, and the youngest son of Emperor Leopold II. Bastiaan Blomhert (letter of 14 March 1994) informs us that autograph piano sketches for an arrangement of Mozart's *Piano Sonata* for 4 hands, K.497, are held in CZ-KRa. We doubt that Archduke Rudolph was entirely responsible for the Harmoniemusik scoring.

RULOFFS (Roeloffs), Bartolomeus (Bartholomäus) *Oct, 1741, Amsterdam-13 May 1801, Amsterdam* His 5 items of military music were written in the early 1780s for "les Compagnies Bourgeoises des M[ess]rs E G van Beaumont."

RUMMEL, Christian (Chrétien) (Franz Ludwig Friedrich Alexander) *27 Nov 1787, Brichsenstadt, Bavaria-13 Feb 1849, Wiesbaden* Christian Rummel is known today, if at all, as the father of the London-based pianist, Joseph Rummel, and as the clarinettist who, indirectly, led to the attribution to Wagner of H Bärmann's Adagio from his Op 23 *Quintet* for clarinet and strings. Rummel was trained in Mannheim and, in 1806, took the post of Bandmaster to the 2nd Regiment of the Duke of Nassau's Infantry. He was a prisoner of war, later freed; after fighting at the Battle of Waterloo, Rummel left the army to found and direct an orchestra for the Duke of Nassau. This he did with great success; when it was disbanded in 1841, he took over its replacement, the Wiesbaden theater orchestra. His music includes arrangements for wind band and novel small works, such as his Op 42 Variations based on Mozart's Variations K.613; these were based in turn on "Ein Weib ist das herrlichste Ding" by B Schack (or F Gerl; both contributed to Schikaneder's *Der dumme Gärtner* [1791], whence it came).

RUSSELL, William *6 Oct 1777, London-21 Nov 1813, London* Organist at several churches in London, notably Lincoln's Inn Fields from 1793-1798; later pianist to Sadler's Wells and Covent Garden. He was a pupil of Samuel Arnold, and a composer of oratorios and pantomimes. His "favourite March" is for the Guildford Volunteers.

RUZITSKA, Georg (György) *1789, Vienna-3 Dec 1869, Kolozsug (now Romania)*   There are several versions of his *Pater Noster, mit einem Praeludium; in C* from 1837 to 1863. Two are accompanied by ca 2cl 2hn 2bn (the earliest wind parts are missing), another by 2cl 2vla vc, and a third by physharmonica, a small organ or harmonium. The 1859 version was written for Baronne de Bántty [sic], née Comtesse Agnes Ezterházi [sic].

RŮZNÍ (Ruzni, Rugni), ( )   Some earlier researchers have mistaken the Czech word for "various" for the actual name of a composer/arranger. *No such person exists.*

RYBA, Jakub Šimon Jan *26 Oct 1765, Přeštice-8 Apr 1815, Rožmitál pod Třemšínem* An early champion of the Czech language, and composer whose varied output included a number of religious works for winds, often to Czech texts. Ryba had to curtail his studies in philosophy in Prague when his schoolmaster father became ill, yet managed to write books on musical theory and a musical dictionary. He took his own life, depressed by small-town life. His funeral works present problems, since the collection copied by František Vaněček, Chorrector of Březnice, Bohemia, includes works not found in other sources; stylistically, they are undoubtedly authentic.

1. J Němeček 1963 *Jakub Jan Ryba. Život a Dílo;* Prague: Státní Hudební Vydavatelství (the thematic catalog is pps 261-356).

RYBAŘ, Jaroslav *b 1942*   His *Sonata* for 10 Winds, **JZR-2,** is recorded by Panton. He has also written a wind quintet *Rozhovor* (Conversation) and smaller works for winds.

RYCHLÍK, Jan *27 April 1916, Prague-20 Jan 1964, Prague*   A musicologist, linguist, mathematician and enthusiastic motorist, who began his musical career playing percussion in jazz bands. His *Africky cyklus* **JAR-2** (1961, 8 winds and piano) is recorded by Supraphon; its novel invention is a metaphoric reminder of Africa. His other music for octet bears the title *Memoires* (1957). Rychlík's smaller works for winds include his 1946 *Wind Quintet* and the chamber cycle *Relazione* (1963-1964) for a-fl ca bn.

SADLO, Franz *(1750)-1829, Regensburg*   His 3-movement *Bantomin* [sic] on the story of *Hamlet* was performed at Regensburg in 1778.

SALIERI, Antonio *18 Aug 1750, Legnano, near Verona-7 May 1825, Vienna*   Salieri's reputation owes more to his associations than to his music: teacher of Schubert and Beethoven; rival and rumored murderer of Mozart; villain of Rimsky-Korsakov's opera *Mozart and Salieri* and of Peter Shaffer's *Amadeus.* So-called demonstrations that Salieri killed Mozart are certainly false; there is evidence that his envy affected Mozart's musical prospects, but little more than is common in an intensely competitive profession. Later, Salieri helped many musicians, both as founder of the Conservatorium in Vienna and vice president of the Tonkünstler-Societät. Nor was Mozart the only composer to have problems; Krommer had difficulties in Vienna at this time, with no hint that Salieri was to blame. Salieri's testimonial for Mozart's son, Franz Xaver, helped the young composer to his first appointment; Salieri was also instrumental in securing da Ponte's position with the Italian Opera in Vienna. Faced with the mixture of contradictions and legends, his music must be judged on its own merits. Some recent revivals show that his success was due as much to fine musicianship as to good politics.

Salieri's brother, a pupil of Tartini, gave him his first grounding in music. After the early death of his parents, Salieri moved to Venice. Here he met Gassmann (qv), previously Kapellmeister to the Emperor of Austria, who took Salieri to Vienna in 1766. When Gassmann died, Salieri helped his family generously. Salieri became Court Composer in 1774. He won commissions from Milan, Venice, and Rome, and in 1788 succeeded Bonno as Kapellmeister to the Imperial Court. A conservative at heart, he stopped composing opera in 1804 because popular tastes had changed in ways he could not approve; the death of his son in 1805 and his wife in 1807 were further reverses from which he did not recover. Yet he remained involved in Viennese music, receiving the city's gold Civil-Ehrenmedaille in 1816 for his 50 years' association with Vienna; at the celebrations, there were performances of works by his pupils, including Schubert. Salieri's reforms of the organization of the Court Music Library were important (1), and his proposals for safeguarding music could well have been adopted more widely. Only in 1824 did Salieri retire; after 50 years' service to the court, he did so on full salary.

AXS-1 *Armonia per un Tempio della Notte,* dated 1794. This extended and dignified movement was composed in Vienna and dedicated to Baron von Braun, who was in charge of the court theaters (cf. Cherubini); it may have been intended for performance at the Baron's residence at Schönau. The central Poco lento appears in the 1795 opera *Palmira, regina di Persia,* based on the 1791 opera *La princesse de Babylone.* The same section was used by P Wranizky, also for winds alone, in his *Quodlibet Symphony,* as did Seyfried in **IXS-1.4.** Other parts may be based on operas as well, perhaps to remind von Braun that Salieri's operas were worth performing. A lovely work, recorded by Il Gruppo di Roma on Frequenz CAP-1.

AXS-2 The several versions of essentially the same material cause confusion. The *Serenata* in Bb **AXS-2.1,** scored for 2cl 2hn 2bn vlne, has six movements (Allegro Maestoso; Minuet & Alternativo; Larghetto; Allegro assai; Adagio; Allegretto/Allegro assai). It is recorded on Frequenz CAP-1. **AXS-2.4** is also recorded on Frequenz CAP-1; it is amiable but undistinguished. The other versions are **AXS-2.2 (-2.5)** *Serenatas 1-4,* each of two movements. Apart from *Serenata 3,* which is new, a Minuet and an Allegro, there are only minor changes from **AXS-2.1.** Thus *Serenatas 1-3* are now for 2fl 2ob 2hn 2bn, and *Serenata 4* is for 2ob 2cl 2hn 2bn and transposed from Bb to C. **AXS-2.6, 2.7** are essentially **AXS-2.2, 2.3,** and were purchased from the estate of Graf von Klenau, c.1820. **AXS-2.8** combines **AXS-2.2** and **AXS-2.3** as a single work for 2ob 2ca 2hn 2bn, and may well be a transcription by Went for the Schwarzenberg Harmonie.

AXS-3 *Picciola Serenata* This relatively simple work was composed in 1778 "per Il Senatore di Roma Il Principe D[on] Abondro Rezzonico Sig Luigi Fuchs." In that year Salieri was producing his opera *Europa riconosciuta* in Milan. The *Serenata* is not unlike early Haydn at times, though it is slightly longer and makes more use of the first horn and second oboe. It is recorded by the Lukas Consort on Campion RRCD 1330.

AXS-1mv A *Parade March,* inscribed "Prägt tief eure Herzen Brüder die Jahrzahl eins acht null und neun," perhaps because Austria declared war on France in 1809.

1. Jane Schatkin Hettrick 1986 Fontes Artis Musicae **33/3** 226-235 *A Thematic Catalog of Sacred Works by Antonio Salieri.*

SALNER, G P *(1770)* His *Slow March* (c.1800) is dedicated to "Capt. Den. Taaffe, Island of St Helena." This work therefore dates from before Napoleon's arrival in 1815.

SAMMARTINI, Giovanni Battista *1700/1701, Milan-15 Jan 1775, Milan* Prolific composer and organist, described by Mysliveček as "the true predecessor of Haydn." Many of his compositions were in the archives of the Pálffy family. He was the elder brother of oboist Giuseppe Sammartini.

SANDRED, Örjan *b 15 June 1964, ?Sweden* His 1991 *Sabda* uses a tabla.

SARO, Heinrich *1827-1891* Bandmaster associated with the Lippe Kapelle, Detmold, known for his marches and as a conductor of massed bands. He arranged for winds the funeral march which forms the slow movement of Raff's *6th Symphony.*

SARTI, Guiseppe *(baptized) 1 Dec 1729, Faeriza-28 July 1802, Berlin* Successful opera composer, whose "Come un agnello" is played by Don Giovanni's wind band. Among his compositions from St Petersburg are an oratorio using a Russian horn band, and a *Te Deum* with cannon and fireworks to celebrate Potemkin's taking of Ochakov in 1788. In his scientific work on acoustics, he fixed the normal orchestral pitch as A = 436 Hz.

SARTORIUS (Sartorus), Georg Caspar *(1770?)* All of his arrangements of operas (by Mozart, Martín y Soler, Paisiello, and others) and works such as Danzi's *Freudenfest* are in D-DS. Most reflect the unusual configuration adopted by the Hesse-Darmstadt Harmonie, with a cbn part added to 2cl 2hn 2bn. The arrangements clearly call for an independent cbn part, which adds a distinctive color. The balance of sonorities is maintained, unlike the often ill-advised modern additions of db to sextet music. Sartorius, who wrote a march for the Hochfürstliche Hessen-Darmstädischen Leibregiment, described himself as General Music Director to Ludwig X (Landgraf of Hesse-Darmstadt from 1790 to 1806 and Grand Duke from 1806 to 1830). Unusually, fair copy scores survive, and show the arrangements to be rather good. They include operas first performed as early as 1774, together with others, like Mozart's, which had become popular before Sartorius began to build this repertoire of wind music. His arrangement of the Overture and five items (including two duets and a terzetto) from Mozart's *Le nozze di Figaro* is recorded by Mozzafiato on Sony Classical SK 53965.

SAUER (Saver), Ignaz *1 Apr 1759, Třebušín-2 Dec 1833, Vienna.* Active as a music publisher in the 1820s, Sauer described himself as "Musikdirector des k.k.Waiseninstitut in Wien," in charge of music in Vienna's orphanage. The titles of his works confirm this. Some are choral works to celebrate specific events, like the award of a gold medal to the teacher, Herr Johann Föls (**IYS–1v**), patriotic works (like **IYS–3v** and **IYS–6v**) and sadder occasions, like the burial of teacher Herr Johann Theodor Persche (**IYS–1t**). The vocal score of **IYS–1v** bears a note on the second section that the Duetto was sung by "Herrn Ferd Schubert [qv] Lehrer an der Hauptnormalschule bei St Anna, und Herrn Ign Hofstädter[,] Lehrer an der Hauptschule im [Waisen]institute."

SAUGUET, Henri Pierre (who also used his mother's name, Poupard) *19 May 1901, Bordeaux-22 Jun 1989, Paris* His 1941 *Alentours saxophonistiques* is for solo saxophone and double wind quintet.

SAVI, Antonio *(1870), active 1901* His *Andante Patetico* is for fl 2cl(C) hn bn tp.

SAXTON, Robert *b 8 Oct 1953, London* His *Paraphrase on Mozart's Idomeneo* was written for performance before the opera at Glyndebourne. It is recorded on EMI CDC 7 54424 by members of the London Philharmonic Orchestra under Andrew Parrott.

SCHACHT, Theodor, Baron (Freiherr) von *1748 Strasbourg-20 June 1823, Regensburg* The Regensburg court owed its prosperity to the postal service which the Thurn und Taxis family had founded in the sixteenth century. Theodor von Schacht's father represented the court abroad, and indeed Theodor was born on such a visit, though he returned to Regensburg from 1756 to 1766 to study music, before moving to Stuttgart as a pupil of Jommelli. Yet music was not von Schacht's main career: he, like his father, was to become an able administrator. After a brief period at Wetzlar as administrator for the Prince von Fürstenberg, von Schacht returned to Regensburg, forging links with the heir, Carl Anselm, who made him his Intendant "with full power in things concerning the regulation of music itself." When Carl Anselm became Prince of Thurn und Taxis in 1773, von Schacht was Administrator of the Court Music and Musical Director of the Court Theater. He held these positions with distinction, and wrote much music for the stage and for wind band. Von Schacht was a capable composer, best known by a symphony which was once attributed to Haydn (Hob I:Es11; its theme for variations was used by Haydn in his *Symphony No 85* [1]). Regensburg, as the seat of the plenary sessions of the Reichstag, the Diet of the Holy Roman Empire, held the 1803 sessions which agreed to Napoleon's reordering of the German territories. Two years later, as an indirect result, von Schacht moved to Vienna, and associated with the circle of Beethoven's friend, Archduke Rudolph. Napoleon heard of von Schacht's music, and commissioned six masses. In 1813, von Schacht retired to the Thurn und Taxis estate at Scheer, Württemberg, returning to Regensburg in 1819. He wrote much church music in his later years. Von Schacht's music for winds is varied: marches, parthias, arrangements, works with chorus, and rarities such as his *Serenada* *d'Eco* [sic] in which the echo is a small wind group.

1. J de la Rue 1959 Music and Letters **40** 132.

SCHAFFNER, Nicolaus Albert *born c.1790*   Schaffner wrote 2 *Suites* of 12-part "Divertissements militaires, polonaises, allemandes et walses" [sic] published by Dufaut et Dubois in 1824. Three of his works, including an *Ouverture de Chasse*, were arranged by Gambaro (qv).

SCHALL, Claus Nielsen *28 Apr 1757, Copenhagen-9 Aug 1835, Copenhagen*   From 1776 to 1792, Schall directed the ballet at the Royal Theater; he became Konzertmeister and later Director of the Copenhagen Opera. The *Carasel Musique [sic]* CNS–1, like that by Anton Wranizky, would have been written for an equestrian tournament. Schall composed the *Schild- und Tanz-tour* music; the other movements are by Skalle.

SCHALLER, ( ) *(?1800)*   Arranger for winds of music from Sacchini's *Oedipe à Colonne* for the Lippe Harmonie, Detmold.

SCHENK, Johann Baptist *30 Nov 1753, Wiener Neustadt-29 Dec 1836, Vienna*   A pupil of Wagenseil (qv) and composer of much music, including operas such as *Der Dorfbarbier*. Schenk was highly regarded as a teacher; he helped Beethoven with formal training in counterpoint when Haydn's supervision was too informal. His wind music includes the attractive *7 Nocturnen* for SATB, fl cl 2hn bn, settings of Italian texts.

SCHERER, ( ) *(?1780)*   The MS parts of his *Adagio in Dis [Eb] mit Variation in B[b]* are marked "Ex Musicalibus Josepha Labler m.p." and "L[adislav] Vaněček" (qv) on the clarinet 2 part. He also wrote a *Harmonie Messe* for chorus and winds.

SCHETKY, Johann Georg Christoph *19 Aug 1737, Darmstadt-30 Nov 1824, Edinburgh*   Cellist and composer, whose visit to London in 1772 led him to settle in Edinburgh. He was a friend of Robert Burns, some of whose verses he set. In 1774, Schetky married the daughter of Joseph Reinagle, senior, father of Alexander Reinagle (whose career took him to America) and Joseph Reinagle, junior (qv). Schetky's son was marine painter to George IV and to Queen Victoria. In 1794 Schetky conducted the Gentlemen Volunteers, which led him to write military music: the *Edinburgh Volunteers' March* of 1795, the 1806 Marches, and the 1800 *Scottish Airs, Reels and Strathspeys*. The modest Scottish works are of interest, both as a foil to traditional Austro-Bohemian serenades and because their careful construction gives them real charm. One cannot reasonably play all 24 items in sequence, but many varied and attractive suites can be constructed.

JGS–1 *A Collection of Scottish Music consisting of Twelve Slow Airs and Twelve Reels and Strathspeys Respectfully Dedicated to His Excellency Earl Moira, Commander in Chief of His Majesty's Forces in Scotland.*   They are scored for 2fl 2cl 2hn bn tp perc, but the trumpet is tacet in the Airs; the flutes are "in Bb" (really Ab, see part 3) so that a piccolo substitutes well for flute I in the faster movements. The early printed version contains many errors.

The contents page of the *Slow Airs* reads [sic]: "N B As the beauty of the Scottish Airs consists in their simplicity the author of this collection has wrote them as he wishes them to be played the slow airs between Largo and Larghetto the Strathspeys, Moderato Allegretto, and the Reels a brisk Allegro." The items are 1 Busk Ye (The Braes of Yarrow) (Eb) ["Busk Ye" means "Get dressed"; Brae means hillside]; 2 The Bush aboon Traquair (Eb); 3 Waly Waly (F); 4 The Broom of Cowdenknows (F); 5 Peggy I must love thee (Bb); 6 Gilderoy (from the Gaelic "gille ruadh"for red-haired boy; C minor); 7 An thou were my ain thing (Bb); 8 The last time I came o'er the Muir (F); 9 Braes of Ballandyne (Bb); 10 Thou art gone awa (Eb); 11 Donald (Eb); 12 Within a mile of Edinburgh (Bb). The Airs may be based on *A Selection of Scots Songs*, published with string accompaniment by Pietro Urbani (qv), from 1792 onwards.

The *Reels and Strathspeys* have a similar note on the contents page: "N B The Bass Drum, Triangle, Tambourine &c will easily be added in the lively Airs as the Judgement of the Leader shall direct." The items are: 1 Short Life to Stepmothers (E♭, Strathspey); 2 Mrs Garden of Troup's Reel (E♭); 3 Miss Herron's Reel (F); 4 Mrs McDonald Grant's Strathspey (F); 5 Mrs Morthland's Reel (B♭); 6 Lady C: Keith's Reel (B♭); 7 Kempshot Hunt (Reel, B♭); 8 Lady Mary Murray's Delight (Strathspey, F); 9 Village Reel (B♭); 10 Jarnovik(i)'s Reel (E♭); 11 Miss Graham of Finty's Reel (E♭); 12 Miss A: McKenzie's Reel (B♭). The title of No 10 comes from the name of the Sicilian violinist Giovanni Mane Giornovichi (1740-1804) whose *Reel* was first published c.1800. The several spellings (Jarnowick is another) are noteworthy because they follow the Norse forms common in Scottish place names. Robert Burns wrote at least four Verse Epistles to Mr Graham of Fintry (not Finty); presumably Miss Graham was his daughter.

The places named are: *Yarrow:* west of Selkirk; *Traquair:* south east of Peebles; *Cowdenknows:* east of Galashiels; *Ballandyne:* probably Ballindean, west of Dundee; *Troup:* west of Fraserburgh, on the Morray Firth; *Fintry:* east of Loch Lomond.

SCHICKELE, Peter, (composing as "P D Q Bach") *b 17 July 1935, Amos, Iowa*
Schickele, as a composer, needs three biographies: as himself, as "Professor Schickele," and as P D Q Bach. Peter Schickele, bassoonist and pianist, taught at Swarthmore College and the Juilliard School of Music. His serious compositions are wide-ranging and inventive. They include music to accompany poetry recited by Joan Baez and music involving winds, such as his *Quartet for Clarinet, Violin, Cello and Piano,* and a *Concerto for Brass Quintet and Orchestra,* commissioned by Canadian Brass.

Schickele is best known for the musical spoofs of his alter ego, "Professor Schickele," Professor of Musical Pathology at the University of Southern North Dakota, at Hoople, who lists his main influence as "plagiarism" (most of his compositions have not a single original note in them) and who tried to hold the position of music critic of the *Hoople Scoop.* The Professor made musical history conducting the first modern performances of the works of P D Q Bach on 26 April 1965 at Carnegie Hall. Despite the efforts of music lovers to suppress them, Professor Schickele has continued to find works by this justly-neglected composer with alarming regularity, and record albums appear just as frequently in a vain attempt to change listeners' first impressions.

P D Q Bach (1807-1742) was, Professor Schickele asserts, the last and certainly the least of Johann Sebastian Bach's children. Having failed with High Baroque and Low Baroque, P D Q Bach found his true level in Gutter Baroque, such that the extended Bach family preferred to deny all knowledge of him. If his home, Wein-am-Rhein, had been closer to Salzburg, perhaps Leopold Mozart would have found his company stimulating. Only fragments of P D Q Bach's third opera, *The Civilian Barber,* survive, including *Perückenstück* (Hair Piece) among the debris. The Suite from the opera (2hn 2bn 2tp tb timp, cellos and basses), consists of six movements in various keys: Entrance of the Dragoons *(tempo di Marsha);* Dance of St Vitus; His Majesty's minuet; Fanfare for the royal shaft; Her Majesty's minuet; Departure of the Dragoons *(tempo di on the double).* Dragoons, the *Definitive Biography of P D Q Bach* observes, are soldiers specially trained to quell disturbances in operas. It is unclear whether *tempo di Marsha* is *March* mis-spelt or a reference to that soldier known as "Puff, the Magic Dragoon."

Two works outside our scope provide an awful warning: the *Schleptet in E♭,* in which the composer believed string players need to take breath, but wind players do not, and the *Royal Firewater Musick.* Closer to our scope, but happily outside it, are the *Grand Serenade for an Awful [sic] Lot of Winds and Percussion* (White Bear Productions 1975) and *Last Tango in Bayreuth* for 4bn, the work Wagner could have written had he known better; composed for the first English performance of P D Q Bach's works on 3 December 1983. His *Octoot à 8* **PXS-2,** recorded in *A Little Nightmare Music,* could bring an end to any concert. If not, perhaps the *Echo Sonata for Two Unfriendly Groups of Instruments* would suffice.

SCHIEDERMAYR, Johann Baptist *23 Jun 1779, Pfaffenmünster near Straubing, Bavaria-6 Jan 1840, Linz* Organist at Linz Cathedral; composer of Singspiels and masses. He wrote two *Harmonies*, marches (one for the "Landwehr im Erzherzogthum Österreich ob der Enns"), Turkish pieces, and much religious music with winds. His *IV Evangelien* for Corpus Christi, published by Haslinger, proved enormously popular. We have traced 14 different local scorings in the Austrian Empire (many do not mention the composer's name), and performances are mentioned as late as 1875.

SCHINN, Georg Johann *14 Sept 1768, Sinzing, nr Regensberg-18 Feb 1833, Munich* Hofmusiker of the Archbishop in Eichstatt. His *Pièces d'Harmonie*, in the Schwarzenberg Harmonie archive, have some parallels with Mozart's *Gran Partita,* for there are 13 instruments, and the 6 movements have a structure similar to the 7 movements of Mozart's work. The 13 instruments differ, for Schinn uses 2fl instead of the second pair of horns, and 2vla instead of 2bthn.

SCHIRINGER (SCHÖRINGER), Karl (Carl) *(1740), active 1767-1790* This *Parthia* for 2ob 2hn bn, c.1770, may well be by Carl Joseph Schoeringer, bassoonist and later flautist at Eszterháza from 1767 until his dismissal in 1790.

SCHMELLING, ( ) *(?1800)* His *Ouverture* was written for the Lippe Harmonie, Detmold.

SCHMETS, ( ) *(1780)* Associated with the Kinský Harmonie at zámek Budenický.

SCHMID, Josef *30 Aug 1868, Munich-after 1904* His *Serenata Op 42,* for 2fl 2ob 2cl 2hn 2bn cbn, is a large-scale work in four movements, consciously in parthia form. It was written in Munich, and its movements are dated: Entrata (20 April 1904), Notturno (26 April 1904), Menuetto Gemachlich (16 May 1904) and Finale (25 May 1904).

SCHMIDT, Jakob *(?1790)* Composer of various funeral songs with winds. All are found in Geras monastery in Austria; some anonymous music there may also be by Schmidt.

SCHMIDT, Ole *b 14 July 1928, Copenhagen* Conductor, and composer of a *Concerto* for tuba and winds.

SCHMITT, Florent *28 Sept 1870 Blamont Meurthe-et-Moselle-17 Aug 1958, Neuilly-sur-Seine* Schmitt wrote much original band music: his Op 44 *Musiques de plein air,* Op 46 *Hymne funèbre* "pour Choeurs et harmonie" (1899), *Marche du 163e Régiment,* Op 48 *Selamlik* and Op 52 *Dionysiaques.* His other works include *3 Chants en l'honneur d'Auguste Comte* Op 71, for chorus and 10 winds. His *Lied et Scherzo, Op 54* FYS-1 "Pour Double-quintette d'instruments à Vent dont un Cor principal," dedicated to Paul Dukas, is a demanding concerto-like work for solo horn. It is in a single movement, but with many changes of tempo. The score gives the date of completion in Paris as May 1910 (Hucher [1] gives 1906). It is recorded by the Sylvan Winds on Koch International 3-7081-2HI and the Amsterdam Wind Ensemble/Blomhert on STH-CD 19053.
1. Yves Hucher 1953 *Florent Schmitt: L'Homme et l'Artiste;* Paris: Plon.

SCHMITT, Georg *(1770)-c.1839* Leader of the Hohenlohe-Örhingen Harmonie, for which he arranged over 100 works, including many operas, some by Mozart. The earliest dated works (arrangements of Beethoven's *Septet* and of *Symphony No 1*) date from 1817, and the latest from the late 1830s. He, with W E Scholz (whose arrangements start in the late 1830s) arranged a collection of 61 dances (Hopwalzer, Walzer, Galopps, Märsche, Cotillons, Polonaisen). Schmitt began his career (1803 to 1815/1816) with the Harmonie of the Elector of Mainz, and many of his early arrangements are to be found at Amorbach, one of the Elector's residences.

SCHMITT, Georg Aloys *2 Feb 1827, Hanover-15 Oct 1902, Dresden* His 1892 *Trauer Cantate* was for the mother of the Duke of Mecklenburg.

SCHMITT, Nicolaus *(1750), active 1778, d c.1802?* We believe Schmitt was the bassoonist resident in Paris. Some of his works were published in 1806, including divertimentos for 2hn 2bn and arrangements of operas by Orlandi and Paisiello.

SCHMITTBAUER (Schmidbauer, Bauerschmitt, Bauerschmidt), Joseph Aloys *8 Nov 1718, Bamburg-24 Sept 1809, Karlsruhe* Orchestra member and conductor for the Margrave of Baden; also a glass harmonica player, though his wind works do not exploit it.

SCHNABEL, Joseph Ignaz *24 May 1767, Naumberg am Queiss, Silesia-16 Jun 1831, Breslau* His religious works for chorus and winds, like the published *Missa Quadragesimalis,* were performed for some time after his death.

SCHNAUBELT, Heinrich *(1810)* A prolific composer, based in Salzburg. His music for winds comprises a *Tantum ergo* (for Christmas, and dated 16 Dec 1838) and two *Marches* for Corpus Christi processions; they are dated 1866 and 1868.

SCHNEIDER, Anton *1773-after 1827* About 1820, the Prince of Thurn und Taxis tried to establish a private army in Württemburg. A military band was formed at Schloss Taxis, near Neresheim (there is no evidence that it ever played at Regensburg). It had few military duties, and rapidly took the role of a Harmonie. At first, its music was bought from defunct ensembles, but these could not provide suitable music for the band when it expanded to fl 2ob 4cl 2hn 2bn tp b-tb serp (violas were added later, and violone replaced the serpent). Probably in 1821 or 1822 Anton Schneider became Kapellmeister. From 1822 to 1827, *on average* he prepared one or more works per week, the composers ranging from Arne to Weber, and the music from single dances to arrangements of complete operas; he also wrote some excellent overtures and bravura sets of variations. A few items may date from his previous employment, for the first pages of most of the bound parts of Sm 17 state "v: Schneider 1813." Yet the date is carefully lined through three times; the numberings follow directly from Sm 16, and the other works in Sm 17 are from 1820 or later. We suspect that Schneider initially augmented the repertoire with earlier pieces, with minor changes for the local forces. If so, the early dates were an oversight by the band's copyist when adding items to a bound volume of music manuscript, and were corrected by Schneider. Unlike most arrangers, Schneider often prepared entire pieces from operas, including recitatives. The viola parts can be important, either as independent tenor parts, or in replacing clarinet "woodles." The violone is an important source of color, with arco and pizzicato markings, and often frees the bassoons from the chore of bass accompaniment. The string parts may also have enabled the band to play works from the pre-1806 Regensburg Harmonie. Flute parts are usually in C, except for dance music, where one finds flutes in D, Eb and F. When there are 4 clarinets, these are usually either 4cl(Bb) or 2cl(C) 2cl(A). The trumpet was expected to double on third horn or posthorn.

SCHNEIDER, Friedrich *(?1800)* Composer of an *Ouverture in Eb.*

SCHNEIDER, Georg Abraham *19 Apr 1770, Darmstadt-19 Jan 1839, Berlin* He studied with J W Mangold (qv) and played bassoon, horn and oboe in court bands at Darmstadt from 1787, Rheinsberg from 1795, and Berlin from 1803. He was Director of the Berlin Royal Theater from 1820. Presumably **GES-16** *Terpodium Concert* mimics Buschmann's 1816 Terpodion, for which Spohr, Weber and Hummel wrote music. The instrument has a 6-octave keyboard, which controls sound produced by friction from a wooden cylinder.

SCHOEN, ( ), Sig *(?1770)* Schoen's name appears on the title page of the MS parts (c.1800) of Krommer's **FVK-2d**, a *Parthia* octet with two solo horns. Krommer's name, added in pencil, appears in the D-Rtt Gardemusik catalog. The MS may have been bought in July 1820 from Scheffauer, Stuttgart, as part of a set of Krommer works, and perhaps the cataloger merely assumed this work was by the same composer. There is a believable but not overwhelming case for the work to be by Krommer (qv).

SCHOENFELD, ( ) *(1760)* His *March for the Army of the Rhine,* 1792, is for the German army, unlike the Marseillaise ("Chant de la guerre pour l'Armée du Rhin").

SCHOENFELD, William C *(?1930)* Arranger for winds of part of a Beethoven Piano Sonata, namely the Presto Finale of Op 10 No 2.

SCHOLL, Nicolaus (Miklós) *(1780)-after 1827* Bandmaster of Prince Esterházy's 32nd Linien Regiment band at Pest. Scholl's *Racouzy March* ("Ragoszÿ" on the parts) was the first written version of the *Rácóczy March*, c.1820. Scholl's opera arrangements start earlier, since NYS-2a was sold to Eszterháza in 1811 (Hellyer, Haydn Yearbook **15** 66), yet (cf. NYS-1a) continue until after 1827. We suspect that Scholl arranged many of the late works which previously have been attributed to Sedlak without verification (including many of the copies by Perschl).

SCHOLZ, W(ilhelm?) E(rnst?) *(1810)* Arranger of over 200 works, including many operas (from Mozart to Verdi), symphonies (Mozart, Beethoven), songs (Mendelssohn), and piano solos (Chopin), for the Hohenlohe Harmonie at Schlawentzitz, Silesia, from c.1837 (when Georg Schmitt was ending his long period of making arrangements) to the end of 1849. The arrangements are good. The ensemble used often adds fl tp b-tb db timp to the standard octet of 2ob 2cl 2hn 2bn. Scholz composed a few original works too, including 23 works for brass ensemble. What is especially interesting is that the dates of starting and finishing arrangements are known. For long periods, a substantial arrangement was expected *each week* (one can understand why, when Scholz considered a work to be complete, he would often use the closing phrase "Mit Gottes Hilfe"). The movements were sometimes reorganized later to make them most effective; it seems likely that works were only put together into a final form after initial performances.

SCHRECK, Gustav E *9 Sept 1849, Zeulenroda-22 Jan 1918, Leipzig* Schreck was a student with Jadassohn (qv) at the Leipzig Conservatoire, later Königlicher Professor at Leipzig University. His Op 40 *Nonet* is an attractive late romantic work.

SCHRIER (Schrejer) *(1780)-post 1807* Composer of a *Messe in C* dated 15-18 June 1807, from the Trenčín (Slovakia) church collection.

SCHROEDER, H B *(1760)* For so prolific a composer of marches, facts are remarkably sparse. Schroeder wrote songs too, including "The Hero of the Sea," celebrating Trafalgar. His many marches include those for the West London Militia, for the Berkshire Militia "at the request of W. W. Jones, Late of the Berkshire Band" and works dedicated to the Duke of York and to The Duke of Clarence. One song with band accompaniment is for the Sussex Yeomanry Cavalry. The text by Arthur Lee, "Since Virgil wrote in Yeoman's praise" does not seem likely to rouse troops for battle.

SCHRÖDER, Hermann *26 Mar 1904, Bernkastel-7 Oct 1984, Bad Orb* His 1962 music for HRS-1 *Das Wort der Bibel* is recorded on Ariola GG (details untraced). His *Sextet* HRS-2 is dedicated to the Kölner Bläsersextett: Franz & Erwin Klein (cls), Gustav Kettwesz & Udo Hansen (hns), Axel Fürch & Wolfgang Sorge (bns).

SCHUBERT, Ferdinand Lukas *18 Oct 1794, Vienna-26 Feb 1859, Vienna* The elder brother of Franz Schubert, headmaster, and organ professor at the Vienna School of Church Music (see under Ignaz Sauer), Ferdinand Schubert also wrote works for voices and winds (1). Two of his motets with winds (**FLS-4v** *Veni Sancte Spiritus* and **FLS-1v** *Salve Regina)* are recorded by Musica Polyphonica/Maastricht Conservatory Chamber Choir/Devos on Erato/RCA ECD 75386. His fine *Salve Regina* in Bb (Op 12, **FLS-1v**) has been attributed to Franz Schubert as D.386. It is scored for SATB chorus, 2ob 2bn 2hn (with 3tb 2tp timp, org ad lib) and was published by Diabelli in 1833 (pn 4523). Distinct from **FLS-1v**, he also provided (ad lib) wind parts for Franz Schubert's *Salve Regina* in F, D.223. He arranged Mozart's *Alma Dei*, K.277, for SATB, fl 2ob 2hn bn tp timp. Two of his works of 1854 are in praise of the Empress Elisabetha Eugenia, making it clear how long into the 19th century such wind music continued.
1. F Spiegl 1956 Music and Letters **37** 240.

SCHUBERT, Franz Peter *31 Jan 1797, Vienna-19 Nov 1828, Vienna* Schubert's prodigious output is even more impressive when one realizes that he began composing seriously quite late in his short life. Music was encouraged in his home by his father, a poor schoolmaster. Systematic studies, including composition, came later, around 1812, when Schubert had already spent several years at the Imperial Choir School. Even at this time, the economies of war and the threat of social upheaval were bringing on a decline of wind harmony; Schubert's contributions date mainly from the early period around 1813, when he was a pupil of Salieri. Like Weber, Schubert wrote other works with winds, often with voices (*Nachtgesang*, D.913, is a superb work for male voices and horn quartet), and much interesting wind writing is found in stage works (1) like *Rosamunde*, D.797 (1823) with its *Geisterchor* for male voices with 3hn 3tb. Schubert's operas contain much for winds alone, including several whole movements.

FPS-1 *Franz Schuberts Begräbniss-Feyer (Eine kleine Trauermusik) D.79* (dated 19 September 1813). Like Purcell, Mozart and Beethoven, Schubert realized the potential of trombones in funeral music, although it is the horns which dominate in this elegiac piece (the horn parts demand six minutes of continuous playing in a high tessitura, so some ensembles may find two pairs useful). It is not known for whom the music was written. The autograph title (Franz Schubert's Burial Ceremony) could mean several things, from a mere description to what a sixteen-year-old felt he would like played when he died; in fact, it was not played at his funeral fifteen years later. Other suggestions are that it marked his departure from choir school the following month, that it was written for his mother (surely wrong; she died on 28 May 1812), or that it was in memory of Theodor Körner, the poet who had encouraged Schubert to persevere as a composer and who had died a few weeks before in the battle at Gadebusch (26 August 1813) in Mecklenburg- Schwerin. Körner was the poet of the War of Liberation whose direct if naive verse caught the spirit of the time; he served with Ludwig von Lützow's "Black Hunters," remembered through Weber's setting of Körner's *Lützow's Wild Hunt*. A simpler possibility is that the title was written in the same spirit as the *Octet* for winds, D.72 **(FPS-3)**. It is recorded by the London Sinfonietta/Atherton on Argo ZRG 916 and Decca 430 362-4DM, and by the Czech Nonet on Praga PR250 087.

FPS-2 A set of six *Minuets, D.2D*, including three scored by Schubert himself (1 and 2 are based on the piano version D995) and three others scored by Weinmann (2).

FPS-3 *Octet D.72* Not to be confused with the *Octet* for wind and strings, D.803, this early work comprises two completed octet movements, dated 18 August 1813, which were meant for Schubert's fellow students. The inscription "By the Master of Music of the Chinese Court of Nanking" would go straight to the hearts of schoolboys. The first of the movements is a Minuet with two Trios, one for oboe and clarinet, the other for horn and bassoon. The Finale, also amiable if perhaps conventional, shows more traces of Schubert's later style. Interestingly, at this time Schubert used to defend the pleasant but rather superficial music of Kozeluch, speaking slightingly of Krommer; these movements are certainly closer to Kozeluch. They are recorded by the Budapest Schubert Ensemble on Naxos 8.550389; London Sinfonietta/Atherton on Argo ZRG 916, Vienna Wind Soloists on Decca 430 516, and the Netherlands Wind Ensemble/de Waart on Philips 6570 205. These two movements do not stand well by themselves. A much more satisfying version results from adding two more movements, completed by Father Reinhard von Hoorickx (a Franciscan musicologist on whom we lack information) and Christopher Weait (qv). In essence, bars 90 to 109 of the first movement survive, and these allow much of the rest to be restored, with a section added based on a *Fantasia* for piano duet. The second movement is an arrangement of a sketch for piano, found on the back of D.990. The full work is recorded by the German Wind Soloists on Marco Polo 8.223356. There are fragments of a second Minuet.

FPS-1v *Gesäng zur Feier des heiligen Opfers der Messe* (Deutsche Messe; German Mass) D.872; with an appendix, *Das Gebet des Herrn* (Lord's Prayer). This setting contains eight sections corresponding to the traditional mass, and was written in 1826-1827 to a text by Johann Phillip Neumann. The timpani are used in the Sanctus and Gloria only, the trumpets only in the Gloria; the organ doubles the winds and may be omitted. The simple, somewhat sanctimonious, style is not the Schubert of his great works. Its first known performance was in 1846. The movements are 1 Zum Eingang (Introit) "Wohin soll ich mich wenden"; 2 Zum Gloria; 3 Zum Evangelium und Credo; 4 Zum Offertorium; 5 Zum Sanctus; 6 Nach der Wandlung; 7 Zum Agnus Dei; 8 Schlussgesang: "Herr Du hast mein Flehn vernommen." Recordings include those by the Bavarian Radio Orchestra and Chorus/Sawallisch (HMV SLS 5254, ASD4415 and SLS 1436073; EMI CMS7 64783), Vienna Pro Musica/Gillisberger (Turnabout TV 34282S), Vienna Symphony/Harrer (Philips 6514 262), Vienna Ophelia/St Augustine (OP 67108), and Vienna choirs/Orchestra of the Age of Enlightenment/Weil on Sony SK53984.

FPS-2v *Herr, unser Gott: Hymnus an den heiligen Geist (Op post 154) D.904,* a Hymn to the Holy Ghost for male voices; a complex and substantial work, first performed in the Landhaussaal in Vienna in March 1829, six months after it was written.

FPS-3v *Glaube, Hoffnung und Liebe D.954* A choral work (Faith, Hope and Charity) for the dedication of a recast bell in the Dreifaltigkeitskirche (Trinity Church). In this church in the Alsergrund suburb of Vienna, Beethoven's body was blessed in March 1827. The recast bell had been cracked in 1805. It was raised again, and rededicated on 2 September 1828, but it does not seem to have been rung for several days. Choirmaster Leitermayer had been a fellow student of Schubert's, and asked him to write the work, which is in three verses. Schubert seems to have had the priests' choruses from Mozart's *Die Zauberflöte* in mind when he wrote it. Stressed wind chords mimic the bell's sound; such effects are, of course, completely lost in any piano transcription.

1. O Deutsch 1978 *Schubert: Thematisches Verzeichnis;* Kassel: Bärenreiter.

2. C Landon 1970 Musical Review **31** 215.

SCHUBERT, Joseph *(1790)* His *Salve Regina*, c.1825, is from the archives of the church at Nymburk, east north east of Prague.

SCHUBERTH, Johann Christian *(1760)* He was associated with the Kinský Harmonie at zámek Budenický.

SCHUESTER (Schuster, Schüster), ( ) *(1730)* Probably associated with Kroměříž; most of his MSS are dated 1766. One long work, **XXS-5,** is in the Clam Gallas archive.

SCHULLER, Gunther *b 22 Nov 1925, New York* Composer, previously horn player. Schuller's *Eine kleine Posaunenmusik* **GQS-1** is recorded on GM 2009.

SCHULTZ, Svend Simon *b 30 Dec 1913, Denmark* His *Divertimento for blaeseroktet* of 1961 is recorded by the Danish Wind Octet on Da Capo 8.22.4002.

SCHUMANN, Robert Alexander *8 June 1810, Zwickau-29 July 1856, Endenich, near Bonn* While Schumann is far better known for his songs, piano works and symphonies, there are a few choral works which exploit winds. Some are within larger works, such as his fairy tale (Märchen) *Der Rose Pilgerfahrt,* Op 112, based on a text by Moritz Horn, in which No 10 is accompanied by 2cl 2hn 2bn and No 15 by horn quartet.

RAS-1v *Beim Abschied zu singen,* Op 84 was written in 1847 or 1848, when Schumann was working on his opera *Genoveva*. It is a straightforward setting of a text by Baron Ernst von Feuchlersleben. The winds merely double the voices. Reinecke (qv) arranged both this work and "Das Schifflein" for winds, timpani and percussion.

SCHUYT, Nico *2 Jan 1922, Alkmaar, Netherlands-1992* Critic; Director of Donemus.

SCHWARZ, A A flautist at Mecklenburg-Schwerin.

SCHWARZ, (?M) *(?1760)* The Trio of the *Marcia* **UXS-1m** includes a posthorn solo. The MS parts are from Langenbruck. Possibly the M Schwartz who wrote two sets of marches published in Vienna c.1814 (**MYS-1m, -2m**).

SCHWEGLER, Johann David *1759, Endersbach, Württemberg-1817, Stuttgart* His 10 *Harmonien* listed in the 1834 Stuttgart Inventory for the Royal Court Theater were destroyed in the 1902 fire. These were probably the works which Jähns wrongly attributed to Weber. The 1807 *Quartets* for 2fl 2hn survive, as do Schwegler's *Deux Marches zur Braut von Messina* (2fl 2ob 2cl 2hn(F, C) 2bn 2tp timp).

SCIARRINO, Salvatore *b 4 Apr 1947, Palermo   Di Zefiro e Pan, Poemetta,* for double wind quintet (including cl(A) cl(B♭)), is recorded on Rusty Records RRCL 606619.

SEDLAK (SEDLACH, SEDLACK, SEDLASH), Wenzel *4 Aug 1776, ?Bohemia-2 Nov 1851, Vienna?*   Clarinettist, known mainly for his excellent arrangements for the Liechtenstein Harmonie. Given his key position in the development of Harmoniemusik, remarkably little is known of his life, especially for the period before he became Kapellmeister to Prince Liechtenstein in 1812. The gaps in knowledge are made worse by the loss of the archives from Feldsberg (now Valtice) in World War II. Attributing works to Sedlak is also a problem. It is now clear that the picture emerging from early studies of a few collections was too simplistic. It is not the case that, after Triebensee's appointment as opera conductor in Prague in 1816, Sedlak dominated the arrangements market until the early 1840s, apart from those few works arranged by Friedrich Starke in the 1820s. The situation was very different, with serious competition from Starke, Scholl, and possibly shadowy figures such as Roser de Reiter.

Nothing is known of Sedlak's early career. *Hellyer* suggests he joined the Harmonie of Prince Auersperg c.1805, only moving to Prince Liechtenstein's Harmonie in 1808. Sedlak certainly began arranging works soon after 1800, mainly for 2cl 2hn 2bn. These early works were probably issued in manuscript from 1803 by T Weigl at his Kunst- und Musikhandlung. Sedlak's first arrangements for 2ob 2cl 2hn 2bn cbn were issued in manuscript at about the same time (1803/1804) by Johann Cappi in Vienna. Copies in the Löwenstein collection provide identifying characteristics for Sedlak's works of this period. These Cappi manuscripts all bear an MS imprint in their titles (probably because they were being sold outside Vienna) and state "Die Musik ist von Herrn ... / über setzt [sic] / Von Herrn Sedlak" in the title. In one case, the name is spelled "Sedlack."

Sedlak's arrangement of Winter's opera *Das Labyrinth* (**WXS-67a**) points to links between key figures, for it is almost certainly a reduction for 2cl 2hn 2bn of Triebensee's octet version (issued in April 1804 as part of the second number of his *Harmonien Sammlung).* Other pairs of arrangements by these two key figures may be related in the same way, notably the arrangements of Cherubini's *Medée.* Sedlak's arrangements for 2ob 2cl 2hn 2bn cbn continued from 1805 to c.1808. There then seems to be a gap of several years. This gap is consistent with *Hellyer's* chronology, and suggests an altered relationship with Triebensee, who may have discouraged arrangements by a new member of the Harmonie. Sedlak's only extant autograph score of this period, his arrangement of Cherubini's *Faniska* (after 25 February 1806) shows he had problems in deciding the most effective order for the movements.

Both Went and Heidenreich made reductions of their octets to sextets. Sedlak may have expanded sextets to octets instead. If so, perhaps he was responsible for the combined versions of the *Journal für Neunstimmige/Sechstimmige Harmonie* published by the Chemische Druckerei in Vienna from 1810, after the Leichtenstein Harmonie was disbanded. Certainly Sedlak arranged the last two numbers (VII and VIII) of the *Journal,* as well as the Chemische Druckerei version of *Der blöde Ritter,* Duport's pastiche ballet of 1812 (1). However, one must be cautious, for the first six of the *Journals* do not name an arranger, and Sedlak's named arrangement of Boieldieu's *Jean de Paris* differs from that in the *Journals.*

Once Sedlak became Liechtenstein'she Kapellmeister, c.1812, five changes are clear in his arrangements. First, almost all manuscripts state "eingerichtet von H[errn]: W: Sedlak, Kapellmeister bei Sr. Durchlaucht dem regierenden Fürsten Johann von und zu Lichtenstein [sic]." Secondly, his arrangements are usually for 2ob 2cl 2hn 2bn cbn with two ad lib trumpets ("mit Begleitung zwei Trompetten" is on most title pages). Thirdly, Sedlak began to number his works only after his appointment, usually in the form "20tes Werk." Separate T[h]eils were given separate numbers, yet, when he also made a sextet version, the *Werke* numbers are the same (e.g., **WXS–52a**). Fourthly, most of his copies sold commercially have title pages lettered in an extremely bold hand, which we designate the "Auswahl Hand" after the three issues of the "Auswahls" comprising excerpts from his arrangements. We believe this copyist was associated with the firm of Mechetti, in Vienna. The Auswahl Hand continues to appear well into the 1820s. We have used several such copyist features in assigning works to Sedlak, including the use of "Fagotti Bassi" for the combined second bassoon and contrabassoon part. Finally, operas were becoming more complicated. One number could contain anywhere from three to more than ten sections, far longer than was usual for a Harmonie arrangement. Sedlak solved this problem in a thoroughly practical way. What he did was to divide pieces into two (or even three) separate sections, with distinct cadences, separate numbering, and usually the direction *Attacca* at the end of each number. Thus, although one of Sedlak's Teils may comprise 12 numbers, the actual number of pieces arranged may be lower.

Between 1812 and 1831, Sedlak's known arrangements amount to over 70 Teils, about three-quarters of his total verified output. Many surviving copies lack *Werk* numbers, so an accurate chronology is impractical. Our own analysis suggests two gaps around 1819-1822, where works may not survive or where anonymous arrangements have yet to be attributed correctly to Sedlak.

We find no evidence that Sedlak was ever a member of the Imperial Harmonie. He played in the Sedlatzek Harmonie-Quintet from 1821 to 1822. This was the Viennese counterpart of Antonin Reicha's Parisian wind quintet; the flautist Sedlatzek (no relation) moved to England in 1826, joining another distinguished wind quintet, Puzzi's "Classical Concerts for Wind Instruments." We cannot say whether Sedlak made any arrangements for the Harmonie-Quintet concerts. He seems to have written only a few original works for one or two clarinets, or for piano (*Weston/MCVP*). In Kroměříž, there is a setting by him (A1382/Br.C.505) of the *Pange lingua* for 4-part male voices and organ. It bears his Kapellmeister style, and so dates from after 1812. There may have been other works, used only locally.

Only five of Sedlak's arrangements are known to have been published in printed form: *Der blöde Ritter* (1), Liverati's *David,* Persuis' *Nina,* Hummel's *Die Eselshaut oder Die blaue Insel,* and Beethoven's *Fidelio.* Some other arrangements published by the Chemische Druckerei may also be his. There are three major collections of manuscripts. That of the Imperial Harmonie (A-Wn) has many added comments ("gut," "sehr gut," "nichts," and so on) from the Harmonie's leader, showing which movements were to be played. That of the Archduke Ferdinand of Tuscany (I-Fc) is mainly of specially-made copies, lacking the arranger's name. The collection of the Augustinian monastery at Brno presents problems, for many copies were pirated from the 2nd Linien Regiment in Brno, and are not always complete versions. Sedlak's arrangement of *Fidelio* is outstanding. It was authorized, perhaps supervised, by Beethoven himself (2). As expected from a virtuoso clarinettist, Sedlak's arrangements are stongly clarinet-driven, with the horns usually taking a more active role than one finds in either Went's or Triebensee's arrangements. The ad lib trumpet parts are not essential, but add depth and excitement to tutti passages. Given the quality and importance of Sedlak's arrangements, it is surprising how little is available in modern editions.

In the past, a number of anonymous arrangements in A-Wn, dating from 1830 to 1842, have been attributed to Sedlak. We believe these attributions are wrong. They are based on two false premises: that Sedlak was a member of the Imperial Harmonie, and that Perschel, the copyist, was a Court copyist. We have found no evidence at all to link Sedlak and Perschel. Moreover, we have found copies of non-Sedlak works in Perschel's hand in other collections. Perschel, a meticulous copyist, invariably includes a Bögen [sheet] count for each part, and his use of cues (usually added in red ink) was clearly intended to maximize his fee. Several such arrangements were made in 1837, well after the first performances in Vienna. Most include a bass trombone part not copied by Perschel, perhaps added at a later date. The arrangements usually include from two to six long numbers, and do not follow Sedlak's practice of splitting multi-section works into separate numbers. The lack of Sedlak's name and title add to our doubts about the attribution. Are these works by Sedlak, or by a competitor? Starke died in 1835, and can be eliminated. Nicolaus Scholl is a different matter. By about 1829, Scholl's output had reached *Werk 58*. His work remains a largely unknown quantity, but we believe that he is the most likely arranger of these anonymous works.

Recordings of Sedlak's arrangements include the following:

WXS-5a Beethoven: *Fidelio*   London Wind Soloists (who play all 11 movements), on Decca SDD 485; Melbourne Windpower (overture only), on Move MD 3110; Octophoros (overture only; original instruments), on Accent ACC 48434 D.

WXS-46.1a, -51a, -53a, -44a Rossini *Il barbiere di Siviglia extracts, and overtures to Matilda di Shabran (as Corradino), Semiramide, L'Italiana in Algeri:*   Netherlands Wind Ensemble: Philips 412369; Mozzafiato, Sony Vivarte SK 53965; Melbourne Windpower, Move MD 3110 (*Il barbiere,* overture only). Sedlak's two Teils of *Il barbiere di Siviglia* were produced three years apart. Teil 1 (his 22nd work) dates from 1819; a bill in the Imperial records shows Teil 2 (his 30th work) was purchased in 1822, the year of a "festival" of Rossini operas in Vienna, with the entire company from Naples. This festival enhanced Rossini's popularity and the demand for his music. The arrangement includes the interpolated theme and variations by Rode (originally for violin) which were used by Madame Catalani as the display piece in the singing lesson.

WXS-56a Rossini *Guillaume Tell* (15 mvts): Consortium Classicum/Klöcker, Claves 50-8804. The flute/piccolo part used here dates from at least 20 years after the original manuscript and is not authentic. Although Sedlak remains the most likely arranger, we note that the copy from the Augustinian monastery, Brno, is both anonymous and incomplete, missing at least the original No 4 of Teil 2.

WXS-62a Weber *Der Freischütz* (16 mvts): Consortium Classicum/Klöcker, MD+G 3267.
1. Duport choreographed this ballet. As usual, the music used varied from city to city, and perhaps from one production to another; the Vienna production included the overture from Steibelt's *La belle laitière* and pieces by Persuis.
2. R Hellyer 1972 *Music & Letters* 53 242.

SEIBER, Mátyás György *4 May 1905, Budapest-24 Sept 1960 Capetown, S Africa*   He was a musician of great versatility, whose career ranged from cellist of the Lenzewski Quartet to ship's musician; he also held several academic positions. His *Serenade* (*Szerenad/Leicht Musik* on the autograph) **MGS-1** is an outstanding work for wind harmony, unduly neglected. It dates from 1925, when Seiber was a student of Kodály. A vituperative quarrel raged in the Budapest Academy of Music between a conservative Director and his supporters on the one hand and Kodály and Bartók on the other. The issue was partly the role of folk music and partly modern ideas on music or, as Kodály put it (1), between "preserving and fostering the ancient treasure of Hungarian music" and the production of "pale imitations of Brahms and Schumann." Seiber's *Serenade* fell victim to the conflict when entered in a competition in Budapest in 1925. The *Serenade* is firmly based on Hungarian idioms, not unlike those of Kodály's *Dances of Marosszék* (1927) and *Dances of Galanta* (1929). Bartók and Kodály were both on the jury, and the *Serenade* was adjudged the best work. Even so, it was not awarded the prize, and Bartók resigned from the jury in protest. Seiber directed the first public performance in Frankfurt in 1926. This original and attractive work makes a ideal foil to 18th-century wind harmony. It is recorded by the Netherlands Wind Ensemble, on Pinnacle COE 812, and the Wind Soloists of the Chamber Orchestra of Europe, on ASV COE 812.

The three movements show features which most Europeans call "Gypsy" and which Hungarians associate with "Verbunkos." The lively opening Allegro moderato is based on two lyrical Magyar themes, ending with an evocative coda. In the middle is a series of exotic cadenzas for the clarinettist in the true Eastern European style. The movement ends with a quiet passage in falling thirds, akin to the Song in Kodály's *Háry János*. The second movement, Lento, has the characteristic alternation of tempo too, with a faster section embedded in it. The last movement begins with a lively march, and again stresses dance rhythms; once more, Seiber uses tempo changes to produce changes of mood. In the middle is a fugue, handled with technical aplomb, but based on a splendidly incongruous subject. What would have annoyed the conservatives even more are the interruptions by what can only be called instrumental sneezes (exactly the sneezes of disbelief one finds in Kodály's *Háry János)*, presumably to express disapproval of the need for a fugue in this competition piece. The sneezes raise a textual point. It is not obvious what the horn should use as the upper note in the trills. Looking at the autographs (there are three autographs in GB-Lbl, Add 62800) one finds no horn trills in the earliest version, trills with that for first horn crossed out in the second version, and trills for both horns on what appears to be the last version. In the context, any trill which sounds like an irreverent sneeze should be acceptable.

1. László Eösze 1962 *Zoltán Kodály: His Life and Work;* London: Collet's, p 31.

SEIDEL, (possibly Friedrich Ludwig) *14 July 1765, Truenbriezen-7 May 1838 Berlin* Seidel's *Salve Regina* is from Rychnov nad Kněžnou, Bohemia.

SEIFF (Sieff), Jacob *(1780)* Father of the first wife of Franz Strauss, the father of Richard Strauss. Apart from marches for the Bavarian National Guard, 3rd Class, his surviving works, both original and arrangements "des Opéras favoris" are for 2cl 2hn 2bn. We have no locations for other reported Harmonie pieces for fl 2cl 2hn bn 2tp.

SEIFFERT, ( ) *(1800)* His *6 Waltzes,* with an Introduction, were written for the Augustinian monastery at Brno, c.1830.

SELLNER, Josef *13 Mar 1787, Landau-17 May 1843, Vienna* Sellner, an oboist, joined the foremost wind band of its time, the Imperial Harmonie in Vienna, in the mid-1830s. His works often have a soloist (e.g. horn or clarinet) and are competent but not inspired, typical of much music of this time. Sellner may have established the individual Viennese oboe sound (1) through his important oboe tutor and his influence during his period as Professor at the Vienna Conservatorium.

1. Hermann Salagar 1978 *Wiener Holzblasinstrumente* Tibia **3** 1-6.

ŠESTÁK, Zdeněk *b 10 Dec 1925, Cítoliby* Šesták has taken a musicological interest in the traditions and archives of Cítoliby. His wind music includes a *Sonata Sinfonica for Winds, Bell and Kettledrum; Sursum Corda; Concerto for Violin, Winds, Harp and Percussion* (1981) and a 1978 *Sonata da Camera* for 2ob 2cl 2hn 2bn.

SETACCIOLI, Giacomo *8 Dec 1868, Corneto, Tarquinia-5 Dec 1925, Sienna* Studied at the St Cecilia Academy in Rome; later Director of the Conservatorio, Florence.

SEXTARIUS, ( ) *(1770)* Active c.1801 in Langenbruck, northern Bohemia.

SEYFRIED, Ignaz Xaver, Ritter von *15 Aug 1776, Vienna-27 Aug 1841, Vienna* Best known as conductor for Schikaneder (1), Seyfried was a pupil of Leopold Kozeluch (piano) and Haydn (theory), an acquaintance of Mozart and Beethoven (for whom he turned the blank pages of the piano part of the *Third Piano Concerto* in 1803), a collaborator with Triebensee in *Der rote Geist im Donnergebirge* (1799), and the teacher of Suppé. Seyfried was encouraged to change from law to a musical career by

Winter, and became conductor at the Theater an der Wien from 1801 to 1826. When Beethoven died, Seyfried adapted one of Beethoven's *Equali* as a Miserere (2) for the funeral. His other funeral songs are more in traditional Austrian and Czech forms.

IXS–1 A cycle of five works to be performed at Hetzendorf for the Austrian Emperor's nameday, 4 October 1805. There are two bands, each essentially 2ob 2cl 2hn 2bn cbn; one may have been the Imperial Harmonie. In the *Canone*, the second band comprises ca cl 2bthn bn cbn, so at least one person played bassethorn who was not one of the clarinettists. The work is on a large scale: (1) March on a theme from Grétry's *Raoul Barbe-Bleu*; (2) Echo Divertimento (one movement); (3) Cantatina [sic] of three movements, the second being the *Canone*. There are SATB vocal parts; "Coro Parti 16" on the MS presumably means four voices per part; (4) A 22-movement Quodlibet, beginning with the overture to Mozart's *La clemenza di Tito* and ending with Haydn's *Emperor's Hymn*, choices suiting the Emperor's nameday. The other movements are from Gluck's *La rencontre imprévue*, Mozart's *Die Zauberflöte* (No 5 "Dies Bildnis ist bezaubernd schön," No 14 "In diesen heil'gen Hallen," No 23 "Zum Ziele führt dich diese Bahn"), *Figaro* ("Non più andrai," No 21), J Weigl's *L'amor marinaro* (No 6), Salieri's *Palmira* (No 19), Paisiello's *La molinara* (No 7) and the anonymous "O du lieber Augustin" (No 20). Ensembles vary from all 18 players to a contrabassoon solo. Score markings suggest that Seyfried only decided which band would play which section at the concert venue itself; (5) March on a theme from Cherubini's *Les deux journées*.

There seem to be no comparable works for other Imperial namedays. Indeed, some evidence suggests the nameday celebrations were relatively low-key. A work on this huge scale would surely take at least four months to organize. What then happened between the last nameday (October 1804) and May 1805 to give rise to this event? We cannot know; one possible conjecture is that the stimulus came from the celebrations of the coronation in Paris of a new Emperor, Napoleon I.

IXS–3v *Libera me* Planned as an extra movement to Mozart's *Requiem*. At what stage it was written we do not know; certainly Seyfried would have known Süssmayr, who completed the work as it is usually heard now.

1. E M Batley 1969 *Preface to the Magic Flute;* London: Dennis Dobson.

2. J Schmidt-Görg and H Schmidt (editors) 1969 *Beethoven;* Hamburg: Polydor. Page 32 shows the trombonists in procession. Novello published Seyfried's arrangement.

SHEEN, Graham *b 18 Feb 1952, Southampton* Professor of bassoon at the Guildhall School of Music, Sheen is co-principal bassoon of the BBC Symphony Orchestra, and principal bassoon of the Academy of St Martin's in the Fields. From 1976 to 1983 he was a member of the English Chamber Orchestra, for whose wind ensemble he made transcriptions and arrangements. The ones recorded on EMI Eminence 41 2053 4 are: **GHS–6a** Debussy: *Three pieces from Children's Corner* First played complete in its original piano form in 1908, the pieces were written to titles apparently suggested by the English governess of Debussy's step-daughter, Claude-Emma ("Chouchou" 1905-1919). The eccentric spelling of "Golliwogg" and of "Jimbo" (presumably from Barnum's elephant "Jumbo", d 1885) is Debussy's. The movements are: 1 The Little Shepherd; 2 Jimbo's Lullaby; 3 Golliwogg's Cake-Walk. **GHS–12a** Mendelssohn: *Konzertstück Op 114* One of two concert pieces for clarinet and basset horn written by Mendelssohn for the Baermanns, father and son; this one dates from 1833. **GHS–18a** Schubert: *16 German Dances, D.783* These short dances were written for piano in 1823-1824. Despite their brevity (two have 24 bars, the others 16 each) and the facts that all are in 3/4, and most in major keys, there is great variety. The quieter, reflective dances are especially effective. Other works, recorded by Ensemble Fidelio on Gallo CD 674, are: **GHS–2a** Bizet: *Jeux d'Enfants* The eight movements incorporate the five of the orchestral suite: Toupie (Impromptu); La Poupée (Berceuse); Les

Chevaux de bois (scherzo); Colin Maillard (Nocturne); Trompettes et tambours (based on a march in Bizet's unfinished opera, *Ivan the Terrible);* Les Quatre coins; Petit mari, petite femme; Le Bal (Galop). **GHS-1a** Bizet: *Suite de Carmen* Aragonaise; Habañera; Intermezzo; Seguedilla; Les dragons d'Alcal (*recte* Dragon d'Alcola); Les Toréadors.

SHERIFF, Noam *b 7 Jan 1935, Tel Aviv* Musician, later assistant conductor, in the Israeli Army Band. His *Music for Woodwinds, Trombone, Piano and Bass* combines Eastern and Western musical ideas, including Jewish liturgical themes.

SHIELD, William *5 Mar 1748, Whickham, Durham-25 Jan 1829, London* Shield's wind music is in his stage works: in the finale to *Robin Hood* **WYS-1e**, to accompany the banquet, and the clarinets and horns below stage in *The magic cavern.* The March in *The siege of Gibralter* [sic] **WYS-1m** was to be "Perform'd by the Military Band [stage band] while the Fleet sail into the Bay." The 1780 production celebrated the temporary relief of a siege of Gibraltar by the Spanish which eventually ended in 1783.

SHORT, Michael *b 27 Feb 1937, Bermuda (now resident in the UK)* The Northern Sinfonia Wind Ensemble/David Haslam gave the first performance of Short's 3 Pieces on 16 January 1982. The suggested seating is ob 1 cl 1 hn 1 bn 1 bn 2 hn 2 cl 2 ob 2.

SHOSTAKOVICH, Dmitri Dmitrievich *25 Sept 1906, St Petersburg-9 August 1975, Moscow* **DDS-1a** *Two Scarlatti Pieces,* Op 17 (1928): Pastorale (D minor), Capriccio (E major). These arrangements, recorded on ASD 165033 under Rozhdestvensky, sound more like Stravinsky's *Pulcinella* than the better-known Shostakovich.

Shostakovich's 1929 incidental music for *The Bedbug,* a "fairy comedy" by Vladimir Mayakovsky, includes several movements for winds or brass, notably the *March* which opens and closes the score. It is recorded by the USSR Ministry of Culture Orchestra/Rozhdestvensky on Olympia OCD 258. Mayakovsky wanted music "of the type played by firemen's bands." The scoring (2cl 2tp 3saxhn cym b-dr) is indeed close to the Fire Brigade band for which Sibelius composed (see Sibelius).

SIBELIUS, Jean *8 Dec 1865 Tavastehus, Finland-20 Sept 1957, Järvenpää* The intense nationalism of works like *Finlandia* stems from Finland's struggle for independence from Russia (1, 2). Some of this feeling is found in Sibelius's early works for *Torviseitsikolle,* a common ensemble of seven brass (2). These were written for the Fire Brigade Band of Loviisa, birthplace of Sibelius's father and grandfather; the band was directed by horn-player, Christian Haupt, as part of his duties as town *Kapellmästar.* Most are recorded by the London Gabrieli Brass/Larkin on Hyperion CDA66470; the *Praeludium* and *Tiera* are recorded by the Gothenburg Symphony Orchestra on BIS CD 448. They are of interest for several reasons, not least as early compositions. First, the band was a town band, whose role was exactly that of the civic Harmonie we describe elsewehere. Secondly, its membership linked civic bands and the uniformed forces (here the Fire Brigade, rather than the army, though Haupt had been a military musician). Thirdly, there are signs of growing nationalism. These included Song Festivals for bands to generate a Finnish repertoire, some requiring competing composers to base their entries on Finnish songs or folk dances. The *Allegro* which Sibelius wrote in 1889 is based on the tune *Epäilevälle* from an 1887 collection of Mäntyharjun songs published by Emil Sivori (a song also used by Armas Järnefelt). Other works were overtly patriotic, like the *Aténarnes sång* of 1898, based on the War Song of Tyrtaeus (see also Dibdin), written in protest against a manifesto of Czar Nicholas II. The *Athenians' Song* was first performed on 26 April 1899, the brass septet being members of the Helsinki Philharmonic. The *Press Celebrations Music* of 1899, was strongly national too, some of its music being re-used in works like *Finlandia.*

It would be wrong to think of Sibelius as a totally serious young man, single-mindedly dedicated to Finnish nationalism. He enjoyed city life, and frequented the fashionable Kamp restaurant. His friends fitted the words "Now I'm off to the Kamp again..." to the delightful neoclassical *Musette* from the *King Christian Suite, Op 27* of 1898. In the original play, it is heard as through an open window (1, p 78-9). In writing the *Musette* Sibelius said in a letter "I have scored it for 2 clarinets and 2 bassoons. Extravagant, isn't it? We have only two bassoon players in the entire country, and one of them is consumptive" (1, p 78). We have not traced a recording of this wind version.

1. H E Johnson 1960 *Sibelius;* London: Faber.

2. Christopher Larkin, notes to Hyperion CDA66470, including a photograph of Christian Haupt with the Loviisa Fire Brigade Band. The 1890s Finnish band (s-crt[or cl] 2crt a-hn t-hn bar-hn tu) is not too different from the 1890s Sedilia Queen City Band for which Joplin played (2cl crt 2a-hn t-hn bar-hn tu), and even the earlier (1818-1849) Besses o'th'Barn band in England (cl[F] cl[C] crt tp 2hn tb 2b-hn b-dr). Czech bands in the 20th century often use similar ensembles (see e.g., Blecha).

SIGL (SIGEL), Georg *(1750)* Composer of 10 parthias and a *Deutsche Messe* with winds.

SIMAKU, Thoma *b 1958, Kavajĕ, Albania* Music in Albania after the death of Stalin was tightly controlled. Despite this, Simaku was able to publish work outside Albania. His visit to England, for work experience with Emerson Edition, led to openings at York University. His *Elephas Maximus* for 13 winds was commissioned by the Elephan Trust and was first performed in York on 10 December 1993. Simaku has also written a *Wind Quintet* and an *Andante and Scherzo* for bassoon quartet.

ŠIMON (Simoni), ( ) His *Partitas* for 2fl 2taille 2hn bn for the Clam Gallas harmonie presumably date from the early phase of wind harmony.

SIMON, Anton *5 Aug 1850, Paris-1 Feb 1916 St Petersburg* After studying at the Paris Conservatoire, Simon worked in Paris till 1871, when he became Superintendent of the orchestras of the Moscow Imperial Theaters. His Op 26 apparently comprises 22 ensemble pieces for winds (4 septets, 4 sextets, 6 quintets and 8 quartets) and probably dates from before 1890. We have no locations for this material, nor for his brass ensemble music (such as Simon's Op 23 Quartets of 1886 for 2crt 2tb).

SIMON, Ladislav *b 3 April 1929, Klánovice, near Prague* A self-taught flautist and a composition pupil of Alois Hába, Simon's musical activities range widely, and include jazz, which he says "is not meant to entertain, but to communicate." His works for winds include *Episodi* (first performed on 19 April 1989 by members of the National Theater Orchestra) for 2cl 2bthn b-cl, and a *Sinfonietta* for 13 winds, first performed on 17 July 1988 in Strasbourg by Solisten Wels and the Czech Brass Quintet.

SIMONET (Simone), François M *(1760)* First horn at the Théâtre Français in 1793.

SIMONI (Simony), P *(1770)* His one arrangement, in the Schwarzenberg archive, Český Krumlov, is for 2fl 2hn basso, an unusual group for the Schwarzenberg ensemble.

SIRLETTI, Ludovica Arranger for winds of two items from Rossini's *Le comte d'Ory.*

SKACEL, ( ) *(1790)* His one arrangement was for the Augustinian monastery, Brno.

SKALLE, ( ) *(1760)* Oboist of the Royal Danish Foot Life-Guards, who wrote marches and the Ring and Kopftour music for ZQS-1. *Carasel Musique,* performed at the Royal Riding Academy, Copenhagen in 1791. C N Schall (qv) wrote the other movements.

SKIRROW, Andrew M *b 15 Apr 1961, Birkenhead, UK* After graduating from London University and Goldsmith's National Centre for Orchestral Studies, Skirrow was a freelance horn player, working with the Chamber Orchestra of Europe, Opera 80, and the Endymion Ensemble. He was a founder member of London Winds, who broadcast some of his arrangements. In 1991, he gave up concert work to focus on writing and arranging. His company, Camden Music, concentrates on performing editions, such as Urtext editions of Mozart's K.375 and K.388, and modern works. Skirrow's arrangement ARS-2a of George Gershwin's *Scenes from "Porgy and Bess"* is a continuous suite, comprising an Introduction (extracts from the overture), Summertime, It Ain't Necessarily So, Here Comes De Honney Man, My Man's Gone Now, Interlude, There's a Boat That's Leaving Soon for New York. He has also arranged three Gershwin songs for brass quintet, and "I Got Rhythm" for wind quintet.

SKLENIČKA, Karel *b 1933*   Composer of *Legendy* (1981) and a *Concerto for Winds*.

SKÖLD, Yngve *29 Apr 1899, Vallby-6 Dec 1992, Ingarö*   The Passacalia of his *Sinfonia de chiesa,* Op 38, 1939, is for winds alone. See also Gunnar Johansson.

SLAVICKY, Milan *b 7 May 1947, Prague*   La voce soave (1981) is subtitled *Omaggio a Mozart*, and is for glass harmonica (or celeste) and octet. Slavický's doctorate in musicology is from Charles University; he also studied composition in Brno. He has been a recording producer for Supraphon. His work includes smaller works with winds.

SLIMAČEK, Jan (Joseph) *b 31 July 1939, Kelč, Moravia*   A tape of his *Etudy* has been broadcast by Czech Radio, Plzeň.

SMART, Timothy (Thymothy) *(?1760)*   Musician with the 1st Regt of Guards (the Grenadiers), and composer of *Twenty four select military peices* [sic].

SMITH, Clement, M.B. *1760, Richmond, Surrey-16 Nov 1826, Richmond*   Composer of a *Favorite March*, "as Performed by the Duke of York's Band" and of *Lady Nelson's Fancy, a Favorite Quick Step* which is printed with Tebay's *Bath Volunteers March*.

SMITH, William *(1760)*   Master, Band of Music of the West Norfolk Regt of Militia.

SÖDERLUNDH, Bror Axel (known as Lille Bror) *21 May 1912, Kristinehamn, Sweden-23 Aug 1957, Leksand*   His Suite *Vagen till Klockrike (The Road to the Land o'Bells)*, is based on music for a film of the novel by Harry Martinson about a 19th century wanderer in Sweden. It is recorded by Camerata Regionalis, on Caprice CAP 1074.

SOLÈRE (Soler), Étienne (Pedro) *4 April 1753, Mont-Louis-1817, Paris*   His *Chant de bataille d'Austerlitz, Grand Marche à l'usage des Musiques Militaires* celebrates the French victory which took place on 2 December 1805, 20 miles east of Brno.

SOLGERT *(1800)*   Composer of a *Salve Regina* in the Rychnov nad Kněžnou archive.

SOLIÉ (Solier, Soulier) Jean Pierre *1755, Nîmes-6 Aug 1812, Paris*   Tenor (later baritone) for whom Méhul wrote; Solié was also an opera composer.

SOLIVA, Carlo Evasio *1792, Casale Monferrato, Piedmont-20 Dec 1851, Paris*   Soliva studied with Asioli (qv) at the Milan Conservatorio. His attractive *Divertimento Pastorale* probably dates from this period. He became conductor at La Scala in 1815, and moved to Warsaw in 1821, then in 1832 to St Petersburg, where he was conductor of the Czar's Chapel Royal from 1834. Soliva returned to Paris in the year he died.

SOMMER, Johann Matthias *(1740)*   Sommer's large 10-movement *Pieze* in D-Rtt is for 13 instruments, but not quite the ensemble of Mozart's *Gran Partita*: Sommer has 2tp rather than oboes, and 2vla rather than basset horns.

SONNENLEITER, Antonius *(1750)*   His *Parthia* is in the Kroměříž archive.

SONNENLEITER (SONNLEITHNER, SONNENLEITER), L *(?1770)*   Arranger of music by Haydn for chorus and winds. Perhaps related to Dr Christoph Sonnleithner, composer and legal advisor to Prince Esterházy, whose works are often found under Haydn's name. His sons, Joseph and Ignaz, and grandson Leopold (d 1874) showed musical talent.

SPÄT, Joseph *d 1829, Schnaitsee*   His *[Hirten] Lied* for Christmas Night is for CAB 2cl 2hn organ; its title calls for vocal parts for two angels and two shepherds.

SPÄTH, Andreas (André) *9 Oct 1792, Rosach, Coburg-26 Apr 1876, Gotha*   His *Six Fantasies* ADS-1 are based on motifs taken from the romances of Prince Albert. They may be associated with Baroness Späth, lady-in-waiting to Queen Victoria's mother. ADS-3 *Sérénade en forme de Pot-pourri*, written c.1827 for the Société de Music à Zuric [sic], includes two long sections for guitar. The guitar's role is purely rhythmical; interestingly, it is written a tone above what it should sound (a guitar in B♭, in fact).

SPENCER, John, [The] Hon[ourable] Capt[ain] *(1760)*   John Spencer's *Favourite Troop* was played by the Oxford Shire [sic] Militia. Lord Charles Spencer (a relative?) was Colonel of this Militia from 1778 to 1798, a period which would have included the regiment's mutiny). John Spencer composed other music, such as a setting of William Robert Spencer; his musical activities are noted *passim* in *Sainsbury*.

SPERGER, Johann Matthias *23 Mar 1750, Feldsberg (Valtice)-13 May 1812, Ludwigslust* An outstanding double-bass player who was a pupil of Albrechtsberger (qv), Sperger began his musical career with Prince Joseph Batthyáni at Pressburg from 1777 to 1783. Here he would have been a colleague of the basset horn player, Theodor Lotz. Contrary to some speculations, there is no evidence that Sperger was at Eszterháza; he seems to have gone directly to the employ of Count Erdödy at Fidisch, near Egerbrau, in the Burgenland. When Count Ladislaw Erdödy died in 1786, Sperger made extensive tours, reaching Prague, Berlin and Parma; in 1789, he settled at Ludwigslust in the orchestra of the Duke of Mecklenburg. He probably took with him music from Batthyáni (**JWS-1**, - **-36, -38, -59** (all dated 1780), **JWS-42** (dated 10 July 1781) and Erdödy (**JWS-47**, dated 1785). Quite a few of the works at Ludwigslust are autograph scores or parts on Italian (rather than North German) paper, with typical Austro-Hungarian copyist calligraphy. Sperger's music includes some with Masonic links. He was a member of the Lodge zum Goldenen Hirschen, Bratislava, as was Konzertmeister Pleyel (1), and Sperger's colleague Lotz took part in a well-known performance at the Crowned Hope Lodge in Vienna on 15 December 1785 for the benefit of basset horn players David and Springer. Some 61 wind works and 3 religious vocal works with winds by Sperger survive at Schwerin.

JWS-1 *Parthia in F* Clearly for the Batthyáni Harmonie, and c.1780 (not 1770, as given by Meier [1]) for it uses 2tp, presumably played by Francis Fabera and Johann Kleppa.

JWS-2 *Cassatio in D* Sperger's own catalog lists this work as given to Herrn Hauer in 1786, and then to Duke Karl von Kurland in January 1788 (2).

JWS-4 *Adagio in E♭* Here horns are used "con sordini"; the movement was also used later with strings as the slow movement of Sperger's *Sinfonia* A38 of 12 Feb 1796.

JWS-5 *Parthia ex b [B♭]* At the end of the score is the remark "March da Capo, wenn es anstatt einer Cassation gemacht wird. Fine." It would seem that, when a parthia was to be used as a cassation (a term of ambiguous meaning), the music was played, some event occurred, and a closing march followed. The dates of Sperger's orchestral *Cassations* suggest some annual event.

JWS-9, -16, -18, -20.2, -22, -23.2 These *Parthias* were performed at a royal wedding in Parma, 1 April 1789, probably in the version for 2ob (rather than 2cl) 2hn 2bn.

JWS-51.2 *Divertimento in C* This work opens with a 6-bar fanfare for trumpet solo.

JWS-3v *Auf, Brüder, ergreifet gefüllte Pokale* This choral work's reference to "Brothers" suggests a Masonic work, but this is not certain.

JWS-1va *Tantum ergo* An arrangement c.1810 of his own version with full orchestra.

1. Zdenko Nováček 1978 *Hudba v Bratislave;* Bratislava: Opus, p 290.

2. Adolph Meier 1990 *Thematisches Werkverzeichnis der Kompositionen von Johannes Sperger (1750-1812);* Michaelstein: Blankenburg. Documentationen-Reprints Nr. 21.

ŠPLICHAL, Jan (Johann) *(1800)* His *Parthia in Dis* JVS-2 is a complex work, its first and last movements containing many tempo changes. The first movement alternates four times between "Adagio con Recitativo" and "All[egr]o." The last movement is a 6/8 Presto, followed by Adagio (2/4, 16 bars) All[egr]o (11 bars, 6/8) and Adagio (3 bars).

SPOHR, Ludwig (Louis) *5 Apr 1784, Braunschweig-22 Oct 1859, Kassel* "Spohr, who sequestres himself among the green woods of Kassel, has an excellent band to write for, and one of the best clarinets I have ever heard" wrote Edward Holmes in 1828 (1). Spohr found fine clarinet players in many places: Conrad Bänder in Kassel, Heinrich Backofen in Gotha, Joseph Friedlowsky in Vienna and Johann Simon Hermstedt in Sondershausen. Hermstedt (qv) inspired much of Spohr's music for winds.

Spohr was a leading violin virtuoso of his time, known more as a serious composer than as an executant to be compared with Paganini (1782-1840), his close contemporary. Spohr was encouraged by Karl Wilhelm Ferdinand, Duke of Brunswick, who supported him from 1799 to 1804; the Duke also supported that prince of mathematicians, Gauss, for over a decade from 1791. In 1805, Spohr became director of the ducal orchestra at Gotha. There he met his future wife, harpist Dorette Scheidler, for whom he wrote the harp-like piano part in his Op 52 *Quintet* for winds and piano when a nervous breakdown forced her to give up the harp. Also at Gotha he met Hermstedt, and Carl Maria von Weber, who helped secure Spohr's Kassel appointment in 1822.

The three courts with which one associates Spohr (Gotha, Sondershausen, and Kassel) straddle the former border between East and West Germany. Yet Spohr travelled widely in Europe, and these journeys are described in an autobiography (2), which depicts the musical scene with insight. Oddly, there is no mention of the *Notturno,* his sole undoubted piece of wind harmony. Most of Spohr's works with winds are for groups of single instruments (occasionally pairs) with piano or strings, like the *Nonet* Op 31, the *Octet* Op 32 (with its variations on Handel's "Harmonious Blacksmith" chosen to suit an English audience), the *Quintet* Op 52, and the *Septet* Op 147.

Spohr wrote two choral works with wind bands. *Vater Unser* (WoO 70, to a text by F G Klopstock) may be an arrangement. *Hesse's Song of Joy,* WoO 68, was written as a festive hymn for the proclamation of the constitution and for the reconciliation of the Elector and Electress. It was first played at Kassel on 9 January 1831, within a play by Niemayr. He exploited wind bands in his operas, often separately from the orchestra. Examples are found in *Alruna* (Gotha 1808; fl 2cl 2bn 4hn), *Faust* (Vienna 1813; 2bthn 2bn 4tb), *Macbeth* (Kassel 1825; 2fl 2ob 2cl 2hn 2bn in the Tafelmusik No 4; pic fl 2ob 2hn 2bn 2tp in the Marcia No 8), and *Pietro von Abano* (Kassel 1827; 2ob 2cl 2bn 2hn hp perc). The winds of the court theater at Kassel were from the Guards' band (3).

The attractive *Notturno Op 34* LXS-1 was first published in 1816. Its form and dedication to Fürst Günter Friedrich Carl I zu Schwarzburg-Sondershausen suggest it was written for Sondershausen, even though Spohr had been in Vienna for three years. Its structure (March - Minuet & Trio - Andante with Variations - Polacca with Posthorn Trio - Adagio - Finale) would have fitted ideally the pattern and woodland setting of the Sondershausen concerts (see part 1), and the clarinet part would match Hermstedt's skill. Was the work really written entirely in 1815, as usually assumed from the note "Carolath im Juni 1815" on the autograph? Or was this just revision of music written between 1809 and 1812 when Spohr was at Gotha? Spohr's next two opus numbers were early works, brought out long after their composition. Moreover, the Adagio (not the variations, as is sometimes said) is based on the start of an aria ("Ich war vereint, ich hatte ihn gefunden") from his unpublished opera *Alruna,* written for Gotha in 1808. The scoring of the *Notturno* is interesting. At the core are fl(pic terz-fl) 2ob 2cl 2hn 2bn cbn, and these suffice for the Variations, the first Minuet and Trio, and the Adagio. Some doublings can be omitted without loss: b-tb for the easier bn parts, and b-hn for cbn in the opening movement. Trumpets and percussion appear only in the opening March and Finale; the Polacca boasts a posthorn and an optional second piccolo. It is recorded by the Little Orchestra of London/Jones on Oryx Romantic 1830, Consortium Classicum/Klöcker on Orfeo 0155 871A, the Detmolder Bläserkantorei/Michaels, on Carus 63118, and (on early instruments) by Octophoros/Dombrecht, Accent ACC 8860D.

1. Edward Holmes 1828 (reprinted 1969) *A Ramble among the Musicians of Germany,* New York: da Capo.

2. L Spohr 1860-61 *Selbstbiographie,* translated 1865, 1878, reprinted 1969 (edited F Göthel); Tützing: Hans Schneider.

3. Clive Brown 1984 *Louis Spohr: A critical biography;* Cambridge: Cambridge University Press.

SPONTINI, Gasparo (Luigi Pacifico) *14 Nov 1774, Maiolati, Italy-24 Jan 1851, Maiolati* Spontini's most famous opera, *La Vestale*, exploits wind bands in several places. The Marche Triomphale "en dehors du théâtre trés éloignée" is largely for winds accompanying Julia and the Choeur des Vestales. The Finale to act 1 ("Le Cortège s'avance") uses a separate wind band, with the orchestral winds entering only after 16 bars. The Finale also includes an Andantino mosso with winds. His other wind works are for large military band, some with male chorus, and date from after 1830.

SPORCK, Georges *9 Mar 1870, Paris-17 Jan 1943, Paris* Pupil of T Dubois and d'Indy.

ŠRAMEK, Vladimír *b 10 Mar 1923, Košice* Composer of a suite for accordion and winds.

STAAB, Kaspar (Caspar) *1717-1798, ?Frankfurt am Main* His arrangements of six arias from Mozart's *Die Zauberflöte* were for the name day of Archbishop Adalbert II.

STADLER, Anton Paul *28 June 1753, Bruck an der Leitha-15 June 1812, Vienna* and **STADLER, Johann Nepomuk Franz** *6 May 1755, Vienna-2 May 1804 Vienna* The Stadler brothers were trained by their father as clarinettists, and their musical careers intertwined. They joined Prince Galitsin's service in the 1770s; presumably this was the source of the Russian themes used in Johann Stadler's *La Russe* for 3bthn. From 1779 the brothers freelanced in Viennese bands, including perhaps that "band of beggars" for whom Mozart's K.375 was written (1). They were founder members of the Imperial Harmonie from 8 February 1782; the instruments bought for them were C clarinets, with B♭ "pièces de rechange." It was during their years with this ensemble that Count Festetics sought Anton's advice on founding a wind band (part 3). In private life, Anton was a dissolute rogue, frequently drunk and usually in debt. His musicianship excused him, but his playing suffered. Johann died of typhus in dire poverty.

1. P L Poulin 1988 *Music and Letters* **69** 49. Anton Stadler wrote to von Beecke on 6 November 1781 (Schloss Harburg, MS Hofmusik II.3.47) to discuss the possibility of the Stadler brothers and Griessbacher joining the Wallerstein band. Poulin notes that the three were out of employment in Vienna at just the time Mozart wrote K.375.

STADLER, Josef de Wolfersgrün ("Guiseppe Stadler di Praga") *(1770)* The *12 Tadeschi [sic]*, **JTS-1**, are dedicated to Count Christian Philip Clam-Gallas. **JTS-1m,** a march with Turkish instruments dedicated to Prince Lobkowitz, is found in the Lobkovic collection in Prague.

STADLER, Maximilian, Abbé *4 Aug 1748, Melk-8 Sep 1833, Vienna* The Abbé Stadler was an organist, scholar, an excellent contrapuntist, a friend of Haydn and of Mozart, and an administrator who saved the astronomical observatory at Kremsmünster. His wind setting of *Hoch du mein Oesterreich* was for the name day of Emperor Franz I (Francis II as Holy Roman Emperor) in 1818.

STAMITZ, Carl (Karl) Philipp *7 May 1745 Mannheim-9 Nov 1801, Jena* Like his father, Johann Stamitz, Carl Philipp, was both a virtuoso violinist and a fluent and original composer. He travelled widely throughout Europe (Mannheim 1762-1770, London 1778-1784, later at Jena) and his music is hidden in collections from London to St Petersburg. Stamitz was fascinated by alchemy, and took treatises with him on his travels. He was not the only composer to be intrigued by the occult; Thomas Arne's son, Michael, had similar leanings. Mozart, writing from Paris in 1778, described the Stamitz brothers as "a pair of musical scribblers and performers, drunkards and debauchees." It is fair to say that Carl Stamitz's music is a good deal better than that remark suggests.

Many of Stamitz's works are presumed lost, including a number of divertimentos for wind sextet and pieces for 10 winds, written for the Czar in 1795 (one wonders if these are just **CPS-1[-7]** retitled) and marches for larger bands, such as sixteen pieces for winds and Turkish instruments apparently written for the Prince of Wales in the last years of Stamitz's life. The titlepage of Thomas Wright's *Marches* (G Goulding, London c.1795) lists *15 Grand Military Divertimentos*, which might be the same works, or could correspond to the 15 movements of **CPS-10(-13)**. We cannot trace the "Sextet Op 14" for 2cl 2hn 2bn said to be in GB-Lbl (Op 14 is a set of string quartets).

CPS-1(-7) *7 Parthias* These cause problems of identification. The main source is D-Dla (1), and Steinquest (2) cites "7 Partite", probably the same works, in D-B. Riemann's thematic catalog (3) gives the incipit of No 1 only. One cannot tell whether there are 7 movements constituting 3 partitas (or even 7x3 = 21 movements), for one finds strange conventions. A further complication comes from the recording (Panton 11 0522 G) of the three-movement No 1, the one whose incipit is in Riemann. The record sleeve shows an octet (no flutes), and indeed no flutes are mentioned; the recording might use an unidentified manuscript for octet only. One can almost imagine what might be flutes in places, but that may indeed be imagination; even if not, the careful listener will deduce, like us, that the flute parts are very modest, if they exist at all. These parthias are in E♭, and they are said to date from 1777. The situation is complicated further by Klöcker's excellent recording of Stamitz works on CPO 999 081-2, where the first item (Parthia No 1, in E♭, not B♭ as stated) is recorded without flutes from what is said to be a Schwerin source, and with a wholly different finale. We note that the Octet No 2 in B♭ on Klöcker's recording is not by Stamitz, but by Gyrowetz (**ADG-2**), which accounts for the differences in style remarked on in the recording's notes.

CPS-9 *Parthia in E♭* Recorded by Klöcker and the Consortium Classicum. This begins with a splendid hunt, with a gradual crescendo as the hunt draws near. The last four movements are also to be found for 2cl 2hn (1)bn at US-BETm, **CPS-11.1(-11.4)** where they form parts of two separate works in a set of four "Divertissements."

CPS-14 *Serenades Op 28, c.1783* Here there are 12 movements, hence confusing references to 4 serenades, though the movements do not group themselves easily (there are 6 Allegros, 2 Allegrettos, 2 Andantes, a Minuet, and an unmarked 3/8 movement). They tend to confirm that flutes do not fit comfortably into classical wind harmony.

CPS-15 *Divertimento in E♭, Op 8 No 2* One might be tempted to guess that the other works of Op 8 were for the same half-harmonie (ob cl hn bn); not so. However, this work is skilful and attractively-written, with a respectable clarinet part for the early 1780s, some interesting high bassoon writing, and delightful use of horn and oboe.

CPS-1m *March* Presumably this is an arrangement (for 2ob 2bthn 2hn 2bn) by Pick or a colleague. Could this be one of Stamitz's marches for the Prince of Wales?

1. J Newhill 1977 Musical Review **40** 90.
2. E W Steinquest 1981 *Thesis: Royal Prussian Wind Band Music 1740-1797;* New York: George Peabody College for Teachers.
3. H Riemann 1915 Denkmäler der Tonkunst in Bayern **28** Jg 15 11.

STAMITZ (Stamic), Johann Wenzel (Ján Václav) *baptized 17 June 1717, Deutsch Brod (now Havličkûv Brod)-27 Mar 1757, Mannheim* A founder of classical orchestral methods and an innovator in the instrumentation, structure, and musical content of the classical symphony. He helped to introduce clarinets into French orchestras, and made Mannheim's "orchestra of professors" famous throughout Europe. His music for 2cl 2hn is quoted in Roeser's pioneering manual (1). He was the father of Carl Stamitz.
1. V Roeser 1764 *Essai d'Instruction ...* (reprinted Minkoff, Geneva 1972; also p 160 of A Baines 1976 *Brass Instruments: Their History and Development* London: Faber).

STARCK, ( ) "Capellmeister;" the arrangement in Donaueschingen of Dittersdorf's *Hieronimus Knicker* attributed to him is actually by Went.

STARK, Wenzel *1670-1757* His *Quartet* for 2cl 2hn (no bn) is in Kremsmünster.

STARKE, Friedrich *1774, Elsterwerde, Saxony-18 Dec 1835, Döbling, nr Vienna* A musician who mastered "all string and wind instruments" (*Thayer* p 525). He studied with Albrechtsberger (qv) and taught piano to Beethoven's nephew Carl. He later played horn in the Vienna Court Opera orchestra. In 1812, Starke's horn playing won praise from Beethoven, who said he had never heard his Op 17 Sonata performed with such shading and with such a fine pianissimo. Beethoven's piano was a semitone flat, so Starke offered to use an E crook instead of an F one; Beethoven felt that this would spoil the effect, and transposed instead. Starke's original works, such as his *Serenate*, **FRS–3** and his sets of variations, are well worth reviving. His arrangements compare well with those of his competitor, Sedlak; indeed, it is often impossible to tell which (if either) made the anonymous arrangements in collections such as CZ-Bm. Starke's version of Rossini's *Zelmira* was published by Artaria to exploit the success of the 1822 Rossini "festival," and is a tour de force for all instruments. Although the 2tp are · described as "as libitum" on the title page, much excitement is lost by omitting them. Starke was an experienced military bandmaster. In 1806, when he published his Op 14 *Marches* and his *10-stimmige Harmonie,* he was Kapellmeister in the 2nd Infantry Regiment E H Ferdinand; in 1812, when his arrangement of Gyrowetz's *Der Augenarzt* was published, he was Music-Directeur [sic] of the kk Infanterie Regiment Colloredo-Mansfield; c.1819, at the time of his arrangement of Rossini's *Otello,* he was "Capellmeister und dumalen [sic; damaliger?] Musik-Directeur" in the kk König-Max.-Joseph Infantrie Regiment. He was well aware of the market for wind music, and exploited it in the *Journal für Militärmusik* (see part 1 for a discussion).

STARZER, Joseph Franz *1726 Vienna-22 April 1787, Vienna*   Violinist and composer, highly regarded in Vienna for his playing (until excessive corpulence forced him to retire), for his string writing, and for his ballet music for the choreographer Noverre at the Kärntnertortheater. He spent ten years in St Petersburg, where he wrote operas and ballets for the choreographers Hilferding van Wewen and Rauprach. Some of his wind music could date from this period in Russia; other works may be later, like the *Concerto* for 2cl 2hn bn (now lost) performed for the Viennese Tonkünstler-Sozietät on 14 March 1780. Mozart's *Le gelosie del Seraglio* (K.135a) contains movements from Starzer, and material from K.135a appears in the wind works K.166 and K.186.

JFS–1 *Le Matin et Le Soir*   A striking work, though more interesting on paper than in performance. The imitations of rural sounds are very realistic for this period. Other features are of more than musical interest. Starzer shows how peasants of the time divided their day without clocks, a feature rarely clear from idealized pastoral works. Starzer's view is both more realistic and less nostalgic than, say, the *Petite Suite Gauloise* of Gouvy, which harks back to a pre-revolutionary period which Gouvy had not experienced. The continuity of real peasant life style is confirmed by comparison with the divisions of the day for Kraków in the 17th century (1).

   The first half of the day, in the Kraków view, consists of Predawn; Dawn; Sunrise; Breakfast time; Forenoon; Cattle time; Noon and Afternoon follow. Starzer's *Le Matin* begins at Daybreak (an adagio, using the motif best known from the finale of Mozart's *Jupiter Symphony)* and The Rooster, followed by the First, Second and Third Calls to the Hunt, and the Departure for the Hunt. The birds awaken, the Cowherd introduces horn yodels. Only then does the Sun rise, and the day continues quietly with lambs imitated by the oboe. The second half of the day, in the Kraków view, starts with Pre-evening; in Starzer's *Le Soir,* the Hunt is Called Home, the Lambs are heard again, and horn 2 imitates the Bull. Mid Evening and Lower Evening follow in the Kraków description; Starzer has the bassoons imitating frogs and toads, then a Serenade, and the two horns respond with an Echo. The Kraków day ends with After Supper, Before Midnight and After Midnight; Starzer repeats his Serenade, ending with an Adagio which (with minor changes) repeats the start of *Le Matin,* so that the daily cycle continues. The MS of the version with cors anglais (**JFS–1.2**; probably an arrangement by Went for the Schwarzenberg Harmonie) includes a printed slip with the title "Morgen und Abend, eine Musik auf 9 [sic; there are only 8 parts] blasende Instrumenten von einem grossen und berühmten Meister gesetzt," followed by a summary of the sections. "Serenade" becomes "Zerstreuung" (Distraction), one of several variants in descriptions.

The origin of this work, with its unusual sound effects, is not known. There are no sound effects in the four anonymous ballets (*Le Matin, Le Midi, Le Soir, La Nuit*) in CZ-K (these may well be the Hilferding van Wewen ballet for Laxenburg in 1775, which was also given in the same year at the Burgtheater, Vienna, as *Les Quatres Parties du Jour en Quatre Ballets Différens (New Grove)*. Since Starzer and the choreographer had collaborated at Laxenburg from 1755, the octet may include material from the ballet, but we have not identified it. Starzer's ballets were among the first works arranged for winds in Eastern Europe: by Asplmayr as movements in his *Partittas,* by Went, by anonymous arrangers, and possibly by Starzer himself (**JFS-1ad, 2ad, 3ad**).

JFS-2 *Musica da Camera Molto Particulare* A note on the manuscript, states it was composed for the "Regina di Moscova," but not whether this "Queen of Moscow" was the Czarina, or just the title of a ballet. The work constitutes the first five movements of the so-called Mozart Divertimento K.187, the remaining movements of which were arranged from Gluck. It is recorded by the Camerata Bern (disc untraced).

JFS-1ad *Les 3 [sic] Sultanes* Possibly based on one of his Russian ballets, and dating from before 1768, during his stay in St Petersburg (2). The first movement was the basis for the first movement of Mozart's *Divertimento* K.186 (**WAM-2**).

1. N Gockerell 1980 *The Clockwork Universe* (edited K Maurice and O Mayr); Washington: The Smithsonian Institution, p 121.

2. Starzer's *Die Fünf Sultaninen,* a ballet for Noverre, was first performed in Vienna in 1772 (see D Lynham 1950 *The Father of Modern Ballet;* London: Sylvan Press). A similar title was used by others, as in Kraus's *Soliman II, eller De tre Sultanninorna* of 1789. *Solimann second, ou Les trois Sultanes* was a play by Charles Simon Favart, after Marmontel, with songs by Paul César Gilbert, performed in Vienna at the Burgtheater (in French in 1765, in German in 1776 and 1782) and at the Kärntnertortheater (in German in 1770). These varied sources may explain the varied numbers of Sultan(a)s.

STEFFANI, Jan (Jean), l'aîné *1746 or 1748, Prague-24 Feb 1829, Warsaw* Composer, conductor and violinist who joined the Kinský orchestra in Vienna after studies in Prague and in Italy. He moved to Warsaw in 1779 as Kapellmeister of the cathedral and conductor of the court orchestra. Here he was an early popularizer of the polonaise.

STEINER, Franz *(?1780)* Kapellmeister for the Löwenstein court, Wertheim am Main.

ŠTĚPAN (Stephani), Josef Antonín *baptized 14 Mar 1726, Kopidlno, Bohemia-12 Apr 1797, Vienna* His music was taken to Ludwigslust by Sperger; most probably it originated in the music for the Batthyáni Harmonie.

STEVENS, Richard John Samuel *27 Mar 1757, London-23 Sept 1837, London* A fine glee composer, organist, and Gresham Professor of Music, London.

STEVENSON, Sir John Andrew *Nov 1761, Dublin-14 Sept 1833, Meath* Composer and organist, vicar-choral at St Patrick's and at Christchurch, Dublin. He wrote much for the stage, many glees, the accompaniments to a collection of Irish melodies to which Thomas Moore wrote words, and *Lord Donoughmore's First Grand March and Quickstep.*

ŠTIKA (Stika), Jan *(1750)* His *Trauer Marsch des Fürsten S[ch]warzenberg* is known only from a copy by Dominik Hübner at Langenbruck, and is not found in the Schwarzenberg archives. The only likely Fürst is Joseph Adam (1722-1782).

STOKMAR, ( ) *(?1790)* The parts and autograph score of a part of his arrangements in the *Oberwittlbacher Fantasie* are from the Wertheim (Löwenstein) archive.

STONEHAM, (Arthur) Marshall *b 18 May 1940, Barrow-in-Furness, UK* A horn-player and professional scientist (Fellow of the Royal Society from 1989; Massey Professor of Physics, University College London) who has made performing versions of the complete

wind music of Weber (including the reconstruction of the *Trauermusik,* **CMW-3v,** with Mark Goddard, qv), Süssmayer and Dibdin, and of works by Matthew Locke and Schetky; he has also written short works for 2cl 2hn 2bn, and made a number of transcriptions.
STORL, Johann Georg Christian *1675-1719*   Composer of a *March* dedicated to Duke Eberhard Ludwig von Württemburg.
STRAUSS, Johann Baptist (the Younger) *25 Oct 1825, Vienna-3 Jun 1899, Vienna*
In 1844, the composer of *The Blue Danube* wrote a *Graduale* "Tu qui regis totum orbem" for SATB, 2ob 2cl 2hn 2bn 3tb timp.
STRAUSS, Richard Georg *11 June 1864, Munich-8 Sept 1949, Garmisch-Partenkirchen*
The length of Strauss's composing career is impressive (1): born when Rossini and Berlioz were still alive, he outlived Bartók and Webern. His father, Franz Strauss, was the composer and horn player for whom much of Wagner's horn music was intended. Richard Strauss had both opportunity and inclination to compose, and began at age six; his last works were written nearly 80 years later, shortly before his death in 1949.

Strauss wrote four main works for wind harmony. Just as there was a gap of many years between his two horn concertos, so there was a long gap between the two early works for winds (the *Serenade* of 1882 and the *Suite* of 1883-1884) and the late ones (the *Sonatina* of 1943 and the *Symphony* of 1944-1945). All show notably idiomatic writing for winds: always effective, though rarely simple, for Strauss wrote for highly professional players. Recordings of these works include those by London Winds/Michael Collins (all works, Hyperion CDA66731/2); the Netherlands Wind Ensemble (all works, Philips 438 733-2PM2); the Harmonie de Chambre de la Musique des Gardiens de la Paix/Dondeyne (all works, Arion ARN 336019); Chamber Orchestra of Europe/Holliger (Philips 438 933-2PH), London Symphony Winds (*Suite, Sonatina,* on HMV ASD2651); Orpheus Chamber Orchestra (Deutsche Grammophon 445 039-2GHS), and Octophoros/ Dombrecht (Vanguard 99702). The *Sonatina* is recorded by the Vienna Philharmonic Winds/Previn on Philips 420 160-1PH, by the Boston Wind Ensemble/Simon on Argo RG 147 and by the Norwegian Winds (who couple it with the *Suite,* Op 4) on Victoria VCD 19045. The *Wind Symphony* is recorded by the London Haffner Wind Ensemble/Hickox on Chandos CHAN9286 and by the Münchener Bläsakademie/Sawallisch on Orfeo 004821. The *Wind Suite* (Op 4) alone is recorded by the Minnesota Orchestra/de Waart on Virgin Classics 91492, the Eastman Wind Ensemble on Mercury SRI 75193, and the London Baroque Ensemble (Pye GSGC 14040; reissue ZCGC 7054), who also recorded the Eb *Wind Symphony* on HMV XLP 30012. The Seattle Symphony Winds/Schwartz have recorded the *Serenade* on Delos DE 3094.

RGS-1 *Serenade in Eb Op 7*   Scored for the standard wind section of the later 19th century orchestra, it was probably written in 1882, though it may have been started the previous year. It was dedicated to Friedrich Meyer, and was first performed by the Dresdener Tonkünstlerverein under Franz Wüllner on 27 November 1882. Strauss himself was rather modest about his *Serenade,* commenting a quarter of a century later that it was "the respectable work of a music student." It was taken up by the eminent conductor Hans von Bülow, who had a formative influence on Strauss. Indeed, it was for von Bülow and his Meiningen Court Orchestra that Strauss wrote his Op 4 *Suite* for winds, and through them that he came to know the work of Liszt and Wagner well. The *Serenade* is a single movement, simple in layout, with a quicker central section. It is unified by a little rhythmic figure, reminiscent of the device used by Mozart in the *Gran Partita's* Adagio and in the slow movement of Dvořák's *Serenade.* The pervading mood is relaxed; even the climaxes are intense rather than dramatic, and there are several lovely moments of repose. The writing succeeds because of the imaginative use of instrumental color and the uninterrupted melodic invention.

RGS-2 *Suite in Bb Op 4*   This grew out of a suggestion made by von Bülow in the winter of 1883 (so Op 4 follows Op 7) that Strauss write a more substantial wind work. Since classical revivals were topical, Strauss should include a Gavotte and a Fugue. The result is in four movements: Allegretto; Romanze; Gavotte; Introduction and Fugue. The opening Allegretto is similar in idiom to the *Serenade,* but less inventive. The more mature Strauss shows in the Romanze, whose motifs appear in the introduction to the Finale. The Gavotte is the most successful of von Bülow's suggestions. It follows tradition in having a short central passage with a drone accompaniment, like the classical musette. The Finale, despite a striking start, develops into something too academic to be really satisfying. The first performance of the *Suite* was on 18 November 1884, in Munich, where the Meiningen Court Orchestra was on tour; von Bülow decided Strauss should conduct the work himself. It was his first experience of conducting in public, like Dvořák's six years earlier with his own *Serenade.*   An orchestra on tour has no time for rehearsal, von Bülow argued, and such an experienced ensemble could manage without. Later, Strauss recalled only that he made no blunders. **RGS–3** *Wind Sonatina. Sonatina No 1 in F "Aus der Werkstatt eines Kranken"* (From the workshop of an invalid) AV.135;   **RGS–4** *Wind Symphony. Sonatina No 2 in E♭ "Fröhliche Werkstatt"* (Happy workshop); AV.143.   Strauss's talent made itself evident more and more as he moved towards large orchestral works and operas. Wind music was put on one side, though clearly absorbed into his other works. Strauss became less content with his early efforts, especially with their balance: four horns (especially Bavarian ones) tended to swamp the pairs of woodwinds. His solution grew out of his operatic experience, although it was Mozart's too: expand the clarinet section. Strauss regarded the bass clarinet as standard from his earliest operas (usually the B♭ instrument, although the A instrument is asked for in later works). The basset horn was a regular feature after *Elektra,* and the bright-toned C clarinet replaced the D clarinet and the shriller E♭ instrument. In the *Sonatina* and *Wind Symphony,* he uses three extra clarinets: a C clarinet, a basset horn, and a bass clarinet. Strauss also deploys instruments differently. There are many places where groups of four or five instruments play in unison, often regrouping to exploit the wider range of color.

The two late works were started in the dark years of the war. In 1942, Germany was moving from victory to defeat, and both Strauss and his wife were in poor health. The stimulus to write again came from a commission from Vienna for brass music, although the wind works were written mainly for Strauss's own pleasure: "wrist exercise," he called them, for he could not play skat (his favorite card game) all the time. Perhaps the main claim of these works is that they set the scene for the late works culminating in the *Four Last Songs.* Musically, the *Sonatinas* are diffuse (the title *Symphony* appeared after Strauss's death). The chronology of completion dates is enlightening. All of the *Sonatina* was written in 1943: 1 Allegro moderato (Vienna 24 March 1943) 2 Romanze: Andante, including a Minuet (Vienna 23 Feb 1943) 3 Finale: Allegro molto (Garmisch 22 July 1943). Strauss wanted the first performance to be given by the Dresden Harmonic Society, which had premiered his Op 7 *Serenade* long before. This caused delays until June 1944, when it was conducted by Karl Elmendorff. By this time, Strauss had written some of the second *Sonatina:* 1, Allegro con brio (6 March 1944); 2, Andante comodo (10 June 1945); 3, Minuet (22 June 1945); 4, Introduction and Allegro (9 January 1944). All the work was written in Garmisch. The *Symphony* was first played on 25 March 1946 by the Winterthur Musikkollegium under Hermann Scherchen.

The last movement of the first *Sonatina* and the first two movements to be completed of the second are all on a huge scale. It is these three movements (plus availability of parts on hire only) which make these very occasional pieces only for the enthusiastic player. There are purple passages of vintage Strauss in each, but there is quite an amount of "workshop practice" too. The parts are technically formidable, and many audiences balk at more than ten minutes of uninterrupted wind playing. No doubt Strauss realized this, for the last two movements to be written are much slighter. Both these movements, like the middle movement of the *Sonatina* in F, have a simple structure, with well-defined, contrasted sections embedded in the main part. Strauss looked back to classical wind music in writing the works. Sometimes Haydn comes to mind, especially when there are cross-rhythms unrelated to the bar structure; Haydn would have enjoyed the half-note themes in the 3/4 movements which end the *Sonatina* in F and start the *Symphony*. Such touches are carried to extremes in the second movement of the *Symphony* where, because of the silent first beats, one can almost imagine one is hearing the echo of another, unheard, wind band. The two neoclassical movements of the *Symphony* give the clarinets, in particular, passages in Strauss's most lyrical vocal style. In the Minuet, the clarinet family has an especially lovely trio; in the Andantino, the gem is the canon, which involves oboe, basset horn, and ultimately the other clarinets. At such times Mozart comes to mind, although there is no attempt to mimic him. Instead, Strauss's own specialty, a floating cantilena from the upper wind is built into a web of sound which rivals Mozart's for subtlety and elegance. There are moments when one is tempted to accept Strauss's own comment "I may not be a first-rate composer, but I am a first-rate second-class composer." But these moments do not prevent Strauss's wind works being among the finest written, and worthy of the dedication over the last movement of the second *Sonatina*: "To the spirit of the immortal Mozart, at the end of a life full of gratitude."

The authenticity of the stage music for *Romeo and Juliet* (AV.86) is in doubt (2 vol 2 p 253). The two items for winds are **RGS–1evd** Vor dem Hochzeitsbette, and **RGS–1ed**: Trauermusik. Written in the middle of 1887, these are the third and fourth items in the incidental music performed at the Royal Theatre in Munich on 23 October 1887.

1. Erich H Müller von Asow 1966 *Richard Strauss Thematisches Verzeichnis;* Vienna: Doblinger.

2. Norman Del Mar 1962 *Richard Strauss;* London: Barrie and Rockliff.

STRAVINSKY, Igor Feodorovich *17 June 1882, Oranienbaum, near St Petersburg–6 Apr 1971, New York* Stravinsky, the son of the principal bass of the Imperial Opera, was brought up in a musical environment. His teachers, Glazunov and Rimsky-Korsakov, helped to form his orchestral skill. Yet Stravinsky's use of winds is different, exploiting harder and more athletic brass styles and jazz possibilities of woodwinds. Perhaps his teachers' approach was more in evidence in the *Funeral Dirge,* Op 5 (lost in the Revolution), written in 1908 for Rimsky-Korsakov and performed under Felix Blumenfeld. Some of Stravinsky's works for winds can reasonably be called wind harmony; others merely make extensive, even dominant, use of winds. The many recordings of the wind music include those by the Netherlands Wind Ensemble/de Waart (Philips 6500841) and the Nash Ensemble/Howarth (Classics for Pleasure 40098). Among his other works rich in use of winds is the *Canzonetta* for cl b-cl 4hn db harp, an arrangement of a string piece by Sibelius from the incidental music in 1903 for Järnefelt's *Kuolema*. Stravinsky transformed it in homage when he became the first recipient of the Sibelius Medal. The slow, lyrical movement (two of the four horn parts are extraordinarily dull) changes character completely. It was published in 1964.

ITS–1 *Symphonies of Wind Instruments* (1 p 48; 2 pp 39-40). **ITS–1.1:** 1920 version. No full score was issued; it is recorded by the New York Philharmonic Orchestra/Boulez, Disques Montaigne TCE 8800. **ITS–1.2:** 1945-1947 version. There are many recordings e.g., NW German Radio Orchestra/Stravinsky, Sony 46290; Nash Ensemble/Rattle on Chandos 6535; London Sinfonietta/Salonen, Sony 45797; Berlin Radio Symphony Orchestra/ Ashkenazy, Decca 436 416; Montreal Symphony Orchestra/Dutoit on Decca Ovation 436 474; London Symphony Orchestra/Nagano on Virgin Classics VCS 45032.

Both versions are recorded by the Endymion Ensemble/Whitfield on EMI EL 749786.
Stravinsky and Debussy met after the first performance of *Firebird* in Paris in 1910. Eight years later, Debussy died. In 1920, the *Revue Musicale* commissioned a volume in Debussy's memory, and including a chorale by Stravinsky. He was not satisfied with it, and enlarged it into the *Symphonies d'instruments à vent à la mémoire de Claude Debussy* later in 1920. This radical work, austerely scored, did not find favor with Otto Kling, director of J & W Chester, and even Editions Russe's efforts were fruitless and without enthusiasm. Nor was Stravinsky satisfied, for the score did not appear, though performances continued. His full revision in 1947 used the same music, but handled the winds differently: the more succulent original sound became much harder with the loss of alto flute and basset horn and with rechording and altered rhythms. The forces are used sparingly, with all 23 players used in only a few bars. The various sections appear and reappear several times in different scorings, and their tempos are related by simple ratios like 2:1 or 3:1.

ITS-2 *Concerto for Piano* (1, p 52; 2, pp 34-35). Written originally in 1923-1924, the concerto is dedicated to Natalie Koussevitsky and was first performed at Koussevitsky's Paris Opéra concert on 22 May 1924 with the composer as soloist. It was performed many times in subsequent years (including one occasion on which the composer, himself the soloist, could not remember how it continued) and revised in 1950, mainly in minor details of dynamics. It is recorded by the Royal Philharmonic Orchestra/Papadopoulos, Hyperion A66167; London Sinfonietta/Crossley, Sony CD 45797; Suisse Romande/ Berman/Järvi, Chandos CHAN 9239; Columbia Symphony Orchestra/Entremont/ Stravinsky, Sony SMK46295. Stravinsky's other concertante works with accompaniment rich in winds include the *Ebony Concerto* (solo cl, b-cl hn 5tp 3tb db pf hp gtr perc) and the *Concertino* **ITS-3** for 12 instruments (vn, vc, fl ob ca cl 2bn 2tp 2tb).

ITS-4 *Octuor (Octet for Wind Instruments)* (1 p 303, 2 p 202) Begun in Biarritz in 1922, the *Octet* was first performed in Paris on 18 October 1923, with Stravinsky directing. Some slight revisions were made in 1952. The dedicatee, Vera de Bosset, became Stravinsky's second wife, although this is not mentioned on the score itself. Stravinsky's own comments are enigmatic. One suggests that he began the octet before deciding on the instruments involved. Another claimed that he dreamed he was in a small room with an ensemble playing attractive music he did not recognize, although the instruments were those of the *Octet*. He also said that all nuances between forte and piano were excluded, which disagrees with the score. It is recorded by the Endymion Ensemble/ Whitfield on EMI EL 749786 and London Sinfonietta/Salonen on Sony CD45965.

Stravinsky's vocal and choral works, present a problem, for most of them use some strings as well as winds. To call such music wind harmony needs explanation. Yet we feel a passing mention is useful because it shows how the wind ensemble developed from being a source of color for Mozart's contemporaries to the reverse, where it is the strings which provide color instead. In the opera buffa *Mavra,* for instance, the scoring shows specific numbers of strings: single first and second violins and viola, three cellos and three basses. Even these strings are used sparsely: not at all until p 17 of the score, not melodically until p 25, and not extensively until page 48.

ITS-1v *Mavra: Opera Buffa* Based on a Pushkin story, *Mavra* is dedicated to Pushkin, Glinka and Tchaikovsky; it was first performed by the Diaghilev Company in Paris on 3 June 1925. Stravinsky said he stressed the wind band "because the music whistled as wind instruments whistle, and also because there was a certain jazz element in it."

ITS-2v *Symphony of Psalms* In 1929 Koussevitzky commissioned Stravinsky to write a work to celebrate the Boston Symphony Orchestra's fiftieth anniversary, which was to be in 1930. However, the Symphony was first performed in Brussels in 1929 under Ansermet and only later, in 1930, in Boston. The work was revised in 1948. A children's choir is to be preferred for the soprano and alto chorus parts. It is recorded by the Wisconsin Conservatory Chorus/Milwaukee Symphony Orchestra/Foss, PRO PAD169; the Paris Orchestra and Chorus/Barenboim, Erato MCE 75494; Christ Church Choir/ Philip Jones Brass Ensemble/Preston, Decca 430346; and many other ensembles.

ITS-3v *Mass for Mixed Choir and Double Wind Quintet*   Written in 1948, and first performed at La Scala, Milan, under Ansermet on 27 October 1948. As with **IGS-2v**, children's voices are preferred for the soprano and alto chorus parts. The Latin text is used, even though Stravinsky had joined the Russian Orthodox church in 1926. The ensemble consists of two wind choirs, rather than a double wind quintet. It is recorded by the Trinity Boys' Choir/Bath Festival Chorus and Orchestra/Bernstein on DG 423251.

ITS-4v *Canticum Sacrum ad honorem Sancti Marci nominis*   Written for the Basilica of St Mark, Venice, and first performed there on 13 September 1956. An austere work, showing the influence of Webern. The use of the few strings (vla, db) is intermittent. Recorded by Christ Church Choir/Philip Jones Brass Ensemble/Preston, Decca 430346; Westminster Cathedral Choir/City of London Sinfonia/O'Donnell, Hyperion CDA 66347.

ITS-5v *Threni: id est Lamentationes Jeremiae Prophetae*   Once more strings are used only intermittently and, in several places, smaller wind bands are singled out for extended periods, e.g., 2fl 2ob cl in the third movement, or fl 2ob 2cl bthn b-cl 4hn which, with pf hp timp, accompany the chorus and soloists in the last movement. The work ends with a quartet of horns and singers. It was first performed, under Stravinsky, on 23 September 1958 in the Sala della Scuola Grande di Santo Rocco, Venice.

ITS-1a *Song of the Volga Boatmen (Chant des bataliers du Volga-Hymne à la nouvelle Russie)*   After the Revolution, the old Russian national anthem (L'vov's "God Save the Tsar") was naturally suppressed. Stravinsky rapidly arranged the "Song of the Volga Boatmen" as a substitute at Diaghilev's request, and it was first performed at a Red Cross benevolent concert after the Tsar abdicated. Stravinsky dictated it to Ansermet in Lord Berners's apartment in Rome in April 1917. Ansermet has recorded the work with the Suisse Romande orchestra on Claves-Albany CD-50 8918.

1. E W White 1979 *Stravinsky: The Composer and His Works;* London: Faber.
2. D-R Lerma 1974 *I F Stravinsky: A Practical Guide to Publications of His Music;* Kent, Ohio: Kent State University Press.
3. Stephen Walsh [sd] *Igor Stravinsky;* London: Chester Music.

STRECK, Peter *(1800)*   Arranger of some music for King Ludwig's Harmonie, Munich.

STREPPONI, Feliciano *1797, Milan-13 Jan 1832, Trieste*   Organist of Monza Cathedral, and father of Verdi's second wife, Giuseppina.

STROUHAL (STRAUHAL), Bernard, *Padre (1770, Bohemia)*   Strouhal was active even before 1800 at Osek Monastery, Bohemia. One of his three sets of parthias has some fascinating titles: **BYS-1** *Le Galline Cioche* (Broody hens); **BYS-2** *Il Cuco* (Cuckoo), where, since "fl traverso il cuco" is a written-out part in the finale, it may be for a real instrument rather than a toy; **BYS-3** *La Parussola* (Parasol); **BYS-4** *La Zampagna* (Bagpipe); **BYS-5** *La Quaglia* (Quail); **BYS-6** The second movement is entitled *Alla Hanaka. Andantino,* with two Trios, the second called *Alla Blazcka* (we do not know why); it ends with *l'Echo con Adieu,* a Finale with echos. The works look charming.

STRUHAL, ( ) *(1770)*   Not Bernard Strouhal (qv) but composer of Turkish music and dances and marches, including ones named for Napoleon's coronation and for Landon, perhaps the Austrian Feldmarschall Laudon (Loudon).

STÜCKEL, ( ) (? Ferdinand STÜCKEL) *(1770)*   Arranger of J Weigl's *Richard Löwenherz* for the Lancut Harmonie.

STUMPF, Johann Christian *1763-1801, Frankfurt am Main*   Bassoon virtuoso and repetiteur at the Frankfürter Komödiehaus from May 1778; he worked under Cannabich at the Frankfurt Opera. Stumpf made his arrangements for two flutes of Roeser's

Suites in Paris between 1780 and 1786. His fine arrangements of 11 operas in 20 Recueils were published by André between 1795 and 1801. A second edition was issued in 1809-1812. The title pages assert that JUS-3(-5) *Pièces d'Harmonie* were "composées par I STUMPF," not "arrangées par," as for the arrangements; they seem to be original works (contrary to RISM). They are structured as suites, in six movements. All end with an Allemande (in 2/4 for Nos 2, 3, but in 3/8 for No 1). Each contains two movements called "Romanza"; JUS-3 and JUS-5 both start with a Marche.

STURMFEDER, Defours   The MS parts of his Eb *Andante* are from Hrádek, near Sušice, and are for the unusual combination of 2ob 2cl 2hn.

SUDA, Stanislav *22 Mar 1896, Plzeň-13 Dec 1969, Plzeň*   Conductor and choirmaster who composed at least four works for solo violin, harp and 2fl 2ob 2cl(A) 2hn 2bn. His *Symfonie* is for large wind band; his march *Michelák* was rescored by Horák (qv).

SÜSSMAYR (Süssmayer), Franz Xaver *1766 Schwanenstadt, Upper Austria-16 Sept 1803, Vienna*   Süssmayr is remembered today almost solely for his completion of Mozart's *Requiem* (and even then as Constanze Mozart's second choice after Eybler). The difficulty of separating Süssmayr's contribution from Mozart's does suggest that Süssmayr might be a somewhat better composer than commonly supposed; witness also Beethoven's and Paganini's uses of Süssmayr themes for sets of variations. Süssmayr, a pupil of both Mozart and Salieri, contributed to at least two other Mozart works: he helped Mozart prepare *La clemenza di Tito* for Prague, and the familiar version of Mozart's *Horn Concerto No 1* was also prepared by him.

Almost all Süssmayr's surviving wind music autographs are in GB-Lbl, a collection including incomplete works, some usable. Looking through them, one notices how often there are errors, alterations, and obscurities, in contrast to Mozart's manuscripts. His *Ovunque io guardo nel giro immenso*, for SSTB, 2tp 3tb, is an attractive short work recently given in a performing version by Marshall Stoneham. Other vocal works with winds seem to be lost. The *kk Oberpostamtzeitung* of 15 February 1794 mentions a "heart-stirring and uncommonly moving German song" with winds, sung by a Prague assembly. On 9 December 1794, the birthday celebrations for Emperor Franz II at Charles University, Prague, began with a folk song composed for the occasion by Süssmayer to a text by Němeček, with accompaniment arranged by Vitásek (qv) for 13 wind instruments. The song was "supremely effective ... very effective and singable, and truly festive ... when the congregation joined in the chorus after each verse." There is no information about other music these 13 winds played. However, there is an 1819 copy in the Langenbruck archive of *Frohnleichnams-Stationen in Deutschen Texte* for CATB, 2fl 2ob 2cl 2hn 2bn cbn 2tp (hence 13 winds) and timpani, **FXS-1.1v.**

Süssmayr was educated at Kremsmünster monastery, where there was much wind harmony. His opera *Moses* was produced at Schikaneder's theater in 1792. Later operas were produced at the Kärntnertortheater, where he became conductor in 1795. One of the most successful was *Der Spiegel in Arkadien,* an attempt to repeat the success of *Die Zauberflöte* (the autograph is in D-B, Mus.Ms.21533). In it, a group of four winds (fl cl hn[C] hn[F]) and harp are conspicuous in the finale to act 2. The march in the cantata *Der Ritter in Gefahr* was published by Eder in 1797 as a march for a Viennese Corps. The cantata includes an extended recitative and aria accompanied by wind octet.

FXS-1m *March, in C*   The title of this *March* is all but illegible, but appears to include the words "Corps der Freywilligen," suggesting it was for one of the volunteer regiments set up in response to the Napoleonic threat.

FXS-2.1m *Marcia Contradanse* (two titles are given) in Bb; Par Franc: Sußmayr [1]793. Very effective, though short; this octet movement has a trio.

FXS-2.2m *Marcia, Allegretto amoroso, in Bb;*   Di me Franc: Sußmayr [1]793. Essentially the same music as **FXS-2.1m,** but largely rewritten to eliminate the oboes.

Another of Süssmayr's orchestral *Contradanses* appears in two forms, each using two orchestras, one being winds alone. The first version divides the orchestra into (2vl 2ob 2hn bn) (2ob 2cl 2hn 2bn); the second is divided as (2vl basso 2ob 2hn bn) (2cl 2hn 2bn).

FXS-1 *(No title; for 2bthn 2hn 2bn, in F)* An unusually scored but usable fragment, clearly part of a larger piece, perhaps Masonic. Despite the use of the basset horns, there seems to be no connection with Süssmayr's work on Mozart's *Requiem*.

FXS-1a *Robert und Kallisto* A most attractive arrangement, consisting of a slow section with a prominent first bassoon part, and a fast movement. It is based on the Singspiel *Robert und Kallisto* (1780) by Paul Kürzinger (1750-1820) for Regensburg.

FXS-1v *Jubelfeyer (Jubilee) Cantate* for 4 solo voices; 2ob 2cl 2bn 2hn, beginning "Sey uns dreymal hoch willkommen" and dated July 1798. The autograph score shows signs of use, with conductor's annotations and the names of the (original?) singers (Jeanette, Grinzirl?, Pepe, Leopold). There are gaps where repeats are clearly expected. It is unlikely that this is based on the 1794 German song mentioned earlier. The title is all but illegible, but mentions the name "Fraulein Anna Maria v Lang."

SURINACH, Carlos *b 4 Mar 1915, Barcelona* Catalan composer and conductor, US citizen since 1959. His 1960 *David and Bath-Sheba* ballet is for winds, perc harp pf 2db.

SUTERMEISTER, Heinrich *b 12 Aug 1910 Feuerthalen, Schaffhausen, Switzerland* Sutermeister's wind music includes a *Serenade No 2* for fl ob cl hn bn tp and a *Suite* for 4 winds. In his **HES-1** *Modeste Mignon* "Nach einem Walzer von Honoré de Balzac," Auber's waltz is the link to Balzac's novel.

SVOBODA, Josef *(1800)* His two Eb *Missa quadragesimalis*, for chorus, winds and organ, were for the first Sunday of Lent. The MS parts are by A J Hoke, "Oberlehrer."

SWEENEY, William *b 5 Jan 1950, Glasgow* Clarinettist and teacher of composition at the University of Glasgow, he wrote **WIS-1** *Fantasias for 13 Instruments* in 1986 for the Paragon Ensemble. As in the music of McGuire, the hint of a bagpipe can often be discerned in his music. Much of Sweeney's chamber music features his instrument, the clarinet. The first Fantasia is based on the English folk song "One Night As I Lay On My Bed"; the second was inspired by Hugh MacDiarmid's poem "By Hauchup Side."

SYDOW, ( ) *c.1700-1754* Composer of a *Concerto in C* for 2ob taille 2bn.

SYLVANI, ( ) van (Van-Sylvani) *(1770)* His *Harmonie* written for and dedicated to Le Prince Waldek **XSV-1a** comprises arrangements of Haydn, Walter and Blasius.

TAFFANEL, Claude Paul *16 Sept 1844, Bordeaux-22 Nov 1908, Paris* French flautist of distinction who founded the Société de Musique de Chambre pour Instruments à Vent in 1879. This ensemble, at first a wind quintet which added extra players, led the revival of wind harmony in France, and stimulated the formation of similar ensembles. He commissioned works from Boisdeffre, Dubois, Gounod, Gouvy, Lazzari and others. Taffanel wrote a *Wind Quintet*, and also arranged Saint-Saëns's *Feuillet d'Album*. This piano duet, Op 81, is an amiable work, elegantly pleasant in the very best tradition of salon music. This is not to damn the piece with faint praise: Taffanel shows here that he knew the value of such items as foils to more serious works in concert programs.

TAG, Christian Gotthilf *2 Apr 1735, Beierfeld, Erzgebirge-19 July 1811, Niederzwönitz bei Zwönitz, Saxony* Kantor, composer and schoolteacher at Hohenstein-Ernsthal from 1755 to 1811; he was a friend of J G Naumann (qv) and of Hasse.

TANEYEV (Taneeff, Taneyef, Taniev, Taneev), Alexander Sergeivich *17 Jan 1850, St Petersburg-7 Feb 1918, Petrograd* Civil servant, rising to Chief Chancellor, and nationalist composer who studied with Reichel in Dresden and with Rimsky-Korsakov.

TANSMAN, Alexandre (Aleksander) *12 June 1897, Łódź-15 Nov 1986, Paris* Composer and pianist who moved to Paris in 1919, where he associated with Ravel, Milhaud and Honegger. His *Four Impressions* date from 1950.

TARCHI, Angelo *1759/60 Naples-19 Aug 1814, Paris* Opera composer, whose works were arranged for winds, for instance by Fuchs.

TAUSCH, Franz Wilhelm *26 Dec 1762 Heidelberg - 9 Feb 1817 Berlin* He was one of a family of distinguished clarinettists, which included his father Jacob (?-1803), his brother Joseph (1763-?) and his son Friedrich Wilhelm (1790-1845). Jacob was employed at Mannheim and later at Munich. Franz settled in Berlin in 1789 as a court musician. He is said to have favored the German school of playing (*Weston/MCVP*), emphasizing beauty and gradation of tone more than the brilliance. In Berlin, Tausch appears to have written marches for the Prussian and the Russian Guards; we presume he was a member of the ensemble which played works by Rosetti and Righini for the Duke of York's wedding feast. Both he and his brother are said to have become excessively stout.

Franz Wilhelm Tausch also wrote a set of 13 *Pièces en Quatuor* Op 22 for 2cl hn bn, forming two suites, and dedicated to Count Charles de Brühl. They were published c.1808. An adagio from this set was used in Tausch's Op 20 *Concerto* for two clarinets. The *6 Quatuors Op 5* **FWT-1** for two basset horns and two bassoons, with ad lib horns, are dedicated to a then well-known amateur bassoonist, Captain Bredow. Composed in 1797, they were published in 1805.

TAUSINGER, Jan *1 Nov 1921, Piatra Neamţ, Romania-29 July 1980, Prague* Tausinger studied first in Bucharest, then in Prague from 1948. His wind music, including several smaller works as well as his 1967 *Prelude, Sarabande and Postlude*, all for winds hp pf perc, dates from the late 1960s and early 1970s.

TAVENER, John Kenneth *b 28 Jan 1944, London* Tavener's recent music owes much to the Orthodox church, and its skilful invocation of the mystical has had wide appeal. His *Credo* of 1960 is for solo tenor, SATB chorus, 3ob 3tp 2tb organ.

TAYLORSON, John Swainton *b 12 June 1923, County Durham* Founder of Castle Music publishers, and arranger of works for flute(s), wind octet and contrabassoon.

TCHAIKOVSKY (Chaikovsky), Peter (Pyotr) Il'yich *7 May 1840, Kamsko-Votinsk-6 Nov 1893, St Petersburg* Tchaikovsky's writings for winds are primarily student works or within large-scale works, like the slow movement of his *Violin Concerto*. His last opera, *Yolanta,* planned as the other half of a double bill with his ballet, *The Nutcracker,* begins with a *Prelude* for winds. The opera, Op 69, has a libretto by Tchaikovsky's brother, Modest Il'yich Tchaikovsky, from a translation of a play by Henrik Hertz; it was first performed in St Petersburg at the Maryinski Theater on 18 December 1892. The opera is recorded under Georgiev on Philips 442 7962.

TCHEREPNIN, Iwan *b 5 Feb 1943, Paris* Grandson of Nikolai Tcherepnin (qv). A student with Boulez and Stockhausen, now active in electro-acoustic music.

TCHEREPNIN (Cherepnin), Nikolai Nikolaevich *15 May 1873, St Petersburg-26 June 1945, Paris* In addition to his *Sonatine* for winds, timpani and xylophone, Tcherepnin also wrote works for voices and horn quartet.

TEBAY, J *(1770)* Composer of the *Bath Volunteers March.*

TELEMANN, Georg Philipp *14 Mar 1681, Magdeburg-25 June 1767, Hamburg* Telemann, a prolific and fluent composer widely respected in his lifetime (1, 2), was the largely self-taught son of a clergyman. He founded a student Collegium Musicum in Leipzig, where he became Organist of the Neukirche in 1704. A series of moves followed, first to Sorau (now Zary, Poland) as Kapellmeister to Prince Promnitz, and to Eisenach. In February 1712 Telemann became director of music to the city of Frankfurt, and Kapellmeister at the Barfüsserkirche; he also directed the Collegium Musicum of the Frauenstein Society, an association of the nobility and of the middle classes, for whom he organized weekly public concerts. Most of Telemann's wind music seems to date from the years at Frankfurt; it was probably for open-air performance, but no details are certain. In July 1721, Telemann was invited to be Director of Music of the five main churches in Hamburg, an appointment he took up three months later.

GPT-1 The *"Älster-Ouvertüre"* (Hoffmann F/11) carries the subtitle *Ein musikalischer Spass*, though the musical jokes are not like Mozart's. Since the wind parts and strings double, it forms a perfectly natural suite for wind alone. The movements are as follows: 1 Ouvertüre; 2 Die canonierende Pallas; 3 Das Älster Echo; 4 Die Hamburgischen Glockenspiele (this movement is missing in some versions); 5 Der Schwanen Gesang; 6 Der Älster Schaffer Dorff Music [sic]; 7 Die concertierenden Frösche und Krähen (mimicking unmusical frogs and crows also appealed to Starzer and others); 8 Der ruhende Pan; 9 Der Schaffer [sic] und Nymphen eilfertiger Abzug.

GPT-2 *Overture* (Hoffmann F/5) or *Suite* for oboes, horns and bassoon(s). It dates from before 1721 and has six movements, one called "La Chasse."

GPT-3 *Ouvertüre* (Hoffmann F/9), sometimes known as "La Chasse." Its five movements include a Passepied, a Sarabande, a Rigaudon and a finale entitled "Le Plaisir."

GPT-4 *La Fortuna* (Hoffmann F/8), a four movement suite, ending with a Gigue.

GPT-5, 6, 7 In these three *Ouvertüres* (Hoffmann D/24, F/18, F/17) Telemann uses oboes d'amore instead of oboes. Hoffmann (1) suggests that the works date from Telemann's Frankfurt period, before 1721, whereas *Whitwell/7* favors composition in Hamburg after 1721. **GPT-5**'s six movement includes a Siziliano [sic], a Paysan(n)e, a Rigaudon and a Harlequinade. **GPT-6** includes a Loure, a movement called "Les Paysans," a Passepied and a final Gigue. **GPT-7** is in seven movements.

GPT-8 *Ouvertüre/Suite à 5* (Hoffmann F/4). This *Suite* is usually performed with violins, but is effective as a wind work; perhaps the original was for oboes (1). The second movement is a Pastorelle en Rondeau.

GPT-9 *Ouvertüre à 5* for the Landgrave of Darmstadt (Hoffmann F/15). The seven movements end with a Forlane, followed by "La Tempête."

GPT-1m *Marche in F, Marsch zum Stückeschiessen der Artillerie (Serenade des Erzherzog Leopolds von Österreich)* Presumably this is the *March* of 1716 referred to in several sources (2, 3). On 10 August 1716, the artillery at Frankfurt am Main fired a salute for the birthday of Leopold, the infant Archduke of Austria. The garrison's six hautbois, smartly uniformed, preceded the troops, playing the *Frankfurt March,* written for the Artillery (Marsch zum Stückeschiessen der Artillerie) "by Herr Telemann, the Kapellmeister famous for his erudition." The "six hautbois" presumably mean the three oboe players, two horn players and bassoonist (since then hautbois implied any military musician), with the two trumpeters counted separately.

1. Adolf Hoffmann 1969 *Die Orchestersuiten Georg Philipp Telemanns*; Zurich: Möseler.
2. Richard Petzold 1974 *G P Telemann* (translated H Fitzpatrick); London: Benn.
3. W Braun, in *Salmen.*

TEMPLETON, Alec Andrew *4 July 1909, Cardiff-28 Mar 1963, Greenwich, Connecticut* Blind pianist, highly successful on radio in the 1940s, playing with top dance bands.

THÄNN, ( ) *(1770)* Composer of a *Partia in Dis [Eb]* in the Langenbruck archive.

THAIM, ( ) *(1770)* Composer of a *Parthia in Dis [Eb]*; possibly Thänn (qv).

THENY, Jan (Joanne) *10 Mar 1749, Jaroměř-7 June 1828 Frenštát* The wrapper of his *Missa in Dis [Eb] deutsch* styles Theny as "Rev D Joanne Theny Paroch Eccles."

THIEL, Ferdinand *(1800)* The collection of Aloys Englische (Karlovice, near Bruntál, Moravia) includes his *Graduale in A am Sonntag Quadragisima "Angelis suis,"* c.1835.

THOMPSON, Thomas *1777, Sunderland-after 1800* Organist of Newcastle upon Tyne; violinist and horn player (performing in the theater at age 12); piano pupil of Clementi. His *March* (c.1799) is for the Sunderland Loyal Volunteer Corps.

THOMSON, Virgil (Garnett) *25 Nov 1896, Kansas City-30 Sept 1989, New York* His American style evolved while he spent 1925-1940 in Paris. There he studied with Nadia Boulanger, and Satie was a strong influence; he also associated with Gertrude Stein.

THOMU, M, Signore *(1760)*   His one work of Turkish music in A-KR is labelled "Nro 1." Some of the anonymous Turkish music in the Kremsmünster archive may be by him.

THURET, ( )   The Nová Říše monastery includes one *Parthia* for 2cl 2hn bn.

TISHCHENKO, Boris (Ivanovich) *b 23 Mar 1939, Leningrad*   A student at the Leningrad Conservatory who studied privately with Shostakovich. His *Concerto for Cello* No 1, with wind orchestra, is recorded (possibly in the full orchestration by Shostakovich) on Melodya C1022267009.

TOCH, Ernst *7 Dec 1887, Vienna-10 Oct 1964, Santa Monica*   Composer, teacher and pianist who moved to the United States in 1934. He wrote several works for wind band and percussion, for instance, Op 39 *Spiel für Blasorchester*, Op 83 *5 Pieces* and Op 97 *Sinfonietta*. The *Pieces for Wind and Percussion* are recorded by the Deutsch Kammerphilharmonic Winds on Virgin Classics VCS 45056-2.

TOESCHI, Carlo Giuseppe *11 Nov 1731, Ludwigsburg-12 Apr 1788, Munich*   Pupil of Johann Stamitz, Toeschi was a violinist at Mannheim, and later Konzertmeister. From 1786, he was private Musical Director to the Elector of Bavaria.

TOJA, Giuseppe *(1800)*   The attractive *Serenata* for fl ob 2cl 2hn bn is dedicated to "Egregio Signore Lorenzo Soncini, dilettante di Clarinetto."

TOMAŠEK, Václav (Jan Křtitel) *17 Apr 1774, Skuteč-3 Apr, 1850, Prague*   Largely self-taught composer who bridged the classical and romantic traditions; very influential in Czech musical life. He was music tutor and composer to Count Georg Buquoy until 1822. His music includes a march, a funeral march, a *Mass* Op 81 for SATB, fl ob 2cl 2hn 2tp t-tb b-tb, and a song for voice and 2cl 2hn 2bn.

TOMASI, Henri *17 Aug 1901, Marseilles-13 June 1971, Paris*   Conductor and composer of Corsican descent, pupil of d'Indy, and radio station music director. His dance suite *La Moresco* HYT-1 is for octet plus clavecin and percussion, including three types of tom-tom. The Moresco, a Corsican dance for armed men, commemorates the wars between the Christians and Moorish invaders, culminating in the Christian victory at Aléria. The movements are: Entry of the warriors; La Monferina (the Corsicans); Moorish dance; La Tarascone; The Moors (allegro frénétique); La Conca; The Moors (segue to) Résa, the victory of the Corsicans, (and then to) Choral and Salve Regina.

TOMLINSON, Ernest *b 19 Sept 1924, Rawtenstall, Lancashire*   Arranger for Arcadia and Mills Music, and founder of the successful Ernest Tomlinson Orchestra and Singers. His 1957 *Concertino* for ten winds should contrast well with classical serenades.

TOUCHEMOULIN, Joseph *1727, Chalons-sur-Saône-25 Oct 1801, Regensburg*   Pupil of Tartini, who was violinist in the Elector of Saxony's orchestra from 1753; he lost this position in 1754 on the death of the Elector, but moved to Regensburg as violinist and Kapellmeister to the Thurn und Taxis orchestra. Here he wrote a *Divertimento per la Tavola*, a 7-movement work to entertain those who were dining.

TRAUTZL (FRANTZL is a misreading of his name), Jan Jakub (who used the pseudonym Saputo), Pater *22 Feb 1749, Židovice-27 Jun 1834, Osek*   Trautzl entered the Cistercian order in 1770, becoming first Succentor at Osek (1778-1783) and then Abbot. He also continued the thematic catalog of music at Osek started in 1752 by E W Sommer. His four surviving instrumental works are a *Parthia in b [Bb]* for 2cl 2hn 2bn, an *Allegro* for 2cl 2hn, a *Parthia* for 3bn vlne, and an incomplete work for fl 2cl bn, possibly an arrangement of "Bei Männern," from Mozart's *Die Zauberflöte*. These apart, he wrote several choral funeral works with winds, including an extensive *Cantata funebris* in 1797. One cantata was written on the death of Anton Fleischer, Abbot of Osek, who died on 28 April 1805; the work was performed two days later. The incomplete work previously mentioned is on the reverse of the first oblong sheet. The score of a further *Cantate funebre,* dated 29[?] May 1805, is inscribed to "P= V= P= [?] Gottroadí Trabac mercatore et defeto Prenobili Leuthenontio Feldkircher [added] d'anno 1806. Hier Mensch, hier lerne, was du bist"

TRIEBENSEE (Trübensee), Josef *21 Nov 1772, Třebon-22 April 1846, Prague*   This Bohemian composer and oboist is a central figure in music for winds (see part 1 for discussion of his journals). He was the son of another famous oboist, (Johann) Georg Triebensee (28 July 1746, Herrndorf-14 June 1813, Vienna). It is not certain which one took part in the premiere of Beethoven's *Quintet* for wind and piano, Op 16 (the other players were Beer, Matouschek and Nickl; Beethoven was the pianist). All the Triebensee wind harmony we know of is by the son; the father's fame was solely as executant. Triebensee *senior* was first oboe to Prince Schwarzenberg at Wittingau, joining the Imperial Harmonie as a founder member in 1782; he was also first oboe at the Burgtheater in Vienna from 1777. At age 17, Triebensee *junior* was a member of the wind octet chosen by Prince Liechtenstein for his hunting season at Feldsberg (Valtice) (1, 2, 3). It was just such an ensemble which the Prince had discussed with Mozart some years earlier, but the project had been shelved. The Prince must have been pleased with the experiment, since the players were offered a year's contract in the following November (4). These contracts seem to have been extended again, since a June 1791 note from the Prince to his secretary states his intention to go to Vienna without the "besondere Harmonie," despite the wishes of his wife (5). At this time Triebensee *junior* was also second oboe at the Theater auf der Weiden from 1791, then at the Kärntnertortheater from 1793; he became known more widely as a soloist.

On 1 May 1794, Josef Triebensee was appointed fürstlichen Kammer- und Theater-Kapellmeister to Prince Louis von Liechtenstein, with further responsibilities for the Harmonie. He continued to lead the ensemble until the entire Kapelle was dissolved in 1809. By 1796, he must have felt the position secure, since he obtained the Prince's permission to marry Went's daughter (6); their daughter's son, Johann Herbeck (1831-1877), was the conductor who did so much to help Bruckner. However, all was not straightforward, for the Prince needed to issue an order warning all members that they would be dismissed if they failed to obey Triebensee's orders (7). It was probably after his appointment as Kapellmeister that Triebensee began his enormous output of original works and arrangements. He may have inherited some of Went's music and could have been responsible for its reissue with contrabassoon parts soon after Went's death.

Josef Triebensee published two large collections of wind music, namely *Harmonien Sammlung: Opern und Ballette wie auch Originalparthien* and the very ambitious series *Miscellannées* [sic; this spelling is used consistently] *de musique.* Despite advertising widely through the *Allgemeine Musik Zeitung*, the first collection lasted for only two issues (November 1803; April 1804; both were issued from Feldsberg). Each issue comprised two Lieferungen, one of original Parthien, the other a complete opera arrangement. Prince Louis Aloys Liechtenstein's death in 1805 does not seem to have affected the Kapelle, though it did lead Triebensee to write a *Trauer Marsch*, JZT-1.1t. We find no evidence for the conjecture that the *Miscellannées* were prepared to offset the loss of income from the impending disbandment of the Harmonie. It is possible that the initial makeup of the *Miscellannées* reflected the musical tastes of the new Prince.

The *Miscellannées* were issued from 1808 through 1813 in at least 32 installments, typically three double issues each year (8). Apart possibly from Oeuvre 5 (an arrangement of Josef Weigl's opera, *Kaiser Hadrian)* Triebensee clearly intended the Oeuvres to be truly varied sets of pieces. Such compilations of popular selections were becoming common at that time. Many of the works in Oeuvres 1-4, 6 and 7 can be found in the piano arrangements issued as Johann Cappi's *Musicalischen Wochenblatt* from October 1806, and Triebensee's arrangements may well have been based on the Cappi piano versions. Cappi did issue music for Harmonie, such as Sedlak's sextet arrangements based on Triebensee's octet originals. The *Miscellannées* would certainly have had the encouragement of Triebensee's father, the Imperial Harmonie and other members of a small, well-knit community of players. However, there are hints that the regimental bands were his best customers (see part 1).

The Liechtenstein Harmonie was disbanded in 1809. Triebensee held a number of appointments, including leader of the wind band of Count Hunyady in Vienna, and opera conductor in Brno. He took over from Weber as Director of the Prague Opera, a post he held from 1816 until his retirement at the end of 1836; his successor was Škroup. In Prague, he discovered singer Henrietta Sontag, who sang in the premiere of Beethoven's *9th Symphony*. Sadly, he wrote no more wind music in these later years.

Unlike Sedlak, whose output consisted almost entirely of arrangements, Triebensee composed much original wind harmony as well. It is really rather good, with enterprising use of instruments, and musical content well above the level of, say, Druschetzky. The Feldsberg archives are lost, so it is hard to assess his full output. It is entirely possible that some of the arrangements issued anonymously in Vienna are his. **JZT-1** *Partita* for 2ob 2cl 2hn bn plus echo (ob cl 2hn bn) and **JZT-2** *Echostücke* for ob cl hn bn cbn plus echo (ob cl hn bn). These are among the best of the partitas exploiting the echo effects of an offstage band. In **JZT-2** the standard nonet has been divided into half-harmony groups, with the contrabassoon adding weight to the onstage band. The instruments are used so as to simulate pairs of winds, with emphasis on ensemble, rather than contrasting individual timbres. One movement of **JZT-2** is recorded by the English Chamber Orchestra winds on EMI EMX 41 2053; it shows touches of humor as the on-stage band tests its echo: (cl, bn; p echoed pp), (band; ff chord, echoed mf), (ob, mf, echoed pp); (bn, bravura, f, echoed p). The closing cadences use the echo cleverly.

JZT-5 *Partitta in E♭* Recorded on Supraphon SUA 1111 2973, this is a well-written, attractive work; it may be this work recorded on Eurosound ES 46.442 (ensemble not known). A different work with the same title and scoring (**JZT-9**) was broadcast in the late 1980s by the Bournemouth Wind Quire.

JZT-6.1 Recorded as by "Hummel" by Consortium Classicum/Klöcker on Dabringhaus & Grimm MD+G 1 3440.

JZT-8 *Nro 3 Parthia in B[♭]* This may have been intended as the third number of the *Harmonien Sammlung.*

JZT-18(-33) There are many ways to select effective divertimentos from these 16 movements for 2ob 2cl 2hn 2bn. A 17th piece in the set in A-Wn, identified as Triebensee's only on the oboe 1 part, has this name scraped off and "Steibelt" substituted. It is just possible that plagiarism was discerned.

JZT-38 *Variations on an Original Theme* The theme is from Triebensee's *Concertino* for piano and winds, **JZT-7**.

JZT-39 *Variations on a theme of Gyrowetz* It is recorded by Collegium Musicum Pragense on SUA 1111 2973 G. It is based on "Mir leuchtet die Hoffnung," No 6 of *Der Augenarzt,* the cavatina where it is discovered that two blind children can be cured.

JZT-1c(-7c) The evidence that these sets of variations are by Triebensee is minimal; the attribution dates from an A-Wn catalog late in the 19th century. We can only say that some of them, notably **JZT-2c**, feel like Triebensee to the players. **JZT-5c** is based on Haydn's "Gott erhalte Franz den Kaiser," which Triebensee used again in **JZT-1m**, "March on the Austrian Hymn." **JZT-7c** uses the theme from the slow movement of Haydn's *Drumroll Symphony,* Hob I:103.ii. **JZT-2c** is based on the Minuet from the ballroom scene in Mozart's *Don Giovanni* (Triebensee had arranged movements from the opera for wind octet, **JZT-39.1a**). The variations are ingenious, attractive, and of exceptional technical difficulty, a real tribute to the skill of the Imperial Harmonie.

JZT-41 the *Grande Quintuor* for cl ca bthn bn pf is dedicated to Joseph, "Prince regnant de Lobkowitz / Duc de Raudniz." It was also published for vl 2va vc pf.

JZT-1.1t *Trauer Marsch for the funeral of Prince Aloys Liechtenstein*   Aloys Joseph, Prince Liechtenstein (1729-1805, known as Prince Louis Liechtenstein), Knight of the Golden Fleece and Chamberlain, founded the Harmonie at Feldsberg (4).

JZT-1a *Figaro* is here a ballet choreographed by Duport for Vienna in 1808, possibly compiled by Anton Fischer. Purebl also made arrangements (**JSP-1a**) of this ballet, which is not based on Mozart's opera.

JZT-18a   An arrangement of the Echo aria from Gluck's *Armide*. Triebensee's instructions emphasize that the four echo parts must be played as from a distance.

JZT-22a   The arrangement of Haydn's *Oxford Symphony* (No 92 in G) is recorded on STH-CD 19053 by the Amsterdam Wind Ensemble/Blomhert as Symphony No 92 in F.

JZT-39.1a   Triebensee's arrangement of Mozart's *Don Giovanni* uses the later Viennese version of the opera, not the original Prague one: "Dalla sua pace" and "Mi tradì" are in, and the duet "Per queste tue manine" replaces "Il mio tesoro." Donna Elvira's part is simplified, and cuts in Leporello's part lose 180 of the Don's conquests. One wonders if these changes were typical of opera performances, or details of the arrangement. Dramatic incidents are missing: a pregnant pause replaces the climax, where Don Giovanni is dragged to hell. The music for Mozart's three ballroom bands, with their different dances and rhythms, is well arranged for octet alone. Unlike Went, Triebensee omits those passages in the original which are largely for winds, like the scene with Don Giovanni's band. The Lobkowitz copy contains many cuts and performance markings made by Krechler. The arrangement is recorded by the Athena Ensemble on Chandos CHAN6597, and by the Netherlands Wind Ensemble on Philips 6833 251.

JZT-42a This arrangement of the first movement of Mozart's *Symphony No 39*, K.543, is recorded by Consortium Classicum on Dabringhaus und Grimm MDG 301 0496-2.

JZT-68a The arrangement of Thaddeus Weigl's *Bacchus und Ariadne* was first advertized in the *Wiener Zeitung* of 16 November 1803. Hummel's catalog for Eszterháza has a cantata with this title by J S Mayr, perhaps linked with Weigl's ballet.

JZT-71a The arrangement of Winter's *Das Labyrinth* was first advertized in *AMZ* in January 1804. Sedlak's sextet version was based on this arrangement (see also part 1).

1. R Hellyer, in the *New Grove* article on Triebensee; see also *Hellyer*.
2. *Liechtenstein Hausarchiv,* Vienna, Fasc. 1789/11, Nr. 34, 2040 ex 1789, 6 July; 2096 ex 1789. Anton Hollmayer was Musik-Direktor, with Friedrich Zinke and Josef Triebensee (oboes), Ferdinand Schliess and Georg Klein (clarinets), Georg Eisner (horn), Johann Harnisch & Franz Steiner (bassoons).
3. Hannes Stekl 1978 Haydn Yearbook 10 164.
4. *Liechtenstein Hausarchiv,* Vienna, Fasc. 1789/11, Nr. 70, 3600 ex 27 November 1789.
5. *Liechtenstein Hausarchiv,* Vienna, Fasc. 1791/11, Nr. 47, 1965 ex 30 June 1791.
6. *Liechtenstein Hausarchiv,* Vienna, Fasc. H-2, Nr. 159, 160 ex 1794, 1 May; 2096.
7. *Liechtenstein Hausarchiv,* Vienna, Fasc. H-2, Nr. 2, 161 ex 1796 (undated).
8. *Liechtenstein Hausarchiv,* Vienna, Fasc. H-2, Nr. 7, 320 ex 26 October 1798.

TROJAN, Václav *24 Apr 1907, Plzeň-5 July 1983, Prague*   At the Conservatory in Prague, Trojan's studies with Novák were complemented by those with Hába and with his interest in other forms, such as folk music (used in his *Wind Quintet*) and jazz. The *Four Caricatures (With One Added)* **VXT-1** are for wind orchestra, percussion and piano, and date from 1974. He has won prizes for his music for puppet theater and films.

TROOP, A, (?pseudonym)   Composer of *Scotch Quick-Steps des Regiments "Duke of Albany Highlanders."*

TROST, J G M Possibly Johann Baptist Matthäus Trost, flautist to the Margrave of Baden-Durlach from 1714 to 1726; not J G M Trost (born c.1630) nor Johann Kasper Trost. At Zwickau is his *Parthia IV* for 2 octavo-bn 2 quarto-bn 2hn 2bn. At Zittau, 100 miles to the west, there are other compositions for rare bassoons (1, 2), including the

set containing the famous *St Antoni Chorale* often misattributed to Haydn.
1. L G Langwill 1965 *The Bassoon and Contrabassoon;* London: Ernest Benn, p 109.
2. H J Hedlund 1958 Galpin Society Journal 11 78-84.

TUČAPSKY, Antonín *b 27 March 1928, Opatovice, nr Vyškov* One component of his career was the study of musicology and music education at Brno University, leading to his appointment as lecturer in Ostrava. His studies at the Janáček Academy of Music in Brno included choral conducting, and this led to his role as chief conductor with the famous Moravian Teachers' Chorus. At Brno, he studied composition privately with Jan Kunc. His *La grande porte de la Thelemme* for chorus, 2ob ca 2bn was commissioned for the Ensemble Philidor in 1995.

TUČEK, J F *(1820, active in Břetislav, near Plzeň)* Arranger of a *Pot Pouri* [sic] in 33 sections; his arrangements include Haydn's *Gott erhalte Franz den Kaiser.*

TUČEK, Vincenc (Tomáš Václav) *2 Feb 1773, Prague-2 Nov 1820, Pest* Composer of two *Pange lingua* for voices and winds. The clarinet parts of one (**VTT-1v**, in "D##" [sic], actually in D) are written on the back of the oboe parts.

TUCH, Heinrich Agatius Gottlob *1768, Gera-1821, Dessau* Two of his works have dedications: that of the *Serenata* **HAT-2** is to Duke Friedrich Leopold von Anhalt-Dessau, the other is on the funeral march **HAT-1t** commemorating the heroic death of the Duke of Brunswick in 1815. We have no locations for his Op 22 *Bläsermusik* (Leipzig: Breitkopf und Härtel 1808) for 2ob 2cl 2hn 2bn.

TÜRK (TUERIC), Daniel Gottlob (Heinrich Anthon Gottlieb) *10 Aug 1756, Claussnitz-26 Aug 1813, Halle* His music is in the archives of the Moravian wind ensemble from Lititz, Pennsylvania. It may have been brought from Europe by David Moritz Michael.

TÜTEL, ( ) *(1790?)* His *Trauermarsch,* from Veselí, uses keyed trumpets.

UMLAUF, Ignaz *1746, Vienna-8 June 1796, Meidling, near Vienna* Violinist, composer of successful Singspiels, and conductor. He was Kapellmeister of the German Singspiel, Vienna, from 1778, and Vice Kapellmeister at the Vienna Court Theater from 1789. In the 1778 Singspiel *Die Bergknappen*, the movement (Musik von Bergleuten) for octet hints at the much later Huntsmen's Chorus from Weber's *Der Freischütz.*

URBANI, Pietro (Peter) *1749, Milan-Dec 1816, Dublin* Singer and composer in London, Dublin and Edinburgh; he arranged many Scottish songs, including settings of Burns's poems, possibly used by Schetky (qv). His publishing firm continued until 1806. He returned to Dublin c.1809, in poverty and with broken health.

VAČKAŘ, Dalibor Cyril *19 Sept 1906, Korcula, Dalmatia-21 Oct 1984, Prague* The son of a popular Czech composer, with whom he wrote a book on the instrumentation of symphony and wind orchestras; he was also a violinist, and a composition pupil of Joseph Suk. He wrote much film music, five symphonies, and many other works. His 1965 *Legend of Man* is a concerto for harpsichord with winds and percussion.

VACTOR, Dan van *1906, USA* Composer of several works for double wind quintet.

VALEK, Jiří *b 28 March 1923, Prague* His early work dates from the 1940s, when Prague was under Nazi occupation. Válek's *4th Symphony, Dialogues with Inner Voice*, for solo voices, winds, piano and percussion, dates from 1969, another troubled time. It comprises settings of Shakespeare. Other music for winds includes the 1963 *Concertino* for 9 winds and piano, and the alternative version of **JIV-1v** *Seven Musical Fables after Aesop* for children's voices and fl 2cl bn perc, recorded on Panton.

VALENTIN (Wallentin), ( ) *(1810)* "Hautboistfeldwebel" at Brno, presumably a leading player or the equivalent of Bandmaster. His opera arrangements are relatively late; the parts for the overture to Lortzing's *Zar und Zimmermann* are dated 1842.

VAN X: such names are listed under X; for example, VAN PRAAG is under PRAAG.

VANDERHAGEN, Armand Jean François Joseph *1753, Antwerp-July 1822, Paris*
Vanderhagen's reputation came both from his arrangements and from his tutors for
clarinet, oboe and flute. He was the son of an organist, and joined the Antwerp
Cathedral choir when he was ten. His musical education expanded when he joined his
uncle (another A Vanderhagen, principal oboe to the orchestra of Prince Charles of
Lorraine) in Brussels. He learned composition from another member of the orchestra
(*Sainsbury* names Paul Van Malder, perhaps the respected composer Pierre van Maldere
[1729-1768], who was in the orchestra from 1758 onwards). His *Suites des Amusants
militaires* for 2cl 2hn 2bn were published in the mid-1770s on a subscription basis (see
part 1). Vanderhagen moved to Paris in 1783, becoming first clarinet, then in 1788
conductor, of the French Guard. Further arrangements for 2cl 2hn 2bn followed from
1783 to 1790, largely unaffected by the first phase of the Revolution. Vanderhagen's
instruction books date from 1798. When the band of the French Guard was dissolved,
he was one of those Sarrette invited to found the Garde Nationale; he remained with
it through its transformations, and earned from Napoleon the Légion d'Honneur for
services in the Prussian campaign of 1806-1807. Many of his arrangements would have
been made while he belonged to this prestigious band. In 1808, he provided the third
Suite de l'airs de l'opéra buffa, the first two being by Fuchs. His *Grande Symphonie
Militaire,* published in 1811, carries the title *La Naissance du Roi de Rome,* and the
work is dedicated to the French army. When the Empire fell, Vanderhagen became first
clarinet at the Théâtre Français, moving down to second clarinet at age 65 in 1818.
VANĚČEK (Vaniček, Waniček), František S (?Z) *(?1800); active 1821-1849* Choirmaster
from 1838 in Březnice (east south east of Plzeň) and some 13 miles from Kasejovice,
where his brother Ladislav (qv) was a teacher. He composed for winds, especially
funeral music, and his enormous output as a copyist preserved much earlier music.
VANĚČEK (Vaniček, Waniček), Ladislav *(?1800)* Teacher in Kasejovice, south east of
Plzeň. Composer and copyist, though apparently less prolific than his brother.
VANHAL (VAŇHAL, Wanhal), Johann Baptist (Jan Křtitel) *12 May 1739, Nechanice
(Neu Nechanitz), near Hradec Králové, Bohemia-26 Aug 1813, Vienna* After an early
career as an organist, Countess Schaffgotsch took Vanhal to Vienna c.1760 to study
under Dittersdorf. Following an Italian journey (1769-1771) he suffered a mental
breakdown, but recovered during a stay with Count Erdödy, the father of Beethoven's
patron. Later, he was well regarded both as composer and as instrumentalist, and he
made a successful visit to England before those of Haydn (*HCRL/2,* pps 380, 389).
Michael Kelly records him as the cellist in a famous "amateur quartet," the other
members being Haydn, Mozart and Dittersdorf. Vanhal died in poverty. His works for
wind fall into three categories. First are those for 2ob 2hn bn (one with added flute).
Secondly, there are small religious works for chorus and winds. These maintained their
popularity for many years, and his works for Corpus Christi were still being used in
Mödling in 1891. Thirdly, there are the works for 2cl 2hn 1/2bn, often very attractive.
JKV-12 *Parthia in Bb* The Finale contains an early furiant, here a fast two-in-a-bar
section reminiscent of the extra movement associated with the G major manuscript of
Haydn's divertimento Hob II:23 **(FJH-4)**. The work is recorded by the Consortium
Classicum/ Klöcker on Telefunken 6.35334. Both clarinet parts are virtuosic and
alternate in leading, so it is sensible to place them on opposite sides of the ensemble.
JKV-7(-11). *Five Parthias (all Eb)* The set in Kiev comprises numbers 1, 2, 4, 5, 6
from the set advertized in the 1771 Supplement 6 to Breitkopf's catalog.
VARÈSE, Edgar *22 Dec 1883, Paris-6 Nov 1965, New York* Varèse's initial studies
were in mathematics and science. He attended the Schola Cantorum with d'Indy (qv)
and Roussel, and the Conservatoire with Widor. He conducted choirs in Paris and Berlin,
and later the Prague Philharmonic Orchestra. Ill health led to his discharge from the

army in 1915; in 1916 he moved to the United States. Varèse championed modern music; he and Carlos Salzedo founded the International Composers' Guild in 1921. His own works were received with hostility at first, but soon were accepted as strikingly imaginative. Varèse preferred the clarity of winds and brass, and many of his works exploit winds extensively. An example is *Intégrales* (for 2pic ob 2cl hn 2tp 3tb 4perc[17 percussion instruments]). Dedicated to Mrs Juliana Force, it is a single movement divided into three sections, and was the first composition for which the term "spatial music" was used. A contemporary review of the first performance in New York in 1925 described it as a "struggle between two groups of instruments, from which the percussionists emerged victorious." Whether this victory was from Varèse's liking for percussion (as in his 1931 *Ionisation* for two groups of percussion) or from strength of numbers is less clear. A representative group of Varèse's works is recorded by L'Orchestre National de France/Nagano on Erato 4509 92137-2. *Hyperprism*, **EXV-1**, scandalized the audience at its first performance in Philadelphia under Stokowski in 1926. Whatever the issue, Kenneth Curwen, present at the International Composers' Guild concert, was sufficiently impressed to offer to publish Varèse's scores.

VAUGHAN WILLIAMS, Ralph *12 Oct 1872, Down Ampney, UK-26 Aug 1958, London* Original and influential English composer, whose fertile interest in folk song did not prevent him writing music that was intensely dramatic, such as his *4th Symphony,* or cold and bleak, such as his *6th* and *7th Symphonies.* His wind music includes some of the best of the military band repertoire, including the *English Folk Song Suite* 1923; *Sea Songs* (quick march) 1924; *Toccata marziale* 1924, and *The Golden Vanity* (quick march) 1933. The *Flourish for Wind Band* (1939) has been arranged by Roy Douglas for the wind section of a standard symphony orchestra. **RWV-1e** *Scherzo alla marcia.* The second movement of the *8th Symphony* of 1956, uses only woodwinds and brass, and may be played by itself. It is a somewhat spiky quick march, with a quieter 6/8 central section.

VENTURINI, Francesco *c.1675, probably Brussels-18 Apr 1745, Hanover* His suites for the court in "Witmar" are concert music for oboe band. All date from June or July 1723, and all include parts for four oboes (two hautbois, hautcontre, taille) and bassoon. *Sainsbury* notes another Venturini, "an excellent performer on the hautboy" based in Vienna in 1772; he died in 1785. Could he be a relative?

VERN, Auguste *(1780)* His *Nocturne in F* takes its title, rare in wind music, from the adagio opening to the first movement. Next is a rustic 6/8, entitled Air Basque. Then follow an Andante espressivo and four variations, and a Polacca, which give flute, cl 1, hn 1 and bn 1 demanding passages. The one surviving early copy was bought from Herr Hauptmann von Vetter (Tischingen 1822), for the Thurn und Taxis regimental band.

VERRALL, John Weedon *b 17 June 1908, Britt, Iowa* Verrall studied with Kodály, Copland and Harris. Many of his works are based on a 9-note scale of two tetrachords on either side of a flexible central note (e.g., C-Db-Eb-E, F or F#, G-Ab-Bb-B).

VERSCHOOR, Onno *b 1965, Netherlands* Composer of an *Oktet* (1994) for 4ob 3bn cbn.

VESELY (Wessely), R P Tadeáš (Tadeās) *(1810)* The manuscript parts of **RTV-1v** *Christmas song,* from Rychov nad Kněžnou, show that the fl 2cl are a later addition to the original accompaniment of 2tp organ and tuba pastoralis. Similarly, the parts of his *Pjseň pokřebný* have alternative instrument parts on recto and verso of the sheets.

VESQUE VON PÜTINGEN, Johann Evangelist (pseudonym: J Hoven) *23 July 1803, Opole, Poland-30 Oct 1883, Vienna* Singer and songwriter, who studied with Moscheles.

VIGNALI, Gabriele His works are mainly church music for TTB 2ob 2cl(C) 2hn bn; the one instrumental work **GXV-1a** is an arrangement, probably by the composer himself, of his *Canzona* GXV-3v. In the arrangement, the oboes are replaced by flutes.

VILLA-LOBOS, Heitor *5 Mar 1887, Rio de Janeiro, Brazil-17 Nov 1959, Rio de Janeiro* While none of the music by this remarkable composer strictly belongs in a book on wind harmony, we felt it proper to mention works which a wind ensemble might wish to try. As a recent review remarked, who could not warm to the composer of a septet for 8 performers, a quartet for 16 and a nonet for 34? The *Nonet* with mixed voices (1923) is for chorus fl ob cl sax hn hp cel perc (18 instruments, many exotic) and was described by the composer as "a rapid impression of the whole of Brazil." The *Chôro No 3,* called *Pica-Pao* (1925) is for male voices cl sax bn 3hn tb. His instrumental works include the *Sexteto mistico* (1917) for fl cl sax hp cel db, the *Quintet* for fl ob ca cl bn, and the *Chôro No 4* (1925) for 3hn tb (recorded on Westminster Gold WGS-8322). Some of the woodwind music is recorded on Etcetera KTC1144.

VITASEK (Witasek, Wittisek), Jan (Matyáš Nepomuk August) *22 Feb 1770, Hořín, near Mělník-7 Dec 1839, Prague* A pupil of F X Dušek (qv) and J A Kozeluch (qv), Vitásek declined the offer of the conductorship of the Court Chapel in Vienna after Salieri's death. He founded the school for organists in Prague, and was Director of Music at St Vitus Cathedral from 1814. In 1794, Vitásek arranged for 13 winds (supervised by the composer) the accompaniment to Süssmayr's *Song of the Bohemians* for the birthday celebrations of Franz II at Charles University, Prague. Vitásek was regarded as an outstanding interpreter of Mozart's piano music, and was known especially for his effective church music; a number of such works with wind accompaniment survive, and appear to have been popular. He was the composer of one of the variations in Diabelli's famous set. In his *Quintet* **JMV-1** (dated 9 June 1813) the sixth movement is an unusual "Jodel Lied." It is recorded by the Brno State Philharmonic winds, on Pronto 0 014, Brno 1993. The *Kriegslied,* **JMV-1mv,** is a march with chorus for the "Landwehr der kk Oesterreichischen Sta[a]ten." The title page bears an instruction to the effect that "the other instruments used in the military music follow the main beats of the bass drum" (a clear acceptance of the inevitable). One of his cantatas, **JMV-1v,** bears the date 29 August 1839; if this was a first performance, he was still composing in his last year.

VITSKA (WITZKA, WITSCHKA), Karl B *(?1750)* His two *Graduales* for Kremsmünster (Beatam me dicent; Exaltabo Domine) are scored for CATB choir 4hn 2bn.

VLAD, Roman *b 29 Dec 1919, Cernowitz (now Chernovtsy), Ukraine* From 1938, he studied piano in Rome with Casella. Vlad's 1942 *Sinfonietta* won the Enescu Prize. His varied music includes much for films. The *Serenata,* his one work for winds, dates from 1959. Since 1960, serialism has been a growing influence in his work.

VLIJMEN, Jan van *b 11 Oct 1935, Rotterdam* Director of the Conservatory in The Hague since 1971. His early influences were Berg and Schoenberg. His two works for larger wind groups, *Per diacasette* (1968) and *Serenata 1* (1964-67) date from the period when he moved to later serial techniques; he has also written two *Wind Quintets.*

VÖLKEL, Franz Composer of two funeral songs and a *Pange lingua.*

VOGEL, Kajetan (Cajetan) *(1750) Konojedy, near Litoměřice-27 Aug 1794, Prague* Pupil of Lolli, and a priest whose religious music was popular. He joined the Servite Order, becoming Chorregent at the monastic church of Sv Mikuláš, Prague. After the the monastic order was abolished in 1786, he became preacher in German at Trinity Church, Prague. His music takes Haydn, Mysliveček and Zimmermann as models; unlike many others, his arrangements are thorough and complete. Thus the 8 sections of the act 2 Finale from his *Don Giovanni* arrangement **KXV-3a** include the three Harmonie items of the original. We assign the anonymous arrangement of *Così fan tutte* to Vogel **(KXV-4a)** because of its thoroughness and its Prague links. His versions of *Figaro* for octet, sextet and string quartet were advertized in the *Wiener Zeitung* of 16 June 1787.

VOGLER, Georg Joseph, Abbé *15 June 1749, Pleichach, near Würzburg-6 May 1814, Darmstadt* Vogler took a civil post at the Mannheim court in 1771. He was given leave to tour Italy, where he studied with Martini. On his return, he founded an outstanding music school, one of several he founded in different countries; because of the school, he moved to Munich five years after the Elector. Vogler was Hofkapellmeister to King Gustavus III of Sweden from 1786, but travelled widely both before and after the King's assassination in 1792 (dramatized in Verdi's *Un ballo in maschera*). Vogler visited Paris in 1794 to hear the choruses with winds for the Fêtes. Vogler's church music with winds is of high quality. He made great efforts in organ design and improvement.

VOGNER, František (Franz)   Teacher in Litomyšl; three of his funeral songs appear in a collection published in Brno in 1881. All have accompaniments of 2cl 2hn basso.

VOGT, Gustave *18 Mar 1781, Strasbourg-3 Jun 1870, Paris*   The oboist in the famous ensemble for which Reicha's wind quintets were written. In 1799, Vogt took the oboe prize at the Paris Conservatoire; after completing his studies, he entered the private band of the Imperial Chapel, serving until 1814, when he was dismissed for Bonapartist sympathies; as a member of the Imperial Guard, he had opposed Louis XVIII. However, Vogt was restored to favor, and later held civil positions of distinction. His *Sérénade* GUV-1 (1816) was composed for the wedding of the Duc de Berry, to whom it is dedicated. It is a potpourri of appropriate pieces from operas by Paer and others.

VOJAČEK (Wojáček, Wolacek), Hynek *4 Dec 1825, Zlín-9 Nov 1916, Petrograd* Chorister and bassoonist at the Augustinian monastery, Brno, from 1838. Most of his wind music was written before he was 20. He moved to Russia, where he became a bandmaster in the Russian army for a year; later, he played and conducted for the imperial theaters and drama school, and then became Professor of theory at the St Petersburg Conservatory. He was an important force in Moravian nationalism, making a valuable collection of folk songs. His arrangements of operas and other wind harmony show how this tradition persisted in Brno into the mid-19th century.

VOLANEK (WOLLANEK) Antonín (Anton) Josef Alois *1 Nov 1761, Jaroměř-16 Jan 1817, Prague*   Arranger for winds of Dittersdorf's *Hieronimus Knicker*, and composer of a *Pange lingua* for CATB, winds and organ.

VOLANEK, Ignace   The "Virbel et Bomba" in his march **IYV-1** are presumably simply side drum (Wirbel) and bass drum.

VOLANS, Keith *26 Jul 1949, Pietermaritzburg, South Africa*   After early studies in Johannesburg and in Aberdeen, Volans moved to Cologne to work with Stockhausen, Kagel and Kontarsky. He moved to Ireland in 1989. His *Concerto for Piano and Wind Instruments* was written for Peter Donohoe and the Netherlands Wind Ensemble.

VOLCKE, F *(1790)*   Composer of military music published in Mainz in 1822/1823.

VOLEDY, ( ) *(?1740)*   Composer of one *Parthia* for 2ob 2hn bn in the Osek archive.

VOLKERT (Folgert), František Jan *4 Feb 1767, Friedlant (Frýdlant)-12 Mar 1831, Králová*   His *Pastorella* **FZV-1** includes a tuba pastoralis. In **FZV-2** *Echo und Russische Arie* the horns play throughout the first movement, muting to produce the echo. There is also a Franz Josef Volket, 12 Feb 1776-22 Mar 1845, organist in Vienna c.1801-1806, later at the Schottenstift; we believe the wind music is by the Czech Volkert.

VON X: such names are listed under X; for example, VON BEECKE is under BEECKE.

VOORTMAN, Roland *b 22 July 1953, Amsterdam*   His *Faustus* (1982) for mezzo-soprano, chorus and winds, is based on Marlowe's tragedy.

VOSTŘÁK, Zbyněk *10 Jun 1920, Prague-4 Aug 1985, Strakonice*   Vostřák studied in Prague in World War II, when he also played for the Prague Radio Orchestra. He taught at the Conservatoire from 1945, also conducting, and was artistic director of Musica Viva Pragensis from 1963 until it was officially abolished in 1973. Official pressure against electronic, aleatoric and other avant-garde techniques (only one part of his output) led to some works having cover-up titles. His 1962 *Crystallization, Op 28* is for twelve winds (there is a piano arrangement); *Sextant, Op 42* (1969) is for wind quintet.

VRBA (Werba, Wrba), ( ) *(1770)* Composer of a *Parthia* for 2cl 2hn bn copied by Dominik Hübner, at Langenbruck, and a *Messe in C*, from Kvasice, for CATB, 2cl 2hn bn org.

VYCPÁLEK, Ladislav *23 Feb 1882, Prague-9 Jan 1969, Prague*   The title *Tuláci* of LXV-1 means "ramblers," and refers to a hiking tradition common in central Europe.

WAGENSEIL, Georg Christoph *29 Jan 1715, Vienna-1 Mar 1777, Vienna*   Wagenseil was an outstanding keyboard player: even in his old age, when suffering from sciatica, he was described by Burney as playing "in a masterly manner and with great fire." He held many posts, including that of Music Master to Empress Maria Theresa. Two sets of Wagenseil's wind music **GCW-1 (-3)** survive. One set (in A-Wgm) is for pairs of oboes, cors anglais, horns and bassoons; the other (in D-SWl) is for pairs of clarinets, horns and bassoons, with piano. A third set, untraced, was auctioned in Vienna in 1953. We believe that the Schwerin set is the original one, partly because Wagenseil himself could have played the keyboard part, partly because the set has consistent titles, partly because there are two extra suites at Schwerin, but primarily because the Vienna scoring is that of the Schwarzenburg Harmonie, formed only in 1775, when Wagenseil was probably too old to write such a substantial set (the set may well be a transcription by Went). We disagree with modern editions which claim that oboes may be replaced by flutes.

WAGNER, ( )   Perhaps the oboist and composer Jacob Karl Wagner, 22 Feb 1772, Darmstadt-25 Nov 1822, Darmstadt

WAGNER, Richard *22 May 1813, Leipzig-13 February 1883, Venice*   Wagner's eventful life is well known, from his appearance as a fairy in a Weber opera (see Ernest Newman, *Wagner* Vol 1) to operatic revolutionary, political revolutionary, and lover. His wind music includes *Huldigungs-Marsch* (March of homage) to celebrate the birthday of King Ludwig on 25 August 1864 (Raff's arrangement added strings) and the *Trauermusik* for Weber. Wagner aimed for grandeur, so his birthday present for King Ludwig is very different from Weber's analogous gifts **CMW-2(-6)** to the Duke of Gotha. In its original form, the *Funeral Music (Trauersinfonie) for the Solemn Burial of the Remains of Carl Maria von Weber* is for about 80 wind instruments and timpani; the minimum ensemble has 20 players, including 1 timpanist. In scale, it matches the works of Berlioz, A Reicha and composers of the French Revolution. Weber had died and was buried in London. In 1844, it became possible to bring his remains back to Dresden, to be reinterred with great ceremony. On their arrival, Wagner wrote the music for a solemn torchlight procession. The *Trauersinfonie* is based on themes from *Euryanthe*. One, from the overture and the final pages, also accompanies the ghost with the accusing finger who appears after the Wedding March of act 3. The other theme is from Euryanthe's cavatina as she prepares to commit suicide. "Despite the volume of sound," Wagner wrote (1, p 364) "I had not forgotten softness and delicacy of instrumentation. I replaced the grim effects of the violas [in the overture] with 20 muffled drums." A most impressive effect, Wagner modestly observed. "In my youth I had learned to love music through my admiration of Weber's music ... to have come into contact with him again and after so many years was an event that stirred the very depths of my being."
1. J Warrack 1976 *Carl Maria von Weber;* Cambridge: Cambridge University Press.

WAILLY, Louis Auguste Paul Warnier de *16 May 1855, Amiens-18 June 1933, Badoux*   Initially a law student and self-taught composer, but later a pupil of César Franck, who influenced him greatly. His *Octet* is scored unusually, for fl ob 2cl hn 2bn tp.

WALCH, Johann Heinrich *1776-2 Oct 1855, Gotha*   Walch's links with North America are shown by the collections of his music in US-BETm, and by the dedication of Livre 27 of his *Pièces d'Harmonie* "Au Corps de Musique de la Vieille-Garde de Washington à Philadelphia." At first sight, several of Walch's *Pièces* appear to be lost. However, his *Potpourris* fill all the known gaps both in Livre number and the C F Peters plate number sequence; further, the few *Potpourris* traced *only* match the gaps in the sequence of *Pièces*. One exception, **JHW-30**, may date from before the periodical sequence was firmly set up; its plate number puts it in the early numbers of the Pièces. Walch's *3 Marches* (fl 2ob 2cl 2bn tp serp; Breitkopf & Härtel, 1809) have not been traced. Walch often specifies terz-flute, Klappenhorn (the new keyed bugle or cornet), and "Cor de Signale" (bugle). In **JHW-4**, the bugle (a small but conspicuous part) also plays triangle. Clarinet 1 is cued for cornet in Book 6, **JHW-6**. Walch's *Trauermarsch* **JHW-1tm** is sometimes misattributed to Beethoven (Kinsky-Halm 13). Book 13 includes a potpourri based on themes of Hummel and Weber, Book 16 variations on an aria from Paer's *Leonora*, and Book 19 arrangements from Rossini's *Le comte d'Ory*. Dedications are revealing. Book 4 (c.1820) of the *Pièces d'Harmonie,* **JHW-4,** is dedicated to "Son Altesse Royale Le Duc de Cambridge, Gouverneur général du Royaume d'Hannovre," reflecting the fact that the Kings of Great Britain were rulers of Brunswick from 1714 to 1837. Book 28 is dedicated (in English) "by permission to His Royal Highness Prince Albert, Duke of Saxony-Coburg-Gotha." The plate number shows it was published in 1841, not long after Prince Albert's marriage to Queen Victoria on 10 February 1840. Many dedications are to bandmasters: Books 10 and 11 to Directors of Music in Stockholm, F C Preumayr and Braun, Book 12 to F Berr (qv) in Paris, Book 14 to Richter (qv, Stuttgart), Book 17 to F Müller (qv) at Rudolstadt, Book 22 to Friedrich Weller (qv) and Book 23 to H Linder (qv). Walch covered the divide between music for large bands and Harmoniemusik; Liv 1, 2 were available for both forms. His *Pièces* comprise marches and dances, with the occasional more serious movement, all of high standard. His periodical probably served as the mainstay of many military bands.

WALTER, ( ) *(1800)* Principal bassoon at the Grand Théâtre, Marseille. His *Grand Walze du Dey d'Alger* [sic] dates from the French invasion of Algeria in July 1830.

WALTER, David *b 21 May 1958, Paris* Oboist, prizewinner and now teacher at the Conservatoire National Supérieur, and arranger of works for double reed ensembles.

WALTER, G (? Johann/Giovanni Ignaz) *31 Aug 1755, Radonice-22 Feb 1822, Regensburg* We note a similarly named G Walter, a violinist in Paris, 1790-1800, and I Walter, a singer at Metz and a pupil of Starzer.

WANEK, Friedrich Karl *11 Nov 1929, Lugoj (Banat), Romania-13 Apr 1991, Mainz* Composer of a *Concert Suite* for double wind quintet and of a set of four *Grotesken* (1981) for 2fl 2ob 2cl 2bn 2hn tp perc, but also known for his valuable arrangements for winds of music by Françaix, Ligeti, Mahler and Orff. Wanek was educated in Romania, but was banned from his profession in 1958. He was denaturalized in 1962, left Romania, and found employment in Vienna. He was reader for contemporary music at B Schotts Söhne, Mainz, from 1966 to 1991, and held lecturing appointments.

FKW-4a *Carmina Burana* Carl Orff's 1937 *Carmina Burana* is unashamedly diatonic, vivid and colorful in orchestration, and its hypnotic use of repetition impresses it on the mind. It sets texts from the 13th century wandering scholars, which touch on both the basic sensual pleasures and the perennial problems of church, state and society. Wanek arranged five items of Orff's original as a very effective suite, often with the same instrumentation and rhythmic impulse, so reproducing much of the highly colored atmosphere of the original. 1 *"Fortuna plango vulnera,"* where Orff's chorus describes the wounds which fate inflicts: But for those who are now at the top of Fortune's wheel: watch out, for it may turn and throw you to the bottom soon. In Orff's original, the music is repeated three times; in Wanek's it is played twice only, but a further repeat of the movement does improve its balance. 2 *"In trutina,"* where the soprano of the original has to choose between modesty and desire. Here the cor anglais likewise succumbs luxuriantly. After 3 *Tanz,* comes 4 *"Amor volat undique,"* the bitter fate of a girl, alone without a lover; 5 *"In taberna"* In the inn, where men drink and win or lose at dice, where they can drink to the whole world together, where they can curse those who plague them. Here a third horn helps in giving the right power in key places.

WARMERDAM, Desiree van *b 1959, Netherlands* Her 1994 *Xystus* is for 2ob obdam ca 3bn cbn.

WATLEN, John *(1770)* Composer of an *Exordium* for the Newcastle Troop.

WAWRA, Wenzel *b 1767, Niemeyez, Bohemia* Wawra's music in Kremsmünster includes a march, funeral music, and a song with winds "Ich bin ein deutscher Jüngling."

WEAIT, Christopher *b 27 Mar 1939, Surrey, UK* Bassoonist, who studied with Robert Reinert at the Crane School of Music, Potsdam, NY; co-principal with the Toronto Symphony 1968-1985. Arranger, and director of wind ensembles in Ohio and in Toronto, where he made recordings of Mozart's K.361, K.375, K.388 with the Toronto Chamber Winds. His completion of **FPS-3** is discussed under Schubert.

WEBB, William *(1780)* Master of the Band of the Royal Victis Light Dragoons (the Roman name for the Isle of Wight was Vectis), and composer of a *Slow March for the Loyal Isle of Wight Volunteers.*

WEBER, Bernhard Anselm *18 Apr 1766, Mannheim-22 Mar 1821, Berlin* Pupil of Holzbauer (qv) and Vogler (qv), and virtuoso of the Xänophika, which (not unlike the terpodion) combined a keyboard with sound produced by friction. He was joint Kapellmeister of the Berlin National Theater, later Royal Kapellmeister. The Stuttgart Hoftheater archive includes several substantial items for winds for the plays *Die Jungfrau von Orleans* and *Deodato*; his music for *Klymemnestra* is in Vienna.

WEBER, Carl Maria Friedrich Ernst von *18 November 1786, Eutin, near Lübeck-5 June 1826, London* A musical career was natural for Weber. His mother and father were musicians: the former a singer, the latter a violinist, violist, double-bass player and a rogue. Weber's grandfather was also the grandfather of the two Webers in Mozart's life: Aloisia whom Mozart rashly wished to marry, and her sister, Constanza, whom he married instead (1). Two of Weber's half-brothers were pupils of Haydn. Weber achieved much in his short life. Ill health from a congenital hip disease and from inadvertently drinking nitric acid, wild company, economic uncertainty, and constant touring could have destroyed him. To Weber, the experience also gave practical skills long before he wrote his best-known works. The travels made him familiar with the whole range of European music; one can easily forget how difficult this once was.

After a short period as a pupil of Michael Haydn and of the Abbé Vogler, he was appointed conductor of the Breslau Opera. His stay was troubled, and he moved to Karlsruhe, then to Stuttgart where, from 1807 to 1810 he served as secretary to King Frederick of Württemburg. The Webers, father and son, were expelled, as the result of one of Weber senior's disastrous misdeeds. Their visits to Mannheim, Darmstadt and Munich were more peaceful. The travels continued to Gotha and Prague; Dresden was his base from 1817 until his death, although all the operas which made his reputation were first performed elsewhere. Weber was one of many composers from continental Europe who died in England; his death deeply moved many English musicians.

At first glance, Weber may seem to have written little wind music. Jähns (2) notes just a single work called *Harmonie* (**CMW-6d**), no wind divertimentos, and no substantial works. Yet there is much wind music: movements for winds from incidental music, arrangements of songs, marches, and choral works. Much of Weber's wind music is recorded, most of the genuine music (**CMW-2[-7]** and the dubious **CMW-4d**) by Klöcker and the Consortium Classicum on Telefunken 6.65366 FK, and much of the dubious (**CMW-1d[-4d]** plus the genuine **CMW-1** and **CMW-7**) by Malgoire on CBS IM 39011.

CMW-1 *March (in C) for the Royal Society of Musicians J307* The last work Weber saw completed. Weber was asked to be Guest of Honor at an Annual Dinner of the Royal Society of Musicians in the Argyle Rooms in London on 13 May 1826. It was the custom to play a march by some eminent composer: in previous years, ones by Haydn, Winter and Spohr had been played. Weber's illness became critical, and prevented him from attending the dinner. Nevertheless, the March was written on 5-6 May. "Lying back in his armchair in his weakness," wrote Weber's son (1) "he dictated the second and third parts of this March to Fürstenau, including what he considered the correct instrumentation." The March was based on one of Weber's early *Six Easy Pieces for Piano* (J13, No 5), though the Trio was new. There is a version which includes a chorus and largely redundant string parts; Weber's involvement in it is unclear.

✳ **CMW-2 (-6)** *Works for Gotha* Weber's brief stay in Gotha occurred when Spohr was in charge of the Ducal orchestra. These pieces are all associated with that eccentric monarch, Emil Leopold August, Duke of Gotha, who enjoyed appearing in female attire, with different-colored wigs for each day of the week. Like his grandson, Albert, Prince Consort of Queen Victoria, the Duke was an able composer; of the works for Gotha, four (**CMW-3(-6)**) are arrangements of settings by the Duke, and date from 1812.

— **CMW-2** The attractive *Waltz, J149,* was written for the Duke's birthday on 17 November 1812. Its trio is based on Weber's song *Maienblümlein.* The trumpet part is unimportant. The next four items constitute an interesting suite, which works best in numerical order. **CMW-3** *Beim kindlichen Strahl des erwachenden Phoebus* (By the innocent rays of the wakening Phoebus, J153). A rich-sounding Andante con moto, which evokes dawn far better than does its title; arranged from a song by the Duke of Gotha. **CMW-4** *Ihr kleinen Vögelein* (You little birds, J150) is a slight but pleasant piece that would pass without comment in a beer garden. **CMW-5** *Lebewohl, mein süsses Leben* (Farewell my sweet life, J151) is sonorously sentimental, in four sections which, one assumes, tell a tale. **CMW-6** *Die verliebte Schäferin* (The shepherdess in love, J152). Another slight but attractive piece; the trumpet part can be omitted without loss.

CMW-7 *Adagio and Rondo in E♭* A splendid pair of movements, written in 1808 when Weber was a colleague of Danzi in Stuttgart; the autograph is now in Berlin. One of the movements is a richly romantic Adagio (6 July 1808), with soft wind murmurings and echo effects in the best *Der Freischütz* style. The Rondo (24 June 1808) is spontaneous and gay, with a short central section and passages foreshadowing his *Bassoon Concerto.* The Rondo was used again in 1818 in the music to Eduard Gehe's tragedy *Henry IV,* though without the conspicuous bassoon passages (3). The movement was reorchestrated for *Euryanthe,* without the contrasting middle section, when the extra ballet music was added in 1825. Recorded also on Marco Polo 8.223356 (German Wind Soloists).

CMW-1e *Abu Hassan J106* This one-act opera, with its *Thousand and One Nights* plot, includes imaginative use of wind and Turkish instruments. The Finale includes a march (strictly within a larger ensemble) for 2ob 2hn.

CMW-2e *Der Freischütz J271* Music characteristic of wind harmony is found within larger ensembles, like the terzett and chorus "O diese Sonne!" and the Bauern-Marsch of the opening scene. There is inspired use of the horns, both in the overture (just two horns set the scene, though four are used later) and in the huntsmens' chorus. In *Scheibenfest von Pirling* by Adalbert Stifter (1805-1865), we find a description of a shooting competition which sets a similar scene: "a platform was built among the branches of pine-trees ... upon which, enclosed by the world of pine-needles, the horn-players sat and, from time to time, played the pieces they had rehearsed."

✦ **CMW-3e** *Preciosa J279* The Gypsy March, which forms the central section of the Overture, is for winds alone, and reappears by itself several times with differences in detail only (Nos 1, 9a and 10a). When it is played as a separate number, the offstage Gypsy music (No 7: 2pic 2hn 2bn perc) can be used as a trio.

CMW-4e *Euryanthe J291* The use of winds is even richer than in the earlier operas, e.g., the horns in the splendid chorus, No 18, where the huntsmen appear just in time to prevent the heroine expiring in the wilderness, and the sprightly flutes, oboes and clarinets (with horns and bassoons) at the start of the act 1 Finale (No 9). On a larger scale, and more original, is the sombre Wedding March (No 23), full of foreboding.

CMW-5e *Oberon J306* This opera shows extensive use of winds: as a separate wind ensemble within items (No 3, No 6), as a separate body (as in the march, No 8) and in many small passages which accompany dialogue between the main numbers (No 9, and in the melodrama before scene 5). No 8, Allegretto grazioso, is a delightful oriental march (2fl 2cl 2hn 2bn tri tamb) which works well by itself. No 14, an Andante con moto, is a typical example of wind music accompanying stage action (Oberon descends in a "car [sic] drawn by swans"); a horn plays the magic motif, and a flute and a clarinet move languorously over a rippling accompaniment of the other flute and clarinet. The smaller pieces are of more interest for the way opera developed than for their contribution to wind harmony. However, they do show how Weber's smaller pieces influenced his major ones, for example, the close relation between the bars after No 10 here and the start of his "Du hoher Rautenzweig" (J271; **CMW-6v**). The 1865 English libretto of *Oberon* gave us unintended pleasures, for the text was clearly retranslated by one with limited command of English and proof-reading: Reiza is advised to "bid loves delusive vonions melk away" and Huon to "Hic thee on bound" [sic].

CMW-6e *Musik zu Turandot* (J75, 1809), was the source of Hindemith's themes for the *Symphonic Metamorphoses on themes by Carl Maria von Weber*. Of the several items (4) is a mere 4 bars of Turkish music for 2fl 2ob 2cl 2hn 2bn, and (7) a short *Marcia funebre* (30 bars including a 10-bar da capo), the funeral march taken up by Hindemith.

CMW-7e *Musik zu Heinrich IV, König von Frankreich* (J237, 1818) The text is by Gehe. The items for winds show how Weber exploited winds in the theater, with works for the stage band (items 2, 3 and 6 are "auf dem Theater") being somewhat longer: 1. 2pic 2ob 2cl 2hn 2bn 2tpt drum, 2x15 bars; 2. pic 2ob 2cl 2hn 2bn, 3x20 bars; 3. 2fl 2cl 2hn, Adagio, 10 bars; 4. 2fl 2cl 5 bars; 5. 2fl 2cl; 6. 2cl 2hn 2bn, 2x36 bars; this Vivace: Allegro is the Rondo of **CMW-7**. The published piano transcription indicates it lacks the bassoon's solo passage; 7, 8. 2pic 2ob 2cl 2hn 2bn 2timp, 16 bars.

CMW-8e *Musik zu Lieb' um Liebe* (J246, 1818) A 1-act Schauspiel, with items for winds: 1. 35 bars, 2cl 2hn; 2. Chor der Landleute (possibly accompanied); 3. Ländlicher Marsch, 16 bars of unspecified "Bläser"; 4. Melodram, 17 bars with 2ob 2cl 2hn 2tp.

CMW-1v *Heil dir, Sappho!* (J240, 1818) A setting of a text by Grillparzer.

CMW-2v *Agnus Dei* (J273) Written on 13 February 1820 for inclusion in Blankensee's tragedy *Carlo,* produced in Dresden. It is substantial, imaginative in execution, yet with a genuinely religious feeling. Jähns's catalog wrongly gives 2hn only (there are 4hn), even though the manuscript in the Jähns collection may be in his (Jähns's) own hand.

CMW-3v *Trauermusik: "Hörst du die Klage?"* (Elegy: "Do you hear the lament?" J116). Written for the funeral of the actor, Max Heigel, although Winter's *Requiem* was used on that occasion, and Weber's work was left incomplete. Extensive sketches in the Jähns collection show that some of the music came from early works (the *Grablied,* **CMW-4v**) or was used in later ones (the E♭ Mass, J224). The work, reconstructed by Mark Goddard, Marshall Stoneham and Robert Eccles, proves very effective.

CMW-4v *Grablied "Leis' wandeln wir"* (Threnody: "Gently we are transported" J37) Composed in Augsburg in 1803 on the death of a Munich friend, and reorchestrated the following year for the funeral of the wife of the theater's codirector.

CMW-5v *Kriegs Eid "Wir stehn vor Gott"* (War Oath "We stand before God," J139). This is a highly patriotic work for unison male voices and a wind band. When it was first sung by the soldiers of Oranienburg Barracks, a few miles north of Berlin, it "brought tears to the eyes of the captain and chaplain" (1). The many verses lack special merit, and it is hard to imagine a suitable musical occasion on which to perform it today.

CMW-6v *Du hoher Rautenzweig* ("Thou lofty spray of rue," J271). The music of "God Save the King" was a favourite of Weber's, and J271 is one of his four arrangements of it. Musically, it consists of a straightforward setting of a verse, with a sensuous introduction and conclusion (see above, where its relation to *Oberon* is noted). When Prince Friedrich August (later King of Saxony; rue is the emblem of the House of Saxony) married Archduchess Caroline of Austria, Weber originally planned an opera, *Alcindor,* for the festivities. This proved abortive and minor works like this were substituted. It was performed on 11 October 1819, three days after it was written, in the Royal Court Theater, Dresden, for the Royal couple's first public appearance together. The text verges on the unintelligible, but the setting is rather nice.

"Weber?": Dubious and spurious works   With the exception of **CMW-6d** (the Harmonie about which Jähns apparently had doubts, and only listed in the Appendix to his catalog) these works are not listed by Jähns. Nor are they referred to in any contemporary writings (apart possibly from ambiguous hints, like the 10 November 1811 diary note that Weber had orchestrated a concerto for the oboist Fladt). Nor are autographs or similar authenticating material available in accessible form at the time of writing. This, of course, does not rule them out completely. However, when reservations are expressed by scholars with a deep knowledge of Weber (3) and when recordings show some to be feeble, or dull, or both, we have little hesitation in labelling them spurious. Much of the material is available in modern editions, and is recorded by Malgoire on CBS IM 39011.

CMW-2d *Six Waltzes*   A very dubious group of 5 waltzes, plus a later waltz based on themes from *Oberon* in a somewhat tasteless way. There is no mention of Weber on the parts. The set is sometimes wrongly confused with the genuine waltz **CMW-2**.

CMW-3d *Theme and Variations on an Original Theme*   An attractive set, of the sort someone like Hermstedt might have written.

CMW-4d *Concertino for Oboe Solo*   This Adagio and Polacca is the best of a modest group, but does not seem to be by Weber, even in the stylish performance by the Consortium Classicum. The manuscript score is in the hand of Friedrich Witt, and the music is probably by him.

Weber: Arrangements by others   The recordings of wind arrangements of Weber's *Der Freischütz,* by the Consortium Classicum/Klöcker are of that by Carl Flachs on Telefunken 6.35366, and that by Sedlak on Dabringhaus & Grimm MD + G L 3267.

1. John Warrack 1976 *Carl Maria von Weber;* Cambridge: Cambridge University Press.
2. F W Jähns 1871 (reprinted 1967) *Carl Maria von Weber in seinen Werken: Chronologisch-thematisches Verzeichnis seiner sämtlichen Kompositionen;* Berlin.
3. L Hirschberg 1927 *Reliquienschrein des Meisters Carl Maria von Weber in seinem hundertsten Todesjahr;* Berlin: Morawe & Scheffelt (there is a copy at GB-Lbl, H.690.t).
4. Dieter Klöcker, Notes to the recording Telefunken 6.35366.
5. John Warrack 1982 Musical Times *123* 420-421.

WEBER, Friedrich Dionys (Bedřich Diviš) *9 Oct 1766, Velichov, Bohemia-25 Dec 1842, Prague*   A founder and first Director of the Prague Conservatory, and inventor of the lever system for tuning tympani. Conservative musically, yet he was a pioneer of Bohemian music, and active in making the first systematic collection of Czech folksong in 1819. He wrote some fine sextets for horns, recorded on Supraphon 11 0348-1 131 G.

WEBER, (Jacob) Gottfried *1 Mar 1779, Freinsheim, near Mannheim-21 Sept 1839, Kreuznach*   Lawyer, musical scholar, and founder of the Mannheim Conservatory.

WEBER, S J *(1770)*   Arranger of works for the Harmonie of the Archbishop of Mainz.

WEBER, Wilhelm *c.1800-c.30 March 1876*   Weber styled himself "Schullehrer" (school teacher) on his two *Leichenlied,* late works using 2cl 2hn 2bn. The performance dates pencilled on the copies range from 1870 to 1898, and include Weber's own funeral.

WEIDEMANN, Charles Frederick *d 1782, London.*   Could this be the "Wiedemann" who (notes *Sainsbury)* "came to England about the year 1726, and was long the principal player on the German flute ... but ... never broke through the bounds of mediocrity to which his instrument seems confined"?

WEIGART, Franz (Francesco) *(1740)*   Composer of *7 Partittas* [sic] for Kroměříž.

WEIGH, John *(1770)* Master of the Band of the Royal Cheshire Militia, who composed a pair of marches for their use.

WEIGL, Joseph *28 Mar 1766, Eisenstadt-3 Feb 1846, Vienna*   The son of Josef Franz Weigl (19 May 1740, Bavaria-25 Jan 1820, Vienna, also a musician), Haydn's godson, and a pupil of Albrechtsberger (qv) and Salieri (qv). He was the conductor who rehearsed *Figaro* and *Don Giovanni* for the Vienna Court Theater, where he signed a permanent contract as Kapellmeister and composer in 1792. His operas and Singspiele were very popular for their simple tunefulness; his *Parthia* JYW-1 is sadly far less successful. He wrote the *Harmoniestück* in the co-written *Pumpernickels Hochzeitstag*. His output includes opera arrangements, and a *Grosse Messe* for soloist, chorus and winds. We cannot trace a *Marsch* for 2ob 2cl 2hn 2bn, said to be in D-HR.

WEIKERT, ( ) *(1770)*   Possibly Weigart (qv); Weikert is named in the copies of a *Parthia* and *Ländler and Trio* made by Dominik Hübner at Langenbruck.

WEILL, Kurt *2 Mar 1900, Dessau, Germany-3 Apr 1950, New York*   Weill's generation experienced the way that war could devastate lives far from battle fronts and how peace could lead to hardship, civil disorder, and injustice. Weill responded with works like *Die Dreigroschenoper*. Brecht's text was set with directness and vividness demanding unconventional instrumentation, an impact which was possible with wind bands. Weill brought together the disparate influences of jazz and of his own teachers Humperdinck and Busoni. Though much of Weill's use of winds is forthright, he has made more subtle use, as in the *Frauentanz,* Op 10, for soprano, fl cl hn bn and va (here, as elsewhere, Weill omits oboes). Yet this cycle of poems from the Middle Ages was written in 1923, only a short time before his best-known works. A small ensemble (in this case fl cl/sax 2tp tb vn pf) is found too in *Konjunktur* of 1928, incidental music for a play, unpublished at the time, though fragments were reconstructed by David Drew as *Oil Music* in 1975. The stage works have a complex copyright position, and several works were issued in more than one version. Some use stage bands.

Der Protagonist Op 15.   In this one-act opera of 1925, there is an on-stage wind octet of 2fl 2cl 2hn 2bn. Its role, among others, is to differentiate the pantomimes from the rest of the opera. The pit orchestra itself has the unusual combination of 2ob 2b-cl 3hn 3tb in its wind section. The two bands play alternately, rarely together. The premiere at the Dresden Staatsoper was outstandingly successful.

Das kleine Mahagonny (Mahagonny Songspiel) later developed into *Aufstieg und Fall der Stadt Mahagonny. Aufstieg und Fall,* one of Weill's largest works, was his most successful realization of his ideas of the new opera. Before it came the *Mahagonny Songspiel,* which combined the same influence of popular song with his individual use of a large but novel orchestra. The *Songspiel* has a small orchestra (cl cl/b-cl sax 2tp tb 2vl pf perc). The later *Aufstieg und Fall* uses a far larger pit orchestra, aided by an onstage band (2pic 2cl 3sax 2hn 2bn 2tp 2tb tu perc piano xylophone/banjo bandoneon). The *Songspiel* is recorded by the London Sinfonietta/David Atherton on DG 423 255-2.

Happy End   This three-act comedy with music, to a text by "Dorothy Lane" (Brecht in disguise) was first performed at the Theater am Schiffbauerdamm, Berlin, in 1929 with a band of versatile musicians (fl/[cl, a-sax] cl/[a-sax, b-sax] 2tp tb banjo/Hawaiian guitar, mandolin, acoustic bass guitar, bandoneon, accordion] pf[harm] perc).

Die Dreigroschenoper of 1928 is perhaps Weill's best-known achievement, a vehicle for the memorable and intentional nastiness of Mack the Knife. The original production exploited the talents of the Lewis Ruth band, whose 8 players played 21 instruments. The opera was an enormous success, like its 18th-century ancestor, *The Beggar's Opera,* on which it is based. The *Kleine Dreigroschenmusik* also dates from 1928, but was first performed at a 1929 Berlin Staatsoper concert conducted by Klemperer. It is scored for (pic[fl] fl 2cl 2sax 2hn tp tb tu pf guitar[banjo, bandoneon] timp perc), and incorporates 10 numbers of the original opera in 7 movements lasting about 22 minutes. It is recorded by the London Sinfonietta/Atherton on DG 423-255-2; Leipzig Radio Symphony Orchestra/Pommer on Ondine ODE 771; St Luke's Orchestra/Rudel, Music Masters 67007, and Amor Artis/Somary on Newport Classic/Rare Records NCD60098.

Concerto for Violin and Wind Orchestra, Op 12 **KYW-2** Composed for Szigeti (who never played it) in 1924, its first performance was by Marcel Darrieux, under Walter Straran, on 11 June 1925. It was next performed at the 1926 International Society for Contemporary Music in Zurich, where it was paired with the Stravinsky *Octuor*. The work was banned in Germany in 1933, and had its German premiere as recently as 1975. Stefan Frenkel has been especially associated with the *Concerto*. The work is is three movements: Andante con moto; Notturno, Cadenza, and Serenata; Allegro molto un poco agitato. The obvious influences are those of Stravinsky (whose *Concerto for Piano and Winds* had its premiere in 1924), Busoni, and perhaps Hindemith, especially in the use of an ostinato rhythm in the Serenata. The Finale is like a tarantella, occasionally military, but reflective towards the end. The work was received coolly; Copland, for example, found it dull. It does lack the immediate impact of much of Weill's music, but its quality shows in recordings like that by Nona Liddell/London Sinfonietta/Atherton; DG 2543 808, Wächter/Leipzig Radio Symphony Orchestra/ Pommer on Ondine ODE 771; Glab/Musique Oblique Ensemble/Herreweghe on Harmonia Mundi HMC90 1422; Aadland/Norwegian Wind Ensemble/Rund on Simax PSC1090; Tanaka, St Luke's Orchestra/Rudel on Music Masters 67007, Tetzlauff/ Deutsche Kammerphilharmonie Winds on Virgin VCS 45056-2, and by Waldman/Amor Artis/Somary on Newport Classic/Rare Records NCD 60098.

Gustav III **KYW-3** The incidental music to Strindberg's 1902 play was written for a production by Victor Barnowsky at the Theater in der Königgrätzerstrasse, Berlin. About half the 15 items survive, from which David Drew has reconstructed a suite.

Berliner Requiem **KYW-1v** Commissioned in 1928 by Frankfurt Radio to mark the death of Rosa Luxemburg and the 10th anniversary of the end of World War I. It is a series of dirges to texts by Brecht on the general theme of death and the effects of war on the city dweller. It was first performed on Frankfurt Radio, 1929, conducted by Ludwig Rottenburg, with soloists Hans Grahl, Johannes Willy and Jean Stern. It was banned in 1933. The movements are Grosser Dankchoral; Ballade vom ertrunkenen Mädchen; Grabschrift; Erster Bericht über den unbekannten Soldaten; Zweiter Bericht; Grosser Dankchoral. It is widely believed to be Weill's masterpiece, but, left incomplete, it was plundered for later works (the "Ballad of the Drowned Girl," for instance, has been recorded several times as a separate number). The completion by David Drew is recorded with the Düsseldorf Symphony Winds/Hartmut Schmidt on Koch Schwann 314050 and by Musique Oblique/Herreweghe on Harmonia Mundi HMC90 1422.

Ballade Vom Tod im Wald, Op 23 **KYW-2v** A setting of Brecht's 1918 poem "Of Death in the Forest," this work was written in Berlin in 1927. Unpublished in Weill's lifetime, its manuscript is now in the Library of Congress; the only known performance in Weill's lifetime was on 23 November 1927 by Heinrich Hemanns, with the Berlin Philharmonic Orchestra conducted by Eugen Lang. It is recorded by Musique Oblique/ Herreweghe on Harmonia Mundi HMC90 1422.

WEILLAND, ( ) (1770) Composer of an enjoyable 3-movement *Harmonie*, one of the rare serious octets to be published in London in the late 1790s. It had been published two years earlier in Paris; Broderip & Wilkinson may have had an agreement with Pleyel.

WEINER, Lazar S *27 Oct 1897, Cherkassy, near Kiev-10 Jan 1982, New York* Musical director of the Central Synagogue, New York, from 1930 to 1975.

WEINLICH, Johann *(1810)* Arranger of *Astraea Tänze* by Johann Strauss the Elder; the arrangement is in the collection of the Augustinian monastery, Brno.

WEINMANN, Alexander (editor) Weinmann has prepared performing versions of a number of marches originally published in piano versions, including one for the *kk Infanterie Reg: Coloredo* sometimes attributed to Haydn.

WEIS, ( ) *(1770)* His *Divertimento* for 2vl 2cl 2hn bn was copied in 1803 by Augustin Erasmus Hübner, at Langenbruck.

WEISGOTT, ( ) *(1770)* His 5-movement *Parthia in Dis [Eb]* was copied by Augustin Erasmus Hübner, at Langenbruck.

WELLER, Friedrich *c.1790, Dessau-30 May 1870, Zerbst.* Dedicatee of Walch's *Livre 22, Pièces d'Harmonie.* Weller's *Ein musikalische Spass* (A musical joke) concerns mimicry of birdsong: a piccolo as nightingale, cock-a-doodle-doo (Kikkikiri) from F trumpets, bass trombone as cuckoo, and a final woodwind conversation of quail (Die Wachtel, F clarinet), hen (oboe) and basset horn cuckoos. It looks charming. Weller also arranged the major part of Weber's *Oberon* for winds. His arrangement asks for large forces, but often uses them sparingly, e.g. sections for 2cl 2hn 2bn only.

WENT (Vent, Wendt, Wend, Wenth, Venti), Johann Nepomuk (Carlo) *27 June 1745, Divice, Bohemia-3 July 1801, Vienna* Went was respected as a fine oboist, as an arranger of distinction, and as a composer for winds. As oboist, he seems to have specialized in lower parts, second oboe and cor anglais, playing in the best ensembles of his time: Count Pachta of Rayhofen's at Cítoliby, Prince Johann Schwarzenberg's, and the Vienna Burgtheater Orchestra. A founder member of the Imperial Harmonie in 1782, he played in the Burgtheater and Court Orchestra for the rest of his career. His output as arranger was large, and he arranged both for the standard octet of 2ob 2cl 2hn 2bn (as for the Imperial Harmonie) and for 2ob 2ca 2hn 2bn (as for the Schwarzenberg ensemble); Went also arranged for 2cl 2hn 2bn and for a few other combinations. There seem to be no works for the Schwarzenberg Harmonie after about 1796. This may be linked with the Napoleonic Wars, for French armies entered Styria on 4 April 1797. Three days later, on 7 April 1797, a concert at the Schwarzenberg palace was cancelled because of this catastrophic war news; Schwarzenberg, as Austrian commander, would have been especially affected. It is likely that there were longer-term effects on the Schwarzenberg Harmonie as Vienna prepared itself for war. Went's daughter married Josef Triebensee, and it is possible that, after Went's death, Triebensee reissued some of Went's works with added cbn parts. Suggestions that arrangements by Went were completed by Triebensee seem to be based wholly on misread handwriting.

As a composer, Went is less well known. Certainly he concentrated on arrangements after joining the Imperial Harmonie. Yet the Partita **JNW-40** has real charm. The 1799 Traeg catalog offered *Pièces alla Camera* for 2bthn 2hn bn. **JNW-42, -44, -48** are entitled *Parthia a la Camera;* perhaps **JNW-42(-46)** are the originals of those which Traeg lists. Went wrote some works for 2ob ca, such as the *Divertimento in Bb* and the *Serenade No 2.* His original works have individual features, like the use of "Alternativo" rather than "Trio" as a title, the fact that Trios are often truly for three instruments, and the use of "Favorito" dance movements, a further sign that his parthias are more in the tradition of early suites than the later symphonic form.

JNW-40 *Parthia Nro. 12 (Eb)* Recorded on Supraphon 1 11 1156 by the Collegium Musicum Pragense. It is an attractive work: a Presto, then a slow, formal Minuet and sadly gentle Trio, a Romance, and a hunting Finale which breaks off in the middle (for refreshment rather than to celebrate a kill?) before continuing the hunt. Inexplicably, the recording omits the second movement, a Favoritto and Alternativo.

Went established himself as an arranger in the 1770s, perhaps during his associations with the Clam Gallas and Pachta ensembles. The bassoon part of Asplmayr's *La sposa Persiana* (**JNW-8a**) is dated 1775. His early arrangements are mainly of ballets, apart from a few works by Gluck. The works which Went arranged can often be traced to the scores of ballets intended for Laxenburg, where Prince Schwarzenberg was Ballet Intendant. Went's arrangements have distinctive features. The octets are strongly led by the 1st oboe; clarinet 1 leads the sextet versions for 2cl 2hn 2bn. Went, an oboe player, knew the physical problems players have in a long evening, and usually gives the oboes a tacet movement, as in both versions (2ob 2cl 2hn 2bn and 2ob 2ca 2hn 2bn) of Joseph Weigl's *Die Reue des Pigmalion* (**JNW-64a**). His dynamic markings include "mezza voce" (or "m: v:") an instruction which Triebensee seems to have picked up from Went. Another feature, surprisingly rare in arrangements, is that Went often arranges finales en bloc, rather than splitting them into sections. At his peak, from about 1782 until 1796, Went arranged two to four operas each year, many very well done.

JNW-24.1a   Kozeluch's ballet *La ritrovata figlia d'Ottone II* (1794); 2ob 2cl 2hn 2bn. One movement is recorded on Panton 11 0552 G.

JNW-27a   Mozart's opera *Die Entführung aus dem Serail* (1782), in two versions: **JNW-27.1a**: 2ob 2cl 2hn 2bn; **JNW-27.2a**: 2ob 2ca 2hn 2bn. By the end of 1782, Went had arranged three operas for the Imperial Harmonie: Gluck's *La rencontre imprévue* (**JNW-17a**), Sarti's *Fra due litiganti* (**JNW-55a**), and Mozart's *Die Entführung*. Went's arrangement came at a time when Mozart was preparing his own wind version. Mozart wrote to his father on 20 July 1782, saying "I am up to my eyes in work, for I have to arrange my opera for Harmonie by Sunday week. If I don't, someone will anticipate me and take my profits." This suggests competition for a critical performance, perhaps that advertized for 18 August in the Neue Markt concert series run by Philipp Jacob Martin. How much Mozart completed is not clear, for Went won the race. But what were the prizes? Went wanted to confirm his position as the leading arranger for Harmonie, and to establish the newly-formed Imperial Harmonie as a force in Viennese music. He needed this stability, for Joseph Adam Schwarzenberg died in 1782, when Joseph Johann Nepomuk Schwarzenberg was only 13 and when his views were less predictable. Mozart was still seeking an appointment, and his remarks on his writing of K.375 show that his approach may have been indirect (see under **WAM-5**). Mozart's views on other arrangers are clearer from his music for Don Giovanni's wind band plays (see under **WAM-2a**).

Optimists have suggested that the arrangement of *Die Entführung* (**JNW-27.1a**) is really Mozart's own arrangement. This does not survive inspection (nor a comparison with **WAM-3a**). The version with cors anglais differs from that for standard octet only in details, such as omitting a few inept bars (implying that the octet with clarinets is the original). Both versions have strengths and weaknesses. The overture is enfeebled by cuts, but the syncopated high horns in Osmin's "Ha, wie will ich triumphieren!" add real vivacity. Both versions exist in modern editions (one of **JNW-27.1a** confuses alto and basso horn parts) and both are recorded: **JNW-27.1a** by the London Wind Soloists on Decca SDD 485 and the Mannheimer Bläser-Soloisten on RBM 3057, and **JNW-27.2a** by the SDR Wind Ensemble (DGG ARC 73150), the Netherlands Wind Ensemble (Philips 650 783), and the Ensemble Philidor on Supraphon SU 3018-2 131.

JNW-28a   Mozart's opera *Le nozze di Figaro* (1786) lends itself ideally to wind arrangement, and Went exploits this. It seems possible at times that he did not have access to the score (although he played in early performances); the finale is so feeble as to be almost useless, and color is lost through the dominance of oboe and bassoon. In the Countess's aria "Dove sono" the contrast of voice and orchestral oboe gives an effect of great poignancy, and much is lost when oboe merely meets oboe in the arrangement. Yet other items are superb: the overture is a tour de force, and the sextet "Risconosci in questo amplesso" (when Figaro learns that he is the son of Marcellina and Bartolo) is very well done, even if the first oboe has to represent five characters in six bars. Went's arrangement, advertized in the *Wiener Zeitung* of 27 August 1791, was not the first arrangement of parts of *Figaro* for winds (Kajetan Vogel advertized a version **KXV-2a** for 2cl 2hn 2bn in the *Wiener Zeitung* as early as 6 June 1787), but it is extremely effective. It is recorded for 2ob 2cl 2hn 2bn by the London Wind Soloists/Brymer on Decca SDD 280 (a marvellous performance), and by the Collegium Musicum Pragense/Vajnár on Supraphon 207782-425.

JNW-29.2a Went's version with cors anglais of Mozart's *Don Giovanni* is recorded by the Ensemble Philidor on Supraphon SU 3018-2 131. Unlike Triebensee, Went did not take on the challenge of three simultaneous orchestras (the Minuet is heard briefly), but he included all of Mozart's wind music for Don Giovanni's band, and also "Protegga il giusto cielo," for which Mozart had provided a marvellous wind accompaniment.

JNW-30.1a *Così fan tutte* (2ob 2cl 2hn 2bn): recorded in part by the Maurice Bourgue Wind Ensemble on Pierre Verany PV 787033. As in *Figaro,* Went has provided only weak parts for the horns, and here bn 2 is essentially a ripieno instrument for forte sections.

JNW-31.1a *Die Zauberflöte* (2ob 2cl 2hn 2bn). Recorded in part by the Maurice Bourgue Wind Ensemble on Pierre Verany PV 787033; **JNW-31.2a**, for 2ob 2ca 2hn 2bn, is recorded by the Ensemble Philidor on CDD9701.

JNW-42a *La molinara*   Went made several arrangements of Paisiello's opera, which itself went through changes after its premiere in Naples in 1788. The 2ob 2cl 2hn 2bn version is based on the 13 November 1790 Vienna version; the 2ob 2ca 2hn 2bn and 2cl 2hn 2bn versions are different. Went is the likely arranger of the versions of Paisiello's operas for 2fl 2cl 2hn 2bn for the Russian Imperial Harmony in St Petersburg.

JNW-1ac Mozart: *Serenade in C minor,* K.388.   We believe that this transcription, which moves from the standard octet to 2ob 2ca 2hn 2bn, is by Went. It is recorded by Ensemble Philidor on CDD9701. This version follows the original closely, except in the fourth movement when the original clarinets play above the oboes. This was clearly outside the cor anglais range, so the oboes in the arrangement continue to take the melody. The work is of especial interest for the many dynamic markings not found in the original. The hn 2 part carries the date "A°: 1791. 18 Juny", so the arrangement was played during Mozart's lifetime.

WENUSCH, Stanislaus *(1810)*   Composer of a substantial body of music, mainly choral music with winds for funerals, but also some opera arrangements; also copyist. From the scoring (e.g., occasional use of the bombardon) they date from the mid-19th century. Parts for **SXW-1tv** *Leichen-Arie* carry dates of performances from 1839 to 1896, and for the *Antiphonien* **SXW-1avd** from 1845 to 1902 (with a guide to Corpus Christi weather too). Wenusch arranged pieces from operas and ballets for cl(E♭) 2cl(B♭) 2hn bn tp(prin[cipale]), the trumpet being optional, and may be the arranger of Josef Weigl's *IV Antiphonen*, whose scoring matches that of his other works for winds.

WERNER (Vernera), ( ) *(1790)*   The parts of his *Salve Regina*, made by Johann Josef Wagner, date from 1825. The instruments include solo clarinet and solo violin.

WERNER, F W *(1810)*   Associated with the Löwenstein Kapelle. His several arrangements use terz-fl (or pic[E♭]) and 2cl(E♭) for the upper instruments.

WERNER, Sven Erik *(b 1932)* **SEW-1** *Combinations* (1967-1969) is for 14 winds, perc. *Catch,* recorded by the Danish Wind Octet on Da Capo 8.22.4002, may be by him.

WERTH, Francis *(1780)*   Master of the Royal South Gloucester Band.

WERTTIG, Joseph   Composer of marches for the Royal Prussian Wind Band.

WESLEY, Samuel *24 Feb 1766, Bristol-11 Oct 1837, London*   A precocious member of a distinguished musical family whose *March in D* was finished on 24 June 1777, when the composer was 11 years old. Sainsbury prematurely noted his decease; Wesley, supposedly dead, responded alive and well in *The Times*, 11 Oct 1824.

WESTERGAARD, Svend *8 Oct 1922, Copenhagen-1988* He studied with Høffding and Petrassi; Director of the Royal Danish Conservatory 1967-1971. His wind music includes *Trasformazioni Sinfonische* for solo piano and wind orchestra (1976), an early *Octet* (1947) for winds, piano and timpani, and two *Wind Quintets*. His musical influences are Barkók and Shostakovich, as well as Sibelius and Nielsen.

WETTICH, F *(1770)* His arrangement of Cherubini's *Les deux journées* uses a quart-bn.

WHETTAM, Graham *b 7 Sept 1927, Swindon* Self-taught composer of many film scores; influenced by Bartók. His three works for wind ensemble are the *Symphonietta* **GYW-1**, the *Concerto for Ten Wind* **GYW-2** and *Fantasy for Ten Wind* **GYW-3**, all for 2fl 2ob(or ob ca) 2cl 2hn 2bn. He has also written a *Sextet* for wind quintet and piano.

WIDDER, Johann Baptist *1797-1863* The large collection of arrangements **YYW-1a** comprises manuscript scores, each separately stitched, the set held at a single shelfmark. The scores may relate to the part books of Legrand's arrangements. Very similar copies are found in other sources, suggesting Widder had substantial business.

WIDLAR, T J *(1970)* Arranger for octet of three of Mozart's string quintets (K.516, K.593, K.614) first played in 1994 by Vent's Wind Harmonie, Prague.

WIDMER, Ernst *b 25 Apr 1927, Aarau, Switzerland* Widmer studied in Zurich, but, apart from a 1954 *Wind Quintet*, his wind music dates from after his move to Brazil: the *Notturno* of 1973, and *Morfose II* of 1974.

WIDOR, Charles Marie *21 Feb 1844, Lyons-12 March 1937, Paris* Famous as organist of St Sulpice, Paris 1870-1934; composition teacher of Honegger and Milhaud.

WIEPRECHT, Wilhelm Friedrich *10 Aug 1802, Aschersleben-4 Aug 1872, Berlin* The civilian reformer of German military bands. Although a virtuoso clarinettist *(Weston/MCVP)*, he furthered the development of the tuba and the design of valves for brass instruments, a move which led to competition with Sax.

WIESER, F *(1810)* Associated with the Löwenstein Kapelle; composer and arranger of music from the operas of Auber, Bellini, and Donizetti and of dances by Labitzky.

WILBY, Philip *1949, Pontefract, UK* A professional violinist at Covent Garden, then Birmingham, now principal lecturer in composition at the University of Leeds. His works for winds have led to an annual residency at California State University, Fresno. *As I move around the Cross* **PXW-1** (1985) is a short concerto, scored for fl fl(pic) ob ca 2cl 2hn 2bn. He has completed a Mozart fragment **WAM-6f** (K.Anh94) for winds.

WILDER, Alec (Alexander Lafayette Chew) *16 Feb 1907, Rochester, New York-24 Sept 1980, Gainesville, Florida* After informal studies at the Eastman School of Music, Wilder worked as songwriter and arranger on the New York jazz scene. In the late 1930s, his works for winds and harpsichord experimented with extended jazz forms. His music for winds usually carries titles, such as *Entertainment* (**AZW-1**), *Walking home in Spring* (**AZW-3**) and *A debutante's diary* (**AZW-4.2**). The *5 Vocalise* **AZW-1v** of 1971 are for soprano with wind ensemble. **AZW-2v**, for narrator and SSAA chorus, bears the title "Childrens' Plea for Peace." The libretto is "by the children of Avon (England)."

WILLIAMSON, Thomas George *(1770)* The *Six Grand Troops*, in piano score, are for identified regiments, some in India: (1) H.M. 61st Regiment; (2) H.M. 81st Regiment; (3) Bengal Artillery; (4) 1st Regiment of Bengal European Infantry; (5) 2[n]d Regiment of Bengal European Infantry; (6) H.M. 91st Highland Regiment. The headtitles contain the notice "NB. This set of Six Troops are [sic] so arranged that Masters may easily form the parts for their Full Bands," and occasional cues for fl, cl hn are given.

WILLY, Jean (Johannes) *(1730)* Associated with the early phase of the Harmonie at Kroměříž. The titles of **JZW-1(-5)** all involve the word Barthia [sic]. **JZW-6** is entitled *Parthia à la Parade*.

WIND, Blasius (pseudonym) *See: MENTNER, Karl*

WINEBERGER, Paul Anton *7 Oct 1758, Mergentheim am Tauber-8 Feb 1821, Hamburg*
Wineberger studied theology and music at the universities of Würzburg and Heidelberg.
After graduation, he took the post of teacher and organist at the Jesuit church,
Mannheim. In Mannheim he studied music theory with Vogler (qv), composition with
Holzbauer (qv), violin with Tearth, and violin, then cello, with Fränzel (qv). In the fall
of 1780 he moved to Wallerstein as cellist, subsequently succeeding Rosetti (qv) as
Master of the Hofkapelle wind ensemble. Wineberger suffered from poor health, but
remained at Oettingen-Wallerstein even after its heyday. He moved to Hamburg c.1798,
becoming a successful music teacher. Most of Wineberger's wind works date from the
1780s. There are several larger works, and **PAW-3** of 1788 and **PAW-13** of 1794 are
associated with the Prince's birthday. Some, like **PAW-5** have complex structures within
movements, several bearing a title such as *Capricioso* [sic]. Others (**PAW-3, 10, 21**) are
on the lines of old-style suites. Still others have unusual titles of movements: "Menuet
Fresco" in **PAW-3, -12,** and "Capriccio" for the finales of **PAW-5, -6, 15, 21. PAW-6,**
Parthia en Chasse, has sections for 4hn which imitate traditional hunting calls. Another
large work, **PAW-10,** has the instruction *volti* at the end of several movements. In this
work, horn 3 is tacet for 6 of the 10 movements. We suspect that the autograph
manuscript score of **PAW-9** was taken to Ludwigslust by Rosetti (perhaps without
permission, given Rosetti's attempts to poach musicians from Wallerstein).

WINKLER, Johann (Jan) *18 Nov 1794, Vsetín-4 Jan 1874, Návsí u Jablunkova*
Composer of two large (14 and 19 movements) untitled suites for 2cl 2hn bn, plus
funeral music with winds (e.g., 2hn or 3tb). Probably Martin Winkler was his brother.

WINTER, Peter von *bapt 28 Aug 1754, Mannheim-17 Oct 1825, Munich* Though first
a violinist, Winter was from 1776 musical director of the Court Theater at Mannheim.
When the court moved to Munich, Winter followed, becoming Kapellmeister in 1798, a
post he held until his death. He had disagreements with his deputy, Danzi. Winter's
operas had a simple tunefulness which led to many arrangements. He made wind band
versions (now lost) of music by Reid (qv). Many of Winter's religious works for the court
are known only from the Hofkapelle's contemporary thematic catalog. Those surviving
(*Veni Sancte Spiritus;* a *Hymne: O könnt ich dich*; the *Chorale: Nun danket alle Gott*)
are often scored for SATB 2fl 2cl 2hn 2bn org. Only No 2 of the *[9] Responsioni pro
defunctis* was thought to survive; the entire set from the Hofkapelle archives is now
in A-Wn. The core band is the same, but 2vc are added, and in No 9 another 2hn.

His *Partita in Bb* **PVW-3** is in three movements, the second a set of variations.
Breitkopf & Härtel advertized it in the January 1805 *AMZ*, but no such edition is
known; perhaps they were acting as German agents for the Viennese Bureau d'Arts et
d'Industrie edition.

PVW-5 *Parthia in Dis (Eb)* The PL-LA copy is inscribed "Eisenstadt den 11 Maj 1803."
The Kinský Harmonie copy (CZ-Pnm) has an extra movement, an Echo: Adagio, with
the horns and bn II as echo; this may not be authentic.

WITT, Friedrich *8 Nov 1770, Nieder Hallenstetten, Württemberg-3 Jan 1836, Würzburg*
Witt's first work for winds, **FZW-1,** is dated 10 March 1790, about the time he was
associated with Oettingen-Wallerstein as a violinist. He became Kapellmeister at
Würzburg in 1802, an appointment which was probably the result of a successful
performance there of one of his oratorios. Perhaps Witt is best known as the composer
of the *Jena Symphony* once attributed to Beethoven (1). The parthias are conventional
four-movement works; several movements use the title Romance (**FZW-1.ii, FZW-3.i,**
ii and **FZW-5.iii**) and three (**FZW-1, -3, -4**) contain a "Menuetto fresco," a description
also used by Wineberger (**PAW-3** of 1788 and **PAW-13** of 1793). His *Pièces d'harmonie*
(Schott c.1826/27) is dedicated to Prince Carl Friedrich von Löwenstein (qv), for whom

he composed and arranged a number of works for winds.

1. H C Robbins Landon 1957 Mus Rev **18** 109.

WITTEK, Adolf *(1820)*   Active in Břetislav, near Plzeň, c.1850.

WITTLINGER, H *(1800)*   Composer of an *Advent Lied* for CCB 2cl 2hn 2bn; the MS parts by the Loritz schoolteacher are dated 5 September 1837.

WITWAR, ( ) *(1740)*   His *3 Parthien* for 2cl 2hn 2bn are in the Nová Říše archive.

WOELFING, ( ) *(1810)*   Probably a member of the Hohenlohe Harmonie at Schlawentzitz, Silesia, who arranged works by Lanner, Strauss (the Elder) and Pixis.

WOELFL (WÖLFL), Joseph *24 Dec 1773, Salzburg-21 May 1812, London*   A pupil of both Leopold Mozart and Michael Haydn, Woelfl was highly regarded as a pianist. After touring Europe extensively, he settled in London, where he published a number of pleasing works for the piano. His *Sonata Nro I* in D **JSW-7** (2ob 2hn 2bn) is the only surviving number of a set of 6 "Sonate. Dedicate al signore Blasio Rauschgat in Hallem," dated 1800, and has been recorded (with added db) by the Consortium Classicum on Koch Schwann 310002. Another set of *6 Sonatas, Oeuv III,* is in A-Sca.

WOLF, Cyrill *9 Mar 1825, Müglitz-21 Oct 1915, Vienna* Organist of St Leopold, Vienna.

WOLF (Wolff), Franz Xaver *(1760)*   Wolf was a clarinettist in the Royal Prussian Hohelohe Regiment, 1797.

WOLF, Hugo *13 Mar 1860, Windischgraz, Styria-22 Feb 1903, Vienna* Wolf's songs are among the great works of their genre. He scored his Mörike setting *Auf ein altes Bild* for soprano 2ob 2cl 2bn in 1889, when he was at the height of his creativity.

WOLLE, Peter *1792-1871* Presumably related to Jacob Wolle (1789-1863), bassoonist of the Moravian wind band in Bethlehem, Pennsylvania.

WOOLFENDEN, Guy Anthony *b 12 July 1937, Ipswich, UK*   Since 1962, when he became associated with the Royal Shakespeare Company, Stratford, England, Woolfenden, now Head of Music, has written incidental music for all of the Shakespeare plays, some several times (1). Some of this music is recorded by the Royal Shakespeare Wind Band on Abbey LPB 657. The scoring is usually single woodwinds with 2hn 2tp tb perc. Exceptions are the music for *All's well that ends well* (2ob 2hn 2bn 2perc) and the excellent *Suite Française* (commissioned in 1991) for 2fl 2ob 2bn 2hn. This, with other music of his for wind band is recorded by the Royal Northern College of Music Wind Orchestra, conducted by the composer, on Doyen DOYCD042.

1. For a full list, see the 5-volume reference Bryan N S Gooch and David Thatcher 1991 *A Shakespeare Music Catalogue;* Oxford: Oxford University Press.

WOOLRICH, John *b 3 Jan 1954, Cirencester, UK* His *Vaucanson's Machine,* a Northern Sinfonia commission first broadcast in 1988, is scored for fl(a-fl) ob ca 2cl(E♭) 2hn 2bn. *Quick Steps* (1990) is for 2ob cl(E♭) cl (B♭) 2hn 2bn.

WORGAN, James (John), the younger *(1770), London*   Son of John Worgan (1724-1790), composer and organist, and nephew of James Worgan (1715-1753), organist. Both elder Worgans were associated with Vauxhall Gardens. The younger Worgan wrote a march for the Loyal Essex Regiment of Fencible Infantry. A brother, Thomas Danvers Worgan, wrote a musical game (see also under Koehler) with cards in 1807.

WRANIZKY (Vranický, Wraniczky, Wranitzky), Anton (Antonín) *13 June 1761, Nová Říše-6 Aug 1820, Vienna*   Composer and violinist, Anton was the brother of Paul Wranizky, who taught him the violin. Anton moved to Vienna where, before 1783, he was employed as a choirmaster. This ended with Joseph II's reforms and abolition of church music. While in Vienna, Wranizky studied with Haydn, Mozart and Albrechtsberger (qv). In 1794, he entered the service of Joseph Franz Maximilian, Prince Lobkowitz, as leader of the Schlosskapelle at Roudnice (*Weinmann*, kk Hoftheater-Musik-Verlag volume). From 1797, he became Master of Music, serving in Vienna and Prague as well as the Lobkowitz country residences at Roudnice and Bílina.

When Prince Lobkowitz took charge of the Vienna court theaters in 1806, Wranizky became Kapellmeister of the Hoftheater. His daughter, Caroline, was the first Agathe in Weber's *Der Freischütz*. Wranizky's marches are interesting and varied, clearly composed with care. The Lobkovic collection includes two further works for winds and voices: one, dated 4 September 1803, is for the Prince's birthday; the other (Eisenberg, 7 September 1808), is a march for the 1st Bataillon, the *Volkslied "Brüder auf!, uns jedem Stande."* He also wrote a trio for 2ob ca.

AYW-1 *Grosser Quadrille Musik zum Karossel [sic]*   The Carrousel was an event in which horsemen tilted at targets (see also Beethoven, **LVB–2m;** at the 1814 Carrousel for the Congress of Vienna, which took place in the Spanish Riding School, the targets were turbaned heads representing Turks (1). Could this large work (18 movements, and apparently two wind bands) have been for this event? The movement titles are often illegible, but include: 1 Marsch Erste Harmonie/Trio Zweyte Harmonie; 2 Marsch; 3 Allegro; 4 La Tarare [= Salieri: *Tarare*] Nro 4 Türkisch Musik; 5 Inslspiel [= J Weigl: *Die isthmischen Spiele*]; 14 La Zingara; 15 Inspiel [cf. No 5]; 17 [in another hand] del Sig Antonio Castellieri. There is a title "Contradanz", but no music, between Nos 17, 18.

AYW-2 *IIda Harmonie zum Karossel*   Another large work for two wind bands, again one which would have been appropriate for the Carrousel at the Congress of Vienna. Movements 1-4 and 7-11 are marches; movements 5 and 12 comprise Erster Harmonie Marsch[,] Zweyter Harmonie Trio[,] Marcia Da Capo erster Harmonie. A further 24 movements, Karossel Nro 1, are: 1-5 Allegro; 6 Allegretto; 7-10 Allegro; 11 Allegro assai; 17-19 Allegro; 20-22 Allegro assai; 23 All'ungarese; 24 Alla Francese Allegro.

AYW-3 *Musique de Grand Carouss.* [sic]   A 15-movement work in the Festetics archive, Keszthely, scored for octet with ad lib trumpet.

AYW-4 *Parthia in F*   Recorded on Supraphon SUA 1 11 0614.

AYW-1.1m(-1.6m) *VI kleine Märsche* (B♭, E♭, C, D, E♭, D minor), of which four (1, 2, 5, 6) are recorded by the Netherlands Wind Ensemble on Philips 6599172.

AYW-2.1m(-2.3m) *3 Marches in the French Style ("auf französischer Art")* (C, F, C). These marches show no obvious French features; they are recorded on Supraphon SUA 111 1839 and Supraphon CD2060 and the Netherlands Wind Ensemble on Philips 6599172.

AYW-3.1m, 3.2m Two hunting marches (*Jäger-Märsche*), the first in the French style, the second with a solo trumpet ("Solo der Prinzipaltrompete").

AYW-4.1m(4.4m) *Four hunting marches* B♭ F B♭ B♭ are scored for 2ob 2hn 2bn in 1,4 and for 2cl 2hn 2bn in 2,3; a second copy of No 3 exists for 2ob 2hn 2bn. There are no special hunting features. Do the scorings imply that the oboists played clarinet too?

1.The event is shown in National Geographic Magazine 1958 **114** 406-7.

WRANIZKY (Vranický, Wraniczky, Wranizky), Paul (Pavel) *30 Dec 1756, Nová Říše, Moravia-26 Sept 1808, Vienna*   Composer and violinist, Wranizky was also a conductor, widely respected and chosen to direct such major premieres as those of Haydn's *Creation* and Beethoven's *1st Symphony*. He studied at Olomouc, then moved to the theological seminary in Vienna in 1776-1777, studying there with J M Kraus. In 1783, Wranizky joined the establishment of Count János Nepomuk Esterházy; he visited Haydn at Eszterháza (but was not, as has been stated, a member of Haydn's orchestra there). In 1790 he became orchestral director of the Kärntnertortheater and the Burgtheater; he was leader of the Court Opera orchestra from 1785 until his death. Wranizky was obviously regarded highly as a person. As secretary of the Tonkünstler-Societät from 1793, he resolved Haydn's quarrels with it (1); he was also a member of the Masonic lodge "Crowned Hope" to which Mozart belonged (2).

Wranizky's music, while both imaginative and competent, does not always live up to expectations; only on rare occasions are there signs of passion, as in his symphony celebrating the French Revolution. His most famous opera, *Oberon*, is attractive, but most of the drama comes between the numbers, not in them. Nonetheless, he was an ingenious composer, and includes in his output a "Hello and Farewell" Symphony (*"Quodlibet" Symphony* [3] dating from 1798). The musicians enter one by one (ambling or hurrying, as instructed), and play warm-up passages until the leader arrives; they tune up (as scored), and start the main music. At the end the musicians leave, one by one, the leader to end alone. The "Quodlibet" of the title indicates extended arrangements of music then popular. These include passages from Mozart and several sections for winds alone, notably No 7, where a quartet from Salieri's *Palmira* (1795) is taken over by two clarinets and two horns (4); the following number, from Weigl's *L'amor marinaro*, begins for 2cl 2hn 2bn, adding strings only in the middle.

PYW-1 *La Chasse, Op 44*   A piano concerto with accompaniment for winds and timpani, comprising a slow introduction and a fast movement. In 1895, Ernst Pauer (5) recommended it as of special interest, remarkable at a time when even Mozart's wind works were unknown or undervalued (surprisingly, Pauer's copy does not seem to survive). It is recorded on Supraphon SUA 1111 1854 H.

PYW-2 *Partita in F*   Published by Simrock in 1802 as by Haydn (Hob II:F7, **FJH-11d**); it is not certain which Wranizky wrote this octet, but Paul seems the more likely; indeed, one might ask whether Wranizky might have written some of the other so-called Haydn divertimentos too (not that with the Choral St Antoni). The work is recorded twice by Klöcker's Consortium Classicum, as Haydn (Telefunken 6.35473) and as Wranizky (Telefunken 6.35334). The D-DO copy has an extra final March. The perceptive writer Tovey remarked (6) "Slight as this octet is, it shows that by the time Haydn wrote it, he could die in peace, if the handling of wind instruments were his only anxiety." Tovey noted both the influence of Mozart and also the absence of the flute "which, as Mozart realized, stands in relation to the rest of the wind as water colour to oil paint." Tovey then pointed to some of the ingenuities in the writing: the choice of oboe and bassoon tessitura, the G minor variation for horn, and the use of the theme in the bass for unison bassoons. In Tovey's case, the wrong attribution to Haydn on the title page meant there was no prejudgment; he needed only Haydn's name to attract his attention, for he was a formidable supporter of lesser-known composers.

1. *HCRL/3.*
2. H C Robbins Landon 1982 *Mozart and the Freemasons;* London: Thames and Hudson.
3. Jan La Rue 1956 Music and Letters **37** 250.
4. Salieri used the same music in his *Armonia* **AXS-1**, there for 2cl 2bn.
5. E Pauer 1895 *The Pianist's Dictionary;* London: Novello.
6. D F Tovey, in *Essays and Lectures on Music* Oxford: Oxford University Press 1949).

WRIGHT, Thomas *18 Sept 1763, Stockton-on-Tees-24 Nov 1829, Barnard Castle* Wright invented a form of metronome and was an early user (c.1795) of the device. He wrote marches for militia in the north east of England: the Volunteer Corps of Newcastle upon Tyne, the The East York Militia, and the First Battalion of West York Militia. Wright was apprenticed as organist to Thomas Ebdon (qv) at Durham Cathedral.

WUORINEN, Charles *b 9 June 1938, New York* Wuorinen's works with winds all involve a soloist: double bass, tuba, violin. The *Chamber Concerto* for tuba, 12 winds and 12 drums is recorded on CRI SD 491. His later music employs a flexible serialism.

WYVILL (Wivill), Zerubbabel *1762 or 1763, Maidenhead-14 May 1837, Hounslow* Singing master at Bray, organist at the Chapel of St Mary Magdelene and Andrew, Maidenhead, later living at Inwood House, Hounslow. His *Berkshire March* was "Composed for the Berkshire Militia at the Desire of the Right Honble. The Earl of Radnor."

YOST, Michel (also pseudonym: J Michel) *1754, Paris-5 July 1786, Paris*   An outstanding French clarinet player, and a popular soloist at the Concerts Spirituels

(Weston/MCVP). His works are generally published under the name "Michel (J)." Several of his works were written in collaboration with J C Vogel, which may explain the claim in *Sainsbury* that all of Yost's works were actually by Vogel.

ZACH, G[eorg] *(1740)*   His *Parthia's* final movement is a Fugue, rare in wind music.
ZAIDEL-RUDOLPH, Jeanne *b 9 July 1948, Pretoria*   **JXZ-1** *Kaleidescope* is recorded on EMCJ 4661831-4.
ZALUZAN (Valuzau), Johann *(1790)*   Active in the last years of the Kroměříž Harmonie.
ZAMEČNÍK, Evžen *b 5 Feb 1939, Frýdek-Místek*   **EXZ-1** is a *Concerto grosso* for small wind ensemble and symphony orchestra.
ZAPF, Johann Nepomuk *(2? 21?) Feb 1760, Mondsee, upper Austria-after 1820*   A pianist based in Graz who published in Vienna c.1800.
ZASCHE (Czasche), Anton (Antonÿ) *(1770)*   Parts of four of his *Parthias* copied by Dominik Hübner are in the Langenbruck archive; there also are his arrangements of Pleyel (two movements from the *Quartet* B.354) and of a *Parthia* by V V Mašek.
ZECH, Markus *1727-1770*   Four of his religious settings with winds are at Einsiedeln.
ZEHM, Friedrich *b 22 Jan 1923, Neusalz am Oder, Silesia*   The conductor does more than conduct in **FXZ-1** *Konzertstück: Schwierigkeiten und Unfälle mit einem Choral: Sonatine für einen Dirigenten und 10 Bläser* (Difficulties and mishaps with a chorale: Sonatina for conductor and 10 wind instruments), 1974. The wind players (2fl 2ob 2cl 2hn 2bn) double on these instruments: fl 1, alarm whistle; fl 2, piccolo and ratchet; ob 1, siren whistle; ob 2, click frog; cl 1, cl(Eb) and bird-pipe; cl 2, hooter; hn 1, cuckoo; hn 2, rattle; bn 2, cbn. The conductor also plays triangle, slapstick and toy trumpet.
ZELINKA, Jan Evangelista *13 Jan 1893, Prague-30 June 1969, Prague*   Czech composer, whose father (1856-1935, of the same name) was well known as church musician and composer. Zelinka (son) wrote much for stage and church, showing an attractive freshness and inventiveness.
ZELLNER, Leopold Alexander *23 Sept 1823, Zagreb-24 Nov 1894, Vienna*   Harmonium virtuoso who completed Beethoven's *Quintet* for oboe, 3 horns and bassoon. He was Professor at the Vienna Conservatorium from 1868, and was the author of a method for the harmonium. He is listed in Hadow's book on Haydn as a Croatian composer.
ZIFRA, Antonio *(1790)*   Composer of works for winds and organ, including two long, single-movement, *Suonatas,* all in I-Vsmc.
ZIHA, ( ) *(1730)*   The Clam Gallas collection includes five early *Parthien* by Ziha.
ZILLMAN, Eduard *1834-after 1909*   Zillman was associated with the Lippe Kapelle, Detmold; presumably it was for it that he arranged twelve anonymous waltzes.
ZIMMERMANN, Anton *1741, Pressburg (Bratislava)-16 Oct 1781, Pressburg*   From 1776, Kapellmeister to Archbishop Batthyáni. Two of his symphonies were attributed to Haydn, which suggests that his music is due for revival. Most of his music for winds survives in the archive of the Augustinian monastery at Brno.
ZIMMERMANN, Bernd Alois *20 Mar 1918, Bliesheim, Cologne-10 Aug 1970, Grosskönigsdorf*   His *Musique pour les soupers de Roi Ubu. Ballet noir* (1966) refers to Alfred Jarry's *Ubu Roi* (1888 and 1896); Jarry's text also specifies a wind orchestra.
ZINEK, ( ) Baron *(1760?)*   Composer of *Marsch mit einen Kriegslied für Oestreichs [sic] Landwehr,* presumably for the wars of 1796-1797. This work was also arranged by Krechler (qv) as Nos 3, 4 of his *Harmonie Lib: II,* **FFK-4a.**
ZINGARELLI, Niccolò Antonio *4 Apr 1752, Naples-5 May 1837 Torre del Greco, near Naples*   Zingarelli was a successful and fluent composer of opera and church music. He travelled widely, but much of his work is associated with Milan. Apart from two marches (possibly arrangements) he wrote an untitled movement for 2fl 2cl 2bn.

ZONCADA, Giovanni *(1760)* A horn player in London in the 1790s. His **GXZ-1** *Partita* in F for solo ob 2cl 2hn 2bn makes use of muted horns.

ZOPFF, Hermann *1 June 1826, Glogau, Silesia-12 July 1883, Leipzig* The only known score and parts of his *Serenade* Op 35 (2fl ob 2cl 2hn bn) were at one time in the possession of the late John Parr, of Sheffield. His ensemble played the *Serenade* at least once. We would appreciate any further information.

ZULEHNER, Georg Carl *20 July 1770, Mainz-27 Dec 1841, Munich* Arranger for winds of Mozart's *(Eine kleine) Freimaurercantate*, K.623. This Masonic cantata was performed on 28 December 1817 to celebrate the birthday of Prince Carl von Hessen, Grand Master of the Freunden in Or Lodge in Mainz.

ZWECKSTETTER, Christoph *1772-1836* His *Salve Regina*, c.1810, is from the church of St Jakob, Wasserburg am Inn.

ZWINGMANN, Johann (John) Nicolaus *28 Dec 1764, Stottenheim-after 16 Sept 1807, London* Trombonist, active in London in the 3rd Regiment of Guards. His arrangement c.1805 of airs and a march from Steibelt's *La belle Laitière* was one of the first such suites published in the United Kingdom. His application to join the Royal Society of Musicians was supported by Caspar Flack (qv) of the 1st Regiment of Guards.

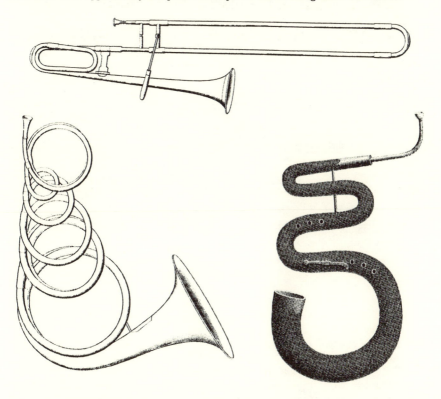

Figure. Wind instruments, as shown in the original steel engravings in Abraham Rees 1806-1820 *The Cyclopaedia; or, Universal Dictionary of Arts, Sciences and Literature;* London: Longman, Hurst, Rees and Orme. A montage from originals in the possession of Marshall Stoneham; the caption labels the instruments as French Horn; Serpent; Sacbut [sic] or Trombone. The trombone would be similar to that used by Zwingmann.

Figure.   The opening bars of the Clarinet 1 parts of two early 19th century arrangements of Mozart's *Gran Partita* K.361 (from originals in the possession of Marshall Stoneham). The upper version is from the Simrock edition pn 994 (*Grande Serenade* on the title page, *Serenata* on the part, c.1813, possibly arranged by Goepfert); the lower version is from the Breitkopf & Härtel edition (Liv I of *Pièces d'Harmonie*, c.1801, pn 61). Note the Breitkopf & Härtel version omits the introductory Largo. Both versions write an appogiatura in the second bar of the Allegro molto, not an acciaccatura. Note the slight differences of dynamics and phrasing. The manuscript additions on the Simrock copy look as if they were made in the 19th century; generally, they bring the arrangement closer into line with Mozart's original.

Part 3

INSTRUMENTS AND PERFORMANCE PRACTICE

Development of Wind Instruments

When Locke celebrated the Restoration of the British Monarchy in 1661, it was with cornetts and sackbuts (1). Trumpets and timpani augmented oboes, horns and bassoons in Handel's 1749 celebration of the Peace of Aix-la-Chapelle. Only in the second half of the 18th century did a standard wind groups emerge (2-9), based on pairs of oboes, clarinets, horns and bassoons. These instruments were also innovations: oboe, bassoon and horn were all more recent than the saxophone is today, and the clarinet was as new then as synthesizers are now. The instruments evolved rapidly alongside major changes in music. Since a player could be composer and instrument improver too, it is important to understand the instruments of the time, their technical limitations and, though this is harder, some notion of the sorts of sounds that they made (10).

Most wind harmony is based on pairs of instruments: a soprano pair (flutes, oboes or clarinets), a tenor pair (horns) and a bass pair (bassoons). Probably the commonest form was the sextet of 2cl 2hn 2bn; perhaps the best-known is the octet, 2ob 2cl 2hn 2bn. In 1799 Anton Stadler (11), replying to a question from the Hungarian Count Festetics about scoring, observed "the so-called wind harmony or table music, usually consisting of 8 instruments, to wit 2 oboes, 2 clarinets, 2 horns and 2 bassoons, also belongs in this category [chamber music] because most pieces for wind are composed in this manner." The soprano instruments varied with time (clarinets replaced oboes in sextets) and from country to country (pairs of flutes were more the choice in Russia and France). At times, there would be just one bassoon, or even two bassoons plus contrabassoon. Nevertheless, the standard format was firmly based on wind instruments employed in pairs, like the orchestral wind section of the time.

Taken together, modern wind instruments span about five octaves. In rare cases, instruments may be fitted with extra keys to extend their range downwards, such as flutes with a low B or bassoons with a low A. Ranges varied with period, and players, writers and composers can differ on what were effective working compasses, especially the highest notes. The use of pairs of wind instruments affects the music in several ways. The homogeneous sound gives a firm, rich effect, hard to achieve with the very individual sounds of single instruments. The mix of woodwinds and horns offered composers more flexibility than the Renaissance and Baroque choirs of instruments, or the later clarinet, saxophone and double-reed choirs. Many composers exploited the special sound of wind bands in operas and orchestral works. However, one major problem with pairs of instruments was that composers were restricted in the keys available, especially with early forms of clarinet or horn. With only one horn or one clarinet, the pull to a single easy key is not hard to avoid, and key contrasts can be made without problems. The pull becomes almost overwhelming with pairs of instruments, which is why so many serenades in E♭ remain in that key unremittingly.

Our convention defining the key of an instrument (e.g., clarinet in D) will be this: If a player, seeing a written C, and without any mental transposition, correctly produces a sounding D (or B♭, and so on), then the instrument is in D (or B♭, and so on). There are other conventions (especially for flutes), but ours is common and logical. Where possible, we give examples from wind harmony of instruments in different keys.

Double-Reed Instruments 1: The Oboe

Both oboe (12) and bassoon were developed by the musicians of Louis XIV's Grand Écurie du Roi in the late 17th century. Both these double-reed instruments have changed significantly since then. The oboe has changed in mechanism as well as in type of reed used: the original wider reed made it easier to use the extreme upper and lower registers, though the narrower modern reed permits wider dynamics in the middle range. Some early oboe parts in marches show how much power was expected in the lower register, presumably at the sacrifice of the upper notes. The tone of the early oboes could be much fuller and far more pungent; Mozart remarked that one player had "such boldness of tone that no other instrument can contend with it." Viennese players still favor instruments closer than usual to this older type, and the distinctive sound suits Haydn's early wind works particularly well (13). Mechanical developments of modern keywork involve the use of extra tone holes, with further keys to bring them under the control of the fingers. Other changes include ring keys: when a player's finger covers a hole, a key closes another distant hole; this improves intonation, and also allows alternative fingerings to make awkward passages easier. These various changes forced players to hold the instrument with their left hand closer to the reed; both possible hand positions are illustrated in early pictures.

Several double-reed instruments extend the range of the oboe to lower registers: the *taille* (a term formerly used for any tenor instrument, not just those of the oboe family), *oboe da caccia* and *oboe d'amore*. Haydn used the cor anglais in the 1760s, Mozart wrote for it in Milan in the 1770s, Went and Fiala used it in the 1780s and 1790s and, as the final stage of respectability, Catel introduced it into the Paris Opéra in 1808. The standard oboe is the *oboe in C*. The *oboe d'amore in A* was largely obsolete when wind harmony was established; a rare example is in Albinoni's *Concerto à Cinque*. Instruments in F include the *taille*, as in Asplmayr's *Parthien*, the *Quintet* **FAR-22** by Rosetti, J C Bach's *Orione*, or Fiala's *Partitas*, **JSF-22, 23**, the *oboe da caccia* common in J S Bach's cantatas, and the *cor anglais* found in much music by Went, Mozart's *Divertimentos* K.166, K.186, Haydn's *Feld-Parthie* Hob II.16 and Fiala's *Partita* **JSF-11**. The *basset oboe* was used to accompany chorales in Calvinist regions of Switzerland. We do not know of any use of Brod's *baritone oboe* in wind music.

Many oboists wrote music for winds. These include (by date of birth) Paisible, Besozzi, Bode, J C Fischer, Went, Fiala, Oliver, Grenser, Schwegler, Krommer, Guenther, C Bochsa, Lang, Feldmayr, Triebensee, Heuschkel, Vogt, Sellner, R C N Bochsa, Hanschke, Chandler, and Gipps.

Double-Reed Instruments 2: The Bassoon

Although a double-reed instrument, the bassoon (14, 15) is only distantly related to the oboe, having developed from the dulcian family rather than the shawms. Its long tube is folded back on itself and has a gently expanding conical bore. Many of the tone holes are drilled at an angle into the thick wood making up the bulk of the instrument, a compromise between acoustical accuracy and comfort of fingering. One result of its construction is that the pitch of many notes varies more from instrument to instrument than on other woodwinds, a phenomenon leading bassoonists to develop individual alternative fingerings for many notes. Early players using simple instruments could often choose whether to rest the bassoon against the left or the right side; this freedom disappeared as key mechanisms improved. Two main types of bassoon exist today: of these, the French or "Buffet" model is closer to the original form than the German instrument. Despite (because of?) its technical problems, the French model is often said to have greater sensitivity in the hands of the best players than the now more common German model (known as the "Heckel system"). As variations between individual bassoons are so great, the question of French or German superiority is questionable. It still remains controversial: Barenboim's insistence that the Paris Opéra bassoonists change from their Buffets led to an uproar as recently as 1989. Some early bassoons, like early oboes, must have had considerable power, for composers did not hesitate to give them important solos above a full accompaniment. One of the most noticeable changes has been the reduction in the size and length of the reed, with a smaller reed giving more control of intonation at the sacrifice of volume.

While the predecessors of the bassoon, like dulcians and Pommers, made up a family of different-sized instruments, most had disappeared from the orchestra by the mid-18th century, with the exception of the *tenoroon* and *contrabassoon*. Little was written for the tenoroon, pitched a fifth higher than the ordinary bassoon and regarded as an alternative to the cor anglais. Outside Paris, acceptance of the cor anglais was slow, especially in centers like Bordeaux (16). When two cors anglais were indicated, often one oboist would transpose the top part and a bassoonist play the other on tenoroon ("basson en fa"). Higher-pitched bassoons tend to lose their characteristic timbre, and so are of less value in a wind band. Fortunately, there is little use of the cor anglais in French wind harmony, so the issue of the authentic tenoroon rarely arises. Yet there is an exception in the 18th-century manuscript at Zwickau (17) of J G M Trost's *Parthia No IV* for 2 Corni in C, 2 fagotti-octavo, 2 fagotti-quarto, 2 fagotti. The concert pitch ranges of the parts are: fagotto-octavo 1: g to f"; 2: e♭ to c"; fagotto-quarto 1: c to c"; 2: G to g'; fagotti 1 and 2: C to g'. Confusingly, some quart-fagott parts are for an alto instrument (e.g., Trost; Heuschkel's 1823 arrangement of Rossini's *Semiramide* includes a movement for bassoons "en Fa," a sixth higher) and others for a bass instrument, closer to a contrabassoon (e.g., Keil, Kopprasch).

It is often unclear (18) whether two bassoons should play when only one part is given, or when there should be no bassoon parts at all (as for Haydn's **FJH-11**). Title pages do not always help: the parts may divide when "fagotto" is named, and there may be just a single part, without divisi passages, when "fagotti" are indicated. Certainly the "single" bassoon parts sometimes divide in J C Bach's *Wind Symphonies* and the *Military Concertos* published by Bremner (**A-67m**). This can happen in larger works, such as Rosetti's **FAR-1**. Yet illustrations show bands with two clarinets or oboes and two horns but no bassoons at all (19); one shows such a small band at Marienberg on the Main in 1790. Some bassoonists might have been expected to read from another part, such as the organ part or a choir part in church music. Occasionally, military music c.1815 lacks separate bassoon parts (e.g., the marches by F Gebauer and J Frey), although there are signs that the bassonists played from the serpent part. Subjective judgments are hard to avoid in deciding how many bassoonists are needed in modern performances.

Bassoonists who wrote music for winds include Besozzi, Eichner, Stumpf, G Schmitt, Braun, Almenraeder, Elgar, W S Elliott, Weait, Gillaspie, Blomhert, Sheen, Goddard.

The Contrabassoon

The contrabassoon, sounding an octave below the bassoon, became valued as bands expanded. It both provided the firm bass line needed for outdoor performance and freed the second bassoon for more paired work with the first bassoon. Again, there are complications. We have examined several hundred manuscripts of original works and arrangements for "octet," as stated on the title page, and have been surprised to find how many contain unannounced divisi in the bn II part. The reverse can happen as well: Viennese publishers reissued Went's arrangements posthumously and anonymously with a "Fagotto Secondo et Contra" part lacking even a single divisi.

The contrabassoon's use was restricted to certain geographical areas until the mid-19th century. The first recorded use in England was announced in the *London Daily Post and General Advertiser* of 6 August 1739, when two "Double Bassoons by Thomas Stanesby the Younger" were demonstrated at a Marylebone Pleasure Gardens concert. Double bassoons also figured in Handel's *L'Allegro* (1740) and *Fireworks Music* (1749), and in the 1784 Handel Commemorations in Westminster Abbey. Contemporary accounts doubted its effect: "At these musical performances Mr Ashley, a sub-director, and first bassoon at Covent Garden Theatre, played for the first time on a newly-invented instrument, called a double bassoon, an appropriate appellation, it being double the size of the common ones. This instrument, which rested on a stand, had a sort of flue affixed to the top of it, similar (with the exception of smoke) to that of a Richmond steamboat. I am ignorant, however, whether it produced any tone, or whether it was placed in the orchestra to terminate the prospect" (20). On the Continent, Mozart's *Masonic Funeral Music* K.477 (1785) and Haydn's music in Vienna in the 1790s exploit the contrabassoon, and Krommer's *Parthias,* composed soon afterwards, make uninhibited use of it. French and German wind bands favored the serpent or ophicleide. Italian bands moved later to wide-bore double-reed instruments (Contrabasso ad ancia), including the larger Rothophones made by Ferdinando Roth (1815-1898) of Milan.

Alternatives to the Contrabassoon

The contrabassoon presents problems of authenticity in wind harmony: early instruments were rare, and string basses common. String basses, usually the violone, are "honorary members" of wind bands, explicit in works from Mozart (K.361) and Rosetti to Dvořák and Stravinsky. Parts for the Wallerstein, Löwenstein and the Thurn und Taxis ensembles include frequent instructions to switch betwwen arco and pizzicato; Florent Schmitt even wrote for Bb string bass in *Selamlik.* Illustrations often show string basses in wind bands; one famous example (21) may show Rosetti playing what seems to be a violone (the bass member of the viol family, rather than the double bass of the violin family). The characteristic underhand bowing is shown too, which gives a strong staccato and clean tone, but less flexibility (22 plate 191). The bass part is often more than reinforcement: Mozart, Rosetti and Dvořák provide independent parts. Yet string basses might be expected even when no explicit part exists. Anton Stadler (11) wrote "the contrabassoon (or the double bass), however, which plays nothing but the fundamental or thorough bass is very effective ... it not only reinforces and completes, but also relieves and assists the wind players. If it is used throughout a piece as in the large scale compositions of Haydn and some other great composers, it can be employed as opportune in suitably adapted solo passages and also as a reinforcement in the main tutti with good effect." This makes sense out-of-doors or for large ensembles; otherwise, discreet playing is relatively harmless. It is *extremely rare* for a string bass to be specified for sextets or smaller groups, since the sound is usually bottom heavy.

One can compare the effects in the fine recordings of Haydn's wind works with a string bass by the Consortium Classicum and without by the London Wind Soloists (23).

The *serpent* supplied the bass in many church bands, moving into military bands in the mid-18th century. German marches with serpents date from c.1750; in England, the serpent became more popular after the arrival of musicians from Hanover in 1794. Serpent parts can be found with occasional octave divisi, which we believe are alternative parts, rather than divisi proper. Occasionally two serpents are called for. In many cases, the serpent is treated as a transposing instrument in Bb. Clearly there were virtuosos of this picturesque precursor of the tuba, since the demands are striking, especially in German court bands c.1790-c.1830. Yet the combination of a tuba mouthpiece and woodwind fingering did not prove satisfactory. The *ophicleide* (bass bugle) became known as the "chromatic bullock" (24). In Germany and France, the *Russisches Fagott* caused confusion. Often called a double bassoon, it is actually an upright wooden serpent in bassoon form, played with a cup mouthpiece. Berlioz remarked (25 p 177) that this "low instrument of the serpent kind" might be withdrawn from the family of wind instruments "without the smallest injury to Art."

Single-Reed Instruments: The Clarinet and Saxophone

The single-reed clarinet (26-30), probably invented by Denner in Nuremburg at the start of the 18th century, was accepted widely within Germany by the mid-18th century. Mayrhofer developed its tenor form, the *basset horn,* in Bavaria about 1770. Like the oboe, the clarinet has evolved over the years. It benefited from Boehm's technical improvements around 1839. However, the most important change was not in key action but in tone, as earlier clarinets could be regarded as substitutes for high trumpets. The bold tone still lingers in early Mozart divertimentos, and, even in the early 19th century, Berlioz wrote of the instrument's epic quality - "the voice of heroic love." The musical links between trumpets and clarinets are distinct from purely verbal confusions of the terms "clarino" or "clarin" and the plurals "clarini" or "clairons." These names can mean high trumpets but, in wind music, they usually mean clarinets. This is clear from the several manuscript sources with more than one wording, cases where trumpets would be wholly unsuitable, and cases where separate trumpet parts exist too (e.g. labelled "Trombe"). The change from the trumpet sound to the soft, idyllic quality expected later began in the 1770s, encouraged by virtuosi like Schwarz and Beer (30). The typical accompanying motifs, usually an Alberti bass or similar repeated rhythmic figure (known [24] as "woodles"), appeared in the 1770s in works by J C Bach, Mysliveček and, par excellence, in Mozart's *Gran Partita* of the early 1780s.

The clarinet spread slowly across Europe, moving into Harmonien and military bands faster than into orchestras. The opera orchestras show the trend: the clarinet appeared in France and England in the late 1750s and early 1760s, in Milan by 1770, Mannheim by 1777, Vienna by 1781, and Berlin by 1787. At around this time, clarinettists began to regard as standard the reed on the lower side of the mouthpiece. In Paris in the 1760s, Stamitz and Gossec used clarinets regularly in La Pouplinière's private orchestra, and it was through Gossec's influence that clarinets were introduced to the Opéra. More isolated courts managed without them, including Eszterháza. Indeed, one feature of Haydn's music until the 1780's is the way he used high horns to fulfil some of the roles of the clarinet. The two Stadler brothers changed Vienna's ideas of clarinet playing, largely through Anton Stadler's collaboration with Mozart. When Anton was pensioned from the Court Orchestra in the 1790s, it was his brother, Johann, who took over and influenced Haydn's later music. Collaborations between individual players and composers speeded the development of the clarinet, and led to differences of approach from one composer to another. Baermann, who inspired Weber, used a clarinet of relatively narrow bore, giving it variety of tone. Hermstedt, Spohr's clarinettist, preferred a larger bore and a modified mouthpiece to provide a fuller sound.

The clarinet is normally a transposing instrument, so a B♭ clarinet part sounds a tone lower than written. Today, most contingencies are met by B♭ and A instruments. In wind harmony, the B♭ and C instruments have the main share, though A, D, E♭ and F high clarinets and low F clarinet (basset horn), E♭ alto, and B♭ and A bass clarinets are found. The brighter C clarinet was common at the end of the 18th century, perhaps partly because it was taking over from the oboe. Certainly, C clarinets are common in music by Went, Sedlak and Triebensee, and appear often in French music after the Revolution. Even in 1812, the formal verdict of the Paris Conservatoire (26 p 90) was that, although the new instruments could play in any key, they had lost the special characters of the sounds of A, B♭ and C instruments. The high E♭ instruments were popular in the early 19th century over much of Europe, often replacing oboes, and were common later in American street jazz bands for funerals. The basset horn and bass clarinet are less common. The soprano and alto E♭ forms are found in clarinet choirs and modern military bands; the F and D forms are found mainly in early band music.

The word "chalumeau" can refer to the precursor of the clarinet (cf. works by Pichl, Gassmann, Dittersdorf and Starzer). Elsewhere, it marks places where the clarinet should sound an octave lower, and relates to the sound of the lower register, as used by Mozart for the Masked Trio (Scene 19) in *Don Giovanni*. Examples include Shield's *The Magic Cavern* (1784-1785; "chalmo unis"), early printed wind music under Mozart's name ("Schalmo" in **WAM-3d**, "Chal(m)" in **WAM-4d**), and music by Went ("Shalmo"). Clarinet parts are written in the tenor clef in Paisiello's *Proserpine,* where the chorus of nymphs (Act 1 Scene 4) is accompanied by 2fl 2cl 2hn 2bn).

Many forms of clarinet are used in wind works. These include the *A♭ (piccolo clarinet)* mainly found in Italian and Spanish military bands or Hungarian Gypsy bands, the *G (piccolo clarinet)* of Viennese cafe bands ("Schrammelmusik"), the *F (soprano clarinet)* found in M J Gebauer's arrangements and Mendelssohn's *Ouvertüre* Op 24, the *E♭ (soprano clarinet)* of Tuch's *Harmonia, Op 35,* and many works of the early 19th century (often alongside a piccolo or terz-flute), the *D clarinet* in Handel's *Overture in D* and J C Bach's Overture to *Orione,* and the *C clarinet* found in the *Divertimento* Hob.II:14 by Haydn, arrangements by Went and Sedlak, Strauss's *Sonatina* and French Revolutionary music. The standard instruments today are the *B♭ clarinet* and the *A clarinet,* both widely used. Mozart's *Concerto* and *Quintet* used a *basset clarinet* with extended range, but it does not seem to have been used in wind harmony music. Lower-pitched instruments include those in *G (clarinette d'amour)* as in J C Bach's *Temistocle,* and used by the Thurn und Taxis Harmonie at Regensburg and by Turkish military bands, and in *F (basset horn)* of Mozart's *Gran Partita,* K.361, and used by Süssmayr, Mayr and Strauss. There are quite a few trios for basset horns, sometimes with bassoons; some possibly Masonic. There are collections in Bohemian archives for cl 3bthn or 3bthn, an ensemble whose nearest modern equivalent is perhaps the saxophone quartet. There is a large collection of music with a pair of basset horns in GB-Lbl. The *E♭ (alto clarinet)* was used in Regensburg in the 1770s and 1780s, and as a replacement for taille parts in early works for the Pachta Harmonie. It was also used in military bands before the saxophone became popular. The *B♭ bass clarinet* is found in Strauss's *Wind Symphony,* as well as Janáček's *Mládi* and Tchaikovsky's *Octet;* the *A (bass clarinet)* is used in Strauss's *Sonatina,* and the *B♭ contrabass clarinet* in Jacob's *"Annie Laurie" Variations.*

Clarinettists who wrote music for winds include Schmittbauer, Roeser, Meissner, Franzmeyer, Michael, Fuchs, Griesbach, A P Stadler, Braun, Yost, J A Stadler, Schulze,

Blasius, Oliver, Schwegler, C Bochsa, Lang, Tausch, Lefèvre, Goepfert, Roth, Purebl, Hammerl, Wolf, K J Krause, Lefèbvre, Küffner, J G Krause, Shaw, J G G Hoffmann, J J Bouffil, P Cremont, G B (V) Gambaro, F Müller, Rummel, Mejo, Bender, Kunze, Birtwistle, van Keulen, and Ruppert.

The saxophone (31) is largely but not exclusively confined to military and symphonic wind ensembles. The instrument is found in quite a few modern Dutch works, and in Koechlin's *Septet* (**CHK-1**), Op 165.

The Horn

The horn (32-34), like the clarinet, is a transposing instrument; as with double-reed instruments, it evolved in France, but many famous players were Bohemians. The problems of transposition are far worse for the modern horn player than for the modern clarinettist. The 18th century player substituted lengths of tubing ("crooks") to change from, say, B♭ basso to A alto horn. The 20th century player transposes mentally as needed. Transposition causes no real problems in 18th and early 19th century music (35). In later chromatic works, the player may have to do work a lazy publisher has avoided. Dvořák's, Verdi's and Wagner's works are notably bad in this respect (36); any competent player can manage, but should not have the worry. The characteristics of the natural horn lie at the root of the matter. Even today the natural horn continues to influence good horn writing; much of the best still exploits phrases based on the notes which are the horn's natural harmonics. Changing crooks within a work takes a minimum time, which can be estimated for experienced 18th century players. The members of Don Giovanni's personal band in Mozart's opera manage the operation in about 8 seconds (their clarinet colleagues switch instruments in this time too).

Crooks used in classical orchestral horn writing range from E♭ alto (e.g. the arrangement by J C [sic] of Weber's *Jägerchor* from *Euryanthe)* to G basso (Arne's *Artaxerxes).* Certain rare sharp keys do not seem to occur: B alto (as in Haydn's *Symphony* No 46), B basso (as in Brahms's *Symphony* No 2), F# (as in Haydn's *Symphony* No 45 "Farewell"), C# (as in Berlioz's *Te Deum*) and A basso (as in Rossini's *Semiramide* overture); there seems to be no case of A♭ alto in wind bands either.

Alto horn crooks required in wind music are *C* (Haydn, *Armide* March for winds in the Finale); *B♭* (Mozart, K 270; Süssmayr: *Robert und Callisto); A* (Dittersdorf, Strauss: *Sonatina).* The normal crooks, rarely called either alto or basso, are *G* (Haydn: Hob.II:3); the now-standard key *F* (Raff: *Sinfonietta); E* (Dvořák *Serenade;* this key is surprisingly rare in wind harmony); *E♭ (= Dis)* Mozart: *Serenade* in E♭, K 375; this key is by far the commonest in classical wind music); *D* (Haydn: Hob.II:D18; Dvořák [horn 3]). The basso horn crooks are those in *C* (Haydn: Hob.II:7 and Arne: *Thomas and Sally);* B♭ (Mozart: *Serenade* in B♭, K.361); and *A♭* (Rossini, *March* **GAR-1m**; Berr).

There were two main traditions of horn playing in the early 18th century. One is associated with trumpeters who, like military bandsmen today, had to be competent on several brass instruments. The results must have been spectacular out of doors (a role implied by the German name *Waldhorn* and Czech name *Lesní roh)* but overwhelming indoors. The second tradition was the Bohemian one, which led to the sound now considered normal. Hand stopping was devised and made systematic by players such as Hampel in Dresden, who domesticated the horn by discovering that a judiciously placed hand in the bell of the instrument mellowed the tone, gave control of the pitch of out-of-tune notes, and transformed the horn into a chromatic instrument. Any attempt at authentic sound has to decide between "bells up" or "hands in bells." Hand-stopping needs hands in bells; Berlioz (25 p 141) quotes Méhul to suggest that bells up was not the Paris manner of the 1790s. One might suggest bells up before 1770, hands in from 1790, and a transition which depended on the sophistication of player, music and venue (37, 38). At this time, players were specialists who achieved remarkable effects on primitive instruments: "high-horn players" worked with the closely-spaced harmonics of the upper register, while "low-horn players" concentrated on agility in the less extreme range. Composers like Cartellieri, Krommer and Pleyel demanded formidable techniques. Krommer (Op 69) and Druschetzky were among those who wrote music in which the second horn has the main interest. Valve horns appeared from c.1815, but took a long time to become the norm. They were adopted in the Royal Artillery Band only in 1840. In the 20th century, there has been a trend to wider-bore, higher-pitched models to make easier the volume and endurance composers have come to expect.

One way to satisfy the composer's wish to modulate without making the horn players change crooks was to have horns using different sets of crooks. Mozart's *Symphony in G minor* (K.550) calls for one horn in G and one in B♭. This approach is very rare in wind harmony unless more than two horns are used. Mozart's *Gran Partita* (K.361) has two horns in F and two in B♭ (though the horns are hardly used melodically, unlike K.375 or K.388); Dvořák's *Serenade,* Op 44, has a horn in D as well as a pair of horns in E. Feldmayr also adds a horn III in another key, but the parts are slight. When there are two pairs of horns, as in Strauss's Op 7 *Serenade,* each pair has its own key.

Horn players who wrote music for winds include Amon, Hiebesch, G A Schneider, Zoncada, d'Indy and Krol.

The Flute

The flute (39) was the earliest of the modern wind instruments to be properly domesticated, replacing its predecessor, the recorder, at the court of Louis XIV at the end of the 17th century. The flute's transverse action gives far greater control of pitch, volume and tone than was possible on the recorder. Like the clarinet, the flute benefited from Boehm's thorough redesigning in the 1840s. Possibly because of its association with smaller-scale indoor music like the trio sonata, the flute appears less commonly in wind bands in the Austrian Empire prior to the 1870s. Its volume and power, except in the highest register, did not compete with a wind octet playing fortissimo. As Stadler noted (11) "Flutes can also be used but most of their parts must be specially written in." This was presumably not the case in Nuremberg in 1804, when eight members of the Theater Orchestra wrote an open letter to Kapellmeister Mainberger complaining about the use of the flute in the military band because its tone was too delicate (40). One can find special parts for flutes as alternatives to oboes (41) but - as in Hoffmeister's FAH-2.1 - the publisher's commercial sense surely overrode his musicianship in suggesting straight substitution. Wind octets in Russia and, later, in France often comprised 2fl 2cl 2hn 2bn, so that flutes replaced the oboes common in German-speaking countries. However, even the Viennese used the flute in sections for winds alone in orchestral music, e.g. in P Wranizky's *Symphony: Joy of the Hungarian Nation.* In the 20th century, the brighter-toned metal flute (as needed in Stravinsky's music) has almost completely replaced the wooden flute in orchestras, influenced especially by French players like Moyse. The issue of vibrato remains contentious, with some of those who argue against the practice clearly using vibrato in their recordings. Flautists who composed music for winds include Kreith, Feldmayr, A Reicha, Taffanel, and Bennett.

The *piccolo* (or sopranino flute) and the *fife* (the band flute or marching flute) both make occasional appearances in wind music, especially in French revolutionary wind bands. Both have great powers of penetration and can easily overwhelm an average symphony orchestra, with or without chorus. It is not always clear what is meant by "Petite flûte en Eb (or Fa)." We have examined many works, and believe these parts are for flutes, rather than piccolos. The *flauto piccolo* of Turkish music c.1780 was usually a simple flageolet (effectively a recorder), and is basically the same as the *flautino* or *fletin* of Prachensky's Turkish works.

Again, instruments in many keys are encountered; indeed, some flautists needed as many as 9 flutes. There can be ambiguity about keys; we shall follow the convention defined at the start of the Chapter. With that convention, the uses of different flutes in wind music include the following: *F, Eb (terz-piccolo)* in music from Wertheim; *Db (piccolo)* in military bands; *C (piccolo)* in Spohr's *Notturno* and Janáček's *Mládí*; *Bb (called "in C")* in marches by Cutler and Guest; *Ab (often called "in Bb")* is used by Schetky; *Eb (flauto terzo)* in Tuch's Op 35 *Harmonia* and Moudrux's version of the Krommer parthias, Spohr's *Notturno*, and many early 19th century works, often alongside an Eb clarinet; *D* and *Db* are found mainly in military bands. The standard instrument is in C though, for various reasons, it is often said to be in D, and is technically better suited to sharp keys; ensembles favoring flat keys often used the terz-flute. The lower-pitched instruments are in *A (flauto d'amore):* Hoffmeister, *Notturno, No 1* and Neubauer.

Brass Instruments

The *trumpet* (42, 43; see also remarks under clarinet about "clarino") has some important appearances, such as Haydn's *March for the Prince of Wales*, and the wind version of the slow movement of his *Symphony No 100*. Appearances in divertimentos are often brief, even if effective, as in Krommer's Op 45 or Sedlak's arrangements. One may wonder why it was included in the first place. Perhaps it was a reminder that trumpet guilds were once powerful. Only in 1810 did Friedrich Wilhelm III abolish the guild system for trumpets in cavalry regiments (44). In many instances the trumpet only takes a low interior harmony part when all other instruments have more important music. One is reminded of Sir Thomas Beecham's quotation of the epitaph for an infant who survived but two minutes: "Seeing I was here for such a short time / It was hardly worth coming at all." Later band music includes keyed or valved bugles and their variants (cornet, flugelhorn, cor de signal à clefs). Natural trumpets persisted for some time: in the Royal Artillery Band, they were replaced by slide trumpets in 1817, and by valve trumpets in 1835. Haydn and Hummel wrote concertos for a Klappentrompette (keyed trumpet), and parts for this chromatic instrument are found occasionally.

The *posthorn* served as a sort of "novelty instrument" on occasion, making a notable appearance in Spohr's *Notturno*. The printed version of the Posthorn Trio in Schwarz's "II Märsche für die ganze Turkisch Musick [sic] oder neun-stimmige Harmonie, mit dem beliebten Posthorn Trio, für das zweyte Bürgerregiment" (MYS-1m) suggests a trumpet in G as a replacement for the higher posthorn, but no alternative for the lower Bb one.

The *trombone* (42) appears in early band music (such as that arranged by Pick) and in much religious music. The bass trombone became an established part of military and Turkish music in Austria and Germany from the 1790s; its use soon spread to civilian bands. In general, the bass trombone's role was limited to ripieno to the contrabasso (contrabassoon, violone, serpent). This was not always a good idea; as Berlioz commented "Means have nevertheless been found to degrade the trombone, by reducing it to a servile doubling, as useless as grotesque, of the double bass part" (25 p 156). By the mid-1810s, works would call for a choir of three trombones, often alto, tenor and bass trombones. Many Löwenstein Harmonie works (c.1800-1820) are scored for 2cl 2hn bn b-tb. In the enormous choral pieces of the French revolutionary Fêtes, trombones were almost invariably employed to double the alto, tenor and bass parts of the male chorus. One unusual example is found in Meyer's *Journal de Harmonie* (Leipzig, 1808) where, strangely, the bass trombone part is printed a semitone below concert pitch. The *Dixtuor* by Arrieu is an attractive modern work using a single trombone.

The orchestral *tuba* is also rare in serenade music, although it commonly replaces the contrabassoon in the *Serenade, Op 7*, by Strauss. The *ophicleide,* invented late in the 18th century, was present in the bands of several armies at the 1815 Battle of Waterloo. The *bass horn* (cf Spohr's *Notturno*) and the *tuba pastoralis,* akin to an alphorn, make rare appearances; the tuba pastoralis can be heard with the Collegium Musicum Pragense on Supraphon 1111 2616. French revolutionary music sometimes imitated ancient Roman instruments by including a *tuba curva* or a *buccina,* whose bell was raised over the players' heads (45), like an early sousaphone. Doubtless the effect was better seen than heard. *Tenor horns* and *bass horns* in the bands of the American Civil War were played over-the-shoulder (46).

Stringed Instruments in Wind Harmony

The roles of violone and double bass have already been mentioned. Violins are found in Haydn's Hob. II:16. A cello combines naturally with a string bass in Dvořák's *Serenade,* (and indeed in Winter's *Responsioni pro defunctis*) and is the soloist in the Ibert and Martinů concertos with winds. The viola is found surprisingly often, especially in German sources, sometimes as an alternative to cor anglais or basset horn parts. Zwing's *Six pièces d'harmonie, Op 2*, includes a part for viola, and other composers who use or allow use of violas include von Schacht (47), Croes, Anton Schneider, V V Mašek (48) and Malipiero (*Serenata Mattutina*, **GGM-1**). The viola parts are not normally substitutes for other instruments, like cor anglais, and their use is puzzling. Paisiello's *Serenata* and Späth's *Sérénade en forme de Pot-Pourri* **ADS-3** offer the guitarist a rare chance to join in wind harmony. The guitar part of the Späth is written a tone higher than it should sound. Works for solo strings with winds include Berg's *Chamber Concerto for Violin and Piano*, several by Hindemith for viola, Martinů's *Concertino for Cello*, Ibert's *Concerto for Cello* and Weill's *Concerto for Violin and Winds*.

Keyboard Instruments in Wind Harmony

The high water mark of wind harmony coincides with the appearance of the forte-piano and the demise of the harpsichord, so that keyboard works with wind harmony were often written with the fortepiano in mind. Sometimes this is explicit, as in Honauer's *Suite de Pièces pour L'Harmonie avec Le Fortepiano*. Concertos for keyboards and wind band include those for one or more harpsichords and/or fortepianos by V V Mašek, and Paul Wranizky's *La Chasse* for pianoforte and winds (49).

Modern works for solo piano and winds include Berg's *Chamber Concerto* for violin and piano (1923-1925), Stravinsky's *Piano Concerto* with winds (1924), and the opening movement of Bartók's *Second Piano Concerto* of 1931-1932. The celesta is used by Malipiero (**GGM-1**), the accordion by Martinů in his *Legend of the Smoke from Potato Fires,* and Friedrich Heinrich Himmel (1765-1814) uses a "Harmonika" (presumably tuned glasses) in his *Terzetto* for voices and winds. Slavický's 1991 *La voce soave: Omaggio a Mozart* asks for glass harmonica or celeste. Piano parts at the bottom of many British military band scores (from the 18th century to the present day; Holst's scores are an example) are simply an aid to the bandmaster, and should not be played.

Timpani and Percussion in Wind Harmony

The importance of percussion in marches should not be underestimated. Sousa himself said "I sometimes think that no band can be greater than its bass drummer, because it is given to him, more than to any person except the director, to reflect the rhythm and spirit of the composition" (50). Performance practices are not always clear. In the 17th century, drums would be expected in cases where there is no explicit part. Recent recordings of Purcell's *Music for the Funeral of Queen Mary* restore these parts (New London Consort/Neary, Sony SK66243; The Sixteen/Christophers, Collins 1425-2). The timpani parts of many later marches were also left for local decisions. From the mid-18th century, the so-called Turkish instruments are especially important. They appeared widely in Europe after full Turkish bands were presented by the Sultan to Poland in the 1720's, to Russia in 1725, and to Prussia and Austria soon afterwards. In British Army bands, one notes the use of cymbals in 1777, bass drum and tambourines in 1782, and a Jingling Johnnie (Pavillon Chinois; Schellenbaum; Padiglione cinese) in 1785. This pole with cross-pieces, on which pieces of metal were loosely fixed, started as a trophy of war; later it was used in American jug and stringbands. It has been a regular member of bands for several centuries. Bass drum and cymbals were included in the 1795 Paris Conservatoire band; triangle and side drum appear in Beethoven's marches of 1809-1810. Castanets (crotolo, crotales) seem to be Spanish in origin.

Names of percussion instruments are very variable and show regional variations (51). In the late 19th century, there were differences from regiment to regiment (51): English soldiers preferred a larger, heavier bass drum than Ghurkas; US bands preferred a bass drum that was 12" deep, rather than the 14" British one. English side-drums were normally less than 15" across, shallower than the French ones, and smaller than the US 16-20" diameters. Composers are often imprecise, especially about sticks. Authenticity is probably a vain hope, so it is more helpful to indicate the main groups here:
Bass drum: Tamburo grosso, tamburo grande, tamburo turco, grosse Trommel, grosse Caisse, gran tambaro, bass drum, long drum, gran cassa, cassa grande. This was usually a tall drum of small diameter, often struck with the right hand by a club-like stick and by the left hand with a switch or birch.
Side drum: Tambour militaire, kleine Trommel, caisse claire, side drum, snare drum.
Tenor drum: Tenor drum, caisse roulante, caisse sourde (also Rührtrommel, Wirbeltrommel, Rolltrommel).
Cymbals: Cinelli, cymbales, Becken, cymbals, piatti. Note that the earlier cymbals were smaller, saucer shaped, and with a definite pitch.

Voices and Wind Harmony

One possible problem concerns the common British and German use of male sopranos and altos in church music, rather than mixed choirs with female voices. A note about Emmert's *Kirchenlieder* remarks "Choirs unable to provide four male voices for these motets may like to note that the first tenor part may be taken by the soprano, and the first bass part by an alto, without detriment to the harmony, indeed in many cases to its advantage." Local judgment was encouraged by Emmert and others as to whether winds should be used alternately or together with the choir.

Aspects of Authenticity

Authenticity and Its Aims

"Sociall Musick," observed Roger North in 1728, "hath two respects: 1. to the Performers, and, 2. the Auditors; for there is a vast difference both in designe and event between these two nations" (52 p 258). Authenticity, too, concerns the making of music and the response of its listeners. Musical authenticity has its changing fashions, whose main components concern the musical text, traditions of performance like repeats and ornamentation, and the instruments used.

Clearly, an authentic musical text is desirable. Wrong notes, wrong phrasings, wrong transpositions, wrong dynamics and wrong bar lengths are all to be found, not to mention illegible printing and, one almost feels, page turns carefully contrived to be impossible (53). We assume that competent composers wrote what could be played, at least by the very best musicians. Where impossible demands are made on the performer, it is the job of the editor to suggest practical solutions. For many important works, no composer's autograph exists. Even when the autograph exists, there can still be ambiguities of ornamentation (54) or even instrumentation. Then one needs both the best scholarship and the best musicianship, always invaluable and sadly rare. Authenticity is not to be achieved merely by using old instruments and observing some superficial differences in technique. Hearing "authentic performances" may well encourage better ones; changing instruments alone is not a panacea.

The traditions of performance - tempos, repeats and ornamentation - are especially open to dispute. Even band layouts - the groupings of players for performance - have changed over the years. Clearly one should try to reduce compromises between scholarly precision and convincing performance. The many uncertainties in scholarship can be seen in relation to performing music of the recent past. There is no single approach to performance in the 20th century, even within contemporary Europe. The sound - the timbre, vibrato and phrasing - of a wind instrument has strong regional variations. One has only to imagine a French group playing Richard Strauss or a Bavarian ensemble playing Milhaud to realize that being contemporaries is simply not enough. Nor are the problems merely those of a forgotten tradition. Many people still alive know the performing traditions of the 1920s and 1930s, yet rarely play works of that period in that style. If the musical text has not altered, the listener for whom it was intended has changed. When the authentic sound is elusive or ill-defined, can one hope to obtain an *authentic* response? Can the effect on the modern listener match that of the original performers on their audiences? Modern listeners, at least subconsciously, know how music has changed, and cannot ignore their added experience. It is not possible to hear music exactly as Mozart did unless, perhaps, one had been isolated from modern sounds and music. Authentic response, in this sense, is a matter for social discussion, not scholarly effort. The proper aim is to be true to the composer's intentions, and to help the audience to respond to the music itself. It is deceptive to think a performance is "better" simply because it claims to be "authentic." The quest for authenticity should also bring out the excitement of early performances. Listeners would have known that what they heard was based on opera, even in an arrangement. Players and audiences would recognize the drama of *Figaro,* or *Don Giovanni,* or *Fidelio.* The best music was not mere background, but a reflection of the opera itself. Players today who know and understand the plot can bring to wind music the same sense of occasion, of power, humor, or nobility. This is especially evident in the recordings of the London Wind Soloists, whose members must have played together in many operas.

Authenticity and Performing Practices

The Problem of Pitch. Today, most players tune to an A of 440 Hz. Lists of data from tuning forks, organs, and other sources (55) indicate that, in the critical period 1750-1814, the same A would have been around 422 Hz, close to the present A♭ of 415.3 Hz (56). Apparently, the rise in pitch began at the Congress of Vienna, 1814, when "the Russian Emperor presented new, sharper, wind instruments to an Austrian regiment of which he was colonel. The band of this regiment became noted for the brilliancy of its tones" (55). Subsequent changes in pitch led to A's as high as 460 Hz, nearly the present B♭ of 466.2 Hz. Thus, in the heyday of wind harmony, the lower pitch was used throughout Austro-Hungary, England, France and Germany: any 18th century composer would expect his E♭ serenade to sound close to what a modern player would call D. By the same reckoning, a brighter sound was expected in the wind octet revival of the 1870s - indeed, Brahms's D was sharp to Mozart's E♭. Some of the worries about the thick textures and muddy sound of the romantics might be resolved if players used the higher pitch then current with an A at about 450 Hz. Recent recordings tend to use lower pitches (typically an A of 420 Hz) for "authentic" performances and pitches up to an A of 450-455 Hz for American, Berlin and Czech orchestras (57).

Composers' Performance Instructions. The instructions composers provide for their performers are illuminating in the way they show how problems were solved. Tempo is an example, for 18th century musicians presumably had views about, say, the speed of "allegro," which were as varied as those of their modern colleagues. Some conventions have changed with time: the 18th century musician would have been clear that "Vivace" was not a tempo marking. The situation is complicated further by copyists using *All⁰* to mean either *Allegro* or *Allegretto.* The metronome, after a confusing start (58, 59), was used by composers like A Reicha, whose ambitiously rapid tempos (up to 144 beats per minute in his wind quintet Op 88, No 3 [60]) are ignored as regularly as Beethoven's apparently eccentric ones. Reicha's care over performance is especially clear in the remarkable preface to his Op 88 quintets (60). This preface was written by the players for whom the quintets were first written, namely, "Membres de l'École Royale de Musique et du Théâtre Royal de l'Opéra." They observe the disparity in quality and quantity between wind and string music, and point to Reicha's conscious attempt to remedy it. They then note what the player can do about this (besides, of course, buying Reicha's quintets). Players should study their parts carefully and rehearse often; they should, further, perfect their ensemble, observe dynamics strictly, and let the melody through. In all, this is an extraordinary comment on Parisian music making. The signatories were Joseph Guillou (1787-1853, flute), Jacques Jules Bouffil (1783-1868, clarinet), Gustave Vogt (1781- 1870, oboe), Louis François Dauprat (1781-1868, horn) and Henri (bassoon). All were eminent players and teachers and all composed for their instruments well enough for their music still to be in circulation; Dauprat, incidentally, was one of the last great virtuosi of the valveless horn. Berlioz, a lively observer of the musical scene, would have been entertained by this Preface, since his *Memoirs* mention Guillou just once - to condemn precisely the liberties Guillou cites: In Gluck's *Alceste,* the lower register of the flute is fully exploited, but Guillou would have none of this: he wanted a solo, and a solo can be heard much better an octave higher (an outrage, Berlioz complained, one which turns an ingenious idea into a trivial one) (61).

Military band music was different, since bandmasters had to adjust to local resources. Few composers expected their works to be played as written. This is shown by some of the handwritten comments which Charles Dibdin made (62, 63) on the autographs of his marches, showing a recognition of what was and was not practical:

"Directions. In military bands that are powerful, the effect of this march may be rendered very strong by the addition of hautboys, and kettle drums, in which case the hautboys may play in unison with the clarinets, and the kettledrums, and indeed every other kind of drums calculated for a grand accompanyment, may be easily regulated by the (bottom) line. If the band be not very full, the trumpets had better be omitted" (62).

"Directions. This march may be played in G (63) according to the foregoing score. In which case the hautboys and flutes may take the place of the clarinetts the flutes only playing the solo passages and if the band should be strong the effect of the trumpet may be ventured. It will however have the best effect if played with clarinets as above."

This sort of guidance appears on the autographs of Gustav Holst's *Suites* and in Kanne's instructions (see **FAK-1m**): *"To the Capellmeister.* If verses are to be sung to these marches, they must be played in D, since they will lie too high for the singers in E♭ and too deep in C. If need be, one can leave out the bassoons."

Musical Tempos.   Altenburg's manual of 1795 (43) observed that the "Heroic Trumpeters' March ... should be played more slowly for the heavy cavalry, in order to express the serious and heroic passions, and more briskly for the Hussars and light cavalry." He does not add, for his readers needed no telling, that for much of the 18th century band music was not normally played on the march. Only simple drums (or fifes and drums) were common when marching. As noted in part 1, marching in step was not normal in the early 18th century, but became common only after changes in military discipline. One should not be surprised that the natural musical speed of some marches does not suit the physical act of marching. Some consistency emerged later; however, only those which give a step length define a speed of marching, and these speeds are usually slow (1-2 mph does not get anyone anywhere fast), even when "the unit is the half note, two beats per measure at the cadence indicated" (64).

Marches are often found in pairs at different speeds (e.g., those by J C Bach). Tempos listed for early marches (64-67, *Grove V* under March, and Paisiello **GXP-1mv, 2mv**) are in line with other information, including dotted quarter note = 84 of the Turkish march in the finale of Beethoven's *Choral Symphony.* Modern British Army quick march tempos (in steps per minute) are 110 for Highland Regiments, 116 for Foot Guards, 120 for Infantry Regiments, and 140 for the Rifle Light Infantry. The British, (French, German) forms are slow march (pas ordinaire; Parademarsch); quick march (pas redoublé; Geschwindmarsch); double-quick march (pas de charge; Sturmmarsch).

How accurate were these tempo markings? Druschetzky's **GYD-20**, probably written c.1817, gives us some idea. The five short pieces demonstrate early devices for setting tempos. Each piece has two markings, one for "Takt Messer" (Vienna Standard Timing Device) and the other for the metronome. The Takt Messer was a simple pendulum, a lead bullet with a string knotted at critical points; in the British army, the corresponding device was a "plummett," lead on a string suspended from a tripod. A simple mathematical check on the numbers shows the two sets of tempos are not consistent internally. *This casts doubts on too precise use of contemporary metronome marks. Errors of as much as 20% seem possible.* If the Takt Messer gives T for the quarter note, for instance, and if the metronome mark (scaled, if need be, to refer to quarter notes) has quarter note = M, then the elementary physics of the simple pendulum tells us that $(T \times M^2)$ should be constant. The actual values of $(T \times M^2)$ are these: 11.5 (for M = 32); 11.7 (for M = 45); 10.4 (for M = 112); 9.7 (for M = 156); 15.2 (for M = 276) in order of increasing pace. Clearly all are inaccurate; faster speeds are the worst, and they can be wrong in either direction. This suggests that the variations in march tempos from one year to another may have little significance.

Table 3.1
March Tempos (Paces/Minute) for Slow and Quick Marches from Contemporary Editions (64–67, *Grove V* under March, and Paisiello GXP-1mv, 2mv)

1759 British	Common	60	Quick	120	
1772 French/Corsican	Common	70	Quick	140	Pas de Routte 90
1775 British	Common	60	Quick	120	
1779 North American	Common	75	Quick	110	
1780s? Italy	Slower	80	Quick	120	
1788 British	Slow	80	Quick	110	
1797 Italy	Slow	80	Quick	120	
1804 British	Slow	75	Quick	110	
1812 United States	Common	75	Quick	100	
1815	Common	90	Quick	120	
1817 German	Slow	80	Quick	114	
1828 Bavarian	Slow	88	Quick	100	
1831 French	Slow	76	Quick	100	
1835 United States	Common	90	Quick	110	
1855 United States	Common	90	Quick	110	
1867 United States	Common	90	Quick	110	
1870 British	Slow	75	Quick	116	
1891 United States			Quick	120	
1935 British	Slow	70	Quick	120	

Other Traditions and Musical Conventions

Use of Dis (D sharp) for works in E♭ (E flat). The use of "Dis" is a common but localized phenomenon, mainly confined to Austria and Germany. Even the program for the first public performance of Beethoven's *Eroica Symphony* described it as "a new Grand Symphony in Dis" (58, p 375). "Dis" seems to be restricted to titles, so instrumental parts have key signatures with three flats. Nothing enharmonic is implied, which may be why the practice did not spread. The French especially can require performers to be pedants (68), even for transposing instruments, for which the need is not clear. Is concert B♯ really usefully written Gx for an E♭ horn part, where the player will surely simply play concert C, adjusted if he or she is subtle? And what about A♯ tied to B♭ over a bar line? The use of D♯ or D## to mean D major (not E♭) is encountered in Schwerin (D-SWl) and Bohemia; A### meaning A is also found.

Dynamics.   One should not presume that modern views on dynamics were standard when wind harmony was at its peak. Certainly dynamic contrast was valued even earlier; as Roger North observed in his "Of Soft and Loud" (52 p 218), "This conduceth much to the delight of musick," continuing "The voice performs this best; next wind musick, as trumpetts and hautbouys;" later, he notes "And this soft and lowd is discretionary, falling under no rule, unless it be that in many parts each must conform." North's description suggests that dynamics strictly given by a composer were the exception and developed out of the needs of larger ensembles before control by conductor was the norm. This is certainly part of the truth: dynamics are found only sparingly in 18th century works, and these tend to be economical in range. Thus "fff" appears first only in Haydn's *Seven Last Words*, and ">" (rather than "*fz*") was modern when Haydn used it in the 1790s (69). Went's "m:v:" (mezza voce) is an individual touch, used only by him and, rarely, by his son-in-law Triebensee. Presumably it comes from opera vocal parts. Went, Triebensee and Sedlak all use "sotto voce." Some dynamics now standard are editorial, not stated desires of the composer, a good example being the start of Mozart's K.361, where the "piano" marking of the second chord is absent in the autograph. In the 19th century, players were keen to assert themselves (i.e. to play loudly to excess, rather than merely to vary dynamic level at will). We have noted the Preface to A Reicha's Op 88 Quintets; we have remarked on odd dynamics (e.g. under Donizetti), but it is simpler to quote a cartoon caption (70) showing an amateur orchestral society in vigorous activity: The Conductor: "Oh, piano, Mr Brown! Pi-an-o"; Mr Brown: "Piano be blowed! I've come here to enjoy myself!"

Basso continuo.   In music before about 1750, a continuo - bass line - was taken not just by a bass "melody" instrument, but also by a keyboard player who provided harmonic variety and color. Usually the player would be guided by figures in the part representing the harmonic progressions (71). We should ask whether any of the earlier works do need keyboard elaboration. Very few cases of wind music seem to need such a continuo. Molter's works for tp 2ob 2hn bn appear to be breaking away from a continuo intentionally (72). Alcock does provide a figured bass for *Let Chearful Smiles*, though it is useful mainly in the choral passages; the passages for 2ob bn alone are complete in themselves. Some individual judgment is needed in performances of earlier composers such as Albinoni, Telemann, Holzbauer and Hertel.

Musical handwriting.   The symbol used now as the acciaccatura, and usually as a short unstressed precursor to its main note, is often found in 18th century manuscripts with different meaning. Examples from Mozart's *Gran Partita* K.361 are given on pps 340, 368. The appoggiatura versus acciaccatura issue extends to the 19th century too, cf. the different recordings of "Was gleicht wohl auf Erden" in Weber's *Der Freischütz*.

Repeats.   Whether repeats were really expected, or merely in the arbitrary hands of the publisher is rarely clear, though one can guess the views of modern music-hire libraries who base charges on performing time. Yet there are practical guides, depending on the type - and hence the pace - of a performance. In a concert, with only short gaps between movements, there is a case for omitting some repeats to help the concentration (and endurance) both of performers and audience; it may even make the structure of a work clearer. When playing for a formal dinner, when audiences will want time to talk, time to eat, and time to digest, longer pauses between movements are needed, and more repeats make sense. This view, which is clear to many players, may be one reason for the differences between the two versions of Mozart's *Haffner Symphony:* the original, for the Salzburg celebrations of 1782, repeats both parts of the first movement; in the 1783 concert version (with added flutes and clarinets) Mozart struck out the repeats.

Should you play it all? Arrangements can have 20 or more movements; suites can be far longer than is reasonable for one performance. There is clear evidence from 18th- and 19th-century parts that performers reorganized the order of movements, or simply left out movements, to suit their needs. Thus in a number of the Vienna Imperial Harmonie's purchased arrangements by Sedlak, movements are marked either "gut," "sehr gut," "X," or, if they were to be omitted, "nicht" or "O." In some cases, cuts are marked in long movements.

Quality of Performance

Modern recordings are great deceivers. They suggest that the most difficult music can be played consistently, free from error, with all problems of balance, tuning, current emotional distractions and cold feet sorted out. The unfortunate player in the 18th century used primitive instruments and handwritten music, perhaps badly copied, and may have had to play for hours in a draughty, poorly lit spot. In Bath, the same minuet was played throughout the Master of Ceremony's introduction of people of rank by precedence so they, one couple at a time, could dance through the complete figure. One understands why the title "The New Bath Minuet" was needed so often, since it was a welcome event to both the musically literate and the musicians involved.

It is a marvel that, with all the difficulties, musicians of this period played well at all. Yet sometimes they did. The ever-critical Mozart wrote of an early performance of his *Serenade* K.375, "The six gentlemen who played it are poor beggars who, however, play quite well together" (73). Holmes, nearly fifty years later, described an itinerant band of musicians as "so clever and eminent in their way as to deserve notice ... these poor fellows will amuse you with such an exhibition of tone and skill as would set up an English artist of the first water" (74). There was an elite to set standards: at Eszterháza, the Viennese courts, at Mannheim and at Paris. How they maintained their quality is shown by the care Haydn took in replacing the second horn of the Eszterháza orchestra following the death of Eisen. The procedure included an audition of applicants by Salieri in the presence of the whole wind band, the decision being based on Salieri's written view and the sealed written votes of all the members of the band (75).

Plenty of musicians fell well below these standards. Rousseau even argued that poor French bands were a military advantage: hearing such bad music, the enemy would think they had raw recruits before them and so would not act with sufficient prudence. He doubted that there was a trumpet in tune in the French kingdom. Certainly many composers worked on this assumption. When Mozart adapted Handel's *Messiah* for Viennese use, he ensured that "The Trumpet Shall Sound" on a horn (a linguistic anomaly made even odder because a trombone, not a trumpet, sounds at the Apocalypse in German-speaking countries). J S Bach needed to criticize the poor oboe tone and trombone technique of his players (15 p 18). At other times, words failed him: "Modesty forbids me to comment on their competence and musicianship." In England, the records of Vauxhall Gardens were more candid: "The Duke [of York]'s band performed very ill - a made-up band." Perhaps the audience was happier another time when "the Duke's band came too late" (76). Burney found the octet in the Golden Ox in Vienna "so miserably out of tune" that he wished them "a hundred miles off" (77). This was not typical of Vienna, but points to the enormous variations in standards of performance.

Did any but the best bands play the notes as written, even when the notes were right? Haydn made changes in his marches between manuscript and printed edition (78) to help his players, and doubtless other players changed notes without sanction. Spohr could not prevent the best wind players in Rome from putting in a cacophony of incompatible, unwritten ornaments at each cadence (79). Standards tended to improve as players and instruments improved. In 1750, the band for the changing of the guard at St James's Park knew only Handel's march from *Scipio;* by 1770, it matched the best in Europe (*Burney* vol 2 p 30). Today, composers tend to assume that the best talent will always be available, so it is a real achievement for amateurs to perform well some of the large modern works.

One can ask what sort of performance audiences deserve. In the 18th century, American opera orchestras had to put up with missiles (80) and persistent spitting (80, 81). In Europe, King Ferdinand of Naples would throw food at the audience (82); Mark Twain described the King of Bavaria's similar use of water (83). Even a keg was thrown at Covent Garden (84). While such extremes were not common, lack of consideration was frequent (85). At a ball in London in 1774 for the King's birthday, the band was asked to play 70 minuets and more (84). Typical 19th century portraits of a famous soloist at work show rapturous audiences, elegantly if uncomfortably arranged. The complaints of Spohr, Chopin, Clara Schumann and Mendelssohn suggest that this was the exception, not the rule. As a Victorian guide to etiquette suggests, "It is usual to listen to the performance, or at least appear to do so; and if conversation is carried on, it should be in a low tone" (86). Small wonder that many players chose music that was safe, flashy, immediately identifiable, or uninterestingly pleasant and banal (87).

Quality depends, of course, on what is necessary. The player with tenure in a small court may play for safety, avoiding risk to his job by performing with bland competence. The soloist a century later may aim to impress by facility rather than musicianship. Even survival was hard for the independent musician in the eighteenth century, with composers like Boccherini, Dittersdorf, Mozart, Mysliveček, d'Ordoñez and Piccinni dying in poverty, and with others like Jommelli discouraged after early success. For some, another solution was to hand, as biographies in *Sainsbury* show: (of F C Neubauer's death in 1795) "Most probably he accelerated it by the intemperate use of strong liquors; for as he was wont, when in the neighbourhood of the Rhine, to excite his imagination with the juice of the grape, the want of it [i.e. imagination] afterwards compelled him to have recourse ... to brandy"; (of Charles Norris's disappointment) "drove him to convivial consolations, in which he indulged to a degree that [they] not only impaired his health but after a while injured his voice, and was greatly detrimental to his fortune"; (of the German bandmaster Rakeman, to whom Parry was subordinate at Denbigh) "being fonder of paying court to Bacchus than Apollo." Modern professional musicians recognize that security takes the edge off the highest performing standards. Yet real deprivation will destroy the best too, and such social difficulties are reason enough for the wide variations in professional standards.

Band Layouts: Where Did They Play?

Illustrations (examples are found in [22] and [38]) show layouts which do not correspond to textbook idealizations. Some bands seem arranged at random, and often players could not see each other. Others were more systematic. *Burney* (vol 2 p 28) described a long line of 18 players in Mannheim in 1770. These players were organised with care, and with enough symmetry (2bn 3tp 4ob 4cl 3tp 2bn) to make possible some interesting musical effects. Early Turkish bands are in neat circles, looking inwards; this layout can still be seen in Istanbul and in small street bands elsewhere in Europe.

In the diagrams which follow, the band faces the bottom of the diagram. Usually, the conductor or audience would be placed at the bottom of the figure.

Bands Standing and Playing

Prague, 1743 (22). We believe the band has stopped.	bn ob ob ob ob ob ob bn hn hn
Austria c.1750 (88)	bn ob ob ob hn hn tp
London 1753? (38, 89)	ob ob ob ob hn hn bn bn
Regensburg, 3 January 1776. A wind band and an oboe band on opposite outdoor stages at the wedding of Prince Hieronymus von Radzivil and Princess Sophia von Thurn und Taxis (90). Band 1 includes what appears to be a then-obsolete Zink. s-bn is a small bassoon (quint-bn?).	*Band 1*　　　　　tp　　　　hn 　　　　　　　ob　　bn　　　　hn Conductor　　　　　　ob　　tamb 　　　　　?Zink　fl　　fl　fl　tp 　　　　　　　　　dr　dr　dr　　cym *Band 2*　　　　　ob　ob　ob　ob 　　　　　　ob　ob　ob　ob　ob (Man, not　　　　　ob　ob　bn conducting)　　s-bn ob　ob　s-bn s-bn
England, 1777 (38); a sensible arrangement with the high winds together, and the lower parts grouped together.	fl ob tp　　　bn ob　　　bn ob cl　cl
Oettingen Wallerstein: the famous silhouette. 1784?-1791? Or perhaps a montage (see Part 1)	fl ob fl　　ob cl　　　hn cl　　　hn vlne　　　　bn
Marienberg, 1790 (91)	drum cym　　　hn tp　　　　hn tp　　　　　　cl? 　　　　　　　cl?
Woolwich, UK, 1826 (38). An odd, casual arrangement, probably bad.	tbn serp bn bugle cl cl hn fl
London Wind Soloists, for a recording session in 1983	cbn bn 2　　　　hn 2 bn 1　　　　hn 1 ob 2　　　　　cl 2 ob 1　　　　　cl 1

Bands Playing on the March. It can be hard to tell if a band has stopped or not, and indeed if it is still playing. The distinguished horn player Alan Civil advised other horn players in marching bands never to let the mouthpiece touch the lips.

Prague, 1741 (22). Brass (the loudest) at the front. We believe that the band is still on the move.	bn fl ob ob hn hn
Funeral, 1751; bassoons and oboes have black crepe (92).	ob ob ob ob bn hn hn bn
St James's, London, c.1790.	fifes drums ob bn hn? hn tp serp
Paris, 1791 (48 p 562). Note the spectacular visual effect of four buccinas at the front as Voltaire's remains are transferred to the Panthéon.	timps [unidentified] [unidentified] [unidentified] [unidentified] buc buc buc buc
London, 1799 (38). Paris chose visual effect; London had the loudest in front.	drummer [5 unidentified] oboes? tp serp hn hn
London c.1821 (ref 38) Coldstream Guards.	[5 unidentified] tps? drum hn hn hn ob ob ob

Mounted Bands. Artistic licence makes it extremely hard to decide whether or not the musicians are actually playing.

London, 1763. (38)	timp tp tp hn hn bn bn ob ob ob ob
Versailles, 1805. (record sleeve source; original location not stated). Again, loudest go first.	bn bn ob ob hn hn tp tp

Seated Bands

Prague, 1794 (22).	bn bn hn hn xx xx xx xx (xx means cl or ob; we cannot tell which).
Vienna, at the Sperlbauer Inn (c.1810?) Note the horns are not placed as a pair. X, Y, Z are hidden players (93).	ob? ob X? Y? Z? hn hn bn
Czech wind quintet c.1810 (22). A posed picture. Could the work be Carl Theodore Theuss, Op 21?	fl ob hn bn hn [oboe and bassoon stand; the others sit at a table, looking uncomfortable].
Charing Cross Fair, London, c.1830 (38). No special order; the trumpet points outwards!	fl tp cl or ob [hidden player] bn hn drum (drummer standing)

Part 3: References and Notes

1. R E M Harding 1971 *A Thematic Catalogue of the Works of Matthew Locke with a Calendar of the Main Events of His Life;* London: Alden and Mowbray; Oxford: B H Blackwell. See pp xxvi, 88 and 132. The relevant works 117-128 and the *Sarabande* of doubtful authenticity (several unpublished) have all been performed and recorded (EMI Electrola Reflexe/Conifer 1C 069 46404).

2. A Carse 1969 *The Orchestra in the Eighteenth Century;* New York: Broude Brothers.

3. R Nettel 1946 *The Orchestra in England;* London: Jonathan Cape.

4. A Baines 1957 *Woodwind Instruments and Their History;* London: Faber.

5. A Baines 1976 *Brass Instruments,Their History and Development;* London: Faber.

6. N Zaslaw 1976-1977 Proc Roy Mus Assoc **103** 158.

7. A Baines (editor) 1961 *Musical Instruments through the Ages;* London: Penguin Books.

8. *The New Grove Dictionary of Musical Instruments* 1984 London: Macmillan.

9. D Diderot and J J R D'Alembert 1751-1765 *Encyclopédie ou dictionnaire raisoné des sciences, des arts, &c.* There are substantial contributions by J J Rousseau.

10. Compare the recordings on authentic instruments and on modern instruments listed in Part 2. Locke's music played on modern brass instruments (e.g., by the Philip Jones Brass Ensemble, Argo ZRG 717) sounds wholly different from its sound on authentic cornetts and sackbuts (e.g. Academy of Ancient Music, Oiseau-Lyre DLSO 507).

11. Anton Stadler's *Music Plan* listing the requirements for a new music school, H-Bn, Fol Germ 1434. See also Dieter Klöcker's notes to Telefunken 6.35473 EX.

12. P Bate 1971 *The Oboe;* London: Benn.

13. Contrast the recordings of Haydn by the London Wind Soloists (Decca STS 15078) and the Vienna Volksoper Wind Ensemble (Amadeo AVRS 6208).

14. L G Langwill 1965 *The Bassoon and Contrabassoon;* London: Benn.

15. C S Terry 1932 *Bach's Orchestra;* Oxford: Oxford University Press.

16. C Pierre 1889 *Histoire de l'orchestre de l'Opéra de Paris;* Paris: Bibliothèque de l'Opéra.

17. R J Hedlund 1959 *A Study of Some 18th Century Woodwind Ensemble Music;* PhD thesis, University of Iowa.

18. *HCRL/2* p 477.

19. A Braun 1983 *Historical Targets;* London: Roydon Publications.

20. L G Langwill 1942 Proc Mus Assoc **68**, citing p 42 of W T Parke, *Musical Memoirs* Vol 1. Langwill cites Canon Galpin's 1910 *Old English Instruments of Music* p 169, quoting an apparently spoof advertizement in the *General Advertiser* of 20 October 1740, "a concerto of twenty-four bassoons accompanied on a violoncello, intermixed by

four double bassoons accompanied by a German flute," cf. the description (*Sainsbury*, under John Ernest Gaillard [1687-1749]) of "a curious piece for twenty-four bassoons and four double basses" said to have been performed in 1745.

21. See part 1, under Oettingen-Wallerstein in the discussion of German Harmonien.

22. T Volek and S Jareš 1977 *Dějiny České Hudby v Obrazech;* Prague: Supraphon. The Czech, German and English captions often contain different information.

23. Consortium Classicum (with string bass, Telefunken 6.35473); London Wind Soloists (no string bass, Decca STS 15078).

24. Fritz Spiegl 1984 *Music through the Looking Glass;* London: Routledge and Kegan Paul.

25. H Berlioz 1843 *Traité de l'instrumentation et de l'orchestration modernes;* translated by M C Clarke 1856 as *A Treatise on Modern Instrumentation and Orchestration;* London: J A Novello.

26. F G Rendall 1971 *The Clarinet: Some Notes on its History and Construction;* London: Benn.

27. *Weston/CVP.*

28. *Weston/MCVP.*

29. Albert H Rice 1991 *The Baroque Clarinet;* Oxford: Oxford University Press.

30. Early Music (1986) **14** contains relevant articles by C Karp, p 545; A Rice, p 552; C Lawson, p 554; see also Early Music (1979) 7 p 351.

31. W Horwood 1980 *Adolphe Sax 1814-1894: His Life and Legacy;* Bramley, Hampshire, UK: Bramley Books.

32. R Morley-Pegge 1971 *The French Horn;* London: Benn.

33. H Fitzpatrick 1970 *The Horn and Horn Playing and the Austro-Bohemian Tradition;* Oxford: Oxford University Press.

34. C S Terry 1932 *Bach's Orchestra;* Oxford: Oxford University Press.

35. Arne indicates changes of clef, rather than changes of crook. That he could assume players were able to read clefs is shown by the printed remark in the 1763 collection of horn duets and trios (GB-Lbl a.18.a) "The Bass or part for the 3d Horn is done in the Treble Cliff for such performers as may not understand the Bass Cliff" [sic]. Another oddity of this period is that Handel's parts in (concert) D are notated for C basso (as in the *Water Music* or *Fireworks Music*) though the obvious notation is used elsewhere (horn parts in F for movements in F). One possible, if bizarre, explanation, is that the same parts were often used also for flutes (41).

36. Wagner's early operas, like *Lohengrin*, show that he thought of valves as a means of rapid crook change, not a means to a chromatic instrument. The many transposition changes within phrases make his original parts virtually unusable.

37. For bells up, see (22) figs 192 (Prague 1741) and 190 (Prague 1743) and (38) (London 1777). For hands in bells, see (22) fig 231 (Prague 1794) and (38) fig 59 (London c 1830).

38. E Croft-Murray 1980 *British Library Year Book,* **4** p 135.

39. P Bate 1971 *The Flute;* London: Benn.

40. *Allgemeine musikalische Zeitung* (AMZ), August 1804.

41. See under Hoffmeister in Part 2. Oboe and flute parts can be written differently, without being strict alternatives (see Part 2 under W F E Bach). Flutes substitute for almost any instrument in smaller works. Thus one finds flutes as alternatives to horns in *Forest Harmony* and the *Sonata di Trompas di Caza* (i.e., hunting horns) *o Flautas Traversier Dal Siniore Giovanni Perussini* (manuscript in El Escorial). One even finds V A Holmes's Op 1 *Twenty-four duets in a pleasing style for two french horns or two guittars as also for two german flutes or two violins* (London, John Fentum c.1763; GB-Lbl, b.4) and Cocchi's *Six Quintets. For two German Flutes, violins, clarinets or hoboys, two horns and a bass* (London: Longman and Broderip, c.1780; GB-Lbl, b.346.u).

42. P Bate 1966 *The Trumpet and Trombone;* London: Benn.

43. Johann Ernst Altenburg 1795 *Versuch an einer Anleitung zur heroisch-musikalischen Trompeter-und Pauken-Kunst;* Halle. Translation by E H Tarr 1974 as *Trumpeters' and Kettledrummers' Art;* Nashville, Tennessee: The Brass Press.

44. W Braun, in *Salmen* p 144, which discusses the effect of introducing a standing trumpeter into the hautboist ensemble of the Prussian-Brandenburgian Regiment, since it intruded on the privileges of the trumpeters' and timpanists' guilds.

45. Simon Schama 1989 *Citizens;* New York: Viking.

46. Over-the-shoulder band instruments are played in the recording *The Civil War: Its Music and Its Sounds* by Frederick Fennell/Eastman Wind Ensemble, Mercury 432591.

47. In several works (Schacht 86/II, 87/II, 160-163) there are two violas plus violone, in addition to the wind band. In Schacht 79/II, violas are asked for, but have not been composed for; this may mean that they were to double other parts, and indeed in Schacht 80/III, the viola parts are marked "con violone" or "con fagotti."

48. Breitkopf und Härtel Catalog, Supplemento XVI (1785, 1786, 1787) *Notturno da MASCHEK a 2C. 2clarinetti. 2fag. 2 viole* [sic]. The work appears to be lost.

49. Wranizky's *La Chasse* is especially recommended by Ernst Pauer in his 1895 *The Pianist's Dictionary;* London: Novello, Ewer and Co, so it is surprising that no copy appears to exist in the United Kingdom.

50. F P Byrne, Jr, in F J Cipolla and D Hunsberger 1994 *The Wind Ensemble and its Repertoire;* Rochester: University of Rochester Press, pp 141 et seq. Byrne cites remarks by Sousa reported in the *Star* (Tucson, Arizona) of 14 January 1924.

51. *Scholes*, under "Percussion Family." See too the notes by N Harnoncourt to *Die Entführung aus dem Serail* (Teldec 8.35673) and Algernon Rose c.1895 *Talks with Bandsmen;* London: William Rider and Sons, especially pp 274 et seq.

52. *Roger North on Music, c 1695-1728;* edited J Wilson 1959; London: Novello.

53. Examples of transposition errors are so common that it is invidious to give examples. Lack of care is clear in the modern facsimile of the Lachner *Octet,* where the correct original B♭ parts are wrongly overprinted as E♭. Examples of print problems include page-turn problems for the clarinets in d'Indy's *Chanson et Danses,* avoidable if there were separate parts for 1st and 2nd clarinets. Often publishers could avoid problems at no extra cost by starting on a left-hand page, not a right-hand one. We note in part 1 that Viennese copyists took great pains to avoid such problems.

54. See W G Ord-Hume 1982 *Joseph Haydn and the Mechanical Organ;* Cardiff: University of Cardiff Press, p 75.

55. A J Ellis 1885, appearing as pp 495-513 of his translation of H Helmholz *On the Sensations of Tone;* reissued 1954, New York: Dover Books.

56. B van der Pol and C C J Addink, 1939 (May 15) *The Wireless World,* p 441. This important article discusses pitch as measured during performances in different countries. It notes, for instance, the spontaneous adaptation by orchestral players to a piano at a somewhat low pitch relative to the orchestral oboe.

57. *The Times,* 7 July 1988.

58. R E M Harding 1938 *The Metronome and Its Precursors;* Henley on Thames: Gresham Books (reissued 1983).

59. *Thayer* pps 686-688.

60. A Reicha, Op 88 1st edition (Jeannet et Cotelle; a copy is at GB-Lbl g.1044.c). Reicha's own guide to tempos is given in the 1st edition of his Op 99 quintets (also Jeannet et Cotelle; GB-Lbl g.1044.c).

61. H Berlioz *Autobiography of Hector Berlioz,* translated R S R and E Holmes 1884; London: Macmillan; translated and edited D Cairns 1977; London: Gollancz, Chapter 15.

62. C Dibdin, GB-Lbl Add 30950 f134 and in his *War Song 1* "Fall and Conquer."

63. C Dibdin, GB-Lbl Add 30953 f180 and in *War Song 2* "The British Heroines." In the autograph G is written but surely C is meant (cf the printed edition).

64. R Camus 1994 in F J Cipolla and D Hunsberger 1994 *The Wind Ensemble and Its Repertoire;* Rochester, NY: University of Rochester Press, pp 57 et seq.

65. *L'Ordonnance pour la Musique de la Légion Corse* 1772; the introductory text to the score of a MS in D-DS, Mus.ms.1186 describes drumming on the march.

66. *Preussens Allerhächste Kabinetts-Ordnung* for 10 February 1817, relating to the collection of approved music (D-B).

67. *Uniformirung und Organisation des Bürger-Militärs in dem Königreiche Baiern* 1807 (GB-Lbl Hirsch III.544).

68. The possible acoustic basis for such pedantry is subject to scientific scrutiny in the paper by B van der Pol 1946 The Musical Review 7 1-25, especially p 25.

69. *HCRL/5* p 201.

70. *Mr Punch in Bohemia* sd; London: The Educational Book Co Ltd, p 40.

71. *New Grove Dictionary of Musical Instruments,* 1984; London: Macmillan, Vol 1 p 477. See also *Scholes* under "Basso continuo" and "Figured bass."

72. Musical Times 1974 **115** 231 review of the Molter *Concertini* MWV VIII 5-7.

73. *Mozart Letters*: See W A Mozart, letter to his father dated 3 November 1781.

74. E Holmes 1828 *A Ramble among the Musicians of Germany;* 2nd Edition, London; reprinted 1969, New York: Da Capo Press.

75. *HCRL/4,* pp 99-100.

76. C Cudworth 1967 Galpin Soc Journal **20** 24-42, *The Vauxhall Lists.*

77. *Burney,* Vol 2 p 114.

78. *HCRL/5,* p 237.

79. L Spohr 1865 *Autobiography* (original Kassel and Göttingen; in translation 1878, reprinted 1959, New York: Da Capo). See also *Scholes* under "Ornamentation."

80. J Mates 1962 *The American Musical Stage before 1800;* New Brunswick, NJ: Rutgers University Press. Even spitting returned to fashion: "gobbing" on the band was a mark of approbation in punk music of the late 1970s.

81. W Frances Trollope 1832 *Domestic Manners of the Americans;* reprinted 1974, London: the Folio Society.

82. A Heriot 1956 *The Castrati in Opera;* London: Secker and Warburg; reprinted 1975 New York: Da Capo Press, p 75.

83. Mark Twain 1896 *A Tramp Abroad;* London: Chatto and Windus, p 78.

84. John Hampden (compiler) 1940 *An Eighteenth Century Journal, Being a Record of the Years 1774-1776;* London: Macmillan.

85. Thomas Wilson 1816 *Companion to the Ballroom;* London, p 232.

86. R Pearsall 1973 *Victorian Popular Music;* Newton Abbott, UK: David and Charles. The *Economist* of 7 September 1996 remarks of the Salzburg Festival "Once inside the auditorium, feel free to chat during the music; it is a Salzburg tradition."

87. Bernard Shaw, reprinted in the collected edition of his writings on music *Shaw's Music,* edited Dan H Lawrence; London: Bodley Head 1981, Vol 1 p 865.

88. G Pätzig 1971 *Historische Bläsermusik des 18. Jahrhunderts;* Kassel: Bärenreiter, pn 4135. The cover shows a picture by C Weigel from the Bildarchiv of A-Wn.

89. H G Farmer 1950 *Military Music;* London: Max Parrish.

90. Information from a print in the Exhibition Hall at Regensburg. The print (Joh: Gottlieb Friedrich Sculpsit et excud. Ratisbonnae / Simon Sorg Statuaris et Architekt) shows the festivities for the 3 January 1776 wedding of Prince Hieronymus von Radzivil and Princess Sophia von Thurn und Taxis. The tambourine is shown held in the left hand above shoulder level and beaten with a stick. One drum is being played with a whisk (left hand) and wooden paddle (right hand); the other drums are played with sticks.

91. A Braun 1983 *Historical Targets* London: Roydon. Figure 25 p 6 reproduces a painting from the Mainfränkisches Museum in Würzburg.

92. From an engraving by J Punt of a picture by P von Cuyuck the Younger (Buser Collection, Billington), reproduced in G Jopping 1988 (translated Alfred Clayton) *The Oboe and the Bassoon;* London: B T Batsford Ltd, p 55.

93. Sleeve (the original source is not identified) for the recording by the London Wind Soloists of the wind arrangement of *Fidelio,* Decca SDD 485.

Figure. Part of the Adagio from Mozart's autograph of the *Gran Partita,* K.361 (courtesy of the Music Division, Library of Congress, Washington DC). Note the last sixteenth-note in the two full bars. It is clearly a sixteenth-note in the oboe 2 part (line 2) but looks more like an acciaccatura in lines 4, 6 (clarinet 2, bassoon 2).

Index

Page numbers in **boldfaced** type refer to main entries.

About the Authors

MARSHALL STONEHAM is Massey Professor of Physics, University College London, a Fellow of the Royal Society, and Chief Scientist of AEA Technology. He has written extensively not only on the physical sciences, but on music as well. He has taken the opportunity to visit libraries in many countries when on travels associated with his scientific work. He is an experienced horn player and the founder and organizer of the Dorchester Wind Players, which, over the past twenty years, has played many works of the genre described in this book.

JON A. GILLASPIE is a freelance musicologist and music cataloger as well as a composer, arranger, record producer, and experienced bassoonist and keyboard player. Born in Potsdam, New York, he studied social anthropology before emigrating to England in 1973. His extensive travels researching into primary sources of wind harmony now total more than three actual years in the field and his own extensive collection includes the former wind harmony of the Löwenstein Kapelle. He has composed and arranged widely for wind ensemble, including many works for the Dorchester Wind Players.

DAVID LINDSEY CLARK was a Music Librarian to Oxfordshire County Libraries, Oxford, England. He has been involved in the revision of the Music Catalogs of a number of libraries, including the Bodleian of Oxford University. Now retired, he continues his bibliographical work, reflecting his interest in exploring the repertoire of music on which he has written over a number of years.